PUTTING GOD FIRST
JEWISH HUMANISM
AFTER HEIDEGGER

PUTTING GOD FIRST
JEWISH HUMANISM AFTER HEIDEGGER

Alick (Alexander Chayyim) Isaacs

gefen
publishing house בית הוצאה לאור גפן Est. 1981
JERUSALEM ◆ NEW YORK

Cover Design: Leah Ben Avraham
Typesetting: www.optumetech.com

ISBN: 978-965-7023-71-6

1 3 5 7 9 8 6 4 2

Gefen Publishing House Ltd.
6 Hatzvi Street
Jerusalem 9438614,
Israel
972-2-538-0247
orders@gefenpublishing.com

Gefen Books
c/o Baker & Taylor Publisher Services
30 Amberwood Parkway
Ashland, Ohio 44805
516-593-1234
orders@gefenpublishing.com

www.gefenpublishing.com

Printed in Israel

Library of Congress Control Number: 2022913319

For our children Hillel, Noam, Talia, Ori, and Hadas,
and our daughters-in-law, Rachel and Noa.

וְעָלוּ מוֹשִׁעִים בְּהַר צִיּוֹן לִשְׁפֹּט אֶת הַר עֵשָׂו וְהָיְתָה לַה׳ הַמְּלוּכָה

— Obadiah 1:21

Table of Contents

Preface

In April 2015 I had the pleasure of participating in an evening at the Hebrew University in Jerusalem dedicated to the memory of Dr. Ze'ev Mankowitz. Though I knew Mankowitz quite well, it was only after I heard his closest colleagues, students, and friends speaking about him that I was able to put his life's work into context. I heard that evening how two key questions concerned him throughout his career.[1] The first is captured in his wonderfully alliterated formulation: "How was the Holocaust humanly possible?" The second (which Mankowitz considered no less mysterious) was perhaps expressed a little less succinctly but is nonetheless of tremendous importance. Mankowitz struggled to explain how so many Holocaust survivors found the spiritual energy to dedicate their lives to – and in some cases even to sacrifice their lives for – the rebuilding of the Jewish state?[2] How was this humanly possible too?

---

1. I am referring in particular to a presentation made that evening by my friend Jonny Ariel entitled "Remembering Zeev, *z"l* – the Humanity, the History, and the Hope." Mankowitz had been a close friend and colleague of my father-in-law, which is how I had originally met him. For a while, I time-shared an office with him at the Melton Center for Jewish Education of the Hebrew University, which gave me an opportunity to get to know him better and to learn from him. But during the excellent panel discussion that was held in his memory, his closest friends, colleagues, and students set out a broad view of his life that was new to me, describing in detail his masterful teaching, his educational vision, and his deeply probing historical research.

2. Z. Mankowitz, *Life between Memory and Hope: The Survivors of the Holocaust in Occupied Germany* (Cambridge University Press, 2009). Of course, not all Holocaust survivors chose to move to Israel and many of those who did were motivated by pragmatic rather than idealistic reasons. All the same, the Zionist fervor among many of them captured Mankowitz's attention and in the context of the argument that I will be making in this book, this is an acute symbol of the wider wonder, which is the reawakening of both national sentiments and practical yearnings for the land of Israel among many nineteenth- and twentieth-century Jews.

These two questions capture the full power of the transition that took place in Jewish life between 1940 and 1950. According to Mankowitz, they are the touchstone of any effort to make sense of the two events – the Holocaust and the foundation of the State of Israel – which he (and of course, many others) considered definitive of twentieth-century Jewish history and which in his mind provided the overarching historical context for contemporary Jewish identity education. Mankowitz insisted that these questions have no final answers. Each one is the opening of a labyrinth that spirals down deeper and deeper, never reaching its bottom. To live after the fateful fifth decade of the twentieth century is to bring these questions to bear on all our efforts to know and understand ourselves as Jewish people and human beings.

Though I am aware that no answer to these questions is ever final, this book is my spiraling attempt to draw philosophical and spiritual conclusions that I believe are especially meaningful for today, from the Holocaust, the establishment of the Jewish state, and the relationship between them. It must be noted that Mankowitz's perspective is a Zionist one. There are three high-impact demographic processes in modern Jewish history that still determine the conditions of contemporary Judaism: large-scale migration to the United States (and other Western liberal democracies), Zionist emigration to the land of Israel, and the Holocaust. Mankowitz clearly sought hope for humanity after the Holocaust in the story of the survivors who came to build the Jewish state and not in the forms of Jewish life cultivated by the immigrants and survivors who made it to America's shores both before and after the war.[3]

In this book I will try to gain more insight into the "human possibility" of the Holocaust but also to address today's crisis of Jewish identity and why it is that neither the State of Israel nor American Jewish life has provided

---

3. We have singled out America here, but our comments should be taken as equally applicable to the smaller but still extremely significant Jewish communities in other Western liberal democracies such as France, the UK, Canada, and Australia, in which Jewish life has prospered since 1945. While the specific cultural and sociological circumstances in each of these communities is of course unique, there are certain general philosophical and political values that characterize all of these societies along with the United States such as commitment to democracy, equality, liberty, and the value of rational science. It was these commitments that united them in opposition to Hitler and the Nazi regime in the Second World War.

solutions to it. Like Mankowitz, my position is indeed Zionist, but unlike him what I mean by this can only be fully understood in religious terms. I will be looking for solutions to the crisis of Jewish identity by seeking to uncover what the post-Holocaust, Zionist era can reveal to us about the meaning of Jewish identity in the Torah. I see this as a profound and immensely complicated philosophical and spiritual journey that has yielded insights for me that I believe are especially relevant for the world today.

The basic premise of this book is that the overly enthusiastic embrace of modern liberalism by the Jewish world is a misjudgement fuelled by an over-optimistic view of liberal opposition to Nazism. This caused most modern western Jews to overlook the fact that key features of Jewish identity – and hence of Jewish statehood – are not commensurable with the values of western liberalism and are unable to prosper in an exclusively liberal environment. I claim that this error of judgement is inherently connected to a profound distinction between Jewish humanism (which is a theological concept) and Western humanism (which emphatically is not). The confusion of the two contributed to what I see as the disastrous effects of widespread Jewish over-integration into western society. This degree of integration has not only undermined the moral viability of the covenantal connection between Am Yisrael and Eretz Israel as a distinctive form of identity, but it has also distorted many other Jewish ideas to such an extent that some of the most basic elements of Judaism's worldview appear both implausible and morally reprehensible when viewed through the prism that most western Jews now associate with Jewish values. It is as if a whole dimension of Judaism is under water.

I shall argue that reclaiming this lost dimension of Judaism is a precondition for finding solutions to many of the problems that the Jewish world faces today. But doing this requires us to reassess the relationship between Judaism and Western civilization and to disentangle Judaism from the Western way of thinking about individual and collective identity, space, time, territory, God, and the Torah. Unfortunately, this already-complex proposal for disentanglement is complicated further by the fact that even the streams in Judaism that consider themselves hostile to Western values are oftentimes no less entangled in them than others. When we see the complexity of this, the enormity of Western influence over Judaism and hence the enormity of our task comes more fully into view.

My strategy for disentanglement will be based upon a broad philosophical analysis, the centerpiece of which will rest on an examination of Martin Heidegger's Nazism and its implications for the future of westernized Judaism. I will be arguing that when viewed through the prism of the ontological system that Heidegger presents in his masterwork *Being and Time*, the rise of Nazism and the resulting Holocaust should be regarded as a reason for Jews to let go of their dependence on Western thinking about identity and to extricate themselves from Western modes of defining collectives, even those that have nothing to do with Nazism. I will propose that *Being and Time* can provide us with a systematic method for disengaging our brains from the constraints of Western thought about identity and give us tools for accessing the Torah's ontology of Jewish identity. I appreciate that this contradicts the overwhelmingly dominant attitude adopted by most Jews in the world today who, since 1945, have progressively become more and more integrated into the Western mindset. But I submit that this is precisely why the Jewish world is in crisis about Judaism's collective particularism, its ethnocentric theology, and its connection to the land of Israel, none of which can be fully justified in Western terms.[4] Through an analysis of the contrast between *Being and Time* and the ontological system that I believe underpins the Torah, I will try to reframe our understanding of Judaism's collective, ethnocentric, theological connection to the land and show why and how the State of Israel provides the Jewish world with a supreme opportunity for rehabilitating Jewish life on non-westernized Jewish foundations.[5]

---

4. Peter Beinart's book *The Crisis of Zionism* (New York: Times Books, 2012) is a powerful example of this. The inside cover is dubbed with the headline "Israel's next great crisis may not come with the Palestinians or Iran, but with young American Jews." In many ways, I began working on this book when I realized that the philosophical framing in which Beinart's analysis of Zionism was based is one that cannot come to terms with the foundations of Israel's claim to the land or Judaism's national ethnocentricity. Western liberal thought has no moral language in which these values can stand up.

5. Much has been written about the legacy of Sephardic Jewish communities and the potential that the long and rich traditions of Jewish learning, thought, and exegesis that they cultivated over the centuries offers for the establishment of contemporary Jewish identity on firm non-Western grounds. See, for example, Meir Buzaglo, *A Language for the Faithful* (Keter Books, 2009) [Hebrew] and Haviva Pedaya, *Expanses: An Essay on the Political and Theological Unconscious* (HaKibbutz HaMeuchad, 2011) [Hebrew] and *The Return of the Lost Voice* (HaKibbutz HaMeuchad, 2016) [Hebrew]. Despite this rich and valuable literature, our focus will not be on non-Western Jewish thought but

I am very much aware that this is an approach to the strengthening of Jewish identity that might be considered hostile to Western values and to the forms of contemporary Jewish identity that seek to emulate them. I hope that I can succeed in demonstrating that this is not the case. I believe that interaction with Western thought has in many ways been immensely important and productive throughout Jewish history. This book is no exception to this rule. Mine is therefore not a hostile analysis; rather, it is a path to formulating a new foundation for a peaceful relationship between two civilizations that in my view remain alarmingly unaware of just how incompatible they are.

The process of disentanglement that I propose will unfold in four stages. These stages comprise the four parts of this book. Each of these parts is named after a classical Jewish concept. The first is Segulah, and it refers here to the particularistic biblical vision of the Jewish people's universal purpose. A preliminary articulation of this will give us what we shall refer to as "a perspective of Segulah" with which we will begin to look afresh at the mindset that Westernized Jews have adopted to *survive* in the modern world and to adapt their institutions to the *systems* that govern and organize Western society. In this part, we will begin to consider the meaning of Jewish purpose, contrasting it with these modes of survival and system. As we begin, we will only be able to talk about the perspective of Segulah from afar, working under the assumption that its viability is essentially concealed from us by our inability to fully embrace the ontological principles on which it is predicated. But we will move toward it by seeking out the traces of its plausibility that shine through certain cracks in the veneer of Western thought – cracks that we will refer to as "sparks of Segulah."

The second concept is Galut, or Exile. In Jewish history the term Galut refers to a time period in which Jewish people are separated from collective life in the land of Israel. However, for many Jewish thinkers, Galut also describes a condition in which Jewish identity is in exile from itself. Our philosophical analysis of Galut will focus on the reassessment of the Western

---

rather on the disentangling of Western Jewish thought from the perceptions of reality that dominate modern Western consciousness. This is primarily because – despite the cultural differences – the Western mindset is so ubiquitous that even Jews of non-Western heritage today are implicated in it.

understanding of the exiled self, looking at deconstruction and the linguistic turn[6] in twentieth-century philosophy from the perspective of Segulah. Ultimately, we will present the linguistic turn as an important opportunity for dismantling the self-assured certainty with which the Western mindset views the world. In a sense Galut or deconstruction is a spark of Segulah too.

The third concept is Churban, or Destruction, which for our purposes is defined in modern historical experience by the Holocaust (but which more traditionally refers to the destructions of the First and Second Temples in Jerusalem by the Babylonians and Romans in 586 BCE and 70 CE, respectively). Our focus here will be to talk about Churban in philosophical terms, resting our discussion of it on Heidegger's method of Destruction (or Destruktion) as outlined in *Being and Time* (henceforth *BT*).[7] In this part, we will discuss this book in detail, looking to penetrate the depths of its complex argument but also to expose its implications for Jewish disentanglement from both inauthentic and authentic understandings of the self as Heidegger described them.

Fourth and finally there is Tikkun, generally translated as "fixing" or "healing" but here as Rehabilitation. Historically, Tikkun is a condition that has yet to be realized but which already exists in the sense that it is the underlying current of Torah in which past, present, and future unite. The philosophical

---

6.   The "linguistic turn" is a term used to describe the shift in twentieth-century philosophy that is often referred to as postmodernism. More specifically, this term is used with reference to philosophers such as Ludwig Wittgenstein, Martin Heidegger, Jacques Derrida, Richard Rorty and others who focused their philosophical attention on exposing and deconstructing the shifting instability that underlies the correlation between language and meaning. For examples of the scholarly use of this term and its application to dominant trends in early twentieth century philosophy, see Richard Rorty, ed., *The Linguistic Turn: Recent Essays in Philosophical Method* (Chicago University Press, 1967) and Richard Rorty, "Wittgenstein, Heidegger, and the Reification of Language," in Richard Rorty, *Essays on Heidegger and Others: Philosophical Papers* (Cambridge University Press, 1991). For an example of a prominent Jewish religious thinker who embraced the linguistic turn and seized its potential for the reconstruction of contemporary Jewish theology, see Rabbi Shimon Gershon Rosenberg (Shagar), *Faith Shattered and Restored: Judaism in the Postmodern Age* (Maggid Books, 2017).

7.   The term Destruction (which might be taken as the precursor of Derrida's similar term Deconstruction) is used by Heidegger to describe his own philosophical method. We will discuss this in detail in chapters 11–16 below. All our citations from Martin Heidegger's *Being and Time* are from the excellent English translation by Joan Stambaugh (SUNY, 1953).

interpretation of Tikkun offered here will follow on the heels of the section dedicated to Churban. Drawing on the juxtaposition of Heidegger's ontology with modern Jewish mysticism, I will try to offer an ontologically explicit description of the early modern and modern efforts to integrate the mystical dimension of *sod*[8] into the public discourse of Jewish individual and collective life. In this context I will try to portray the meanings of certain key concepts in Jewish thought in ontological terms, the definitions of which will be based on an inversion of Heidegger's system of thought in *BT*. In this way I will try to access the meaning of Jewish collective life and its connection to the land of Israel in disentangled, non-Western Jewish terms.

The stages of this book are like stepping-stones that are designed to help Jewish thought let go of principles that should have been discredited by the Holocaust. By dealing with each of these concepts philosophically, we will try to grasp onto a viable way of leaving behind what Western epistemology says about human identity while rehabilitating the Jewish ontological system that underpins the Torah. I will look to describe a disentangled or rehabilitated version of Jewish identity in which both the Torah and Zionism are seen to stand on a foundation of *sod* that Churban – represented by Heidegger's method of Destruction – can help us reveal.

A Note on the Use of Italics and Capitalization

According to standard practice, I will use italics to indicate the titles of published works in both the text and footnotes of this book. I will use an initial capital letter to mark the ontological concepts (in Heidegger and in Jewish thought) that are the building blocks of my argument. Many of these are Hebrew terms (such as Segulah, Galut, and Churban, which have already

---

8.   *sod* is a Hebrew word which literally means "secret" or "concealed" but which is widely and generally used to refer to the use of a mystical or esoteric paradigm in the interpretation of the Torah. One of the central arguments that we will be developing in this book is that the possibility of inverting Heidegger's philosophical system makes it a powerful tool for interpreting this dimension of biblical exegesis outside the confines of Western epistemology. For an introduction to the hermeneutics of *sod* in Jewish biblical exegesis, see Michael Fishbane, *Sacred Attunement: A Jewish Theology* (Chicago, 2008), 102–8 and his extensive discussion of the four levels of biblical exegesis known as the *pardes* (a Hebrew acronym in which the last *s* stands for *sod*) in his introduction to *The JPS Bible Commentary: Song of Songs* (JPS, 2015).

been mentioned above). Some words, such as *being, care, useful,* and others appear both in italics and in regular text. When the word is italicized this indicates that the ontological term is implied; in regular text the word reverts to its normal meaning. All other uses of italics are in quotations where the italics appear in the original.

On the Use of the Plural

Except for this Preface, the narrative voice of this book is in the first-person plural "we." There are several reasons for this. First, this is my way of acknowledging the fact that the thought that went into the composition of this book was in many ways a collective effort. While I take total responsibility for all interpretations, lines of argument, and errors, I feel that true recognition of the significant contributions of those friends and colleagues mentioned in the acknowledgments below requires me to adopt a plural voice throughout. Second, I've structured this book like a journey that I am trying to share with my fellow travelers (you). The plural voice expresses the shared experience that I hope to create. Finally, one aspect of Jewish identity that will be discussed in this book is its fundamentally collective nature. In this spirit, the use of a plural voice seems like a fitting gesture.

Acknowledgments

This book was not authored in isolation from the busy routine of my life. The time that I was able to dedicate to the writing process was embedded in a schedule filled by meetings and conversations with friends, family, students, and colleagues. Whether I was aware of it or not, the deposits that others left in my mind each day surfaced during the precious hours I was able to find for writing and left me with debts of gratitude that are not always easy to pin down. This is where I hope to express my gratitude for the people with whom I share my life and whose generous gifts of thoughts, wisdom, and knowledge have shaped the chapter of my personal development that this book seeks to express.

I would like to begin with Sharon Leshem Zinger and Professor Avinoam Rosenak, with whom I cofounded an NGO called Siach Shalom (Talking Peace). We have been on a profound journey together since 2009 looking for the hidden secret of "peace." The philosophical insights that we have coauthored and the methods for bringing unlikely combinations of people peacefully together in the Israeli, Palestinian, and Israeli/Palestinian contexts have changed and even defined my life. The debt that I owe each of them is beyond measure, and (as I mentioned above) it is one of the reasons why this entire book is written in the plural voice. Our countless discussions about the differences between Jewish and Western conceptualizations of peace were the first stimulus for the inner journey that this book describes, and while I do not wish to impose upon them views that they do not share or mistakes that are not theirs, their voices were in my mind every step of the way. I have no measure for the gratitude that I owe them for the spiritual companionship that we share and for the ideas, texts, and concepts they taught me. Their influence appears in one way or another on almost every page of this book.

I would like to thank Rabbi Isadore Rubenstein, the administrative director of Siach Shalom, for the long hours of conversation that we share on a weekly basis. We discuss the practical side of Siach Shalom but also delve together into the ideas and beliefs that animate our work. His personal companionship is of immeasurable importance to me, and without his active support and encouragement, this book would never have been published.

I am a member of the "Yakar" community in Jerusalem. This is a special place which I share with a close circle of friends who walk a spiritual path of prayer and study together. My dear friend Professor Elie Holzer has been a constant presence in my life for over twenty years. We have shared a conversation for decades about Judaism and hermeneutics, many aspects of which are reflected in part 2 of this book. Elie also introduced me to the Torah of the Sefat Emet and from there opened the door for me to the wonderful world of Hasidic teachings that are so central to the discussion of Tikkun in part 4. Also, at Yakar, Professor Yehuda (Jerome) Gellman has been an inspiration for me. In his writing and teaching he grapples with the tensions and contradictions between Judaism and Western philosophy, offering elegant, creative, brilliant, and brutally honest solutions that he wraps up in his incomparable humility. Yehuda also read several chapters of this manuscript, offering his insights, corrections, and comments. Gabi Strenger, Dr. Elie Schoenfeld, and Dr. Ari Akerman, all members of the same community, read different chapters of the manuscript, sharing reactions and suggesting improvements for which I am also extremely grateful.

I would like to mention my students at the Rothberg International School and the Melton Center for Jewish Education, both at the Hebrew University, where I have taught multiple courses, each of which addressed a different aspect of this book. I learned more than I can say from their reactions, questions, papers, and class (and after class) discussions. Moreover, I found that teaching greatly enriched the writing process. It enabled me to refine the articulations of complex ideas and formulate many of the metaphors that I use throughout. I want to express my gratitude also to the academic and administrative staff of Melton and Rothberg for giving me the opportunity to teach that I value so much.

I would like to thank my friends Robbie Gringras and Jonny Ariel for introducing me to the work of Jonathan Haidt and George Steiner, respectively and to Professor Jeffery Perl who read a very early draft of the first two sections of the book and sent me his copious detailed and extremely helpful comments. A very special thank-you to my son Hillel, with whom I studied Rav Kook and the Maharal in *chavruta* and whose insights and sharp understanding added greatly to the readings offered in part 4. Thank you to Mark Bilski, Joe Pryzant, and Ofer Levin for generous gifts that aided the publication of this book. I would like also to thank my dear friend Marilyn Hassid for her constant support of every project I undertake and for making the first introduction to the Gefen Publishing House. Thank you to Ilan Greenfield for agreeing to publish and to Debbie Ismailoff for her superb editing.

Finally, I thank my wife Shuli for being the soul of my life. There are no words that I can write here that could possibly capture the depth of my gratitude and love for her. In the words of the Rabbis, "mine and yours is hers." I want to dedicate this book to our children Hillel, Noam, Talia, Ori, and Hadas and to our daughters-in-law, Rachel and Noa. My deepest desire is that you will be blessed to live your lives joyfully while putting God first.

INTRODUCTION

~

Beginning with Separation
in Order to End in Unity

The Identity Conflict between Jews and the West

After the Enlightenment and the emancipation of Western Jews in the eighteenth and nineteenth centuries, it perhaps appeared that an ancient conflict between Western civilization and the Jews (which arguably began around the third century BCE and continued throughout the Christian Middle Ages and beyond) was finally over. Given the sense of hope and security that this situation created, it is understandable that the turn of the tide against the highly integrated and prosperous Jews of Germany in the 1930s came as such a terrible shock. A conflict that had seemingly been resolved rose from the ashes with a more venomous and lethal effect than had ever been seen before.

Despite the overwhelming power of this shock, the Holocaust did not actually dislodge – for most Jews – their sense of security in the ideals and values that the Enlightenment seemed to offer. Indeed, after the Holocaust and the defeat of the Nazis in 1945, Jewish confidence in the West was quickly restored when the liberal democracies of Europe and the United States embraced the Jewish communities as never before and the United Nations momentously voted for the establishment of a Jewish state in the land of Israel. Even though the problems facing the Jewish people were far from solved, it once again seemed that the age-old conflict with the West had truly ended.

Though it is not our intention to play down the crucial importance of the advantages that Western modernity has held out to the Jews, we tend to ignore the fact that the philosophical foundations of the postwar alliance between Jews and the liberal democratic values of the West are still to be found in the humanism of the Enlightenment and not only in the lessons learned after the Holocaust. Given this, it is perhaps uncomfortable, but nonetheless appropriate, to connect the conditions that enabled Nazism to the continuing complications that still threaten Jewish identity in the West. This is perhaps most disturbingly visible in acts of antisemitism that continue to involve open hostility toward Jews. But, more controversially, we suggest that it is also connected to the demographic threat posed by the alarmingly high rates of assimilation in all Western Jewish communities. Similarly, despite the legitimate grounds for criticizing some of the State of Israel's policies, it is still true to say that a complex intermingling of anti-Zionism and antisemitism intoxicates public opinion about Israel, calls into question the legitimacy of the Jewish connection to the land, and places an additional and even threatening burden on the Middle East peace effort.

Our hypothesis in this book is that these phenomena and others reveal a continuing identity-based conflict[1] between the idea of collective Jewish identity as covenantal collective chosenness and Western understandings of how individuals form collectives and become connected to the land they inhabit.[2] More poignantly, our point is that this is a conflict which the aftershock of the Holocaust has not resolved. Though many assume that this conflict has ended, we suggest that addressing the flaws of contemporary humanism more stridently poses one of the most profound challenges to any effort at resolving many enduring remnants such as antisemitism, assimilation, antisemitic anti-Zionism, the conflict in the Middle East, and others.

Essentially, what we are proposing is that the specific problems still faced regarding the maintenance and legitimization of Jewish identity in the West (and this includes the State of Israel) can be better understood and most effectively tackled when the philosophical depths of the difference between

---

1.　I would like to thank Jay Rothman for introducing me to the concept of identity-based conflict and to its implications for understanding the challenges facing the State of Israel in today's Middle East. See Jay Rothman, *Resolving Identity-Based Conflict in Nations, Organizations and Communities* (Jossey Bass, 1997) and *From Identity-Based Conflict to Identity-Based Cooperation* (Springer, 2012).

2.　For a powerful reckoning with the contemporary meaning of covenantal chosenness, see Yehuda (Jerome) Gellman, *God's Kindness Has Overwhelmed Us: A Contemporary Doctrine of the Jews as the Chosen People* (Academic Studies Press, 2012).

Jewish and Western philosophies of identity are brought out into the open. Since for the most part Western Jews live alongside their neighbors in relative peace, our accentuation of difference might sound like a disruptive if not cantankerous thing to do. It must therefore be clear that our intention is not to exacerbate tensions. Rather, we are placing an a priori emphasis on disparity because we believe that this is the way to move toward peace and understanding. This emphasis echoes Rabbi Abraham Isaac Kook's inversion of the words that appear in the *Zohar* when he says that "the way of holiness is to begin with separation in order to end in unity"[3] (my translation[4]).

The Individual and the Collective

In our attempt to tease this disparity out into the open, we shall explore at length what the meaning of the individual self is and how its relation to the idea of the collective in Western humanist terms differs from and indeed conflicts with the way the Torah frames the meaning of Jewish collectivity. We shall suggest that because of the fundamental difference between the Jewish and Western framing of this relationship, a robustly distinctive Jewish identity is not viable when Western thinking is applied to the solution of many of today's most challenging Jewish problems. In exposing the deeper aspects of this, we will pay special attention to what Germany's falling prey to Nazism can teach us about the struggle in Western thought to reach an authentic understanding of human (individual and collective) consciousness. At its heart, this book will offer a close reading of Martin Heidegger's reckoning with Western anxiety about authentic humanist identity in *BT* (1927). We will argue that *BT* tells us something definitive about Western philosophy's portrayal of the individual and his or her relationship with the surrounding world while showing, at the same time, why the argument presented in *BT* must be understood in the context of what Heidegger wrote as late as 1953:

---

3. Rabbi Abraham Isaac Kook, *Lights of Holiness*, vol. 1 (Jerusalem: Agudah Lehotzaat Sifrei Harav Avraham Yitzchak HaKohen Kook, 1938) 15 [Hebrew]; see also *Zohar*, Mishpatim 95a.

4. Unless otherwise stated, all translations of Hebrew texts throughout this book are my own.

The works that are peddled about nowadays as the philosophy of National Socialism but have nothing whatever to do with the inner truth and greatness of this movement have all been written by men fishing in the troubled waters of 'values' and 'totalities.'[5]

If, as Heidegger seems to suggest, his philosophy is an enduring statement about the inner truth and greatness of Nazism's remedies for the sicknesses of Western civilization, we propose that a close reading of *BT* can offer unique insights not only into Nazism itself but into the broader and long-term implications of Heidegger's Nazism for Jewish efforts to define Jewish identity in Western terms.

Klippat Yavan[6] – The Hellenistic Shell

As we mentioned in the preface, our strategy for healing the deep structure of Jewish/Western relations is to try to disentangle Jewish from Western notions of individual and collective identity. Using a kabbalistic term, we shall refer to this as an effort to remove Klippat Yavan (the Hellenistic shell) from the way in which the nature and meaning of the Jewish people is understood in Jewish thought. By emphasizing disentanglement and the removal of a shell we are taking a position that self-consciously runs against the grain of the overwhelming embrace of the Western values that seemingly won the day after 1945. It also deviates from the predominantly liberal response of world Jewry to the West since the Enlightenment and most especially since the end of the Second World War.

---

5.   See George Steiner's discussion of this statement in "Heidegger Again," in *Salmagundi*, nos. 82–83 (Spring/Summer 1989): 31–55. On the substantial evidence found in Heidegger's so-called "Black Notebooks" that testifies to his lifelong commitment to Nazism, see Andrew J. Mitchell and Peter Trawny, eds., *Heidegger's Black Notebooks: Responses to Anti-Semitism* (Columbia University Press, 2015).

6.   Klippat Yavan is a kabbalistic term that refers to the mental concealments imposed upon the human capacity to recognize God in this world by classical Greek philosophy and the epistemological frameworks that it provided for philosophical reflection. For a brief explanation of the traditional understanding of this term, see, for example, Rabbi Chayim HaKohen and Rabbi Reuven Sasson, *Talelei Chayim: Introductions and Gateways to the Inner Torah and the Service of God: Ana Bakoach* (2003), 40–41 [Hebrew].

But, our approach to disentanglement will not be directed in any way against the West or against Westernized Jews. Our path will be to follow a journey inward in which we shall try to elucidate the differences in the ways in which traditional Judaism and Western thought have sought to access the inner dimensions of human consciousness, thought, and feeling. This makes philosophical analysis especially important. Only after the inner psycho-philosophical dimension of identity has been disentangled will it be possible to look outward at questions concerning the political, social, cultural, and spiritual realities of Jewish life and relations with the West.

In our philosophical discussions we shall try to remove powerful obstacles that block our ability to encounter the inner identity of the individual and collective self as Jewish thought seeks to access it. Our strategy for removing these obstacles will be to start with some of the processes of deconstructive self-criticism that characterize much of the philosophy written in Europe during the twentieth century. As we already mentioned, we will look closely at Heidegger but also at Ludwig Wittgenstein, Jacques Derrida, Michel Foucault, George Steiner, Bruno Latour, Jonathan Haidt, Daniel Kahneman, and others. In reading their work we will seek to present our understanding of what Heidegger's concept of Destruction and Derrida's concept of Deconstruction can contribute to the task of removing Klippat Yavan from the Jewish conception of the individual and collective self. Through our discussion of these thinkers, we shall try to disengage Western ontology from the ontology of Jewish theology, giving us a fresh point of access to concepts such as Tzelem Elohim (humanity in the image of God), Nefesh (the psyche), Neshamah (the soul), and Da'at Hashem (intimate Knowledge of God) as these and others are outlined in early modern and modern Torah texts.[7] We shall argue that these terms belong to a uniquely Jewish network of ontological (onto-theological) concepts that we shall seek to rehabilitate as part of our effort to address our identity crisis meaningfully.

---

7. The concept of Tzelem Elohim, i.e., that humankind is created in the image of God, first appears in Genesis 1: 26–27. We will discuss this concept in detail in chapter 15 below. The vision that the imperfect world will reach its state of perfect resolution when it is filled with Da'at Hashem, i.e., the inner awareness of God, appears, for example, in Isaiah 11:9. Again we will return to a detailed analysis of this concept in chapters 15 and 16 below.

The Methodology of Segulah

Though Torah texts will be discussed in detail only in the last section of the book, it is necessary for methodological reasons to say something now about the Jewish religious ideas and concepts that provide the platform on which our analysis is built. What we say here will perhaps sound like a personal statement of religious faith – and in many ways it is. All the same, since the purpose of this book is to detach its own methodological principles from the meanings and categorizations that modern Western culture gives them, the justifications for introducing religious faith into what we mean by an analytical methodology – which is something that this whole book aims to accomplish – will have to wait until our argument is more developed. So, we will simply begin.

Throughout this book we shall refer to our outlook on the relationship between Jewish identity and Western philosophy from a point of view that we shall refer to as "the perspective of Segulah."[8] This is a traditional Jewish articulation of the purpose of Jewish covenantal chosenness which, in the words of the Aleinu prayer, is *"tikkun olam bemalchut Shaddai* (the rehabilitation of the world in the Kingdom of God)."[9] This vision of collective Jewish purpose is one that charges the Jewish people with the task of bringing about a fundamental revolution in the way in which human beings experience their individual/collective identities and their consciousness of the world. Tikkun Olam is a prophetic or messianic idea that culminates in a form of peace and

---

8. Segulah is a biblical term that describes the purposeful nature of Jewish collective identity. It is generally translated as "chosenness" but is taken here as referring more pointedly to both the purpose and the spiritual capacities required for the fulfillment of that purpose which God attributed to the children of Israel in the Bible, as in Exodus 19:5 or Deuteronomy 7:6.

9. The Aleinu prayer closes the regular Jewish prayers recited three times each day. The tradition attributes its composition to the biblical Joshua Bin Nun at the time of the conquest of Jericho. Modern scholarship suggests alternatives, including the early and later rabbinic periods. See A. Z. Idelsohn, *Jewish Liturgy and Its Development* (New York, 1931); Ismar Elbogen, *Jewish Liturgy: A Comprehensive History* (Philadelphia: JPS, 1993), 72; Barry Freundel, *Why We Pray What We Pray: The Remarkable History of Jewish Prayer* (Urim, 2010), 232; Joseph Hertz, *The Authorized Daily Prayer Book with Commentary, Introductions, and Notes*, revised American edition (New York: Bloch, 1948), 209; Stefan Reif, *Judaism and Hebrew Prayer: New Perspectives on Jewish Liturgical History* (Cambridge, 1993) and "Jewish Liturgical Research, Past, Present, and Future," *JJS* 35 (1984).

unity that is forged in the image (or the Kingdom) of God. This vision is realized in the world – again, in the words of the Aleinu prayer – when

> all will recognize and know you...for every knee will bend down before You and every tongue will swear allegiance to You. And it will be said, "God is King of the whole earth!" And on that day, He will be One and His name will be One.[10]

A secular or liberal-religious humanist might be easily forgiven for reeling away from this vision. It seems to describe a theocracy in which human liberty is quashed by the demands of an overpowering God (or worse still, by those who claim to act in His name). However, from within the perspective of Segulah, nothing could be farther from the truth. The sovereignty of the divine that Jews pray for daily comes as a true source of relief from the burden of detachment. It is at the same time the quintessential symbol of freedom from even the most delicate forms of political oppression. It releases human consciousness from its flawed perception of the relationship between inner selfness and external reality. In psychological terms we speak about crises of identity and flawed perceptions of reality that cause anxiety, jealousy, misery, and confusion. These in turn breed selfishness and callousness that harden our hearts to the feelings of others and often lead to meanness and violence. People are often needy and mistaken, overconfident, oppressive, tyrannical, unable to find inner peace through self-understanding and compassion for the world. As a result, our societies, which are indeed filled with beauty, kindness, and generosity of spirit, are also plagued by incessant struggles over power, ego, and self-assertion. Though *tikkun olam bemalchut Shaddai* is a release from all this, the vision of peace and completion that it offers goes way beyond alleviating the suffering caused by the disquieted human psyche alone. From the perspective of Segulah, self-understanding is a vessel in which the awareness that "all is, always has been, and always will be One" can reside. The effect of this realization changes the whole human perception of

---

10. Quoted from the Aleinu prayer.

nature, as in Isaiah's vision that the wolf will lie down with the lamb and the whole world will be filled with Da'at Hashem (intimate Knowledge of God).[11]

There are Jewish thinkers who explain that the human crisis of identity is caused by the ego. Because our sense of self is egotistical it blocks our consciousness of the Oneness of all *being* from our awareness.[12] This blocking is what the perspective of Segulah identifies as the distancing or concealment of God. And it is the distancing of God from human awareness that is ultimately responsible for the separateness, competition, and enmity that cause suffering, strife, and injustice in the world. Biblical and kabbalistic images that portray God sitting on His throne or uniting His *being* and His name refer to a state of mind in which the united conscious *being* of the world is recognized. The principal purpose of the perspective of Segulah is to enable a shift in the way we see the world from a consciousness of separateness to one of God's unity; this, too, is an idea that the deceptively simple phrase quoted above, "we begin with separation in order to end in unity," captures beautifully.

From the perspective of Segulah, Judaism fulfills its purpose of Tikkun Olam by creating a national community in the land of Israel whose collectivity

---

11. This is a reference to Isaiah 11:9. To appreciate the meaning of this phrase it is important to underline the connection between the word *da'at*, which literally means knowledge and its more intimate or even erotic connotations, for example, in the verse "And Adam knew Eve his wife" (Genesis 4:1). Da'at also connotes ingestion, joining things together, and in this verse, intercourse. In this sense the kabbalistic tradition understands the fruit of the Tree of Knowledge as having this joining equality, and as such, the result of Adam and Eve's eating from the fruit of the tree is more about the joining or mixing together of good and evil than understanding the difference between them. In a similar vein, the knowledge of God is understood as an intimate and internal dimension of human consciousness that recognizes the aspect of the divine that is joined with or inside the world. In this sense, Da'at Hashem is a state of mind in which God is discovered from within. For a brief and accessible discussion of these themes in Jewish thought, see Avraham Sutton, *Spiritual Technology* (Shamir Inc., 2013), 40–48.

12. The principle that the self blocks our ability to recognize God in the world is connected to the notion that the egotistical self is incompatible with the purely altruistic nature of the divine. In order to recognize the divine, it is therefore necessary for the self to be like the divine and overcome its egoism. This is a central premise in kabbalistic thought and especially in the teachings of Rabbi Yehuda Ashlag. For an extensive discussion of this theme in Rabbi Ashlag's writings, see Michael Laitman, *Self-Interest vs. Altruism in the Global Era: How Society Can Turn Self-Interest into Mutual Benefit* (Toronto: Laitman Kabbalah Publishers, 2011).

is defined by its shared inner participation in an onto-theological fascination with the unity of *being* itself. This unity is experienced individually by each member of that community as an inner reality that corresponds with and complements the unified reality of the community and ultimately of all *being*. The charge of making this encounter real in the collective consciousness of all Jews is the purpose of the Covenant or chosenness that ties the Jewish people to each other and the land of Israel through the Torah. Internalizing the Torah through study and the observation of its commandments is the task that makes this state of *being* possible. The choice to embrace a unified consciousness of *being* is broken down into all the free choices that Jews must make day after day as they choose to follow the life of Torah and thus to encounter the source of all life. In order to internalize the Torah in this way they must freely choose the life of Torah repeatedly every day; even when its light is concealed by any number of individualistic or self-serving desires. Choosing the life of Torah is what is meant by accepting the burden of God's kingdom. If a unified intimate consciousness of *being* is what the knowledge of God means, the saturation of our daily experience of life with this consciousness is what the life of Torah accomplishes. The name and the throne are thus both metaphors for an immanent ontological theology that represents God's presence in the world as equivalent to humanity's cumulative, collective experience of the world across time. The infinity of space and time captured in the word "world" (and more specifically in the Hebrew word *olam*) is thus the revealed dimension of God's *being*. The *Zohar* teaches that the unity of *being* and the world (which is again what the image of God sitting on His throne represents) is also the meaning of the unity of God and His name that the Aleinu prayer describes.[13] When this unity of name and *being* is experienced, human beings will finally be able to see beyond the illusions and misunderstandings that our self-misunderstanding causes and

---

13. See, for example, the *Zohar*'s commentary on the closing words of the Aleinu prayer cited above: "And on that day He will be One and His name will be One." The *Zohar* writes, "Just as the above unite in Oneness so She (i.e., the Shechinah or the indwelling spirit of the divine) unites below in the mystery of Oneness to be One; One with those above; One receiving One. The Holy One, blessed be He, who is One above does not sit upon His throne of glory until She too is transformed with the mystery of Oneness that they become One within One. This is the secret of God is One and His name is One" (*Zohar*, Terumah, 163–66).

which distort our perception of the world. Tikkun Olam occurs when every individual finally discovers what the nature of humanity's inevitable collectivity is supposed to feel like from within. It is this that allows the good and the pleasure of life to flow freely between us all without blurring our differences.

The Jewish tradition describes two stages for the political completion of this vision of Tikkun Olam.[14] Again, these two stages reveal yet another dimension of meaning that is condensed into the idea of "beginning in separateness in order to end in unity." In the first stage the Jewish people must remain separate from others. As a people, it is their distinctive task to gain a collective awareness of the world as an expression of God's *being*. This stage focuses on the particularistic commitment of the Jewish people to the practice of Torah. But the purpose of this is not self-serving for Jews. Thus, from the perspective of Segulah, overt expressions of Jewish collectivity such as contemporary Jewish nationalism are not simply the claim of a people to the right of self-determination in their historical homeland. Jewish national collectivism is better described as a matter of purpose: Jews are separate only for the purpose of the greater unity that follows. The separateness of the Jewish collective from the rest of the nations of the world and its covenantal connection to its land is a kind of halfway position on the road to universal unity that comes to deconstruct the illusion of separateness and set the microcosmic collective (or national) self on the path to its ultimate macrocosmic, all-inclusive purpose. This is the path that leads toward the fulfillment of a covenantal unity across difference between all peoples and all lands.

In other words, given the a priori condition of human consciousness – in which the gap between our natural state of selfness or separateness and

---

14. The idea that the Jewish project for the world begins with a particularistic stage before entering its universal stage appears widely in Jewish thought from the Bible to the modern day. This is captured, for example, when God says to Abraham that his descendants are to be a blessing to all the nations of the world in Genesis 12:3, or that the children of Israel are to serve the world as a kingdom of priests, as in Exodus 19:6, or that the Jewish Temple in Jerusalem will serve all the nations of the world, as in Isaiah 2:2 and 56:7. Modern articulations of this are ubiquitous. See, for example, Martin Buber, "The Spirit of Israel and the World Today," in *Israel and the World: Essays in a Time of Crisis* (Schocken Books, 1963), 183–94; Michael Rosenak, "Children of Two Covenants," in *Tree of Life Tree of Knowledge: Conversations with the Torah* (Westview, 2001), 217–29; J. D. Levenson, *The Universal Horizon of Biblical Particularism* (New York, 1985).

our desired state of unity and Oneness is too large to bridge – the covenant seeks to condense the gap and focus the task of closing it by singling out one people (Am Segulah) and one land (Israel) to achieve in microcosm the inseparable unity of immanent and transcendent *being* that ties all people to one another and to the world. The experience of the unified *being* as well as the unity of the people and the land is often referred to in Jewish literature as "light" which thus becomes accessible to all *being* in the world. This is what the prophet Isaiah refers to as a "light unto the nations."[15]

Given this understanding of the perspective of Segulah, it follows that our analysis of the relationship between Judaism and Western civilization must focus on the arena of human consciousness, the collective, and the self. Despite the many virtues of Hellenism and humanism, the humanist/individualist consciousness on which they depend is essentially at odds with the ethnocentric Jewish alternative to it. Thus, Klippat Yavan has sought to undermine the otherness of the Jewish collective and its covenantal connections to the Torah and the land in different ways for thousands of years. This is the deep source of the correlation between antisemitism (aggressive opposition to the otherness of Jewish collectivity), anti-Zionism (aggressive opposition to the otherness of the Jewish connection to the land), and Hellenization/assimilation (cultural opposition to the otherness of Jewish identity). This is also the source of deep inner confusion about the moral, ethical, and epistemological viability of this view of the world.

So far, the perspective of Segulah has been described as a statement of faith. As our argument unfolds, we shall seek to understand its viability as a grounded portrayal of human experience that provides us with a methodology for analyzing the distinctive nature of Jewish identity in terms that we can base in human experience.

---

15. Isaiah 49:6.

PART I

SEGULAH

CHAPTER 1

Tikkun Olam from the Perspective of Segulah

Fixing the World

The purpose of the biblical covenant and hence of the Jewish people is often cited as Tikkun Olam, but what this concept actually means is often significantly limited and misunderstood. From the perspective of Segulah the concept of Tikkun Olam has public, collective, global, and cosmic implications. It means no less than rehabilitating and healing the entire world.[1] Tikkun Olam is most often taken as referring to individual or communal acts of charity and social justice.[2] But this is not the definition with which we are concerned. The scope of this term that we are interested in is connected to the full cosmic meaning of the Hebrew word *olam*, which connotes the eternity of the world in both time and space and the concealment of that eternity. This concept suggests that the world as we know it obscures a deeper eternal truth that it is our task to disclose.[3] Tikkun Olam is therefore the recovery

---

1. Literally the word *tikkun* means "fixing," "healing," or "setting on it proper foundations," and *olam* refers to the whole world or even the eternal universe in both space and time.

2. One of the striking features of modern liberal Judaism, particularly (though not exclusively) in the United States, is the way in which it has embraced the idea of Tikkun Olam as the central value of Judaism. However, this has come under severe criticism. Liberal Judaism is seen by many as having reduced this concept almost entirely to a consensual American liberal value that serves the Left's agenda of social equality and social justice in ways that clash with particularist Jewish values. For a controversial but illuminating example of this critique, see Jonathan Neumann, *To Heal the World: How the Left Corrupts Judaism and Endangers Israel* (New York: St. Martin's, 2018).

3. The word *olam*, meaning "universe," also refers to eternal time and to something that is hidden, as in the Hebrew word *ne'elam*, meaning "missing" or "concealed." In this sense the idea of Tikkun Olam is connected to healing the human incapacity to see the eternity of space and time that is concealed in our finite and mortal experience of life

3

of a perspective that is connected to the eternity of time and space and to the hidden nature of this eternity. When understood in this way, it becomes clear that introducing the seemingly popular value of Tikkun Olam into our sense of purpose in public, collective, or even political life requires us to face the theological challenge of speaking plausibly about the idea of God's accessibility – or even visibility – within the confines of our finite experience. This is not an easy thing to do, and it is especially complex in our context, in which public political space is generally explained in predominantly secular humanist terms.

Though God's involvement in the life of the collective is central to Jewish thought, it is also far from simple to talk about in modern terms. The presence of God in public life does not align easily with the rationalist-humanist political tradition alongside which Judaism has evolved since the Enlightenment. As we try to grasp Tikkun Olam in public political terms, we must therefore face the obstacles that prevent God from reentering public political discourse appropriately. This reentry is blocked by the privatization, or individuation, in liberal society, of the choice "to believe," and as such, a theologically driven notion of Tikkun Olam can accomplish its higher munificent goal only if the reality of God is somehow made apparent to eyes of flesh.[4] For now, this is inconceivable, which means that – from the perspective of Segulah – the possibility of fixing the world by Tikkun Olam, i.e., "revealing what is concealed," depends on pushing aside the veils, constructions, and piles of rubble that block the possibility of encountering the divine from emerging into the light.

---

in the world. Tikkun Olam is therefore related to a spiritual healing process in which human consciousness in its condition of inauthenticity is transformed into a state in which the divine presence of God that is concealed as the world and in the world (but which also lies beyond the world) is recognized.

4.   The regular daily and weekly Jewish liturgy contains frequent references to the idea that God will be recognized and seen in the world. In addition to the passages that we discussed from the Aleinu prayer in our introduction above, some additional examples of phrases in the Hebrew liturgy that carry this message include "And our eyes will see when You return to Zion in mercy" that appears in the Shemoneh Esrei prayer; "Appear from Your place and be our King…and our eyes will see Your kingdom" from the Shabbat morning Kedushah prayer; and "May every existing being know that You made it and may every creature know that You created it and may everything that has breath in its nose proclaim, 'The Lord God of Israel is King and His kingdom rules over all!'" that appears in the Musaf service of the High Holy Days of Rosh HaShanah and Yom Kippur.

Before we begin, we might ask, "Does the world need fixing?" Is there a need for Tikkun Olam? A fair answer to that must of course acknowledge that not everything is broken. Much of what there is works well, but not well enough. We know that the world as it is embodies a mix of good and evil, function and dysfunction. Yet we are conscious that the line that divides them is not the same one that divides success from failure, happiness from misery, prosperity from calamity. The misplacing of these lines presents a greater challenge than the mere existence of evil. Virtually every religious tradition is puzzled not simply by evil itself, but by the fact that the world seems to reward good and evil indiscriminately.[5] We seem to live in a world in which we are obliged to stay with good even when it does not pay off. This is a tough demand, and we quite naturally seek to circumvent it, whether by sinning or by creating meritocratic societies that defy the way of the world and try to reward only the deserving. Indeed, this latter effort is the heart of Western ethics. And yet, despite our best intentions, we know that the practical project of building ethical societies fails. Corruption seeps in from outside the limited boundaries we construct, and we remain with the tragicomic intermingling of hope and disappointment that characterizes the human condition. In our struggle to comprehend and overcome the reality in which it is possible for evil people to prosper and for good people to suffer,

---

5. This question, which is broadly referred to as the question of "theodicy," is a concern in many religious traditions. It is one of the central themes in the biblical book of Job, which has been the subject of exegetical investigation by Jewish, Christian, and Muslim scholars. See, for example, P. Koslowski, ed., *The Origin and the Overcoming of Evil and Suffering in the World Religions* (Netherlands: Springer, 2018). See also the classic work of Gilbert Chesterton, *The Book of Job with an Introduction by G. K. Chesterton* (London, 1907), or for a more recent study, see Gustavo Gutiérrez, *On Job: God-Talk and the Suffering of the Innocent*, trans. M. J. O'Connell (Orbis Books, 1987). The theme of theodicy in Christian theology was tackled by some of the greatest writers and thinkers of the twentieth century, including, for example: C. S. Lewis, *The Problem of Pain* (London: Collins, 1966); Paul Ricoeur, *Evil: A Challenge to Philosophy and Theology*, trans. John Bowden (New York: Continuum, 2007); and Simone Weil, *Waiting for God* (London: Harper Perennial 2001). Two examples of many that appear in the work of Jewish writers include Zvi Kolitz, *Yosl Rakover Talks to God* (New York, 2000) and Elie Wiesel, *Night* (1960), (New York: Hill and Wand, 2006). For a discussion of theodicy in Buddhist thought, see John Ross Carter, *Dharma: Western Academic and Sinhalese Buddhist Interpretations: A Study of a Religious Concept* (Tokyo, 1978); for an example of Islamic analysis of theodicy, see Nasrin Rouzati, "Evil and Human Suffering in Islamic Thought – Towards a Mystical Theodicy," in *MDPI* (2018).

we seek to demystify and give a rational account of the relationship between cause and effect in every possible feature of life. The recruitment of human logic and science to this project of demystification is the heart of modernity. It is, as we shall see, at the core of the worldview that banishes God from the public sphere of life.[6] This is the rubble that we must move, and the tenacity of its justification for staying put should never be underestimated.

Faith in the Bible offers an elegant alternative to all this confusion. The Torah tells us that the world as created by God is good – but also that the final perfection of the world requires a shift in the state of human consciousness, which is the task of humankind. The imperfection of the world as we know it is thus its perfection-in-our-making. As we have stated, from the perspective of Segulah, the mechanism of global perfection is the internalization of Torah, by the Jewish people, living in the land of Israel according to the Covenant of Sinai. This is the meaning and purpose of divine election. From the perspective of Segulah, this is God's strategy for helping humanity to fix and heal the world. History, in this spiritual-political discourse, is the process through which the ever-deeper or inner meanings of the Torah are internalized, realized, and thus revealed in human action. Ultimately, when the people of Israel gather together in the land of Israel and observe the law, they will unite their external reality with a new light, a new collective inner consciousness that is a vessel for an awareness of God so tangible that His *being* becomes visible in the utter unity of the whole world. In Jewish faith, it is this visibility that solves the crisis of human identity and allows the world to unite in perfect harmony.[7]

---

6.   In chapter 2 below, we will discuss William Cavanaugh's historical discussion of the wars of religion and his understanding of the connection between Western modernity and the exclusion of God from the public sphere in politics. See William T. Cavanaugh, "A Fire Strong Enough to Consume the House: The Wars of Religion and the Rise of the Nation-State," in J. Milbank and S. Oliver, eds., *The Radical Orthodox Reader* (London: Routledge, 2009). In chapter 3 below, we will discuss Jonathan Haidt's analysis of moral psychology. Of particular relevance to our point here is his discussion of the evolutionary reasons for moral psychology and Haidt's detachment of human morality from religion. See Jonathan Haidt, *The Righteous Mind: Why Good People Are Divided by Politics and Religion* (Vintage Books, 2012), 3–30, 256–83.

7.   For an example of this vision, see Martin Buber, "The Spirit of Israel and the World of Today," in *Israel and the World: Essays in a Time of Crisis* (New York: Schocken Books, 1948), 183–95.

The problem here is that this system of thought requires us to deviate from the critical standards that we apply to other aspects of our lives. For this reason, while it appears meaningful and exciting for many, for a lot of others the biblical logic is hard to see working in the world. As such, even believers in God find it hard to embrace depictions of reality that they cannot normally gain access to. Doing so is usually presumed to require a counterintuitive inversion of the rational or logical order of things. Acceptance that precedes comprehension (as in the baffling notion of "We shall do then we shall hear" – Exodus 24:7) seems to directly contradict the sequence of modern deductive thought. Comprehension that is confined to pre-scribed parameters is generally suspicious. Most troubling for some, the irrationality or concealed logic of God's ethnocentric election of Israel is both defiantly and problematically mysterious. This was perhaps best expressed by William Norman Ewer in his infamous epigram "How odd of God to choose the Jews!" Many moderns have a hard time making sense of this without drifting – one way or another – into fanaticism.[8]

This is how the vision of Tikkun Olam appears when the rubble and the veils are not removed or cleared away. But the problem that this vision creates for any who wish to take it seriously is tenacious. For skeptics, its connection to reality as we know it is delusional. For people of faith, its inner workings are concealed from our point of view. One might imagine that it is something that you can choose to believe if you want to, but that you are equally free to reject. But neither proposition is satisfactory, since they both offer only partial engagement in a vision that is, by its very nature, both universal and holistic. It can be fully rejected only on the incomplete grounds of its irrefutability. Conversely, it can be accepted only after a leap of faith that overlooks the intense critical effort that must be dedicated to understanding its inner logic in a way that makes it genuinely accessible. Either way, the path to Tikkun Olam, if it exists, is lost to the world. When we step over this

---

8. The two forms of fanaticism that we are referring to here are antisemitism from the one side – in which the irrationality or concealed logic of the Jewish claim to chosenness breeds irrational or even pathological hatred for Jews. The reverse side of this is rooted in a similar form of irrationalism which breeds a kind of mystical philo-Semitism that is characteristic of many Evangelist churches. When applied to Jews, a similarly irrational kind of Jewish chauvinism emerges that is characteristic of certain streams in Orthodox Judaism.

problem, we breed fanaticism. In extreme cases, Jews who believe it entirely cultivate a fanatic hostility to the rest of the world, while Gentiles who reject it entirely build upon it a fanatic hostility toward Jews.

We shall take extremely seriously both the significance of this hostility and the seriousness of the challenge that the rubble poses. When choosing to investigate the inner meaning of Tikkun Olam, we must be careful not to disentangle ourselves from or destroy values that we know and trust as we proceed. In this sense, the danger of fanaticism demands the disqualification of anything that undermines such things as liberty, equality, justice, and truth that currently serve us tolerably well. Similarly, we must steer away from ideas that cultivate hate, harm, violence, racism, sexism, persecution, and oppression. We take these values as guidelines that we must not deviate from as we ask: Can the discourse of Tikkun Olam be retrieved and rehabilitated?

Galut, Churban, and Tikkun

Our strategy for answering this question essentially provides us with the overall structure of this book. We will try to follow a meta-historical but also psycho-philosophical path that – following our initial attempts to grasp the "perspective of Segulah" – will unfold in three stages. In these stages we will engage in philosophical reflection seeking to elicit inner experiences of Galut (Exile), Churban (Destruction) and Tikkun (Rehabilitation). On the meta-historical scale, these concepts correspond to the exile of the Jewish people from the land of Israel, the Holocaust, and the return of the Jewish people to the land. On the psycho-philosophical level each of these terms requires a slightly more detailed initial explanation:

1. Galut, or Exile, is detachment from the state of consciousness in which we might honestly experience the world in the way that the vision of Tikkun Olam describes. It is a condition of being separated from unity and hence in constant conflict. Since this notion of separateness and individuality is heavily associated with the philosophical concept of the "res cogitans" or "the knowing self," the condition of Exile is one that is connected to epistemology and to the limitations of the "normal" or ontic state of human consciousness. Our

effort to really recognize that we are in Exile is therefore closely connected to the philosophy of deconstruction and its interrogation of how human beings erroneously construct their images of the world.

2. Churban, or Destruction, refers to a collapse or to the falling away of the foundational conditions that make survival in Exile possible. As we shall try to experience it, Destruction creates a condition of openness to a shift in attitudes about the deeper potential of human consciousness. It is the huge crisis and collapse that allows us to see things differently. What we shall seek to "destroy" is no less than the disproportionate faith that modernity in the West has placed in what human beings think they know when they look through their own eyes at the surrounding world. This disproportionate faith in human rationality is what Charles Taylor referred to as "extremist humanism" that allows the tangible visibility of the world to overshadow and discredit the experiences that Taylor refers to as "beyond life."[9]

The only language generally available for speaking about what is "beyond life" is inadequate and rarely does it give us access to a spiritual perspective that is simultaneously capable of offering an appreciable account of cause and effect in physical, social, and political activity. Most efforts at this are spiritually flaky and hard to convey. More intellectually rigorous approaches tend to be strong on their "deconstructive" side and weak when it comes to proposing alternatives. Destruction is therefore also a process that requires us to generate a language in which we can talk about the inner experience of historical identity on a different foundation from the dominant models provided by Western humanist epistemology. Our efforts to accomplish this goal will rest quite heavily on the neologisms, terms, and concepts that Heidegger developed in his laborious efforts to establish the priority of *being* (ontology) over knowing (epistemology) in his work *Being and Time* (*BT*). But after reading Heidegger and attempting to extract from his philosophy a new understanding of his reasons for supporting Hitler, we will endeavor to invert

---

9.   Charles Taylor, "A Catholic Modernity?" in *A Catholic Modernity? Charles Taylor's Marianist Award Lecture with Responses by William Shea, Rosemary Lulling Haughton, George Marsden, and John Bethke Elshtain* (Oxford University Press, 1990).

his terms and use them to rehabilitate the concepts and images that certain choice examples of early modern and modern Jewish literature employ in their efforts to convey their own vision of inner consciousness. In this sense, Destruction is but a prelude to a process of Tikkun or Rehabilitation in which we will try to offer a philosophical lexicon for understanding and internalizing the meaning of the encounter that takes place between God and humankind when we consider our inner human condition through the prism of the Torah.

3. Tikkun or Rehabilitation is uncovering the reasonableness of a full-bodied system that already exists in the Torah and which can be experienced and accessed when the heart and mind are opened to it. The challenge here is to see how much of it we can successfully extract from concealment and allow to be seen by the critical eye as offering a plausible account of the workings of the world as we observe and know it.

As we already said, the point of this process is not to compromise the values that humanism has served well. However, it should also be clear that the politics of Tikkun Olam does not and will not accept these same values on Western humanist terms. The path to Tikkun Olam that we shall follow ultimately leads nowhere if the values that humanism champions well are lost. But it accomplishes nothing if it does not both supplement them and advance their more successful implementation by significantly changing them. In sum, Exile, Destruction, and Rehabilitation combined are the attempt to fix the world by removing Klippat Yavan from the perspective of Segulah, thus positioning the Covenant of Sinai on a publicly visible path that leads to global and even cosmic healing, compassion, stability, happiness, prosperity, freedom, justice, truth, holiness, and peace for the Jewish people and through them for the whole world.

Survival, System, and Segulah

Since the rise of modern humanism, Jewish people have developed a tendency to talk of their own existence as a problem. This is the so-called "Jewish problem" that, in our view, takes its present form as a result of the integration between Jewish and Western conceptualizations of individual and collective identity. Many of the modern forms of Jewish life that have evolved, particularly in the West, are in one way or another attempts at tackling the problems that this integration causes. The result is that many Jews have instrumental-ized Jewish life itself and have begun thinking of Judaism, Jewish education, Jewish family, Jewish community, and Jewish statehood as problem-solving mechanisms that seek to preserve a threatened identity. In this book we shall try to face these issues differently.

At this stage, we simply want to introduce a term that we have come up with as a kind of shorthand for our framing in very general terms of what we mean by westernized forms of Jewish life. The term is Survival and System (or the politics of Survival and System), and it is our way of denoting a kind of modern Jewish "realpolitik" in which the correlation of political cause and effect in Jewish life and history is seen in Western humanist terms. This is our term for a perspective that has enjoyed near-to-ubiquitous dominance in Jewish communal and political thought since the Enlightenment and is in many ways completely intuitive to all modern Jews. We coined this phrase by grafting together two ideas that we see as central to post-Enlightenment Jewish humanism. When contrasted with Segulah, the alliteration of the three *s*'s has its appeal too.

By Survival, we mean the dominant concern of many modern Jewish institutions in the last two hundred years. For many, it is also the very raison d'être of the Jewish state. In its own self-perception, Survival looks at the problems of the present and the future from a perspective that is rooted in the traumatic memories of the past. Thousands of years of persecution and suffering have – with abundant justification – convinced Jews that their very survival is always in doubt. In the context of the discourse of Survival, Jews worry about such things as physical defense against antisemitism and anti-Zionism in the Diaspora; existential threats to the security and well-being of the State of Israel (such as terrorism, illegal immigration, financial insecurity, international delegitimization, nuclear weapons, etc.), and cultural defense against nonacceptance of Jews or assimilation and the corrosion of Jewish identity.

System refers to the values of the institutions that govern Western society and are duplicated by Jewish institutions. Outside of Israel, the concerns of System affect the running of communal institutions. Questions of System might concern curricular choices in Jewish education or questions of strategy messaging and ideology that inform the ways in which Jewish communal institutions represent their interests, values, and concerns in public. On a larger scale, these problems of System might concern attitudes to Israel's democracy, the policies of AIPAC and J Street, or the rulings of a halachic committee on gay marriage, intermarriage, conversion, or women's involvement in the liturgy. In Israel questions of System can, of course, be found on a small local community scale too, but the more obvious discussions of System affect such things as government policy, democratic procedure, occupation of/settlement in the West Bank/Judea and Samaria, religious and secular divides in society, social justice, crime rates, military service, government corruption, immigration, trade, religious freedom, human rights, fair economy, the tension between Jewish nationalism and democracy, and so on. In sum, System is concerned with the effective and ethical running of the institutions that are central to Jewish collective living. System is focused on values and with practical outcomes. Together, Survival and System comprise a comprehensive ethical system that seeks to define and protect the value of Jewish existence in Western humanist terms.

At the core of the Jewish problem that Survival and System seek to resolve is the question of Jewish identity – over which Jews fuss, worry, invest, build, and despair. The argument that we shall develop in this book is one in which the effort to resolve all these concerns will leave behind both the problem definitions and the problem-solving mechanisms of Survival and System. Instead of thinking of the Jewish identity question as concerned with the identification of Jews with Judaism or of individual Jews with the Jewish collective, we shall consider the problem of modern Judaism as rooted in the concealment (through implausibility) of the nature and inner purpose of Jewish life. We shall try to see the point of Jewish identity as neither Jewish survival nor the improvement of the systems of Jewish organizations but as the fulfillment of covenantal purpose. We shall argue that in order to appreciate this, the notion of Jewish collective identity must be understood as connected to the deeper meaning and structure of the collective term Segulah. The core of the problem of Jewish identity – as we shall try to understand it – is the incompatibility of Am Segulah with any of the modern categories used to replace it. It is not an accident that

Am Segulah resists and defies the concepts of "religion" and "nation." These are the terms that humanist political philosophy proposed for modeling the separation of church and state. The categories and the separation they engender are entirely foreign to the methodological approach represented by the perspective of Segulah.

Segulah is a counterintuitive soteriological category which is geared toward the fulfillment of Jewish purpose and Tikkun Olam. But the path to a practicable politics of Tikkun Olam is hard to find. As a mode of political problem solving, it is hard to trust. The result is that the soteriological purpose of the Jewish people has produced virtually no reliable or recognizable problem-solving mechanisms in the world of modern Jewish national and institutional politics. For the narrative of Segulah to become viable as a mechanism for uniting the Jewish people and healing the world, it needs Rehabilitation. Since this is the overall problematic that this book will try to address, we cannot yet summarize what we mean by this. But we can perhaps find an approximation of the problem and the desire for a solution to it in the connection that Martin Buber draws between Zionism and Jewish chosenness. For Buber, the meaning of Zionism was inextricably connected to the notion of Jewish election. However, Buber insisted that the Jewish people were not elected for preferential treatment, ethnic advantage, power, or even divine favor. In his words, "the Jewish conceptualization of election is unique because though every great People regards itself as the chosen people...the nature of our doctrine of election is entirely different from that of other nations.... Our doctrine is distinguished from their theories, in that ours is completely a demand."[10]

According to Buber, this demand is to heal the world by creating unity and peace. The political implementation of this is what Buber understood as the true purpose of Zionism. When we look at Zionism and the challenges facing the State of Israel from this perspective, we almost immediately encounter the obstacles and concealments that make the inner significance of this brand of Zionism difficult to see in the world. If the project of Zionism is to be viably described as universally beneficial, a great deal must change and develop. To begin to move the State of Israel in the direction of fulfilling

---

10.   Martin Buber, "Hebrew Humanism," in *Israel and the World* (1948), 241–45.

the politics of Tikkun Olam, it must first be clear that the logic of Buber's formulation is currently blocked from view.[11] As Buber himself intuited, the place to start is with the internal dynamics of Jewish life. As such, the terms with which we begin our analysis – Survival, System, and Segulah – all point inward.

Paradigm Shifts and Operating Systems

When we suggest that the politics of the State of Israel or of the Jewish communities in the Diaspora might be conceptualized in terms of Segulah, we introduce terminology into a public discourse of communal and national politics that lies outside the boundaries of rational or social-scientific verification. As such, these terms feel inappropriate, inapplicable, or threatening – functioning in a setting in which they have no normal place. When we extend Tikkun Olam beyond the context of activism for social justice and refer to it as a form of spiritual politics, it remains virtually without intelligible political meaning. In other words, in its fuller meaning, Tikkun Olam in the cosmic sense is either meaningless or it belongs to a paradigm that is not yet public. For this idea to emerge as plausible in public life, we must bring about a "paradigm shift." This is an idea that we need to explain in order to clearly define our objectives going forward.

"Paradigm shift" is a term coined by Thomas Kuhn. In his landmark historical study of revolutions in science, Kuhn suggested that scientific progress and innovation involve a process akin to religious conversion that cannot be described in purely rational terms.[12] Kuhn insisted that science is an activity that takes place in human communities – communities

---

11. Rather than engaging in the full process of disentanglement that we shall pursue, Buber proposed his notion of Hebrew Humanism as a corrective that embraces both the humanist and the uniquely Hebraic political traditions. It seems clear that Buber feared religious fanaticism and sought to guard against it by reusing the accomplishments that first made the humanist response to medieval politics plausible. The equitable result seems to have been inadequate to the task at hand and perhaps inaccessible to the Zionist leaders for whom he articulated it. In many ways, we would not like our position to be seen as a critique of Buber's but rather as an attempt to carry on from where he and others like him left off. For Buber's notion of Hebrew Humanism, see Buber, ibid.

12. Thomas Kuhn, *The Structure of Scientific Revolutions* (University of Chicago Press, 1970).

of scientists – whose allegiances and convictions are affected by social and political processes. While new evidence and reasoning accumulate to suggest why a new theory gives a better account of observed phenomena than an older one, the complex matrix of social interactions between scientists – looking for the truth about the world but also for tenure, peer approval, research grants, and other such "extraneous" concerns – creates the social reality in which a theory is either validated or rejected. When it is validated, it wins new adherents. It is at this stage that a paradigm shift occurs. However, while two competing theories coexist in a community that has yet to reach its final decision, a condition of "incommensurability" exists. When this happens, scientists who adhere to different theories evolve such considerably different allegiances that it is as if they speak two (admittedly recognizable yet) significantly different languages. At this stage members of two separate camps can no longer collaborate or communicate effectively with one another.

Similarly, one might imagine two operating systems in a computer. It is perhaps possible that a program might run tolerably well on both. But, as each system becomes more elaborate and complex, users who wish to operate programs that belong to one system (such as Mac) on a computer running on another (such as Microsoft Windows) will encounter increasing degrees of difficulty. And yet, both systems work, and both seek to serve the same functions. But they do not interface well, and it is here that collaboration fails.

The distinction between the language of Survival and System on the one hand and Segulah on the other is a difference of this sort. The ability to translate terms and concerns that are currently understood in the language of Survival and System into the language of Segulah requires a paradigm shift. It might perhaps be helpful to frame the questions of this book in the following way: Can the "operating system" of Segulah continue to support all the programs that ran well on the operating system of Survival and System? What additional benefits come with the system of Segulah that the politics of Survival and System were unable to accomplish? Most importantly, how is the shift between the paradigms to be accomplished?

The Need for a Paradigm Shift

Let us begin answering these questions by establishing the premise that there is in fact a need for a shift. Our primary argument is quite simply that the rise of Nazism in Germany and the establishment of the State of Israel have far wider long-term implications for the relationship between Judaism and the West than most Jews have so far considered or imagined. If we were truly to appreciate the implications of the Holocaust for the Jewish-Western relationship, this would yield an enduring realization that the conflict between Judaism and Klippat Yavan cannot be resolved according to the paradigm of Survival and System. Similarly, the State of Israel and even Zionism itself would be more fully understood as a shift away from Klippat Yavan in the sense that they represent a powerful impulse to move away from "Western" soil in order to reclaim Hebraic land, language, and identity and are not – as many assume – a huge collective project of integration into a humanist international community with a tendency to blur identity boundaries beyond recognition.

There are, of course, Jewish thinkers and scholars who have, in different ways, struggled with this issue. Perhaps a few examples will suffice: The sense of ambivalence about overidentification with Western values is what Ahad Ha'am injected into the heart of secular Zionism,[13] while a handful of twentieth-century "postliberal" Jewish writers – among them: George Steiner, Theodor Adorno, Max Horkheimer, Ernst Cassirer, Gershom Scholem, Martin Buber, Hannah Arendt, Emmanuel Levinas, Jacques Derrida, and Abraham Joshua Heschel – expressed this most poignantly in the aftermath

---

13. Asher Tzvi Hirsch Ginsberg, who was known as Ahad Ha'am, was one of the key leaders of the Zionist movement. His form of cultural Zionism was particularly focused on the idea that the Jewish state must be founded on the revival and reinvigoration of Hebrew culture and not exclusively on the values of the post-Enlightenment West. See, for example, Ahad Ha'am, *The Jewish State and Jewish Problem* (JPS, 1897) and Hans Kohn, ed., *Nationalism and the Jewish Ethic: Basic Writings of Ahad Ha'am* (Schocken Books, 1962).

of the Holocaust.[14] Many of these will be discussed in more detail and will help us to formulate the central arguments of this book.[15]

---

14. Most, though not all, of the writers in this list will be discussed in this book. Some will be dealt with in detail while others will receive more cursory mention. For example, we will discuss George Steiner in chapters 2 and 9; Jacques Derrida in chapters 6, 7, and 8; and Abraham Joshua Heschel in chapters 17 and 18. We will mention and briefly discuss Hannah Arendt and Ernst Cassirer in chapters 2 and 9, Adorno and Horkheimer in chapters 2 and 5, and Gershom Scholem in chapter 15. What these thinkers share is their uniquely Jewish rethinking of the relationship between Jewish identity and Western politics after the Holocaust. The texts that we will be discussing or mentioning in this connection are George Steiner, *In Bluebeard's Castle: Some Notes towards the Redefinition of Culture* (Yale University Press, 1971); Jacques Derrida, *Writing and Difference*, trans. Alan Bass (University of Chicago Press, 1978), *On the Name*, ed. Thomas Dutoit and trans. David Wood, John P. Leaver, Jr., and Ian McLeod (Stanford University Press, 1995), and *The Beast and the Sovereign*, vol. 1, trans. Geoffrey Bennington (Chicago University Press, 2009); Abraham Joshua Heschel, *The Sabbath* (New York: Farrar, Strauss and Giroux, 1951); Max Horkheimer and Theodor Adorno, *Dialectic of Enlightenment: Philosophical Fragments* (English Translation; Stanford University Press, 1987); Ernst Cassirer, *Myth of the State* (Yale University Press, 1946); Gershom G. Scholem, *Major Trends in Jewish Mysticism* (Schocken Books, 1946). See also *On Jews and Judaism in Crisis: Selected Essays* (Schocken Books, 1976); David Biale, *Gershom Scholem: Kabbalah and Counter-History* (Cambridge, MA and London: Harvard University Press, 1982); "Zionism: Dialectics of Continuity and Rebellion – An Interview with Gershom G. Scholem," in Ehud Ben Ezer, *Unease in Zion* (Quadrangle/The New York Times Book Company and Jerusalem Academic Press, 1974), 269; Gershom G. Scholem, "On What Point Do They Disagree," in *Od Davar* (Am Oved, 1987), 57–59 [Hebrew]; Hannah Arendt, *The Origins of Totalitarianism* (Benediction Classics Edition 2009 [1950]), Martin Buber, *Israel and the World: Essays in a Time of Crisis* (New York Schocken Books, 1948); for Emmanuel Levinas, see *Totality and Infinity: An Essay on Exteriority*, trans. Alphonso Lingis (Duquesne University Press, 1969).

15. While it perhaps goes without saying that nonliberal and ultra-Orthodox writers held this position even before the Holocaust and expressed severe opposition to modernity and the Enlightenment, what these thinkers have in common is a brand of skepticism about the post-Enlightenment worldview that can be attributed specifically to lessons learned from the rise of Nazism. For example, Arendt's notorious association of Nazism and communism crossed the lines that were drawn to form the alliance between the United States, Great Britain, and the Soviet Union in the war. While she remained deeply hopeful about American democracy, this is nonetheless a dramatic reevaluation of the way the relationship between communism and Nazism was viewed until the publication of her monumental book on totalitarianism. Moreover, her work stands out for the extensive attention that she gives to the role of the Jewish minority in the evolution of the twentieth-century totalitarian regimes. See Arendt, *Origins of Totalitarianism*, chapters 1–4. Similarly, Steiner's demand for a total review of Western culture in *Bluebeard* (as we will see in detail in chapter 2 below) rests upon the

We are also aware of contemporary political concerns that underline the need for the shift we are proposing. For example, Western Judaism is having a progressively harder time defending the ethics of circumcision, the ritual slaughtering of kosher animals, the resistance to intermarriage, and Jewish practices concerning the status of women in marriage and divorce, etc. Likewise, the irresolvable paradox of the democratic State of Israel's insistence on its collective national Jewishness is a constant source of strife. Were there no underlying currents of Segulah, from the perspective of Survival and System the option of dispensing with the uncomfortable features of the tradition or of the problem of Jewish ethnocentricity would seem far more natural. Even the ethical complexity of justifying the right of the Jewish people to return to the land of Israel creates a crisis of values. The language of Survival and System offers no universally plausible articulation of the Jewish people's special claim to the land. While no effective and equitable solution to this problem has emerged from the religious community – some of whom display a lack of sensitivity to Palestinian needs that is at best insensitively hawkish and at worst blatantly racist – the Judaism of Survival and System will inevitably falter in the face of a Palestinian landowner holding a valid document of purchase. What moral language can there be to express meaningfully the vitality of the Jewish connection to the biblical land in such a situation?

The language of Survival and System perhaps faces an even greater challenge as Western civilization lives through a modern era of constitutional crisis. In the last few decades, most of the primary institutions in every democratic society have come under attack in one Western country or another. Skepticism and misconduct have plagued electoral processes, discredited courts, and politicized the press. Corruption and bad conduct run rampant at all levels of local and national government while many of the international federations such as the EU, the UN, and NATO have faced crises of cohesion as well. The idea that our global world order is undermining the

---

assumption that the entire project of the Western humanities failed between 1933 and 1945, with cultural and political implications that reach as far as the United States and Great Britain. Similarly, in his work *The Myth of the State*, Cassirer rethinks the whole idea of the state following the failure of Germany, while Adorno and Horkheimer see the rise of Nazism and the Holocaust as a reason to expose the underlying myth and deceit upon which the Enlightenment was founded.

viability of the planet is also a powerful warning sign, since the lion's share of pollution comes from industrial democracies as well. All the constitutional upheavals and challenges that we have witnessed in the United States, the United Kingdom, Greece, Spain, Italy, Hungary, and other nations have their parallels in Israel, which has had its fair share of misconduct, institutional corrosion, and corruption to deal with. The result is that in both rhetoric and practice people are openly worrying about the survival of democracy and its viability in the future. The Covid-19 crisis exposed how the ego-centric nature of interest-based politics, when facing an actual or perceived existential threat, goes into survival mode at the expense of others rather than cooperative mode together with others. In short, at a juncture when the tension between nationalist particularism and universalism is high, the time has come to question the viability of liberal humanist globalism and the perspective of Survival and System that depends upon it.

Does Jewish thought have another world vision? Or must we remain content with Churchill's quip that "democracy is the worst form of government except for all the others." Such a claim – such an acceptance of unsatisfactory results – marks the boundary of a paradigm. This is a boundary that cannot be crossed until we find the means of shifting away and making room for a nonmutant, nondistorted, nonfanatical, genuinely progressive form of Segulah to safely emerge. But the luxury of postponing this effort and the rethinking that it demands is no longer an option.

We propose that since historical events alone have not brought about the required shift we can only do so when we move inward and tackle the conceptual obstacles that continue to prevent this from happening. We must see if, by philosophically recognizing the impact of Klippat Yavan on Jewish thought, we can make the need for this shift into a compelling concern. To do this, the argument must enact the shift itself. It is for this reason that our three-stage path is long. It is an attempt to experience Galut, Churban, and Tikkun from the inside in order to pick up the trail where the perspective of Segulah leads.

Misappropriation and Distortion

So far, we have suggested that Segulah is concealed and that for the politics of Segulah to emerge a realignment (paradigm shift) that touches all the institutions of Jewish political life is required. This necessitates the reconceptualization of the individual, the family, the community, the public political sphere, and the international political arena all in terms of Segulah. Without this broad paradigmatic structure, the language of Segulah defies intuitive understanding like a program that malfunctions on a foreign operating system. The simultaneous mixture of comprehension and bemusement that this malfunction elicits is counterproductive in either useless or damaging ways.

Let us now touch briefly on one illustrative effect of this that perhaps underlines our point about the need for a paradigm shift in a deeper way. The case studies of this side effect are perhaps politically obscure, but crucially significant to the clarification of our point. What we are referring to are the scholarly representations of some of the thinkers whose ideas this book hopes to rehabilitate. Our claim is that without the necessary psychological, philosophical, historical, and political infrastructures to absorb what these thinkers have to say, the radical impact of their teaching is lost. Our argument is that this loss is the deliberate outcome of a mode of scholarship that is itself predicated on the same philosophical assumptions as the politics of Survival and System. In this sense, Survival and System has a vested interest in pasting over certain ideas using mechanisms of resistance or immunity that we shall refer to as Structures of Concealment, or Klippot. Let us briefly consider two examples of these structures:

1. Acceptance through misappropriation
2. Rejection through distortion

We shall take a brief look at one example of each: The writings of Abraham Joshua Heschel and their reception in the liberal Jewish communities of North America are an excellent example of the former, while the teachings of Rabbi Abraham Isaac HaKohen Kook and their long-term impact on Israeli politics exemplify the latter.[16] As we discuss each case, we shall do nothing more at this stage than briefly rehearse arguments that have already been

---

16. At a later stage we shall return in much greater detail to both Rabbi Kook and Heschel (chapters 16 and 17 below). For now, the purpose is to establish the need for the processes we are referring to as Destruction and Rehabilitation and not to deal more significantly with the implications of their teachings.

presented and supported by others. In the case of Heschel, we shall follow his student Byron Sherwin, and in the case of Rabbi Kook, we will consider the thesis of Avinoam Rosenak.

Heschel

Byron Sherwin insists that the association of Heschel with the liberal project of Tikkun Olam (in its more limited sense as a form of social justice) is a categorical error. This error stems from the primary project of post-Enlightenment Jewry in Europe and America, which has been that of evolving a successful synthesis between the Jewish tradition and the universal claims of humanist rationalism (i.e., Survival and System). Sherwin makes the claim that

> from a sociological point of view, "prophetic Judaism" and its spinoffs culminating in "coalescence" were developed to further Jewish integration in the post-Emancipation era. However, as sociologist Charles Liebman already wrote in the early 1970s, "More than ever before, the values of integration and survival are mutually contradictory." He continues, "With particular reference to universalistic ethics and political liberalism in the 1960s, Liebman observed that Jewish religious values are not unambiguously liberal; "they are folk-oriented rather than universalistic, ethnocentric rather than cosmopolitan." Writing in the 1990s, he observed that liberalism "fails as a strategy for Jewish survival because it lacks the resources to justify Jewish cohesion and particularism."[17]

The argument here underlines what is problematic about the strategy of Survival and System and the inevitable continuum that it establishes between cultural and social assimilation. However, more specifically, Sherwin insists that Heschel's writings, rather than trying to facilitate that synthesis are in fact a fierce attempt to break away from it. A prime example of this is Heschel's warnings against cultural assimilation, which were directed not only at Jews

---

17. Byron L. Sherwin, "The Assimilation of Judaism, Heschel, and the 'Category Mistake'" *Judaism* 53, no. 3 (June 2006): 40–50. See also Einat Ramon, "Abraham Joshua Heschel's Critique of Modern Society," *G'vanim* 6, no.1 (2010): 28–41.

who intermarry but also at those who live right at the epicenter of committed Jewish life. Cultural assimilation for Heschel did not simply refer to loss of Jewish identity. He fought against the contamination of Jewish culture that the synthesis with secular humanism represented. Heschel's opposition to this synthesis was directed at all forms of integration that extended the limits and boundaries of "Jewishness," even when these take place among the innermost circles of those deeply committed to Torah scholarship. Sherwin reports that

> Heschel considered attempts — medieval and modern — to forge a synthesis between Jewish thinking and that of the dominant culture to be a mistake, inevitably leading to a distortion of authentic Jewish thinking, to the creation of a grotesque hybrid. Rather than applying the universalistic approach of Western thinking to particularly Jewish issues, he advocated the application of a particularly authentic Jewish way of thinking both to Jewish and universal social, ethical and spiritual issues. In his view, a form of Judaism rooted in foreign soil was a distortion, a fraud. "It is a situation of 'the voice is the voice of Esau and the hands are the hands of Jacob...'; physically we are Jews, but spiritually, a fearful assimilation is raging. Jewish leaders talk about social and political problems with the voice of Esau, when the world is hungry instead to hear a new spiritual word in Jewish terminology – a Jewish approach to problems." "This I surely know," wrote Heschel, "the source of creative Jewish thinking cannot be found in the desire to compare and to reconcile Judaism with a current doctrine."[18]

The crucial feature of these complaints is that they apply equally to Mordechai Kaplan and Rabbi Joseph Baer Soloveitchik.[19] Indeed, they could apply to

---

18. Sherwin, "The Assimilation of Judaism," 40–41.

19. Heschel's concern about speaking outside the tribe or in a language that is dictated by thinking that comes from outside the tribe is directed at even the greatest of Torah scholars, such as Rabbi Joseph Baer Soloveitchik, whose idea of Torah and Madda involved the alignment of Jewish religious thought with the epistemological and rational standards of modern Western science. Rabbi Soloveitchik arguably dedicated many of his most significant philosophical works to this question and to the challenge of evolving religious categories that would raise our understanding of Torah to meet modern

almost every form of committed Judaism in the world today. The threat of speaking in the voice of Esau is not simply about identification outside the tribe. It is about the pollution of Judaism's soteriological purpose. Put differently, Heschel is obviously critical of Jews who assimilate, but he is equally concerned about those who assimilate Judaism into the discourse of scientific humanism (Survival and System) while accepting the universal validity of Western philosophy's truth claims. In this sense, Heschel must be understood as rejecting the notions of scientific truth that pop up in Rabbi Soloveitchik's formulation of Torah and Madda (Torah and Science) and that have most prominently dominated modern Western thought since Newton and Kant.

This passage, like many others in Heschel's oeuvre, allows us to see his reticence about the all-pervading structure of humanist thought that obscures the politics of Segulah from view. It allows us to see his life's work as an attempt at creating a Jewish language of politics, free from the Hellenistic influences that stifle and conceal the true meaning of what he ironically chose to call "divine pathos."[20]

Using our terminology, we might say that Sherwin wishes us to see Heschel as an Eastern European Hasidic thinker who, because he grew up in an environment that was deeply saturated in the discourse of Segulah, was bemused by the Survival and System thinking that surrounded him in the United States. One might surmise that he thought the calamity of the Holocaust was, on its own, enough for the power of his own soteriological point of view to emerge. Perhaps his mistake was that he did not anticipate how resilient the structures of humanist thought could be. By his reckoning,

---

scientific standards without compromising halachic commitment. This is indeed the foundation of the stream in American Judaism that calls itself Modern Orthodoxy. See, for example, Rabbi Soloveitchik's treatise *Halachic Man* (trans. Lawrence Kaplan, [Jerusalem: Sefer VeSefel], 2005), and see also *The Halachic Mind* (Seth Press, 1986). It perhaps goes without saying that this critique is voiced with greater vehemence still against liberal Jewish thinkers who reconstituted and reinterpreted the Jewish tradition in order to present its principles as particularistic expressions of universal values. A striking and highly significant example of this is Mordechai Kaplan's *Judaism as a Civilization: Toward a Reconstruction of American Jewish Life* (JPS, 1981 [1934]).

20. The irony here is of course that the term "pathos" is not Hebrew but Greek. All the same, this is a central theme in Heschel's understanding of biblical prophecy and is discussed throughout his classic work *The Prophets* (New York: Harper Collins Perennial Classics, 2001 [1962]). See especially part 2, chapters 1 and 3.

the generation that witnessed the Holocaust could not but be ready to speak or at least hear the politics of Segulah. Heschel addressed the Jews of America in this language using his own terms, such as "the politics of eternity built in a palace of time,"[21] the "authentic Jewish voice," the "voice of Jacob," and – perhaps most famously – the voice of "divine pathos." But these terms, all of which are attempts at pointing toward the language of Segulah, lay beyond the experience of his audiences. Heschel felt deeply frustrated and mourned the shattered world he left behind, a world in which the Hebrew antecedents of these words had once resonated with full-bodied meaning. Heschel's fear that a second Holocaust was taking place in America only makes sense if he is understood in terms of Segulah. It is only in this language that the physical and spiritual survival of the Jewish people can never be separated from each other. Similarly, his attitude to the State of Israel was ambivalent because he felt unsure that the leaders of Zionism understood the significance of the events taking place around them.[22] The mixed messages of Israel's ideological leaders on the spiritual uniqueness of the Jewish state left Heschel simultaneously hopeful and skeptical. Like many, he was mesmerized by the miraculous victory of 1967 but never completely convinced that its soteriological significance had been appropriately appreciated.[23]

---

21. The relationship between time and space in Jewish thought that this image suggests is central to Heschel's argument in his book *The Sabbath* (see note 14 above). We will return to discuss this image in detail, tracing its connections to Hasidic thought, in chapters 17 and 18 below.

22. Like Martin Buber, Rabbi Yehuda Ashlag, Aaron Samuel Tamaret and many other intellectual/spiritual leaders, there was a great deal of ambivalence in Heschel's writing between his tremendous enthusiasm for Zionism and the State of Israel and his concern that the modern Jewish state and the form that it was taking was in fact a Western violation of a sacred idea rather than its Hebraic embodiment. For Heschel this was connected to the confusion that he identified in Zionism about the relevant significance of space and time. See also Lawrence Kaplan, "Time, History, Space, and Place: Abraham Joshua Heschel on the Religious Significance of the Land of Israel," *Journal of Modern Jewish Studies* 17, no. 4 (2018): 496–504. We have written about this ambivalence in the writings of Buber, Ashlag, and Tamaret in Alick Isaacs, "Shlomzion," *Common Knowledge* 20, no.1, Duke University Press (Winter 2013–14).

23. Heschel most enthusiastically expresses this albeit ambivalent sentiment after Israel's victory in the Six-Day War in *Israel: An Echo of Eternity* (1967). See Kaplan, "Time, History, Space, and Place."

Our point here is not so much the discussion of Heschel himself as it is the tragedy of his distortion by liberal Judaism. It seems that Heschel's inner pathos prevented him from gauging correctly the hearts and minds of even his most ardent disciples, for whom German culture collapsed only temporarily after the Holocaust and for whom American culture despite its flaws (racial segregation, religious intolerance, and the war in Vietnam stood out for Heschel in particular) never really collapsed at all. With no access to the language of Segulah they approximated as best they could what they heard their teacher say. But, for the most part, what they heard was American Jewish liberalism. Heschel struggled against racism, senseless war, religious intolerance, and political injustice – espousing a politics of Segulah. As Sherwin insists, his activism grew from the belief that God is involved in the political redemption of the world through the Covenant of Sinai. But he was misappropriated as the founding father and prophet-in-chief of a Jewish secular liberalism that panics at the very mention of Jewish election.

Rabbi Kook

The fate of Rabbi Kook's teachings has been no less dramatic. Avinoam Rosenak's extensive research into Rabbi Kook's writings underlines the significance of the "unity of opposites" to Rabbi Kook's instruction.[24] When Rosenak began writing about Rabbi Kook, he entered a field of scholarship that puzzled over the contradictions between the expansiveness of the latter's philosophy and the stringency that characterized many of his halachic rulings. The effort to systematize the meta-halachic principles that explain when his rulings are either lenient or stringent seemed hopeless, as did the search to make sense of his apparent openness to the secular Zionists in the context of his deeply entrenched and conservative positions on territory, Jewish law, and Jewish-Arab coexistence.

---

24. This theme is central to Rosenak's extensive writing about Rabbi Kook. For a few examples of this, see Avinoam Rosenak, "Hidden Diaries and New Discoveries: The Life and Thought of Rabbi A. I. Kook," *Shofar: An Interdisciplinary Journal of Jewish Studies* 25, no. 3 (Spring 2007): 111–47; "Prophecy and Halakha Dialectics in Rabbi Kook's Meta-Halachic Thought," *Jewish Law Annual* (2011); *Prophetic Halachah: The Philosophy of Halachah in the Teaching of Rabbi Kook* (Jerusalem: Magnes, 2007) [Hebrew]; *Cracks: Unity of Opposites, the Political, and Rabbi Kook's Disciples* (Resling, 2013) [Hebrew].

Rosenak shows how the rationale that accounts for Rabbi Kook's system of thought is embedded in the theological principle of God's unity. It draws upon the contradictory nature of prophetic revelations as they are recorded in the Bible and then duplicated in rabbinic disagreement. Indeed, the insistence on polarity and paradoxical contradiction is one of the hallmarks of Segulah. It can be found in Heschel where it emanates from the Bible, through Rabbinic Judaism, kabbalah, and Hasidic teaching. The same principle is the key to understanding how Rabbi Kook's universalism manages to condense a limitless concern for the entirety of humanity into the particularistic welfare and private concerns of one nation, bound to one land, chosen among others to be the kernel or the heart of the world's inner unity.

This rationale defies the logical consistency of humanism. It contradicts the fundamental rule that two opposing statements cannot both be true. The notion that all contradicting truths emanate from – and ultimately converge in – the same source is incomprehensible to the system of rational thought and alien to all forms of political legalism, which predicate the possibility of either legislation or action upon the resolution of disagreement through either deliberative decision-making or judgment. Rabbi Kook seems to sanctify indecision and contradiction and in doing so, as Rosenak has shown, is often both decisive and decisionist. He insists on holding the bull by both horns. If indecision is the opposite of decision, then the higher unity of these opposites requires a lower expression of each. His broad-based tolerance or openness similarly requires both intolerance and reticence by its side in order to remain truly open to that which is genuinely closed. All emanates from the oneness of God and thus has a place in the "unity of opposites."[25]

As with Heschel, the fuller explication of this concept in the context of Segulah is not accessible without a paradigm shift that discloses the system of logic that allows this principle of unity to make sense. As with Heschel, our point here is of a more preliminary or preparatory nature, and it is to demonstrate the mechanisms that in this case accomplish their purpose through rejection.

---

25. For our discussion of this theme, see Alick Isaacs, "The Concept of Peace in Judaism: The Vessel That Holds a Blessing," in Georges Tamer, ed., *The Concept of Peace in Judaism, Christianity, and Islam* (*Key Concepts in Interreligious Discourses*, vol. 8) (Berlin: De Gruyter, 2020).

Rabbi Kook, like Heschel, believed that the time had arrived when the rehabilitation of Segulah in the public political arena had finally become possible. Unlike Heschel, the impetus for Rabbi Kook was not the Holocaust. He died in Jerusalem in 1935, before the atrocities that defined Heschel's sense of himself as a living ember from a destroyed world had ever taken place. For Rabbi Kook, the decisive and definitive event was the Zionist awakening of the Jewish people that, in his terminology, made possible the reawakening of Torat Eretz Yisrael (the Torah of the land of Israel). The return of Jews to the land allowed for the emergence of prophetic *halachah*, a form of holistic political Jewish practice that drew its energy from the immanent presence of God in the Holy Land. Rabbi Kook intuited that within the context of this land's special saturation in the sanctity of God's presence, a politics of Segulah, rooted in the multilayered mystery of God's paradoxical oneness, was finally possible. In this context the land of Israel is not just the geographical setting for the drama of the Jewish state to unfold, nor is it one of the Jewish people's natural resources. It is not merely a historical homeland and it is not a birthright. The land is a living institution of the state in the same way that a humanist might think of a parliament or a supreme court. It is the institution that gives the politics of Segulah its opportunity to emerge from concealment. Asking a disciple of Rabbi Kook to compromise this value for the sake of peace is like asking a liberal to give up on the legal system or the right to vote.

Rosenak's analysis of the distortion of Rabbi Kook's thought by both Rabbi Kook's disciples and his academic critics is eye-opening. Drawing upon Ernst (Akiva) Simon, he distinguishes between what Simon calls a "Catholic" and a "Protestant" conceptualization of Judaism.[26] Whether or not these labels faithfully represent their original Christian meanings in this context is immaterial. For Simon and now Rosenak's purposes, the Protestant point of view is one that accepts the privatization of religion in the context of post-Enlightenment state politics, while the Catholic view seeks to imbue the entire political arena with sacred significance. Roughly speaking, the distinction

---

26. Ernst (Akiva) Simon, "Are We Israelis Still Jews?" *Commentary* (April 1953). See Rosenak, *Cracks*, 28–40 and "Modernity and Religion: New Explorations in the Light of the Union of Opposites," in *Rabbinic Theology and Jewish Intellectual History* (2013), 133–61.

parallels the terms we have been using. The Protestant point of view is related to Survival and System in its post-Enlightenment context,[27]while Catholic perspective corresponds to the politics of Segulah.[28] In Rosenak's analysis, the academic scholarship dedicated to Rabbi Kook operates on Protestant assumptions and is therefore unable to accept the rationale-defying principles of immanent sanctity and the unity of opposites. The result is that Rabbi Kook is approved of when one side of his paradoxical thought complies with Protestant or humanistic ethics. These evaluations dictate the conditions for the academic reading of his thought and distort the fullness of what the unity of opposites seeks to reveal. The upshot of this is that Protestant scholarship gives Rabbi Kook credit for his openness to secular Zionism and is baffled by the disturbingly tenacious presence of his "darker" side, which, in their view, is always to his detriment.

Among Rabbi Kook's more Catholic disciples, the difficulty of maintaining a durable balance of opposites in practice distorts the language of Segulah too. The outcome is the more fanatical form of religious Zionism that many associated with Rabbi Kook's son Rabbi Tzvi Yehuda Kook. Rosenak defies the common wisdom in the field that sees Rabbi Tzvi Yehuda as an unworthy disciple of his father's teaching. Rosenak insists that the blueprint of Rabbi Kook's thought is successfully passed on, through the instruction of his son, to the next generation of religious Zionist rabbis who after 1967 spearheaded the settlement of Greater Israel with messianic pathos.[29] Rosenak does not deny that there is indeed distortion, but its cause is not the deliberate betrayal of the father by the son. Distortion occurs when the values that Protestant humanism champions well are sacrificed to a form of Catholicism that must make historical decisions in the arena of political action. The burden of equilibrium that the unity of opposites demands is hard to maintain when choosing a definitive course of action. In a full and detailed study, Rosenak measures the religious Zionist responses to the crucial events that have shaped Israel's destiny (from the Six-Day War in 1967 to the disengagement

---

27. This is meant in the sense that the strategy of Survival and System includes both the integration of humanism and Judaism and the acquiescence of the public sphere to secular discourse.

28. Rosenak, *Cracks*, 28–40.

29. Ibid.

from Gaza in 2005), showing how the theoretical structure of the unity of opposites continues to permeate religious Zionist thought but fails the test of politicization. The result is that the internal dynamics of Israeli politics are conflicted, because, in practice, the implementation of the unity of opposites is distorted by those who consistently advance the hard-line and uncompromising commitments of "Catholicism" in a way that only ever comes across as hard-line nationalist ethnocentrism.

Again, at this preparatory stage, the point here is not so much the discussion of Rabbi Kook's thought as the tragedy of its distortion by "Protestant" and "Catholic" Jews alike. As with Heschel, Rabbi Kook is correctly understood by his disciples. But his politics of Segulah are unable to emerge reasonably within the context of a Western-minded secular state. On the other hand, without the preservation of the values that humanism serves well, religious Zionism appears more "fundamentalist" than it actually is. Sometimes this appearance confuses and misleads its own adherents, driving them to take positions that, in the context of Survival and System, cannot be resolved with reason. Just as often, religious Zionists face moralist accusations from the outside that are entirely unfounded or unfair. In order to resolve the incommensurability that this situation illustrates, the analytical experience of Exile and Destruction must precede any attempt at rehabilitating the political language, inner structure, and practical paradigm of Segulah.

In the long, down-spiraling analysis that follows we shall try to create an experience of the collapse or falling away of the political structures of Survival and System so that, after disentangling Jewish conceptions of identity from their Western counterparts, the language of Segulah might emerge as both reasonable and practical. If this can be achieved successfully and meaningfully, what will remain is the attempt to salvage and restore the notion that Judaism is neither a religion nor a people but a reasonable and viable spiritual-political project. It is a spiritual-political project focused on Jews but with the truly universal purpose of Tikkun Olam.

CHAPTER 2

Sparks of Segulah

Cracks in the Politics of Survival and System

Since its inception, the State of Israel has justified its existence in terms of Survival and System. There is no doubt that the biblical heritage of the Jewish people and the ancient connection to the land have played an important role in the formation of Israeli identity. These are also highlighted in the State of Israel's Declaration of Independence.[1] From the perspective of Survival and System, the viability of the State of Israel in the world depends on its being both Jewish and secularly democratic. The image of Israel as the only democracy in the Middle East has served its foreign policy well and has been the foundation for its alliance with the United States. This is an alliance that has played a crucial role in Israel's strategy for survival and which has also depended since the 1990s on Israel's commitment to the establishment of a Palestinian state. In this context, Zionism must articulate (and traditionally has articulated) its legitimacy by running concepts such as the ingathering of the exiles and the biblical connection of the Jewish people to the land of Israel

---

1. The Declaration of the Establishment of the State of Israel begins with the statement: "The Land of Israel was the birthplace of the Jewish people. Here their spiritual, religious and political identity was shaped." But the declaration goes on to frame the calamity of the destruction of this ancient republic and the beginning of a two-thousand-year-exile in terms that are then echoed in the declaration's attitude to the Holocaust: "After being forcibly exiled from their land, the people kept faith with it throughout their dispersion.... the catastrophe that recently befell the Jewish people – the massacre of millions of Jews in Europe – was another clear demonstration of the urgency of solving the problem of its homelessness by reestablishing in Eretz Israel the Jewish state..." The parity between these calamities is an example of how the problem that the State of Israel's establishment comes to address is understood in terms of Survival and its solution in terms of System.

(both mentioned in the Declaration of Independence) on the "operating system" of secular humanist politics. Outside of Israel, the axiomatic principles of social and communal life that predicate political or communal legitimacy on the principles of post-Enlightenment humanism also play a crucial role in delineating the boundaries of what it is plausible to say and do to protect Jewish interests and institutions.

As we mentioned in the previous chapter, the self-evident nature of the principles of humanist politics is experiencing a time of crisis in the Western world. This is perhaps an opportune moment to look back at how some of the most axiomatic ideas of Survival and System have already been called into question in Western philosophy and scholarship. It is not our purpose in this chapter to offer an exhaustive survey of this phenomenon, but rather to look closely at two examples that we shall refer to as Sparks of Segulah. The "sparks" that we will consider concern: (1) rethinking the exclusion of God from Western political thought and (2) the irony of humanism after Nazism.

Rethinking the Exclusion of God from Politics – The First Spark

From the perspective of Segulah, the rehabilitation of God's role in politics is an urgent concern. Our first spark is essentially an example of how the possibility of God's presence in politics is taking new forms. We will present what we mean by this by closely reading one article that belongs to the intellectual trend known as Radical Orthodoxy. Radical Orthodoxy is a movement in Christian scholarship that has offered revisionist historical accounts of how the exclusion of God from politics was accomplished and of how it came to be inextricably associated with the definition of both *intra-* and *inter-*national peace. The example that we have chosen is William T. Cavanaugh's essay "The Wars of Religion and the Rise of the Nation-State."[2] In this essay Cavanaugh provides a historical account of how and why the exclusion of God from politics was so central to the soteriology of the Enlightenment and suggests a way of reversing the trend.

Cavanaugh's essay begins with a report of a document issued in 1993 by the Parliament of the World's Religions in Chicago. The statement condemned

---

2. Cavanaugh, "Fire Strong Enough ," 314–37.

acts of violence committed in the name of religion and "called for the exclusion of religion which is used to legitimize violent and bloody conflicts."[3] The statement goes on to say that "the members of the parliament are 'disgusted' by the aggression, fanaticism, hate and xenophobia that leaders and members of religions incite."[4] Cavanaugh observes sardonically that, while violence perpetrated in the name of religion is condemned, state violence remains beyond censure. Indeed, "[the statement] stops well short of calling religious people out of the armies of the world." The obvious conclusion drawn from this is that "only killing in the name of religion is damned; bloodshed on behalf of the state is subject to no such scorn."[5] Thus, Cavanaugh's point of departure is to expose how a constructed ethical distinction between the use of violence in the name of the secular state and its use in the name of faith is the key to the exclusion of God from politics on disingenuous ethical grounds.

Cavanaugh traces two connected processes. First, the construction of a liberal narrative in which "liberalism…was born out of the cruelties of the religious civil wars, which forever rendered the claims of Christian charity a rebuke to all religious institutions and parties."[6] This gave rise to the insistence that religion is a private concern; "if the faith were to survive at all, it would do so privately."[7] Second, the privatization of religion allowed for the secular state to emerge as the vehicle for world peace.

Beginning with the first process, Cavanaugh shows how the historical emergence of liberal religion was crucial to preserving the modern secular state's monopoly on ethical violence. The maintenance of this monopoly required religion to be rational and confined. Between the fifteenth and eighteenth centuries, "Religion" evolves as "a set of beliefs which is defined as personal conviction and which can exist separately from one's public loyalty to the State."[8] In 1474, in a work entitled *De Christinia Religione,* Marcilio

---

3.   Ibid., 314.

4.   Ibid.

5.   Ibid.

6.   Judith Shklar, *Ordinary Vices* (Cambridge, MA: Harvard University Press, 1984), 5 and Cavanaugh, "Fire Strong Enough," 315 and note 4.

7.   Ibid.

8.   Cavanaugh, "Fire Strong Enough," 320.

Ficino presents religion "as a universal human impulse common to all."[9] Cavanaugh argues that through universalization, religion is humanized and thus "interiorized and removed from its particular ecclesial context."[10] By the sixteenth century, Guillaume Pastel had articulated an argument in favor of religious liberty "based on the construal of Christianity as a set of demonstrable moral truths, rather than theological claims and practices which take a particular social form called the Church."[11] In this form, religion is made recognizable to the universalist claims of humanism and prevented from interfering with them. Following on Jean Bodin's advocacy of liberal religion, Cavanaugh shows that "religion for Bodin is a generic concept; he states directly that he is not concerned with which religion is best. The people should be free in conscience to choose whichever religion they desire. What is important," Cavanaugh insists, "is that once a form of religion has been embraced by a people, the sovereign must forbid any public dispute over religious matters to break out and thereby threaten his authority."[12]

Cavanaugh goes on to show how, in the crucially influential political projects of both Hobbes and Kant, redefining the place of religion in the state is fundamentally connected to peace. For Hobbes, "without universal obedience to but one sovereign, civil war between temporal and spiritual powers is tragically inevitable." Cavanaugh suggests that the inevitability of this conflict lies in Hobbes's "ontology of violence.... The soteriology of the state as peacemaker demands that its sovereign authority be absolutely alone and without rival."[13] Similarly, Kant's vision of a "Perpetual Peace" rests upon the universalization of humanist rationalism and on the assertion that peace is best served politically by the secular republic. In Cavanaugh's words, Kant's idea of the modern republic "is the agent for bringing about perpetual peace because it will allow people to transcend their historical particularities, e.g., Lutheran vs. Catholic, and respect one another on the basis of their common rationality."[14]

---

9. Ibid., 321 and note 33.
10. Ibid., 321.
11. Ibid.
12. Ibid., 322.
13. Ibid., 323.
14. Ibid., 326.

The flaw in Kant's identification of the state as guarantor of freedom and peace is that human rationalism is neither universal nor uniform. The result, as Cavanaugh correctly points out, is that the state itself becomes a primary or particularistic value. If the state is an end in itself that claims to be an absolute value, it cannot tolerate any violence or rebellion directed against it. The state therefore takes the form of an ultimate good which preserves for itself the exclusive right to "defend its prerogatives coercively."[15] This is why the state, far from coming on the scene as a peacekeeper, is actually the ultimate ideologue of state-controlled violence. When rebellion comes from within or a threat looms from without, the state enjoys an unprecedented entitlement to defend itself against dissenting citizens from within and enemy states from without. The irony of war, of course, is that the state reserves the right even to "send its own citizens out to kill and die in exchange for protection from violence both internal and external to the state's borders."[16] In other words, it is the myth of the state as peacemaker that gives it "unlimited access to our bodies and possessions to fuel its war-making."[17]

So, in Cavanaugh's analysis, the state is the ultimate mechanism of war and violence which, through the privatization of religion, has accorded itself exclusive moral and ethical entitlement to the use of destructive force. This is a radical reversal of the common wisdom that dominates politics and international relations in most of the Western world today. In Cavanaugh's words,

> Liberal theorists such as Rawls, Shklar, and Stout would have us believe that the state stepped in like a scolding schoolteacher on the playground of doctrinal dispute to put fanatical religionists in their proper place. Self-righteous clucking about the dangers of public faith...ignores the fact that transfer of ultimate loyalty to the nation-state has only increased the scope of modern warfare.[18]

---

15. Ibid.
16. Ibid.
17. Ibid.
18. Ibid., 325.

Ultimately, Cavanaugh is arguing that we should no longer see the "wars of religion" as the events which necessitated the birth of the modern state. Rather, "they were in fact themselves the birth pangs of the State." His point is that the state was never a messenger of peace, because it was crafted in the crucible of war. Moreover, in modern politics, war is the bloody ritual that, ex post facto, provides the moral justification for the existence of the state. It is not the problem that state intervention finally came to alleviate. When you look at the state from this angle, what the privatization of religion allows for is "revulsion to killing in the name of religion [in order] to legitimize the transfer of ultimate loyalty to the modern State."[19] Rather than having constructed the apparatus that would bring peace to the world, as the modern liberal myth would have it, Cavanaugh insists that the political institutions of the Enlightenment invented the most destructive myth the world has ever known: the idea that peace depends upon the exclusion of God from politics on ethical grounds.

Thus far, Cavanaugh's argument is of crucial importance to our project. However, he does not stop here. The continuation of his discussion is no less important but for a very different reason. The final stage of his essay exemplifies our claim that intellectually rigorous attempts to revise humanist politics tend to be strong on their deconstructive side and much weaker when it comes to proposing political alternatives. When attempting to imagine the rehabilitation of religion in politics, Cavanaugh is less imaginative and less successful than he is as a historical deconstructor of the secular state. There genuinely is no reason to be negative about this, since his effort is extraordinarily brave. But we must also appreciate that his failed attempt here underlines the importance of the claim that the exclusion of God from the public sphere cannot be justified in the name of peace.

In the final section of his essay, Cavanaugh tries to imagine how religion might return to redeem the state of its inherent violence. He cites Richard John Neuhaus, who in *The Naked Public Square* makes the case for the public reentry of religion into the political sphere. Neuhaus draws on Clifford Geertz to argue that religion is the ground or depth level of culture and must

---

19. Ibid., 314.

therefore be present in building a common political consensus.[20] Cavanaugh's final suggestion seeks a place for religion in building this consensus. But, here too, as in the rest of his historical argument, his thrust is primarily deconstructive. The need to break down an existing consensus in search of a new one is enough, in his mind, to make room for the re-emergence of religion in public. However, Cavanaugh's vision cannot be seen in any way as an attempt to reconstruct the modern state as a political cathedral. He offers no drastically new paradigm. Cavanaugh proposes that we imagine a brotherhood of Christian disciples dedicated to Christ's doctrines of peace and love and ready to bring these into the public sphere in a civil space that religion may occupy. This idea is a lot like Charles Taylor's suggestion that a sense of what is beyond life might play a role in dampening the overstated pretenses of extremist humanists who imagine that they have it all figured out.[21]In both cases what is being offered is a deconstructive politics that draws upon religion to limit the confidence of secular government without sacrificing its accomplishments. Cavanaugh's strategy for doing this is to create a middle space – a third realm between the private and the public – where religion can meaningfully reside.

The idea that religion can enter the public sphere in a deconstructive role is modeled on a common portrayal of the biblical relationship between the prophet and the king. In this model, the role of religion is basically to "speak truth to power." However, even though religion is much more visible in this model, all the power remains in the same place. In other words, what follows Cavanaugh's brilliant analysis of the secular state is yet another mechanism that seeks to perpetuate the secular state's hold on political power by placating one of its most threatening rivals from within. The reasons for this conservatism are clear. One cannot but fear the new cycles of enmity that the seizure of power by religion would spark. Who could blame the deposed secularists for fighting back when the power they once enjoyed is usurped?

---

20. Ibid., 327 and note 60.

21. Charles Taylor, "A Catholic Modernity?" in *A Catholic Modernity? Charles Taylor's Marianist Award Lecture with Responses by William Shea, Rosemary Lulling Haughton, George Marsden, and John Bethke Elshtain* (Oxford University Press, 1990). See also our discussion of this theme in Alick Isaacs, *A Prophetic Peace: Judaism, Religion, and Politics* (Indiana University Press, 2011), 10–12.

It seems so much better to create a third realm neatly tucked in between the private and the public, than to run the risk of simply perpetuating cycles of revolution and counterrevolution that must be kept at bay.

Cavanaugh is therefore paradigmatically critical of the state, but too fearful of the imaginable alternatives to it to suggest a true reversal of the process his essay most vehemently condemns. Without a full-blown theory of religious politics guiding him, Cavanaugh's critique of the secular state does nothing to generate an alternative that he is prepared to commit to. The essay emerges as a corrective to an existing paradigm rather than a turn toward something entirely different. This is not his fault. It is endemic to the ongoing stalemate in Western politics that has struggled with conflicting notions of religion and state since the earliest origins of Christian political history in Byzantine Europe. This is why, despite all the distance covered in this essay, at the end we are catapulted back – as if we were tied by an elastic leash to our point of departure – to a position that still sees the exclusion of God from politics as ethically indispensable.

It is here that the definitive importance of our critique emerges. General guilt for the mutation of humanism into Nazism, if it can genuinely be established, has the power to provide sufficient grounds for a process of destruction that allows religion to emerge with more in its hands than the rather lame claim that it is no less trustworthy than anything else. By balking at the notion that humanist politics truly falls significantly short of the promise that religion offers, Cavanaugh reveals the crucial hold of faith in post-Enlightenment humanism on Western political thinking. Had he considered humanism more responsible for Nazism, his perpetuation of the myth that even the partial exclusion of God from politics is ethically indispensable would have meant taking a risk that no one of right mind can afford to take. Since this partial exclusion is indeed an organic part of the political history of Christian Europe, it is hard to imagine an escape route from it emerging from anything other than a post-Holocaust Jewish perspective. This assertion, if it becomes plausible, is the first spark of Segulah.

The Irony of Humanism after Nazism – The Second Spark

After Nazism, humanism continues to dominate the entire project of Jewish life in the West. Preparing for a paradigm shift from the perspective of Segulah therefore requires us to seek out the possibility of questioning the plausibility of post-Enlightenment humanism after the Holocaust.

Before beginning the explication of this extremely complex and delicate issue, it should be clear that our purpose is not to blame Christianity, humanism, or liberalism for the Holocaust. The point is also not to blur the differences between the progressive liberal democracies of the West today and Nazi Germany.[22] Neither should we confuse the issue by suggesting that the Allied forces, that joined together to resist Nazism, were no different from the Nazis they defeated. While Hannah Arendt notably made this argument about Stalinist Russia in her monumental *Origins of Totalitarianism*, she correctly avoids even the remotest suggestion that her analysis applies to either the United States, the United Kingdom, Australia, New Zealand, Canada, or others.[23]

To move closer to an understanding of what we are referring to as a second spark of Segulah, we must for the time being direct our gaze away from Nazism itself. Our focus is on the mechanism that exonerates humanism from a broader sense of guilt for the Holocaust. The facts are that Jews in humanist societies today believe (with ample justification supported by the many virtues of democratic politics) that they enjoy unprecedented power and prosperity and, moreover, that the State of Israel's redeeming quality is its affiliation to and alignment with the humanist principles of the West. Similarly, from this viewpoint, the greatest flaws in Israel are to be found in those areas in which its regime does not keep up with the moral standards

---

22. That said, it is pertinent to consider modern criticism of Winston Churchill and his racism. After the killing of George Floyd by a police officer in Minnesota on May 29, 2020, the resultant protests that targeted Confederate monuments in the United States provoked similar assaults on monuments and statues in the United Kingdom. The targets in the UK were monuments that commemorated the contributions of British Imperial and Colonial heroes, many of whom were slave owners. This list included the famous statue of Winston Churchill opposite the British Parliament building in Westminster. In a wave of widespread criticism, Churchill's legacy faced accusations of racism, white supremacy, and even mass murder. While this position is far more extreme than ours, it underlines how the cracks in the veneer of liberal humanism's legacy are emerging to the surface of public debate and an ironic consciousness about humanism after Nazism is beginning to take hold.

23. More to the point, Arendt ends up looking toward America as the ultimate alternative. See Arendt, *Origins of Totalitarianism* and our comments in chapter 1 above.

set by the International Red Cross, Amnesty International, Human Rights Watch, the UN, the US, the EU, and others. Despite the hold that the point of view espoused by these powerful organizations has over us, if a broader sense of accountability for Nazism were assigned to the political-philosophical principles on which they all operate, attempts at rehabilitating Jewry after the Holocaust on their terms (i.e., on the terms of Survival and System) would seem far more problematic and dubious than they otherwise do.

The hold that keeps world Jewry on the trajectory determined after the Enlightenment is maintained by saturating in a taboo of extremism the very suggestion that humanism is stained with Nazism's guilt. Without this taboo, we would experience our contemporary situation very differently. We might only look on with shock and bewilderment at the perpetuation of political humanism after its presumed expiration date on May 5, 1945. But this is not easily done. Given all the sacrifices made by millions to defeat Hitler, is this taboo not justified? Why and how should it be broken?

If we look at the way this taboo works from the perspective of Segulah, we see the importance of asking a question that the politics of Survival and System dare not ask: How is humanism absolved of so much of the blame? The truthful answer to this question, an answer that does not betray the millions who fought for the Allied forces in World War II, is that neither the Holocaust nor the rise of Nazism was humanism's fault. For the crimes of the Holocaust we must blame the likes of Hitler, Himmler, and Goebbels. But after recognizing that, and honoring it, we are now obliged to notice how the virtue of this truthful answer also conceals the locus of humanism's wider guilt. By way of an analogy, we might say that humanism need not share any more of the blame for Nazism than an oncologist for cancer. However, the fact that the doctor is not to blame for the disease should not confuse us when he stands accused of administering an inappropriate cure. In this case, we might hold the doctor fully responsible for misdiagnosing the patient or for believing in a presumed cure which turned out to have devastating side effects. This formulation explains much more clearly why humanism should not be exonerated from the full burden of its guilt for what went wrong in Nazi Germany.

Breaking the hold of the Enlightenment on the modern world was perhaps the most dramatic philosophical project of the twentieth century. The shift that took place particularly in France is generally associated with linguistic-turn philosophy, deconstruction, and post-modernity.[24] We shall return to discuss these and their meaning from the perspective of Segulah in detail in the next section of this book. But first we shall focus our attention on a more pristine or direct Jewish reaction to the Holocaust that few would associate with postmodernism. This specifically Jewish and directly post-Holocaust phenomenon is a turn of tide with reference to the Enlightenment that grew more directly and organically from the stark realization of the Holocaust's meaning in the personal lives of some of its indirect victims.[25] One strikingly eloquent example of this is George Steiner's masterful but controversial little volume, *In Bluebeard's Castle: Some Notes towards the Redefinition of Culture.*[26]

Bluebeard is tellingly subtitled to echo T. S. Eliot's *Notes towards the Definition of Culture.*[27] At the outset of this extended book-size essay, Steiner asks how it was possible for Eliot, writing in 1948, to consider a redefinition of culture without paying detailed attention to the Holocaust. This is the question of the book, and in many ways, it is the question of an era. How could humanist culture continue defining and redefining itself without experiencing the Holocaust as the watershed event that puts an end to its history? The same question appears in different formulations. Steiner asks how was it possible "for the libraries, museums, theatres, universities and research centers, in and through which the transmission of the humanities and of the sciences mainly takes place, to prosper next to the concentration camps?"[28] Again he asks how are we to understand "men such as Hans Frank, who administered the final solution in Eastern Europe, but at the same time

---

24. For a brilliant analysis of the connection between the linguistic turn in Western philosophy, disarmament, and peace, see Jeffery Perl's editorial preface to Jeffrey Perl, ed., *Peace and Mind: Civilian Scholarship from Common Knowledge* (Davies Group Publishers, 2011), vii–xxviii.

25. See chapter 1, notes 14 and 15.

26. Steiner, *In Bluebeard's Castle.*

27. T. S. Eliot, *Notes Towards a Definition of Culture* (Faber and Faber, 1948) and Steiner, *Bluebeard*, 3.

28. Steiner, *Bluebeard*, 77 This quotation from Steiner has been slightly altered to fit our text. His interrogative statements have been converted into a question form but the author's intentions have not been distorted.

were connoisseurs and in some instances performers of Bach and Mozart?"[29] He continues, "We know of personnel in the bureaucracy of the torturers and of the ovens who cultivated knowledge of Goethe, a love of Rilke. The facile evasion: 'such men did not understand the poems they read or the music they knew and seemed to play so well' will not do. There is simply no evidence that they were more obtuse than anyone else to the humane genius, to the enacted moral energies of great literature and art."[30] This is the question that the Holocaust forces us to ask of liberal humanism. Steiner is urging us to understand that it is the definitive question of a generation.

In the British academia of the 1960s and 1970s, Steiner had to make a case that the Holocaust was a question at all for British culture. His intuitive reaction to Eliot's omission is disbelief. But Eliot was no exception to the rule. The response of most British intellectuals to Steiner was tellingly abrasive. In her excellent intellectual biography, Catherine D. Chatterley admits that there were many reasons that Steiner was not liked in England. His arrogant, argumentative, and judgmental style did not go down well in elite British circles. Many thought he was superficial and journalistic. He was clearly a foreigner and an outsider. As a polyglot, his tendency to consider the English literary tradition within a broader European perspective grated against Anglophonic isolationist leanings and perhaps made some Oxbridge dons feel uncomfortable with the difficulties they had learning foreign languages. His undervaluing of British literary icons did little to enhance his popularity, and his distaste for Zionism hardly endeared him to Anglo-Jewish circles. Despite all this, Chatterley's point is that the general irritation with Steiner ran deeper. For the British who paid such heavy prices fighting the war against Nazism, the accusation of culpability for its crimes against humanity was infuriatingly insufferable.

Chatterley's argument illustrates powerfully the hold of post-Enlightenment (rather than post-Holocaust) humanism over postwar England. In her words, "His early study of the Holocaust, placed at the center of his study of Western culture, further compounded Steiner's isolation from English

---

29. Ibid.
30. Ibid., 77–78.

colleagues who did not share his interest in the subject."[31] But the problem was more than a lack of interest. It involved the very powerful impulse of denial. Chatterley cites Anne Samson, whose biography of F. R. Leavis broadly traces Leavis's impact on the academic study of English literature in postwar England. Samson writes,

> The wartime experiences of many had been cataclysmic and had roused in them a spirit of seriousness and idealism; a need to find point and value in human life and to work actively for a better society. This search, combined with long-held notions about the value of English Studies, invested many of the students…with an almost religious belief in its value as a civilizing, humanizing force outside the confines of the academy.[32]

A wholehearted faith in the humanizing tendencies of English literature defined what was good about the Allied side of the conflict and distinguished it from the barbarianism of the Nazis. Like the town elders in Deuteronomy, chapter 21, the leaders of post-Holocaust British culture protested their innocence, saying, "Our hands did not spill this blood." Indeed, while biblical law is inclined to believe the townspeople, it still holds them accountable. Steiner's exasperation with the English literature crowd at Cambridge has something of this spirit in it when he says, "Unlike Dr. Leavis, I find myself unable to assert confidently that the humanities humanize."[33]

Steiner's interrogation of humanism thrust a spear into the bleeding heart of British postwar rehabilitation, and it was insufferable to British ears. In Chatterley's words, Steiner "works hard to convince [his] English colleagues that they too, as members of Western civilization, must wrestle with the meaning of the Holocaust in their evaluation of the function of literature in the humanities." But this was too presumptuous for British tastes and Steiner was understood as either "bizarre or subversive."[34]

---

31. Catherine D. Chatterley, *Disenchantment: George Steiner and the Meaning of Western Civilization after Auschwitz* (Syracuse University Press, 2011), 44.

32. Ibid., 52.

33. Ibid., 54.

34. Ibid., 53.

For Steiner, as for others in his generation of Central European Jewish émigré intellectuals, his question comes from the direct experience of personal crisis. People who once enjoyed the high culture of European civilization and excelled in its practices, who grew up believing that the humanities humanize, were now bewildered by the discovery that they had been wrong. What is striking about these émigrés is how gracious so many of them are about it. One can feel the desire to save the world from itself coursing through the veins of Arendt in her *Origins of Totalitarianism*. The same spirit yielded Ernst Cassirer's *Myth of the State*. Leo Strauss's entire oeuvre – represented by his symbolic distinction between the formative political impacts of Athens and Jerusalem – is of the same heart. Max Horkheimer and Theodor Adorno's *Dialectic of Enlightenment: Philosophical Fragments*[35] is perhaps the most learned and eloquent expression of this view. In all these cases, the search for a way forward is so much more powerful than what might quite understandably have poured out as a venomous desire for revenge. Their combination of rigorous honesty and gentle soteriological sensibility is a spark of Segulah, a step on a path to Tikkun Olam that we must sniff out and follow.

Bluebeard begins with a portrayal of the great ennui, the deep feeling of boredom that Steiner sees as the prelude to self-destructive calamity.[36] In the gardens of England and Western Europe between the 1820s and 1915, an unprecedented era of prosperity ushered in by the Enlightenment yielded an age of "a high and gaining literacy. The rule of law; a doubtless imperfect yet actively spreading use of representative forms of government.... The achievement, occasionally marred but steadily pursued, of peaceful coexistence between nation-states."[37] Boredom is the poison secreted into the blood of this period. "No string of quotations, no statistics, can recapture for us what must have been the inner excitement…unleashed by the events of 1789 and sustained…until 1815." In this period, "the pace of felt time" palpably accelerated. The excitement generated a rhythm that pulsed through literature and music. Human experience became denser, less patient with history as heightened expectations of progress, confused and intertwined

---

35. See chapter 1, note 14 above.

36. Steiner, *Bluebeard*, "The Great Ennui," 1–25.

37. Ibid., 9.

with personal ambitions, gradually mutated into a spirit of self-destruction. Typically, Steiner traces these phenomena with broad sweeping brushstrokes flitting between Beethoven's tempi, Hegel's phenomenology, and sexual metaphors that surface in Wordsworth and Keats. The forces and energies that created progress and realized the dream of tranquil prosperity produced a quickening of time and a new, revolutionary, vehement sense of anticipation that spread throughout Europe. What followed was a long spell of stasis and ennui, a drop in tension, a collapse of revolutionary hopes into a stable, sluggishly advancing civilization that sank – only ever uneasily - into the presumed security of its home-manufactured cradle of assurance. Steiner portrays the expansion of industrialism and grand-scale urbanization that brought with them yet another layer of self-contradictory complexity. The culture of Enlightenment, which sought progress and advancement, used for its tools the great equalizers of "categorization" and "rational analysis," only to discover that they too were the apparatus of domination and conquest. The dramatic energies and impulses that planted the garden of rational tranquility that Kant crowned sovereign of world peace were uneasy in their own pastures. The engines of progress were the same as the darker forces of self-destruction. The era became itchy and uncomfortable with this luxury and developed a fascination with the idea of global conflict.

For Steiner, this process is the end of culture. From here on, the world has struggled with the abandonment of culture and must learn, in post-culture, to do without it. The humanities lose their potency, language is emptied of all nuance, and science sucks in the best minds and creative talents. One might have expected Steiner to hold a more optimistic view of post-culture or perhaps, contrarily, to have suggested that the new era simply taught us that the history of culture had been an illusion all along. But this is not his view. His position here is remarkable and of crucial importance.

Steiner draws on T. S. Eliot. Like Eliot, Steiner thinks of culture itself as inextricably tied to sanctity. In his book-length essay on "Tolstoy and Dostoevsky," Steiner ties both ethics and aesthetics to the sacred demands of Western civilization.[38] In Chatterley's words, he shows there that "the rejec-

---

38. George Steiner, *Tolstoy or Dostoyevsky: An Essay in the Old Criticism* (Yale University Press, 1959).

tion of religious belief and the process of secularization in Western culture…
do not result in our liberation from violence and superstition as promised by
the philosophies of the Enlightenment. Instead, the absence of formal religion creates a feeling of emptiness in the lives of people, a void of meaning
and purpose, which they attempt to fill with secular imitations."[39] It is this
void that generates what Steiner refers to as "Nostalgia for the Absolute" that
pours out in mass adherence to total systems of thought that vary in range
and scope from Marxism to Freudian psychoanalysis and Levi-Straussian
anthropology. These movements, along with many others that built upon
the methods and truth claims of post-Enlightenment secular science, make
demands on their adherents that are "profoundly religious in strategy and
effect."[40] They represent what Steiner sees as a deep-seated nostalgia for a
broad mythology that answers our need to explain the world and our place
within it.

Enlightenment did not do away with this mythology. Horkheimer and
Adorno's central thesis is that the mythology of the absolute is already embedded within the heart of Enlightenment, and Enlightenment therefore "reverts
to mythology." As such, in their words, "Enlightenment is totalitarian."[41] It
is totally powerless to defend against its own deepest destructive passions.
The Second World War is therefore not a struggle of good and evil. It is complicit collaboration in a ritual of self-destruction. The British and American
involvement in the war answers a powerful post-Enlightenment urge to rally
round and to be drawn in.

Nazism for Steiner is an organic expression of the Enlightenment's project
to divorce itself, through self-destruction, from religion. In what is perhaps
the most striking section of *Bluebeard,* he describes Auschwitz and Treblinka
as Enlightenment's most potent weapon in this struggle. The divorce from
religion cannot be complete without the demystification of hell. Unable to
break free of the shackles of an image that has regulated Christian ethics for
centuries, post-Christian culture learned to make hell *immanent,* "to build

---

39. Chatterley, *Disenchantment,* 72.

40. Chatterley, *Disenchantment,* 79 and note 133 there.

41. Max Horkheimer and Theodor Adorno, *Dialectic of Enlightenment: Philosophical Fragments,* English Translation. (Stanford University Press, 1987), 4.

it and run it on earth…a few miles from Goethe's Weimar."[42] By building "Hell above ground, we have passed out of the major order and symmetries of Western civilization."[43]

Steiner is disturbed by Eliot's failure to address the Holocaust directly. But he is persuaded by the claim that the collapse of culture must be set in the framework of the psychology of religion. This framework accounts for the construction of Hell above ground and provides the deeper meaning of Nazism's obsessive focus on the destruction of Jewry. Without it, one cannot account for the "active indifference – active because collaboratively unknowing – of the vast majority of the European population."[44] The replacement of religion is also crucial to understanding "the deliberate decision of the National Socialist regime, even in the final stages of economic warfare, to liquidate the Jews rather than exploit them." Steiner's explanation for these baffling choices against self-interest and survival is found in what he calls "the blackmail of transcendence." This term denotes and beguiles the unrelenting demands of morality the Jews impose upon humanity.

As Chatterley describes it, "According to Steiner, the Jewish people are responsible for creating three separate systems of human perfectibility by which they are perceived to blackmail humanity: Mosaic monotheism, Christianity, and Marxism…. Jewish ethical demands, which flow from these three systems, are beyond the grasp of humanity and the psychic stress produced by this failure eventually leads to resentment and hatred for the people responsible for it." In *Bluebeard*, Steiner writes, "By killing the Jews, Western culture would eradicate those who had 'invented' God, who had…been the declarers of his unbearable absence…. to become man, man must make himself new, and in so doing stifle the elemental desires, weaknesses and claims of the ego."[45]

Steiner's point here goes to the heart of the challenge that is essential to the perspective of Segulah: This is to face the realization that the power of ego cannot be relied upon to attain the desires of the soul. Steiner's explanation of

---

42. Steiner, *Bluebeard*, 55–56.

43. Ibid., 56.

44. Ibid., 35.

45. Ibid., 41.

antisemitism in this context is most telling. He says, "We hate most those who hold out to us a goal, an ideal, a visionary promise which, even though we have stretched our muscles to the utmost, we cannot reach, which slips again and again just out of range of our racked fingers." From his point of view, this is a psychological truism. Deep loathing builds up against those who shame us. The results are primordial and murderous. But from the perspective of Segulah, the crucial point here is slightly different. The denial of the Jew whose presence reminds us of the relentless demands of Segulah erupts when we recognize how helpless we are to face a higher vision of morality on our own – unassisted by an appropriate point of contact with God. We fail time and again and become resentful but are still unable to reject the higher moral calling of man "because," as Steiner himself agrees, "we fully acknowledge its supreme value."[46]

With no culpability for the genocide itself, Allied compliance in the war provided the cover for Hitler to carry it out. With no guilt for the building of Auschwitz, the blackmail of transcendence poisoned the blood of Europe, yielding both the radical and the milder forms of antisemitism. With no part in the systematic killing of millions, humanism's desire to break free of religion left humankind to quarry the vast recesses of inner ego and to discover in its empty heart technologies that gave it the power of God and dominion over nature. Steiner finishes *Bluebeard* with the shocking idea that Enlightenment has given humankind the capacity to discover truths about the world that it cannot handle. Humankind faces a crisis of confidence, knowing that it can indeed build both heaven and hell on earth. Worse still, after the Holocaust, it now realizes that, when left to its own devices, human power is not equal to the task of telling the two apart.

Steiner provoked his English audiences by telling them that Nazism was a phenomenon of Western culture that implicated them. This was a spark of Segulah that could not be borne. It contradicted the deepest humanist fantasies and impulses. It seemed to throw out the baby with the bathwater, insisting against the grain of popular will that if hell had been made imma-nent by the Nazis, the human project of building a democratic liberal heaven

---

46. Ibid., 45.

was doomed. If the road to hell is paved with good intentions, then it follows that the human desire for good is the accomplice that keeps evil close at hand.

From the perspective of Segulah, we can begin to see here that the belief in humanism is a mechanism of denial. This denial takes hold of the humanistic West, placing unreasonable constraints on its moral vision. It takes hold of post-Enlightenment privatized religion – which willingly complies with the tyranny of rationalism – and forces religion's deepest intuitions about its role in public politics underground. Cloistered in communal gatherings, performing rituals of prayer and limited if kindly acts of charity, religion remains imprisoned in apologetically first-person subjective semantic fields. It dares not venture beyond the confines of personal belief. From inside these constraints, the public professing of faith dare not threaten the ubiquitous "objectivity" of humanist ego, and the politics of Tikkun Olam dare not extend its vision beyond the consensual boundaries of ritual, charity, and social action.

Returning to Arendt, our point is perhaps connected with her famous idea that even the most glaring forms of evil are banal.[47] In her coverage of the Eichmann trial, Arendt observes that evil is all too recognizable in and to humanity. It coexists indiscriminately with acts of kindness and gentility and is quite natural to the humane. The general significance of this observation seems to apply far beyond the context in which it was originally uttered. More than the mere normality of Adolf Eichmann's appearance sitting in a glass box while on trial in Jerusalem, more than even the chilling normality of his polite daily routine as an SS officer following orders and organizing train timetables, the banality of evil bespeaks the normality of his humanity.

The familiarity of Eichmann's humanity stands in stark contrast to the superfluously monstrous portrayals of villains in art, theater, literature, and cinema. The satanic monstrosities of Western art were designed to keep evil away by portraying it at an almost unattainable distance. Melodramatic representations of evil allow us to believe that evil is grotesque in its abnormality and that we are not readily implicated in it. Arendt's point is that, despite

---

47. This term, though not used in any of her books, is of course taken from the notorious subtitle of Arendt's account of the Adolf Eichmann trial held in Jerusalem in 1961. See Hannah Arendt, *Eichmann in Jerusalem: A Report on the Banality of Evil* (Penguin Classics, 1963).

its better intentions, the Enlightenment, by allowing humanism to police humanity, brought the evils (which banal humans are eminently capable of) much closer. Rudely awakened from the enchantments of her cultured Jewish German youth, Arendt gasped at the sudden realization that the most monstrous forms of evil imaginable were quite familiar to her.

Arendt's "banality of evil" is arguably an adaptation of her onetime lover and teacher Martin Heidegger's concept of everydayness.[48] In our discussion of Heidegger's *BT*, we will look to experience his philosophy as a form of Churban. From the dark depths of a descent into the heart of his thought, we will experience why humanity, when left to its own devices, cannot be trusted. This is a realization that has widespread and far-reaching implications for how we think about the culpability of humanism in the Holocaust. And we shall address this in our discussion of Heidegger below. But for now there is a more immediate conclusion that must be drawn, and it is this: From the perspective of Segulah, the fact that humanism survived the World Wars must come to be seen as unreasonable. If humanism is a device for the human being to trust him- or herself, the crucial lesson of the Holocaust must be that – without assigning guilt for the cause of evil itself – humanism is nonetheless unforgivably culpable for masquerading as its cure.

The Untenable Conclusions of Survival and System

Our analysis now reaches the point from where we can begin to see how the politics of Survival and System errs by drawing untenable conclusions from both the Holocaust and the foundation of the State of Israel. The former insists that Jews learn vigilance from the Holocaust. This is the source of contemporary Jewish victimhood. The Holocaust is taken as an ultimate sign of how vulnerable Jewish life is, and, as a result, the meaning of Jewish identity becomes predicated on the insistence that nothing like the Holocaust may ever be allowed to happen again. In this context, the Zionist movement is understood by the politics of Survival and System as the ultimate weapon of post-Holocaust Jewish self-defense. It provides a rational humanistic political

---

48. We will return to discuss in detail Heidegger's concept of everydayness in chapters 10–14 below and will make some specific references to the connection between that concept and Arendt's notion of the banality of evil in chapter 14.

answer to both the physical and cultural threats that Jews today are resolved to fend off. This line of argument must now be seen as unreasonable.

The blackmail of transcendence points to the relationship between Steiner's three historical "Jewish" proposals for the perfection of humanity and their impact on the rest of the world. In Steiner's view, the "crime" of the Jewish people is that they held the world to a higher standard. But for all the good they accomplished, they were also a provocation. Ultimately, by applying impossible pressures on the limits of humanistic morality, they unleashed the energies that provoked human beings to think of building hell above ground. Rather than accepting the limitations of their ego's capacity (or incapacity) to achieve perfection, post-Enlightenment humanists turned to the denial of God and to the violent hatred of His elected people. This is the challenge that the politics of Survival and System seeks to face. The conclusion they draw is that Jews must gain humanist political power (Survival) and handle it humanely (System) in order to survive and prosper.

A different conclusion is that the power of human ego cannot be relied on to attain the desires of the soul. Steiner's arrival at this insight from within a critique of the Enlightenment – is indeed a spark of Segulah. But this is something that Steiner himself saw in a very particular way. Steiner's analysis misses the connection between the inadequacy and unreliability of ego and the calamity that ensued from the blackmail of the transcendent because he fails to appreciate the particularistic dimension of Segulah's strategy for fixing the entire world. Steiner's misconception of this strategy has a long history that can be traced back at least as far as Paul. It is this misconception – Paul's misconception – that backfired, with the calamitous results that Steiner observes.

Let us consider this further: The idea that the power of ego cannot be relied upon to answer the needs of the soul is at the heart of the Covenant of Sinai, whose purpose is to allow God, through the agency of the Jewish people, to fix or heal the entire world. According to Steiner, the mechanisms of denial that render the ego powerless to achieve political perfection indeed generate a pathology that has no doubt played a role in the emergence of antisemitic sentiment throughout Christian history. However, the heart of this pathology does not apply to the Covenant of Sinai itself, as Steiner suggests. The pathology emanates from the premature extension of the covenant's demands to the whole of humankind. Steiner's observation about the diverse effects of, "blackmailing the transcendent" apply only to systems of human perfectibility that make demands on others. The Covenant of Sinai never does this; it addresses itself to Am Segulah alone. By universalizing morality to a single standard, Christianity, Marxism, and the other so-called "Jewish" moral systems that Steiner mentions make a crucial mistake that cannot but backfire and create bitter resentment with calamitous results. The direct appeal to humankind involves skipping over a highly particularistic stage which is inherent to the concept of Segulah. This first stage is most often misconstrued as chauvinistic ethnocentrism, and it has no doubt played a role in generating resentment against Jews. Paul jumped over this first stage when he presented the Gospels of Jesus as a Jewish message for the whole world.[49] This was the crucial development in the evolution of Christianity that sealed its fate as separate from Judaism.[50] Once it became married to the politics of the Byzantine Empire, Christianity emerged not only as separate from Judaism but as a "religion" in the first place. By way of contrast, from the perspective of Segulah, Judaism is not a religion that gains its identity from the contrast between religion and politics. In Judaism there is no such contrast. Judaism is not a religion, a system of belief, or even the religion of a nation. No combination of these terms can help. There is no sociological vocabulary in Hellenistic or humanistic thought that is capable of capturing the collective spiritual mission with which the Jewish people are charged and for which they must continue to exist. Only the rehabilitation of Segulah makes sense of the idea that the Covenant of Sinai's universal meaning is embedded in Israel's particularistic separateness.

This is an idea that contradicts humanistic logic, in which particularism is the opposite of universality. This leads to a misconception that the project of Western Judaism finds embarrassing. Using an economic analogy, one might erroneously compare the universality of Jewish internality with the

---

49. For an excellent discussion of Paul's attitude to Jewish particularism, see E. P. Sanders, *Paul, the Law and the Jewish People* (Fortress, 1983).

50. The argument that Paul's revelation that led to the mission to the Gentiles is the turning point in the separation of Judaism and Christianity is well known. Like Sanders, Daniel Boyarin also argued that this process was complex and slow, taking place over several hundred years. See Daniel Boyarin, *Border Lines: The Partition of Judaeo-Christianity* (University of Pennsylvania Press, 2004).

attempts to construct economic strategies that serve the common or general good by cultivating the prosperity of a select few. One might conclude that the strategy of Segulah involves a kind of moral capitalism: if you invest in the elite, that is how – through them – you will benefit the many. Presenting the Jewish people as spiritual elite in this way is a cause of great discomfort to those who adhere to the paradigm of Survival and System. But this is a misconception and it is extremely hard to really see this correctly.

From the perspective of Segulah, Jewish particularism serves a universal good, not because the Jewish people are somehow parallel to the industrial elite in which an extreme capitalist economic policy would have us exclusively invest. The particularism of Am Segulah is inherently universal by virtue of the fact that through the Jewish people's particularistic relationship to the Covenant of Sinai, all of humanity attains access to God. The election of the Jewish people emerges as a strategy that does not limit in any way the "universal" implications of God's munificent design for the entire world. On the contrary, it is the conduit that the Bible refers to when it describes the Jewish people as a kingdom of priests and a holy people with a purpose for the world.[51]

In conclusion, both Cavanaugh's critique of the exclusion of God from politics and Steiner's powerful articulation of the Holocaust's deeper meaning for the project of humanism are – as we have said – sparks of Segulah. They are sparks because they point in the direction of Segulah from within the language of humanist scholarship. Their deepest importance cannot be found in universalistic articulations or conceptualizations of the general role of religion in government. Similarly, their significance is not embedded in the shift they may bring about in our general attitudes toward the capacity of the humanities to humanize. Counterintuitive as this undoubtedly sounds, from the perspective of Segulah, the broadest and most dramatic universally significant conclusions that must be drawn from these crucial theses find their meaning in the internality of Jewish political discourse. Their importance lies in their capacity to begin the work of releasing the particular hold that the politics of Survival and System has on the internal mechanisms of Jewish political life. What we wish to show is that the nature of humanism's hold on

---

51. Exodus 19:6.

the internal workings of Jewish life is problematic even when we talk about it in purely Western, humanistic terms. More specifically, this means two things. First, by virtue of their election, it is the Jewish people who must learn from the first spark ignited by Cavanaugh, to discover the unreasonableness of the humanist strategy for peace. This has immensely important implications for Israel's foreign policy and its involvement in Middle East peace efforts. Second, it is Am Segulah who must awaken to the unreasonableness and short-sightedness of allowing humanist politics to survive the Holocaust, through contemplating the second spark ignited by Steiner, i.e., his critique of humanism in light of the Holocaust.

Setting the Course for the Rehabilitation of Segulah

At this initial stage of our analysis we are in a position to catch only a first glimpse of some of the final outcomes that we will be able to reach when our discussion runs its full course.

As we move toward imagining the meaning of Jewish statehood in the land of Israel from the perspective of Segulah, we take our first steps by becoming open to the reasonableness of breaking our axiomatic commitment to a political value-system that does not deserve the unflinching loyalty that it currently commands. For now this suggestion demands only that we become skeptical about the ethics of Western humanism, wary about the best intentions of our own political egos, and open to the possibility that – in the context of a still-concealed politics of Segulah – the entire struggle of religion in politics can be constructed differently. Breaking with the assumptions that dominate Western Jewish life means that we can dare to let go of our unconditional fear of religion in politics. It means replacing the Western concept of "religion" in politics with the Jewish concept of Segulah and becoming open to what can be learned from Jewish traditional yearnings about the inner depths of collective spirit. These Jewish political yearnings, themselves a spark of Segulah, were the impetus for Rabbi Kook, who was convinced by them that a process of spiritual Rehabilitation was already underway in his lifetime.[52]

---

52. This is a central theme in Rabbi Kook's writing and in his support for Zionism. He saw the return to the land and the effort to make it productive as a sign of redemption. One striking and famous example of this appears in his preface to *Orot HaTeshuvah*,

Second, to construct a politics of Tikkun Olam, Jewish political life must draw from the lessons of the Holocaust the strength to wean itself off humanistic ego and steer itself away from the kind of political power that the ego craves. This requires us to question our assumption that Western politics can truly serve an ultimate greater good. This questioning, as we stated in our introduction, applies to internal Jewish politics as much as it does to the interaction between Jews and others. Ultimately, we must go so far as to call into question the axiomatic assumption that the Jewish people and the Allies were on the same side of the Second World War. We must come to appreciate that the deeper implications of Steiner's critique of humanism after the Holocaust suggest that it is inappropriate for the Jewish people to overalign itself with the values of the liberal West just because it was the Allied forces who successfully defeated Hitler. Ultimately, it is this that will allow us to recognize with sadness that despite the rapprochement that followed the Second World War, the identity-based conflict between Judaism and the West has not yet ended.

If the basic principles of humanist politics are genuinely allowed to collapse, the idea that the State of Israel should emulate the moral and political standards dictated to it by the West is little short of scandalous. Admittedly, the alternative construction of a politics of Tikkun Olam has not as yet been made plausible. But making the case for the feasibility of the vision of Segulah is something that, in our view, can be done only after we have cleared away many more of the objections to it than we have done thus far. To this we will dedicate the continuation of our discussion. However, at this stage, we have come far enough to offer a first glimpse of what we might consider our final political objective. This is to build a politics that speaks the language and

---

or *Lights of Repentance*. In a section entitled "At the Foundation of Everything: The General Explanation of the Certainty of *Teshuvah*," he writes about the energies of general penitence that are healing the world in the following terms, "And all of these things in all of their details reach the practical level of life…raising up every fallen spirit in the people of Israel, a beloved and holy nation wherever it is, at whichever fallen level, from the deepest depths of the land, whether though action or thought to the highest level – the light of life bringing them joyfully…to the day of redemption that progressively appears before us each and every day in the land in the land of life…where the hilltops are being planted and worked and the trees are bearing fruit." See Rabbi A. I. Kook, *Lights of Repentance*, ed. Rabbi Z. Y Kook (Or Etzion, 1986) [Hebrew].

articulates the vision of Segulah with an understanding of the mechanisms of cause and effect that operate it. If we are able to arrive at a practical understanding of this, we will at last be able to examine the claim that the form of sovereignty implied by the vision of Segulah is qualitatively different from – indeed, antonymous to – the power used in humanist politics. This is a far cry from a full political explanation of what is meant by the idea that "on that day God will be One and His name will be One." But it is a start.

Our conclusions thus far allow us to say that, without sacrificing the values that humanism serves well, the sparks of Segulah allow us to appreciate why it is reasonable to imagine that the viability of the State of Israel's political future is far from ensured by its Western regime. Moreover, we can now appreciate more fully why it is intolerable to compare the morality of Segulah with the notions of ethics and morality adopted by the politics of Survival and System.

Without more access to the language and politics of Segulah, it is not yet possible to ask what kind of politics, morality, and sovereignty the Jewish State of Israel should seek to embody. But the very suggestion of such a replacement at this stage already allows us to begin the process of realigning our expectations of Israel's Western democracy. The axiomatic assumption that for the foreseeable future secular Western democracy must do is not enough. We must by now be able to imagine that after the Holocaust and the foundation of the State of Israel, it is a matter of urgency that the perspective of Segulah lead Israel toward something better.

In order to be completely clear, let us mention once more that our purpose here cannot be to jeopardize the prosperity that Jews have enjoyed under circumstances where humanist power has dealt kindly with them. Neither can it be to undermine the moral and ethical standards that humanism has served well. In addition, our purpose is most certainly not to reinforce the culture of victimhood that the post-Enlightenment politics of Survival and System pinned to the Holocaust. Undermining Jewish faith in humanist power is not designed to rekindle trauma or encourage xenophobic hate of others. In an era defined by both the destruction of the Holocaust and the remarkable opportunity for rehabilitation presented by the State of Israel, our purpose must be understood in a more hopeful light. After the foundation of the Jewish state, it is now possible to consider undermining or destroying Survival and System because these may now be seen as obstacles, false constructions, and mechanisms that perpetuate Jewish crisis and block the path to the greater project of Tikkun Olam that our current situation makes possible.

In sum, our questioning of Survival and System's axiomatic assumptions and our discussion of the two sparks of Segulah in this chapter call into question the most basic principles on which Jewish collective life is most commonly based. Whether applied to the strategy of Jewish survival in the Diaspora or to the humanistic political foundations of the Jewish state, it is our contention that these principles should be seen as unreasonable after the Holocaust and unnecessary from the perspective of Segulah.

In the next chapter we will discuss developments in the field of moral psychology and heuristics that support our claims about the inability of the rational ego to dominate human conduct or to yield stable or truthful understandings of the world. Releasing the ego from the agony of responsibility for morality and truth can help us uncover the elaborate mechanisms of denial with which it defends itself and conceals – above all from itself – its inadequacies. This is a crucial step toward understanding the nature of the inner transformation that fulfilling the vision of Tikkun Olam requires.

CHAPTER 3

~

The Psychology of the Rational Self

Questioning the Morality of Humanism

In the previous chapter we discussed George Steiner's observation that left to its own devices the human ego cannot be relied upon to attain the higher desires of the human soul. We thought of this as a significant spark of Segulah which paves the way for a fresh conversation about the monopoly of secularism in the public sphere. It is hard to be specific about what Steiner means by the "higher desires of the human soul," but even without aspiring to the greatest heights, it is clear that individuals and societies aspire to higher goals than they (as individuals and as collectives) ever live up to. This is as true today as ever, and it poses a huge challenge to the idea that a moral system based on humanism could ever attain the goal of Tikkun Olam.

In this chapter we shall look at the psychological questions that parallel Steiner's philosophical concerns about the failure of the humanities to humanize human beings. Given the fact that humans habitually fail to live up to their own moral standards, moral psychology asks how and why this happens. The ubiquitous scale of this problem extends the implications of Steiner's concept "the blackmailing of the transcendent." Civilizations that make unreasonable demands on people's behavior while relying on rationalism to hold people to a higher moral standard are all likely to experience failure and to cover it up, leading to the attrition of morality itself. The "blackmailing of the transcendent" is therefore not just a problem with the Jews, as Steiner suggested. The problem is humanist, and it can lead to the undermining of all leaders, governments, and societal institutions that fail to live up to the standards they impose on others. While there are many very relevant conclusions that we can draw from this, the issue that concerns us here is the emerging viability of the perspective of Segulah. In this context, this observation supports Steiner's claim that rethinking the moral "self" after the Holocaust must go beyond the boundaries of the societies implicated in its perpetration. This is what it means to face the full force of Mankowitz's question about the human possibility of the Holocaust.[1]

In this chapter we will not yet develop the religious implications of this argument. Rather we will focus on some of the support that psychological research can provide for Steiner's observation. We will do this by offering an analysis of two books: Jonathan Haidt's *The Righteous Mind*[2] and Daniel Kahneman's *Thinking, Fast and Slow*.[3] In light of these books we shall consider three themes. First, contrary to the principles of post-Enlightenment moral philosophy, Haidt's psychological analysis calls into question the idea that rational thought can and even should dominate human choices. Second, despite the incredible achievements and benefits of modern science, Kahneman's research forces us to rethink the basic assumption that rational thought can provide the means for making a moral distinction between truth and untruth. Finally, in the last section of this chapter we will consider the implications of Haidt's and Kahneman's research for our understanding of liberty, calling into question the extent to which the moral standards of liberty that humanist societies claim to offer are in fact maintained in the type of free choice they extend to their citizens.

Can/Should Rational Thought Dominate Human Action?

In his book *The Righteous Mind,* Jonathan Haidt sets out to offer a psychological analysis of how different moral sensitivities divide people over issues of politics and religion. In many ways, the book is an unusually honest attempt by a frustrated Democrat writing in the Bush era to figure out why the "other" side keeps winning the US elections. Haidt, who, like many liberals, confesses to having felt a sense of moral outrage at the persistent choice of Americans to side with the "less advanced" political and religious viewpoints proposed by Republicans, begins the book by backing down from

---

1.   See prologue above.

2.   Jonathan Haidt, *The Righteous Mind: Why Good People Are Divided by Politics and Religion* (Vintage Books, 2012).

3.   Daniel Kahneman, *Thinking, Fast and Slow* (Farrar, Strauss, and Giroux, 2013).

his own judgmental approach. Instead of moral outrage, Haidt tries to figure out what he and his frustrated political allies are failing to understand about the realities of human nature. It is from here that he introduces his reader to the field of moral psychology.

What Haidt calls the "righteous human mind" is an evolutionary mechanism of human domination over other species that – when turned inward – can also pose an ominous threat to human survival by becoming a source of human conflict. In his view, the purpose of moral psychology is to understand the workings of this mechanism correctly, and in so doing, "to help people get along."[4] His hope is that the three crucial observations he offers in his book will help "drain some of the heat, anger and divisiveness"[5] out of the debate about religion and politics and create a world in which, "competing ideologies are kept in balance, systems of accountability keep us from getting away with too much, and fewer people believe that righteous ends justify violent means."[6] Haidt dedicates a section of the book to each of his three observations or principles and supplies a metaphor as well as ample empirical evidence to illustrate and support the validity of each one.

The first of these principles is the most important of the three for our purposes, and it is from it that the other two ensue. This first principle states, "Moral intuitions arise automatically and almost instantaneously, long before moral reasoning has a chance to get started."[7] When Haidt began his research in moral psychology, he found that the field was dominated by Kohlberg's and Turiel's graphs of cognitive moral development. In his studies, Haidt found that children were sensitive to moral intuitions about disgust, pollution, sanctity, group loyalty, and disrespect that have no place in Kohlberg's scale of moral development. He argues that Kohlberg's findings accurately represent only the moral sensitivities (and the stages of development that these sensitivities undergo) that children are able to describe cognitively. In other words, they traced the developmental processes of "moral reasoning" in children but did not capture the broader range of moral and ethical

---

4.   Haidt, *Righteous Mind*, introduction, xii–xiii.

5.   Ibid.

6.   Ibid.

7.   Ibid., xiv.

responses that children and adults feel intuitively. Haidt's research endorses Joe Heinrich, Steve Heine, and Ara Norenzayan's critique of Kohlberg and their categorization of WEIRD (i.e., Western, Educated, Industrialized, Rich, and Democratic) societies as not indicative of the moral norms that operate in most human societies.[8] These researchers claimed that psychological studies are disproportionately concerned with a narrow sector whose culturally conditioned capacity for moral reasoning is significantly narrower than the range of moral intuitions that most people innately feel.[9] Haidt insists that in other "less WEIRD" cultures, language for articulating a broader range of moral concerns is, in fact, readily available. This observation goes to the heart of his second principle, to which we shall return. But the crucial point here is his conclusion that inside WEIRD cultures, consistent reactions to moral concerns that lie outside the confines of Kohlberg's graph suggest that morality does not primarily come from reasoning. Rather, reasoning is an ex post facto, culturally conditioned phenomenon.

Haidt traces the Western preference for reason as the source of moral conduct back to Plato's *Timaeus*[10] and continues to follow what he calls "a direct line running from Plato through Immanuel Kant to Lawrence Kohlberg."[11] This line, which Haidt dubs the "rationalist delusion,"[12] sanctifies the claim that the passions are controlled by reason, which simultaneously binds its adherents to this way of thinking and blinds them to possible alternatives and refutations. Haidt provides substantial empirical evidence, obtained through thousands of field interviews and questionnaires, to support David Hume, who wrote in 1739 that "reason is, and ought only to be, the slave of the passions and can never pretend to any other office than to serve and obey them."[13] What this means for Haidt is that moral reasoning is not there "to

---

8.   Ibid., 96. See also J. Heinrich, S. Heine, and A. Norenzayan, "The Weirdest People in the World?" *Behavioral and Brain Sciences* 33 (2010): 61–83 See Hume's (1739) *A Treatise of Human Nature* (Penguin Books: London, 1969).

9.   Haidt, *Righteous Mind*, 96.

10.   Ibid., 28; Plato, *Timaeus*, trans. D. J. Zeyl, in J. M. Cooper, ed., *Plato: Complete Works* (Indianapolis: Hackett, 1997).

11.   Haidt, *Righteous Mind*, 28.

12.   Ibid., 88–92.

13.   Ibid., 25. See also note 30, in which Haidt offers an account of some unpublished research which documents how subjects in an experiment struggled to find rational

reconstruct the reasons why we ourselves came to a judgment." Rather, the evolutionary function of moral reasoning is "to find the best possible reasons why somebody else ought to join us in our judgment."[14]

The metaphor that Haidt proposes to describe this condition is that of the righteous human mind as "divided like a rider on an elephant.[15] The "elephant" – perhaps an allusion to the expression "elephant in the room" that everybody notices but is too polite to mention – is a carefully chosen image. Elephants are bigger and more powerful than horses. They are also smarter and extremely adept at doing what all animals who have endured the arduous tests of natural selection (i.e., survival) are programmed to do best. Here, the elephant refers to the moral judgments that take place through emotional and intuitive processes of cognition. "Intuition" is a term that is used here as "the best word to describe the dozens or hundreds of rapid, effortless moral judgments and decisions that we all make every day." These are the "flashes of condemnation or approval" that "flit through your consciousness" when you read a newspaper, watch the news, or walk down the street. The "rider," on the other hand, is responsible for the "controlled processes" that we know consciously as reasoning. Though it is possible to reach decisions and judgments through reasoning, these systems work much more slowly than the "automatic processes that run the human mind, just as they have been running animal minds for 500 million years."[16] Intuitions (elephants) are powerful survival mechanisms finely tuned to take over and control human reactions to situations of danger, to align us with allies, and distance us from threats. Reasoning is a later development that followed upon the evolution of the human capacity to speak. When this happened, "the brain did not rewire itself to hand over the reins to a new and inexperienced charioteer. Rather,

---

articulations for moral convictions that were clearly not the products of rational thought processes.

14. Ibid., 44. See also note 36, in which Haidt refers to a number of philosophers who have made the argument that "reasoning should be understood as playing social and justificatory functions." He refers there to A. Gibbard, *Wise Choices, Apt Feelings* (Cambridge, MA: Harvard University Press, 1990) and C. L. Stevenson, *Ethics and Language* (Yale University Press, 1960).

15. Haidt, *Righteous Mind*, 44.

16. Ibid., 45.

the rider (language-based reasoning) evolved because it did something useful for the elephant."[17]

Haidt's rider has certain cognitive advantages that allow him to learn and avoid future danger. But his most crucial function is a social one. The rider allows the elephant to represent himself rationally to others. "The rider is skilled at fabricating post hoc explanations for whatever the elephant has just done, and it is good at finding reasons to justify whatever the elephant wants to do next."[18] Thus, when confronted with moral dilemmas, the judgments of the elephant respond most quickly and definitively. Expanding the metaphor, Haidt describes these intuitive judgments as "the elephant leaning"[19] in a particular direction. Once this leaning has taken place, the function of the rider is to continue steering the elephant in the direction that it has already determined for itself. This steering serves a strategic social function. It helps with such things as "managing your reputation, building alliances, and recruiting bystanders to support your side in disputes."[20] It is possible for mechanisms of rational reasoning to mull over a particular choice or think through a problem and convince the elephant to change its direction. But it is far more common for such shifts to emanate from challenges that have come at the elephant from the outside. These force the rationale to shift along with the elephant while providing reasonable defenses for its new position, moving from one point of view to another (in order to remain safe from a perceived threat or receptive to a potential source of benefit). Such shifts can allow the rational mind to find justifications for almost anything, making "cruelty seem acceptable and altruism embarrassing," all the while remaining powerfully oblivious to evidence that might disconfirm initial judgments that the rider only rarely makes.[21]

---

17. Ibid., 45–46.

18. Ibid.

19. Ibid., 46.

20. Ibid.

21. Ibid., 55. Although this is not the focus of Haidt's interest here, it is important for our purposes to point out that this capacity of the elephant to lean in an "immoral" direction – and of the rider to justify and defend it – supports the claim we make below that Haidt's portrayal of moral intuition allows for the separation of moral intuition from the substance or values of moral content as generally described in moral philosophy.

Haidt's first principle suggests a number of significant conclusions. First of all, human morality does not originate in reason, neither is it controlled by it. This does not and need not lead Haidt to the conclusion that human beings are inherently immoral. But it does suggest that moral decision making takes place elsewhere – in which case this analysis provides compelling support for the claim that emerged in our discussion of Steiner, that rational free choice cannot in fact be relied upon to control human behavior. Second, and most importantly, it suggests very clearly that reason – whether it is powerful enough to control moral decision making or not – is not a moral force in its own right. On the contrary, its primary function is social, political, and potentially combative. Without moral content of its own, reason is therefore an ethically unreliable resource for moral decision making.

The full force of these conclusions is supported by the research that furnishes Haidt with the second and third principles of the book. The second principle is built upon an empirical description of the kinds of moral intuition that can be seen in studies conducted around the world.[22] It states, "There's more to morality than harm and fairness."[23] The argument here is multilayered, and for our purposes it is best to present it in three stages. First, Haidt introduces what he understands as six fundamental moral intuitions, which include liberty/oppression, care/harm, fairness/cheating, loyalty/betrayal, authority/subversion, and sanctity/degradation. The central metaphor that he uses to illustrate this point is: "the righteous mind is like a tongue with six taste receptors."[24] These six receptors comprise a complex

---

22. For example, Haidt opens the book with the story of a family whose dog was killed by a car in front of their house. They had learned that dog meat was delicious, so they cut up the dog and cooked it and ate it for dinner. Nobody saw them do this. After hearing the story, subjects in a study had their physical, emotional, and intuitive responses to the event recorded. Then they were asked to explain what was wrong. It is here, for example, that Haidt discovered considerable gaps between moral reason and moral intuition. In his words, "If you are like most of the well-educated people in my studies, you felt an initial flash of disgust, but you hesitated before saying the family had done anything *morally* wrong. After all, the dog was dead, so they didn't hurt it, right? And it was their dog, so they had a right to do what they wanted with the carcass, no?" (ibid. 5). See also J. Haidt, "The Emotional Dog and Its Rational Tail: A Social Institutionist Approach to Moral Judgment," *Psychological Review* 108 (2001): 814–34.

23. Haidt, *Righteous Mind*, 98.

24. Ibid., 121–27.

matrix of moral intuition that Haidt refers to as his Moral Foundations Theory. Second, Haidt constructs an analysis of why many of these "taste receptors" are excluded from the moral language available to educated citizens of the liberal West. Third, he considers the political implications of the gap between moral intuition and moral reasoning, which he illustrates with examples from modern American politics.

Beginning with the six moral taste buds, Haidt's notion of them as foundational operates on the principles of Darwinian natural selection. In this analysis, each of the six moral "tastes" functions in the human brain like "cognitive modules" that evolved over time in order to attune the mind's sensitivity to fundamental social and environmental needs that must be processed "intuitively," i.e., effortlessly and at high speed in order for the human species to survive.[25] Here he sniffs out the adaptive challenges that would allow the identification of "universal cognitive modules upon which cultures construct moral matrices."[26] The outcome of this sniffing is a graph of six "adaptive challenges,"[27] each of which responds to an "original trigger" and a "current trigger." These triggers stimulate "characteristic emotions" that carry "intuitive cognitive knowledge" about moral intuitions and hence stimulate virtuous behaviors.

For example, the cognitive module of care/harm faces the adaptive challenge of protecting and caring for children. The original trigger for this module is the suffering or distress of one's child. A broader range of current triggers that stimulate related emotional responses might include pictures of cute animals suffering from the damaging effects of global warming or even a cute cartoon character on the wrapping of a commercial product. These emotional responses are the broader moral matrix associated with such moral virtues as caring and kindness.[28] Similarly, the module of sanctity/degradation serves the adaptive challenge of avoiding contaminants. It is originally triggered by the waste of valuable resources or contact with diseased people

---

25. Ibid., 123.

26. Ibid.

27. This graph appears in ibid., 125.

28. Ibid.

and can be more broadly associated with current triggers such as taboo ideas.[29] The emotion that these triggers stimulate is disgust, which is the most basic intuitive expression of such moral virtues as temperance, chastity, piety, and cleanliness.[30]

Haidt understands Moral Foundations Theory as offering a broadly pluralistic and evolutionarily biological (i.e., scientifically verifiable) portrayal of the full range of functions that morality serves for the human species. But this portrayal also calls into question the discourse of moral philosophy that modern Western civilization is based upon. Haidt offers a summary description of Bentham's utilitarian principle, "which approves or disapproves of every action whatsoever, according to the tendency which it appears to have to augment or diminish the happiness of the party whose interest is in question."[31] Haidt then moves on to summarize Kant's categorical imperative, which, resting upon the rational principle of non-contradiction, states that one should "act only according to the maxim whereby you can at the same time will that it should become a universal law."[32] Despite the range and variety of different perspectives that each of these principles suggests, Haidt's focus is on their limiting effect on the discourse of morality in Western civilization. What they share in Haidt's view is their rejection of Hume and their insistence on the rational systemization – one way or another – of moral reasoning.

Hinting lightly that Kant and Bentham might both have suffered from high-functioning Asperger's syndrome (while carefully steering clear of an ad hominem argument against either one), Haidt's allusion is strong enough to

---

29. Taboo ideas can be culturally conditioned. In some societies the taboo might be directed against racism, in others against feminism, religion, communism, homosexuality, or semitism. Whatever the content of the taboo, according to Haidt, the emotional reactions of disgust and outrage are similar.

30. A full description of these moral matrices is the subject of chapter 6 of Haidt's book, especially 123–127.

31. Ibid., 118. Also see note 16 and Haidt's reference to Jeremy Bentham's 1789 work *An Introduction to the Principles of Morals and Legislation* (Oxford: Clarendon, 1996), chapter 1, section 2.

32. Haidt, *Righteous Mind*, 119. See also note 22 and Haidt's reference to Immanuel Kant's 1785 *Grounding for the Metaphysics of Morals*, 3rd ed., trans. J. W. Ellington (Indianapolis: Hackett, 1993), 30.

leave the distinct impression that, in his view, Western civilization in general is suffering from a form of moral autism. In other words, the attempt to subjugate the elephant of moral intuition to the rational principles generated by the rider provides not only an inaccurate representation of the varied moral pallet (because the rationalist description of moral processes is empirically wrong); it is also responsible for deficiencies that cause strife and conflict. Kant wanted to discover timeless, changeless principles about humanity and in order to do so he turned to pure reasoning. Haidt is suggesting that this move is not only misguided, it actively obscures information – or observable data about moral behavior – from view.

The critique of reasoning as opposed to observation as a source of moral knowledge runs deeper. Haidt traces the cultural differences that cause mutual outrage, anger, insult, and disgust – between competing civilizations, cultures, or even political parties – to the narrowing of moral sensitivity that moral reasoning causes. Against the backdrop of this evolutionary argument, Haidt's portrayal of the struggle between Republicans and Democrats seems a little trivial. But it actually serves as a powerful tool for illustrating his claim that the debate between the two parties has deteriorated because the deeper differences between them are culturally conditioned and not political. Haidt insists that, though the same moral pallet is available to all people, cultural circumstances can condition – i.e., hypersensitize and desensitize – different modules or buds in the range of tastes. He argues that this possibility accounts for the differing moral sensitivities in different regions of the world. More specifically, the two competing parties in American politics operate on different sets of moral intuitions that stimulate different cognitive modules. In its campaigns, each party triggers different emotional/moral responses that serve its interests. Due to the hypersensitizing and desensitizing of different modules, these two sets of moral range are incommensurable with each other – which is where, in Haidt's view, campaigning gets ugly.

Haidt chalks up the repeated successes of Republican politics to the claim that the conservative worldview speaks more effectively to the elephant by triggering all six of the moral taste buds.[33] Admittedly, most Republican moral arguments downplay the nodes of care and liberty and place a stronger

---

33. Haidt, *Righteous Mind*, 181–84.

emphasis on loyalty, authority, and sanctity, but the full range is one way or another generally traceable in every Republican campaign.[34] Conversely, Haidt claims that Democrats suffer from an electoral disadvantage because they speak more narrowly, placing an almost exclusive emphasis on the two modules of care and liberty. Hence they are often baffled and literally lost for words when confronted with moral arguments that inconceivably allow for the suppression of liberty and care at the expense of such things as loyalty, patriotism, and authority.[35]

Our interest here is not the same as Haidt's, and the importance of this argument to us is not connected to the efficacy of Republican or Democrat electoral campaigns. His overall conclusion that understanding the truth about moral intuition and moral reasoning will help us all get along better is also not the nub of our interest. The crucial point here is the access that this analysis gives us to the powerful mechanism of concealment that prevents the concept of Segulah from resonating in the moral discourse of Survival and System. Using Haidt's matrix of Moral Foundations Theory, we can suggest that, precisely because rationalism cannot control moral intuition, humanist thought surrounds moral concerns that lie outside the confines of humanist discourse with a blanket of perceived irrationality. In other words, the incapacity of rational discourse to control moral intuition is compensated for by its very potent capacity to obscure a whole range of human moral sensitivities. More significantly, it is the hold that moral reasoning has on moral language that conceals or obscures the viability or reasonableness of alternative (nonconventionally rational) sequences of cause and effect – of action and result. The concealment of the reasonableness of these sequences conditions us to see the truth claims of Segulah as irrational or inadequately verifiable.[36]

---

34. Ibid., 156–81.

35. Ibid.

36. Examples of sequences such as these abound and can include many of the passages in the Torah which deal with divine involvement in history, reward, and punishment that many modern readers might find irrational, unreasonable, incommensurate with reality (as they perceive it), or in some cases even immoral. A great deal of modern liberal Jewish scholarship is dedicated to resolving these incongruities, and this is what Heschel referred to as the assimilation of Jewish values. See our discussion of this in chapter 1. A significant example of modern scholarship of this sort is Moshe Halbertal's

This is the mechanism that explains why, as we mentioned above, the values of Judaism are "underwater."[37]

This brings us to Haidt's third principle, which states that "morality binds and blinds."[38] The evolutionary function served by the capacity of the rider to blinker the elephant is linked to survival. Social and political gains are made through rejecting the logic (or semantic sequences) of "irrational" moral reasoning. The elephant succumbs to having his moral intuitions selected and narrowed down because the politicization of the moral pallet serves a powerful human need to join groups and align with others. In one of the most passionate chapters of the book, Haidt presents the evolutionary significance of this. It is the incredibly powerful (and according to Haidt, uniquely human) capacity for "shared intentionality" that accounts for the human domination of the other species on the planet.[39] In a discussion of what he calls the "hive switch," Haidt states that "human beings are conditional hive creatures with the ability to transcend self-interest and lose ourselves in something larger than ourselves."[40] This "switch," which Haidt describes in terms of the hormones and neurons triggered by certain social, situational, and narcotic stimulants, is responsible for special moments of great happiness in which people transcend the mundane and profane aspects of life and "transit to the sacred world in which we become simply a part of the whole."[41] This capacity is responsible for the deepest religious impulses, the desire to transcend limitations and find the value of our existence in a shared sense of spiritual purpose.

The empirical evidence that Haidt marshals to substantiate his three theses potently reinforces the idea that rational thought cannot be relied upon to

---

Commentary Revolutions in the Making: Values as Interpretive Considerations in Midreshei Halachah (Magnes, 1997) [Hebrew].

37. See preface.

38. See Haidt, *Righteous Mind*, 189. This is an argument that has also been made by Yuval Noah Harari in *Sapiens: A Brief History of Humankind* (Vintage Books, 2011), 21–44. Here Harari focuses on the role of language and throughout the book on what he refers to as the imagined order, by which he means the uniquely human ability to share beliefs in the same fictional or imagined entities.

39. Haidt, *Righteous Mind*, 189–220.

40. Ibid., 244.

41. Ibid.

regulate moral behavior. From the first of his principles we can conclude that moral reasoning ("the rider") does not and cannot control moral intuition ("the elephant"). From the second, we can conclude that moral reasoning cannot control moral decision making because ultimately that is not its function. Instead it accumulates political and social power while actively blinding itself to a fuller range of possible moral intuitions. Finally, the evolutionary psychobiology on which Haidt's theory of moral psychology is built suggests that our most powerful spiritual experiences – those that transcend the normal plane of human experience and invigorate our sense of a greater whole – ultimately serve social and political functions of survival. It is these functions that motivate people to act beyond the boundaries of rational thought and engage in communal rites and practices that create bonds of security. For all their virtues, bonds such as these are also responsible for blinding us to the convictions of others and thus create enmity. One way or another, there seems little connection between them and the greater human impulses that might inspire people to cultivate systems that take the project of perfecting human society seriously.

In sum, one might say that Haidt offers a forceful and appropriately ambivalent portrayal of human morality as a socio-political-survivalist mechanism. Human beings are capable of greatness, transcendence, altruism, and virtue. However, the very same faculties that allow these are not easily controlled and are also responsible for conflict. It is Haidt's hope that a better understanding of the empirical psychology – rather than erroneous philosophies of moral reasoning – will indeed help people to get along. Again, it is not this conclusion that commands our interest. Rather we are concerned with relaxing the hold of humanism – and by way of extension, of Survival and System – by establishing the following four crucial points:

First, as we have already said, since moral reasoning is not in control, the claim that the rational faculty of the ego self can be relied upon to guide human beings toward attaining the higher desires of the soul can be seen to fall away. From the perspective of Segulah, the importance of recognizing this is an acute and urgent concern, as we have said.

Second, Haidt's evolutionary analysis debunks the rational functionality of morality as we know it by detaching the rational principles and purposes upon which humanist morality purports to be based (human betterment) from the substantive meanings, purposes, and functions that actually comprise the empirical reality of moral intuition. This detachment allows us to conclude that, without moral reasoning, there is nothing substantively "moral" (in the idealistic, elevated, and altruistic sense that rationalist moral philosophy generally intends) about the actuality of human moral intuition. If moral intuition is an evolutionary survival mechanism that is detached from and in control of moral reasoning, the very concept of morality proposed by humanist moral reasoning is a delusion. Indeed, when the need arises it can lead us to think that "cruelty [is] acceptable and altruism embarrassing."[42] Again, the acute significance of this claim is reinforced by the perverse performance of moral reasoning that made it possible for Nazi propaganda to actually appeal to the morality and values adopted by so many Germans and others between 1933 and 1945.

Third, Haidt's analysis of the alliance-forming role that rational discourse plays in fulfilling the evolutionary function of social morality underscores the connection between rational moral discourse (i.e., selective cultural sensitizing and desensitizing of our moral "taste buds") and our portrayal of humanistic morality as conflict. After imposing limitations on certain moral sensitivities, moral reasoning constructs social and political arguments in which certain behaviors come to be seen as direct causes with clear moral effects. Enemies are those who irrationally reject our sense of how the world works and allies are those who succumb to our logic. Rather than offering a path toward the attainment of higher human goals, moral rationalism emerges as a mechanism for forming alliances based on the moral confines dictated to it by moral intuition whose leanings it does not and cannot control. The perpetual uphill struggle against conscious wrongdoing – which becomes an end in itself – emerges as the primary outcome of the interactions between moral reasoning and moral intuition. This is not a path to moral improvement.

Fourth, Haidt's claim that the narrowing of the moral pallet is most acute in liberal (WEIRD) societies – or on the liberal leaning end of the political spectrum – reinforces the suggestion, often associated with Michel Foucault,[43]

---

42. See note 20 above.

43. This is a central idea in much of Michel Foucault's historical writing. This, for example, is his argument regarding the suppression of irrational behavior by the modern mental health care system, of crime by the modern prison system, of sexuality by modern

that the liberal humanist tradition is implicated in the construction of mechanisms of suppression, concealment, delusion, and denial that prevent moral intuitions outside its range from staying in view. This observation brings us back to our earlier insistence that despite liberal humanism's many virtues, it is in this context that the vision of Segulah is most stubbornly blocked from emerging plausibly into public discourse.

Haidt's conclusions allow us to show that the use of rationalism's concealing and manipulative power to establish moral independence undermines its claim to serve moral purposes and implicates it in arbitrary uses of power that one might correctly associate with contriving politics at best and perhaps even tyranny. It is therefore no longer reasonable to imagine that human moral power – understood as inextricable from the competing functions of moral reasoning and moral intuition – is equal to the task of preventing the suffering caused by conscious wrongdoing. Ultimately, it is the very "morality" (in the idealist or Kantian sense) of humanist morality (in the sense that the reality contradicts the ideal) that must now be seen to fall away. If the rational self cannot be relied upon to control moral behavior, the question is which faculties of the self can. This is a topic to which we will return when we reach the stage of Tikkun, or Rehabilitation.

Does Rational Thought Provide a Moral Distinction between Truth and Untruth?

Maintaining a monopoly over the truth is vital to the successful outcome of the rational self's ongoing campaign to hold our trust. The notion of verifiable truth is a powerful asset in the struggle of post-Enlightenment humanist thought to convince us to let the rational faculties of the mind lead. If this claim is not justified, then it follows that the demand that rational science can distinguish truth from untruth will also fall away.

---

attitudes to individual privacy, and of illness by modern medical care. For examples of each of these, see Michel Foucault, *The History of Madness*, trans. Jonathan Murphy and Jean Khalfa (Routledge, 2006); *Discipline and Punish: The Birth of the Prison*, trans. Alan Sheridan (Vintage Books, 1995); *The History of Sexuality*, 4 vols., trans. Robert Hurley (Random House and Vintage Books, 1978); *The Birth of the Clinic: An Archaeology of Medical Perception*, trans. Alan Sheridan (Tavistock, 1973). We will discuss Foucault in detail in chapters 4, 6, and 8.

It is perhaps a little ironic, but Haidt's rejection of Kantian moral reasoning is ironized (if not actually contradicted) by his use of scientific method to establish the three central claims of his argument. In providing empirical evidence to support his thesis that moral intuitions are more powerful than moral reasoning, Haidt builds a scientifically verifiable truth claim that relies on the epistemological assumption that reasoning in general can and should control intuition. The irony here of course is that it is this foundational methodological assumption that actually "holds up" the idea of moral reasoning over moral intuition because moral reasoning gains its prestige from reasoning in general.

Put more broadly: within the context of post-Enlightenment humanism, the preference for reason and rationalism in moral psychology (which Haidt rejects) itself draws a great deal of its strength and reinforcement from the demonstrable successes of modern rationalism in the field of natural science (which Haidt implicitly accepts). It is in this field that, since Newton, rationalism has most effectively established its supremacy by convincingly demonstrating its power to distinguish between truthful and untruthful accounts of how the world works. The attempt to extend this success into the human sciences (including psychology as well as many other humanistic disciplines such as history, literature, and so on) has had a decisive effect on the development of modern humanist civilization. It has also had a crucial impact on political, religious, psychological, economic, ideological, and other fields in which every idea or proposal is subject to empirical testing. In some way or another, the moral validity of each of these systems is determined by its capacity to present "truth claims" that can be rationally evaluated and verified. Thus, the verifiability of a truth claim according to scientific standards is no technicality. It is a moral principle of modern life. The price paid for failure to live up to the morality of truth dictated by post-Enlightenment scientific culture is exclusion from the public sphere. The privatization or radicalization of rationally nonverifiable truth claims has, of course, had a key impact on the role of religion in public life. But it has also had an influence on a broad range of other fields in which assumptions supported by "subjective belief" alone are marginalized and considered legitimate only in the realm of personal choice. Even here, in the sphere of private life – where the right to convince others on the outside is severely restricted – toleration for the adverse effects of a belief system's convictions about the truth is significantly lower than it might be elsewhere. Violations of the almost universal liberal ethic of care/harm are significantly more acceptable, for example, in a hospital than they are in an acupuncturist's parlor.

We shall consider the monopoly of empirically verified truth claims on morality by discussing the work of Nobel Prize–winning psychologist Daniel Kahneman to establish the claim that the human psyche is not structured in such a way as to prioritize rational thought. Daniel Kahneman was the first psychologist to win the Nobel Prize in Economics.[44] The prize was awarded primarily for the work that he conducted with Amos Twersky on heuristics in decision making. In our exploration of the rational self's capacity to control the psyche's notion of verifiable truth, our discussion will focus on Kahneman's book *Thinking, Fast and Slow*.[45]

Kahneman begins by introducing two fictional characters, each of which represents a different set of functions performed by the human psyche. The first of these, which he calls System 1, is designed to think fast, while System 2 is the one that thinks more slowly.[46] The relationship and interplay between these two functional systems is the subject of the book.

Kahneman starts out by telling us that "System 1 operates automatically and quickly, with little or no effort and no sense of voluntary control."[47] In many ways, this system parallels the "elephant" of moral intuition except that its primary function is not moral judgment so much as intuitive calculation. System 1 is responsible for a broad range of automatic activities, such as to "detect that one object is more distant than another; orient to the source of a sudden sound; complete the phrase "bread and…"; make a disgusted face when shown a horrible picture, answer 2 + 2 =; read words on large billboards,

---

44. Deborah Smith, "Psychologist Wins the Nobel Prize for Economics," *Monitor 33* (December 2002): 11, 22.

45. Daniel Kahneman, *Thinking, Fast and Slow* (Farrar, Strauss and Giroux, 2013).

46. Kahneman attributes Keith Stanovitch and Richard West with the first use of these terms. See Kahneman, ibid., 20 as well as note 20 on page 450. See also Keith Stanovitch and Richard West, "Individual Differences in Reasoning: Implications for the Rationality Debate" *Behavioral and Brain Sciences* 23, no. 5 (2000): 645–65.

47. Kahneman, *Thinking, Fast and Slow*, 20.

drive a car on an open highway."[48] These tasks are performed by System 1 effortlessly and at high speed. Some functions of System 1 develop naturally from birth. Others are more complex and must be acquired. These might include driving a car or – for an expert doctor – noticing a telltale symptom or for an expert pianist playing the *Moonlight Sonata*. All these tasks perhaps require practice and effort but once mastered can be performed with ease.[49]

System 2 "allocates attention to the effortful mental activities that demand it, including complex computations."[50] The activities of this system "require attention and are disrupted when attention is drawn away." Examples of these functions include "bracing for the starter gun in a race; focusing on the voice of a particular person in a crowded and noisy room; maintaining a faster walking speed than is natural for you; monitoring the appropriateness of your behavior in a social situation; counting the occurrences of the letter *a* in a page of text; checking the validity of a complex logical argument,"[51] and so on.

The currency of the relationship between the two systems is "attention."[52] The capacity to "pay attention" is limited, and so the demands made on attention by the performance of complex tasks by System 2 can inhibit and even obscure the capacity of System 1 to perform its basic functions. For example, walking down the road without falling over is a function, which in the case of a healthy person is performed effortlessly by System 1. However, if you are asked at the same time to calculate the answer to a complex arithmetical question, System 2 will draw on the reserve of attention available to System 1, with the result that many people cannot keep walking while performing the calculation. Kahneman offers a more extreme example of the same phenomenon: "Intense focusing on a task can make people effectively blind, even to stimuli that attract normal attention." He cites an experiment conducted by Christopher Chabris and Daniel Simons who showed a short film of two teams passing a basketball between them. One team wore black,

---

48. Ibid., 21.
49. Ibid., 22.
50. Ibid.
51. Ibid.
52. Ibid., 31–37.

the other wore white. The viewers of the film were told to count the number of times the members of the white team passed the ball between them and to ignore the black team. In the middle of the film a woman dressed in a gorilla suit appears on the screen for nine seconds, stands in full view and bashes her chest with her fists. Due to the drain on attention that following the ball passing between the players on the white team caused (and due also to the focus of attention on the color white rather than black), of the many thousands of people who were shown the video, approximately 50 percent did not even see the gorilla appear on screen.[53] The point here is that, while Systems 1 and 2 are both very good at what they do, the finite resource of attention that they share can cause one to override or inhibit the performance of the other, with striking effects.

System 2 does have some ability to control the actions and responses of System 1 by "programming" its normally automatic functions. For example, when looking at a map, you can "set" your memory to look for cities beginning with the letter N and you can prepare yourself to search in a crowd for women wearing blue hats. But, despite this, Kahneman's point is to show that normally, it is System 1 that is in control. In order to perform all of these tasks (including counting the number of times the ball passes between the members of the white team in the case of the gorilla), you are asking your mind to do something that does not come naturally, and soon you will find that you must continue programming and reprogramming it in order to stay focused. This requires "continuous exertions of at least some effort."[54] The difficulty involved in maintaining this effort reveals the crucial feature of System 2, which Kahneman refers to as its "laziness." The central characteristic of this "laziness" according to Kahneman is that System 2 will not act unless it is triggered to do so by System 1. Alas, since it is often not called upon, it often remains excluded from those very mental processes that it is most capable of performing effectively.

When we are awake, both systems are operational. System 1 runs automatically, and System 2 is normally in a comfortable low-effort mode, in which only a fraction of its capacity is engaged. System 1 continually generates

---

53. Ibid., 23-24. See also Christopher Chabris and Daniel Simons, *The Invisible Gorilla and Other Ways Our Intuition Deceives Us* (New York: Crown, 2010).

54. Kahneman, *Thinking, Fast and Slow*, 23.

suggestions for System 2: impressions, intuitions, intentions, and feelings. If endorsed by System 2, impressions and intuitions turn into beliefs, and impulses turn into voluntary actions. When all goes smoothly, and this is most of the time, System 2 adopts the suggestions of System 1 with little or no modification. You generally believe your impressions and act on your desires, and that is fine – usually. When System 1 runs into difficulty, it calls on System 2 to support more detailed and specific processing, "System 2 is mobilized when a question arises for which System 1 does not offer an answer…as happens when you encounter the multiplication problem 17 x 24."[55] Again, this is also an example of an effective and satisfactory division of labor between the two systems. When you need to activate System 2, it springs into action to help you adapt. Thus, "you can also feel a surge of conscious attention whenever you are surprised. System 2 is activated when an event is detected that violates the model of the world that System 1 maintains…. In summary most of what you (your System 2) think and do originates in your System 1, but System 2 takes over when things get difficult, and it normally has the last word."[56]

However, and this is the crucial point, the capacity of System 1 to act before System 2 has been stimulated is often responsible for highly problematic errors of judgment. System 2 is very often not called upon to perform functions of which it is capable because it is dominated by the functions of System 1. The qualities that dominate are what Kahneman refers to as the "biases" of System 1. These cause "systematic errors that it is prone to make in specified circumstances." System 1 "sometimes answers easier questions than the one it was asked, and it has little understanding of logic and statistics. One further limitation of System 1 is that it cannot be turned off. If you are shown a word on a screen in a language you know, you will read it – unless your attention is totally focused elsewhere."[57]

The biases and mistakes of System 1 are "cognitive illusions,"[58] which like (and indeed including) "optical illusions" draw us to conclusions about

---

55. Ibid., 24.
56. Ibid., 26.
57. Ibid., 27.
58. Ibid., 29.

reality that are not in fact true. These illusions are products of misleading leads or telltale signs that System 1 picks up on and processes at high speed and without reflection. Thus, when interviewing a candidate for a job, we are likely to form a favorable impression that is based on qualities that have nothing to do with the available information that might inform a better judgment of character or suitability for the post. For example, we are easily misled by a person's appearance or accent or by the mention of previous employment in a company whose products we happen to like. The problem here is not simply that System 1 can often get it wrong and fail to review more helpful data that is in fact available. The issue is that even through very conscious acts of will, the functioning of System 1 cannot be turned off. Problems are solved and decisions are made before the system more capable of performing them has been stimulated into action. In Kahneman's words, "Because System 1 operates automatically and cannot be turned off at will, errors of intuitive thought are often difficult to prevent. Biases cannot always be avoided because System 2 may have no clue to the error.... System 2 is much too slow and inefficient to serve as a substitute for System 1 in making routine decisions."[59]

The adverse effects of this are extremely significant. Kahneman traces the many stimuli that can impair the judgment of System 1without triggering the corrective mechanisms of System 2. In the more trivial cases, we are presented with uncomplicated calculations or logical sequences that seem to have intuitive answers or lead to simple conclusions. When System 1 is left to its own devices, it quite naturally reaches incorrect answers without setting off any of the alarm bells of doubt or uncertainty that might stimulate System 2 to check. In one study with graver implications, Kahneman shows how cases were presented to eight Israeli parole judges in random order. The judges spent an average of six minutes on each one. Kahneman reports how "the authors of this study plotted the proportion of approved requests against the time since the last food break" and found that the results "spiked after each meal when about 65% of requests are granted."[60] The study has disturbing implications for the truthfulness or justice of court rulings, and these results were therefore checked and rechecked to uncover other variables that might

---

59. Ibid., 45.
60. Ibid.

have affected the outcome. All the same, Kahneman concludes that "the best possible account of the data provides bad news: tired and hungry judges tend to fall back on the easier default position of denying requests for parole."[61] Presumably the same tendencies can apply to doctors choosing treatments, CEOs making investment choices, and scientists evaluating data in a lab.

The stimuli that either block System 2 or misguide it are referred to by Kahneman and Twersky as "heuristics and biases."[62] Their early research in this field totally altered the value of intuitive decision making, drawing a thick line between the capacity of experts and that of others to rely on the judgments of their System 1. In many cases, especially those that concern the financial market – where there is often no expertise available – understanding how System 1 is affected by heuristics and biases to the exclusion of System 2 has huge implications. The exhaustive analysis provided in Kahneman's book focuses on the broad range of stimuli that cause decision-making processes to fall between the cracks of the two systems. Other examples show how System 1 finds shortcuts for making elementary mathematical calculations in which relatively simple errors go unnoticed.[63] These results and more enabled Kahneman and Twersky to call attention to the flaws in the decision-making practices that make the business world spin and to suggest regulatory methods based on their finding that System 2 is more readily stimulated when called upon to monitor the choices of others. It is therefore a crucial element of their argument that companies and organizations in general need to develop System 2 stimulating mechanisms and procedures – ranging from checklists to external monitoring – that can heighten the probability of recourse to System 2 when decisions must be made.

---

61. Ibid.

62. Ibid. "Heuristics and Biases" is the title of part 2 of the book.

63. For example, System 1 draws conclusions by making inappropriate but readily accessible associations between sets of data which cause people to jump to erroneous conclusions based on inadequate evidence. System 1 is an expert at substituting difficult questions for easier ones and supplying immediate, intuitive answers. System 1 can cause overconfidence and disorientation when it is primed (or stimulated) to factor in irrelevant information while making a decision or choice. System 1 can fail to return to the correct baseline when comparing options, as is the case in the famous bat and ball exercise described there on pages 244-45 and 417.

These findings are of crucial importance to our analysis of the axiom which attaches moral weight to reliance on the power of the rationale to distinguish truth from untruth. We do not wish to suggest that human beings are neither rational nor capable of rational thought and action. We certainly do not want to deny the achievements of science that have significantly improved quality of life for billions of people. What we are concerned with is evaluating the capacity of the human mind to be controlled by its eminently accomplished rational faculty and the morality of a system for improving society that depends on it.

Indeed, as Kahneman himself insists, it is not the purpose of his research to portray the human mind as inherently irrational. Neither is it his purpose to question the capacity of rational thought to establish scientifically verifiable truths. Thus, there is no need here to call attention to any kind of ironic gap between his reliance on scientific methodology and the substance of his psychological findings. Though the struggle against System 1 is presumably a constant in all (including Kahneman's own) research, the availability of a conscious capacity to construct mechanisms that stimulate System 2 into action supplies psychological research with enough methodological coherence to justify the study. Given this, it is Kahneman's observations about the "positioning" of this capacity in a subordinate role inside the workings of the human mind that is of crucial significance to our analysis. This observation allows the claim that System 2 can be relied upon to take control of our conception of the truth to fall away. Though that control is hypothetically possible, it requires a degree of consistent effort that few if any individuals can maintain over time. The methods that allow us to stimulate System 2 and attain truthful outcomes are significantly impaired when directed at the rational self. Willpower is insufficiently supplied with the fuel or currency of "attention" to constantly keep control of the mind, and thus the priority we give to rationalism emerges as something that teeteringly balances on the capacity of System 2 to monitor the actions, behavior, and thought processes of others. This leads us to conclude from the implications of Kahneman's study that the moral priority of rationally verifiable truth is far from stable. Given the dependence of the priority of moral reasoning on the priority of reasoning in general, the morality of the domination of reasoning over intuition collapses alongside its plausibility. If it is not plausible for reason to dominate, a system in which manufactured conditions allow the impression that reason dominates cannot be moral either. This is indeed one of the key intuitions of the entire movement in twentieth-century philosophy that we call deconstruction.

Using the metaphorical terminology that we have learned from Haidt and Kahneman, we might summarize this argument as follows:

(a) Since the rider cannot control the elephant, (b) the impression that the rider can control the elephant must be seen as an illusion held in place only by the fact that System 2 is capable of performing tasks that System 1 cannot. (c) Since System 2 cannot be relied upon to control System 1, (d) System 2 cannot be relied upon to perform the tasks of which it is capable. (e) Since System 2 cannot be relied upon, the morality of the claim that external mechanisms might be used to secure the control of System 2 over System 1 collapses alongside the morality of the claim that the rider should control the elephant.

From this sequence we can conclude that the humanist system of morality that blocks the viability of Segulah from emerging into view is built upon the priority given by humanist anthropology to the rational mind. Prioritizing in this way, humanist morality gives license to the rational mind to use whatever means available to it to exert its control over the human self. The illusory morality of this license is held in place by the capacity of the rational self to know the truth. Without yet denying the plausibility of this capacity, we can still say that due to the unreliability or the laziness of the rational self, the morality of its right to dominate is far from self-evident.

As we try to make space for the possibility of the perspective of Segulah to gain plausibility, what must be seen to fall away here is the idea that social or political systems that rely upon the capacity of the individual to exert rational control over the human psyche are morally viable. What seems to work is perhaps more a product of the use of power than of moral improvement.

Freedom of Choice and the Morality of Human Liberty in Humanism

Kahneman and Twersky's research had a wide impact on economic theory for a number of reasons. One of these is because they significantly challenged

Milton Friedman's insistence that the market should be "free to choose."[64] Their research suggests that if the market were left entirely to its own devices it would fall prey to the unreliable but inevitable control of heuristics and biases, i.e., System 1. Friedman's convictions were based on the fundamental assumption that the definition of rationality is coherence and that coherent choices would ultimately serve the best interests of the common good. But, as Kahneman says, "this definition is impossibly restrictive, it demands adherence to rules of logic that a finite mind is not able to implement."[65] Thus, although System 2 is clearly rational, "human beings often need help to make more accurate judgments and better decisions."[66] Friedman would no doubt have objected to this notion of "help" on moral grounds. Given the reality of the human psyche, we might now understand how people may be convinced to acquiesce.

This leads us to the simple observation that the right to choose freely is limited just as "liberty" is limited in any free society. The operational meaning of liberty is therefore culpable for limiting what liberal societies claim to mean by freedom. The limitations that social realities inevitably impose on absolute liberty come in the form of impositions and coercive mechanisms that are determined by those who have coercive power. The irony is clear. But political coercion that uses power to produce desirable results has the advantage of demonstrable efficacy. Basing ourselves for now only on what we have learned from Haidt and Kahneman, we can see that the moral claim that the individual has the right to freely choose and evaluate the truth as he or she sees fit emerges as founded on an unrealistic and implausible evaluation of how human beings actually think. This is because the right to choose is only really accorded to those who exercise it coherently in ways that are recognized by the rational self. While alternatives are not necessarily persecuted or punished, they can be, and they are easily and readily pushed out of the public sphere. Sometimes this occurs on the left wing of society; at other times it occurs on the right. Either way, the phenomena of conservative moral censorship and radical political correctness are a limitation on the freedom of choice

---

64. Milton Friedman with Rose Friedman, *Free to Choose: A Personal Statement* (Harvest, 1980).

65. Kahneman, *Thinking, Fast and Slow*, 411.

66. Ibid., 402.

that is supported by Kahneman's observation that System 2 is more likely to act effectively when it is triggered by an external stimulus. As Foucault famously argued, such things as police forces, criminal justice systems, and mandatory medical procedures for the mentally ill are all products of rational government. But the raw coercive power that they conceal is fearsome to say the least.[67]

Our point is that what is true about the regulation of markets is true about the regulation of other aspects of political life. The psychology of rationalism shamelessly convinces us to acquiesce to its rule in the public sphere even though we can know that its main reason for doing so is its failure to dominate human behavior from within. Ultimately, the observation that System 1 and not System 2 is in control debunks the moral principle that freedom of choice is given to all by virtue of humanism's appreciation of the human capacity to identify truth. The interface in decision making between Systems 1 and 2 leads Kahneman to the conclusion that, in the interests of reaching closer approximations of the truth, we are best advised to impose upon the "freedoms" of System 1, which cannot be trusted on its own. Taking the laziness of System 2 into account, it now falls upon others – whether they are government institutions, market regulators, or other systems of coercion – to intervene.

The idea that rationalism (represented by System 2) expresses and protects freedom of choice is therefore an illusion. Since System 2 is slow and perhaps reluctant to act, we may conclude that this illusion functions as a mechanism which conceals the threat posed to humanist values by the psychological realities that dictate the preferences and choices of the human mind. As Kahneman shows in tremendous detail, the human mind naturally and repeatedly chooses against knowable truths. The result is that the human mind works in a way that blocks us from choosing rational truth even when we have the capacity to know it. This is the case simply because rationality is not always available to us. This is a problem that no act of will can permanently overcome – certainly not on a public or political scale. The amount of attention and regulation needed would destroy our very humanity. This insight poses a very new and significant question to the problem of objective

---

67. See note 42 above.

science. Rather than claiming that the mind cannot find the objective truth at all, Kahneman's study suggests that it can but is most often programmed not to. This thesis exposes the Achilles' heel of humanism – i.e., the uncontrollable subject – and conceals the realm in which free will can function meaningfully. As we shall see in the next chapter, this form of concealment or obstruction was a purposeful feature of Kant's strategy in establishing the priority of epistemology over ontology in philosophy. As such it was a deliberate strategy of the philosophy of the Enlightenment.

The ironic outcome of this analysis is that rather than emerging as the champion of liberty, the rational capacities of moral reasoning and System 2 are responsible for the mechanisms of coercion that construct the moral justifications that allowed rationalist humanism to impose itself on society and politics at large. The struggle with the self that the rider and System 2 are powerless to win on the inner battleground of the human psyche is futile because here the elephant and System 1 rule supreme. The battleground of humanist politics is therefore transposed to the public sphere where the coercive tools and mechanisms at the disposal of System 2 – which is most effective when applied to the monitoring of others – can take control. This is how the illusion that a rationally run society is a free society is constructed.

Entitlement to the power to restrict liberty in the public sphere is therefore the ironic foundation of post-Enlightenment politics. The same basic principle is also the basis of Cavanaugh's notion of privatized religious thought. The history of the struggle between the rational and irrational aspects of the self is long. One of the great projects of medieval religious philosophy was the evaluation of reason and its capacity to exercise control over the other willful forces in the self. But the struggle to demonstrate the nonviability of sin or crime and "convince" the adherent or the citizen that choosing goodness is always in his or her better interest has rarely succeeded in overcoming desires, passions, and impulses that do not seem to give themselves over to rational persuasion. The transposition of this struggle over the soul to the public sphere where object-focused mechanisms can engineer society through the use of coercive power is at the heart of secularism, and it drives the culture of science and technology, which build machines and gadgets to perform functions for the body from the outside.[68] The exposure of the manipulations that hold up this Structure of Concealment must now be seen to fall away in order to make space for the perspective of Segulah, which seeks to improve society through inner spiritual transformation, to become plausible.

Psychology, politics, and religion have all had to face the irrational and subconscious elements of the human self that rational argument does not seem to penetrate. But, in doing so, they seem to run against the grain of the human psyche. This running against the grain is an uphill struggle and it is an act of will. Thus, structures of coercion and mechanisms of imposition can be seen as ways of serving the willful interest of System 2 that bypass and manipulate human consciousness and restrict, rather than liberate, its inner freedom. The fact that this can be done only from the outside is crucial to our understanding of Segulah as a force that operates from within. There is only so much that you can enforce from the outside without something untouchable rebelling from within. Read stories of heroism and resistance such as Primo Levi's *Moments of Reprieve*[69] or Hans Fallada's *Alone in Berlin*[70] and you can know that Inner Segulah survived the tyranny of Nazism's quest for total control. The grotesque coherence between the barbaric imposition on human freedom manufactured by totalitarian regimes and the concealing mechanisms of rational politics allows us to move closer to an encounter with the meaning for Segulah of the elephant's dominance. The elephant cannot be shut down. It acts immediately and at speed. Even after the Holocaust, the elephant remained intact. The meaning of the elephant's dominance is therefore to be found in its connection to inner dimensions of the self that the perspective of Segulah is based upon. It is toward the discovery of this inner map that we will orient our present process of investigation.

---

68. This theme is developed in Jacques Derrida, *The Beast and the Sovereign*. We shall return to discuss this argument in detail in chapter 8 below.

69. Primo Levi, *Moments of Reprieve* (1981; trans. Ruth Feldman, 1985).

70. Hans Fallada, *Alone in Berlin*, trans. Michael Hofmann (Penguin Books, 2010).

PART II

GALUT

CHAPTER 4

~

Structures of Concealment as Klippot

Klippot and Concealment

In this chapter we will begin our philosophical analysis of Galut, or Exile. The first stage of this is to delve more deeply into the concept that, drawing on Heidegger, we have been referring to as "concealment."[1] This discussion is a necessary prelude to our discussion of deconstruction because we wish to equate these concealments with the constructs that the philosophy of deconstruction interrogates. We might think of them as the "constructions" of thought that the modern, scientific, or positivist movements in philosophy sought – ironically – to establish as self-evident truths or universal values. In our analysis of these concealments from the perspective of Segulah we shall equate them with the kabbalistic concept of Klippot.

Klippot (Klippah in the singular) is a kabbalistic term that is generally translated as "husks" or "shells." In kabbalistic thought these shells are barriers in our consciousness that block primordial awareness or "light" from view. We can experience them as obstacles and distractions that prevent us from knowing or sensing things that we do indeed know and sense and they can take the form of impulses, temptations, emotions, misconceptions, and more. In certain "porous" moments, when the membrane of the Klippah becomes permeable, we experience anxiety, pangs of conscience, and inner conflict or perhaps great love, fear, tears, or inner peace when our consciousness is troubled by what it is preventing itself from seeing or hearing.[2] These

---

1. See our discussion of concealments in *BT* in chapter 10 below.

2. This description rests heavily on Heidegger's concept of *attunement*, a term that basically refers to a mood or an ontological state of mind that discloses to us how we feel about the way in which we experience *being in the world*. This topic is of central importance to

are moments in which we are powerfully spurred to return to ourselves. They can generate waves of Teshuvah or Returning/Repentance without which the politics of Tikkun Olam cannot spread openly through the world.[3] More often, however, our Klippot are more tightly sealed. Using artificial psychological and cognitive constructions, they limit our consciousness and conceal from us what we, perhaps, most long to encounter. The specific features of post-Enlightenment humanism that we see as Klippot are the subject of this chapter.

Structures of Concealment and Post-Enlightenment Philosophy

Thus far we have argued that post-Enlightenment humanism made a crucial contribution to the dominance of rationalism over modern society's understandings of moral behavior, truth, and liberty. Finally, we have mentioned how this domination is an outcome of natural science and its newfound ability to represent its methods as geared toward establishing universal, rationally verifiable truths. This chapter will be dedicated to explaining more precisely what this Structure of Concealment consists in. We shall consider Structures of Concealment within the context of post-Enlightenment thought, giving special attention to the impact of Immanuel Kant. Our purpose here will be to clarify the implications for the Jewish politics of Survival and System of the priority given to epistemology over ontology in post-Enlightenment thought.[4] Ultimately, this analysis will allow us to draw four crucial inferences

---

our analysis, and the idea that these *attunements* disclose something to us that we know but also conceal from ourselves is essential to the claim that such things as concealments exist. We will discuss Heidegger's analysis of this concept in detail in chapter 13 below and will return to consider its meaning from the perspective of Segulah repeatedly throughout our discussion of Jewish texts in chapters 15–18.

3.   We will suggest in chapter 15 that Heidegger's concept of *attunement* is a powerful tool for interpreting the Jewish concepts of Middot Nefesh and Middot Neshamah. In this passage we allude to the idea that certain flashes of inspiration can be experienced as calls from within to bring our conscious experience of our own *being* closer to an experience of *being* that is grounded in the experience of all *being* (including our own) as God's *being*. Again, these are themes to which we will return in detail. However, at this point it is pertinent to mention that our description of this experience here is a deliberate echo of the way in which this idea is expressed by Rabbi Kook in his teachings about Teshuva, or Repentance. See Rabbi A. I. Kook, *Orot HaTeshuvah*.

4.   The idea that epistemology takes priority over ontology is central to Kant's thought, and as we will see, it is central to Heidegger's critique of Kant. See, for example, Karl

or meditations that will guide our efforts to understand the implications of linguistic-turn philosophy from the perspective of Segulah.

The philosophical questions of the Enlightenment were in many ways responses to breakthroughs in the natural sciences that posited rationally comprehensible accounts of cause and effect in the physical world. The spectacular progress made in natural science by Newton and others suggested that rational thought gave humanity the power to describe, observe, and predict the workings of the physical world without depending upon authoritative traditional or religious doctrines. Scientific experimentation and verification established the capacity of human thought to interact reliably or stably with the world outside of human consciousness. It made it possible to focus on the objects of the world and to know about them without obsessing over the ontological *being* of the knowing subject.

While the spirit of the Enlightenment was not geared toward the replacement of religion with science, the new methods did seem to suggest that the demonstrability of scientific findings about the world enabled humanity to progress toward the solution of its problems on its own. This assertion of human independence from God was not intended to annihilate religion, though its impact upon it was inescapable. What it meant was that "truth" now meant "rationally demonstrable, universally valid and verifiable truth" alone. Truth no longer corresponded directly to the content of either inner intuition or revelation. While the culture of the age had not turned its back on traditional structures of authority, it now faced the challenge of justifying them on new grounds. Scientific accomplishment required the subjugation of religion's truth claims to the principles of rationalism.[5]

Two significant philosophical problems emerge here. The first is a new chapter in the complex relationship between rationalism and religious faith in which attention was now urgently called to the futility of medieval philosophy's endeavor to provide rational proofs for God's existence. The second and more strictly "philosophical" problem concerned the viability of metaphysics

---

Ameriks, "The Critique of Metaphysics: Kant and Traditional Ontology," in Paul Guyer, ed., *The Cambridge Companion to Kant* (Cambridge University Press, 1992), 249–79.

5. See, for example, Paul Guyer and Allen W. Wood, eds., *Immanuel Kant, Religion and Rational Theology*, trans. Allen Wood and George Di Giovanni (Cambridge, 1996).

(i.e., the realm of pure abstract concepts and ideas which lie outside the confines of scientific experimentation and verification) in philosophical method. The problem here was that the philosophical methods that have recourse to metaphysics were themselves an extrapolation of rational thought. But faced with the meaning of rationality as defined by the new science, this rational outgrowth (i.e., metaphysical propositions) now seemed irrational. In order to align philosophy with scientific standards of truth, philosophers had to either dispense with the problems that generated the need for metaphysics in the first place or provide a scientifically defensible account of how metaphysical categories may still be used in philosophical method.

If we state this in slightly different terms, we might say that science's success in accounting for (and even predicting) observable phenomena seemed to force philosophy to dispense with its investigations into the mystery of the human subject. The mystery of the human subject that lies behind – and thus interprets or decodes – sensory perception generated the foundations of philosophical questioning. Thus, the importance of Thales's suggestion that the entire world is water quite obviously has nothing to do with scientific accuracy.[6] The point is that his skepticism inaugurated a kind of inquiry geared to uncovering a deeper or more fundamental, stable, universal reality than the one we know most naturally through the use of our senses. This deeper reality was the one that was believed to be more rationally coherent than the transient observable world. Metaphysics was crucial because it allowed the unstable, unreliable subject (the "I" of every first-person sentence) to journey toward clarity and perfection-of-understanding by penetrating beyond unstable, tangible reality. Thought moved past irrational appearances into the rational coherence of an abstract realm in which metaphysical truth was appreciable. What the mind could be trained to see through philosophical deduction was beyond the world, but it allowed for a rational account of the knowledge and information gleaned from the world as it appears to the senses.

After Newton, it seemed clear that rational science could do away with the need for metaphysics. As a collective enterprise, the new science demonstrated how multiple subjects could all see the same scientific truths. One

---

6.   This claim is famously reported by Aristotle in his *Metaphysics*, 983b17–984a5.

could therefore conclude that scientific knowledge did not originate in the experience of the subject but in the objects themselves. The universality of the stable truth that was now discoverable in the "laws of nature" required no metaphysics. The universal truth of the object was now a demonstrable physical or this-worldly reality.[7]

In the late Enlightenment period, philosophy struggled to absorb these claims. This was not just an attempt to keep up. The new methods presented philosophical problems that science on its own could not solve. First, the philosophical struggle to rationalize faith was not only a response to a historical, social, or cultural clinging to familiar values. It was philosophically essential in order to maintain the liberty of the human mind from the laws and rules of scientific determinism. While religion accounted for the possibility of sin, the laws of nature could not be broken. The freedom of choice that the Enlightenment had ultimately cultivated as an ideal was therefore in danger of being sacrificed to the irresistible certainty of scientific proofs. Within such a context, morality and ethics could lose their meaning if the license to choose them was somehow limited too. Second, while science and technology continued to steamroll ahead, philosophy had to confront its reservations about the possibility of bypassing the role of the subject in cognition. Somehow the subject needed to be resurrected but without elevating subjective thought to the level of metaphysics. Philosophy reached an impasse. Calling into question the capacity of the subject to participate as an "understanding self" in science was futile. Traditional metaphysics was no longer an option. Something new was called for. In its search for this innovation, post-Enlightenment philosophy moved into an age of crisis.

Structures of Concealment and the Critiques of Immanuel Kant

In the face of the demonstrable progress that scientific objectivism was making possible, the insistence that objective reality could be perceived only through the philosophical perception of a metaphysical world was no longer reasonable. The laboratory and the real world-itself seemed to own up with

---

7.   See Gale E. Christianson, *Isaac Newton and the Scientific Revolution* (New York: Oxford University Press, 1996).

such enthusiasm to the laws, rules, and equations that science was discovering in (or perhaps imposing upon) them, that philosophy had no choice but to comply. Thus, philosophy could not but provide its own explanations and accounts for the unstoppable momentum of scientific discovery. What now demanded explanation was how – despite the undeniable limitations of the subject – rational objective knowledge ultimately works. How could this newfound objectivism be brought back to the objective comprehension of the subject? Moreover, could the subjugation of comprehension to the discoverable systems of objective knowledge provide clarity and guidance in questions of morality, ethics, society, and religion?

It is in the context of these questions that the so-called "critical" period in Immanuel Kant's philosophical career is so important. Kant's purpose was neither to reject religion nor to undermine science. He sought to present a full-blown, broad philosophical system that could acknowledge the primacy of rational thought while at the same time maintaining the moral freedom of the human subject to resist the kind of determinism that scientific comprehension imposed on its descriptions of objective physical reality. Kant sought a philosophical system that was sufficiently rational to comply with the dictates of scientific objectivism and yet free enough to allow for an ethics and faith rooted in human liberty. Kant's primary mechanism for resolving this philosophical conundrum is a crucial example of concealment. Kant's Structure of Concealment provided him with a system of thought that insisted that the limits of existence are defined by the limits of human knowledge (of existence). He did this while at the same time making room for both the expansion of knowledge and the protection of the subjective liberty that gave moral and religious choices their rational meaning. Ultimately, it is this Structure of Concealment that provided the philosophical support for science's noncontemplative drive toward the objectification of epistemology.

While a detailed discussion of Kant might perhaps be called for at this stage, we shall confine ourselves to some general remarks alone. It is not our purpose here to present a systematic study of Kant but instead to grasp the general structure of objective philosophical rationalism that is both the foundation of Survival and System and the object of deconstruction's criticism.

Kant famously distinguishes between two forms of reason. He refers to the first as "pure" reason and to the second as "practical" reason.[8] In his *Critique of Pure Reason*, Kant seeks to establish a stable philosophical foundation for mathematics and physics by restricting the scope of the phenomena in the world that rational science can ever gain access to.[9] As such, Kant suggests that the world is comprised of phenomena that are accessible to rational observation.[10] These phenomena submit themselves to mathematical and physical laws that are recognizable to and commensurate with the a priori or internal mental structures of human cognition. Like Copernicus, who first posited that all the stars in the sky (and the world too) are spinning in perpetual movement, Kant inverted the way in which philosophy understood human comprehension, moving metaphysics from outside the world to the inner compartments of the mind. Like the spinning earth and the stars in Copernican physics, Kant aligned the dynamics of the outside world as we know it with the inner mind, suggesting that both share the same condition of relative perpetual motion. The knowable world is accessible to comprehension because it is structured in the same way as the inner "metaphysics" of the knowing mind. In reverse, one might say that the world can be known mathematically because what is seen reflects the instruments of observation. We might put this as follows: what we do know is an image of what we can know because of how we know.

However, beyond the knowable phenomena of nature, Kant posits inaccessible regions of knowledge which he refers to as noumena.[11] Noumena are the

---

8.   This distinction is essentially reflected in the two major works of Immanuel Kant's critical philosophy. These are *Critique of Pure Reason* (1781), trans. Marcus Weigelt (Penguin Books, 2007) and *Critique of Practical Reason* (1788), trans. Mary Gregor (Cambridge, 1997).

9.   This idea is central to Kant's *Critique of Pure Reason*. See, for example, the introduction, section 3, "Philosophy Requires a Science That Determines the Possibility, the Principles and the Range of All *A Priori* Knowledge," 40–43 and a later section, "Of the Ground of the Distinction of All Objects in General into Phenomena and Noumena," 251–64.

10. Kant, "Of the Ground of the Distinction," in *Critique of Pure Reason*, 251–64.

11. Ibid., 258: "If by noumenon we mean a thing insofar as it is not an object of our sensible intuition, and make abstraction from our mode of intuition, it may be called a noumenon in a negative sense of the term. If, however, by noumenon, we mean an object of a non-sensible intuition, and admit thereby a special mode of intuition, namely, the intellectual mode – which, however, is not our own, nor one of which we

things in the outside world "as they are in themselves." These exist outside the confines of space, time, and substance, to which human knowledge is bound. They lie beyond comprehension because there is nothing in human cognition that can detect them. Noumena are not necessarily distant in the physical sense but, unlike the ideas of classical metaphysics, they are entirely inaccessible to pure reason. Noumena are objects of the universe "in themselves" and not as they are perceived. They are outside of knowledge because their mode of *being* need not conform to the categories of human cognition. Since the ontological *being* of noumena is meaningless, all that matters about objects is that – and how – I know of them. The upshot of this is that, since this knowing conforms to the metaphysics of cognition, the possibility of objective knowledge is now understandable as stable. Everything that can be known to human comprehension must comply with the parameters of understanding – or "forms of intuition"[12] – that are objectively shared by all phenomena, while the *being* of anything that does not comply with these parameters cannot be known at all. It is this that establishes the priority of epistemology over ontology. Epistemology is relevant to and definitive of philosophical inquiry because philosophy deals only with how we know what can be known. Ontology, which is concerned with the *being* of "things in-themselves," is relevant only once an epistemological foundation of "know-ability" has first been established.

Ostensibly, what Kant is arguing is that rationalism is a structure of the mind that conforms with phenomena in the world. But this a priori structure recognizes only the elements of external reality that are recognizable to it. Phenomena are objects that abide by the same rules that are present within the mind.[13] The mind is therefore capable of discovering knowable phenom-

---

can understand even the possibility – then this would be the noumenon in a positive sense of the term."

12. The centrality of intuition to Kant's philosophy of knowledge is one of the themes that attracted Heidegger's attention, and we will return to it in the context of our discussion of his critiques of Kant. The theme of intuition is central to the *Critique of Pure Reason* as exemplified by the key role that Kant attaches to it in cognition. For example, he begins his analysis of the transcendental aesthetic in the first part of the *Critique* with the following methodological statement, "Whatever the process and the means may be by which knowledge refers to its objects, intuition is that through which it refers to them immediately, and at which all thought aims as a means." See ibid., 59.

13. In Kant's thought, the a priori structures are the frameworks of thought that allow human experience of the world in thought to correspond to the reality of the world.

ena as they are – objectively – in the world of human cognition. In this sense, there is no mystery about the way phenomena are rationally known. Thus, cognition involves demystification. On the other hand, things "in themselves" that do not conform to the a priori structures of comprehension are liberated from the demystification of "pure" reason and continue to hold mystical significance.

In offering this portrayal of cognition, Kant believed he had accomplished a "Copernican revolution" in philosophy. This so-called "transcendental turn"[14] was designed to show how we can give an account of objective knowledge. Prior to Kant, philosophy which had thought that objects might be grasped as they are could not avoid the conundrum of the subject's *being*. Kant's epistemology, on the other hand, does not seek to demystify noumenal reality "in itself." Instead he sought only to establish a system that would allow truthfulness about objects as phenomena to be stably conceived. For Kant, the a priori knowledge that is embedded in the rational faculty of the mind before comprehension ensues is what makes possible the pure abstractions of metaphysics. The correlation of these a priori structures and the world of phenomena is perceived by Kant as allowing for a form of transcendentalism that is metaphysical only in the sense that it is the habitat of pure reason.

The significance and meaning of noumena to this philosophical system emerge in Kant's *Critique of Practical Reason*.[15] Practical reason is concerned

---

In order to clarify the meaning of this idea, Kant relies upon the notion of the a priori structure to distinguish between pure and empirical knowledge. See his discussion of this in the *Critique of Pure Reason*, 38–43.

14. The Transcendental Turn is a term coined to describe Kant's suggestion in the *Critique of Pure Reason* that cognition is made possible by a kind of structural correspondence between our thought and the objects of our attention in the world. The *Critique* is dedicated to what Kant refers to as "Transcendental Aesthetics," "Transcendental Logic," "Transcendental Analysis," "Transcendental Deduction," "Transcendental Dialectic," etc. This approach to philosophy is a turn in the road in the sense that henceforth the dominance of our knowledge of the world over the being of the world itself is secured as the primary and hence most fundamental human experience.

15. As Kant states in his Preface to the *Critique of Practical Reason*, this book comes to address the misunderstandings that his comments about the un-knowability of noumena caused in his analysis of pure reason. In his words, "I also understand why the most considerable objections to the *Critique* that have so far come to my attention turn about just these two points; namely, *on the one side* the objective reality of the categories applied to noumena, denied in theoretical cognition and affirmed in practical, and

with the freedom of the will and with the possibility of founding moral action on reason. For Kant, moral action could not be guided by utilitarian concerns. It required the free election of a moral path that is grounded in an eternal value that lies outside the confines of space and time. Essentially, morality for Kant was a religious term. But it required rationalization. Here Kant distinguished between the pure knowledge that is accessible to pure reason and the practical knowledge that is accessible to practical reason. The limitations that Kant imposed upon our capacity to know things in-themselves through the application of pure reason provide the groundwork for the meaning of noumena in practical morality. Kant insists that noumena cannot be known. But after insisting on the limitations of pure reason, he proceeds to build upon it his account of the human capacity to ground moral behavior on principles higher than those of desire. Kant's famous insistence that the existence of God cannot be proven allows him to speak of God, immortality, and pure freedom as rationally knowable.[16] This is because these noumena are knowable as non-verifiable articles of faith. However, as such, they become postulates of reason endowed with practical significance. It is the withdrawal or the concealment of noumena from know-ability that allows them to function as unimposing values or agents which inspire rational moral judgment without impinging upon human liberty. However, as agents in practical reason, the values in themselves become observable (though not verifiable) through empirical testing. Thus, Kant will insist that a principle

---

on the other side the paradoxical requirement to make oneself as subject of freedom a noumenon but at the same time, with regard to nature, a phenomenon in one's own empirical consciousness, for, as long as one had as yet formed no determinate concepts of morality and freedom, one could not conjecture, on the one side, what one was to put as a noumenon at the basis of the alleged appearance, and, on the other side, whether it was at all possible even to form a concept of it, since all the concepts of the pure understanding in its theoretical use had already been assigned exclusively to mere appearances. Only a detailed *Critique of Practical Reason* can remove all this misinterpretation and put in a clear light the consistent way of thinking that constitutes its greatest merit" (Kant, *Critique of Practical Reason*, 5–6).

16. Kant makes this argument in his essay "Religion within the Boundaries of Mere Reason," which appears in Allen Wood and George Di Giovanni, eds., *Kant, Religion within the Boundaries of Mere Reason and Other Writings*, Cambridge Texts in the History of Philosophy (Cambridge University Press, 1998), 31–191. For a valuable discussion of this evolution in Kant's religious thought, see the introduction to *Religion within the Boundaries* by Robert Merrihew Adams, vii–x.

of moral value cannot express whim or desire. It must conform to a "categorical imperative."[17] Through the categorical imperative, the value of good or righteousness as it is "in-itself" can be tested rationally and empirically for its universal applicability. Thus, only maxims of free will that can also hold up a principle of universal legislation conform to the practical law. Similarly, through practical experience, noumena can be comprehended empirically as universal moral laws that can be known in the world as phenomena. This capacity of noumena to become phenomena is how Kant accounts for the demonstrable growth of the phenomenal knowledge accessible to pure reason through scientific discovery.

The significance of this short account of Kant to our analysis is twofold. First, it allows us to recognize that the all-important supremacy of rational epistemology is accomplished through a construct. Second, it enables us to uncover the irony that is inherent in the Jewish politics of Survival and System. Let us briefly rehearse the broader significance of the first of these conclusions, after which we will dedicate a separate section to the second:

The philosophical account of the capacity of rational thought to establish verifiable stable truths is dependent upon the concealment of things-in-themselves. Phenomena are objectively known only because a curtain has been drawn which conceals noumena. But this concealment – which is an integral part of Kant's philosophical system – is not morally neutral. Without prior knowledge of noumena we cannot claim that we know nothing about them. Similarly, in order to describe our knowledge of phenomena as rational we must posit them. Kant therefore had to write the *Critique of Practical Reason* in order to account for his philosophical capacity – as a thinking subject – to exclude noumena from cognition in the first place. In other words, he must know about something he claims he cannot comprehend in order to exclude it from comprehension. It is this knowing about what cannot be known that makes this Structure of Concealment manipulative.

---

17. The categorical imperative for Kant refers to the principle that one should "act only according to that maxim whereby you can at the same time will that it should become a universal law." This formulation of the categorical imperative, quoted in Wood and Di Giovanni, *Religion within the Boundaries*, first appears in Immanuel Kant (1785), *Grounding for the Metaphysics of Morals: On A Supposed Right to Lie because of Philanthropic Concerns*.

The crucial point here is that the possibility of this manipulation exposes the constructed nature of post-Enlightenment rationalism. So whatever is gained by setting truth and morality free of the subject is lost by the constructed nature of the manipulative mechanism required to do it. If the morality of constructing this curtain is called into question, the morality of the distinction that rational thought provides between truth and untruth – which depends on its universal applicability to the world of phenomena – collapses. Likewise, if the notion that ties human liberty to morality is constructed manipulatively, it too loses its moral meaning.

The manipulative mechanism that we are referring to as a construct operates on the possibility of reversing deduction and induction. Through induction (which here is a philosophical equivalent of the psychological term "priming"[18]), the representation of the universal truth can be seen to appear even though it has not been discovered. It can be seen because it can be generated and disseminated through industrial mass production and distribution. In other words, what is seen as "empirically true" in the world need not be what is known but can also be what is "made known."[19] It is planted into public consciousness as empirical truth through the mass production of corroborative evidence for rational findings. This is a lot like the dual principle upon which the marketability of technology operates: on the one hand, need is the mother of invention. On the other, need itself can be generated in order to market inventions. The possibility of this inductive reversal (i.e., of constructing need or truth) is corrupting, and it is what Adorno and Horkheimer refer to as the "mass deception" of the Enlightenment. In their words,

---

18. The concept of priming refers in psychology to the ways in which subliminal messages enter into a person's consciousness without their paying attention to them. This has a decisive impact on decision making and choice. The theme is discussed by Daniel Kahneman in his *Thinking, Fast and Slow*, 52–58.

19. This comment is similar to Jacques Derrida's analysis of performative speech as a kind of speech that instead of reporting rather involves "making known" what is being politically promulgated by the speaker or reporter. We will return to this theme in chapter 8. See Jacques Derrida, *The Beast and the Sovereign*, vol. 1, ed. Michel Lisse, Mari-Louise Mallet, and Ginette Michaud, trans. Geoffrey Bennington (Chicago, 2009), 34–36.

Kant's conceptions are ambiguous. Reason as the transcendental, supraindividual self contains the idea of a free co-existence in which human beings organize themselves to form the universal subject and resolve the conflict between pure and empirical reason in the conscious solidarity of the whole. The whole represents the idea of a true universality, utopia. At the same time, however, reason is the agency of calculating thought, which arranges the world for the purposes of self-preservation and recognizes no function other than that of working on the object as mere sense material in order to make it the material of subjugation. The true nature of the schematism which externally coordinates the universal and the particular, the concept and the individual case, finally turns out, in current science, to be the interest of industrial society. Being is apprehended in terms of manipulation and administration….The senses are determined by the conceptual apparatus in advance of perception; the citizen sees the world as made a priori of the stuff from which he himself constructs it."[20]

Similarly, the attempt to ground morality in reason draws upon a manipulation that undercuts the moral viability of the whole project of practical reason. In this vein, Adorno and Horkheimer continue,

In confirming the scientific system as the embodiment of truth – the result arrived at by Kant – thought sets the seal on its own insignificance, because science is a technical operation, as far removed from reflection on its own objectives as is any other form of labor under the pressure of the system.[21]

Rational truth and morality appear plausible because they are technically manufacturable. However, with no capacity to reflect on their own objectives, they are inherently synthetic and prosthetic. They are servants to the

---

20. Horkheimer and Adorno, *Dialectic of Enlightenment*, 65.
21. Ibid., 66.

human capacity to mass produce them. They originate in captivity, not in the freedom of the mind.

Such is the curtain that Kant draws to cover up noumena. Since the curtain – i.e., the distinction between phenomena and noumena – itself is already an artificial construction, its moral viability can be manipulatively constructed too. Thus, the escape from the subject to the object that rational philosophy seems to accomplish is really an eminently marketable or manu-facturable delusion for which laboratories and other factories of information readily supply lavish layers of evidence. In this way "scientific progress" is really a sequence of trends replacing trends and cover-ups replacing cover-ups until the illusion of objective progress is complete. In other words, since the escape from the confines of the subject was never authentic, the mech-anisms of concealment that made it possible are really only a re-covering up, achieved again and again as the curtain that conceals the subjectivity of objective method is repeatedly drawn and redrawn for repeated profit. Given this, we can now understand how the regenerative and repeatable mechanism of concealment – which constructs the notion of rational truth – manages to seem stable. The mechanism that delineates the boundaries of the "know-able" truth according to an a priori metaphysics of rational cognition appears permanent only because it continually regenerates itself and thus lives on and on at the heart of post-Enlightenment humanism. Ultimately, as we shall see, it is this mechanism or Structure of Concealment that is the object of deconstruction's assault.

Klippot and the Jewish Politics of Survival and System

Before moving on with our philosophical deconstruction of post-Enlight-enment humanism, we must first clarify the significance of Kant's Structure of Concealment to the Jewish politics of Survival and System. There are multiple ironies that attend upon the consistent and repeated clinging onto Kant of the European Jews whose politics, thought, and religion is rooted in Survival and System. While Kant was not exactly the most philo-Semitic of Enlightenment thinkers, the Structure of Concealment that he provided played a crucial role in founding the premises of Jewish integration in post-Enlightenment Europe. In its simpler versions, the priority given to the rational mind as the knowing self in post-Enlightenment thought was taken by many as a reliable invitation to the Jews of Europe to become fully fledged members of their societies.[22] Given their acculturated capacity for rational thought, Jews were given the chance to integrate if they successfully faced the challenge of articulating rational parameters for their faith. Alternately, they might now discover how to abandon their burden of faith without compromising their moral convictions. Either way, the various attempts to create a balance between secular and religious rationalism, Jewish particularism, and rational universalism led the Jews of Western Europe into a crisis of identity. We might say that the dilemmas generated by the Enlightenment give us the axes of a graph upon which we may plot the evolution of the modern Jewish denominations in the West, from secular to ultra-Orthodox and everything in between. The irony here bespeaks itself.

Our point is that these developments – and not the lessons learned from the Holocaust – are the birthplace of the post-Enlightenment Jewish politics of Survival and System. From the perspective of Segulah, the sociological disintegration of European Jewish life is an expression of the angst and panic that follow the (ironically self-inflicted) imposition of Klippat Yavan on the identity of Am Segulah. From this perspective we can see the politics of Survival and System as an anxiously self-delusional strategy of survival that embraced the Enlightenment's Structures of Concealment at a devastatingly high price. The empirical nature of science and liberty (i.e., as the rational meanings of truth and free choice, respectively) was understood as the foundation for a form of universal humanism which presented itself "hospitably" to the Jews of Europe. It allowed them to belong as acculturated European Jews.

Even though this was also a period of rising antisemitism in Western Europe, the Jews of Europe consciously "bought into" the Structures of Concealment that made their inclusion possible while burying their heads in the sand. On the one hand, it is perhaps only with the full benefit of post-Holocaust hindsight that we can now see how devastatingly naive this

---

22. A striking example of this in the popular culture of the period is Gotthold Ephraim Lessing's play *Nathan the Wise*, which has a Jewish protagonist whose character is largely molded on the model of Moses Mendelssohn. For a discussion of this, see Paul Mendes-Flohr and Jehuda Reinharz, *The Jew in the Modern World: A Documentary History* (Oxford University Press, 1980), 55–60.

delusion really was. On the other hand, the persistence of Survival and System in today's Jewish world suggests that the problem here was and is deeper. It suggests that knowledge was and is an act of will and therefore that the choice of a system laced with a visible Structure of Concealment was a willful one. In this sense we can say that the politics of Survival and System is not only self-delusional; it is rooted in a strategic acceptance of visibly disturbing concealments. One possible historical illustration of this is the troublingly little evidence of contemporaneous Jewish indignation about the visible underbelly of the new rationalism's conduct in the colonies. Jews consciously allowed post-Enlightenment rationalism to define morality and virtue even as the "rational" and "morally enlightened" peoples of Europe entitled themselves to oppress and trample down the human liberty of every colonial "wog" and native "savage" who got in their way.

In philosophy, the strategically self-conscious Jewish allegiance to Kant is perhaps symbolized by the seminal impact of Jewish thinkers on the neo-Kantian movement. Though in the early nineteenth century German philosophy after Hegel had moved away from Kantian transcendentalism, by the end of the century neo-Kantianism was the dominant voice that summoned German philosophy consciously "back to Kant." This call was first articulated by Otto Leibmann, and it was followed by champions of neo-Kantianism such as Hermann Cohen and Ernst Cassirer, all three of whom were Jews.[23] Cohen and Cassirer understood the emphasis that Kant

---

23. For a rich and detailed collection of neo-Kantian texts in translation, including detailed bibliographical references to original German publications, see Sebastian Luft, ed., *The Neo-Kantian Reader* (NKR) (Routledge, 2015). See there, for example, Hermann Cohen, *Das Prinzip der Infinitesimal-Methode und seine Geschichte* (Berlin: Dümmler, 1883), partially translated as *The Principle of the Infinitesimal Method and Its History*, by D. Hyder and L. Patton, NKR, 101–16, and *Kants Theorie der Erfahrung* (1885), partially translated as *Kant's Theory of Experience*, by D. Hyder, NKR (1919), 107–16; *Die Religion der Vernunft aus den Quellen des Judentums* (Leipzig: Fock), translated as *Religion of Reason: Out of the Sources of Judaism*, by Simon Kaplan (New York: Frederick Unger, 1972). See also Ernst Cassirer, "Kant und die moderne Mathematik," *Kant-Studien* 12:1–40 (1907b); *Substanzbegriff und Funktionsbegriff. Untersuchungen über die Grundfragen der Erkenntniskritik* (Berlin: Bruno Cassirer, 1910), translated in *Substance and Function and Einstein's Theory of Relativity*, by Swabey and Swabey (Chicago: Open Court, 1923); "Hermann Cohen and the Renewal of Kantian Philosophy," trans. Lydia Patton, in NKR, 221–35; *Kants Leben und Lehre* (Berlin: Bruno Cassirer, 1918), translated as *Kant's Life and Thought*, by James Haden (New Haven: Yale University Press, 1981); *Zur Einstein'schen Relativitätstheorie*

placed on phenomena as moving philosophy and culture closer to the rigorous objectivity of the natural sciences. As Peter Gordon puts it, "Taking the riddle of the Kantian 'thing-in-itself' as his point of departure, Cohen attempted to show that Kant's chief aim was to develop a theory of scientific discovery in which the thing-in-itself surrendered its metaphysical status to become, instead, a purely methodological idea, as the 'task' (Aufgabe), or the as-yet unexplained, of expanding scientific knowledge."[24] Cohen proposed a system that ultimately dispensed with metaphysics altogether in which

> the thing-in-itself was accordingly abandoned in favor of a purely conceptual coherentism that replaced the empiricist model of truth as correspondence to an independent object, with a purely intellectualistic model of truth as the systematic coherence among concepts.[25]

The Jews in the neo-Kantian movement sought to steer European philosophy back to objectivism because they believed that scientific rigor would protect them from the demons in the dark. The debate between Cassirer and Heidegger at Davos in 1929 is a case in point that provides us with a setting for exploring the fullness of this phenomenon.[26] Politically speaking, the neo-Kantian movement resurrected the post-Enlightenment hope that Jews may enjoy full integration in German society. The notion of a rationally negotiable and discoverable truth was understood by many as an invitation for Jewish ideas to compete on an even playing field in the context of a universal discourse. Though, as we have said, Kant was notoriously unsympathetic to Judaism, there were adequate reasons for the Jewish thinkers of the Enlightenment to believe that rationalism was an opportunity. Strategically,

---

(Berlin: Bruno Cassirer, 1921), trans. Swabey and Swabey as *Substance and Function and Einstein's Theory of Relativity*; *Determinismus und Indeterminismus in der modernen Physik* (Göteborg: Göteborgs Högskolas Årsskrift, 1936), 42, trans. O. Theodor Benfey as *Determinism and Indeterminism in Modern Physics* (New Haven: Yale University Press, 1954).

24. Peter E. Gordon, *Continental Divide: Heidegger, Cassirer, Davos* (Cambridge, MA: Harvard University Press, 2012), 52.

25. Ibid., 53.

26. We shall return to discuss this debate and Gordon's account of it in detail in chapter 8.

bringing the schools of German philosophy back to Kant can therefore be seen as a necessary companion to Cohen's attempts to reconstitute Jewish thought in nonmetaphysical, rational terms. Cohen's famous claim that neo-Kantian philosophy is authentically and originally a Jewish idea suffices to illustrate the point.[27]

From the perspective of Segulah, the significance of the historical role Jews played in neo-Kantianism is an expression of the angst that motivates the politics of Survival and System. This is not an angst that originates in the lessons learned from the Holocaust. It is an angst which suppresses or conceals the inner desire for Teshuvah (i.e., full self-disclosure of identity) by redirecting it toward a need to be part of the Enlightenment. It is this neediness that accounts for the willing embrace of the Structures of Concealment that may cover over the demons for a while – but at the terrible price that Jews have paid and continue to pay in the modern era. Just as the concept of Teshuvah requires the extraction of light from Klippot, the philosophical journey that we shall seek to undertake in order to rehabilitate the perspective of Segulah will begin with the attempt to remove the Structures of Concealment outlined in this chapter. For this task, we will turn now to the philosophy of deconstruction.

---

27. This is Hermann Cohen's key argument in his *Religion of Reason out of the Sources of Judaism* (1919); see note 23 above.

CHAPTER 5

Deconstruction and De-con-struction:
Introduction and Overview[1]

Galut and Churban

The following chapters will be dedicated to an analysis of deconstruction.[2] We are interested in grasping the ways in which this mode of "doing philosophy" can help expose the Klippot that hold up the strategic choices of Survival and System. By talking about deconstruction and reading examples of deconstructive texts we shall try to experience how concealments work and see if we can destabilize their hold upon us. Before we enter a detailed discussion of the texts that we have chosen, we shall offer here a short conceptual framework that guides our reading and gears us toward accomplishing our specific purpose.

Our interest in deconstruction is in the type of exilic consciousness that it engenders. This is the element that offers us the insight we are seeking into the experience and meaning of Galut. While Exile is a negative term,

---

1.   In this chapter we will provide an overview or condensed version of the argument that will unfold through the rest of part 2 of this book. As such we shall withhold bibliographical details and textual support for any of the claims made here. These will be provided in ample detail in the following four chapters.

2.   Throughout our discussion of Galut we will be using the word "deconstruction" in three distinct ways. The first is a general reference to this approach to philosophy, and we will indicate this meaning by the use of a lower case d – deconstruction. The second use refers specifically to the concept of Galut as it is connected to the philosophy of Ludwig Wittgenstein and for this, we will use a capital D – Deconstruction. Finally, the third use refers specifically to the concept of Galut as it relates to the philosophy of Martin Heidegger. This will be written, De-con-struction.

in our case, it is something we are looking for. The Exile that we seek is the experience of disentanglement from the most basic and seemingly intractable assumptions of post-Enlightenment humanism, and it is these assumptions that must be seen to fall away before we can draw the necessary conclusions from the process of Churban, or Destruction, that lies ahead.

Conventionally, Churban refers to the destruction of the two ancient Jewish Temples in Jerusalem. The first was destroyed by Babylonia in 586 BCE and the second by the Romans in 70 CE. But the term can be used to denote historical calamity in general, and that, of course, includes the Holocaust. What we are proposing is an idea that emanates from the Jewish tradition or from what we have referred to as the perspective of Segulah. The idea is that the historical calamities of the Jewish exile are opportunities for finding a path toward Tikkun. More specifically, our proposal is that these opportunities are missed when the inner experience of their meaning is not precise. In the case of the Holocaust, what we are suggesting is that its implications for the relationship between Jewish and Western identity are lost when Jews are too attached to the West to appreciate them. For this, as we have said, Churban must be preceded by Galut.

Galut means Exile and refers to both the historical exile of the Jewish people from the land of Israel and to the experience of inner exile from the self. In both cases, the experience of an exilic consciousness is there to make us yearn. Our suggestion is that the wholesale adoption of Western humanism has concealed from the Judaism of Survival and System the proper object of its yearning. But Galut is also a protective shell. It is a place where we know we are in the shadows. Galut is therefore a condition, one in which esoteric spiritual or discredited traditional intuitions are pushed beyond the boundaries of public life. In Exile we can only yearn for their revelation and vindication.

Two Genealogies of Deconstruction

The inner experience of Exile that we are seeking is one that we have chosen to approach and hopefully grasp through philosophical reflection. And it is to this that we now turn. We will do this by trying to experience the inner intuition of the need for disentanglement from post-Enlightenment humanism that we propose motivated the philosophy of deconstruction. We shall make no attempt here to offer a comprehensive academic portrayal of deconstruction in the context of twentieth-century thought. Rather, we shall draw upon illustrative examples that will help us get at the meaning of deconstruction's exilic nature.

Our discussions of deconstruction will focus on Michel Foucault and Jacques Derrida – arguably the most emblematic, influential, and best known practitioners of deconstructive thought. We will try to see certain passages from the writings of each as belonging to two separate forms of exile. We want to distinguish between them by referring to them as two separate genealogies of deconstruction that we shall refer to as Deconstruction and De-con-struction, respectively. The first meaning or genealogy of Deconstruction will highlight passages in which Foucault and Derrida seem to be reacting to or extending the impact of Ludwig Wittgenstein on their thought. In this Wittgensteinian sense, Deconstruction means exile from the metaphysical meaning of language. De-con-struction will be understood as a post-traumatic, philosophical reaction to Heidegger. In this sense De-con-struction is a conscious insistence on exile, motivated by (and a defense against the reoccurrence of) the horrifying experience of coming face-to-face with the primordial abyss that is exposed when transcendental epistemology gives way to (or is demolished by) an egocentric ontological being that is totally obsessed with the inevitability of its own demise.[3]

We shall begin by dedicating the rest of this chapter to laying out a densely packed overview that will show where each of these two trails leads. We will also compare them, outlining the overlaps and distinctions between them. In the following chapters we will return to each point mentioned here and retrace it with detailed textual illustrations and explanations that for now will be left out.

Deconstruction and De-con-struction

Since we are using both Deconstruction and De-con-struction to describe the philosophical methods of the same thinkers, it is clear that the meanings that we are ascribing here to the two terms will necessarily overlap. However, because of the two different genealogies we are tracing for them, there are also

---

3.   These slightly oblique references to Wittgenstein and Heidegger will be fully explained in the coming chapters.

important distinctions between them. The principal point of overlap is that both De-con-struction and Deconstruction conduct philosophical interrogations of the priority given to the rational mind as the knowing self in post-Enlightenment thought. Moreover, both De-con-struction and Deconstruction assault the elevated status accorded to epistemology in Western thought since Plato (and more specifically since Kant). The principal distinction between them is in the different strategies used to conduct this assault. De-con-struction proceeds by overthrowing the priority accorded to epistemology in post-Enlightenment philosophy. It does this by establishing the philosophical precedence of ontology. In this sense, De-con-struction rests on the assumption that all knowledge is dependent upon a subject who's *being* primordially *is* before understanding ensues. By contrast, Deconstruction seems to accept the priority of epistemology in post-Enlightenment humanist philosophy – i.e., Deconstruction proceeds from the assumption that the world *is* only insofar as we consciously *know* it. However, instead of claiming that this knowledge is absolute or universal, Deconstruction insists that the inevitable instability of language as we use it undermines the whole project of philosophy itself. Deconstruction is thus epistemologically antiphilosophical while De-con-struction is ontologically antiepistemological.

If we now turn to the thinkers we will be discussing, we might rephrase the previous paragraph as follows: Both Jacques Derrida and Michel Foucault assault post-Enlightenment rationalism. However, the question is whether their philosophical genealogy should be traced back to Ludwig Wittgenstein (Deconstruction) or to Martin Heidegger (De-con-struction). In the scheme that we are building, it is Wittgenstein who represents the struggle against "philosophy (as epistemology) in general," while Heidegger destroys the priority of epistemology in philosophy by claiming that authentic human thought can be accessed only through ontological analysis of the mortal self, which he refers to as Dasein. The plausibility of connecting Derrida and Foucault to both Heidegger and Wittgenstein is the overlap between Deconstruction and De-con-struction. The fundamental gulf that divides Heidegger from Wittgenstein – first-degree Jewish Mischling from second-degree Nazi – is the distinction.[4]

---

4.   It is very important to be clear that we do not mean to imply here that Heidegger is a second-degree philosopher. On the contrary, it is the vital accomplishment of his career that makes the process of Churban possible. For now, our intention is more neutral.

In our analysis of Deconstruction, we shall present the assault on the priority of rationalism in humanist thought in antiphilosophical terms, focusing on the so-called "linguistic turn" in twentieth-century thought and its implications for the destabilization of rational knowledge. Without presuming to offer anything approaching an exhaustive or even adequate summary of the "linguistic turn" (and without referring in any detail to more than a handful of the numerous careers that were dedicated to it), we shall trace how Deconstruction can be seen as having put an end to the philosophical attempts at modeling human language on mathematics in the human and social sciences. Starting from the other end, as it were, we will also follow the attempts of Thomas Kuhn and Bruno Latour to expose the linguistic contingencies of even the most mathematical truth claims in the natural sciences.

Our purpose here is to emerge from this discussion with an analysis of Deconstruction that, when applied to metaphysics and theology, will allow us to experience the exilic Deconstruction of positivist objectivist truth claims. Following this, we shall move on to ask whether the same contingencies that apply to "truth" with reference to the human sciences apply also to the natural sciences, the point being to demonstrate the seemingly inescapable plausibility of both "subjectivism" and "objectivism" in humanist thought. The inescapable plausibility of the subjectivism insisted upon by Deconstruction is honest, relentlessly integral, and chaste, but only insofar as it refuses – on moral grounds – to desist from exposing the concealments that enable objectivist claims and constructions to stand up. In this sense, Deconstruction is chaste, but antipolitical and prudish. It is perennially counterintuitive and tied to powerlessness as a matter of principle. It offers freedom and liberty but only in silent exile. More problematically, it can hardly keep up with the relentless pace of construction (or "discovery") that objectivism demonstrates

---

By that we mean only that, despite Heidegger's lasting importance and prominence in the world of philosophy, in the Nazi hierarchy he did not enjoy similar fame. He was certainly not among the political thinkers such as Adolf Hitler and Joseph Goebbels who formulated the National Socialist political manifesto. He was also not counted among Alfred Baeumler and Alfred Rosenberg as one of the philosophers most highly valued by the Reich as an academic spokesman of the Nazi ideology. We will return to a discussion of Heidegger's career and moral standing in the next chapter and again in chapter 9. We will dedicate chapters 10–14 to a close analysis of his masterwork, *Being and Time*.

each day as the roller coaster of scientific progress hurtles forward at break-neck speed.

In light of these observations, we shall voice the critique that Deconstruction is insufficiently troubled by the ease of construction and by the willingness of human nature and the natural world to yield to the scalpel that objectivist natural science takes to them daily. It is the easy viability of constructions – which from the perspective of Deconstruction is perhaps perennially suspect as artificial, technological, manipulative, and prosthetic – that must also be seen as inescapably plausible. The inescapable or undeniable plausibility of construction demarcates the boundary between what has and what has not been discovered about the truth of the world, and it is here, at this boundary of language and silence, that the inner self can feel what is unsatisfactory about the condition of Galut. It is from here, as Derrida himself acknowledged,[5] that the exiled self feels the need to yearn.

Here Deconstruction brings us to a terminus in exile, where we may indeed choose to stop and resign ourselves to our condition, warily protecting ourselves from crossing the boundary of thick silence that delineates the limits of rational argument. What lies beyond the boundary of rational argument is an infrangible silence Beyond this silence there are no words. From here we can only yearn that what lies beyond the boundaries of human consciousness will make itself known to us. In the words of Derrida, it is from here that we can pray, "*Viens!*" (Come!)[6]

This condition is perhaps of intrinsic value, but in the unique historical context that follows the Holocaust it is also intolerable. The path forward that we are proposing is one in which we switch modes and prepare to learn the lessons that are concealed in the experience of Churban. What we are suggesting is that this becomes possible when we begin by thinking afresh about Deconstruction but this time, we must explore its meaning as De-construction. De-con-struction conceals the horror that perennially threatens to shatter its exilic condition in calamity. The silence that we reach at the end of the path of De-con-struction, as we shall see, is of a different order from the inviolate silence of Deconstruction. This is a silence that can be broken – but

---

5.   See John Caputo, *The Prayers and Tears of Jacques Derrida: Religion without Religion* (Indiana University Press, 1997), 42–44.

6.   Ibid.

only at a very high price. The journey back to Churban that the breaking of this silence sets into motion is dreadful – but possible.

De-con-struction frames the genealogy of Derrida, Foucault, and the "linguistic turn" as a reaction to Heidegger. In retracing the genealogy of De-con-struction back to Heidegger, Deconstruction's relentless insistence on antipolitical powerlessness will be presented not as a silence enforced upon us by the limits of language but as a post-traumatic reaction to the encounter that Heidegger gives us with the aspect of the inner self that he calls authentic Dasein. In *BT* Heidegger strips away the concealments that maintain priority of rational, transcendental epistemology over ontology. The significance of the destabilization and re-subjectification of the truth accomplished here is that it refocuses philosophical attention back to the inner mystery of human consciousness. But what is discovered there is the overwhelmingly definitive experience of death that shapes and informs every moment of human *being*. Heidegger frames the experience of the self in the inevitable Holocaust that awaits the self and which the self must embrace and face in order to know truth. Heidegger motivates the philosophy of De-con-struction as its dooms-day prophet.

As a post-traumatic response to Heidegger, De-con-struction exposes the contingencies that attend upon the humanist claim to control stable notions of the truth as a prophetic warning against the inescapably imminent threat of the notion of truth that Destruction proposes. In De-con-struction the humanist construction of objectified truth is seen to rely upon the manipulative concealment of ontological mystery through the inauthentic and perhaps even dishonest assignation of philosophical priority to epistemology. This concealment, which according to Heidegger was first perpetrated by Plato himself, was the philosophical strategy of the Enlightenment that Heidegger believed he had discovered in his readings of Kant.[7] From Heidegger's perspective, Kant's re-concealing of the question of *being* obscured the significance of Dasein and its structures of *being* as the ultimate opportunity for finding authenticity. By leading back to the question of *being*, Heidegger exposes the constructed or "laboratory" nature of human knowledge, opening up an

---

7. This is the theme of Heidegger's discussion of Kant in Martin Heidegger, *Kant and the Problem of Metaphysics* (1929), trans. Richard Taft (Indiana University Press, 1997). We will return to discuss this argument in chapter 8 below.

abyss in which manipulative willpower runs rampant. Facing the haunting awareness of this abyss square on is, perhaps, the most honest philosophical accomplishment of Heidegger's *BT*, and it is echoed in Carl Schmitt's portrayal of political sovereignty.[8]

In this analysis, De-con-struction emerges as unable to accept the morality of an ontology whose only coherent political expression is necessarily tyrannical and obsessed with death. The philosophers of De-con-struction (again, Foucault and Derrida) - for whom Heidegger's ontology was inescapable – therefore invented a radically antipolitical philosophy which set up a line of defense against the true nature of ontologically honest politics. The deep purpose of De-con-struction is therefore to prevent the "breaking out" of Heidegger's ontophilosophical consciousness and its political aspirations. This is accomplished through the relentless interrogation of every political structure from the grandest of colonial empires to the most delicate of syntactical sequences while staying pristinely clear of the inevitable ontological contamination that any and every constructive alternative to De-con-struction must inhere. The silence that De-con-struction imposes on itself is therefore a strategic part of its post-traumatic struggle to prevent the inevitable calamitous outcomes of Dasein running rampant. Unlike the more pristine silence of Deconstruction, this self-imposed post-traumatic silence is breakable but only if you have the stomach for it. We shall argue that this "stomach" comes from Churban after which the yearning to break free from Galut is no longer practical. After Churban there is no turning back, and the way forward is Tikkun.

In sum, both Deconstruction and De-con-struction are desperate attempts to prevent (a reoccurrence of) Destruction. Neither offers a constructive path to Rehabilitation because they are both equally reticent about construction. This is their overlap. But they are exilically silent and reticent for different reasons. Deconstruction is tied to Galut by the inviolable rigor of a silence that lies beyond language, while De-con-struction is paralyzed at the edge of Galut where it maintains a self-imposed discipline that struggles to keep the

---

8.   See Carl Schmitt, *Political Theology: Four Chapters on the Concept of Sovereignty* (1922), trans. George Schwab (University of Chicago Press, 1985). We are offering this citation here because, unlike the other thinkers mentioned in this chapter, we will not be returning to Schmitt in any detail later on.

destructive power of authentic Dasein at bay. While the silence that the limits of language impose upon Deconstruction is borne of an encounter with the ineffable, De-con-struction is silent because it has faced the unspeakable. While the articulation of the ineffable is nonsense, speaking the unspeakable is indeed possible. Ensconced in the ineffable, there is no sensible (i.e., non-nonsensical) path to Rehabilitation. On the other hand, bespeaking the unspeakable is a moral calling

This initial statement of our analysis was necessarily dense and compact, and it is not complete. But the point we have just reached is the point that we must reach again in order to begin the process of Destruction. On our second run we shall repeat this analysis in more detail. But before we embark upon this fuller explication of Deconstruction and De-con-struction, it is worth returning briefly to the politics of Survival and System. More poignantly, it is worth returning to the story of the Jewish people who continued to choose the politics of Survival and System even as the scarred tissue of their skin smoldered from the flames of historical Churban and Holocaust.

Faced with a brutal choice between delusional concealment and the abyss of Destruction, the navigators, who steered the path of the Jewish people toward a political strategy that rested upon the politics of Survival and System, chose concealment. Their unflinching commitment to the axiomatic conviction that humanism does not bear the full burden of guilt for the emergence of Nazism concealed from them the delusional irony of their decision to choose Kant instead of confronting Heidegger.[9] From the perspective of Segulah we can see how the politics of Survival and System have been defined by a commitment to the concealment of the illusion (or delusion) about the humanist conception of human *being* that the primacy of epistemology over ontology holds up. Despite the complex prices paid for this choice (the costliest of which have been the Holocaust and today's enduring crisis of Jewish identity), the politics of Survival and System built an elaborate strategy for ensuring Jewish prosperity on the very structure of thought that we seek to unhinge.

---

9. We shall consider a significant example of this when we discuss Peter Gordon's excellent analysis of the debate between the Jewish philosopher Ernst Cassirer and Heidegger that took place in Davos in 1929. See chapter 8 (below).

In the final outcome, our analysis of Deconstruction will expose this Structure of Concealment and allow the humanist illusion of rationally verifiable truth (on which the politics of Survival and System relies) to fall away. Following this, our analysis of De-con-struction will reveal the grotesqueness of the manipulation that ties the rational construction of verifiable truth to our emotionally charged moral intuitions (the elephant). This analysis will finally allow the illusion that the rational meaning of free choice gives us liberty to fall away too. It is in the horrifying unconstructed primordial abyss that is exposed when rationalist epistemology gives way to (or is demolished by) ontology, it is in this Auschwitz of the human consciousness, that De-con-struction will lead us back to the path that we shall ultimately follow to the locus of Destruction from where the path to Rehabilitation can emerge into view.

CHAPTER 6

~

Deconstruction as Galut

Deconstruction and Truth

We shall now turn to the task of presenting the meaning of Deconstruction as Galut. Here we shall begin by focusing on Deconstruction as distinguished from De-con-struction (as explained above).

Deconstruction tolerates no attempts at reconstruction and will offer no opportunity for Rehabilitation. However, it provides us with a crucially important account of the meaning of Galut, which in epistemological terms refers to "a condition of chaste exile from ultimate or universal propositional truth." In this sense, Deconstruction is closely connected to (though not the same as) negative theology and apophasis. The importance of Deconstruction is in its capacity to call our attention again and again to what is inevitably left unsaid in any and every proposition.

Deconstruction weighs heavily on the tongue; it forces us to stammer, to contradict and repeat ourselves, to push polished articulations back to the primal state of khôra in which they originate so we may see their constructed nature. Deconstruction's value is not to be found in what it posits but in what it prevents. Deconstruction looks on with yearning at an absolute and ultimate truth. But it knows that it can never reach it. This deep knowledge takes an active form; it requires perpetual reaffirmation. In this sense Deconstruction requires a commitment to exposing and overwhelming all propositional attempts at stating stable truths and to calling attention to the inadequacy of their pretenses. Deconstruction only knows that it does not know anything completely and is therefore keenly sensitized to the not-knowing of those who claim to know more than they really can. It notices the

115

constructions that make the illusion of stable knowledge appear reasonable and bombards them with questions that undermine their plausibility.

This is not done without remorse. Deconstruction is tortured with angst. Deconstruction is a killjoy, but perhaps it only kills the joy that in the first place is had at the expense of others (though it is possible that, for Deconstruction, all joy is somehow at the expense of someone). Deconstruction can be painful because it is the work of privileged people who must renounce profit or benefit for chastity. In this it shares something with Tolstoy and Marx and has, with some justification, been readily associated with radical politics. But of more significance to us is the fact that Deconstruction is not a system of human perfectibility in the sense that it cannot venture any image of perfection. Its gaze is fixed on the superfluities that recall unnoticed or under-dignified imperfections. It gradually and slowly refines imperfection by tearing down and peeling away the layers of falsehood that conceal the partial perfections and the "good-enough" standards of constructed politics, philosophy, economics, law, and religion. It overwhelms the rational management of thought, drowning it in obstacles that upset and obstruct its advancement along the smooth, clear path of progress. It tells us that the path itself is a construction and that it is paved on someone else's field.

Methodologically, Deconstruction begins with the rejection of ontology's claim to the foundations of philosophy. This means that philosophy is bound to clarify only what we know without venturing near what is not and cannot be known. Philosophy is limited by language and we can speak only of what we know. All that *is* in *being* is relevant to philosophizing only insofar as it is known to *be*. In Kantian terms, we might say that Deconstruction is concerned only with phenomena and that it is more chaste than Kant about noumena because it is unwilling to posit the un-knowability of something that cannot be known. It is more chaste also about the knowability of phenomena, insisting that their complete range of forms and manifestations can never find a stable place to settle on the tumultuous soil of the knowing "I." The soil is indeed soil. It is a ground. But it is like the soil on a riverbed that is constantly unsettled by the rush of water all around it.[1] The knowing "I"

---

1.   This is an image used by Ludwig Wittgenstein in *On Certainty* (ed. G. E. M. Anscombe and G. H. von Wright [Harper, 1969], 15e, 97): "The mythology may change back into a state of flux; the river-bed of thoughts may shift. But I distinguish between the

is in turmoil and can only know that it does not fully know and that the very notion of its stable *being* is itself a water-swept riverbed. This is not to be confused with doubt or even with uncertainty. The non-knowing of Deconstruction is a condition of flux, a sensitivity to the movement of the world and its perpetually undulating rhythmic movement through space and time that never stands still long enough to *be* any single truth. But this epistemological rejection of ontology should not be confused for an acceptance of philosophy as epistemology.

To the extent that we may describe Deconstruction as philosophical, it endorses the claim that knowledge is always given – in some way or another – to articulation. As Kjell S. Johannessen put it (in terms that deliberately echo Wittgenstein),

> Knowledge and language are woven together in an indissoluble bond. The requirement that knowledge should have a linguistic articulation becomes an unconditional demand. The possibility of possessing knowledge that cannot be wholly articulated by linguistic means emerges, against such a background, as completely unintelligible.[2]

Put simply, "saying it back" is proof of comprehension. Insofar as Deconstruction is philosophical it acknowledges the principle that all knowledge is reliant on language. Since language is the medium of knowledge and of all meaningful thought, all of epistemology depends on it.

However, Deconstruction insists that language is not stable. It rejects the notion that philosophical inquiry into the precise meaning of words can allow thought to transcend the "physical" realm in which these words are used. Though this reservation about metaphysics is not new, it faced an acute crisis when, without (even Kantian) metaphysics as its refuge, philosophy had to support its propositions about knowledge in the post-Newtonian world.

---

movement of the waters on the river-bed and the shift of the bed itself; though there is not a sharp division of the one from the other."

2. Kjell S. Johannessen, "Rule Following, Intransitive Understanding, and Tacit Knowledge," in *Essays in Pragmatic Philosophy II* (Norwegian University Press, 1990), 104–5.

The language of philosophy, with all its extremities and complexities, had to face the precision and elegance of Galileo's claim that "the book of nature is written in mathematical language."[3] While the recognition that "language is not mathematics" is at the core of the crisis of all modernist philosophy, Deconstruction stands out as a radical response to the failed attempts of philosophers like Russell and Frege to redeem philosophy by elevating the logical precision of philosophical language to equal that of mathematics.[4] Deconstruction represents a change of strategy or a "turn" in the plot of philosophy's handling of this crisis. In this sense, Deconstruction is antiphilosophical. If philosophy believed that it had to evolve the mathematical logic of language in order to attach mathematical precision and certainty to philosophical propositions, Deconstruction is nothing less than the deliberate subversion of this effort. If philosophy sought redemption through the finessing of philosophical language, Deconstruction insisted on inexorable exile. Given the inescapability of language and the undeniable possibility of communication that it provides, Deconstruction abandons philosophy's meta-lingual aspirations and chooses in their place language itself. It actively insists that all knowledge can be communicated – i.e., known – only within the logically flawed boundaries of language as it is. As we shall see, this claim is extended

---

3. This famous pronouncement of Galileo's appears in his book (1623) *The Assayer*, trans. Stillman Drake, in *Discoveries and Opinions of Galileo* (New York: Doubleday, 1957), 237–38.

4. The elevation of the philosophy of language to the logical level of mathematics was the project that Bertrand Russell tackled in his primary works of logical and analytical philosophy. These most famously include his *Principia Mathematica* (1910–13), written in conjunction with Alfred North Whitehead, and his earlier work, *The Principles of Mathematics* (1903), in which he published his famous paradox. Put succinctly, Russell discovered in 1901 a flaw in Cantor's set theory which defined a set as a collection of elements with a common property. Gotlob Frege extended this definition to the realm of logic, referring to a "set of sets" as something that can be expanded into a "set of all sets." Within this type of set one can include a "set of all sets" that includes a "set containing itself" as one of its properties. If, for example, we think of a set of all numbers, this set is not in itself a number and is therefore not contained within itself. Given this, a set of all sets of numbers that includes itself paradoxically cannot exist. Thus, Russell concludes that self-reference will always function paradoxically in language, as in the case of someone who says, "I am lying." It of course follows that if he or she is lying then he/she is not; and if he/she is not lying, then of course, he/she is. From Russell's perspective this discovery had a shattering impact on the possibility of language finding its logical foundation in mathematics.

to include the destabilization not only of language but of mathematics too. Methodologically, Deconstruction therefore directs its attention to the instability of language. It calls attention not only to what language is and to how it works but also to what it is not. As such, given the obvious recognition that Truth, Justice, Good, Evil, God, Morality, Peace, and Perfection are all words, Deconstruction determines to find their meaning inside the confines of truth's exilic existence (Galut).

This description of Deconstruction as Galut is saturated with unmarked allusions to Wittgenstein, Foucault, Derrida, and many others. Though for the purposes of our overall argument our coverage of this field need not be exhaustive, it is necessary to draw out some of these allusions by looking closely at a handful of select texts, each of which will serve only as an illustration of Deconstruction's antiphilosophical linguistic method and its connection with Galut. We shall begin with Michel Foucault and with his discussions of unity and contradiction in *The Archaeology of Knowledge*.[5]

Michel Foucault, Unity and Contradiction

Foucault's book *The Archaeology of Knowledge* begins with a discussion of what he refers to as the "unities of discourse."[6] These "unities" are an example of what we have been calling Structures of Concealment, which Foucault tells us "may not have a very rigorous structure, but they have a very precise function."[7] That function is to create the illusion of continuity where it need not necessarily exist. Continuity depends upon the construction of an illusion of sameness. The illusion of sameness — across either space or time — ties together disparate phenomena in a sequence of interconnections that can then be seen to comply with a kinetic logic of cause and effect. In Foucault's words,

> Take the notion of tradition: it is intended to give a special temporal status to a group of phenomena that are both successive and identical (or at least similar); it makes it possible to rethink the

---

5.   Michel Foucault, *The Archaeology of Knowledge and the Discourse on Language*, trans. A. M. Sheridan (New York: Pantheon Books, 1971).

6.   Ibid., chapter 1, "The 'Unities of Discourse,'" 21–30.

7.   Ibid., 21.

dispersion of history in the form of the same; it allows a reduction of the difference proper to every beginning, in order to pursue without discontinuity the endless search for the origin; tradition enables us to isolate the new against a background of permanence, and to transfer its merit to originality, to genius, to the decisions proper to individuals.[8]

The illusion of sameness transmitted in time allows us to speak of historical processes as if they were a protracted single event that has somehow been triggered by an extraordinary act of genius whose seminal impact is seen to travel across time. The discovery of a point of origin provides a rationale for the historical phenomena that are seen to emanate from it. But Foucault insists that the notion of a tradition can be held up only by reducing the difference caused by every new beginning to an act of passive duplication. In other words, to hold up this logic, the illusion of tradition must be constructed. Tradition requires a metaphor in which some kind of a diachronic time-ether or time-matrix is assumed. Against the backdrop of this construction, events can be seen to originate in moments of greatness or genius and appear to travel across the surface of time like ripples on the surface of a pond. To imagine a tradition, we must think of time as offering no resistance. In it, sequences of events duplicate their point of origin in the same way as a ball in outer space retains the energy with which it was first thrown. Historical processes, like the ball, continue to move in a set direction until a new source of energy forces them to change their course. Similarly, the notion of influence,

which provides a support – of too magical a kind to be very amenable to analysis – for the facts of transmission and communication; which refers to an apparently causal process (but with neither rigorous delimitation nor theoretical definition) the phenomena of resemblance and repetition; which links at a distance and through time – as if through the mediation of a medium of propagation – such defined unities as individuals, oeuvres, notions, or theories. There are the notions of development and evolution: they make

---

8.   Ibid.

it possible to group a succession of dispersed events, to link them to one and the same organizing principle, to subject them to the exemplary power of life (with its adaptations, its capacity for innovation, the incessant correlation of its different elements, its systems of assimilation and exchange), to discover already at work in each beginning, a principle of coherence and the outline of a future unity, to master time through a perpetually reversible relation between an origin and a term that are never given, but are always at work.[9]

Foucault exposes the construction that makes the notion of influence – like the notion of tradition – appear plausible. Influence is made possible by the Structure of Concealment that blinds us to the mystery and magic of transmission and communication by discovering for us a principle of coherence. Coherence blinds us to the mystery of the world. It provides a rationale that conceals the magical mechanisms of cause and effect that somehow generate similarities. In place of magic it manufactures coherent "unities" such as the "individual" or the "theory." Rational methods of analysis such as grouping, collecting, and categorizing create perceptions of reality that conceal the knowing subject from its own crisis of identity and shield the similarity-searching ego from the trouble of assimilating true diversity.

Finally, in this sequence Foucault discusses a spirit or a geist which enables us to establish between the simultaneous or successive phenomena of a given period a community of meanings, symbolic links, an interplay of resemblance and reflexion, or which allows the sovereignty of collective consciousness to emerge as the principle of unity and explanation.[10]

Foucault identifies unities as constructions of coherence and draws our attention to the inconsistencies and the disunities that contradict and overwhelm the illusion of coherence that is made possible only through their concealment.

Deconstruction (though this is not the term Foucault uses here) requires us to question those ready-made syntheses, those groupings that we normally accept before any examination, those links whose validity is recognized from

9. Ibid., 22.
10. Ibid.

the outset; we must oust these forms and obscure forces by which we usually link the discourse of one man with that of another; they must be driven out from the darkness in which they reign. And instead of according them unqualified, spontaneous value, we must accept, in the name of methodological rigor, that, in the first instance, they concern only a population of dispersed events.[11]

The origin of the Structures of Concealment is in the a priori mechanism that facilitates the possibility of understanding phenomena. For Foucault, understanding is itself a form of construction. It will inevitably require a form of recognition. When one recognizes, one assimilates what is "out there" with what the subject can know. As the subject engages in the act of knowing the object, it is already familiarizing and rationalizing it. This rationalization is how understanding works, and so knowing is also its own opposite. To know is to relinquish the not-knowing that is always possible. To understand is to compress the unqualified dispersion of things into the tightly knit narrowness of coherence. To not-know demands the possibility of a framework in which contradictory points of view can coexist. In the third chapter of the fourth section of the same book Foucault continues:

> The history of ideas usually credits the discourse that it analyses with coherence. If it happens to notice an irregularity in the use of words, several incompatible propositions, a set of meanings that do not adjust to one another, concepts that cannot be systematized together, then it regards it as a duty to find, at a deeper level, a principle of cohesion that organizes the discourse and restores to it its hidden unity. This law of coherence is a heuristic rule, a procedural obligation, almost a moral constraint of research; not to multiply contradictions uselessly; not to be taken in by small differences; not to give too much weight to changes, disavowals, returns to the past, and polemics; not to suppose that men's discourse is perpetually undermined from within by the contradiction of their desires, the influences that they have been subjected to, or the conditions in which they live; but to admit that if they speak, and if they

---

11. Ibid.

speak among themselves, it is rather to overcome these contradictions, and to find the point from which they will be mastered.[12]

Deconstruction generates contradiction and dissent. It vigilantly protects the right of the minority, the delicate difference, the incompatible proposition to resist the violence of being shoved into coherence. The discourse of men, the hegemonic discourse, is perpetually threatened and undermined from within by the contradictions that obstruct the fulfillment of its desires. To maintain a contradiction is to protect the subtleties of difference from the oppressive mastery of sameness. The "archaeological analysis" of contradictions sees them as

> objects to be described for themselves, without any attempt being made to discover from what point of view they can be dissipated.... archaeological analysis does not try to discover in their place a common form or theme; it tries to determine the extent and form of the gap that separates them. In relation to a history of ideas that attempts to melt contradictions in the semi-nocturnal unity of an overall figure.... archaeology describes the different *spaces of dissension*.[13]

Spaces of dissension are antipolitical spaces. They are the isolated communities where dissenters huddle together in exile. They are built to provide refuge for those who would otherwise be melted down into a seminocturnal unity. A seminocturnal unity is a Structure of Concealment. Or rather, Structures of Concealment are seminocturnal. They are visible and noticeable, but dark and opaque. In a space of dissension, something more dignifying of difference is allowed. The matrix of difference or the community in exile in which the contradictions promulgated by dissenting minorities can survive is what Foucault calls a "discursive formation":

> A discursive formation is not, therefore, an ideal, continuous, smooth text that runs beneath the multiplicity of contradictions,

---

12. Ibid., 149.
13. Ibid., 155.

and resolves them in the calm unity of coherent thought.... It is rather a space of multiple dissensions; a set of different oppositions whose levels and roles must be described.[14]

In a discursive formation, oppressive explanation is replaced by descriptive mapping. Differences and dissensions are somehow contained in this space because it is here that they are encouraged to go forth and multiply. Endless interrogation produces the proliferation of difference. In spaces of dissent these differences can all belong because belonging entails no more than being plotted on a web or a matrix that resists coherence and serves only to maintain the contradictory structure of simultaneous negation and affirmation.

> Archaeological analysis, then, erects the primacy of a contradiction that has its model in the simultaneous affirmation and negation of a single proposition. But the reason for this is not to even out oppositions in the general forms of thought and to pacify them by force, by a recourse to a constructing *a priori*. On the contrary, its purpose is to map, in a particular discursive practice, the point at which they are constituted, to define the form that they assume, the relations that they have with each other, and the domain that they govern. In short, its purpose is to maintain discourse in all its many irregularities.[15]

Foucault's a priori analysis of knowing, recognition, comprehension, and coherence corresponds closely to Kant's. In this genealogy of Deconstruction, we can therefore understand Foucault as accepting the notion of philosophy as epistemological in the Kantian sense. But from there, Foucault turns away from philosophy. He conjures up magic in place of coherence; not-knowing in place of knowing. He constructs a chaste place in which the contradictions inherent in not-knowing can live free of coercion and in exile.

Deconstruction requires the courage not to know; to know through embracing Galut as the condition of not-knowing. Galut is a condition of

---

14. Ibid.
15. Ibid., 155–56.

discourse in which contradictions endure and conflicting points of view coexist while resisting the political impositions of governing bodies or general forms of thought that seek to pacify them by force. The reversibility of knowing and not-knowing is a product of rigor. Exile is not passive anticipation of redemption. To refuse the illusion of knowledge, to defy the constructions of rational thought, is not simply the resignation of the knowing self to the incomprehensibility of surrounding chaos. To not-know is to interrogate and to question. It is to be actively overwhelmed by more and more non-correlated observations and encounters. It is to detoxify the knowing subject and wean it off its neediness for coherence. It is to protect it from being lulled into a stupor in which it will resign itself – a resignation that does not contradict the activity of vibrant research and construction – to the illusion of stable truths.

Jacques Derrida, Negative Theology, Apophasis, Difference, and Ellipsis

Though Foucault and Derrida are often lumped together (and indeed the similarities between them are significant), an academic analysis, conducted with the purpose of evaluating their respective roles in twentieth-century philosophy, would have to pay significant and detailed attention to the differences between them. In the same vein, an adequate discussion of Derrida and Foucault, or indeed of either one separately, would require much more detailed attention to the varieties and developments that occur over time in their work. However, this kind of academic scholarship is not our purpose here. We are concerned with drawing upon Foucault and Derrida in order to give philosophical depth to the concept of Deconstruction as Galut and to the significance of its meaning within the language, narrative, and politics of Segulah. And it is with this very specific purpose in mind that we shall focus on the overlap between the two thinkers. We shall now turn to consider two small illustrative slivers of Derrida's writing.

In his later career, though to an extent this is also true of his earlier writing, Derrida acknowledged the connection between Deconstruction and negative theology. While he insisted that Deconstruction was not the same as negative theology, the correspondence between them and the apophatic dimension they share was a theme that concerned him. In "Sauf le Nom (post scriptum),"[16] Derrida writes,

> – ...
>
> – Sorry, but more than one, it is always necessary to be more than one in order to speak, several voices are necessary for that...
>
> – Yes, granted, and par excellence, let us say exemplarily, when it's a matter of God...
>
> – Still more, if this is possible, when one claims to speak about God according to what they call apophasis [*l'apophase*], in other words, according to the voiceless voice [*la voix blanche*], the way of theology called or so-called negative. This voice multiplies itself, dividing within itself; it says one thing and its contrary, God that is without being or God that (is) beyond being. The *apophasis* is a declaration, an explanation, a response that, taking on the subject of God a negative or interrogative form (for that is also what *apophasis* means), at times so resembles a profession of atheism as to be mistaken for it.[17]

We shall begin our reading of this passage from the middle and then work our way back to the beginning because Derrida is suggesting here that this passage – and perhaps all passages of writing – can only be read if they are also read backward. Apophasis is reading backward, and it is all reading because of the principle of the reversibility of meaning that applies to all words. Deconstruction exposes this reversibility. It draws out the multiple meanings that must have been compressed into the use of a word for it to assume a singular meaning. It exposes the instability in all truth claims that is inevitable due to the fact that they are inevitably expressed in language.

For Derrida, it is an omnipresent feature of language that words assume meaning by standing in place of what they mean and by therefore *not being* what they mean. They are always meaningful through apophasis. If this is

---

16. Jacques Derrida, "Sauf le Nom" (1993), in *On the Name*, ed. Thomas Dutoit, trans. David Wood, John P. Leavey Jr., and Ian Mcleod (Stanford University Press, 1995), 35–85.

17. Ibid., 35.

ubiquitously true of language itself, it is acutely true of that family of words in language (what Wittgenstein calls a language-game) that we call "theology." Therefore, what Derrida is saying and doing in this passage should not be confused with more conventional forms of negative theology. Derrida is not resorting to negative language because we cannot and do not know enough about God to say anything propositionally valuable about Him. Neither is his insistence on negativity to be confused with reticence about anthropomorphosis. For Derrida, in this passage, God is negative not because He *is not* a body or *is not* an outstretched arm. God is spoken of negatively because "God" is only a word. "God" is a name. Apophasis is required because of the temptation to speak of God as something other than His name. God, as we can speak of Him, is part of language, and because of this He cannot be spoken of – or propositionally known – in anything other than language. Since this is the condition of all language, it is also the condition of God as He appears to us through the medium of language.

But "God," if the word is to refer to anything, can also mean what is not in the word. What the word does and does not say about God must be simultaneously sounded if the notion of the unsaid in language is not to be crushed. Speaking is also not-speaking for Derrida (much in the same way as knowing was not-knowing in our discussion of Foucault above). Derrida insists here that the voice that speaks multiplies itself as it speaks. Its utterance triggers a proliferation of connotations and an escalation of meanings which flood the air every time a word is spoken. If the word is uttered with a singularity of purpose, it is the duty of Deconstruction to resist. Deconstruction prevents the intended meaning from colonizing the word. The escalation of meanings that Deconstruction exposes inevitably generates contradictions. If only one single sound is spoken, even that sound itself must already contain its own contradiction. A word can mean what it means only by pointing away from what the speaker has chosen for it not to mean. Language means what it means by not meaning what it is not. Singularity and clarity of meaning are possible only by the suppression of connotation and allusion. Conversely, metaphor is metaphor (and not meaning) only when it senses the distance between itself and that which it metaphorizes. In this sense, because there is always a distance or a difference (Derrida uses the auto-deconstructive

misspelling différance) between the word itself and its meaning, all language
is metaphor.

It is with this conception of language that we can understand the sliding movement of words in our passage. "Speaking" and "declaring" slide
into the realm of negating. Speaking slides toward silence while the declaration of God slides toward atheism. Derrida is suggesting that speaking
itself is in exile. It is in exile from itself and from the whole realm of signals
that we can associate with meaning. By sliding from negative theology to
atheism, Derrida is also suggesting that, due to the barrier erected by the
apophatic dimension of language, God too is in exile. Deconstruction
is the insistent exposition of this condition of exile. Deconstruction is
neither constructive nor destructive. It is chaste; willing – in the name of
this chastity – to sacrifice the vindication and self-satisfaction of *chercher
le mot juste*. Deconstruction does not undermine communication and
meaning. It does not come to either affirm or deny truth claims about
God. It merely comes to call attention to the reversibility that is inherent in the use of language and that emerges as the gaps between words
and their meanings are made visible. Theologically, it protects God from
being confused with the word "God" or from being reduced to the mono-
lithic monotony of the graphological sign "GOD" or, for that matter, the
sound of its utterance.

Next to the sound of speech there is also silence, and next to the mark
on the page there is the ellipsis. This now takes us, in an apophatic movement, back to the beginning of our text. Derrida makes room in this text
for the gaps and the silences, the contradictions and the double enten-
dres – the hidden meanings and the unaccounted-for connotations – by
resisting the violence that is concealed in the reader's desire for rational
coherence. Derrida insists on contradiction. But contradiction is required
not so much by the variety of experiences that language seeks to describe
as by the instability of language itself. Language speaks necessarily in more
than one voice. To avoid contradiction is to deny access to what is inevitably said in, by, through, and around every word. For Derrida this denial is
an act of political violence. It is an act of repression. To avoid violence one
must invite the inconsistency of plurality into the act of speech. One must
sacrifice precision for diffusion, coherence for chaos, strength of purpose

for timidity of spirit. To simply say "God" is to violate God. So, Derrida constructs this whole text in two voices that together "save the name" from desecration. These two voices are not in conversation. Neither are they in contradistinction. They are just both there, speaking in turns, beside each other.

One might expect otherwise, but in the world as we know it, to speak without violence is actually a little rude. It is to stammer clumsily, an inconvenience for which Derrida apologizes,

— Sorry, but more than one

It will take more than one voice to be honest and chaste and to make sure that you, the reader, are not fooled into believing there ever can be one voice at all. This calling of attention to the self-dividing multiplicity of voices in language is auto-Deconstruction. It is the explanation of Derrida's writing style which chooses chastity over clarity, apophatic, negative not-saying over violently constructing an illusion of the truth. It remains chastely in exile. This exile slides into a form of silence, which is why Derrida begins to "speak" about God and about the naming of God without words. He begins with ellipsis. Even before there ever are two voices, there is ellipsis, and before that there is silence. The dash and the ellipsis are perhaps the most honest thing that can/cannot be said about God from a condition of exile. This is a condition in which truth is too final and too narrow a term to use broadly without violence. God cannot be spoken of as merely a truth. Were we to speak of God this way, we would be making Him a victim of our violence. God is a mere word standing in for something that might only be honestly not said in the chaste silence of an ellipsis.

— Yes, granted, and par excellence, let us say exemplarily, when it's
a matter of God . . .

Derrida slides in and out of words. He begins with a dash, ends with an ellipsis, and thus slides from silence into language and back into silence. By enveloping the name of God in silence, Derrida is "saving" the name. "Save the name" is perhaps an inadequate translation of the duality of *sauf le nom*. To save the name is to save it from being named. But it is also to protect it by saying everything about it except for the name itself. Everything can be said, "save the name" – except for the name. Saying the name is saving the name by saying it only against a backdrop of the impossibility of saying it. Saving the name is to save the possibility of not-saying it.

Sauf le nom begins with two voices and the speaking of the two voices begins with an ellipsis. Meaning is in exile from singular speech and speech is in exile from silence. The text reads backward. It reads apophatically. All of its words read back to the ellipsis that is its beginning.

An earlier essay of Derrida's, which first appeared in his collection *L'écriture et la Différence*, is dedicated to the theme of the ellipsis.[18] Derrida's essay "Ellipsis" is basically a reading of Edmond Jabès's *Book of Questions* in which Derrida explores the confines of "the book" and the limitations that apply to the written word. A book is a finite entity, but it is also cyclical. "To write is to have a passion for the origin," but it is also an endless quest for "the lost writing of the origin."[19] Writing in the book is ultimately an attempt to reach beyond the book into that which cannot be contained by the book, into what "succeeds the book":[20]

> Here or there we have discerned writing: a nonsymmetrical divi-
> sion designated on the one hand the closure of the book, and on
> the other the opening of the text. On the one hand, the theologi-
> cal encyclopedia and, modeled upon it, the book of man. On the
> other a fabric of traces marking the disappearance of an exceeded
> God or of an erased man. The question of writing could be opened
> only if the book was closed.... And yet did we not know that the
> closure of the book was not a simple limit among others? And
> that only in the book, coming back to it unceasingly, drawing all
> our resources from it; could we indefinitely designate the writing
> beyond the book? Which brings us to consider *Le retour au livre*

---

18. Jacques Derrida, "Ellipsis," in *Writing and Difference*, trans. Alan Bass (University of Chicago Press, 1978), 294–300.

19. Ibid., 295.

20. Ibid., 294.

(The Return to the Book). Under this heading Edmond Jabès first tells us what it is "to abandon the book." If closure is not end, we protest or deconstruct in vain,

God succeeds God and the Book succeeds the Book.[21]

This passage, like the rest of this short essay, is elusive. It is hard to know what is being said, and in this sense its use of language, though opaque, is gentle. It invites the reader to jump into the cycle of the book and to seek closure. But also, to see the closure opening up as the text unfolds again. How may we read this passage intelligibly?

The passage seems like an invitation to read it beyond itself. It suggests that we must bring our own associations to it and come to it unceasingly so that we may read it without bringing closure to it. Since we bring ourselves to the reading, we are conscious (and perhaps guiltily so) that we can never even aspire to a faithful reading of the text as it is "in itself." It is not "in itself." It is written in such a way as to resist having an "in itself." This is why as the reader reads, the author is "erased" in the reading. By writing in such a way as to ensure that the text cannot be read without erasing the author, Derrida suggests that all reading is like this. Though concealments may allow us to ignore this, Derrida's style gives us no such reprieve.

However, this is the meaning of chastity here. Chastity is adjusting our expectations honestly to our condition of exile. To read the text honestly is to submit oneself to it. From our perspective and in this case, what this means is not ignoring the kabbalistic allusions conjured up by Derrida's choice to write elliptically about Jabès. Jabès consciously draws on kabbalistic and Jewish themes in his writing. Indeed, his first book of questions is comprised of conversations between imaginary rabbis answering each other. Even though the elusive style of the text is not really to be unraveled, the rabbinic and kabbalistic references; combined with the elliptical cyclical reading of "the Book" that succeeds "the Book" in the context of a negative theology in which God succeeds God, emboldens us to venture an author-erasing reading.

---

21. Ibid.

The Book that is read over and over is plausibly read as referring to the Torah. The Torah is a book that has been read and reread too often for us to speak of it as simply readable. It is only rereadable. The ritual cycle of reading that has continued without end or beginning for thousands of years is surely a passion for the origin. The reading of the book, which is not book but scroll of text, words that are free of the boundaries put on them by their physical inscription in letters, words that in their Hebrew original resist monotone and insist on being read differently and variously, with no vowels and no punctuation to rein them in, is comfortably understood as delving into the "encyclopedia" of a disappearing God – a self-concealing God – who has indelibly inscribed Himself into the "Book of man." This is a book to which we return unceasingly. It is the book from where all our resources are drawn. It is in the Torah and with the Torah that life is lived. The life lived explains the Torah, and the Torah explains the life lived. The cycle is never ending. It is a cycle of endless return that ties Torah to life and life to Torah. It is a cycle in which the Book succeeds the Book.

The meaning of ellipsis in Derrida's writing is the absence of closure. Deconstruction resists the possibility of closure and prevents the stabilization of language or knowledge in finite terms. There is no end. There is no universal truth. There is only a quest, a journey, and a move toward an end that cannot be reached. Standing on the edge of a cliff and beseeching God to come is prayer only for so long as God does not come. Deconstruction yearns for the impossible. It is theological atheism because it believes in a God that can matter only if He is impossible. But it is the possibility of that impossibility – and the refusal to accept any kind of finite closure – that keeps the faith in the possibility of the impossible alive in the first place. This is a condition of exile in which Segulah is protected from being converted into idolatry. God cannot speak without auto-Deconstruction. No man can speak for God without auto-Deconstruction. No stable, finite, or final truth claim can be asserted at all without owning up chastely to the multiplicity that it connotes and to the violence to which it must acquiesce in order to be more simply understood.

By underlining the connection between the experience of reading the book and of living life with Torah, we can understand more deeply how the destabilization of language through perpetual Deconstruction is a mechanism that maintains Jewish life in Galut. The cycle of Torah reading which accompanies the crossing of history in exile is the heart of the mechanism that enables the Jewish people to continue yearning in Galut. This cycle deconstructs historical experience and cyclically reinvigorates the conviction that "this is not the end." The last word has not been said because, living *in* and *with* the cycle of reading, one knows that the last word only precedes the next reading of the first. Subjugation to the rhythm of this cycle is honest and chaste resignation to the condition of exile. With each cycle new connotations and associations from life become attached to the words. The cycle of reading that absorbs into the text the historical experience of life as it has been lived draws out new dimensions of repressed and unnoticed meaning over and over until we reach the stage – which Derrida describes – when we may know that "if closure is not end, we deconstruct in vain."[22] This place of exile in exile, the point at which we no longer deconstruct in vain, is not one we can ever reach without sacrificing the chastity and honesty with which we resign ourselves to our condition of exile. We cannot leave exile from here without compromising or damaging the pristine chastity of prophetic vision. In other words, from the perspective of a world dominated by post-Enlightenment humanism, we cannot protect ourselves against the constructions and the concealments of rationalism without confining our resistance to them to negative terms. This leaves us with the endless task of deconstructing every closure in order to stay true to our expectant yearning for true Rehabilitation. It is a vigil against false Messiahs. From here we can only pray for something nonpropositioned to come. We can only pray for its incoming as we prepare ourselves to recognize it when it does. This is the prayer for the end of Galut that we can pray only from within Galut. This helpless prayer for the end of exile is Galut itself. The will to keep praying it in Galut is kept alive by the apophatic protection in silence of whatever it is we hope for that lies beyond our language. Galut here is the tireless determination to keep the continual yearning alive.[23]

---

22. Ibid.

23. This sentiment echoes the twelfth of Maimonides's thirteen principles of faith: "I believe with complete faith in the coming of the Messiah, and even though he tarries in waiting, in spite of that, I will still wait expectantly for him each day that he will come."

Orienting Deconstruction to the Perspective of Segulah

From the perspective of Segulah, our analysis of Deconstruction thus far can be seen to offer the following insights:

First, the dominance of epistemology is responsible for a crisis of identity in the subject because we are trapped in agnosticism about the capacity of the subject to know truth. We have described this crisis as the yearning of the knowing subject for not-knowing. This yearning is the condition of Galut. The subject actively seeks to know and speak outside the boundaries of coherence and in the spaces in which it will not be coerced or violently pacified into resolving difference and submitting itself to the calm unity of coherent thought. In Galut, the inner self stays awake to the possibility of non-knowing by remaining skeptical and agnostic about the capacity of the rational self to know the truth. The inner self yearns for a type of redemption that it cannot find in Galut. But it takes comfort in the knowledge that Galut will protect it and deflect from it the illusions that would quiet its yearning and subdue its vibrant capacity to continue with its dissent.

Second, the identity crisis of the subject is not one that can be reliably or stably resolved in the object without recourse to manipulative constructs (i.e., concealments). Therefore, as we walk along the path before us, we must carry in our backpacks a healthy skepticism about the value of rationally constructed truth itself. In the state of Galut we know that our crisis is also our hope for ingathering.[24] In Galut, the inner self stays hypersensitized to the constructions, illusions, and Structures of Concealment that surround it and, though no clear vision of the truth can present itself in exile, it need not worry that its skepticism about specific truths will ever breed cynicism about its undying hope for the final ingathering and Rehabilitation of all truths.

Third, since universal, rational truth is exposed as a manufacturable illusion, its destabilization through Deconstruction is not something to be feared. As it lives out an ever-lengthening history of exile, so long as it continues to yearn, the struggle against manipulative constructions is one that gives the perspective of Segulah a home in communities of dissension.

---

24. This echoes the famous story about Rabbi Akiva, who laughed when he saw the destruction of the Temple in Jerusalem and the beginning of the exile. It was only when he saw the prophecy of exile fulfilled that he knew for certain that redemption would come. See Babylonian Talmud, *Makkot* 24 a–b.

Fourth and finally, the rejection of false truths refines our approximation of truth. This cumulative experience is an apophatic process, i.e., it is accomplished backward, as it were. The collective outcome of this struggle is – in the deepest sense – the meaning of time endured in Galut and the purpose of its length. Galut is not pointless endurance.

CHAPTER 7

The Genealogy of Deconstruction as Galut

Exile, Antiphilosophy, and the Linguistic Turn

As we already stated, the meaning of Deconstruction is distinguished from De-con-struction by considering its genealogy in terms of Wittgenstein's philosophy. It is to the "exilic" or "destructive" element in Wittgenstein's thought that we now turn in order to understand what it is that the apophatic or negative side of Galut is protecting against. Again, what we shall present here does not qualify as a full discussion of Wittgenstein. This is not our purpose and so we shall confine our analysis to illustrations that allow us to advance our argument alone.

The point of connecting Deconstruction to Wittgenstein is to show how the apophatic or negative dimension of Deconstruction is designed to protect against the dangers of metaphysics. More specifically, in the context of post-Enlightenment humanism, Deconstruction as Galut protects against the concealment that allows us to believe that scientific truth claims expressed in mathematics and pure logic are more plausibly universal than classical metaphysics. It was Wittgenstein who showed that nothing is gained for philosophy by replacing classical metaphysics with pure logic or mathematics. Moreover, since Wittgenstein believed he could show how ordinary language works without conforming to the dictates of either scientific logic or metaphysics, his work also suggests that the recourse to either one is responsible for a great deal of damage. This damage is "philosophy" itself, and it is on account of his opposition to it that we describe his position as antiphilosophical.

To gain a fuller appreciation of the exilic dimension of Wittgenstein, we can start by considering him in the context of Bertrand Russell's efforts to provide philosophy with a language of pure logic. In our discussion of Kant,

136

we considered the importance for philosophy of duplicating the success modern physicists had with the cultivation of mathematics as the dispassionate and impersonal language of objective science. If fulfilling the redemptive promise of modernity depends on escaping from the prison of the subject into the freedom and certainty of the object (i.e., the domination of ontology by epistemology), Kant believed that philosophy must provide the sciences with an account of how the knowing self is capable of scientific objectivity. To Russell, this meant solving the philosophical question about the subjective nature of human knowing, which could only be done if the media of knowing, i.e., language and mathematics, could be shown to succumb to a fundamentally logical account of themselves. The project of modern philosophy for Russell was therefore the construction of a philosophical language that offered a logically coherent account of the foundations of both language and mathematics. This effort can be seen broadly as an extension of the redemptive project started by Kant, continued by the neo-Kantians, by the positivist school,[1] the Vienna circle,[2] Frege,[3] Whitehead,[4] and – in a different though related way – Sigmund Freud.[5]

---

1. The positivist school refers to the thinkers who sought to align philosophy and the human sciences in general with the principles of logic that apply to mathematics and rational science. Some of the prominent thinkers and scholars in this school are August Comte, Wilhelm Dilthey, and Leopold von Ranke.

2. The Vienna circle is a reference to a group of Viennese intellectuals that included Moritz Schlik, Friedrich Waismann, Rudolf Carnap, and Herbert Feigl. For a brief but helpful discussion of this circle and the relationship between its members and Wittgenstein, see Ray Monk, *Ludwig Wittgenstein: The Duty of Genius* (Penguin Books, 1990), 241–45.

3. Gotlob Frege, who wrote, among other works, *The Foundations of Arithmetic* (see Blackwell edition, 1950) and *Philosophical and Mathematical Correspondence* (see Blackwell edition, 1980), was considered by Russell as one of the founders of analytic philosophy whose work had significant implications for the philosophy of language in particular.

4. Arthur Whitehead coauthored with Russell *The Principia Mathematica* in 1910–13 (see chapter 6, note 4 above).

5. The comparison with Freud is based on the assumption that the attempt to define a precise language of knowledge can be compared to the scientific attempt to map what we might refer to as the inner grammar of the human psyche. Again, the notion of the enlightened state of mind that Kant believed rational thought could accomplish has its similarities to Freud's idea that a fuller understanding of human consciousness (that included both conscious and subconscious thought) was the key to the proper or healthy understanding of the self and hence to the healing of neurosis.

Wittgenstein inherited the mantle of Russell's efforts when the latter desisted from them after running into the conundrum that became known as Russell's Paradox.[6] After discovering the paradox, Russell joined forces with Whitehead in the composition of the "Principia Mathematica," a project which, despite the mammoth effort that both men dedicated to it, Russell ultimately believed had failed to accomplish its goal. Russell's unsuccessful attempts to find the logical foundations of language and mathematics left him exhausted. To Wittgenstein's chagrin, Russell gave up (what Wittgenstein considered) "serious philosophy" and planted his greatest expectations on the shoulders of his most brilliant protégé.[7]

The drama of the "linguistic turn" – a drama that we understand as a turn away from modernism's project of redemption and toward an insistent acceptance of exile – is captured in the vignette of Russell's severe disappointment with the outcome of Wittgenstein's efforts. The *Tractatus Logico-Philosophicus*, a book that Wittgenstein believed had "found on all essential points, the final solution of the problems,"[8] was introduced to the reader by Russell as one that left him "unable to be sure of the rightness of a theory merely on the ground that I cannot see any point on which it is wrong."[9] Russell is baffled by Wittgenstein's departure from the path he was expected to follow. He is perhaps impressed by the brilliance of Wittgenstein's new path, but he is neither convinced by nor satisfied with it. In his notoriously cool and reluctant introduction to the *Tractatus,* Russell writes, "Whether or not it should prove to give the ultimate truth on the matters with which it deals, [it] certainly deserves, by its breadth and scope and profundity, to be considered an important event in the philosophical world."[10] Unlike the members of the Viennese circle who (as Wittgenstein himself insisted) admired the *Tractatus*

---

6. See chapter 6, note 4 above.

7. For this transition in Russell's work and the effect it had on his relationship with Wittgenstein, see Ray Monk, *Ludwig Wittgenstein: The Duty of Genius*, chapters 3 and 4, entitled "Russell's Protégé" and "Russell's Master," respectively. See Monk, *ibid.*, 36–90.

8. Ludwig Wittgenstein, *Tractatus Logico-Philosophicus*, trans. D. F. Pears and B. F. McGuinness (London: Routledge, 1972), 4.

9. Ibid., "Introduction by Bertrand Russell F.R.S.," xxv.

10. Ibid., ix.

for all the wrong reasons, it seems clear that Russell's disappointment had nothing to do with misunderstanding. He simply didn't like it.

What Russell didn't like was Wittgenstein's turn away from the search for the first premises that Russell believed were essential to articulating a logical foundation for human thought. Wittgenstein instead turned to ordinary language as it was, adopting a dismissive position toward both foundational mathematics and pure logic. From our perspective, Russell's disappointment is an indication or a symptom of Wittgenstein's unveiling a Structure of Concealment which delivers a fatal blow to the post-Enlightenment project of redemption through science. Wittgenstein pulls the plug on this redemptive project by stating unequivocally in his preface to the *Tractatus* that "the aim of this book is to draw a limit to thought, or rather to the expression of thoughts."[11] This limit is placed at the boundary of normal language, a boundary that is positioned at the edge of silence.[12] The *Tractatus* demonstrates how the mathematicization of thought is itself a Structure of Concealment.

As we move on to illustrate this more fully, it is important to state clearly our position on the question of the consistency across the different stages of Wittgenstein's philosophical career. Though much has been said and written about the philosophical differences between Wittgenstein's earlier and later work, our perspective – while not denying the many strategic changes in his methods (which Wittgenstein himself alludes to in his introduction to the *Philosophical Investigations*[13]) – will emphasize the consistent thrust that drives both his early and his later philosophy. While his approach and method in the *Tractatus* are perhaps much more visibly engaged with

---

11. Ibid., 3.

12. Wittgenstein famously wrote in his preface to the *Tractatus*, "The whole sense of the book might be summed up in the following words: what can be said at all can be said clearly, and what we cannot talk about we must pass over in silence."

13. Ludwig Wittgenstein, *Philosophical Investigations*, trans. G. E. M. Anscombe (New York: Macmillan, 1953), preface, viii: "Four years ago I had occasion to re-read my first book.... It suddenly seemed to me that I should publish those old thoughts and the new ones together; that the latter could be seen in the right light only by contrast with and against the backdrop of my old way of thinking. For since beginning to occupy myself with philosophy again...I have been forced to recognize grave mistakes in what I wrote in that first book."

logic – and with Russell's notion of an atomic foundation of linguistic logic – than the *Philosophical Investigations*, the overall concern of both seems to be to show – as Wittgenstein stated in the preface to the *Tractatus* – "how little is achieved when those problems [i.e., the problems of philosophy] are solved."[14]

The antiphilosophical claim that little is solved by the solutions to philosophical problems is connected to Wittgenstein's basic intuition – common to both books – that philosophy itself is a product of the misconception of how ordinary language works. In the *Philosophical Investigations*, the attempt to overcome ordinary language and to provide a rational or logical account of it is presented as a dead end in philosophy. Wittgenstein writes,

> It is easy to get into the dead-end in philosophy, where one believes that the difficulty of the task consists in our having to describe phenomena that are hard to get hold of.… Where we find ordinary language too crude, and it looks as if we were having to do, not with the phenomena of every-day but with ones that "easily elude us, and, in their coming to be and passing away, produce those others as an average effect." (Augustine: Manifestissima et usitatissima sunt, et eademrusus nimis latent, et nova est invention eorum.)"[15]

Similarly, Wittgenstein suggests that philosophy must promote a return to ordinary speech. He writes,

> If it is asked: "How do sentences manage to represent?" – the answer might be: "Don't you know? You certainly see it, when you use them." For nothing is concealed.[16]

Our point about the consistency between the two books emerges when we see that this theme is also central to the *Tractatus*, where Wittgenstein writes, "The book deals with the problems of philosophy, and shows, I believe, that

---

14. See Wittgenstein, preface to *Tractatus*, 4.

15. Wittgenstein, *Philosophical Investigations*, 129e, paragraph 436.

16. Ibid.

the reason why these problems are posed is that the logic of our language is misunderstood."[17] If the correct meaning-making mechanism of language can be demonstrated, philosophy's proposed subjugation of language to logic can be understood as prone to regenerating all the problems with which philosophy is already redundantly occupied. It was because Wittgenstein recognized this that he dared to make the otherwise seemingly preposterous claim that he had solved "all the problems of philosophy."

In Wittgenstein's view, philosophy generates its own problems when it seeks to go beyond language to create either a system of logic or metaphysics that will account for meaning in language. This traveling beyond language is completely hopeless, because all language is a thing of this world and not external to its confines. This basic conviction, which guides both Wittgenstein's earlier and later work, is summed up succinctly in the infamous phrase "What can be said at all can be said clearly, and what we cannot talk about we must pass over in silence."[18] Indeed, this is the point at which Wittgenstein brings the *Tractatus* to its climactic end:

> 6.54 My propositions serve as elucidations in the following way: anyone who understands me eventually recognizes them as nonsensical, when he has used them – as steps – to climb beyond them. (He must, so to speak, throw away the ladder after he has climbed up it.)
>
> He must transcend these propositions, and then he will see the world aright....
>
> What we cannot speak about we must pass over in silence.[19]

It is undeniably true that the *Tractatus* and the *Philosophical Investigations* offer two very different strategies for explaining how ordinary language works. But, despite these differences, they share the conviction that language is not a mystery. In fact, it is so non-mysterious that we all know how to use it. It is only when it is examined with the wrong premises in mind that we

---

17. Wittgenstein, *Tractatus*, 3.
18. Ibid.
19. Ibid., 89.

become confused about things that are already out in the open and in plain view. This confusion is a crime that philosophy has perpetrated, and it has caused a great deal of damage along with it.

The crucial substantive point here is that, as a thing of this world, language does not point toward something that is beyond itself or outside of itself. Rather, language is self-referential. It creates meaning by something that it does and not by something that it says. In his later philosophy, Wittgenstein understands that the role of philosophy must be to show this doing instead of trying to explain it. In his earlier work, while the objective is the same, his method is more explanatory. In the *Tractatus*, language is an object of the world that can be used to create images of other things in this world. It is the logic of this imaging that creates the effect of meaning. Wittgenstein offers several different metaphors to demonstrate this point. He suggests that language is like a picture, a map, or sheet music. In the latter case, the music written on a score is not sound and it does not mean sound, but it does correspond to it by virtue of an "inner similarity" that it has with it:

> 4.0141 There is a general rule by means of which the musician can obtain the symphony from the score, and which make it possible to derive the symphony from the groove on the gramophone record, and, using the first rule, to derive the score again. That is what constitutes the inner similarity between these things which seem to be constructed in entirely different ways. And that rule is the law of projection which projects the symphony into the language of musical notation. It is the rule for translating this language into the language of gramophone records.[20]

The image of music on a score is but one expression of Wittgenstein's *bildung* or picture theory. More broadly, Wittgenstein suggests that language mimics other elements of reality and corresponds to them. In this sense, language is like a picture. This is perhaps most obvious in hieroglyphic script, "which depicts the facts that it describes."[21] But this quality continues into more

---

20. Ibid., 24.
21. Ibid.

complex forms of language and writing, because "alphabetic script developed out of it without losing what was essential to depiction."[22]

Wittgenstein suggests that we think of language as a picture which has an internal grammar that corresponds to the grammar of facts and the relationships between them elsewhere in the world. There is no mystery of meaning here, merely a recognizable correspondence that is somewhat similar to the correspondence between the actual streets we walk in and a map we use to navigate them. The map must correspond to the streets, but we only know that it corresponds to them by virtue of its not being them. Because of its self-referential quality – i.e., because it is a map and not the streets – it can exist alongside the streets as a means of helping us find our way around. Similarly, language is a picture of other things in the world that functions and gains its meaning by not being them. It is a thing itself that corresponds to them and somehow "reaches out" to them:

> 2.1511 That is how a picture is attached to reality; it reaches right out to it.[23]

It is the precise nature of this "reaching out" that is perhaps the primary point in the *Tractatus* that Wittgenstein revised in his later philosophy. At this early stage of his thinking he adopted Russell's notion of an atomic level of correspondence between pure logic and reality. He suggests that at this atomic level, language could be seen to line up against reality "like a measure."

> 2.1512 It is laid against reality like a measure

> 2.15121 Only the end-points of the graduating lines actually touch the object that is to be measured.

> 2.1513 So a picture, conceived in this way, also includes the pictorial relationship, which makes it into a picture.[24]

---

22. Ibid., 24.

23. Ibid.

24. Ibid., 10.

Wittgenstein turns to what he calls the "pictorial form" of the picture to provide an elemental or atomic feature of the picture which corresponds to the reality that the picture depicts. Similarly, he equates the pictorial form of the picture with a grammatical structure in language which mimics the grammatical or relational structure of the reality that propositions describe. But this level of correspondence leaves Wittgenstein dissatisfied for two reasons. First, because he has no instances of any words and their corresponding realities that are elemental enough to serve as examples of it, and second, because it is not intended to stick as a permanent part of his thought. Already in the *Tractatus,* Wittgenstein undermines his own reliance on this sub-atomic metaphysics as part of his strategy. This is the meaning of his closing, in which he suggests that his propositions are a ladder that ultimately needs to be thrown away in order to see the world aright. Indeed, it is the awkwardness of having to build the ladder only to throw it away that he later sees as the primary flaw of his earlier work. But it was his initial ability to envisage getting rid of the ladder as part of his method that convinced him that all the problems of philosophy had at once been resolved.

This flaw is overcome in the *Philosophical Investigations* by his notion of "language-games" and by his unique understanding of the function of grammar. Both allow Wittgenstein to develop an entirely new method in philosophy in which the art of showing how language works is perfected. Language-games represent circles of contexts in our experience of the world in which certain words coexist by association. This association is somewhat akin to what Wittgenstein calls a "family resemblance," and it is this resemblance that allows us to bunch together words such as pen, ink, and paper in a language-game that designates the tools of writing. However, the language-game is not a provider of meaning. Meaning derives not from what the words stand for but from the ways in which we use them. The observation and description of how this usage creates the effect of comprehension is what Wittgenstein means by grammar. We know and associate words in a language-game because we use them together frequently and not because we understand their shared underlying essence. Thus, we are perfectly capable of using words in different ways without worrying about the logical consistency that accounts for their multiple meanings. Since we derive the meanings of words from their usage, philosophy must survey that usage and notice its multidimensional workings correctly in order to see how the grammar of our daily use of ordinary language works.

Overall, the *Philosophical Investigations* is a survey of observations that all correspond to the ways in which we already know how to use words. This survey allows Wittgenstein to construct a grammar of language that is neither systematic nor stagnant. Instead, grammar captures the actual elements of a word's use that convey its specific and intended meaning during the act of communication. In this sense, to know the meaning of a word is not to have access to the essence of an underlying abstract philosophical concept but to have developed a competence in the appropriate use of that word in multiple linguistic situations. This is true of words and it is true of sentences which, with different intonations and punctuations, can be questions, statements, expressions of bewilderment, orders, etc.

While this portrayal of the working of language is fundamentally different from the one developed in the *Tractatus*, our primary concern is with the basic thrust, which, as we have mentioned, is the same. For example, in light of what we have said about the *Philosophical Investigations*, consider the intuition with which Wittgenstein refutes the possibility of subjugating language to a foundational logic in the *Tractatus*. There he writes of logical propositions that

> 4.064 Every proposition must *already* have a sense; it cannot be given a sense by affirmation. Indeed, its sense is just what is affirmed. And the same applies to negation, etc.[25]

This crucial remark demonstrates Wittgenstein's early commitment to the notion that language derives its meaning from usage and not the other way around. To put it into its original context, this remark follows a more extensive account of Frege's notion of a truth-value. Considering the possibility of determining a logical truth about a piece of paper with black and white points on it, Wittgenstein insists that the logical sequence whereby the positive or negative affirmation of propositions about whether or not a particular point is black or white – and whether or not a statement about a selected

---

25. Ibid., 29.

point's color is true – depends on our first determining the meaning of black and white. "If we do not know what black and white are," then any proposition we make about the points on the page makes no sense. In other words, Wittgenstein inverts the relationship between truth and logic, insisting that the notification of something as true or false depends first on knowledge of how to use the words "true" and "false" and not on the logic that the words come to serve. Wittgenstein therefore concludes that

> 4.063 The verb of a proposition is not 'is true' or 'is false', as Frege thought; rather, that which 'is true' must already contain the verb. The sense of the proposition is therefore affirmed by logic or exemplified by it rather than established by it.[26]

This is a powerful early example of the "linguistic turn." Wittgenstein insists here that it is the linguistic use of the terms of language that allow the human pursuit of logic and not the other way around. It is therefore entirely possible for language to contain falsehood, fantasy, and flagrant violations of its own rules. This, for example, is the case with all lies, most fiction, and much of poetry, respectively. Similarly, even when we focus our attention on language, we must not think of grammar as a set of rules that dictate the limits or the boundaries of use to us. Grammar is merely a language-game inside language that describes usage of words:

> 496. Grammar does not tell us how language must be constructed in order to fulfill its purpose, in order to have such and such an effect on human beings. It only describes and in no way explains the use of signs.[27]

If we return now to think about the climactic conclusion of the *Tractatus,* we might see how its deepest purpose is fulfilled most fully in the *Philosophical Investigations,* in which Wittgenstein painstakingly shows how to observe language use descriptively and without explaining it. This descriptive method

---

26. Wittgenstein, *Tractatus,* 29.
27. Wittgenstein, *Philosophical Investigations,* 138e.

is one that Wittgenstein recalls in the introduction to the *Philosophical Investigations* where he alludes to the metaphor of the picture from the *Tractatus*:

> The philosophical remarks in this book are, as it were, a number of sketches of landscapes which were made in the course of these long and involved journeyings.... Thus this book is really only an album.[28]

The pictures in this album, we are told, "criss-cross in every direction."[29] Wittgenstein confesses that he failed to provide an organized structure for the book because his thoughts "were soon crippled if I tried to force them on in any single direction against their natural inclination. And this was, of course, connected with the very nature of the investigation."[30] In other words, the form of the book demonstrates how confused philosophy becomes when it tries to force language to subdue itself to a higher system, since it can only be communicable or "make sense" within the context of language as it already functions. When one sees this, one sees the futility of all efforts to defy it. When the non-logically regimented mechanisms of ordinary language are understood as the true boundaries of expression, the significance of the *Tractatus*'s conclusion – i.e., of casting away the ladder and looking beyond language in absolute, resolute silence – emerges into view.

Likewise, the method of the *Philosophical Investigations* can now help us get at what Wittgenstein was trying to say in the *Tractatus* when he insisted that philosophy is not one of the natural sciences. The natural sciences in which logic and mathematics are useful are confined to the organized structuring of true propositions about the natural world. As Wittgenstein writes in the *Tractatus*,

---

28. Wittgenstein, *Philosophical Investigations*, preface, vii–viii.

29. Ibid.

30. Ibid.

> 4.11 The totality of true propositions is the whole of natural science (or the whole corpus of natural sciences).[31]

He returns to this theme in the famous penultimate entry in which he says,

> 6.53 The correct methodology in philosophy would really be the following: to say nothing except what can be said, i.e., propositions of natural science – i.e. something that has nothing to do with philosophy – and then whenever someone else wanted to say something metaphysical, to demonstrate to him that he had failed to give a meaning to certain signs and propositions.[32]

These propositions, the things we can know about natural science and which we can describe using language, logic, and mathematics, have no foundation beyond the usages of language that human beings intuitively learn to know as ordinary. They will always return to language's this-world-liness and remain subject to it. Thus, the attempt of modern philosophy to draw upon the modern accomplishments of the natural sciences in order to construct an escape from the confines of the knowing subject is pointless and not essentially different from classical metaphysics. By way of extension, Wittgenstein's distinction between philosophy and natural science under-lines his claim that mathematics functions well as the language of the natural sciences only when it is treated like an ordinary language, i.e., as "something that has nothing to do with philosophy." In other words, the attempt of logicians to free the logical principles of mathematics from axiomatic assumptions is ultimately no less doomed than the effort to regulate the language of philosophy. As such, for Wittgenstein, natural science and ordinary language belong to the same plain of this-worldly pursuits. Ultimately, the point of the *Tractatus* is that Russell's attempts to transcend these restraints are equally hopeless and damaging. It is no wonder that Russell did not take kindly to this.

---

31. Wittgenstein, *Tractatus*, 29, 4.11.
32. Ibid., 89, 6.53.

Wittgenstein's ultimate blow to the project of post-Enlightenment positivism is therefore embedded in the claim that the quest for a universally valid logic is no different and no less damaging than the classical quest for metaphysics. Both are flawed if they seek out essences in the vain hope of stabilizing a universally valid system of thought that claims to "explain everything." Or, in Wittgenstein's words,

> 6.371 The whole modern conception of the world is founded on the illusion that the so-called laws of nature are the explanation of natural phenomena.

> 6.372 Thus people today stop at the laws of nature, treating them as something inviolable, just as God and Fate were treated in past ages.

> And in fact, both are right and both wrong: though the view of the ancients is clearer in so far as they have a clear and acknowledged terminus, while the modern system tries to make it look as if *everything* were explained.[33]

The problem that natural science shares with philosophy is its presumption to posit universally valid truth claims. The illusion that modern logic is somehow different from metaphysics is a Structure of Concealment that Wittgenstein exposes in the hope that the problems of philosophy will be solved by the recognition that the whole enterprise is a mistake. By showing the workings of ordinary language, Wittgenstein demonstrates why the whole effort in philosophy to posit universal truth claims is unnecessary. Not only that, he establishes why the presumption that this can be done must be experienced as entirely futile if philosophy is to atone for the damage caused by claiming that the search for the stable foundations of objective truth should be undertaken. It is here that we can see the genealogical ancestry of Deconstruction as Galut in Wittgenstein's thought most clearly.

---

33. Wittgenstein, *Tractatus*, 85.

Wittgenstein and the Meaning of Deconstruction as Galut

As we have said, Wittgenstein's insistence on philosophy remaining within the confines of language (whether mathematical, ordinary, or logical) imposes a chaste silence on anything that seeks to move beyond language. From the perspective of Deconstruction as Galut, it is this boundary that Deconstruction comes to protect. This silence belongs to a mysticism that is observable – only apophatically – from the top of the ladder. The ladder represents what can be said in ordinary speech, logic, or mathematics. The top of the ladder is the limit of speech from where something else can perhaps be seen, yearned for, or silently prayed for.

From the perspective of Segulah, we must see that this silence is the terminus of Galut from where no progress toward the Promised Land can be made. The tip of the ladder is the tip of Mount Nebo. All and any venturing beyond that point into a presumed metaphysics or universal logic in which language will somehow preserve or accomplish its fullest meaning is nonsensical and is therefore a violation of the terms and conditions of Galut. Given this, we must understand that any appearance of having done so must be recognized as an illusion accomplished through the manipulative utilization of concealment. From the perspective of Deconstruction, those who crave the power to extract themselves from Galut inevitably abuse power and those who construct elaborate Structures of Concealment to conceal their abuse will readily turn to power (as Foucault observes) and even violence (as Derrida argues) to hold up the illusion. More significant still, self-extraction from Galut is also an invasion of the inviolate silence that Deconstruction comes to protect. It is the silence that is protected by exposing the incapacity of language to transcend its boundaries. It is this silence of Galut that demands we abandon all hope of self-redemption through rational thought.

From a Wittgensteinian point of view, antiphilosophy turns the rational mind against itself, applying its unique capabilities to the project of protecting humanity from its (i.e., rationalism's) darker ambitions. Through Deconstruction, rationalism can be trained to protect us from believing that rational thought is the propositional foundation of truth and liberty. It restores our right to "not know" by relentlessly interrogating and deconstructing the imprisoning structures of thought that the rational mind no less persistently constructs. This endless uphill struggle against construction is the philosophical condition of Galut. Putting rationalism to its proper use is the Tikkun (healing mechanism) of the rational mind.

Yearning and the Possibility of Construction

There are two final points that we wish to address with reference to Wittgenstein because they are crucial to gaining a full understanding of the purpose and meaning of Deconstruction as Galut from this perspective.

We have already seen that Galut is a place of hopeless yearning. But this yearning also generates the desire to get out. Given the inescapability of this trap, our first point concerns the meaning of that hopeless yearning to the ongoing process of Tikkun. Put simply, if it is hopeless and even potentially damaging to yearn, what is the meaning and purpose of that yearning?

Our second point is closely related to the first, and it concerns the meaning and possibility of construction. If the purpose of Deconstruction is to harness rationalism to the task of protecting us from believing that rational thought can provide the propositional foundation of truth and freedom, what is the purpose of rationalism's darker side? Why is rationalism capable of creating the illusion that the inviolate silence can be broken? Why is it capable of constructing the Structures of Concealment that make this illusion seem plausible? What is the mechanism that seemingly defies the boundaries of Galut to make this construction possible?

Let us turn to the first of these points: Wittgenstein spoke most eloquently about yearning and the meaning of its hopelessness in the closing passage of his "Lecture on Ethics":

> You will say: Well, if certain experiences constantly tempt us to attribute a quality to them which we call absolute or ethical value and importance, this simply shows that by these words we don't mean nonsense, that after all what we mean by saying that an experience has absolute value is just a fact like other facts and that all it comes to is that we have not yet succeeded in finding the correct logical analysis of what we mean by our ethical and religious expressions. Now when this is urged against me I at once see clearly, as it were in a flash of light, not only that no description that I can think of would do to describe what I mean by absolute value,

but that I would reject every significant description that anybody could possibly suggest, ab initio, on the ground of its significance.

That is to say: I see now that these nonsensical expressions were not nonsensical because I had not yet found the correct expressions, but that their nonsensicality was their very essence. For all I wanted to do with them was just to go beyond the world and that is to say beyond significant language. My whole tendency and, I believe the tendency of all men who ever tried to write or talk Ethics or Religion, was to run against the boundaries of language.

This running against the walls of our cage is perfectly, absolutely hopeless. Ethics so far as it springs from the desire to say something about the ultimate meaning of life, the absolute good, the absolute valuable, can be no science. What it says does not add to our knowledge in any sense. But it is a document of a tendency in the human mind which I personally cannot help respecting deeply and I would not for my life ridicule it.[34]

The tendency that Wittgenstein cannot help but respect deeply is the hopeless yearning that pushes us to run up against the walls of our cage. This cage is language, and the walls represent the outer limits where the inviolate silence of Galut inevitably begins. When we push the limits of language up against these walls, we encounter "nonsensical expressions" of the kind that we know from the end of the *Tractatus*, where Wittgenstein referred to them as steps on the ladder which we must ultimately push away. The experience of this yearning, for Wittgenstein, is a temptation to speak nonsense. For example, when we speak within a consciousness of language's limitations, we can know that "absolute" is simply a word in a language-game of qualifiers that can make perfect grammatical sense in usage. However, when we are confused by this, and drawn to imagining an absoluteness of good that lies outside our language-game and belongs to an imaginary higher realm of expression, we might then be struck – as Wittgenstein was – by the light of recognition that tells us that there is no description of this absoluteness that

---

34. Ludwig Wittgenstein, "Lecture on Ethics" (1929), first published in *Philosophical Review* 74:1 (1965), 3–12.

we would not reject. There is therefore no knowledge to be gained from this yearning and no escape.

What we are left with is a tendency to yearn that reminds us of the hopelessness of our exilic situation. The meaning and the purpose of this hopeless yearning and prayer is to prevent our embracing the condition of Galut as an ideal. If escape from Galut is hopeless, we might be tempted to make our final home in it. Yearning comes to prevent this. Hopeless yearnings and prayers remind us of this and keep us faithful to our continued dissatisfaction with Galut. Despite the dangerous tendencies that they are responsible for, these yearnings for the impossible must be respected deeply. When dissatisfaction gives way to satisfaction in exile, our condition – and here we are also alluding to the condition of the Jewish people in exile – is perilous.

This intuition about yearning lies at the heart of John Caputo's analysis of Derrida's religion.[35] According to Caputo, this is a religion without Religion. Religion of this sort is exilic. It is a religion of relentless, hopeless hope, dedicated to determining the impossibility of redemption so that the possibility of praying for the impossible may remain plausible. In Caputo's words, for Derrida,

> "God" is given only in praying and weeping.... we would say for him here that "God" is given not in theological analysis but in religious experience, in a certain passion for the impossible.[36]

The total otherness of God for Derrida demands that no concretization of His meaning can pass for knowledge. Ensuring this is the negative theological work of Deconstruction. But this resistance also reveals the heart of the religious meaning that Derrida found in the prayer that he uttered throughout his life, "*Viens!*" (Come!) This prayer, which captures Derrida's dissatisfaction with the condition of exile, touches the core of what Deconstruction adds to our understanding of Galut. If there were no yearning for self-redemption, the finality of the truly inescapable exilic experience of Galut would not be accessible. Without this combination of hopelessness and yearning, there

---

35. John Caputo, *The Prayers and Tears of Jacques Derrida: Religion without Religion* (Indiana University Press, 1997).

36. Ibid., 42–44.

would be no passion to drive forward the process of Tikkun, part of which is achieved through the relentless struggle of Galut.

Our second point which concerns the meaning of construction is closely related to yearning. The hopelessness of yearning is duplicated by the hopelessness of construction. Both draw our attention back to the inescapability of the condition of Galut and promote our dissatisfaction with it. However, the possibility of construction poses powerful questions that mere yearning does not, and Deconstruction seems inadequately concerned with these. For all its chaste insistence that escaping from Galut is impossible, Deconstruction must give an account of construction which, though neither chaste nor redemptive, demonstrates rationalism's extraordinary capabilities each day as the roller coaster of scientific progress and technological innovation hurtles forward at breakneck speed. Inattention to this capability weakens Deconstruction's capacity to demonstrate the importance of the task it performs. Moreover, the success that construction has improving the lives of millions through technological advance weakens the power of Deconstruction to resist it.

This weakness is a little like that of non-scientific medicine, which demands too much patience from its patients, who are happy to violate its rules and who run to doctors to have stone-filled gall bladders and ruptured spleens removed, saying, "Do anything – just so long as you make the pain go away!" Few will endure the effort and the discomfort of curing damaged organs from within in order to maintain the flow of qi and the energetic balance of the natural whole. Similarly, many will choose a prescribed chemical solution to their anxiety and are happy to take it each morning with a glass of water without coming near to the underlying causes that demand inner transformation as a precondition to lasting healing. High death rates in childbirth and the pangs of agony that accompany infertility sweep aside the naturalists' reservations about obstetric delivery rooms and UVF treatments. Efficiency, high-speed communication, effortlessness, and sheer prestige make the temptations of technology irresistible, as are the protective covers, benefits, and services offered by the massively constructed political and social systems of modern society. As many have predicted, it is only a matter of time till we all agree to have bionic organs, chips, nanotechnology, and artificial intelligence implanted in our bodies and brains so we can keep up with the times, live safely on the moon, and enjoy a better quality of life.

If a healthy sense of dissatisfaction with the condition of Galut is to be maintained, Deconstruction must offer a plausible account of why and how all these constructions and concealments are possible.

There are three crucial strategies of analysis that must be employed to address this concern. Each performs a different function and all three are required. The first is Deconstruction itself. As we have already discussed, Deconstruction can be used to call attention to the prices paid for constructions. This is an ethical argument that most often focuses its attention on the problem of the violence we do to our own humanity. It is an extension of the analysis of Deconstruction as Galut that touches the very purpose of deconstruction and helps demonstrate the philosophical importance of its task. However, as far as the question at hand is concerned, this argument is not helpful in explaining the meaning of construction – it merely opposes it. It also offers no better alternatives to violent construction and therefore does little to change social or political reality.

Second, Deconstruction can be extended to demonstrate the contingencies that limit the truth claims upon which scientific constructions are built. The central insight of this strategy brings us to recognize how the constructive processes of research and verification that take place in scientific laboratories are themselves human activities. As such they are necessarily contingent upon the limitations that confine the knowing self to its condition of Galut. The exposure of this contingency is of crucial importance, but not because it undermines the practicability of science. Understanding science as a human activity, i.e., as a construction that does not in fact rest upon universal truth claims, allows us to understand construction as a feature of Galut and not as part of a project of self-redemption. In other words, it brings us back to the unredeemed knowing subject and away from the delusion that the inviolate silence of Galut has somehow been broken.

This insight is captured in Bruno Latour's book, *We Have Never Been Modern*.[37] Latour's analysis of the social and human interactions that permeate our knowledge of science owes a great deal to Thomas Kuhn's *The Structures*

---

37. Bruno Latour, *We Have Never Been Modern* (1991), trans. Catherine Porter (Harvard University Press, 1993).

of Scientific Revolutions.[38] Kuhn demonstrated how scientific progress was not simply the product of the cumulative piling up of shared consensual objective knowledge but the result of sociological processes that affect the community of researchers engaged in the study of that knowledge. Scientific revolutions are as much the product of funding and trends as they are of refined theoretical propositions and improved techniques for validating them. A charismatic, well-endowed, or brilliant leader in a field of research might win the faith of scientific disciples and form a new paradigm of thought. However, this paradigm must create a shift in scientific thinking in order for it to take hold. The circumstances that bring about that shift are often as dependent on social dynamics as they are on objective evidence. This is something that we can all recall from our own various experiences of being either convinced or of remaining unconvinced by the same evidence when it is presented to us by different people. The importance of the social element to the gradual growth of credence that creates a new consensus about the laws of nature underlines how far the "discovery of the laws of nature" is from the redemption of the knowing subject in the knowledge of the object. And yet, the natural world yields to our analysis and to our theories. As such, something is discovered. But whatever it is, and this is Latour's crucial point, it is not evidence that we are "Modern." To capture this point, Latour refers to the discoveries of science and indeed of social science as "quasi-objects". In his words,

> As soon as we grant historicity to all the actors so that we can accommodate the proliferation of quasi-objects, Nature and Society have no more existence than East and West. They become convenient and relative reference points that moderns use to differentiate intermediaries, some of which are called 'natural' and others 'social', while still others are termed 'purely natural' and others 'purely social', and yet others are considered 'not only' natural 'but also' a little bit social.[39]

---

38. See Thomas Kuhn, *The Structure of Scientific Revolutions* (University of Chicago Press, 1970).

39. Latour, *We Have Never Been Modern*, 85.

Quasi-objects are what we know when we grant historicity to all the actors in the drama of scientific discovery. These actors must be plotted on a complex graph in which society, time (i.e., different periods in history), and the natural world interact. It is in this context that such terms as East and West can attain useful meaning as reference points that, from within a historical and social context, say something about the world. They are neither a purely fictional construction nor are they objective points of reference that reach out and somehow touch the objective reality of the globe. Plotting the social, natural, and temporal together allows us to construct a quasi-objective description of something. Similar limitations apply to all scientific propositions, all of which are generated within the complex multidimensional context of the variables on this graph. The attempt to reduce the nature of this graph to any single one of its variables, whether social, natural, or historical, will inevitably produce a one-dimensional portrayal that is of no use.

Latour's critique of modernism and its belief in redemption through knowledge of the object is also directed at the radical relativism produced by deconstruction that, to his mind, pays insufficient attention to the object (Nature) and reduces everything to the realm of the subject (Society). Latour says that

> the great masses of Nature and Society can be compared to the cooled-down continents of plate tectonics. If we want to understand their movement, we have to go down into those searing rifts where the magma erupts and on the basis of this eruption are produced – much later and much farther off, by cooling and progressive stacking – the two continental plates on which our feet are firmly planted.[40]

Quasi-objective knowledge is knowledge that stands on two feet. The first is the foot of Deconstruction, which ties us to our condition of exile; the second is the common-sense recognition of the external world. This second foot plays the crucial role of undermining the absoluteness of deconstruction's counterintuitive denial of external reality. The result of this awareness is not simply that we are not in exile from the absolute truth, but rather that

---

40. Ibid., 87.

modernity was never really a serious attempt at getting us out of it. Instead we must see the flight to the object as part of the inescapable condition of exile. Latour asks,

> Are you not fed up at finding yourself forever locked in language alone, or imprisoned in the social representations alone, as so many social scientists would like you to be? We want to gain access to things themselves, not only their phenomena. The real is not remote.... Doesn't external reality abound right here among us?
>
> Do you not have more than enough of being continually dominated by a Nature that is transcendent, unknowable, inaccessible, exact and simply true, peopled with entities that lie dormant like the Sleeping Beauty until the day when scientific Prince Charmings finally discover them?[41]

Finally, he answers,

> Real as Nature, narrated as Discourse, collective as Society, existential as Being: such are the quasi-objects that moderns have caused to proliferate. As such it behoves us to pursue them, while we simply become once more what we have never ceased to be: amoderns.[42]

Latour's notion of "amodern" knowing as the non-redemptive knowing of quasi-objects by quasi-subjects is plotted on the complex graph of Nature, Society, and Time which no one can escape. This portrayal of knowledge is no less chaste about the impossibility of self-extraction from Galut than Deconstruction. However, it adds a dimension to our account of Galut since it allows us to accommodate the possibility of construction – or perhaps we might now call it quasi-construction – within the context of Galut. His title, "We Have Never Been Modern," captures this insight. Though modernity believed it threatened the foundations of the exilic existence of humanity by

---

41. Ibid., 90.
42. Ibid.

utilizing the tools of logic and mathematics to tunnel the way out, it was in fact engaged in a form of construction that – while it threatens deconstruction – does not contradict the project of Deconstruction as Galut. On the contrary, it is part of it. As such we have never really been modern at all.

Latour also gives us a far better account of the meaning of yearning in Galut. The yearning to no longer remain imprisoned in Nature that Latour describes is duplicated in a similar yearning to no longer remain imprisoned in Society. Neither is a route of escape. Both underline the conclusion that Society and Nature, subjectivity and objectivity – even in their most pure and most extreme theoretical forms – are still part of Galut. Finding a balance between subject and object, plotting them both on a graph, placing our feet on both tectonic plates and quasi-building a quasi-existence as quasi-subjects interacting with a quasi-objective external reality, is the condition of Galut. Latour's account is a fuller description of Galut. It provides us with an account of the meaning of the cycle of relentless interrogative Deconstruction and no less persistent construction that is the condition of the rational mind in Galut.

At this point, we can bring our analysis of Deconstruction as Galut to a close, drawing the conclusion from our discussion of yearning and construction that neither one indicates a path to self-extraction from Galut. They both serve a purpose *in* Galut, which is to maintain our discontent *with* Galut. This discontent must also counter the temptations of Galut, because here we have indeed reached a terminus. This is a place where we may choose to stop and remain with our "quasi" faith, resigned to our condition, wary of crossing the boundary of thick silence that delineates the limits of rational argument and of what we may say about what is "out there" in the world. At this point the idea of Segulah can find a form of stable legitimacy in seclusion and build a community of subscribing members. But it cannot be publicly conveyed as a firm foundation for the construction of a shared social, public, or political consciousness.[43] It lives, but only in a cloistered mystical silence characteristic of Jewish life during the thousands of years of its exilic existence.

---

43. This is essentially where William James leaves us with a notion of legitimate but voluntary faith in his 1896 classic, *The Will to Believe and Other Essays in Popular Philosophy* (New York: Dover, 1956). We will return to discuss James's argument in more detail in chapter 10.

Beyond the boundary of rational argument that we have reached there is only an uninfrangible silence. From this inescapable Galut our yearning for rehabilitation must be left in "Other" hands.

It is here, at this point of terminus, that the crucial importance of our third strategy emerges into view. The third strategy necessarily follows from the second. However, it addresses a question which, from the perspective of Deconstruction as Galut, must remain unanswered. If science is a human activity that is both contingent and flawed, we must gain an understanding of how the inarticulate world with which natural science is concerned yields to those contingencies. In other words, if science does not rest on redemptive truths or absolute laws of nature, we must understand the meaning of the natural world's compliance with science's constructive exploits. What is there that lies beyond the quasi-objects, which allows itself to be described by the quasi-subject? Why do "natural phenomena" show up in laboratories and comply with the constructions of researchers? Put in slightly different terms (without resorting to Kant's notion of noumena): What is it about the natural world that allows Wittgenstein's notion of natural science and the plausibility of yearning not to be imprisoned (not only by Nature but also by Society as well) to take hold? If we cannot know what is out there, what is it that is out there that contributes to our feeling that we do?

As Latour himself suggests, this is an ontological question and not an epistemological one.[44] It is a question that cannot be addressed from the perspective of Deconstruction as Galut, because, as we said above, this perspective is chastely antiphilosophical and not merely anti-epistemological. In order to answer this, we must first shift our analysis to an ontological plain. We shall begin to do this in the next chapter, starting with the second genealogy of deconstruction as De-con-struction.

---

44. Latour's discussion of this question appears in a section entitled "Variable Ontologies," in Latour, *We Have Never Been Modern*, 85–88.

CHAPTER 8

De-con-struction and the Edge of Galut

The Historical Importance of Heidegger to De-con-struction

We shall now turn to the task of presenting the meaning of De-con-struction and take up the path that it allows us to follow, to a place that we shall refer to as the edge of Galut. This involves redefining the terminus point of deconstruction, placing it at the edge of an ontological possibility that it does not want to explore. It is from here, i.e., from the place where the idea of Galut metamorphoses into something intolerable from the perspective of Segulah, that we will seek to gain our first glimpse from afar of the locus of Destruction or Churban. This point is the place where we recognize the humanity of the Holocaust in our own. It is a place, perhaps, where extraordinary evil seems "banal."

Though Wittgenstein famously wrote of his philosophy, "I destroy, I destroy, I destroy,"[1] the hyphenation of the term De-con-struction is deliberately designed to connote the connection between deconstruction and Heidegger's – not Wittgenstein's – notion of Destruction (Destruktion). As such, De-con-struction is an aspect of deconstruction that becomes most visible when the debt of Derrida, Foucault, and others to Heidegger is emphasized. Whereas in our discussion of Deconstruction as Galut we highlighted deconstruction's pristinely chaste insistence upon the impossibility of self-extraction from Galut, we shall now delve into the meaning of deconstruction as a post-traumatic line of defense against a known horror that lies beyond.

---

1.   See Ludwig Wittgenstein, *Culture and Value*, ed. G. H. von Wright with Heikki Nyman, trans. C. G. Lukhardt and Maximillian Aue (Chicago University Press, 1982), 21e: "It came into my head today as I was thinking about my philosophical work and saying to myself: 'I destroy, I destroy, I destroy.'"

From the perspective of De-con-struction, the chaste opposition to self-extraction from Galut that we have already discussed in Derrida and Foucault is now best understood as an act of radically conservative resistance to the threat of reencountering the experience of that horror. For De-con-struction, the prospect of self-extraction from Galut (that Deconstruction chastely excludes from the realm of possibility) can in fact be pursued. However, the path that leads out of Galut is one that De-con-struction seeks desperately to block. It should be clear that the mission of deconstruction as De-con-struction is no less chaste than that of Deconstruction – i.e., De-con-struction does not understand its insistence on perennial exilic yearning as the deliberate rejection of a redemptive option. In its own consciousness, De-con-struction insists on its exilic existence because it knows that the only alternatives to it are considerably worse. It struggles incessantly against the impulse of self-extraction from Galut in order to block a path that it knows leads only to Churban. To understand what is meant by this prior knowledge of the path that leads to Churban, we must add a historical dimension to our philosophical analysis of deconstruction. This historical dimension is twofold and must be seen simultaneously on both its microchronological and broad historical planes.

De-con-struction can lead us to the edge of Galut because it arrives at this point on its way back from an encounter with the unspeakable. In other words, it knows the Churban that lies beyond because it has already seen it. It is this prior encounter that we are referring to as the product of a microchronology: the chronological order in which Martin Heidegger, Michel Foucault, and Jacques Derrida lived their lives. However, in order to grasp the point that we need to get at, this microchronological sequence must also be seen in an expansive historical context. In broad historical terms, the association of deconstruction with Heidegger (that our term De-con-struction underlines) is designed to highlight the connection between developments in philosophy and the radical change of tide that the world wars brought about in the history of post-Enlightenment nationalism. The calamity of world war – compounded by the tyranny of Nazism – called into question the ethical legitimacy of the massive resources of power that post-Enlightenment politics had allowed nation-states to accumulate. The invention of the atom bomb and the beginning of the nuclear arms race only added to the rising sense of anxiety about the increasing destructive potential of the nation-state.

While liberal political philosophy in the postwar era set about the task of designing fail-safe political mechanisms for monitoring and regulating the handling of state power, the radical philosophers associated with deconstruction became openly suspicious of power in general and set about the task of calling attention to the ways in which power is invisibly manipulated by political institutions. Though the inner philosophical connection that we shall seek to discover between Heidegger and De-con-struction is not dependent on Heidegger's political affiliation with Nazism, the nexus where his politics and his role in the internal development of philosophy meet is nonetheless of great importance. Historically, the parallel between the line that connects the exaggerated use of state power with radical anti-power politics and the line that connects Heidegger's Destruction with both Foucault's radical suspicion of power and Derrida's hypersensitivity to violence is crucial to our understanding of the Holocaust's implications. It is this parallel that will allow us to appreciate why the Holocaust is a definitive historical event that forces us to reject the possibility of continuing the Jewish/Western relationship on the foundation of post-Enlightenment humanism.

The supplementation of our philosophical analysis with an awareness of historical sequence leads us to the trail that will allow us to see how De-con-struction finally enables Survival and System's axiomatically humanist assumptions about the implications of the Holocaust to fall away. De-con-struction's suspicion of all forms of power (at least of all the forms of power that it knows) undermines the legitimacy of a strategy for Jewish survival that rests upon the cultural and spiritual alliance of Judaism with humanist politics. But, more significantly, exposing the absolute overlap between the meaning of power as understood by both De-con-struction and Heidegger will bring us a step closer to discovering the single form of power worthy of exemption from De-con-struction's suspicion. This power is life itself as understood from the perspective of Segulah, and to this we will return in our discussion of Tikkun.

Through our discussion of De-con-struction we shall see how Derrida and Foucault tried to uncover the ubiquitously destructive human capacity that expressed itself most fully in the Holocaust and which undermines the viability of the entire humanist project. In order to get closer to this, we must now move beyond Deconstruction's exposure of the structures that conceal human non-knowing of the object and delve more deeply into those structures that conceal from view the ontological *being* of the subject. Our analysis of De-con-struction will lead us to the recognition that destructiveness inheres in the human capacity to construct. Though construction and destruction present themselves as opposites, the macrohistorical process that places De-con-struction in the dark shade of the Holocaust, and the microhistorical process that places Derrida and Foucault in the shade of Heidegger, together, allow us to see that human construction and human destruction are grounded in the same soil.

Ontology and Epistemology

To see this soil more clearly, we must recognize how Heidegger influenced the evolution of deconstruction. Since we have reversed the chronological order in our analysis and are dealing with deconstruction first, we shall not yet offer a detailed analysis of Heidegger in this chapter. All the same, a few initial comments are a necessary preliminary to the more detailed analysis of De-con-struction that follows.

Heidegger's philosophy is dedicated to rediscovering the question of *being* that must provide the soil upon which all knowledge is built. Heidegger's basic concern is perhaps best described as an attempt to address the "*being* of being."[2] This "*being* of being" is the primordial experience of *being* that allows the everyday form of being (which Heidegger calls "ontic facticity" and to which we all readily refer every time we use the verb "to be" in ordinary conversation) to disclose itself to us in the world. If we think of this in terms of Descartes' *cogito*, we might refer to the "*being* of being" as the *being* that inheres in the first "I" in "I think therefore I am." While the second "I"

---

2.   We will of course be returning to offer a detailed analysis of this and other central themes in Heidegger's *BT* in chapters 10–14 below. For a specific analysis of this concept, see Thomas Sheehan, "Introduction: Heidegger, the Project and the Fulfillment," in Thomas Sheehan, ed. (1981), *Heidegger: The Man and the Thinker* (New Jersey, 2010). As we stated in our prologue, we are using italics in the body text of this book whenever our intention is to highlight the ontological meaning of the word in the Heideggerian sense. In this case the *being* of being (in which the first use of being is italicized and the second is not) is a case in point.

is by virtue of the first "I"'s thinking, in the *cogito* the *being* of the first "I" remains unexplained. Put differently, Heidegger's question of the *cogito* is: How *does* the *am* of the first "I" that thinks (in the sense in which "I think" means I *am* thinking) *be* in order for the *am* of the second "I" that *is* (in "therefore I am") to *know* that it *is*? This question deconstructs the priority of knowing (epistemology) over *being* (ontology). It insists that in order to focus its energies on knowledge, philosophy has concealed – from the world and perhaps even from itself – the primordial experience that discloses the *being* of human consciousness in the first place. Heidegger's answer to this problem is that the primordial meaning of *being* is only accessible through the analysis of the single being (the human "I am" renamed as "Dasein") that is aware of its own *being* and that the horizon of this being's *being* is time. The primordial experience of time for Heidegger is the condition of our own mortality, which he refers to as *being-toward-death*. Though we shall explore the precise meaning and implications of this idea only when we come to it in our systematic reading of Heidegger, for now we shall bear in mind the fact of this insight, as it will prove important in understanding, as it were from afar, the exposed Structure of Concealment that De-con-struction protects against.

Exposing and dismantling the long history of the concealment that secures the priority of epistemology in philosophy is what Heidegger means by "Destruction." He sees the origin of this in Plato and goes so far as to argue (perhaps unconvincingly) that Kant uncovered it and then reconcealed it in the revisions he made to the second edition of the *Critique of Pure Reason*. This is an argument that Heidegger made in his book *Kant and the Problem of Metaphysics*[3] and which he first presented orally in the lectures that he delivered at Davos in 1929. We shall follow this argument with the assistance of Peter Gordon's account of this lecture in *Continental Divide: Heidegger, Cassirer, Davos*.[4]

---

3.   Martin Heidegger, *Kant and the Problem of Metaphysics*, trans. Richard Taft (Indiana University Press, 1990).

4.   Peter E. Gordon, *Continental Divide: Heidegger, Cassirer, Davos* (Cambridge, MA: Harvard University Press, 2012). In this book Gordon provides an excellent account of the context in which the Davos debate between Heidegger and Cassirer took place. He describes the history of the neo-Kantian movement in German universities in the context of the attempt to heal Europe after the calamity of the First World War. Gordon's analysis of Heidegger's lectures on Kant at Davos appear in chapter 3, 124–30.

As Peter Gordon explains, the thrust of Heidegger's lectures on Kant at Davos was to discredit the neo-Kantian reading of the Critiques, which set out to demonstrate the absolute grounding of human thought in rationality. In Gordon's words, "It is this...interpretation of Kant's philosophy – as an epistemological propaedeutic to natural science...that Heidegger most wished to combat."[5] Gordon continues,

> The essential difference lay in the fact that the neo-Kantians saw the first *Critique* as an epistemological investigation (that is, a study of the formal conditions for empirical knowledge) whereas Heidegger now claimed the *Critique* must be understood as a preparatory investigation into the conditions for *ontological* understanding. As justification, Heidegger noted that Kant's point of departure was the set of concerns known as "traditional metaphysics" (i.e., knowledge of the three super-sensible beings: the world-totality, the immortal soul, and God). But Kant's question, "How is such knowledge possible?" depends in turn on the more foundational question as to the possibility of beings in general.

According to Gordon, what Heidegger argued in Davos was that the key to Kant's metaphysics is not to be found – as the neo-Kantians understood – in the generative independence of the mind. Rather, the metaphysical origin of Kant's a priori structures of thought (that enable the rational recognition of phenomena) is found in Kant's own presentation of the human capacity for intuitive or sensible receptivity to the world. Heidegger argues that Kant claims that "knowledge is always born of an orientation toward the world and a dependency upon its world by means of intuitions."[6] What this means for Heidegger is that the *Critique* predicates its notion of rational knowledge upon an a priori metaphysics that originates in an ontological experience of what Heidegger referred to as *being-in-the-world*. Gordon continues,

---

5.   Ibid., 127.
6.   Ibid.

A proper assessment of the first *Critique* was therefore possible only if one first acknowledged the essence of finite knowledge in general and the basic character of finitude as such. For Heidegger this meant that one must attend primarily to Kant's theory of sensibility.

Gordon observes here that Heidegger is undercutting the Kantian credentials of the neo-Kantian absorption of "the intuition of being" into "understanding." If we place this back into the context of Davos, in this lecture Heidegger was preparing his audience for his subsequent debate with Hermann Cohen's disciple, Ernst Cassirer. He took advantage of his lecture on Kant to unleash a preemptive strike on the Kantian(!) credentials of Cohen's claim that "being itself is the being of thought."[7] In place of this, Heidegger argued that "sensibility should be granted its foundational role not as a merely "sensual" or "psychological" faculty but as a truly "metaphysical" foundation for experience."[8] Gordon goes on to show how Heidegger justified his interpretation of the "Critiques" as a "groundlaying for metaphysics" by remarking on the crucial differences between the first and second editions of the book. The nub of this argument is Kant's idea that "time is the formal condition a priori of all appearance whatsoever." What this meant to Heidegger was that Kant had somehow discovered that ontological knowledge is tied to time and that the possibility of explaining the meaning of *being* is dependent upon the primordial sensual capacity of human consciousness to know itself in time. This primordial sensual experience of receptivity precedes rational knowledge.

From Heidegger's perspective, Kant's discovery of the ontological mechanisms (or a priori schemata) that give philosophy access to the primordial human experience of *being-in-time* should have constituted the highlight of Kant's argument. However, after claiming that the schemata are "nothing but a priori determinations of time in accordance with rules," Kant goes on to say that "this schematism of our understanding with regard to appearances and their mere form is a hidden art in the depths of the human soul, whose true operations we can divine from nature and lay unveiled before our eyes

---

7.   Ibid.

8.   Ibid., 129.

only with difficulty."[9] For Heidegger, this step back in Kant's argument is of crucial importance. In Gordon's words,

> Just why Kant should have admitted ignorance at so pivotal a moment in his argument has been a subject of long-standing debate. The further question was why Kant later went back to revise his later classification of the transcendental imagination: In the 1781 edition he classified it as a "third" faculty, but later (in his personal copy) he renamed it a "function of the understanding." For Heidegger this revision was not merely a textual curiosity. It was integral to the broader issue of how Kant had revised the transcendental deduction itself so as to secure the sovereignty of reason.... In Heidegger's view the change did not signal that Kant had actually improved upon his earlier position. Rather it betrayed the fact that Kant had momentarily discerned the radical and potentially disruptive implications of his own argument and had moved swiftly to conceal them from view.[10]

Heidegger's claim that Kant had deliberately concealed these discoveries from view is one that, Gordon tells us, Cassirer later convinced him to retract.[11] However, his acceptance of Cassirer's claim that Kant had reached no conscious conclusion about the "potentially disruptive implications of his own argument" does not refute Heidegger's overall contention that

> precisely *because* modern philosophy in general and neo-Kantianism in particular *neglected* the true character of metaphysics as a "natural disposition of human beings," they remained trapped within the self-deceptive tradition of metaphysical rationalism.[12]

---

9.   Ibid.; see also note 41.
10. Ibid., 129–30.
11. Ibid., 161.
12. Ibid., 132.

This condition of remaining trapped within a self-deceptive rational tradition is indeed a Structure of Concealment that Heidegger wishes to expose. However, we will totally miss the meaning of this if we construct it in epistemological terms. Heidegger is not making a deconstructive argument about how philosophers choose not to know what they can know. From his point of view, his insight is far more fundamental than that.

In order to see the key innovation of Heidegger's argument here, we must understand that within the system of Heidegger's thought, a Structure of Concealment must be seen as an ontological condition of *being*. Self-delusion and denial are not cognitive functions. They are ontological states of *being*. The form of *being* that allows the self-deceptive tradition of metaphysical rationalism to endure and to present itself as plausible is what Heidegger refers to in *BT* as inauthentic or everyday Dasein.[13] This inauthentic form of *being* is an ontological potentiality in which false or delusional constructions of reality are possible. From Heidegger's point of view, they represent a degenerated state of *being*. Again, this degeneration is not an expression of a lower state of knowledge. Neither should it be understood as ethically degenerate. Indeed, in *BT* Heidegger makes a point of not passing ethical judgment upon it. The degeneration is ontological. It refers to a depleted state of authenticity or of fullness in the consciousness of *being* itself.

Heidegger is interested in discovering how all states of *being* are disclosed to Dasein in the world. The truth or ethics of what is concealed is less important than discovering the primordial mechanisms that make the concealment and disclosure of phenomena recognizable to ontological analysis. In ontological terms, the self-delusional capacity to construct - whether Kant's amended text is an example of it or not – must be seen as a possibility of *being* that is generated by the *being-subject*'s (Dasein's) potentiality to go into hiding from itself while assuming an inauthentic identity. It is this going into hiding of Dasein that lies at the epicenter of De-con-struction's concerns.

---

13. As with all references here to themes and concepts in *BT*, we will return to discuss these in detail in chapters 10–14 below.

De-con-struction and Dasein

In his later philosophy, Heidegger emphasized the connection between the potentiality of Dasein to go into hiding and what he referred to as *technik*.[14] This term designated the broader Structures of Concealment that distract human attention from the degenerated condition of Dasein by expanding the technological capabilities and dependencies of modern man. From Heidegger's ontological perspective, technology is an inauthentic or prosthetic extension of Dasein into space. Technology covers or conceals the distance between inauthentic Dasein and the realization of Dasein's fuller capabilities by building machines or subduing animals or manufacturing contrived conditions of living that allow Dasein to believe it is more capable, fuller, or more expansive than it actually is. Technology conceals a deep anxiety about human powerlessness that it cannot heal. A weapon cannot make a person stronger, and a plane cannot enable him to fly. A drug can no more bolster resilience to pain or enhance the natural capacity to fight depression than a computer can make people smarter. Neither can a house or a hearth help humanity cultivate its ability to resist the cold. All of these are technological or prosthetic extensions of the human body which expand the scope of inauthentic Dasein in space. Dependence on any of these makes humanity vulnerable whenever its tools are out of reach and dependent when they are nearby. More importantly, human dependence on technology stifles the cultivation of authentic human capability, because the plane and the tank do nothing to relieve us of the fantasy of flying like a hawk or of fighting like a tiger. Both fantasies (and many more) continue to haunt us from within. The degenerative effect of these prostheses only underlines the pathetic condition of humanity as it really is while authentic Dasein is left in concealment. Through the "breaking out" of authentic Dasein we may finally come to recognize our condition and do something about it. If we can manage to see ourselves as the true Wizard of Oz (the little old man that hides behind the curtain) who has degenerated, we might finally manage to crawl out from

---

14. The topic of Heidegger's attitude toward technology has been discussed broadly and extensively in the scholarly literature. See, for example, Michael E. Zimmerman, ed., "Beyond 'Humanism': Heidegger's Understanding of Technology in Thomas Sheehan" (1981), in *Heidegger: The Man and the Thinker* (New Jersey, 2010), 219–27; for references to Heidegger's writings on this theme, see note 1.

under the cover of the pyrotechnic projections that inauthentic technological capability has enabled us to build and to attain true greatness.

From De-con-struction's perspective, Heidegger's ontological analysis of technology brings into view the soil that connects the human capacity to construct with humanity's destructiveness. Despite Heidegger's criticism of technology, his analysis of it reveals that the underlying ontological identity of the human capacity for construction is a form of Dasein's *being*. Dasein's capacity to assume an inauthentic form is essentially indicative of its capacity to go into hiding. Again, from De-con-struction's perspective, it is in this hidden form that the fundamentally destructive mortal anxiety that motivates Dasein in all its forms (and that is openly expressed in authentic Dasein) manages to operate in the world under the cover of a benign exterior. Under the cover of humanism, technology, rationalism and enlightenment, inauthentic Dasein appears to make progress. However, from De-con-struction's perspective, when this ontological soil remains undiscovered, Dasein is dangerously free to prowl the world while the destructive consequences of its constructive activities are left unnoticed. De-con-struction keeps a watchful eye out for the expressions of Dasein's constructive desire and directs its suspicion against the palaces and cathedrals of post-Enlightenment humanism that seem to do nothing more malicious than celebrate the liberty of the subject and the enlightened redemptive promise of scientific objectivity.

One of the central arguments of this book, i.e., that the Jewish world has misjudged modernity, rests on the idea that Dasein's ability to go into hiding poses a primary threat to the well-being of the world. This recognition is crucial to appreciating the ontological significance of Dasein's yearning for self-extraction from Galut. The sinister side of Dasein's desire "to find a clearing in the forest"[15] is that the mood or the experience of total self-discovery that Heidegger describes is filled with anxiety and resoluteness and is connected at its core with a destructive impulse. These are claims that we cannot explain until we have engaged more deeply with the relevant passages in *BT*. But we can begin to catch our first glimpse of them from afar when

---

15. This is a term that Heidegger used to describe the moments of clarity in which Dasein experiences its authentic self. See John Sallis, "Into the Clearing," in Sheehan, *Heidegger: The Man and the Thinker*, 107–15.

we consider the shadows of Nazism and the Holocaust that are reflected in Derrida's and Foucault's writing.

The Beast and the Sovereign

Once again, our discussion of De-con-struction in Derrida and Foucault need not be exhaustive. All the same, it is necessary to draw out some of our allusions to their work by looking closely at a handful of texts each of which will serve only as an illustration of De-con-struction's ontological anxiety about power and its connection with the condition of clinging to the edge of Galut. This time around, we shall begin with Derrida and with some selected passages from a seminar that he delivered at the École des hautes études en sciences sociales, in Paris. These seminars were delivered from the fall of 2001 to the spring of 2003 and were published posthumously in 2009 under the title *The Beast and the Sovereign, Volume 1*.[16]

In *The Beast and the Sovereign,* Derrida explores themes that are central to the overall statement of his oeuvre about religion and politics. In our analysis of De-con-struction, it is in the context of the theological-political that we shall seek to understand Derrida's resistance to the notion of a sovereign. More specifically, it is in the connection between power and the stabilization of political sovereignty that Derrida's anxiety about power in general becomes visible.

We shall begin by pointing out that in this lecture series, as in so much of Derrida's writing, Heidegger features prolifically as one of the philosophical foundations of his thought. Derrida's attitude to Heidegger is not dismissive. On the contrary, it is extremely approving. This approbation is a crucial feature of De-con-struction's strategy, which is also apparent in the appreciative attention that Derrida lavishes, here and elsewhere, on the political philosophy of Carl Schmitt. This demands some explanation, since both Schmitt and Heidegger spoke out openly in favor of Hitler. Though neither of them was particularly prominent in the internal hierarchy of the Nazi intelligentsia, these are the two most prominent "Nazi" thinkers who have found an

---

16. Jacques Derrida, *The Beast and the Sovereign, Volume 1*, trans. Geoffrey Bennington (Chicago, 2009).

enduring place in the Western philosophical canon. Derrida, who was a Jew, was not blind to this.

Derrida's approbation of Heidegger and Schmitt does not contradict his anxiety about the "breaking out" of authentic Dasein. On the contrary, it is an expression of it. The uncovering of hidden power-mechanisms is made possible by the philosophical projects of these two thinkers, who sought to pull out into the open authentic Dasein (in Heidegger's case) and exceptional sovereignty (in Schmitt's). De-con-struction operates on a premise of "gratitude" to philosophical Nazism for bringing to light the fullest potentialities that were embedded in post-Enlightenment humanism from its origin. One might say that Derrida is grateful to Heidegger and Schmitt for exposing the devil, since the devil you know is a more manageable source of existential anxiety than the devil you don't. It is in this sense that Derrida writes of Heidegger's letter "On Humanism,"

> Heidegger wants first of all to show that the determination of man as a *rational animal* is insufficiently humanist, as it were, that it misses the humanity of man, what is proper to man. And what thus misses the essence of man is metaphysics.[17]

The phrase "insufficiently humanist" here illustrates the point and suggests that something more sufficiently humanist would involve a greater exposure of authentic Dasein. Moreover, it is clear that what Derrida is referring to as metaphysics is that same "self-deceptive tradition of metaphysical rationalism" that Heidegger sought to expose. By following Heidegger's efforts at driving humanism to its edge, Derrida hopes to expose the destructive truths that go unnoticed when Dasein is left, in its hidden forms, to appear civilized.

The line between what is and what is not civilized is the focus of these lectures. Derrida is concerned with the sovereign and the beast, with the sovereign as beast, and with the beastliness that post-Enlightenment sovereignty projects upon beasts. In the effort to expose the nature of this correlation, Derrida deconstructs the political-zoological lexicon in which terms such as

---

17. Ibid., 321, note 19, and 322. See also Martin Heidegger, "Letter on Humanism," trans. Frank A. Capuzzi and J. Glenn Gray, in: *Martin Heidegger: Basic Writings*, ed. David Krell (New York: Harper, 1977), 213–66.

the "social animal" and the "Leviathan" are used by the humanist political philosophers who carved out the political categories of the Enlightenment. It is these basic categorical distinctions that allowed the Enlightenment to distinguish between the rest of creation and civilized humankind; between civil and savage, nature and nurture.

Derrida begins to tease out the bestiality of sovereignty by giving special attention to the symbolic significance of the wolf,

> Many wolves will, then, be crossing the stage of this seminar. We are going to show in a moment that one cannot be interested in the relations of the beast and sovereign, and all the questions of the animal and the political, of the politics of the animal, of man and beast in the context of the state, the *polis*, the city, the republic, the social body, the law in general, war and peace, terror and terrorism, national or international terrorism, etc., without recognizing some privilege to the figure of the "wolf"…where man tells himself the story of politics, the story of the origin of society, the story of the social contract, etc.: *for* man, man is wolf.[18]

The wolf is important because of its stealth, as in the phrase *peut-être à pas de loup* (perhaps stealthily like a wolf). The wolf approaches but is not heard. It moves in close, but, as the double entendre packed into the word *pas* suggests (i.e., *pas* is both a step and a form of the negative) it – that is, the step and the wolf – is not there, as in *il n'ya pas*.[19] Derrida identifies in the wolf a symbol of the hiddenness of sovereignty. It is there, but it is not. It creeps up and devours you without your knowing. Derrida cites Rousseau, who writes, "So, here we have the human race, divided into herds of cattle, each one with its chief who keeps it in order to devour it." Derrida comments,

> Notice the "in order to devour it"…and the devouring wolf is not far away, the big bad wolf, the wolf's mouth, the big teeth of Little Red Riding Hood's Grandmother-Wolf. Notice then the "in order

---

18. Derrida, *The Beast and the Sovereign*, 9.
19. Meaning "it is not" in French.

to devour it" in Rousseau's text…he, the chief, does not keep the beast by *devouring* it, he does not first keep the cattle and then, subsequently, devour said cattle, no, he keeps the cattle *with a view to devouring it*, he only keeps the cattle *in order to* devour it.[20]

This "in order to devour" is the reasoning of the sovereign. Devouring is the rationale of sovereignty. The sovereign is beast. The sovereign becomes sovereign by becoming beast and by devouring that which he can render bestial.

> We will keep trying to think through this becoming-beast, this becoming-animal of a sovereign who is above all a war-chief and is determined as sovereign or as animal faced with enemy. He is instituted as sovereign by the possibility of the enemy, by that hostility in which Schmitt claimed to recognize, along with the possibility of the political, the very possibility of the sovereign, of sovereign decision and exception.[21]

Within the social contract, citizenship and the political also reduce the human to beast. Sovereignty over humans is therefore a sovereignty that is accomplished through the subjugation of the beast under cover of what Rousseau refers to as "the right of the stronger." It is this right that reduces the citizen, unbeknownst to himself, to beast, "and the originary community of men to an animal community."[22]

The idea that this right, which is brute strength, is also reason, is central to La Fontaine's fable "The Wolf and the Lamb," where the wolf appears on the stage to say,

> The reason of the strongest is always the best; as we shall shortly show.[23]

---

20. Derrida, *The Beast and the Sovereign*, 12.
21. Ibid., 10.
22. Ibid., 11.
23. Ibid., 7, and see note10 for a discussion of Jean de La Fontaine and the fable of the wolf and the lamb.

Similarly, Pascal writes,

> *Justice, force.* It is just that what is just be followed; it is necessary
> that what is strongest be followed. Justice without force is impo-
> tent; force without justice is tyrannical.… Justice is subject to dis-
> pute; force is easy to recognize and indisputable.… And thus not
> being able to make what is just, strong; one made what is strong,
> just.[24]

Derrida's point is to show how Rousseau's *Social Contract* endorses the view
that reason and justice are inextricably tied to brute power. Power generates
them and masters them, but it also defines them, as Derrida puts it, "in fact":

> Rousseau's thesis is thus both that "the reason of the strongest" is
> *in fact* the best, that it has prevailed and prevails in fact…but that
> if *in fact* the reason of the stronger wins out, *by right* the reason of
> the strongest is not the best.[25]

The mutual dependence of strength on reason and reason on strength is
definitive of the modern state. The principle of reversibility that operates
between the two is the same as the one that ties the sovereign to the beast and
pushes them both outside of the law and into a realm in which the law – as
something violently constructed – becomes visible:

> For the current representation, to which we are referring for a start,
> sovereign and beast seem to have in common their being-outside-
> the-law. It is as if both of them were situated by definition at a
> distance from or above the laws, in non-respect for the absolute
> law, the absolute law that they make or that they are but that they
> do not have to respect.[26]

---

24. Derrida, *The Beast and the Sovereign*, 8.
25. Ibid., 13.
26. Ibid., 17.

The sovereign (perhaps because it creates the law, is the persona of the absolute law, or is protected by the law), is outside of the law. The beast, like the criminal, is in violation of the law. But despite the fact that using obviously Heideggerian language Derrida says that "these different modes of being-outside-the-law can seem to be heterogeneous among themselves," Derrida insists that "the fact remains, sharing this common being-outside-the-law, beast criminal, and sovereign have a troubling resemblance."[27] While the beast and the sovereign may appear to occupy two opposite poles of society "and seem to be situated at the antipodes, at each other's antipodes," Derrida points out that,

> it happens, moreover — brief reappearance of the wolf — that the nickname "wolf" is given to a head of state as Father of the Nation. Mustapha Kemal who had given himself the name Ataturk (Father of the Turks) was called the "gray wolf" by his partisans, in memory of the mythical ancestor Genghis Kahn, the "blue wolf."[28]

The interconnection of the beast and the sovereign through power is cause for anxiety. The beast and the sovereign both devour. They devour the law because they are not bound to the law. The law is bound to them. It is defined by their exemption from the law. The beast is not beast unless he is outside the law. His violation of the law is where we can see the law. The sovereign (which refers of course to the abstract state and not necessarily to the person who is head of state) is not sovereign unless he can express his sovereignty over the law. And this correlation between the beast and the sovereign, a correlation that expresses the law, is a source of mesmerizing anxiety about the nature of the law:

> I believe that this troubling resemblance, this worrying superposition of these two beings-outside-the-law or "without laws" or "above the laws" that beast and sovereign both are when viewed from a certain angle — I believe that this resemblance engenders

---

27. Ibid.
28. Ibid.

a sort of hypnotic fascination or irresistible hallucination, which makes us see, project, perceive, as in an X-ray, the face of the beast under the features of the sovereign; or conversely if you prefer, it is as though, through the maw of the untamable beast, a figure of the sovereign were to appear.[29]

The beast holds on to the sovereign in our imagination and vice versa. They are hostage to each other and they host each other, "the one inhabiting or housing the other, the one becoming the intimate host of the other."[30] They coexist in each other rather like Kantorowicz's image of the king's two bodies, one of which represents the man; the other, the state.[31] Here, the state is the beast and the beast is the state. Together,

> in the metamorphic covering-over of the two figures, the beast and the sovereign, one therefore has a presentiment that a profound and essential ontological copula is at work on this couple; it is like a coupling, an ontological, onto-zoo-anthropo-theologico-political copulation: the beast becomes the sovereign who becomes the beast; there is the beast *and* [*et*] the sovereign (conjunction), but also the beast *is* [*est*] the sovereign, the sovereign *is* [*est*] the beast.[32]

This association is extended into international law and politics. It extends beyond the relationships that operate inside the state and gives force to the tensions that exist between states. The criticism of one state by another is the extension of an anxiety about the bestiality of a state that expresses itself in the projection of an image whereby the sovereignty of that enemy state is bestial. Following Chomsky, Derrida offers a brief analysis of the beast of

---

29. Ibid., 18.

30. Ibid.

31. The image of the state being represented by the king's two bodies (his own and that of the state) is the central metaphor in Ernst Kantorowicz's classic study *The King's Two Bodies: A Study in Medieval Political Theology* (Princeton University Press, 1957). For a fascinating analysis of Kantorowicz's attraction to Nazism despite his being Jewish, see Norman F. Cantor, *Inventing the Middle Ages* (New York, 1991), chapter 3.

32. Derrida, *The Beast and the Sovereign*, 18.

states, which is named the "rogue-state."[33] The "rogue-state" is given this name by the would-be sovereign, i.e., by the other state that would extend its sovereignty over the rogue if only it could. But here again a principle of reversibility comes into play because the would-be sovereign is made beast by naming the rogue state "rogue." Rogue states, Derrida explains, are

> delinquent states, criminal states, states that behave like brigands, like highway robbers or like vulgar rapscallions who just do as they feel, do not respect international right, stay in the margins of international civility, violate property, frontiers, rules and good international manners, including the laws of war (terrorism being one of the classic forms of this delinquency, according to the rhetoric of heads of sovereign states who for their part claim to respect international right).[34]

Derrida's analysis turns on the association of the word "rogue" with the bestial. The association here is etymologically English since the term was first used in international politics – and hence it was coined in English – by the United States. In Shakespeare the rogues are elephants, lions, and tigers. The term connotes also the hippopotamus and, most generally, carnivorous animals who defy the law of the pack. "The rogue is the individual who does not even respect the law of the animal community." Famously, so-called rogue states frequently turn this accusation back on the accuser, which is where the principle of reversibility is established,

> The United States, which is so ready to accuse others of being rogue states, is in fact allegedly the most rogue of all, the one that most often violates international right even as it enjoins other states (often by force when it suits it) to respect the international right that it does not itself respect whenever it suits it not to.[35]

---

33. Ibid., 19; see also note 28. Derrida refers to Chomsky's *Rogue States: The Rule of Force in World Affairs* (Cambridge, MA, 2000).

34. Derrida, *The Beast and the Sovereign*, 18–19.

35. Ibid., 19.

The inextricable association of moral and legal judgment with immorality and flagrant violence is embedded in the constructive power that enables the human manipulation of force. It is in this sense that the capacity of the United States to label a terrorist regime is essentially the same capacity that is duplicated by that regime when it accuses the United States of state-sponsored terrorism. Ultimately, the only response is power and force. The moral distinction between the two can be made only by monopolizing the right to master an ever-escalating technology of destructive power. The accumulation of this power and the propagation of the morality that justifies it are all products of anxiety about the bestiality of the other, which is combated with fear and force – the bestiality of the self. It is impossible to escape the capacity of those who have been censured by power from turning that censure back. The accused accuses because the accuser only does so with the raw power that, despite its best efforts to appear moral and constructive, it cannot conceal. This is where law and morality become visible as force, and it is where the beast and the state cannot avoid being each other. This condition is what Derrida calls the "ontological copula of the two." The point here is not to provide support for moral relativism. Rather, it is to show how the inescapability of power that connects the beast to the state simultaneously makes a beast of the state and a state of the beast. This points in ontological terms to the human capacity to construct, and it is an inevitable feature of humanist rationalism that this capacity is inseparable (and sometimes even indistinguishable) from the monstrous power to devour and destroy.

> Just where the animal realm is so often opposed to the human realm as the realm of the non-political to the realm of the political, and just where it has seemed possible to define man as a political animal or living being, a living being that is, on top of that, a "political" being, there too the essence of the political and, in particular of the state and sovereignty, has often been represented in the formless form of the animal monstrosity, in the figure without figure of a mythological, fabulous, and non-natural monstrosity, and artificial monstrosity of the animal.[36]

---

36. Ibid., 25.

This monstrosity, which is also the state, is the Leviathan. Derrida's reading of Hobbes takes his analysis beyond the bestiality of the state to touch the constructed nature, not only of the state, but of the bestiality of the state. The monstrosity is not the animal itself. The animal itself is long forgotten. The beast that is sovereign is a human beast. The sovereign that is beast is a human sovereign. They are constructions that extract humanity, through its manipulation of its own rhetoric about the beast, from the world of the beast. To the extent that the human is a social animal, its "animal-ness" is not animal at all. In other words, the animal is a construction or a prosthetic extension of the human into the world of the animal. The rhetoric of the beast – whether rogue or Leviathan – is the colonization of the animal by the human. By operating the same principle of reversibility that applies to all of Derrida's deconstructions, the bestiality of the state is also a construction. The beast, the sovereign, and the coupling of the two are only there because they are extensions of something that is being concealed. In this sense they are artificial or inauthentic technologies.

Derrida makes this point most clear when, amid his analysis of Hobbes's *Leviathan*, he "interrupts" the flow of his analysis to make a crucial clarification,

> Let me interrupt for a moment...to emphasize [that]...sovereignty is the artificial soul: the soul, i.e., the principle of life, vitality, vivacity of this Leviathan, and so also of the state, of this state monster created and dominated by the art of man, artificial animal monster which is none other than artificial man, says Hobbes, and which lives as a republic, state, commonwealth, *civitas* only through this sovereignty. This sovereignty is like an iron lung, an artificial respiration, an "Artificial *Soul*." So the state is a sort of robot, an animal monster, which in the figure of man, or of man in the figure of the animal monster, is stronger, etc., than natural man. Like a gigantic prosthesis designed to amplify, by objectifying it outside natural man, to amplify the power of the living, the living man that it protects, that it serves, but like a dead machine, or even a machine

of death, a machine, which is only the mask of the living, like a machine of death can serve the living.[37]

Derrida goes on to describe the prosthetic extensions of the human body in the state. The state has a head; it has a humanoid physiology in which each limb corresponds to an arm of the state's mechanism. This is the "prosth-State," which, when noticed and understood, should hail the end of the states. The state, as a body that has turned upon itself in war, is as much a machine of death as it is of life. It is as destructive as it is constructive. It has turned against the humanity it protects, and in the case of civil war, it turns against itself.

This interruption comes to underline Derrida's insight that the colonization of the bestial by the human is only one (albeit central) example of a wider phenomenon in which the human capacity to construct is discovered as the human capacity to artificially extend the range of human power. Derrida feels compelled to point out that the extension of power into the realm of the animal that he is analyzing is the same as the extension of human power into the political. In other words, Derrida feels compelled to interrupt his discussion of Hobbes's *Leviathan* to point out how the prosthetic nature of the state underlines the connection between the construction and the accumulation of destructive capability. But Derrida's analysis does more than expose this irony. It connects the constructive and destructive accumulation of power with the existential anxiety that the state comes to alleviate. This leads him to a dramatic insight about the Leviathan state's presumed immortality.

Derrida's portrayal of the state as a prosthesis of the body deconstructs and undermines the supposed immortality of the state. Derrida shows that Hobbes's vision of the immortality of unending succession in power that is the state – the gapless presence of the state in the time of the state – came to answer the fundamental human fear of death. In other words, the state is a human made machine that defies the boundaries of death by defining the sovereignty of the state as a god. Derrida deconstructs the fantasy that the state represents an endless cycle, in which the power of the state is transferred without gaps or interruptions in time from head to head, from prime

---

37. Ibid., 28.

minister to prime minister from president to president, by showing that the state is only a prosthState. The crucial point here is that this fantasy of the immortal succession of power (embedded in the state itself and in the offices of the state rather than in the hands of the people who occupy them), plays a central a role in the political philosophy of even the most liberal modern democracies. Derrida insists that this fantasy cannot go without scrutiny. By deconstructing it, Derrida shows how the notion of the state as prosthState emerges as yet another "object" on which the subject projects an extension of itself into space as it tries to escape the crisis of knowing its own mortality. This is a theme that we have already encountered on the epistemological plane and that we must try to understand in ontological terms:

Just as Deconstruction calls attention to the epistemological delusion of fleeing to the object, De-con-struction undercuts the ontological anxiety of the "subject" whose fantasy is to protect his *being* from the threat of death by extending it into the artificial externality of the sovereign state. Both the object and the state are projections of the subject. They are what Heidegger called *Technik*. They are prosthetic, robotic, or technological extensions of the self into the space that is around. And like the human image in which they are built, they can die. In Derrida's words,

> It follows that law, sovereignty, the institution of the state are historical and always provisional, let's say deconstructable, essentially fragile and finite or mortal, even if sovereignty is *posited as immortal*. It is posited as immortal and indivisible precisely because it is mortal and divisible, contract and convention being destined to ensure for it what it does not have, or is not, naturally.[38]

In this passage Derrida closely echoes Heidegger's ontological resistance to technology. However, the upshot of Derrida's analysis comes to replace the Structure of Concealment that claims that the exclusion of God from politics is justified by rational argument. According to Derrida, rationalism is not even interested in disproving the non-rational abstract, nor is it troubled by the difficulty science has with religious ideas about an infinite or immortal

---

38. Ibid., 42.

being. Instead, he suggests that the expulsion of God from the public sphere is motivated by something more ontologically primal than that. Post-Enlightenment humanist politics expelled God from the public sphere so that it could keep all competitors away from its own contender. The idea of the immortal God is banished from politics because it threatens the exclusive plausibility of the state's delusional claim to immortality. On this reading, underlying anxiety about the illusion of the state's immortality is the force that provided the impetus for secularism. This idea, which is also central to Derrida's reading of the Tower of Babel, is a response to Carl Schmitt's proposal that the modern state is an expression of the human project to transfer the authority of the divine to the human sphere of the political. It is this that justifies the sovereign's right to take away life, to declare war, and to make exceptional decisions when faced by a mortal enemy. Sovereignty for Schmitt is most purely visible for what it really is only when the coverings and concealments are stripped away, when the sovereign seizes the pure and immortal power to declare war and send its citizens to death. From the perspective of Segulah, this is where we catch our glimpse of Churban.

In Heidegger's terms we might say that the Structure of Concealment that drives humanity to create states is the ontological condition of Dasein in hiding. Only a political state of *being* that can face its own mortality and exist in a condition of *being-toward-death* can bring Dasein out of hiding. From Derrida's perspective, Schmitt's notion of the secular state answers the primordial need, which Heidegger discovers, to face death. The liberal state that cannot own this perception of its own identity lives with itself by keeping God at a distance so that He cannot expose or spoil the illusion of immortality that Dasein (in hiding) has constructed and which the prosthetic (and hence mortal) politics of the state struggles so desperately to conceal.[39]

In order to see this point more clearly, we must return to the chronological sequences that underpin the historical dimension of Derrida's analysis. We

---

39. This analysis adds a very interesting perspective to William Cavanaugh's thesis discussed in chapter 2 above, in that it offers a philosophical dimension to Cavanaugh's historical claim that the wars of religion were the birth pangs of the modern state. See Cavanaugh, "Fire Strong Enough," 314–37. This theme is also central to Carl Schmitt's notion of political theology in which the state replaces God and seizes the ultimate power to make decisions in matters of life and death for its citizens. See Carl Schmitt, *Political Theology.*

must see how the micro-chronology that runs from Heidegger and Schmitt to Derrida is intertwined with the trauma of the Holocaust. De-con-struction is therefore a political endeavor. It makes space for a kind of politics that Derrida considers safe enough to work in an era that has seen the "breaking out" of Dasein in two world wars, two brutal totalitarian regimes (Soviet Russia and Nazi Germany) and in the philosophy of both Heidegger and Schmitt. All these phenomena (and more like them that preceded them and become more visible after them) disclose the true nature of sovereignty. They uncover it for the beast that it is and heighten our suspicion of it when we encounter its more concealed or civilized forms. Derrida shows us the "beast," the "troubling resemblance," the "worrying super-opposition," and the "ontological copula." The making public of this hidden Dasein is Churban. It is humanism's great trauma and it must be definitive of all the politics that follows it. If it is not, the idea that Survival and System continues poses an existential threat to Judaism.

For this "post-traumatic" era Derrida looks for a new politics whose first principle is that human beings can no longer subject themselves to the potential tyranny embedded in all forms of prosthetic sovereignty. However, at the same time, Derrida understands he has no alternative to sovereignty. As such, all Derrida can propose is the perennial condition of what we have called De-con-struction's clinging to the edge of Galut. At the edge of Galut he hangs on for dear life, deconstructing anything and everything for fear of slipping into the horrific certainty that lies beyond. In Derrida's own terms, this is a politics that engages in "a slow and differentiated deconstruction" of all forms of sovereignty. In Derrida's view, this is the inevitable and only choice that faces the generation that has seen "the beast." Western civilization has no choice but to self-deconstruct, and in his mind this is indeed what is happening,

> This deconstruction is what is happening, as I often say, and what is happening today in the world — through crises, wars, phenomena of so-called national and international terrorism, massacres that are declared or not, the transformation of the global market and of international law — what is happening is so many events

that are affecting the classical concept of sovereignty and making trouble for it.[40]

There are two points that we would like to underline here. The first is that liberalism (i.e., the politics of the side that vanquished Nazi Germany in World War II) does not present a way forward for Derrida. This is because in Derrida's view liberalism is a potently self-deceiving mechanism that lures the released mind back into the very delusion that exposure to the beast should have shattered. This idea totally deconstructs the world order since 1945 because it disavows the claim of the Allied forces in World War II to use their extraordinary power morally and police the world.[41] Second, the disclosure of the beast, horrific and unbearable as it is, is all the same something to be thankful for. This is why Derrida is grateful to Heidegger, Schmitt, and (in passages that we have not discussed) Machiavelli.[42] In Derrida's political thought, these thinkers are the ones who uncover and expose the inner meaning of the broad historical processes through which the raw and blatantly tyrannical side of sovereignty becomes comprehensible. It becomes clear that what is worthy of incredible note is not that human sovereignty is capable of bestial cruelty but that the anxiously destructive existential force of authentic Dasein is so deftly capable – like a wolf – of going stealthily into hiding while it waits for its next opportunity to creep up and pounce. This threat is so concealed and alluring that you must be careful not to be tempted. Derrida warns,

> It goes without saying that, while taking this argumentation of Schmitt's seriously, but without subscribing to it through and through, what I am seeking elsewhere but in particular in this seminar, is a prudent deconstruction of this logic, and of the

---

40. Derrida, *The Beast and the Sovereign*, 76.

41. This is a radical claim in that it is directed specifically at the liberal democracies that fought against Germany in World War II. It perhaps goes without saying when applied to Stalin's USSR in which case Derrida can be seen here as calling our attention to the underlying irony that the inclusion of Stalin in the alliance suggests. This, of course, is also the ironic implication of Hannah Arendt's thesis in her analysis of totalitarianism.

42. Derrida, *The Beast and the Sovereign*, 82–85.

dominant, classical concept of nation-state sovereignty (which is Schmitt's reference), without ending up with a depoliticization, a neutralization of the political, but with another politicization.[43]

Behind the lure and seduction of Schmitt's rhetoric all sovereignty is indicted. It is this indictment that provides the meaning of Schmitt's value. In a strikingly candid passage Derrida brings together the appeal of Schmitt's argument and the indictment of liberalism when he says,

> Whether or not one agrees with these propositions of Schmitt's, one can understand why, even though they come from a right-wing Catholic who was more than compromised a few years later with Nazism and anti-Semitism, they should have seduced, and still today retain their power of seduction on the Left for all those who are ready at least to share this vigilance with respect to "humanistic" and "humanitarian" ruses and allegations, which constitute the rhetorical weapon but also the weapon pure and simple, and sometimes a highly murderous weapon, of new political or economical imperialisms.[44]

Schmitt is there to be learned from. He tells us what sovereignty is. He is not there so that we can subscribe to his pure logic. From this we must stand guard and remember our purpose is the quest for an alternative. But this is an alternative that De-con-struction cannot and does not know. The best positive proposition Derrida can offer, as we have already seen, is yearning. It would be ideal if a new politics were possible, but Derrida is categorically (chastely) insistent that, as far as he can see, it is not. He rejects the plausibility of a "depoliticization" of human society and is skeptical about the possibility of a "neutralization of the political." What he wishes for is

---

43. Ibid., 75.
44. Ibid., 77.

a repoliticization that does not fall into the same "ruts" of dishonest fiction – while what an "honest fiction" can be and on which concept of fiction one is relying remains to be found out.[45]

With no redemptive option, Derrida offers a permanent condition of deconstructive vigilance. The perennial deconstruction of sovereignty at least allows the citizen to know that he or she is being made subject to something that is only mortal. "Recognizing that sovereignty is divisible, that it divides and partitions, even where there is hardly any sovereignty left, is already to begin to deconstruct a pure concept of sovereignty that presupposes indivisibility."[46] With this mission in mind, De-con-struction turns to the plight of the oppressed. It exposes colonialism and chauvinism, racism, bigotry, and blindness and all the forms of oppression under sovereignty that expose the fiction of the right to rule as a façade for bestiality. It exposes, but it does not replace. It knows it is in Galut but insists on offering no way out. All it can do is hope to spread a consciousness that will make life in Galut more tolerable.

In sum, Dec-con-struction remains at the edge of Galut because it knows that any and all attempts to create a "better" sovereignty will fall subject to the mortal anxiety of Dasein. There is no escape because, from De-con-struction's post-traumatic perspective, one form of Dasein or another is the only thing that awaits you if you push past the boundaries of exile. By embracing an apophatic and negative identity of powerless exilic opposition to all forms of construction, De-con-struction erects a wall of silence – a line of active deconstructive resistance – that it believes will protect against the alluring logic of sovereignty itself. This is how and why it conceals from us the path. But this is the path that we must follow even in the knowledge that the only place it leads is back to the locus of Churban where the beast lies waiting.

The Birth of the Prison

As before, our discussion of Foucault is only an illustration of an idea and not its proof. Similarly, though Derrida and Foucault are very different from one another, we shall turn to both to illustrate the same basic idea. What is

45. Ibid.
46. Ibid., 76.

gained by reading Foucault after our discussion of Derrida is the historical perspective that he provides. Ultimately, what we hope to add through our next discussion of Foucault is a richer understanding of the role played by the Holocaust in generating the historical conditions that allow the plausibility of rehabilitating Segulah to emerge into view.

Like Derrida, Foucault is concerned with the hidden or dark side of the use of power in modern politics. However, Foucault seeks to ferret this out by telling, in copious detail, the story of the invention and evolution of some of post-Enlightenment humanism's most seemingly benevolent institutional innovations. In particular, Foucault is interested in the darker side of how modern societies "take care" of deviants, utilizing a façade of benevolence (which can still be appreciated at least in part as truly compassionate) to suppress and repress the social forces that pose a mortal threat to the constructed security of modern political life. In particular, Foucault seeks to expose the mechanisms that conceal and suppress the Achilles' heels of human potentiality – the "unreasonable" or "rogue" *states-of-being* which infringe upon the inviolate preconditions that must be met in order to ensure the security and stability of modern political society. The point here is not to ascribe simplistically sinister intentions to progressivism but to underline the inevitability of the sinister outcomes of progress and air the anxiety that drives the "rational" sovereign to keep them hidden. As such, Foucault is interested in institutions that have walls that conceal societal procedures that were once conducted out in the open.

In order to consider Foucault's historiography from the perspective of De-con-struction, we shall emphasize the ontological dimension of his analysis looking at historical case studies as portrayals of *conditions-of-being*. Let us briefly consider two examples of ontological subjects that are vital to the modern state's capacity to function effectively. The first of these is the condition of *being-subject-to the law*, while the second is the condition of *being-subject-to reason*. Foucault wants us to see these *conditions-of-being* as the nation-state's constructions of the subject. Like Derrida, the methodology that he uses to expose this is negative and apophatic which in Foucault's case means that he brings phenomena into view by tracing the historical construction of their ontological opposites. These too are *states-of-being*; the condition of *being-in-violation-of the law* that characterizes the modern criminal and the condition of *being-in-violation-of reason* that characterizes the modern mentally insane.

Foucault's work shows that these *conditions-of-being* are constructed through the state's manipulation of two simultaneous and inverted disciplinary technologies. These are the state's capability to extend the boundaries of sovereignty through the construction of "docile bodies" and "permanent coercions" in the public sphere and its power to construct "panoptic" conditions for the confinement of deviance. On the one hand, the state demonstrates its sovereignty to its subjects by projecting its image of the subject onto the behaviors that are normative to the public sphere. On the other hand, the state assumes the right to exclude the deviant subject from public view and subjects it to endless examination. These two conditions must be differentiated from raw law enforcement and the execution of criminal justice. While both were carried out in the premodern village square, the modern state created new conditions for these functions. It is these conditions and not the functions themselves that are served, according to Foucault, by the construction of institutions such as the penitentiary and the asylum.

For Foucault, these institutional innovations of the modern state, even though they do indeed serve and protect public interest, are mechanisms for wielding state power. In this sense they not only protect the public sphere; they construct it as the sphere in which the state is demonstrably effective. Demonstrating its efficacy is how the state seizes power. The asylum, as such, creates the ontological condition of the madness that it institutionalizes so that the state is the demonstrable protector of public sanity. Similarly, the prison generates the unique conditions of modern criminality that establish the rule of law outside its walls. Ultimately, though these two cases are at the extremes of society, the mechanisms of sovereignty that they display are the very ones that everywhere construct normative social behavior. Thus, Foucault asks,

> Is it surprising that the cellular prison, with its regular chronologies, forced labor, its authorities of surveillance and registration, its experts in normality, who continue and multiply the functions of the judge, should have become a modern instrument of penality?

Is it surprising that prisons resemble factories, schools, barracks, hospitals, which all resemble prisons?[47]

In the construction of the prison, Foucault finds traces of the state's need to dominate its subjects' experiences of time, to define and monitor normality and to establish its authority over normative behavior. However, while these mechanisms of coercion are perhaps most visible in the prison, his deconstructive historical analysis makes the duplications of these same mechanisms in the freer and less concealed institutions of state even more noticeable.

A broad look at Foucault's work allows us to see how he traces the construction of modern normativity through the extension of sovereignty and the exclusion of deviance in almost every sphere of modern life. He traces the processes whereby practices that once belonged to the visible spheres of social life are repositioned behind the walls of institutions such as the education of children in schools, sexuality in the nuclear family home, childbirth in the obstetric ward, the treatment of the sick in the hospital, the treatment of the insane in the asylum, and more. In order to make the point that is important to us clearer, it is sufficient to look, in a little more detail, at just one example (which we have already begun referring to): the invention of the modern prison which Foucault describes in *Discipline and Punish: The Birth of the Prison*.[48]

The heart of Foucault's thesis in *Discipline and Punish* is that a principle of reciprocity moves between the body of the sovereign that is violated by crime and the violation of the criminal's body through punishment. The book begins with a blood-chilling account of the public drawing and quartering of Robert-François Damiens, who attempted the assassination of Louis XV in 1757. According to Foucault, the public display of Damiens's torturous execution exhibited

the extreme point of penal justice under the Ançien Régime [which] was the infinite segmentation of the body of the regicide; a manifestation of the strongest power over the body of the

---

47. Michel Foucault, *Discipline and Punish: The Birth of the Prison*, trans. Alan Sheridan (Vintage Books, 1977), 227–28.

48. Ibid.

greatest criminal, whose total destruction made the crime explode in its truth.[49]

Damiens's public torture corresponded to the sovereign's perception of the crime as a violation of the sovereign body. As chilling and disturbing as Damiens's public execution was, Foucault's main purpose in the book is to question the humanity of the process of "humanization" that brought the public spectacle of penal torture to an end. Foucault explores the more complex nature of the modern sovereign body as it becomes visible in the new treatments of the body in the modern criminal justice system. The modern prison is in many undeniable ways more humane than its medieval predecessors. However, as we saw above with Derrida's reading of Heidegger's "On Humanism," the nature of that humanity is complex and diverse, and its fullest expressions are necessarily tainted. While the externality of its humaneness is genuine, Foucault insists that the modern criminal justice system makes no superfluous concessions to clemency. On the contrary, on close analysis, the seemingly progressive leniency of the modern penal system conceals its careful design as a highly efficient tool for fending off – with maximum precision – the true threats that modern criminality poses to the rule of law.

Though the physical torture of Damiens's public execution was more severe than any of the disciplinary practices used in the modern prison, in prison the modern criminal now finds himself subject to endless scrutiny and examination. The fact that this scrutiny represents an idea of the state is central to Foucault's thesis:

> The ideal point of penality today would be an infinite discipline: an interrogation without end, an investigation that would be extended without limit to a meticulous and ever more analytical observation, a judgment that would at the same time be the constitution of a file that was never closed, the calculated leniency of a penalty that would be interlaced with the ruthless curiosity of an examination, a procedure that would be at the same time the permanent measure of a gap in relation to an inaccessible norm

49. Ibid., 227.

and the asymptomatic movement that strives to meet in infinity. The public execution was the legal culmination of a procedure governed by the Inquisition. The practice of placing individuals under "observation" is a natural extension of a justice imbued with disciplinary methods and examination procedures.[50]

The criminal is subject to scrutiny and examination from within. The prison not only expels him from society; it subjects him to endless processes of psychological examination, judgment, socialization, and penitent reeducation. In modern society it is no longer the action of the criminal's body that the system seeks to punish but the defiance that places him into the ontological condition of deviance that is perhaps best expressed by the notion of crime as the profession of the criminal. The mind of the professional criminal represents a *state-of-being* that will not become subject to the conditions of lawfulness imposed on it by the sovereign. This *state-of-being* is intolerable primarily because, like the behavior of the insane, it can be restrained only with raw power alone. In other words, stubborn deviants force the state to show its bestial face and crack the veneer of rationality on which its ideal interactions with its subjects rely. Bringing this power into public view threatens the reasonable foundations upon which the state earns the willing compliance of its citizens to the rule of law.

This is why both the modern asylum and the modern prison seek to restore order without resorting to pure power alone. They do this by treating, curing, and reeducating the mentally or criminally insane. The benevolence of these objectives provides a cover that enables the violent invasion of the prisoner's *inner-being* that "institutional correction" requires. The use of institutional correction facilities to provide the remedy for social deviance is what Foucault refers to as "calculated leniency." This leniency allows the state to present its progressive criminal justice system as concerned with the well-being of the criminal.

Alongside this leniency Foucault emphasizes the state's anxious curiosity about the prisoner's state of mind. Here the state's surveillance and examination of the prisoner is described as "ruthlessly infinite." This infinity echoes

---

50. Ibid.

the state's self-image as immortal and underlines the endlessness of its struggle to protect itself. The ideal criminal justice system of the state enters endlessly into the criminal-being in an anxious attempt to penetrate it and establish the state's monopoly over power from within. Behind the prison walls, the state extends its coercive capabilities and aggressively scrutinizes the prisoner's time, behavior, and even his thoughts. The prison protects society from the threat posed to it by the criminal. But more importantly, it closes in on the prisoner, taking its license to reeducate the prisoner from the prisoner's violation of the rule of law – as defined by the social contract. In private, behind the prison walls, a new state is constructed, and the prisoner is constructed from within as its subject.

This feature of prison is perhaps the key to its stability as the penalty par excellence in modern society. The self-evidence of the prison's legitimacy is built into the fabric of society, because the methods that it uses are extensions of that same fabric. That the "deprivation of liberty" should be the punishment par excellence in a society in which "liberty is a good that belongs to all" perhaps goes without saying,

> but the self-evidence of the prison is also based on its role, supposed or demanded, as an apparatus for transforming individuals. How could the prison not be immediately accepted when, by locking up, retraining and rendering docile, it merely reproduces, with a little more emphasis, all the mechanisms that are to be found in the social body? The prison is like a rather disciplined barracks, a strict school, a dark workshop, but not qualitatively different.[51]

The prison is thus a visible mechanism of power that is built in the image of the state's body. However, the modern criminal must be seen to pose no real threat to the physical mortality of the state. As such, it is the condition of the criminal's insubordinate behavior that must be made subject to the norms of life in the social body. In essence, the modern prison's leniency is actually an expression of its consistency with the hidden mechanisms that abound

---

51. Ibid., 233.

elsewhere in the limbs of the social body – such as the strict school, barracks, or workshop – where the state takes similar unnoticed liberties in conditioning the behavior of seemingly law-abiding citizens.

For Foucault, the fact that the modern criminal justice system takes upon itself the responsibility for the correction and reeducation of prisoners is of extreme importance. In particular, he wishes to underline how this objective is itself transformed by being tied inextricably to the notion of punishment. In Foucault's words,

> This double foundation – juridico-economic on the one hand, techno-disciplinary on the other – made the prison seem the most immediate and civilized form of all penalties.[52]

However, at the same time, the technical transformation of individuals that the prison sought to accomplish "immediately forms part of the institutional framework of penal detention."[53] The point is that the use of enlightened corrective methods as part of punishment implicates social reform and reeducation in all of its forms in what Foucault refers to as "procedures of domination" that are characteristic of "a particular type of power."

> A Justice that is supposed to be "equal," a legal machinery that is supposed to be "autonomous," but which contains all the asymmetries of disciplinary subjection, this conjunction marked the birth of the prison, "the penalty of civilized societies."[54]

For Foucault, the concealment of punishment under the cover of reeducation is a sinister expression of the hidden anxiety of the state. The externality of benevolence and equality before the law provides the cover that makes the maximum exertion of state power against the criminal possible. Moreover, the institutionalization of the criminal and his expulsion from the public

---

52. Ibid.
53. Ibid.
54. Ibid., 231–32.

sphere facilitates the duplication of practices that rest on the same double foundation of reform and punishment in society at large. The marginalization of the criminal, therefore, represents the hold of the state on the normative public sphere. The criminal is locked up in individualized cellular space in which an alternative and blatantly invasive regime of law is enacted especially for him. This is not the rule of law. It is the rule of the prison to which he must now totally surrender the freedom of his being. But, while this system is indeed more gentle, humane, and benevolent than its medieval predecessors, Foucault is concerned with underlining the mechanisms that serve a far greater purpose than the reeducation of the criminal and the protection of the public sphere from the danger that he poses to it. It is these mechanisms that he refers to as the "carceral archipelago." This term refers to the surveillance systems and technologies in general used in modern societies to gain social control and to establish discipline in all areas of social life. These constructions are not only mechanisms that the state turns against the citizen. They are accessible to private citizens who protect their homes and use private investigators to accumulate knowledge about others. These can be used to keep criminals in, as in prisons, and to keep them out, as in gated communities built by the rich to construct a safe environment for their children to play in after school.

The ironic and dark associations conjured up by Foucault's choice of phrase "the carceral archipelago" expresses the destructiveness that is inherent in the human capacity to construct. Foucault's analysis of the prison and the asylum demonstrate this same inevitable Dr. Jekyll that accompanies the Mr. Hyde of social reform and progressive justice wherever he goes. Foucault demonstrates the danger that the accumulation of power by the state poses from within, i.e., to the very citizens it protects. In the same way that the world wars show how readily the power accumulated by the nation-state in order to keep the peace can be turned into the destructive power of state-sponsored war, Foucault shows how the benevolent desire to protect law, order, health, and morality can erupt into an anxious crisis in which the munificent mechanisms of the state declare war against its citizens.

This theme is particularly pronounced in his analysis of the treatment of delinquents. As we already saw above, the delinquents are the rogues who will not conform even when power is directed against them. It is here, when the threat to the power of the state becomes raw, that the state declares "a permanent state of conflict." This is a war against crime that is promulgated, generated, and maintained by the press through the popular genres of crime reports, crime novels, and newsreels that have their early modern origin in the journalist genre known as the *fait divers*:

> The criminal *fait divers*, by its everyday redundancy, makes acceptable the system of judicial police supervisions that partition society; it recounts from day to day a sort of internal battle against the faceless enemy; in this war, it constitutes the daily bulletin of alarm or victory.[55]

The *fait divers* is itself a construct of the perception of the law as generated by the state. But it is also a reeducator that allows the lines of the state's entitlement to power to be redrawn and to create an almost paranoid anxiety about crime, deviance, and insanity. Deviants and criminals are casted in the role of a faceless enemy, an enemy who is all around and who must be vanquished in battle.

Foucault closes his analysis of carceral mechanisms saying that ultimately,

> what presides over all these mechanisms is not the unitary functioning of an apparatus or an institution, but the necessity of combat and the rules of strategy. That, consequently, the notions of institutions of repression, of rejection, exclusion, marginalization, are not adequate to describe, at the very centre of the carceral city, the formation of the insidious leniencies, unavowable petty cruelties, small acts of cunning, calculated methods, techniques, "sciences" that permit the fabrication of the disciplinary individual. In this central and centralized humanity, the effect and instrument of complex power relations, bodies and forces subjected by multiple mechanisms of "incarceration," objects for discourses that are in

---

55. Ibid., 286.

themselves elements for this strategy, we must hear the distant roar of battle.[56]

Ultimately, Foucault has reached his glimpse of Churban. It is here that the balanced and complex account of the multifaceted matrix of forces that compete with each other for dominance over the production of social justice in humanist politics is stripped down to the raw power and enmity that lie at the root of sovereignty and gain their only pure expression in the destructive carnage of the battlefield. He signs off eerily and ominously,

> At this point I end a book that must serve as a historical background to various studies of the power of normalization and the formation of knowledge in modern society.[57]

It is hard not to wonder what these various studies must study. And even though Foucault leaves his intentions shrouded in mystery, it is hard not to imagine that this portrayal of the evolution of the criminal justice system that we know and recognize, that resonates for us with the gangster wars in the thirties, with the penitentiaries of Pennsylvania as well as with the modern histories of the evolving criminal justice systems all over Europe, is somehow a "middle ground" on a sliding scale that has at one extreme the unmentioned inmate whose *being* has been so invaded by the state that Primo Levi wonders if he is even a man[58] at all, and at the other extreme, the unnamed prison or *lager* we call Auschwitz.[59]

---

56. Ibid., 308.

57. Ibid.

58. This is a reference to Levi's classic account of his experiences as an inmate in Auschwitz. Primo Levi, *If This Is a Man*, trans. Stuart Woolf (New York: Orion, 1959).

59. For a discussion of Foucault's silence about the Holocaust especially in the context of his analysis of the prison but also in his discussion of the modern state's power to control life and death (which appears in his classical study of modern sexuality), see Alan Milchman and Alan Rosenberg, "Michel Foucault and the Genealogy of the Holocaust," in *Post-Modernism and the Holocaust* (Radopi, 1998). See also Michel Foucault, "Right of Death and Power of Life," in *The History of Sexuality*, trans. Robert Hurley (Vintage Books, 1978).

De-con-struction at the Edge of Galut and the
Meaning of Churban

Our path has taken us to the edge of Galut from where (though the chronological order has been reversed) we can catch our glimpse of Churban. This is a place or a locus that we have sought to understand in both philosophical and historical terms.

In philosophical terms, what this means is that our ontological analysis of deconstruction (as De-con-struction) has allowed us to recognize the danger posed to humanity by the post-Enlightenment strategy of using rationality to conceal bestiality. Thus far, our discussion of De-con-struction has allowed us to recognize or see from afar the "fact" of this, though we have not yet comprehended or encountered its core meaning from within. The "fact" of this *condition-of-being* is attested to, as it were from afar, by De-con-struction's traumatic recoiling from the project of humanism. This recoiling or conservatism is motivated by the horrific realization that the humanist project is a Structure of Concealment that establishes the priority of epistemology in modern thought in order to obscure the destructively anxious existential *condition-of-being* of the being, the Leviathan wolf, that is in hiding. The ontology of this being or Dasein takes two forms, an authentic form and an inauthentic form. In each case it is plagued with a fundamental or existential anxiety about its own *being* that is rooted in the fact of human mortality.

In its inauthentic forms, Dasein builds the prosthetic structures of modern society in which it manufactures its object-based account of science, truth, and even liberty. Despite the fact that these structures generate progress and improvement, they are constructions that both build and destroy. With the manipulatively grotesque skill of the rational "rider," this is what Dasein works hard to conceal.

In its authentic form Dasein seeks to blow off the covering and reveal the power of the beast. When this happens the forms of thought, society, sovereignty, and power that are consistent with authentic Dasein's *resolve to come fully into being* become political realities and take the form of the total state. With the temptation of *resolve* that offers the power of *coming fully into being*, the total state lures its citizens into surrendering their liberty. To come fully into *being* is to resolutely surrender the totality of human liberty to authentic

Dasein. To resist this is to confront head-on the deathly and destructive underbelly of the total state's determination to establish itself in full.

The philosophical encounter with Dasein's *coming-fully-and-resolutely-in-to-being* creates a philosophical state of mind in which Dasein in all its inauthentic forms becomes visible all around. The Structures of Concealment are blown open and Dasein's consciousness of itself becomes disclosed. An ontological notion of the truth becomes visible as Dasein recognizes the ways in which the *truth-of-being* allows itself to be manifest in the world. By way of analogy, we might say that the truth of Dasein in its inauthentic forms becomes visible after the encounter with authentic Dasein in the same way, perhaps, that the shard of a broken vessel is recognizable to someone who has seen the vessel whole. Once you've seen it you recognize it in everything.

Like the vessel whole, the political expressions of authentic Dasein allow the inauthentic expressions of Dasein in all the liberal forms of humanist politics to be disclosed. By coupling the philosophical analysis of Dasein with the history of modernity and the Holocaust, De-con-struction explains how the *conditions-of-being* that underlie the entire post-Enlightenment humanist project are disclosed and made recognizable by National Socialism. It is this realization that constitutes the glimpse of Churban.

After this glimpse, Survival and System is just no longer plausible, which makes sense of the widespread anxiety that so many people feel about the possible recurrence of the Holocaust. In our view, Survival and System is anxious because it knows that it is in an unstable relationship with a political civilization that has a destructive edge that is capable of "breaking out." To understand the nature of this more deeply, we must turn to the method that we propose offers us a path we can follow toward an inner understanding of Churban.

PART III

CHURBAN

CHAPTER 9

Heidegger's Nazism and the Methodology of Churban

The Importance of Heidegger's Support for Nazism

Our proposed method of Churban depends on the argument that Heidegger's masterpiece *BT* adds greatly to our understanding of the psychological and philosophical depths of National Socialism. This book, which was composed in the same years as *Mein Kampf*, does not by any means provide us with a full picture of Heidegger's philosophy, which, quite naturally, developed and changed throughout his life.[1] It is arguably his most important book, and it is indeed concerned with the question of *being* that stayed with him throughout his career. But it is not the sum of his work, nor is it his last word on any of his philosophical concerns. We have singled out *BT* for special attention because it is an extraordinary window into the thoughts of a man with a brilliant mind writing in the thick of the milieu in which the ideas that germinated into Nazism took form.

But in order to proceed with our analysis, we need to provide a little support for this claim. We also need to move aside the danger of having the idea – which is essentially the methodological linchpin of our whole discussion of Heidegger – reduced to a banal comment on the tone of Heidegger's rectorial address in Freiburg in May 1933,[2] his membership in the Nazi party, the now-extant evidence of his lifelong loyalty to National Socialism,

---

1. For a detailed philosophical biography of Heidegger, see Rüdiger Safranski, *Martin Heidegger: Between Good and Evil*, trans. Ewald Osers (Harvard University Press, 2002).

2. The rectorial address, which is considered notorious for its ominously Nazi sentiments, was delivered by Heidegger on his appointment by the Nazis as rector of Freiburg

or even the blatant antisemitism that came to light with the publication of the so-called "Black Notebooks" in 2014.[3] While this evidence is clearly important to us, our method does not, by any means, depend on it alone. Rather, we are concerned with the analytic of Dasein and its meaning as an independent testimonial to the redemptive appeal of National Socialism and its power to resolve the crisis of human identity as Heidegger understood it.

One of the problems that our approach faces is that it runs up against the assumption that Nazi science is pseudo-science, Nazi philosophy is pseudo-philosophy. The challenge here is that this otherwise laudably dismissive approach to Nazism's intellectual legacy makes it difficult to accept the seriousness of Heidegger's Nazism and his philosophy together. Conventionally, you can't really have it both ways. Either serious philosophy or seriously Nazi, but not both together. The position we want to adopt is beautifully summed up in an oral statement that is attributed to Levinas, who supposedly said, "Heidegger was a Nazi. He was also the greatest thinker of our century."[4]

The literature that deals with Heidegger's Nazism is vast and varied, and it tends to focus on the question of his attitudes to the Jews or his use of antisemitic and fascist rhetoric. Victor Farias, Hugo Ott, Otto Pöggeler, Hans Sluga, Richard Wolin, Tom Rockmore, and Emmanuel Faye believe that *BT* is so poisoned with Nazi bluster that we must disqualify it from the

---

University in 1933. For a detailed description of the events leading up to this address, including an analysis of the address itself, see ibid., 238–47.

3.　　The Black Notebooks are a set of Heidegger's personal notes, composed between 1889 and 1976. They were first published by Peter Trawny in 2014 and have since reignited the debate about the connection between Heidegger's philosophy and his Nazism. See, for example, Andrew Mitchell and Peter Trawny, *Heidegger's Black Notebooks: Responses to Anti-Semitism* (Columbia University Press, 2017).

4.　　Emmanuel Levinas was a French Jewish existentialist philosopher who was among Heidegger's students at the Davos debate with Cassirer. It is not clear whether he said this or not, but there is no doubt that he dedicated much of his career to opposing Heidegger's philosophy. This suggests not only his rejection of Heidegger but his appreciation of his importance as well. See, for example, Emmanuel Levinas, *Time and the Other* (1947), trans. Richard A. Cohen (Pittsburgh, 1987) and Levinas, *Totality and Infinity: An Essay on Exteriority* (1961), trans. Alphonso Lingis (Pittsburgh: Duquesne University Press, 1969).

Western philosophical canon.[5] But many other scholars, including Hannah Arendt, Jacques Derrida, Jürgen Habermas, Hans Georg Gadamer, Richard Rorty, Karl Moehling, and Emmanuel Levinas,[6] rank Heidegger among the greatest thinkers of the twentieth century, separating his character flaws from their overall evaluation of his work.[7]

Before we dive into reading *BT* from the perspective of Segulah, we wish to analyze more closely the meaning of this attitude to Heidegger's Nazism. Rather than offering a wide survey of the opinions and nuances in the literature, we will look closely at two texts. The first is by Richard Rorty and it illustrates our problem. The second is by George Steiner and it will help us establish the premise on which our methodology of Churban is based.

---

5. See Victor Farias, *Heidegger and Nazism*, ed. Joseph Margolis and Tom Rockmore (Philadelphia, 1989); Hugo Ott, *Martin Heidegger: A Political Life*, trans. Allan Blunden (London, 1994); Otto Pöggeler, "Heidegger's Political Understanding," in *The Heidegger Controversy: A Critical Reader*, ed. Richard Wolin (New York, 1991) and Pöggeler, *Martin Heidegger's Path of Thinking* (Atlantic Highlands, NJ, 1987); Hans Sluga, *Heidegger's Crisis: Philosophy and Politics in Nazi Germany* (Harvard University Press, 1995); Richard Wolin, *The Politics of Being: The Political Thought of Martin Heidegger* (Columbia University Press, 1990) (the hardback edition of this volume [2016] includes a new preface that addresses the effect of the Black Notebooks on our understanding of the relationship between politics and philosophy in Heidegger); Tom Rockmore, *On Heidegger's Nazism and Philosophy* (University of California Press, 1997); Emmanuel Faye, *Heidegger: The Introduction of Nazism into Philosophy in Light of the Unpublished Seminars 1933–1935* (Yale, 2009). For a very specific but highly nuanced analysis of Heidegger's Nazism with specific reference to the climactic section 74 in *BT*, see Johannes Fristche, *Historical Destiny and National Socialism in Heidegger's Being and Time* (University of California Press, 1999).

6. For a discussion of Hannah Arendt's attitude to Heidegger's Nazism after the war, see Safranski, *Martin Heidegger*, 370–89; see also Jacques Derrida, *Of Spirit: Heidegger and the Question*, trans. Geoffrey Bennington and Richard Bowlby (Chicago, 1989); see Jürgen Habermas, *Philosophical-Political Profiles*, trans. Frederick G. Lawrence (Cambridge, MA: MIT Press, 1983) 53–60; see Hans Georg Gadamer, *Hegel-Husserl-Heidegger* (Tubingen, 1987) and Safranski, 130–34. Richard Rorty outlines his specific attitude toward the relationship between Heidegger's philosophy and his Nazism in his essay "On Heidegger's Nazism," in Richard Rorty, *Philosophy and Social Hope* (Penguin Books, 1999). We shall return to offer a close analysis of this essay in our discussion below. See Karl A. Moehling, "Heidegger and the Nazis," in Thomas Sheehan, ed. (1981), *Heidegger: The Man and the Thinker* (New Jersey, 2010), 31–43.

7. Safranski, *Martin Heidegger*, 370–89.

Richard Rorty and Heidegger's Nazism

In the opening pages of his *Philosophy and the Mirror of Nature*, Rorty famously dubs Heidegger (along with Wittgenstein and Dewey) "one of the three most important philosophers of our century."[8] Tellingly, Rorty makes no mention of Heidegger's involvement with Nazism. He deals most explicitly with this question in an astonishing piece originally published in the *London Review of Books* and reprinted in his *Philosophy and Social Hope* under the title "On Heidegger's Nazism."[9]

In this short essay Rorty is most concerned with the project of separating Heidegger's work from his essentialist pretenses. In this sense, he is perhaps trying to save Heidegger from himself. In Rorty's view, "Heidegger's suggestion that he always followed a single star" is "self-deceptive flattery."[10] Heidegger would no doubt have found Rorty's selective and anti-essentialist way of reading his books exasperating. But Rorty insists that rummaging through a mixed bag of chaff and pearls is all there is. There is no Archimedean point or overarching principle that can be singled out in either the life or the writing of a great philosopher that can then be used to place all his work in a single coherent context. Instead, there is a toolbox in which one might find both good tools and bad. It is the job of the contemporary reader to pick out what is good and useful and reject the junk. This selection must be based on intellectual merit and detached from unreasonable pretensions about how and why one tool or another might have an impact on the world. Rorty therefore sees Heidegger's multiple projects in both his life and his work as varied and as connected only in the sense that they are "chance events." Rorty's distinction between life and work brings him to his comment on the significance of Heidegger's Nazism. He is not dismissive of it. He simply recommends that "for those of us who wish to continue to pick over the tools in Heidegger's box, the fact that the man who designed these remarkable tools was first a Nazi and later a cowardly hypocrite is just one of history's many ironies."[11]

---

8.   Richard Rorty, *Philosophy and the Mirror of Nature* (Princeton University Press, 1979), 5.

9.   Rorty, *Philosophy and Social Hope*, 190–97.

10.   Ibid., 191.

11.   Ibid., 192.

Rorty goes on to allow that there are certain key characteristics in a man's personality which single him out and remain constant throughout his life. These traits are not enough to determine the paths that our lives take. But, in varying historical circumstances, they can prove important. In Heidegger's case Rorty concedes, "Whereas I do not believe that there is such a thing as the essential Heidegger; I think that the critics are right only to the following extent: Heidegger was anti-egalitarian throughout his life, and never cared the slightest for the liberal project of increasing the sum of human happiness." As unpleasant as these qualities are, Rorty doubts that they would have been of any interest to Heidegger's readers had he not become a Nazi. Instead he insists that there is no necessary connection between them and his Nazism and finds a rather extraordinary way of making his point.

Rorty suggests that under different circumstances, "chance events" could have taken a man with the very same personal traits and the same philosophical career down a very different road. To illustrate the idea, he composes what he calls "an independent variation of Heidegger's life story," which goes as follows:

> I can clarify what I mean by 'chance events' and 'independent variation' by sketching a slightly different possible world – a world in which Heidegger joins his fellow anti-egalitarian, Thomas Mann, in preaching resistance to Hitler. To see how this possible world might have been actual, imagine that in the summer of 1930 Heidegger suddenly finds himself deeply in love with a beautiful, intense, adoring philosophy student named Sarah Mandelbaum. Sarah is Jewish, but Heidegger barely notices this, dizzy with passion as he is. After a painful divorce from Elfride – a process that costs him the friendship of, among other people, the Husserls – Heidegger marries Sarah in 1932. In January 1933 they have a son, Abraham.
>
> Heidegger jokes that Sarah can think of Abraham as named after the patriarch, but that he will think of him as named after Abraham a Sancta Clara, the only other Messkirch boy to make good. Sarah looks up Abraham a Sancta Clara's antisemitic writings in the library stacks, and Heidegger's little joke becomes the

occasion of the first serious quarrel between husband and wife. But by the end of 1933, Heidegger is no longer making such jokes. For Sarah makes him notice that the Jewish Beamt, including his father-in-law, have been cashiered. Heidegger reads things about himself in the student newspaper that make him realize that his day in the sun may be over. Gradually it dawns upon him that his love for Sarah has cost him much of his prestige and will sooner or later cost him his job.

But he still loves her, and eventually he leaves his beloved Freiburg for her sake. In 1935 Heidegger is teaching in Berne, but only as a visitor. Switzerland has by now given away all its philosophy chairs. Suddenly a call comes from the Institute for Advanced Study in Princeton. There Heidegger spends two years slowly and painfully learning English, aching for the chance once again to spellbind seminar rooms of worshipfully attentive students. He gets a chance to do so in 1937 when some of his fellow émigrés arrange a permanent job for him at the University of Chicago.

There he meets Elizabeth Mann Borgese, who introduces him to her father. Heidegger manages to overcome his initial suspicion of the Hanseatic darling of fortune, and Mann his initial suspicion of the Black Forest Bauernkind. They find they agree with each other, and with Adorno and Horkheimer; that America is a reduction ad absurdum of Enlightenment hopes, a land without culture. But their contempt for America does not prevent them from seeing Hitler as having ruined Germany and being about to ruin Europe. Heidegger's stirring anti-Nazi broadcasts enable him to gratify a need to strike a heroic attitude before large masses of people – a need that he might, under other circumstances, have gratified in a rectorial address.

By the end of the Second World War, Heidegger's marriage is on the rocks. Sarah Heidegger is a social democrat to the core, loves America, and is a passionate Zionist. She has come to think of Heidegger as a great man with a cold and impervious heart, a heart which had once opened to her but remains closed to her social hopes. She has come to despise the egotist as much as she admires the philosopher and the anti-Nazi polemicist. In 1947 she separates from Heidegger and takes the 14-year-old Abraham with her to Palestine. She is wounded in the civil war but eventually, after the proclamation of independence, becomes a philosophy professor at Tel Aviv University.

Heidegger himself returns to Freiburg in triumph in 1948. There he gets his old friend Gadamer a job, even though he is acidly contemptuous of Gadamer's acquiescence in the Nazi take-over of the German universities. He eventually takes as his third wife a war widow, a woman who reminds all his old friends of Elfride. When he dies in 1976, his wife lays on his coffin the Presidential Medal of Freedom, the medal of the order Pour le Merite, and the gold medal of the Nobel Prize for Literature. This last had been awarded him in the year after the publication of his brief but poignant elegy for Abraham, who had died on the Golan Heights in 1967.[12]

Rorty's parallel universe is carefully crafted in many places to echo the true story of Heidegger's life. The betrayal of Elfride for a young Jewish philosophy student recalls the story of his affair with Hanna Arendt; the distaste for America (which here throws him into the company of prominent Jewish refugees) recalls his actual attitude to capitalist decadence; the miscalculated antisemitic joke captures the vulgar side of Heidegger's gruff and often insensitive humor; and most obviously, the stirring anti-Nazi radio broadcasts explicitly parallel the rousing political rhetoric of his infamous rectorial address. Rorty wants us to see how easily the same bag of contradictory personal traits, in another universe, might have guided the same philosopher, Martin Heidegger, to a very different sequence of choices and outcomes in his personal life story.

But, reading this astonishing story, one wonders if Rorty would have been able to design a similar parallel universe for Adolf Hitler. Would it be considered feasible for the character traits and works of this "political philosopher" to encounter each other only as "chance events"? Would Rorty have said the

---

12. Ibid., 193–95.

same of Goebbels or of Alfred Baeumler and Alfred Rosenberg or Hans Frank the music connoisseur?[13] The question is not cynical or facetious; it merely comes to delineate the boundary of Rorty's argument. It underlines the significance of his premise (or implicit insistence) that what is of enduring value in Heidegger's philosophy cannot coincide with his Nazism. When discussing the real life of Martin Heidegger, Rorty does not shy away from criticizing his indifference to the suffering of his Jewish colleagues whom he "watched... being dismissed from their jobs and then...disappear to a fate about which he could easily have learned."[14] He echoes Derrida and Habermas, who in his view, "were right in saying that the really unforgivable thing is the post-war silence" but then goes on to insist,

> I agree that this silence was unforgivable, but I am unable to deduce this silence from the content of Heidegger's books, or even to see it as a sign of something that should make us suspicious of these books. This is because I take a person's moral character – his or her selective sensitivity to the suffering of others – to be shaped by chance events in his or her life. Often, perhaps usually, this sensitivity varies independently of the project of self-creation that the person undertakes in his or her work.[15]

There are three crucial points to be made here. First, the emphasis on Heidegger's silence is disturbing because it shifts our attention away from the key issue, which is his affiliation with and support for Nazism. Moreover, what makes Heidegger different from Carnap, Sartre, and the many other great thinkers who put themselves behind fatefully anti-egalitarian political causes is not his postwar silence about the Holocaust. It is his active political and intellectual role in the Nazi project, which Rorty does not see.[16] Next to this, Heidegger's postwar conduct seems little more than a minor misdemeanor. To think otherwise is to put him in the wrong company. Indeed, he

---

13. This is a reference to a comment by George Steiner in his work *In Bluebeard's Castle*, which we discussed in chapter 2; see note 27.
14. Rorty, *Philosophy and Social Hope*, 193.
15. Ibid.
16. Ibid., 193.

was perhaps, as Rorty says, "the only eminent twentieth-century writer…
to have remained unmoved by the Holocaust"[17] (though others such as Carl
Schmitt do come to mind). But he was by no means the only Nazi after the
war to stay silent and express no remorse! Whether or not he was influential
and highly regarded by the Nazis, in this context, is immaterial.

Second, the comment about the impact of "chance events" on Heidegger's
life draws on a second unpalatable suggestion offered by Habermas and
Derrida. Rorty cites their having said that "any of us might, given Heidegger's
background, have thought that Hitler was Germany's only hope in 1933."[18]
In other words, Heidegger's membership in the Nazi party was forgivable;
following Hitler in 1933 was a reasonable mistake!

The third point is not so much about Rorty as it is a comment about our
assumptions going forward. Rorty suggests that we treat Heidegger like "any
one of us" when our point is that in fact he is not. We are not naïvely suggesting that Heidegger should have known better because he was a philosopher!
Clearly not, and in that sense Rorty is correct to keep his expectations low.
All the same, Heidegger is not like any one of us because of the specific substance of the philosophy he was writing and teaching in this crucial period.
In *BT*, Heidegger sought to lay bare the question of *being* that he maintained
Western philosophy was busy concealing. It is this crucial and central ambition that connects his philosophy, with enduring significance, to Nazism.
Heidegger saw Hitler as a partner in the struggle to tell and live out the truth
about the condition of humankind. To deny Heidegger's Nazism is to miss
the true importance of what is disclosed about humanity – what is disclosed
about how the Holocaust is humanly possible – in his work.

In the coming chapters, we shall offer a reading of *BT* that seeks to substantiate this claim. We shall look at *BT* as a one-of-a-kind opportunity to
peer into the existential angst that drove forward Nazism's deepest inner
struggle. From a methodological point of view, we have singled out *BT* for
special attention, because Heidegger's historical analysis of Dasein is perhaps
the most penetrating example in writing of what people were thinking, feeling, or intuiting both before and during the Nazi period. Without suggesting

---

17. Ibid.
18. Ibid.

that Heidegger's thought had any influence on the unfolding of political events, the fact that the "chance events" of his life-story in 1927 placed him at the heart of the milieu in which the collective consciousness that ultimately perpetrated the Holocaust began to grow is of providential import. More important still as we shall show, Heidegger's philosophy is an act of complicit inner participation in Nazism's struggle against inauthenticity. And it is to this idea that we now turn our attention.

George Steiner and Heidegger's Nazism

George Steiner's controversial monograph, simply entitled "Martin Heidegger," presents a more complex and painfully ambivalent picture of Heidegger's Nazi affiliation.[19] Like Rorty, Steiner identifies Heidegger's post-war silence as his principal offense. Indeed, in what one must assume is a slightly zealous jab at Derrida (with whom, as we mentioned, Rorty's position concurs), Steiner takes care to make it clear that it was he who first pointed out the importance of the postwar silence. However, on close reading, the meaning and significance of this silence for Steiner is very different from that of Rorty and Derrida. Steiner is less concerned with Heidegger's failure to show empathy and speak out. His rebuke is more carefully directed at what Heidegger's postwar silence tells us about the degree to which his own thought is enduringly caught up in the Nazi project. Beyond Heidegger's membership in the Nazi party, his rectorial address, his deceitful postwar interviews, and even his passionate participation in the Nazification of the German university world, Steiner identifies Heidegger's involvement in Nazism in the substance of his philosophical writing. Indeed, in Steiner's view, Heidegger's special genius in *BT* is most powerfully displayed as a "struggle" (i.e., Kampf) that runs parallel to the deepest aspirations of Nazism.

This struggle is a theme that runs like a thread through Steiner's monograph whenever he talks about *BT*. He deals with many other issues and touches upon the connection between Heidegger and Nazism in many other – and perhaps more conventional – ways. *BT* is not the sole focus of

---

19. George Steiner, *Martin Heidegger: With a New Introduction* (University of Chicago Press, 1989).

his analysis, but it is this leitmotif that appears when Steiner discusses *BT* that has captured our attention and which we shall try to tease out into the open.

In the spring/summer edition of *Salmagundi* (1989), Steiner published a piece entitled "Heidegger Again" that was subsequently attached as a new introduction to the second edition of his monograph on Heidegger under the title "In 1991."[20] Steiner wrote this piece in the wake of the substantial new evidence exposed by Ott, Farias, and others about the true extent of Heidegger's Nazi involvement.[21] Though he does not hold the philosophical understanding of these authors in high esteem, Steiner is disturbed by this new information. It drives him to reassert some of the arguments already contained in the original monograph and, in so doing, to highlight this idea about Heidegger's struggle in a new and bolder light.

Beyond the fact of Heidegger's Nazi association, Steiner is concerned with how the Nazism that is inherent to his philosophy can somehow be reconciled with the undeniable genius of his work. Steiner proposes, for example, that the true force of Heidegger's writing can only really be appreciated when his books are read out loud.[22] When Steiner comments that Heidegger's writing is primarily based on his famous lectures, he implies that his resounding rhetorical skill mesmerized his students in much the same way as Hitler's oratory captured the hearts and minds of the German people.[23]

This hint of a similarity between Heidegger's oratory and Hitler's is made more explicit when Steiner talks about *BT*, grouping it together with half a dozen other books written in the German language which, in his words, are "unlike any others produced in the history of Western thought and feeling."[24] Each of these books was composed during "the nine short but critical years between 1918 and 1927." Each one in its own way represents what Steiner calls "a metaphysical discourse on chaos."[25] The books are all voluminous, prophetic, total, and apocalyptic. This list includes Ernst Bloch's *Geist der Utope*, Oswald Spengler's *Decline of the West*, the initial version of Karl Barth's

---

20. Ibid., vii–xxxv.
21. See Ott and Farias, note 3 above.
22. Steiner, *Martin Heidegger*, xv.
23. Ibid., 123.
24. Ibid., viii.
25. Ibid.

Commentary on Romans, Franz Rosenzweig's *Stern der Erlösung* and – though with some reservation – the two volumes of Adolf Hitler's *Mein Kampf.*[26] In Steiner's words,

> these writings out of the German ruin are, indeed, meant to be read either by men and women doomed to decay, as in Spengler, or by men and women destined to undergo some fundamental renovation, some agonizing rebirth out of the ash of a dead past. This is Bloch's message, Rosenzweig's and, in a perspective of eternal untimeliness, that of Barth. It is Hitler's promise to the *Volk.*[27]

Germany's shameful defeat in 1918 lurks in the shadows for each of these writers. It is an experience that each one seeks in his own way to purge. The books propose a path of apocalyptic destruction for Germany, in the faith that this will finally clear the ground and annihilate even the ashes – the remnants of a previous and now embarrassingly exposed inauthenticity – before a new horizon can come into view. It is painful (perhaps provocatively so) to see Rosenzweig's *Star of Redemption* in this list. One hopes that the tone and the passion of this very Jewish book might not really be compared with *Mein Kampf.* All the same, Steiner's way of thinking about this list echoes the relationship between Churban and Tikkun that Rosenzweig's and Heidegger's philosophy do indeed share. Steiner is an advocate of Diaspora because for him Churban is basically the inevitable outcome of every attempt at Tikkun. This is the ground upon which his famous objections to Zionism stand, and this is the ironic foundation upon which the speech that he puts in the mouth of Adolf Hitler in his philosophical novel, *The Portage to San Cristobal of A.H.* is built.[28] However, in the context of Steiner's treatment of Heidegger, the importance of this association is that it allows us to see how, in Steiner's view,

---

26. Ibid.

27. Ibid., ix.

28. This fictional speech by Hitler fills chapter 17 of George Steiner's philosophical novel *The Portage to San Cristobal of A.H* (University of Chicago Press, 1979), 161–70. Steiner's fictional Hitler claims in his defense that he took the idea of the master race from the Jews. He goes on to blame the Jews for the blackmailing of transcendence – an argument that Steiner makes in the analysis discussed in chapter 2 above. Finally, Steiner's Hitler suggests that the Jews should be grateful to him, since without him there

both Heidegger's and Hitler's brands of Nazism are inextricably tied to the modern project of self-redemption from inauthenticity. As partners in this project, they implicate each other in the full extent of its flaws. If *Mein Kampf* is a redemptive political proposal for Germany, *BT* is the philosophical handbook to understanding this proposal's inner depths. We extrapolate from this that Steiner concurs with our suggestion that *BT* can be read in search of the philosophical depths of Nazism that no one with lesser powers than Heidegger's could have managed to articulate. *BT* takes on Nazism's struggle for a free modern Germany. Heidegger's method of Destruction throws off the shackles of the past and takes on the heroic struggle to free humanity of its incapacity to think about its own *being* beyond the limitations (or concealments) imposed upon it by the bourgeoise, inauthentic, transcendental epistemology of the Enlightenment.

Like Hitler's struggle against the shackles of modern liberal convention, Heidegger's is a violent one. Indeed, according to Steiner, all the books in this list are violent. Each one is haunted by its massive scale, its prophetic tenor, its invocation of apocalypse, and by what Steiner refers to as a "specific violence."[29] The calls for exaltation, the actualization of sublimity and a new order of the psyche generate a violent and expectant pitch that preaches revolution. In the case of *BT* this violence is perhaps more subtle than it is in *Mein Kampf*, but it is no less important. At the time when Hitler sought to force his will on the German people, Steiner sees violence in the way in which Heidegger seeks to impose his will on the German language.

Steiner points out Heidegger's unique capacity "to follow the etymological arteries into the primal rock of language."[30] This is something that, as a German speaker, he feels is not accessible to the many who read Heidegger in translation. But it is, in his view, the most important feature of his work. This linguistic probing is Heidegger's principal tool in his heroic attempt to think about the imminence of *being* without recourse to theology. In Steiner's view, the critical question in Heidegger's work is therefore "Could there, in fact,

---

would have been no Jewish state. We return to discuss this speech and its implications for understanding Jewish ethnocentrism in more detail in chapter 18 below.

29. See Steiner, *Martin Heidegger*, ix.

30. Ibid., xiii.

be a communicable, an arguable, intelligible articulation of an ontology of pure immanence?"[31] The answer to this is yes, but only with the use of force.

In Steiner' reading of *BT*, Heidegger's massive effort to articulate his "ontology of pure immanence" is inescapably connected to his lifelong struggle to beat back the presence of the "old God" in philosophy. Heidegger's violence with language is therefore part of his struggle – and indeed of a larger modern struggle – to replace "the old God" as the posited foundation of *being* with Dasein. Violence against "the old God" is in Steiner's view the link that connects Heidegger's neologism with the totality of his ontology. Heidegger recruits the full force of German etymology to "hack out a path to the clearing, to the luminous thereness of what is."[32] This involves a purgation of a web of literary associations from which Heidegger, in Steiner's opinion, is ultimately unable to break free.

> In the Heideggerian dialectic, A is defined as A in a tautological imperative which, consciously or not, generates a counterstatement to the tautological self-definition of the transcendent as it speaks out of the Burning Bush. The "I am what I am" or "I am that which is" of the Mosaic Deity is exactly counter-echoed in Heidegger's definitions of Being *qua* Being, in his strenuous refusal to allow the definitional dispersal of Beings in beings.[33]

This struggle to escape the divine through the invention of a new set of terms is ironically and exasperatingly hopeless. "As everywhere else in Heidegger, the thought and speech experiment which is demanded in order to 'think being, independent of extants, of that which actually and existentially is, proves abortive.'"[34] It is the frantic determination with which Heidegger does battle with the "old God" that Steiner identifies as perhaps the most enduring and significant contribution of his work. But, according to Steiner, it is this

---

31. Ibid., xviii.
32. Ibid., xix.
33. Ibid., xviii.
34. Ibid.

very heroic failure that creates the frantically violent pitch that connects *BT* most profoundly with Nazism.

This analysis reminds us of Steiner's understanding of Auschwitz as a frantic expression of the human determination to demythologize hell by building it on earth.[35] Just as the effort to imagine and articulate culture without religion is ultimately hopeless, Heidegger is trapped in the inescapability of the divine "I am" that courses through the words he must use to hack his way toward the clearing. The result is that what Steiner identifies as the Nazi struggle to be free of the "old God" and His people is paralleled by Heidegger's effort to overcome philosophy's "involuntary reversion to the theological." In his words,

> One need only replace "*Sein*" with "*God*" in all the key passages of *BT* and their meaning becomes pellucid.[36]

Ultimately, Heidegger fails to accomplish this goal in *BT* because the auto-deconstructive and self-referential nature of language constantly and inevitably connects the analytic of *being* with the biblical "*I am.*" Yet *BT* is an assault not only on the biblical God but also on humanity. Steiner comments on the impersonality of the word "Dasein," suggesting that Heidegger invented impersonal language to denote the self in the same way that the Nazis invented euphemisms and stamped numbers on the arms of their victims to cover up (or conceal from themselves) their unspeakable brutality. In contrast to Rorty's declaration that there is nothing in Heidegger's philosophy that should make us suspicious of his connections with Nazism, Steiner asks,

> Are there in Heidegger's incomplete ontological *summa* categories, advocacies of inhumanism, eradications of the human person, which in some sense, prepare for the subsequent program of Nazism? Is Heidegger's play with and on Nothingness (a play intimately analogous with negative theology) a nihilism *in extremis* rather than, as it professes to be, an 'overcoming of nihilism'? …

---

35. This is the theme of Steiner's chapter "A Season in Hell" discussed in detail in chapter 2 above.

36. Ibid., xix–xx.

Secondly, there is the famous urgency of death, of the will to and motion toward death in Heidegger's analysis of felt-being, of human individuation…. Can we say that this … inflects Heidegger's and his readers' attitudes toward the macabre obsessions of National Socialism?[37]

While Steiner prudently leaves these questions unanswered, his articulation of them is sufficiently suggestive to leave an impression. He is reluctant to posit a historical argument that traces Heidegger's impact on the unfolding of Nazi inhumanity. But even if such an argument were plausible, it might still be less important than the broad indictment of Western thought that Heidegger's philosophical Nazism implies. It is Heidegger who champions philosophy's struggle to honestly articulate a language of *being* that does not rest upon untested metaphysical or mythological assumptions. In this basic desire to free thought from mythology and metaphysics, Heidegger is not alone. But if his accomplishment is of value, it must be recognized that it is connected to Nazism, since his work shows that confronting myth and metaphysics inevitably involves embracing a form of inhumanity that – philosophically speaking – destroys layers of meaning that humanity has embedded in language and thought over time. Politically, it makes space for the inhumane.

Steiner carefully strings a web in which the inhumanity of Heidegger's ontology is presented as an inherent outgrowth of Western civilization's crisis of *being*. By becoming the hero of an epic struggle against all that is inauthentic in the thinking of *being*, Steiner suggests that Heidegger is consciously doing battle shoulder to shoulder with the more visible political struggle of Nazism against inauthentic living. In other words, assuming that Heidegger was not naïve, in Steiner's view he must be held accountable for no less than consciously leading the charge for Nazism on the battlefield of philosophy. Arguably, Heidegger felt some discomfort with the barbarism of Nazism that had already become obvious as early as 1934. However, to the very deep extent that Heidegger was a Nazi in 1927, he remained so till the end of his

---

37. Ibid., xxv.

life. This is the cause of his silence, and this is the reason why Steiner considered it so insufferable. In 1953 Heidegger wrote,

> The works that are peddled about nowadays as the philosophy of National Socialism but have nothing whatever to do with the inner truth and greatness of this movement have all been written by men fishing in the troubled waters of 'values' and 'totalities.'[38]

Steiner comments, "Thus, [in 1953] Heidegger still believed that the inner truth and greatness of the Nazi movement stands affirmed."[39] The inner truth and greatness of the struggle to free *being* of its in-authenticity is so central to Heidegger's entire philosophical project, both before and after the war, that speaking out against it was simply never an option.

We shall conclude with a passage in Steiner that stands out for the force and the passion of his concomitant feeling for the genius of *BT* and his horror at its endemic Nazism:

> The evidence is, I think, incontrovertible: there *were* instrumental connections between the language of *Sein und Zeit* [*BT*], especially the later sections, and those of Nazism. Those who would deny this are blind or mendacious. In both…there is the presumption, at once mesmerized by and acquiescent in, of a nearing apocalypse, of so deep a crisis in human affairs that the norms of personal and institutional morality must be and shall inevitably be brushed aside. There was in the pseudo-Messianism of the Hitler phenomenon a confirmation of some of Heidegger's most shadowy but deep-seated apprehensions. Both Nazism and the ontological anthropology of *Sein und Zeit* stress the concreteness of man's function in the world, the primordial sanctity of hand and body. Both exalt the mystical kinship between the laborer and his tools in an existential innocence which must be cleansed of the pretensions and illusions of abstract intellect. With this emphasis

---

38. Ibid., 120.
39. Ibid.

goes a closely related stress on rootedness, on the intimacies of blood and remembrance that an authentic human being cultivates with his native ground. Heidegger's rhetoric of "at-homeness," of the organic continuum which knits the living to the ancestral dead buried close by, fits effortlessly into the Nazi cult of "blood and soil." Concomitantly, the Hitlerite denunciation of "rootless cosmopolitans," the urban riffraff, and unhoused intelligentsia that live parasitically on the modish surface of society, chime in readily with the Heideggerian critique of "theyness," of technological modernity, of the busy restlessness of the inauthentic.

Heideggerian *resoluteness* (*Entschlossenheit*) has more than a hint of the mystique of commitment, of self-sacrificial and self-protective élan preached by the Führer and his "hard-clear" acolytes. Both enact the heightening of personal fate into national and ethnic vocation which is analyzed in *Sein und Zeit*. In there is, logically and essentially, an exaltation of death as life's purposed summit and fulfillment.... but above all, there is the idiom of *Sein und Zeit* and that of National Socialist jargon. Both, though at obviously different levels, exploit the genius of German for suggestive darkness, its ability to give to (often empty half-baked) abstractions a physical presence and intensity. There is in Heidegger's supposition, itself at once metaphorical and mesmeric, that it is not man who speaks where language is most fully effective, but "language itself through man," an ominous hint of Hitler's brand of inspiration, of the Nazi use of the human voice as trumpet played upon by immense, ruminous agencies beyond the puny will or judgment of rational man. This motif of dehumanization is key. Nazism comes on Heidegger precisely at the moment in his thinking when the human person is being edged away from the center of meaning and of being. The idiom of the purely ontological blends with that of the inhuman.[40]

The tone of this passage, as powerful as it is in isolation, does not reflect the central thesis or thrust of Steiner's monograph. He is generally more forgiving

---

40. Ibid., 121–23.

of Heidegger (especially in light of the more lyrical turn that characterizes his later thought) than he sounds here. He remains troubled and disturbed but cannot resist the lure of Heidegger's genius and of his word craft. All the same, the significance of the leitmotif that we have discussed sets a crucial precedent for us. Steiner, here as in *Bluebeard,* helps us to understand that after Nazism there is no stable future for Western humanism until it manages to free itself from the volatile and unstable substance of the self/Dasein that inhabits its core.

CHAPTER 10

Concern and the Ontological Meaning of Faith

The Inner Drama of Heidegger's *BT*

In this chapter we will begin our systematic reading of Heidegger's *BT*. Over the next five chapters we shall make the case for our reading of *BT*, which we ultimately see as an exploration of the self and its capacity to conceal or deny the true nature of its own *being*. In *BT*, Heidegger offers an ontological analysis of mortal *being* as the foundation of humanism. He takes us to an inner world in which human *being* is defined by the contours, shifting scales, and limits of our capacity for self-deception. Our argument is that here, in this inner world, Heidegger leads us to reflect on the nature of our own inauthenticity and to find authenticity in our resolve to convince ourselves that death can take priority over life. It is here, in the depths of Heidegger's inner world, that mortality prevails, and the battle is fought between God and humankind. We shall begin in this chapter with a close reading of Heidegger's introduction to *BT.*

Destruction as Retrieving the Question of *Being*

Heidegger opens *BT* with a section dedicated to "the necessity of an explicit repetition of the question of being." Likewise, the book begins with the words "The question of being has been forgotten."[1] He goes on to insist that the question of *being* must be formulated and proposes a process of Destruction

---

1. Martin Heidegger, *Being and Time*, trans. Joan Stambaugh, revised and with a foreword by Dennis J. Schmidt (SUNY Press, 2010), 1.

which, for him, underlines the need to move aside the obstacles in philosophy that obscure the question of *being,* so that philosophy can start over.

For Heidegger, the question of *being* was a uniquely Greek question. The very nature of the Greek language called for an analysis of the question of *being.* The sense of the importance of this question began to emerge into view through the ontological reflections that originated in Plato and in Aristotle. However, these were lost to the history of philosophy when the concept of *being* was concealed by three crucial prejudices.[2]

First, Heidegger argues that Aristotle understood *being* as a universal concept and not as a lower-level genus. As such, it indeed presupposed all forms of being in his thought. However, in subsequent philosophical analysis, *being* was emptied of all meaning. Ontological *being* came to be understood as something that draws its content from the lower forms of ontic being that are readily visible in the world (such as the being of material content). Under these circumstances, the unified universal meaning of *being* that made all *being* accessible became completely obscured from view.[3] Second, the universality of the concept of being meant that *being* itself was indefinable. As such, philosophical investigation that sought to define observable phenomena pulled back from the investigation of *being* itself.[4] Third and finally, ontic being, in the sense in which we are nonetheless aware of it, was understood as a self-evident concept ("the sky is blue" and "I am happy").[5] The appreciable being of things such as blue skies and happiness was seen to delineate the boundaries of philosophical interest and concealed the question of the *being* of that being from view. Rather than becoming the object of philosophical inquiry, being meant the self-evident condition that qualified other things as eligible for analysis.[6]

This state of affairs in itself calls for a process of rethinking the history of philosophy that Heidegger calls "Destruction." However, the problem ran deeper. Reflecting on his earlier concerns with the ontology of medieval

---

2. Ibid., 2.
3. Ibid.
4. Ibid., 3.
5. See ibid., 3. These examples are Heidegger's own.
6. Ibid.

religion, Heidegger discovered that the religious history of medieval thought was ultimately responsible for the further concealment from view of the question of *being*. The problem here is not with the idea of God. It is with the philosophical nature of the inquiry into the question of His existence. The plausibility of a language of cause and effect that sees *being* as an active presence in this-worldly processes is concealed by an overwhelming predisposition to see the question of God's *being* in terms that Heidegger identified as epistemological or ontic. In other words, medieval religious philosophy failed to explore the question of *being* because it worried about the verifiability of God's existence instead of seeking out a path that leads to the primordial human experience of *being*. In the context of medieval religious thought, if philosophical investigation had sought out this latter path it might perhaps have discovered how to make God's *being* visible as something that originates equiprimordially with our own experience of human *being* in this world. However, the plausibility of this path was covered over by a rationalist-religious language of cause and effect that even in the medieval period depended upon science and social science (Heidegger deals specifically with mathematics, physics, historiography, anthropology, psychology, and biology)[7] for its methods of observing and explaining social, historical, and political processes. In Heidegger's view, the question of God's *being* is therefore obscured, not by denial of God, but by the absence of an ontological analytic that allows the lost question of His *being* to emerge into view.

Put differently, we can say that the deep problem that pushed Heidegger away from religion can be appreciated only when we realize that the question of God's *being* is obscured – rather than revealed – by faith. Rationalism per se does not insist that God, as a subject of private and even collective voluntary belief, be excluded from the public sphere. Belief in God and the practice of religion can be tolerated, accepted, and even actively encouraged as they were even in the most rationalist circles throughout the medieval period. Similarly, religion can clearly be a powerful force for good within rationally governed societies. However, the mechanism that accounts for the visible workings of that force in the world will always depend on notions of efficacy

---

7. Heidegger returns to this theme of how the rational systems of thought used in the various scientific disciplines covered over the ontological dimension of human *being* in several places in the opening passages of *BT*. See for example, *BT* 9, 19–25, 44–49.

(i.e., of cause and effect) that do not rely on God's *being* for the first principle of their logic. Rather, in the religious (and even the pre-Enlightenment religious) humanist context, faith in God's *being* must be understood as a second tier of knowing in which an epistemologically unverifiable proposition can be ethically viable only within the realm of individual free choice and good behavior. Free choice cannot be surrendered to it without turning a blind eye to something that remains dark and mysterious. In this paradigm, God can enter the public sphere only when the fact of His *being* is enforced tyrannically through the use of power (as it was in much of medieval religious politics and still is in modern fundamentalist contexts) or when the possibility of His *being* is gently wrapped in the non-verifiable subjective convictions of those who freely choose to let Him be (as in modern liberal religion). This is also the case in societies where faith is ubiquitous, since even there, God has no independent presence that makes itself indirectly and undeniably irresistible to human *knowing*.

This conclusion prompted Heidegger to reject God as the foundation of *being* on what he understands as phenomenologically sound – or one might even say "scientific" – grounds. The flaw he points out is not to be found in either the implausibility or the plausibility of God as an idea, but rather in the second-tier nature of the knowledge that belief in God demands we accept. After rejecting the notion of either a theology or a philosophy that builds its foundation on this second tier, Heidegger's analysis of Dasein seeks to retrieve the question of *being* as a first-tier or primordial human experience. This first-tier encounter is what he refers to as the "being of being."

This is an idea that has paradigm-shattering ambitions, and as such, it is worth pausing briefly to allow it to stand out by comparing and contrasting it with the lesser ambitions of thinkers who have sought to put an end one way or another to the debate about the epistemological plausibility of faith. Again, our frame of reference here is not designed to deal exhaustively with this question but rather to illustrate – by way of a brief comparison – what is uniquely significant here about Heidegger.

Let us take Richard Dawkins's "new atheism" as an example and contrast it with William James's "will to believe." At the outset of *The God Delusion*, Dawkins explicitly states that his intention in writing the book is that "religious readers who open it will be atheists when they put it down."[8] Dawkins believes that the scientific certainty on which he bases his claims entitles him – on rational or scientific grounds – to undermine or disapprove of the moral right of people to freely choose faith. In Dawkins's view, the morality of faith is as questionable as surrendering one's freedom to the sovereignty of a cult. At first glance this might seem like an ambition not dissimilar to Heidegger's. However, on closer reflection this is not at all the case.

The strategy of Dawkins's argument is much more similar to that of William James, who conversely argued against the rational/moral right to absolutely deny faith. In *The Will to Believe*, James reaches the conclusion that in plain reason, *"a rule of thinking that would absolutely prevent me from acknowledging certain kinds of truth if those kinds of truth were really there, would be an irrational rule"* (italics in the original).[9] James and Dawkins thus share the sense that, in the face of an unsupported hypothesis, one must cut one's losses by acquiescing to a default or zero-sum option. James argues that without sufficient evidence to refute faith, the empirically observable "fact" of God's appeal to so many people requires that we remain open all the time to the viability of the claims made by faith and to the possibility that sufficient evidence of God's existence will at some time in the future become available. Similarly (though conversely), Dawkins argues that since there is no evidence to prove the existence of God as an object of knowledge, it is not reasonable to posit the axiom of faith in God. (Incidentally, Dawkins backs up this claim with what he sees as overwhelming scientific data that supports the verifiability of natural selection, the evolutionary roots of morality, the effect of psychological priming upon the dissemination of religious faith,

---

8.   Richard Dawkins, *The God Delusion* (Bantam, 2006), 28.

9.   See William James, *The Will to Believe and Other Essays in Popular Philosophy* (New York: Dover, 1956), 28. On page 30, James goes on to insist that a rationalist, empiricist perspective that can offer no final proof that a viable religious belief (in James's terms, a belief that for whatever personal, autobiographical, or subjective reason one experiences as a "live option") is not true cannot be rejected out of hand without unjustifiably impinging upon the mental freedom of others. Moreover, human awareness of the limitations of our own understanding must insist that this remain the case even if the evidence available to support that belief is still wholly insufficient.

the genetic evolution of the human propensity to believe falsely, and more.)[10]
Despite the opposition between their attempts at moving beyond the human
right to either freely hold out for or discount faith, James and Dawkins actually share a perspective that is rooted in the conditions that conceal the ontological dimension of philosophy. The question that they are both evaluating
is whether or not it is rational to hold onto a religious belief when the objective evidence that supports or refutes it is incomplete.

Our point is that both Dawkins and James remain completely tied to the
assumption that both verification and refutation of the proposition of God's
existence are dependent upon the rational perception of objective phenomena that present themselves one way or another to human comprehension.
The uniqueness of Heidegger's premise comes into view when we realize that
the finality of the decision that is reached when this assumption is followed
remains on the second tier of how humans encounter knowledge. In the context of his effort to grasp the first tier of the human experience of knowledge,
Heidegger's rejection of God is built on an entirely different foundation.

Heidegger identifies the dominance of philosophy by epistemology as
a concealment that blocks the "I" from accessing the first tier of thought.
It presupposes the *being* of this "I" by proposing that the "subject" can be
redeemed from the mystery of its *being* by fleeing to the pole of the supposedly scientifically verifiable "object." This is true even when the object of
inquiry is the thinking "I" itself. Heidegger insists that this is plausible only
so long as the question of *being* is submerged. As such, Dawkins's and James's
rational inquiry into the verifiability (or the refutability) of God's *being* is
one that is necessarily conducted within the confines of an epistemology that
remains in exile from stable propositional truth claims about God. This is
because God is an epistemological mystery. To suggest otherwise would be a
categorical error, since the content of God's *being* as portrayed even by those
who believe in the idea of God is posited as rationally unknowable. One
might say that any attempt to resolve the question of God's verifiability on
these grounds can only produce results that must fall somewhere between
atheist skepticism and willful faith, both of which round up (or down) a

10. Dawkins, *The God Delusion*. The evolutionary purpose of faith is also discussed from a
    psychological point of view by Jonathan Haidt, who refers to it as the "hive switch." See
    his discussion of the "biology of the hive switch" in Haidt, *Righteous Mind*, 221–45.

condition of uncertainty to a preferred conclusion. No attempt of this sort can yield the kind of first-tier certainty that lies beyond.

The importance of Heidegger's effort to move beyond this position has already been alluded to in the previous chapters. Placed into the larger context of this book, his rejection of God as the foundation of *being* is the Churban that is paralleled by the Nazi rejection of the Jewish people's right to exist. From the perspective of Segulah, after the crisis of the Holocaust – at a time when exilic theology is intolerable – an encounter with God that offers a qualitatively different justification for the continued *being* of the Jewish people is a matter of moral urgency. Historically, what this means is that the conditions of Jewish life defined by the Holocaust can no longer tolerate the state of human *being* that is disclosed by the Holocaust. Moreover, the very idea of "*God*" after the Holocaust can no longer tolerate the parameters for its meaning that were defined by the humanism that failed to restrain the hands of its perpetrators. In his struggle against God, Heidegger exposes the equi-primordiality of the onto-theology that he rejects and inadvertently opens a path to its Rehabilitation. This path is dependent upon the replacement of the deficient epistemological concept of faith with the ontology of Sorge (meaning "care" or "concern").

The First Premise for an Onto-theological Analysis of Dasein

Heidegger believed that the German language was uniquely capable of generating the linguistic tools required for his philosophy. In his view German has the same linguistic malleability that enabled people who thought in Greek to mine the depths of human thought. His own knowledge of Greek was a crucial guide, as was the historical conviction that the second-tier notion of the subject, represented by the word "I," was in desperate need of rejuvenation. This may be seen against the backdrop of the historical calamity that befell the German people in the First World War. As such, Heidegger's drive for ontological certainty can be understood as a self-redemptive attempt to rehabilitate the crisis of the German "subject" that experienced a post-trauma of its own in the Weimar era. Perhaps it was the infamous "stabbing in the back" at the end of World War I that created a sense of political urgency. But whatever the cause, what Heidegger demanded was the retrieval and the rehabilitation of the undeniable essence of human *being* in its specific and uniquely Germanic form. He believed that through the agency of the German language, he could give the German people access to something concealed and buried in the mental recesses of ancient Greece. This depleted and lost "something" was the ontological "subject" that Heidegger referred to as Dasein.

The depleted condition of Dasein demanded the destruction of the concealments that prevented an authentic sense of *being* from shining in the world. For Heidegger, the destruction of the concealments that shamed Dasein by defeating its spirit in the war was essential to the rediscovery of the power that would ultimately decorate it in triumph. The psycho-philosophical methodological premise with which this redemptive analytic begins is the capacity of Dasein to show what Heidegger refers to as *concern* or *care* for its own *being*. This is what makes Dasein unique, and it is from this first premise that his analysis ensues.

As Heidegger says close to the outset of his analytic of Dasein, "Dasein is ontically distinguished by the fact that in its being this being is concerned *about* its very being."[11] It is its "being concerned with *being*" that distinguishes Dasein from every other form of being. Therefore, Dasein is a being that can serve as a window through which the *being* of being can be disclosed. However, the reliance of this disclosure on Dasein's capacity for *concern* with *being* generates a methodological problem that occupies Heidegger almost from the outset of his two-chapter introduction to *BT*. The idea that the nature of *being* can be disclosed only through the assumption of Dasein's *concern* for its own *being* suggests that the analytic of Dasein might be inevitably circular and hence flawed. In other words, if, in order to get at the question of *being*, one must first formulate a question that itself emerges from the quest for *being*, one is in danger of simply rediscovering or reenforcing the bias or the conceit that was already there before the analytical process began.

The way in which Heidegger addresses this problem is of crucial importance to his attempt to establish a solid scientific or phenomenological point of departure for his ensuing analysis. This point of departure or grounding is essential for us because it also allows us to redefine the nature of faith and clarify the distinction between a second-tier notion of faith as the "rounding

---

11. Heidegger, *BT*, 11.

up" acceptance of something unknowable and a first-tier ontological experience of it.

Heidegger explains the grounding of his analysis as follows:

> Every questioning is a seeking. Every seeking takes its lead beforehand from what is sought. Questioning is a knowing search for beings in their thatness and whatness. The knowing search can become an "investigation," as the revealing determination of what the questioning aims at. As questioning about...questioning has *what it asks about.* All asking about...is in some way an inquiring of.... Besides what is asked, what is *interrogated* also belongs to questioning. What is questioned is to be defined and conceptualized in the investigating, that is, the specifically theoretical, question. As what is really intended, what is to be *ascertained*, lies in what is questioned; here questioning arrives at its goal. As an attitude adopted by a being, the questioner, questioning has its own character of being. Questioning can come about as "just asking around" or as an explicitly formulated question. What is peculiar to the latter is the fact that questioning first becomes lucid in advance with regard to all the above-named constitutive characteristics of the question.[12]

The question to be *formulated* is about the meaning of being. Thus we are confronted with the necessity of explicating the question of being with regard to the structural moments cited.

> As a seeking, questioning needs prior guidance from what it seeks. The meaning of being must therefore already be available to us in a certain way. We intimated that we are always already involved in an understanding of being. From this grows the explicit question of the meaning of being and the tendency toward its concept. We do not *know* what being means. But already when we ask, "What *is* being?" we stand in an understanding of the *is* without being able to determine conceptually what the "*is*" means. We do not

---

12. Heidegger, *BT,* 4.

even know the horizon on which we are supposed to grasp and pin down the meaning. *This average and vague understanding of being is a fact.*[13]

In this passage Heidegger elucidates the distinction between epistemological and ontological questioning. He maintains that all questioning is "questioning about something" that is discovered. Discovery is questioning "arriving at its goal." In this sense, the prior knowledge of what is sought inevitably determines the possibility of the question since what is questioned is the thing that the question itself seeks. When viewed in epistemological terms, the method that relies on this assumption is indeed undermined by the flaw of its circular logic. As such the problem of epistemological solipsism (i.e., the inevitability of circular argumentation in all quests for knowledge in which the "I" is perceived as the "as yet unknowing subject" and the sought-after knowledge as the "as yet unknown object") is the key to Heidegger's destruction of a system of philosophical inquiry that gives priority to questions about knowledge over the question of *being*.

In Heidegger's terms, the thing that is found is indeed "always already" there in the question that leads to it. But this does not mean that the thing that is sought in the question is necessarily knowledge about an object that *is*. If it were, the circular method of such an investigation would indeed be problematic. If the thing that is supposedly not known remains to be discovered, the questioning that inevitably discloses prior knowledge of it cannot be other than disingenuous and biased. More importantly, if all questioning begins with prior knowledge of what is questioned, no form of knowledge gained through questioning can be treated as a truly original encounter with something that independently *is* an external – "yet unknown" – object. Thus, the philosophical priority of epistemology is destroyed by the claim that all theories of knowledge can be founded only on a second-tier encounter with how human beings think.

If, on the other hand, the questioning is understood as the state of *being* of the questioner, the quest for first-tier knowledge can find its philosophical feet. In Heidegger's view, if questioning is understood as a state of *being*, the

---

13. Ibid., 4.

questioner need not pretend that he or she is simply "asking around" in the hope of stumbling into something not previously known. Rather, investigation itself can be seen as *concerned* with the state of *being* that is already experienced "vaguely" or "averagely" by the questioner. Thus, the questioner is a being that "*is, with questions*" (in the same way as one might say of a pregnant woman that she "*is, with child*") who seeks to bring his or her *questioning-state-of-being* more consciously into view.

For Heidegger, the *questioning-state-of-being* that characterizes the experience of the being that is concerned with its *being* is itself *the fact* that demands elucidation. This *fact* is *always already* in place when any question is raised. But it is not the "thatness" or the "whatness" of the thing in question that is disclosed by the questioning. Rather, what is disclosed is the condition of *being-with-question* (i.e., the condition of being a questioner) that the questioner can now hold onto and unravel. Thus, the existential experience of *being-with-question* emerges as the starting point for the investigation that follows. In other words, *being-with-question,* when noticed by the questioner, is like a crack of light shining through a wall that the questioner may now open up, expand, or excavate around, until it becomes a larger gap or window through which he or she may gain a fuller glimpse of his or her own *being*. Thus, the ontological *being* of the questioner and not the epistemological content of the question is the *fact* that the questioning of *being* seeks to draw out of vagueness or hiddenness into what Heidegger calls "a developed concept of being."[14]

This is how Heidegger establishes the priority of *being* over knowing, i.e., by absorbing all the mechanisms by which knowledge is sought, gained, and held and redefining them as states or conditions of *being*. In his words,

> Regarding, understanding and grasping, choosing, and gaining access to, are constitutive attitudes of inquiry and are thus themselves modes of being of a particular being, of the *being* we inquirers ourselves in each case are. Thus, to work out the question of being means to make a being – one who questions – transparent in its being.[15]

---

14. Ibid.
15. Ibid., 6.

This is not a move that defends sloppy scientific research against claims of tendentiousness and bias. What it does is to single out the question of *being* as one that is uniquely exempt from the accusations that are otherwise leveled (with ample justification) against circular arguments. In Heidegger's words, "Circular reasoning does not occur in the question of the meaning of being."[16] This is because the *fact* that *is* "out there," i.e., the fact that the question of *being* seeks to ascertain, is *already there* in the state of *being* that the questioner *is in* when the *being* of the questioner is first disclosed by the act of questioning. This condition of *being* is a naive form of Dasein that is experienced at the outset of all questioning and which Heidegger refers to as an "average, vague or indeterminate" understanding of *being*. This naive state of *being* is one that is required for the question of *being* to unfold, and as such it is a natural or neutral state of Dasein.[17]

In this vague or average state of *being* Dasein is *concerned* with its experience of what Heidegger later refers to as its own "throwness." To explain this term, we might compare the vague consciousness of *being* in which a question is asked, to an arrow that Dasein shoots into the dark. As the investigation unfolds, Dasein moves out from its point of departure into the darkness in search of the arrow that it has already "projected." When Dasein arrives at the arrow it inevitably discovers that – since the arrow has *always already* arrived at its point of landing before Dasein finds it – it (i.e., Dasein's consciousness of self) has *always already* been where it now finally arrives. In Heidegger's words, "Dasein has a mode of being in which it is brought before itself and...disclosed to itself in its throwness."[18] This cycle of throwness, projection, and arrival is the movement that allows Heidegger to present Dasein as something that exists factically in the world. Thus, "throwness is the mode of being of a being which always *is* itself its possibilities in such a way that it understands itself in them and in terms of them (projects itself upon them)."[19]

---

16. Ibid., 7.

17. This is not the condition of being that Heidegger refers to as inauthentic Dasein in which Dasein is actively involved in the concealment and suppression of itself. This second form and the concealments that allow it to *be* are the ones that Heidegger seeks to destroy and overcome.

18. Heidegger, *BT*, 175.

19. Ibid.

At the moment of arrival, when the fullness of these possibilities is made accessible to Dasein, it develops the capability of facing them and of gaining an authentic awareness of its own *being*.

To return to the methodological premise with which Heidegger begins: the *always already*-ness of the primordial encounter with *being* (i.e., the arrival at the landing point of an arrow that was *always already* known vaguely even when the arrow was first held in hand and shot into the dark) that necessarily precedes the consciousness of *being* is presented by Heidegger not as the outcome of his philosophical analysis but as the solid methodological foundation from which the analysis itself must proceed. As such, the nature of the questioning that guides the analytic of Dasein *always already* assumes the structural form of Dasein. Though the analysis of the structure of Dasein will develop significantly as *BT* continues, at this stage of our reading what we know of this structure from Heidegger's opening remarks is essential to the whole argument that unfolds in the rest of the book.

So, to clarify the point: The first principle of *BT* is that Dasein is a being that is *concerned* about its own *being* as *throwness*. Similarly, the *fact* of the question is the *fact* of the *being* that is disclosed in the question by the *being* of the questioner. The answer to the question of *being* is therefore an escalation of the clarity with which the *being* of the questioner is made progressively more accessible or "transparent" to him- or herself. This escalating clarity is what the continuation of Heidegger's analytic seeks to accomplish.

Ultimately, Heidegger will move on to show that this journey (from the "shooting of the arrow" to the moment when it is retrieved) is a progression that takes time and that therefore attains its fuller meaning in time. But this is something to which we must return in much greater detail only after we have attained a more complete understanding of what Heidegger refers to as "the spatial dimension of Dasein." For now, what we can say is this: Heidegger's methodological premise is that no mode of interrogation that is not modeled on the structure of Dasein can give the questioner access to the question of *being*. Because it is modeled on the structure of Dasein's *throwness*, Heidegger's method can now be seen to stand on solid philosophical ground. Heidegger's way of saying this is to insist that "ontology is possible only as phenomenology."[20] By this he means that philosophy that deals with the disclosure or the self-showing of phenomena is plausible and reliable only when the beings that are disclosed present themselves in the way that is proper to them. Because the structure of Dasein includes its *concern* for its *throwness*, there can be no method of disclosure that does not reflect that *concern*. This is the crucial methodological conclusion of *BT*'s introduction, and it contains within it the structural heart of the entire book.

Concern and the Perspective of Segulah

And now a few words about the path that Heidegger inadvertently opens to the rehabilitation of faith. We shall refer to this path intermittently at each stage of our discussion of *BT* though we will begin to treat it systematically only in the final section of this book.

Thus far Heidegger's phenomenological disclosure of *being* provides the perspective of Segulah with a stable methodological foundation for describing faith in "God" in ontological terms. This description presents us with a concept of "God" that is significantly different from the notion of the supreme persona that Dawkins rejects. The idea that "God" can be approached in ontological terms is underlined by the close linguistic relationship between most of the Hebrew words for "God" and the Hebrew verb "to be," *havayah*.[21] Thinking about Havayah in light of Heidegger's analysis allows us to begin to see the value or credibility of a circularly structured onto-theological proposition. Rather than defining a theological hypothesis as a piece of tentative knowledge about something "out there" that awaits verification, we can now describe it as a state of *being-with-question* that awaits its own arrival, escalation, culmination, or full disclosure in time. Heidegger's portrayal of a hypothesis as a *questioning-state-of-being* inadvertently discloses the existential or ontological plausibility of faithfulness to an *always already* but not yet encountered idea of God. This, we propose, is a useful approximation of the

---

20. Heidegger, *BT*, 33.

21. Havayah is a term that we will be using throughout. It simultaneously means "being" and "God." The root letters of the Hebrew verb "to be" are *yud*, *heh*, and *vav*. Many of the biblical names of God such as Eheyeh (as in Exodus 3:14) Yah, and the tetragrammaton (YHVH) are built upon these same root letters. The centrality of this to the onto-theology of Judaism will occupy us in the final section of this book.

Hebrew term Emunah. Emunah means faith, but it also connotes the idea of faithfulness and loyalty (*ne'emanut*) to the viability of a vague or indeterminate encounter with a *being* that can become completely visible only in the fullness of time. This yearning awareness or Emunah is an inner experience, and as such, it suggests that we come to know God through knowing our own *being* more closely. As we learn from Heidegger how the inner process of circular questioning creates an existential sense of disquiet in the knowing self, we find the methodological starting point for self-disclosure as the disclosure of God's *being*. In its most simple form, it is the vague or indeterminate experience that Dasein has of itself as alive – as in contact with its point of life. As such, Emunah can be defined as a state of *being* in which Dasein is tentatively or questioningly conscious of its proximity to the source of its aliveness. Emunah is a state of *being* in which the same circular condition of *questioning-being* that allows Dasein to show concern for its own *being* might also allow Dasein to loyally, consistently, and persistently (i.e., with *ne'emanut*) seek out the possibility of its own *being* culminating in the experience of its own *throwness* as *concern* (not for its own mortal *being* but) for the living *being* of everything across all of space and time.

Arguably, this is the idea of God with which Heidegger wishes to do battle. The battleground is *concern*, and Heidegger's most powerful weapon is his claim that since Dasein is mortal, it is exclusively *concerned* with its own *being* alone. The alternative to this that Heidegger rejects is the idea that Dasein's *concern* for its own *being* is subsumed by its concern for the *being* of everything that *is*. It is this *being* of everything that *is* that the theological language of Segulah refers to as Havayah.

CHAPTER 11

~

The Spatiality of Dasein:
from Galut to Churban

The De Facto Structure of BT as Galut and Churban

In the final section of the introduction to *BT*, Heidegger presents his proposed outline for the entire work. As is well known, Heidegger never completed the treatise as planned. His original proposal divided *BT* into two sections, each of which was supposed to comprise three subdivisions. Of all this, the final form of *BT* published in 1927 included only the first two intended subdivisions of the first section. The third one and the entire second section were never completed. In Heidegger's original plan, the first section was to be concerned primarily with "Dasein on the basis of temporality [Zeitlichkeit] and the explication of time as the transcendental horizon of the question of being."[1] The second was supposed to deal with the implications of his insights about temporality for the general destruction of the history of ontology. Given this overall structure, it seems clear that, as the title of the work suggests, the overall primary concern of Heidegger's ontology is time.

However, in the form in which *BT* was published, since the third subdivision of the first section (which was to be dedicated to time and being) and the entire second section are missing, only half of the extant book is in fact about Dasein's temporal dimension. The first half, which Heidegger initially planned as only a "preparatory fundamental analysis of Dasein," is dedicated to the ontological encounter with *being* as a spatial concept. This spatial analysis foreshadows very closely the structure of the temporal analysis

---

1.   Heidegger, *BT*, 37.

and as such it is indeed a "preparatory fundamental analysis" for what was supposed to follow. All the same, as things now appear, there is an inevitable discrepancy between the deemphasis that Heidegger intended for the spatial dimension of his analytic and the emphasis that the published work actually gives to the reader.

Intended or no, this final structure of the book is significant, since it invites us to consider the two existing parts of the work as almost equally divided between an analytic of Dasein in space and an analytic of Dasein in time. This is useful because the de facto structure of the book corresponds in quite a balanced way with the two elements of Galut and Churban. Broadly speaking, our reading of Heidegger's spatial analysis will seek to reap a new and penetrating articulation of the critical problem of Galut as a state of *being*. After this, we will be able to read his temporal analysis of Dasein with the intention of discovering as direct a portrayal as possible of why his path of redemption from Galut is Churban.

In more conventional philosophical language, the problem dealt with in the first section is – as we have already said – the dominance of epistemology in the history of the human effort to understand the first tier of human consciousness. The crucial accomplishment of Heidegger's articulation of this problem here is that he succeeds in presenting epistemology very compellingly in ontological terms. He does this by explaining how the dominance of knowing over being is itself an ontological state of *being* in which authentic Dasein is submerged. In this section Heidegger gives us an insight into what we might refer to as his broad epochal state of mind. Strictly speaking, what he writes about is his deep dissatisfaction with the state of academic philosophy as a field. To his mind, philosophy is asking the wrong questions because it has misunderstood the true nature of its "subject" (pun intended). But if for a moment we look at this frustration beyond the strict limits of Heidegger's academic mudslinging, it seems that he is no less frustrated with inauthentic Dasein as a social, cultural, and political force in the world. We mention this because the possibility of tapping into Heidegger's broader frustrations can allow us to frame our understanding of his philosophical project in the context of Nazism's wider ambitions for Germany.

Heidegger knew that he could only destroy and rehabilitate the history of philosophy, if he could present the phenomenon of philosophy's domination by epistemology as a form of *being* or as a possibility of Dasein. This means that the conventional portrayal of the subject (i.e., the "I" of I know/I think/I am) must be accounted for from within the general structure of the analytic of Dasein. In order to understand this more fully, we must follow closely how Heidegger presents inauthentic Dasein as responsible for creating the illusion of the subject or the thinking/knowing "I." Grasping the full meaning of Heidegger's requirement that we treat inauthentic Dasein as a form of its own authentic *being* adds significantly to our understanding of Galut. We have already suggested that the central characteristic of Dasein in all its form is its capacity for self-deception. Showing how this applies to authentic Dasein requires a separate argument to which we shall return in our discussion of Heidegger's temporal analysis. Here, self-delusion is Heidegger's straightforward characterization of inauthenticity. From his perspective, our most natural way of thinking about ourselves is a self-delusional construction of the self, in exile from the self, and hence in exile from the surrounding world.[2]

One more comment on the de facto structure of the book. The analytic of the second extant division of *BT* that conceives of Dasein temporally (and which we know from the proposed outline of *BT* was to be considered of greater importance) is where Heidegger lays out the foundations for his redemptive solution. In his words:

> Time must be brought to light and genuinely grasped as the horizon of every understanding and interpretation of being. For this to become clear we need an *original explication of time as the horizon of the understanding of being, in terms of temporality as the being of Dasein which understands being.*[3]

---

2.   This argument connects with our discussion of De-con-struction, where we commented on the implications of Latour's understanding of science as a human activity, i.e., as a construction that does not in fact rest upon universal truth claims. Science emerges as a feature of Galut, as an example of the possibility of construction within Galut but not as part of a project that leads beyond Galut. In other words, it brings scientific knowledge back to the unredeemed knowing subject and warps it with the flaws of inauthentic self-awareness.

3.   Heidegger, *BT*, 17. The italics here are in the original.

We mention this reference to temporality here only in order to differentiate between the spatial and temporal dimensions of *BT* as these appear in the structure of the published text. For the rest of this and the next two chapters our attention will be focused on comprehending what Heidegger tells us indirectly in this passage about the spatial nature of inauthentic Dasein. From this passage we can deduce two principal points. First, that inauthentic Dasein is a form of *being* of Dasein which does not understand its own *being* in terms of an authentic temporality. Second, in this condition of not understanding temporality authentically, inauthentic Dasein is both absorbed in and submerged by its own spatiality. Again, these two features of inauthentic Dasein are of crucial importance to our understanding of Galut as an ontological condition of *being* absorbed in spatiality.

Being-in-the-World

The spatial analytic of Dasein begins with the concept of *being-in-the-world* (*In-der-Welt-sein*). *Being-in the-world* in general, as the fundamental constitution of Dasein, is the subject of the second and third chapters of *BT*. We will begin with the second chapter, which deals primarily with the discrepancy between the authentic spatiality of Dasein and the fact of inauthentic experience.

Heidegger kicks off his discussion of *being-in-the-world* by apologizing for the awkwardness of the terminology that he uses to ensure that his analysis remains on track. (Perhaps we might offer a similar apology because what lies ahead is not simple reading!) In his words,

> With regard to the awkwardness and 'inelegance' of expression in the following analyses, we may remark that it is one thing to report narratively about *beings* and another to grasp beings in their *being*. For the latter task not only most of the words are lacking but above all the 'grammar'.[4]

On the one hand, Heidegger feels awkward about the expressions he must use. The inelegance of his neologisms is excused by the total absence of

---

4.   Ibid., 36.

vocabulary and grammar for the analysis that follows. On the other hand, the possibility of inventing the – albeit inelegant – terms that Heidegger goes on to use demonstrates, in his view, both the unique malleability of the German language and its special capacity to allow German philosophy to pick up from where the Greeks left off. Moreover, since, as Heidegger says, "the area of being to be disclosed ontologically is far more difficult than that presented to the Greeks, the complexity of our concept-formation and the severity of our expression will increase."[5] Thus, Heidegger prepares his readers for the bumpy ride ahead as each concept is painstakingly explained, assiduously distinguished from possible alternative understandings to it (which might lead the analysis astray from the path it must follow), and carefully worked into the overall conceptual lexicon that he builds in order to allow the fullest possible view of Dasein's topology to emerge.

The primary reason for the inelegance of the language that Heidegger uses is his insistence that each and every term used must reflect or remain faithful to the structure of Dasein itself. This is something we already encountered in the Introduction to *BT* but which we can now explore in greater depth and detail.

Literally the term "Dasein" means "being-there" or "being-with," and *being-with* is a term that has a specific structure that is echoed throughout *BT*. This structure is central to Heidegger's replacement of "I" as the subject of philosophy because it inherently describes the subject's experience of things in the world as originating in its primordial experience of itself as "there with" them. In this sense the subject and object of conventional philosophy are never apart. They originate together as Dasein becomes aware of itself *with* objects in the world. The unification of subject and object in this concept of *being-with* is the methodological linchpin of Heidegger's proposal for the liberation or redemption of the subject from its condition of exile from truth. Ultimately, Heidegger will argue that the redemptive potential embedded in an analytic that follows the structure of Dasein is reached only when Dasein appears in its authentic form. In these preparatory chapters, Heidegger is engaged in the complex work of both explaining how Dasein comes to assume an inauthentic form and of showing how our managing

---

5.   Ibid., 37.

to understand the true nature of this form can lead on to redemption from it. Heidegger argues that the truth about Dasein – even in its inauthentic form – is that it is entangled in or distracted by its own spatiality. This spatiality is intricately connected to Heidegger's concept of the *world* in which Dasein (as opposed to the illusory subject) actually *is*. As we shall see, for Heidegger, *world* is a difficult idea, and Dasein's entangled relationship with it is indeed very hard to tease out.

The discussion of *being-in-the-world* starts with the "vague" idea that "world" is the most general description of space that gives access to Dasein as a *being* whose consciousness is always situated. In other words, *being-in-the-world* is a fundamental spatial category that captures the structure of Dasein as a being whose *is*-ness is always situated in the world or *with* things that are *there*, i.e., *in-the-world*. The awkward cramming together of the words in the form of the neologism conveys Heidegger's insistence on the equiprimordiality of Dasein and its encounters with the world. In this way the term shows how Dasein first knows itself or shows *concern* for its own *being* "along with" (rather than prior to) encountering things in the world. This is because it only knows itself as a being that *is-with* the things in the world. Heidegger repeatedly insists that Dasein must always be somewhere; it cannot just be in a pure, abstract, or not-situated form. "World" represents the spatiality that gives Dasein its situation as *always being* somewhere in the world. However, in order to fully appreciate Dasein's spatiality, all the possibilities of Dasein's forms of *being* in the world need to be explored or unraveled. This unraveling or unfolding is as endless as the number of situations in which *being* can *be*. Nonetheless, Heidegger seeks to categorize and arrange them by offering as full a range as possible of different forms in which Dasein can *be with* the *world*.[6] His analytic of Dasein is therefore not concerned with the attributes or the characteristics of this being or that. Dasein does not encounter these beings as it somehow scours the world looking for them. Dasein actively *is* in different forms, each of which is determined by the thing that its structure of *being-with* is with. Since, as we have said, a full account of this is impossible, Heidegger's focus is the various forms of *being* in which *being is*. Heidegger presents these forms as an ontological expression of the diverse encounters

---

6.   Ibid., 41.

that allow Dasein to experience the world as a range of what he calls Dasein's own "possibilities of *being* in the world."

This is only an initial sketch of "world" which does not yet explain how the world itself exists in the form that makes it accessible to Dasein. Heidegger offers his portrayal of how the existence of the world as an object is ontologically possible only at a later stage of his analysis.

The Inauthentic Meaning of *World*

Having proposed a spatial analytic that begins with the *being-in* of Dasein as the point of departure for solving the problem of how the knowing self knows things in the world, Heidegger now shifts the tack of his argument. He does this in order to retrace the difficulty that allowed Dasein to lose track of its knowledge of self and assume an inauthentic form in the first place. What concerns him here is the inauthentic form of *being-in-the-world* in which Dasein allows itself to hide away from its consciousness of the true nature of its own *being*. As we said above, Heidegger's insistence on showing why things do not seem as they are is of crucial importance to him in *BT*. Though the authentic notion of "world" has not yet been elucidated, Heidegger insists that we gain an understanding of it only after securing a clear account of its inauthentic form.

The distinction between authentic and inauthentic Dasein first appears at the beginning of the first chapter of *BT*:

> The two kinds of being of authenticity and inauthenticity...are based on the fact that Dasein is in general determined by always being-mine. But the inauthenticity of Dasein does not signify a "lesser" being or a "lower" degree of being. Rather, inauthenticity can determine Dasein in its fullest concretion, when it is busy, excited, interested, and capable of pleasure.[7]

The problem posed by inauthentic Dasein is deeper than a superficial judgment of it as a lesser degree of *being* would imply. Rather, the inauthentic expressions of Dasein indicate that Dasein must somehow be actively sought

---

7.   Ibid., 42.

after and resolutely smoked out of its deliberate hiding place. The nature of this active or deliberate hiding is characterized by Heidegger as ontological *indifference*. What this means is that inauthentic Dasein is a full-blown condition of *being* in which Dasein's form of *being* is one in which it is actively *indifferent* to its own *being*. This condition of *indifference* is characteristic of what Heidegger calls the everydayness of average or vague Dasein. "But," he insists, "the average everydayness of Dasein must not be understood as a mere aspect." Even in its everyday or average state, "Dasein is concerned in a particular way about its being to which it is related in the mode of average everydayness, if only in the mode of fleeing *from* it and of forgetting *it*."[8] When Dasein "flees" and "forgets" itself in this way, it experiences itself as a knowing "I" that meets the world, that knows the world, or that knows about the world. This fleeing is responsible for the subject/object illusion on which epistemology is based. It is the ontological or existential possibility of this illusion that Heidegger insists we must understand in authentic terms. In his words,

> Because knowing has been given this priority, our understanding of its ownmost kind of being is led astray, and thus being-in-the-world must be delineated more precisely with reference to knowing the world, and must itself be made visible in an existential modality of being-in.[9]

In this condition Dasein creates for itself the illusion – familiar to philosophy – that the subject is somehow a primordial entity of consciousness that originates on its own and without a world. As we have said, it does this actively through fleeing and forgetting. This is its *indifference*. In Heidegger's words, "The evidence for this is the interpretation of knowledge, still prevalent today, as a relation between subject and object which contains about as much truth as it does vacuity."[10] He goes on to say that Dasein's ability to hide led philosophy to erroneously imagine the self as a theoretical proposition – a

---

8.   Ibid., 43.

9.   Ibid., 59.

10.   Ibid., 60.

subject or abstract "I" – that then goes out into the world to discover what is there. If we wish to construct a full portrayal of Dasein we must be aware of this, since it is a form of Dasein. And if we wish to overcome this *indifference,* we must be aware that we are struggling to destroy an illusion that Dasein itself actively creates. This requires us to see ourselves as Dasein and not as subjects so that we can guide our own thinking along the right path. We need to understand that "subject and object are not the same as Dasein and world."[11] In order to see this, to think of ourselves as Dasein, the illusory relationship of subject and object must be unpacked. We need to see the subject as a form of Dasein or as way in which Dasein *indifferently is.* Likewise, the illusion of the object must be destroyed and replaced with a concept of "world" that truly reflects the form of Dasein's experience of it.

Heidegger goes on to insist that the condition of Dasein in which Dasein is submerged

> must not be interpreted as a "procedure" by which a subject gathers representations about something for itself which then remain stored up "inside" as thus appropriated, and in reference to which the question can arise at times of how they "correspond" with reality.[12]

The condition that allows (even inauthentic) Dasein's encounter with the world is one in which Dasein is equiprimordially caught up with the world. It does not know itself independently of the things that it encounters and does not orient itself toward them in order to grasp them. Rather, "in its primary kind of being, it is always already 'outside' together with some being encountered in the world already discovered."[13] In this sense, we might think of Dasein as hiding in the world and somehow exiled from itself in the everydayness of its awareness of its *being-in-the-world.* Later in the same paragraph Heidegger elaborates on this point:

---

11. Ibid.
12. Ibid., 62.
13. Ibid.

Again, the perception of what is known does not take place as
a return with one's booty to the "cabinet" of consciousness after
one had gone out and grasped it. Rather, in perceiving, preserving,
and retaining, the Dasein that knows *remains outside as Dasein…* in
knowing, Dasein gains a new *perspective of being* toward the world
always already discovered in Dasein.[14]

In this passage Heidegger adds a new dimension to his presentation of *indifference*. He describes the nature of spatial *throwness* as the mechanism that
enables Dasein's *indifference* to be active. It is the spatial *throwness* of Dasein
into the world that allows Dasein to actively hide in the world. Given the
extent of the effort that Heidegger puts into explaining and accounting for
the possibility of inauthentic Dasein's hiding at every step along the way
of *BT*, it is clear that he attaches a great deal of significance to his explanations of why the encounter between subject and object in the world does not
appear to us to take place as he claims it does. On one level, he must do this
to be convincing. Otherwise, we might simply ask why things do not appear
as he says. Indeed, we may ask this with the entire history of philosophy on
our side. However, on a second level, this feature of *BT* is essential to the task
that lies ahead. Without a deep familiarity with Dasein's methods of camou-
flage, subterfuge, and stealth, the task of seeking out Dasein must surely be
an impossible one.

Heidegger's attention to Dasein's exile mirrors for us the nature of Galut.
These statements that prepare us for what lies ahead sharpen our understanding of the questions that emerge from the ontological condition of Galut.
But, on a deeper level, this stage of the analysis gives us a powerful psycho-philosophical reflection of what Steiner referred to as the "active indifference – active because collaboratively unknowing – of the vast majority of
the European population"[15] during the Holocaust and this gives us pause.

Heidegger's quest for authentic Dasein puts the humanity of his milieu
on display. It also adds vital insight to our efforts to understand why Galut
is morally intolerable after the Holocaust. His efforts to smoke out the

---

14. Ibid.
15. Steiner, *In Bluebeard's Castle*, 35.

mechanism that allows us to be distracted from our own potential to emerge from Galut are also crucial. Without a complex (and unfortunately intricate) understanding of inauthentic Dasein's hiding mechanism, Heidegger's quest for authentic Dasein is lost. By the same token, without a similarly deep, complex, and intricate understanding of how Churban takes place in the context of Galut, our hope for Tikkun has no path to follow.

The Worldliness of the World

Having identified the importance of accounting for Dasein's hiding mechanisms and *indifference*, Heidegger begins to construct a fuller analysis of "world" that conforms to the structure of Dasein. As we saw, Dasein is hidden because it is caught up with the world into which it is *thrown*. But this statement of *throwness* as Dasein "remaining outside"[16] in the world leaves us with only a preliminary understanding of the problem. In order for this account to stand up, Heidegger must explain the ontological nature of the world in which Dasein's knowledge is *always already* caught up. If inauthentic "knowing" is to be understood as a mode of Dasein which is founded on *being-in-the-world*, the conception of Dasein's knowing about the world must be founded upon what Heidegger calls "a prior interpretation of the world's worldliness." This prior interpretation of worldliness is the subject of the third chapter of *BT*.

Heidegger's discussion of what he calls the "worldliness of the world" is designed to disclose the primordial form of Dasein's spatiality. He begins with an interrogation of the nature of the world in which Dasein's ontological form of *being-in-the-world* ostensibly *is*. In laying out the terminology of this analysis, Heidegger distinguishes between an ontic concept of the world that "signifies the totality of beings which can be objectively present in the world" and an understanding of "the world '*in which*' a factical Dasein 'lives' as Dasein."[17] The former represents the illusory world, which is an object perceived by a subject. The latter is Dasein's primordial ontological experience of the world that corresponds to its structure of *being*. In the ontological sense, "worldly" therefore means "a kind of *being* of Dasein." This is distinguished

---

16. Heidegger, *BT*, 62.
17. Ibid., 65.

from things in the world, in the ontic sense, which Heidegger refers to as "innerworldly" or as "things that belong to the world."

The ontic notion of "world" with which we all intuitively start to think understands the concept of "the world" as representing the sum total of innerworldly *beings*. This is the world as we most naturally perceive it. It is comprised of the innerworldly beings of which Dasein – in its hidden or ontic form, i.e., as the conventional subject – is most naturally aware. Heidegger points this out because his method is based on the premise that our intuitive or normal encounters with everyday objects in the world can lead us to an appreciation of the total ontological concept of "world." But innerworldly beings can disclose the ontological notion of "world" as a totality only when our understanding of these beings conforms with the structure of Dasein. Heidegger therefore proceeds by presenting to us an understanding of "world" as the world in which Dasein *is* in the way in which Dasein *is*. We might say that this understanding of "world" refers to the world of Dasein. It is Dasein's surrounding world which Dasein "takes *care* of" (Sorge). This is the world in which Dasein is engaged in *being-with*.

Thus far, what Heidegger means by the worldliness of the world is still not clear. The next step is to see innerworldly objects as beings that announce the worldliness of the world to Dasein.[18] Heidegger tells us that beings of this sort are ones that Dasein most primordially experiences as *at hand*. Things that are *at hand* disclose themselves to Dasein as *useful* to it. *Useful* here is an ontological term that should not be confused with its conventional meaning. Things that are ontologically *useful* are not useful in the same way perhaps as a hammer and nails are useful for hanging paintings on a wall. In Heidegger's terminology, the *use* of innerworldly beings refers to how they reach out to Dasein and are *together-with* it. The *usefulness* of innerworldly beings is the pure expression of their being *relative* to Dasein. They are *useful* because they are *at hand*. This is an ontological state of *being* that is still there even if it is disclosed by uselessness. It is in this sense that *usefulness* can allow Dasein to *be-with* a broken hammer and a bent nail whose ontological *use* takes the form of *being useless* for hanging paintings on the wall. This double-sided nature of *usefulness* is the feature that distinguishes the ontological

18. Ibid., 72.

from the epistemological. The hammer and broken hammer are *useful* to the same degree when their *use* is defined in terms of their capacity to be *useful* to Dasein that wants to *be-with* them. Through this *usefulness*, innerworldly objects might be said to populate Dasein's sense of "world."

To clarify the point, the *handiness* or *usefulness* of things that are in the world does not point at the objective faculties of objects. Rather, "handiness is the ontological categorical definition of beings as they are "in themselves.""[19] In this form, they *are* in the sense in which they are disclosed to Dasein as ways of *being-with* Dasein. Thus, they can stand out in the world, showing themselves to Dasein as things it can *be-with*, in forms that Heidegger refers to as "conspicuousness, obtrusiveness and obstinacy." It is these forms that allow objects to come to the fore of Dasein's tapestry of "world." In the sense in which they bring things to the foreground of the tapestry of the world, "conspicuousness," "obtrusiveness," and "obstinacy" are breaches in the totality of world that Dasein can notice or have "announced" to it in the form of things that are *at hand* and thus inside the spatiality of its consciousness of *world*.[20]

This mode of *being* that allows objects in the world to be announced to Dasein is one that Heidegger refers to as *being-in-itself*. The *being* of objects *at hand* discloses their *worldliness* to Dasein but only as things that are in the world of Dasein. The point here is that while *being-in* the world of Dasein is indeed a form of *being-in-itself*, this form of *being* still does not account for the general category of *world* on which their being *at hand* as objects in the world necessarily relies. In Heidegger's words, the problem arises when we realize that "when we are primarily and exclusively oriented toward that which is objectively present, the 'in itself' cannot be ontologically explained at all." The idea of objects' *being-in-themselves* in Dasein's *world* does not give us an account of how they are "out there" in the world that enters into Dasein's consciousness from beyond.[21] Driving forward toward a phenomenology of *world*, Heidegger continues, "The foregoing analysis makes it clear

---

19. Ibid., 71.
20. Ibid., 75.
21. This is a reference to the problem of whether unperceived existence is possible. The most famous articulation of this problem is attributed to George Berkeley, who famously asked whether a tree that falls in the woods with no one there to hear can still

that the being-in-itself of innerworldly beings is ontologically comprehensible only on the basis of the phenomenon of world."[22] But this phenomenon of *world* has not yet been explained.

The way forward is to offer an ontological analysis of *world* that discloses the relative relationship of the world in general (and the innerworldly objects that have the character of *being-in-itself*), to the *being-with* of Dasein. Heidegger's formula for this is as follows,

> World is always already predisclosed for circumspect heedfulness together with the accessibility of innerworldly beings at hand. Thus, world is something "in which" Dasein as being always already *was,* and world is that to which Dasein can always only come back whenever it explicitly moves toward something in some way.[23]

We have already said that Dasein does not know itself temporally because it is absorbed in the world. What we can now add is that the mode of this absorption is a mode of Dasein's *being* which discovers the possibility of having an encounter with innerworldly beings – or objects that are *at hand* in the world – by actively overlooking the concept of *world*. It is this overlooking that gives meaning to the condition of *being-in-the-world* because, at the same time that it is clear that the world is being overlooked, it is the overlooked *worldliness* of *being-in-the-world* that ultimately makes those encounters with innerworldly beings possible. This occurs because Dasein is *always already* engaged in the world in which innerworldly beings announce themselves as usefully *at hand*. Thus, we might say that Dasein is distracted from the world by its own experience of *being-with* beings that have the character of *beings-in-themselves* in the world. In order to move forward, the hidden notion of *world* that allows Dasein to encounter innerworldly things in this way must be teased out of hiding. In Heidegger's words,

---

be said to make a sound. See his (1710) *A Treatise Concerning the Principles of Human Knowledge*, Hackett Classics (1982).

22. Heidegger, *BT*, 75.

23. Ibid.

According to our foregoing interpretation, being-in-the-world signifies unthematic, circumspect absorption in the references constitutive for the handiness of the totality of useful things. Taking care
of things always already occurs on the basis of familiarity with the
world. In this familiarity Dasein can lose itself in what it encounters within the world and be numbed by it. With what is Dasein
familiar? Why can the worldly character of innerworldly beings
appear? How is the referential totality in which circumspection
"moves" to be understood more precisely?[24]

What Heidegger is saying here is that the encounter with innerworldly beings
is possible for Dasein because beings that are *at hand* only present themselves
to Dasein after the totality of the *world* that appears to it is breached. It is
this breaching that allows the presence of beings that are less than the world
to be thrust to the foreground of Dasein's awareness of the world.[25] But this
in turn is only possible because of Dasein's primordial familiarity with the
concept of *world* that gives meaning to the fuller form of *being* that is *being-
in-the-world*. What Heidegger wants is to recall the attention of Dasein to
its own primordially familiar reality (a reality that is *always already* known
to Dasein and which makes Dasein's encounter with innerworldly beings
possible) in order for it to assume an authentic consciousness of the mode of
its own *being* in the *world*. It is within the context of what is made possible
by this authentic consciousness that Dasein can assume its inauthentic forms.

In order to draw this point more clearly into the open, Heidegger offers
what he calls "a concrete analysis of the structures in whose context a phenomenological analysis of worldliness can be possible."[26] He calls the structures that he singles out for this concrete analysis *references*. Just like all
innerworldly beings, *references* are known to Dasein as *useful* and *at hand*.
However, their structure of *being* is unique and worthy of special attention
because *references* – in addition to being themselves – also have a pointing
capacity as *signs*. On account of this, *references* are innerworldly objects that

---

24. Ibid.
25. Ibid.
26. Ibid.

disclose the broader context of the world in which they assume their meaning. Heidegger defines *signs* as "initially useful things whose specific character as *useful* things consists of indicating."[27] Examples of these kinds of *references* or *signs* are abundant and include such things as traffic lights, road signs, flags, military insignia, and so on.[28]

Heidegger's analysis of *signs* hinges on the way in which they function as *referents*. Here we can distinguish between two ways or modes in which *signs* communicate with us and tell us about the things they *refer* to. First, the *sign* presents itself to us as *useful* or *at hand*. It is *useful* to us as a form of *referent* that indicates something to us. However, in this the *sign* is not distinguished from any other object that is *useful* to Dasein when encountered. Second, the *sign* discloses to us what Heidegger calls a "circumspect overview of the surrounding world." This is an encounter in which information is communicated ontologically. In this sense the *sign* discloses a sense of *world* to Dasein which can be distinguished from the notion of an object giving over knowledge to a subject as follows:

> A sign is *not* really "comprehended" when we stare at it and ascertain that it is indicating a thing that occurs. Even if we follow the direction which an arrow indicates and look at something which is objectively present in the region thus indicated, even then the sign is not really encountered…circumspect overseeing does not *comprehend* what is at hand; instead it acquires an orientation within the surrounding world…. Here the arrow's specific character of being as a useful thing need not be discovered. What and how it is to indicate can remain completely undetermined and yet what is encountered is not a mere thing.[29]

This analysis of the *sign* is well illustrated by the famous image of the laughing Buddha Hotei pointing at the moon. There are two ways in which we can view this image. In the first scenario, what you see is a man pointing at

27. Ibid., 76.
28. Ibid.
29. Ibid., 78.

the moon. In this case, the man pointing appears as an innerworldly being who stands out against the backdrop of the world as *useful*. His *use* is that he points out the moon for us. In the second scenario the man who points at the moon is not seen. Rather one sees only the moon. In this case the man who points at the moon discloses the moon as *useful*. It is only after we are already familiar with the moon that we then return to the man and understand his meaning as the one who pointed out the moon for us.

In order to understand Heidegger's point, we must recognize that the first scenario (in which we see the man pointing) is possible only because of the second. Even when we pay no attention to the moon and see only the man pointing at it, we can see him as a man pointing at the moon only because we have *always already* seen the moon. This is why we are able to then see his meaning as a *sign* that points to the moon. Thus, for Heidegger, "the meaning of signs lets what is at hand be encountered."[30] *Signs* "let their context become accessible in such a way that heedful dealings get and secure for themselves an orientation."[31] In the same way that the disclosure of the moon discloses for us the meaning of the man who points at the moon, "useful things explicitly bring a totality of useful things to circumspection so that the worldly character of what is at hand makes itself known at the same time."[32]

With this description of two things happening at the same time, Heidegger constructs a synergy that, once again, unites or combines the separate functions of subject and object in Dasein. Innerworldly beings are known to Dasein as *useful* or as *at hand*. In this capacity, they function as *signs* which disclose the *usefulness* or the *handiness* of the world. Thus, "what is taken as a sign first becomes accessible through its handiness."[33] But ultimately, this *handiness* is itself a disclosure of the *world* (the moon in our analogy) that enables innerworldly beings to function as *at hand* within it. In this way, an object that assumes the character of *being useful*

---

30. Ibid.
31. Ibid.
32. Ibid.
33. Ibid., 79.

takes over the "work" of *letting* things at hand become conspicuous…. But even as conspicuous things, they are not taken as objectively present arbitrarily, rather they are "set up" in a definite way with a view toward easy accessibility.[34]

What is *at hand* discloses how an object that is ontically useful "functions at the same time as something which indicates the ontological structure of handiness, referential totality and worldliness."[35]

Up until this point Heidegger's analysis has not yet given us access to the meaning of *worldliness*. What we have really gained so far is a sense of how *reference* has the ontological structure of *handiness*. First, we know that things *at hand* are encountered within the world. Second, we know that the *being* of this *handiness* is related to the world. Third, we understand that this relation exists because the world is *always already there* in all things that are *at hand*. *World* is therefore the *referent* that allows things that are *at hand* to *be at hand* for us. As we said, this is possible because *world* allows itself to be encountered by freeing objects or breaching its totality so that they may stand out. It does this by allowing innerworldly objects to appear before us as components of the world through the innerworldly structure of *reference*. What we must now discover is how this happens. Once innerworldly objects are understood through *reference* as accessible openings that allow the disclosure of the *world* (in the same way that *signs* call attention to things other than themselves), the nature of Dasein's encounter with the world will be seen to depend on our finding the ontological structure of *reference* itself.

The Ontological Structure of *Together-With*

The next step that Heidegger takes is to show the structure of *being* that allows *referents* to be encountered as *relevant* to their referees. The concept of *relevance* refers to the way in which a *sign* is encountered as *relevant* to the perception that it facilitates in the same way that the man pointing, and the moon, are *relevant* to each other. Here, the finger pointing at the moon is *relevant* to Dasein because it plays a role in making possible its encounter

---

34. Ibid.
35. Ibid., 81.

with the moon. The ontological structure of this *relevance* is what Heidegger refers to as *together-with*. In his words,

> Beings are discovered with regard to the fact that they are referred, as those beings which they are, to something. They are relevant *together with* something else. The character of being of things at hand is relevance. To be relevant means to be together with something else.[36]

By introducing the structure of *together-with*, Heidegger assigns to *reference* the ontological structure of Dasein. *Relevance* therefore emerges as the *being* of innerworldly beings for which they are freed from the overall tapestry of *worldliness*. They become accessible to Dasein as *relevant* because, through the encounter, they are *together-with* it. One might say that they disclose themselves to Dasein by having meaning for Dasein as ontologically *relevant* to it. They populate its experience of *being with* objects that *are* in the world. Again, it is important to remember that "relevant" is being used here as an ontological term that is not captured by the conventional meaning of the word. *Relevance* as a form of *together-with* can also refer to a state of *being* in which *relevant* objects can assume a form of *being-together* with Dasein that is defined by their *irrelevance*. Just as a *useful* tool can be *at hand* for Dasein in the form of *uselessness*, an object of *relevance* to Dasein points to the possibility of the encounter with objects that are not of *relevance*. This is a crucial point, because in this way the structure of *together-with* points beyond itself and toward a far greater sense of worldliness than a conventional idea of *relevance* can possibly capture. This is what Heidegger describes as "a totality of relevance which is always already in ontological relation to the world."[37] In other words, just as the disclosure of an object *at hand* (the finger pointing at the moon) requires a prior disclosure of *handiness* (the moon), the totality of *relevance* (which includes *irrelevance*) must *always* be *already* related to — or *together-with* — the totality of the world in order for it to disclose something as *relevant* within the world. In Heidegger's words,

---

36. Ibid., 82.
37. Ibid., 83.

As that for which one lets beings be encountered in the kind of being of relevance, the wherein of self-referential understanding is the phenomenon of world. And the structure of that to which Dasein is referred is what constitutes the worldliness of the world.[38]

Since Dasein is the point of consciousness within which the world becomes known or understood, the world *is* only in the sense that it *is together-with* Dasein. This is what Heidegger refers to as the "self-referential understand-ing" of Dasein's *being-with* the world. The kind of *being* that is characterized as *relevance*, i.e., the condition of something *being-relevant to* something else and thus *together-with* it, is therefore necessarily connected to the existence of the object as *relevant* to Dasein and to Dasein alone. So the totality of *relevance* is always something that exists exclusively within the structure of *relevance* to Dasein. If this is the case, the totality of world that is *relevant* to Dasein (which in order to be total must also include beings that are irrelevant to Dasein) is always defined in reference to Dasein. This is how *relevance* dis-closes to Dasein the worldliness of the world. In sum, worldliness is defined by – and indeed is dependent upon – the familiarity that Dasein has with the world as *relevant* (in either the positive or negative form) to its own *being*.

If we condense this, what Heidegger is saying here is that Dasein's encounter with the world is defined by its understanding of its own *being*. It is through understanding the *being* of Dasein and the full potentiality of that *being* that the totality of *being* in the world is disclosed. This is because that disclosure is always a disclosure of what is significant to Dasein,

> In its familiarity with significance Dasein is the ontic condition of the possibility of the discovery of beings with the kind of being of relevance (handiness) which are encountered in a world and that can thus make themselves known in their in-itself. As such, Dasein always means that a context of things at hand is already essentially discovered with its being. In that it *is,* Dasein has always already

---

38. Ibid., 85.

referred itself to an encounter with the world. This dependency upon being referred belongs essentially to its being.[39]

Heidegger is clearly grappling for words that will not be confused for a description of Dasein as a subject that encounters the world as object. But despite the difficulty of the language he uses, it is crucial to acknowledge that he is ultimately successful. What he is saying is that there is a mirroring relationship between the way in which Dasein knows itself *together-with* the objects it encounters in the world, and the way the world is disclosed as *together-with* Dasein. This mirroring depends upon Dasein's unique capacity to show *concern* for its own *being* and for nothing else. Because of this, Dasein serves as the screen upon which all disclosure of *being-in-the-world* must necessarily be projected. All forms of *being* that the world may assume are therefore forms of the world's *being-with* Dasein. More precisely, these might be referred to as forms of Dasein's *being-in-the-world* that transcend the limited or ontic consciousness of what Dasein knows about the world at any given time. Heidegger concludes that the possibility of discovering innerworldly beings in general is what discloses the worldliness of the world.

Orienting the Analysis of Spatiality to the Perspective of Segulah

As we saw above, in presenting the nature of *worldliness*, Heidegger makes a concerted effort to explain why everyday Dasein does not notice the world ontologically. In his words, "an interpretation of the worldliness of Dasein and its possibilities and ways of becoming worldly, must show *why* Dasein skips over the phenomenon of worldliness ontically and ontologically in its way of knowing the world."[40] This question leads him into a detailed reckoning with what he calls the "traditional ontology" of Descartes and Kant that he ultimately seeks to disallow.[41] From Heidegger's perspective, the primary flaw of this traditional ontology is that it addresses presumably ontological questions from a primarily epistemological perspective. In other words, it speaks about the *being* of the subject in terms that do not correspond to the

---

39. Ibid., 85–86.
40. Ibid., 75.
41. Ibid., 87–99.

structure of Dasein as *being-in-the-world*. Moreover, the nature of the world is fundamentally blurred by the relentless urge to characterize it as the totality of objects "out there" that the subject comes to comprehend in what we referred to above as a second-tier way.

In the analysis of Dasein's spatiality that lies ahead, Heidegger will lay out the foundations that he will develop into his solution to the problem of the subject's knowledge of the world's existence. This is the question that underlines the problem of human exile from the truth. In turn it is the human sense of crisis and anxiety about the instability of truth that drives forward the effort to secure a stable foundation for human knowledge about the world. Heidegger's handling of this problem will rely heavily upon the terms that have been established thus far in his analysis. And it is therefore interesting and indeed important that Heidegger interrupts the flow of *BT* at this point to take stock of the conventional understandings of ontology that he has already rejected.

Though we shall not describe the discussion of Kant and Descartes that Heidegger offers in this digression, we should note that it indicates that we are about to cross a threshold. We have reached a point that Heidegger identifies as crucial to his effort to see philosophy step away from its flawed and hopeless efforts to redeem the subject from its exile at the pole of the object. Heidegger's philosophy (and, in his view, philosophy in general) is predicated on the assumption that this can be accomplished only through pure thought. Sensory perception is suspect when considered as anything other than a form of thought, since all sight, sound, touch, taste, and smell are only finally experienced inside the human mind. Therefore, a primordial understanding of how humans appear to know things can be reached only through thoughts about thought. These thoughts can occur only at the pole of the subject and are therefore of an ontological rather than an epistemological nature. Thus, Heidegger returns us to the idea that redemption from illusory and erroneous perceptions of the world is to be found through cultivating the subject's ability to discover the truth about how he/she most primordially thinks.

Our stated purpose in this analysis is to follow Heidegger's mapping of the primordial experience of Dasein as part of an effort to find a path to Tikkun Olam. At this stage, it is important to take stock as Heidegger does and to meditatively re-orient ourselves toward the ontological perspective that we are seeking. To begin with, we can do this by returning to what we have already discovered about the character of Galut. We can recall that, in our discussion of deconstruction, we considered how an ontological perspective allows us to progress from the exilic silence of Wittgenstein's philosophy to the edge of Galut and beyond. The journey from exilic silence to the edge of Galut was made possible by the notion that the relentlessness of yearning in exile and the possibility of construction demand an explanation of how "natural phenomena" show up in the world and comply quasi-objectively with the constructions of observers.[42] At this juncture we can also dig deeper into the significance of self-redemptive efforts and how they tend to lead to Churban rather than Tikkun.

Despite the perennial condition of yearning that we described as essential to the experience of Galut, the Babylonian Talmud (*Ketubot* 111a) issues an injunction against self-redemptive construction in Galut in the form of two oaths. According to these oaths, Am Segulah is sworn not to go up from exile to the land of Israel and not to rebel against the sovereignty of the nations. A third oath in the same passage requires the nations of the world not to subjugate and oppress the Jewish people excessively. Together, these three oaths represent the terms and conditions of exilic existence.

Placing our discussion of Heidegger into the macro-historical context generated by the Holocaust and the return to the land allows us to consider these terms and conditions afresh. The injunction against construction in exile that the first two oaths represent draws its special importance from the perennial fear that self-redemptive projects will inevitably bring about catastrophic results. Such is the case, for example, in Numbers, chapter 14, when the children of Israel seek to go and conquer the land after the sin of the spies, saying, "We are here and will go up unto the place which the Lord has promised, for we have sinned."[43] The fear of catastrophe and the imperative of avoiding it delineate the boundaries of what is reasonable in exile. From Moses' reply, "Do not go up, for the Lord is not among you,"[44] we learn that these boundaries depend upon the accessibility of God's *being* (Havayah) to

---

42. Latour, *We Have Never been Modern*, 85–90.

43. Numbers 14:40.

44. Ibid., 42.

the people. Without the renewal of revelation, there can be no access to the Promised Land. In Galut, Zionism is not an option.

In terms of our macro-historical reevaluation of the plausibility of self-redemptive projects, the Holocaust represents the violation of the third oath by the nations, and hence the Jewish people is released from its obligation to the first two.[45] This suggests that after the Holocaust, Survival and System in Galut is no longer viable. But, staying on the macro-historical level, the question of the return to the land is indeed supported by a justifiable fear of construction in exile and the catastrophic consequences that follow self-redemptive projects. It is here that the psycho-philosophical path we are pursuing comes into play. What is disclosed in Heidegger's portrayal of Dasein is the precise psycho-philosophical condition of Galut in which we become aware of what we lack when we recognize how our absorption in the *worldliness* of the *world* conceals from us the nature of our own *being*.

The Devouring Spatiality of Dasein's *Being-in-the-World*

The fundamental structure of Churban is outlined in Heidegger's discussion of time, but his preparatory discussion of this in terms of spatiality is made apparent in what we shall call "the devouring spatiality of Dasein." In the three sections that, following the discussion of Descartes's and Kant's ontology, bring the third chapter of *BT* to a close, Heidegger presents his understanding of three dimensions of Dasein's spatiality that he refers to as follows:

1. The spatiality of innerworldly things at hand
2. The spatiality of being-in-the-world
3. The spatiality of Dasein and space

In general, these three sections are dedicated to determining how the feeling that we have of "space" in the world is constitutive for the concept of "world" that has the structure of *being-in-the-world*. What Heidegger wants

---

45. Many different arguments were made by the supporters of Zionism to justify the suspension of the injunction against returning to Israel implied by the three oaths. The idea that this is permitted because of the violation of the third oath by the nations of the world was one of these. See, for example, Chaim Waxman, "Messianism, Zionism and the State of Israel," *Modern Judaism* 7 (Oxford, 1987).

is to present a notion of space that is distinguished from the ontic notion of space and that he calls "insideness." Insideness is a "spatial container" that somehow delineates the boundaries of something extended in which the subject *is*. Since this notion of space does not have the structure of Dasein, it cannot capture the primordial experience of space in the world that Dasein must *always already* know for the second-tier illusion of space as "insideness" to seem to appear.

As we saw above in Heidegger's discussion of "world," the disclosure of space to Dasein must begin with its encounter of space as breached or freed. It is this breaching or freeing that allows space to be noticed or come to the foreground of Dasein's *being-with*. In this characteristic, space is no different from innerworldly beings that are *at hand*. We have already said that Dasein discovers the *worldliness* of the *world* as the "freeing of beings for a totality of relevance."[46] This freeing, which lets something be *relevant* (again as we have already said), is made possible by or grounded in a previous understanding of *reference* and signification that is *always already* there. What Heidegger must add in order to offer an ontological understanding of space is the category that he refers to as *directedness* or *being-towardness*. He introduces this category as follows:

> The spatiality of Dasein, which is essentially not objective presence, can mean neither something like being found in a position in "world space" nor being at hand in a place. Both of these are kinds of being belonging to beings encountered in the world. But Dasein is "in" the world in the sense of a familiar and heedful dealing with beings encountered within the world. Thus, when spatiality is attributed to it in some way, this is possible only on the basis of this being-in. But the spatiality of being-in shows the character of de-*distancing* and *directionality*.[47]

De-distancing and *directionality* are the key terms in this passage. What they evoke is descriptive of how Dasein allows things in the world to come to the

---

46. Heidegger, *BT*, 102.

47. Ibid.

foreground of its attention. Heidegger portrays coming to the foreground of attention as movement in space. By calling this movement *de-distancing*, Heidegger is not referring to the conventional drawing near of an object through physical movement across space. Rather, when Dasein notices an object, it draws nearer in what Heidegger calls "an active or transitive sense."[48] What he means by this is that the actual encounters through *concern* that Dasein has with innerworldly objects are themselves given a spatial dimension. It is the encounter or the experience of "noticing" that Heidegger refers to as assuming the ontological form of *being-near*. In this sense, to notice is itself to draw near. *De-distancing* is therefore an essential feature of Dasein's *concern*. To be conscious of an innerworldly object – to have it disclosed in the context of *being-in-the-world* – is to *de-distance* the object. Or, in Heidegger's words, "Dasein is essentially de-distancing. As the being that it is, it lets being be encountered in nearness."[49] Thus, when an object is noticed, even if that object lies at a distance, both the object and the distance that separates the object from Dasein are encountered through *de-distancing*. Dasein and the object may be said to "merely have a measurable distance between them which is encountered in de-distancing."[50] He continues, "De-distancing does not necessarily imply an explicit estimation of the far-ness of things at hand in relation to Dasein. Above all, remoteness is never understood as measurable distance."[51]

This portrayal, which perhaps sounds a little counterintuitive at first, is in fact one of the most common features of our modern, everyday experience of the world. Writing this passage, Heidegger is perhaps one of the first thinkers to comment on the phenomenon that we now call globalization. The image of the global village is a perfect example of how Dasein primordially encounters space as an essential feature of its *being-with*. This is an experience of space that is clearly not defined by epistemological knowledge of "distance in space" that somehow hangs out there as an innerworldly thing in itself. In Heidegger's words,

---

48. Ibid.
49. Ibid.
50. Ibid.
51. Ibid., 103.

All kinds of increasing speed which we are more or less compelled
to go along with today push for overcoming distance. With the
"radio," for example, Dasein is bringing about today a de-distancing of the "world" which is unforeseeable in its meaning for
Dasein, by way of expanding and destroying the everyday surrounding world.[52]

The primordial experience of space that Heidegger describes here is in fact
the one with which we live. If we stop in our cars on a highway to ask for
directions, it makes perfect sense to us to hear that we are "nearly there," even
if the destination we seek is still several miles away. Similarly, on a plane we
understand what the pilot means when he tells us that we are coming into
land even when the screen in front of us indicates that we still have as much
as fifty or even a hundred miles to go. On foot, it is natural to hear that we
are a long way from where we wish to be when we are in fact only a mile or
two away. There is no incongruity, because our actual experience of distance
depends upon our particular inner experience of it in a given circumstance.
Similarly, in an example that Heidegger offers,

For someone who wears spectacles which are distantially so close
to him that they are sitting on his nose, this useful thing is further,
in being used, further away in the surrounding world than the
picture on the wall across the room.[53]

Thus, "the circumspect de-distancing of everyday Dasein discovers the *being-
in-itself* of the 'true world' of beings with which Dasein as existing is always
already together."[54] By way of extension, Dasein itself is not positioned at a
point that may be referred to as "here" and therefore at a measurable distance
from what is "there." Rather, "here" is a term that is understood by Dasein
according to the structure of its own *being*. In this sense, "Dasein understands
its here in terms of the 'over there' of the surrounding world. The 'here' (i.e.,

---

52. Ibid.
53. Ibid., 104.
54. Ibid.

the place where Dasein factically is) does not mean the 'where' of something objectively present, but the where of de-distancing *being-with*."[55] "Here" is therefore the direction in which *de-distancing* progresses while "there" is the direction from which *de-distancing* must *always already* begin. This is how the breeching occurs that draws Dasein's attention in the direction of an inner-worldly object that then becomes conspicuous or noticeable as something that is "there."

This analysis finally brings us to the question of space itself. When we speak of directionality and *de-distancing*, we seem to be speaking of it in the context of a spatiality in which these movements and rearrangements of proximity take place. However, since space is not a thing in the world, it cannot take the form of an innerworldly being. It can also not be the same as "world," because it does not constitute the world and because the world, in the total sense of the word, is ultimately a thing. Finally, space cannot be a form of Dasein because if – unlike "world" – it is not a thing, it cannot have the kind of *being* of Dasein. As such it should not be possible for awareness of space to be disclosed to Dasein.

Heidegger's solution to this problem is the spatial precedent for the tem-poral idea that is ultimately the most important argument of *BT*. It is an argu-ment that sets the precedent for Derrida's analysis of the devouring beast and which we refer to as the "devouring quality of Dasein." Heidegger explains that space emerges as accessible to Dasein because spatiality (or devouring space) is an essential feature of how Dasein *is*. Devouring space is essen-tial to the structure of Dasein's *being-with*. The *de-distancing* of *being-with* is an essential characteristic of Dasein's mode of *being-in-the-world*. This is because the structure of *being-in-the-world* always has a quality of directional-ity. It is this quality that brings Dasein and innerworldly objects into contact with each other. Dasein's inner experience of directionality discloses space to human consciousness in a way that then appears as a thing in the world. In Heidegger's words,

> Letting innerworldly beings be encountered, which is constitu-tive for being-in-the-world, is "giving space." This "giving space,"

---

55. Ibid., 105.

which we call *making room*, frees things at hand for their spatiality. As a way of discovering and presenting a possible totality of places relevantly determined, making room makes actual factical orientation possible. As a circumspect taking care of things in the world, Dasein can change things around, remove them or "make room" for them only because making room – understood as an existential – belongs to its being-in-the-world…. Space is initially discovered in this spatiality with being-in-the-world. On the basis of the spatiality thus discovered, space itself becomes accessible to cognition.[56]

What Heidegger is saying here is that space, as we know it ontically – as we measure it and experience it as something that feels like a thing in the world – is visible to us only because we first *always already* encounter it as the *de-distancing* and the *directionality* of Dasein's *being-in the-world*. Space is not part of the subject's inner experience of the world and it is not a thing that somehow contains the world. Space is not an innerworldly being, but it can also not be detached from the world. The world cannot be imagined without it. The experience of space and spatiality "co-constitutes the world in accordance with the essential spatiality of Dasein."[57] Space is thus essential to the disclosure of the world (and of all innerworldly beings) because it is an inevitable dimension or movement that occurs in the experience of Dasein's *being-with*. It is Dasein's essential spatiality; Dasein's experience of *being-in-the-world* inevitably involves *de-distancing* and directionality that disclose ontic space to it. This disclosure most primordially occurs in what Heidegger calls an unthematic way. All the same, the unthematic disclosure of space becomes known to us only when space is thematized. Thematization is what happens when space is measured or allocated in a way that we can see it. Thus, unthematic space becomes thematized when we call it a distance or a room or a field. Heidegger's point here is that the experience of space as distance or as room can only be disclosed to Dasein because of the unique un-thematized

---

56. Ibid., 108.
57. Ibid., 110.

spatiality that is *always already* essential to the mode of Dasein's *being-with*. This is because Dasein is always with or in the world, spatially.

Heidegger's portrayal of Dasein's spatiality offers a fundamental preparatory analysis for his discussion of temporality. This will become clear when we discover the parallel between the structure of *directionality* and *de-distancing* in space and the structure of Dasein's ontological experience of time. As we shall see, Dasein's experience of time involves its "spending" that time, or "expending" it in such a way that past and present devour the incoming moments of future. In his spatial analysis here, Heidegger lays the ground for his temporal thesis by showing how *de-distancing* and *directionality* are essential features of Dasein's mode of *being-with*. Through *de-distancing* and *directionality*, Dasein must always "spend," "expend," or "devour" space in order to *be* in the form of Dasein's *being-in-the-world*. The distances which Dasein crosses in order to allow objects in the world to become *conspicuous* are distances that it has *always already* crossed in its prior encounter with them through *throwness* and *projection*. If this encounter is one in which space is *always already* devoured, Dasein's inauthentic state of absorption in its own spatiality is somehow to be understood as a trance of distraction from this devouring process.

Devouring Spatiality from Galut to Churban

Heidegger's analysis of spatial *being-in-the-world* yields for us a crucial insight into the relationship between the concepts of Galut and Churban. What we need to emphasize here is the role of authentic Dasein in the genesis of its own inauthentic form. Dasein experiences space in an inauthentic way in order to avoid feeling the devouring or the spending of its essential spatiality. Dasein generates active *indifference* because it does not want to face itself as a devouring consumer of the very space in which it experiences its own *being*. The devouring of the space that Dasein needs to live is a source of anxiety that Dasein represses. Imagine a fish that must drink water in order to swim. From an environmentalist perspective it is not hard to imagine the horror of facing the anxiety that this fish would experience were it to realize that its very mode of living drains the resources on which its survival depends. Instead of facing this, Dasein chooses to become absorbed in an inauthentic experience of space which is far less threatening. It does this even though it knows – on the most primordial level of its own authentic experience of *being* – that it can experience the ontic illusion of space only because space is disclosed to its consciousness by the essential form of its authentic, inner, devouring, spatiality. In its anxiety, Dasein needs to make artificial space (or Lebensraum) for itself to live in.[58]

In its inauthentic form, Dasein can stay away from the inherent association of its spatial essence with the destruction of space. It does this to avoid the anxiety of knowing itself as a force in the world that is constantly engaged in devouring, shrinking, condensing, and using up the space that it needs in order to *be*. Inauthenticity allows it to find a way of being in which *being* is not permanently saturated with the angst of self-Destruction. However, this requires Dasein to hide. It does this by assuming the form of the knowing subject that exists with a consciousness that conceals from itself the authentic form of its own spatiality. It hides by deliberately creating a situation of Galut in which Dasein conceals from itself the fact that it is always and inevitably engaged in the self-devouring process of Churban Olam.

The deliberately disturbing point that we wish to make here is that this condition of *being* is Heidegger's description of the spatiality on which the idea of Survival and System is predicated. Indeed, our allusions to the destruction of the world's resources and the systematic denial of it underline how powerfully this portrayal of Dasein describes the self of modern Western civilization. On this ground, we return to our suggestion that a Jewish identity predicated on Survival and System is self-delusional and untenable. Our argument is that it must be replaced by a form of Jewish identity that is based upon an onto-theological alternative to Heidegger's description of human *being*. But in order to confront Dasein, we must first need to find it. For that, we need to discover how it manipulates its capacity for self-distraction in order to hide itself from us. Dasein's hiding mechanisms are the subject of the next chapter.

---

58. Lebensraum, or "living space," was the colonial policy of expanding the space occupied by the German Reich. It was an ideological principle of Nazism that motivated the expansionism and conquests that ultimately sparked off the Second World War. See, for example, Holger Herwig, "Geopolitik: Haushofer, Hitler and Lebensraum," in Colin Gray and Geoffrey Sloan, eds., *Geopolitics, Geography and Strategy* (London, 1999).

CHAPTER 12

Hiding in Society

Dasein's Social World

While we have already identified the role of "devouring spatiality" in motivating Dasein's hiding, we have yet to look closely at how or where Dasein hides. In chapters 4 and 5 of *BT*, Heidegger's answer to this is that Dasein hides in society. In order to appreciate the ontological significance of this answer, we will need to acquire a richer understanding of what is meant by Dasein's social world. To do this, we must bore our way back into the evolving pattern of Heidegger's methodology and understand how chapter 4 builds upon what we have already learned in chapters 2 and 3.

Thus far, Heidegger's analysis of spatiality has shown how the phenomenology of *world* can been given a structure that corresponds to the *being-with* of Dasein. However, at the beginning of chapter 4, Heidegger points out that *being-with* has become available to us only in the sense that it is absorbed in the *world's worldliness*. What this means is that the phenomenology of *being-in-the-world* has thus far only explained for us how innerworldly objects are *together-with* Dasein. It has not yet given us a clear sense of how Dasein's capacity for *being-with* is *together-with* them. Without a fuller understanding of this, the phenomenology of *being-in-the-world* is necessarily incomplete.

In order to bring out into the open a fuller view of *being-in-the-world*, Heidegger sets about the task of giving ontological clarity to the question of who Dasein *is*. What he is looking for in asking this question is a way to begin his analysis of the "self" of Dasein as the subject of the *being* referred to in the neologism *being-in-the-world*.[1] Heidegger refers to this "self" as

---

1. Heidegger, *BT*, 111–12.

Dasein's *being-a-self*. The recognition that a full discussion of *being-in-the-world* requires an analysis of Dasein's *selfhood* is essential in order for the notion of the *world* in which Dasein *is* to yield for us a sense of how Dasein goes about *being-a-self* (i.e., a subject) in that world. Furthermore, the notion of Dasein's *being-a-self* as the subject of *being* suggests that Dasein's mode of *being* has what we refer to as a "social" dimension: *World* is the company that *being* keeps in the context of its *being-in-the-world*.

To understand more specifically who Dasein *is* as a social *being*, we therefore need to understand inauthentic Dasein, as a subject of *being*, more clearly. Methodologically speaking, in this analysis Heidegger sticks to his insistence that descriptions of the everyday or inauthentic conditions of the self all correspond to the overall structure of Dasein. As such, inauthentic forms of Dasein are modes of *being* that can only be recognized and identified from within a perspective that is geared toward the recovery of Dasein's complete authentic form, because inauthentic Dasein only *is* as an expression of authentic Dasein's deliberate hiding.

Since inauthentic Dasein is a form of authentic Dasein and authentic Dasein is not readily accessible to us, Heidegger's analytic of inauthentic Dasein is possible only because of authentic Dasein's repressed desire to "break out." Authentic Dasein can be discovered only because in hiding it is like a child looking to be found in a game. In Heideggerian terms, this desire to be found is called *anticipation*, which as a "fact" has the seemingly circular structure (that we discussed above) of *throwness* and *projection*. This structure allows us to ground the analysis even if this "grounding" is based upon something that has not yet been disclosed.

The experience that has not yet been attained is what we referred to above as the landing point of an arrow which has been shot into the dark. To see this grounding, thought must peer into the darkness – as if through a keyhole – in order to follow the flight path of the arrow. This is something that can be accomplished only through thought, and in Heidegger's view, this discovery of the self is the purpose of philosophy. The point of philosophizing is to gain intelligence, as it were, from inside the cave, about what life in the cave looks like from above the cave. The complexity of this is what demands Heidegger to invent his neologisms. His descriptions in complex language of Dasein's inauthentic forms are therefore to be read as a kind of ex post facto account of his own keyhole preview of his own *being* from the perspective of an imagined authenticity that lies beyond. This circularity between inside and out is what is meant by immanent metaphysics.

The experience of reading Heidegger is therefore akin to following a map he has drawn of the ground inside the cave. But a map of the inside which is drawn from the ground inside the cave has the perspective of what can be seen outside and above. This map reimagines the journey into the cave on the grounds that anticipation is a primordial memory. In this sense, Heidegger's neologisms presume to name experiences that we ourselves must *always already* know from within. Their purpose is to help us navigate our way through terrain that our primordial consciousness has *always already* flown over in the dark.

This is confusing and difficult. But as we previously saw in our discussion of the introductory chapters, the circular structure of this method is supremely important because it gives the analysis of Dasein the same structure as Dasein's *being-in-the-world*. Since we are all ostensibly Dasein, giving the thematic analysis of Dasein the structure of Dasein is methodologically vital to the grounding of the analytic in our own authentic or primordial experiences of thinking. By virtue of this circularity, it becomes possible to build observations about Dasein on the foundations of those inauthentic expressions of Dasein's *being* in which its authentic forms are most submerged. Dasein's *anticipation* of being discovered (like a child playing hide and seek) is a clue to where Dasein can be found. *Anticipation* of being found is a thumbprint of authentic Dasein that leaves its mark on all Dasein's inauthentic forms. It enables us to recognize inauthentic forms of *being* for what Heidegger believes they really are – for what they conceal. In short, it allows us to recreate the experience of going into hiding and thus tease Dasein out of its lair.

Dasein-With and Being-With

Following his assertion that inauthentic Dasein has *always already* had an authentic form, Heidegger insists that a well-grounded ontological analysis of Dasein must begin with Dasein's most readily familiar everyday or inauthentic expressions of itself. In order to take the next step toward authenticity Heidegger starts with an everyday reflection on how we think of the "self" in order to begin an ontological analysis of Dasein's *being-a-self*.

The difficulty getting started here is that beginning with the everyday self requires us to explain how the inauthentic subject is generated by Dasein. It is for this reason that the approach that Heidegger takes must be geared toward discovering the subject's most primordial experience of itself within a context that contradicts its most readily available experience of selfhood. In order to remain consistent with the circular methodology outlined above, we must begin by identifying the concealment that authentic Dasein uses to invent its inauthentic form.

In Heidegger's words, the subject most naturally experiences itself in its everyday form as "the being that I myself am."[2] Given this, we might say that it is Dasein that I am referring to when I refer to myself as "I." Thus we might say that "the who is answered in terms of the 'I' itself, the 'subject' the 'self.'"[3] Dasein is therefore the sense of self that "maintains itself as identity throughout the changes in behavior and experiences"[4] that every individual has. In other words, insofar as we think of ourselves as the same person throughout our lives – despite both the physical and psychological changes we experience – Dasein is a constant that provides the basis for the changes that occur. It is because of this constant that we may think of change as something that repeatedly happens to the same "me."

Now, if this intuitive or everyday answer to the question of who Dasein is describes an inauthentic sense of self that has *always already* encountered itself in an authentic way, our next task is to discover the method that will enable us to see this depiction of the self as a Structure of Concealment. This will allow us to see how and why it was constructed. To do this, the constant of the "being that I myself always am" must be reformulated in accordance with the structure of Dasein. Heidegger toys with such ideas as the "human soul" and the "thingliness of consciousness" as names for this constant of *being*, but what he is trying to get at here is an experience that we know and cannot explain. This experience is the intuitive idea that people have of themselves as possessing an "objectivity of person" that can be posited in a form

---

2.   Ibid., 112.

3.   Ibid.

4.   Ibid.

which reasonably allows one to speak of something whose *being* retains the meaning of "objective presence" throughout the course of our lives.

Having crystallized this description, we now know what we are looking for. All the same, the description of the self as a constant of *being* is not sufficient for our purposes since it does not yet have the structure of Dasein. To bridge that gap, Heidegger must demonstrate the inadequacy of what has been said thus far. He argues that while it perhaps seems most natural and appropriate to consider who Dasein is in the terms that are most familiar to Dasein when it speaks of itself, this approach underestimates the power of everyday Dasein to conceal itself even from itself. This argument is methodologically grounded in the claim that it is Dasein's hiding that leads to our perplexity. Thus, Dasein's capacity to conceal itself from Dasein accounts for its capacity to conceal itself from us. Put differently, it is our perplexity about who we are which pushes us in the first place to search outside of Dasein's most familiar experiences of its own *being* for the constant of objective presence. This is indeed a powerful argument that provides a solid methodological justification for the analysis that follows, since it is rooted in our own everyday experience of what it is like to *be*. On this foundation, it becomes entirely reasonable to posit that the existential answer to the question of Dasein's identity is not consciously known to Dasein when it asks itself in an unthematic way who in fact it is. In Heidegger's words,

> Just as the ontic, self-evident character of being-in-itself of inner-worldly beings misleads us by convincing us of the ontologically self-evident character of the meaning of this being and makes us overlook the phenomenon of world, so too does the ontically self-evident character that Dasein is always my own, harbor the possibility that the ontological problematic inherent in it might be led astray.[5]

Dasein's already established ability to overlook *world* is evidence enough for Heidegger that Dasein is also capable of overlooking or hiding from itself. In addition, the implausibility of the isolated "I" forces us to return to what we

---

5.   Ibid., 114.

have already discovered about the way in which the subject is in fact given to us in the context of the *world's worldliness.* All this leads Heidegger to the conclusion that the way forward is to continue the analytic from the established and grounded starting point of *being-in-the-world* and – starting with the subject that is phenomenally visible to us – interpret it in an ontologically appropriate way.[6]

The point of departure for this analysis is to say that "Dasein is always only itself in existing."[7] It is neither body, soul, nor any combination of the two. The constant of Dasein's objective presence is the fact of its existence. Dasein is therefore the pure fact of the self's *existence.* This *existence* is the most primordial element of what Dasein points at when it says "I," because the "I" that Dasein points to always *is.* The task now is to make this existence ontologically accessible by giving it the structure of Dasein's *being-with.* Heidegger says that the way to do this is to think of who Dasein is as the "whom" for "whom" innerworldly beings are *relevant.* We have already established that objects in the world that are *at hand* must be *useful* for Dasein. Now we must invert this in order to see that it is Dasein's complicit participation in the *being-with* of innerworldly objects that reveals *who* Dasein *is.* Heidegger offers several cases to illustrate this point. For example:

> The boat anchored at the shore refers in its being-in-itself to an acquaintance who undertakes voyages in it, but even as a boat which is unknown to us it still points to others. The others who are encountered in the context of useful things in the surrounding world at hand are not somehow added on in thought to an initially merely objectively present thing, but these "things" are encountered from the world in which they are at hand for the others. The world is always already from the outset my own.[8]

In this portrayal, the direction of *being-in-the-world's de-distancing* is reversed. We now come to see Dasein as the being whose *being* is indicated by the

---

6. Ibid.
7. Ibid.
8. Ibid., 115.

capacity of innerworldly objects like boats to be *relevant, at hand,* or *useful* for Dasein. Dasein emerges out of its place of hiding when we think of its existence as indicated or *de-distanced* by the very *usefulness* of things that are *useful* for someone – a, *for whom* or a *who* – that *exists-with* them. We are invited to ask, "For whom are innerworldly objects *useful?*" If the answer to this question is Dasein, this might be described as Dasein hosting or giving company to the innerworldly objects that draw the ontological meaning of their *being* from Dasein's capacity to *be-with* or *de-distance* them. This form of *being-with*, which captures the very existence of Dasein – i.e., it captures the ontological rather than the ontic sense of *usefulness* – uncovers or indicates the *being* of Dasein as the being whose *being* (or *is-ness*) has the structure of *existence-with* innerworldly objects. Heidegger refers to this form of *being-with* (that discloses who Dasein *is* in the context of its encounters with innerworldly objects), as *Dasein-with*, or in his words, "The innerworldly being-in-itself of others is *Dasein-with*."[9]

The importance of the step forward that has been taken here becomes clearer when we consider how this description of *Dasein-with* allows us our first real glimpse of the Structure of Concealment that Dasein creates to generate its own inauthentic form. The inversion of *being-in-the-world* and the personification of the *being who is* in the world (in the form of "for whom"), gives us a vital clue to understanding how Dasein constructs itself as "I." We can begin to follow that clue by expanding our view of *world* to include other beings that are themselves Dasein. Up until this point, Heidegger's discussion of *world* has addressed only how Dasein frees beings that have a character unlike Dasein's from the tapestry of *world* and makes them conspicuous for Dasein by giving to them the characteristics of *handiness* and objective presence. Because Dasein has now been personified as the "for whom" of *being*, the "*who*" of Dasein (whose structure of *being* is not like that of innerworldly objects) is also made conspicuous against the backdrop of its *with-world*. After freeing Dasein in this way, it now becomes possible to consider Dasein's interactions with other beings that are also Dasein. In Heidegger's words, what we may now consider is how Dasein frees beings

---

9.   Ibid., 116.

which are not completely different from tools and objects but which themselves in accordance with their kind of being as Dasein are themselves "in" the world as being-in-the-world in which they are at the same time encountered.[10]

Heidegger calls Dasein's mode of interaction with other beings that are like Dasein "*being-with.*" This is a specific term and it must be clear from now on that Dasein's capacity for *being-with* is not the same as its capacity for *being-in*. *Being-in* is the mode of *being* that makes innerworldly objects accessible to Dasein's *with-world*. *Being-with*, on the other hand, is an extension of Dasein's capacity to serve as the "for whom" of the *being* of innerworldly objects into the realm of Dasein's encounters with other beings that are also Dasein. In other words, *being-with* is the "for whom" of other Dasein and it is therefore the essential mode of Dasein's social interactions. As Heidegger puts it, "The Dasein-with of others is disclosed only within the world, and so too for beings who are Daseins with us, because Dasein in itself is essentially being-with."[11] In this way, Dasein identifies the "being-with" of other Daseins as they engage in *being-in-the-world*. But this identification of other Daseins does not take the form of *being-with* them but rather of *being-with* them as *Dasein-with* others. In this sense, Dasein, other Daseins and innerworldly objects are always *together-with* Dasein in its surrounding *with-world*. Even when Dasein is alone it is never without them. Thus, "the being-alone of Dasein, too, is being-with in the world."[12] It is this structure and the complex interchange between *Dasein-with* and *being-with* that will now reveal for us the Structure of Concealment that generates inauthentic Dasein's sense of itself as "I."

The Construction of Dasein's Inauthentic Self as an Object

Our challenge now is to use the tools of *being-with* and *Dasein-with* to understand both how and why Dasein goes into hiding. Only then can we account for how Dasein generates the illusion of the "I." So far, these tools have

---

10. Ibid., 115.
11. Ibid., 117.
12. Ibid.

elucidated for us the nature of Dasein's social dimension. What we must now understand is how Dasein experiences its social spatiality. This is important because Dasein's reasons for hiding are intrinsically connected to the anxiety that this social spatiality generates. To proceed, we need to understand who Dasein *is* in the context of its sociality.

Dasein's social dimension is intrinsically connected to who inauthentic or everyday Dasein *is* for three reasons. First, the conditions of *being-in-the-world* that apply to the encounters between beings that have the form of Dasein are an indispensable part of Dasein's mode of *being*. Without them, we would have no understanding of Dasein's encounters with others, and as such, our portrayal of Dasein would simply not be complete. Second, the structure of *being-with* tells us how Dasein goes about *being-together-with* others. It therefore shows us how Dasein discovers itself as the subject or person of its social condition of *being* when it is with others.[13] The point is that, since we are all Dasein, a methodologically grounded answer to the question of who Dasein *is* therefore depends upon our reaching an ontologically appropriate understanding of how Dasein knows itself in society. In effect these are one and the same thing. Third, the structure of *being-with* shows us how the encounter between beings that have the form of Dasein allows them to be the "for whom" of each other. When we apply this structure to our own Dasein, we can ground the answer to the question of who Dasein *is* in our own inner experience of ourselves as the answer to the question of "for whom."

This is difficult because the "for whom" of our own Dasein is a Structure of Concealment. The key to making this structure visible is embedded in the similarity between *Dasein-with* (i.e., Dasein's capacity for being the "for whom" of innerworldly objects) and *being-with* (i.e., Dasein's capacity for being the "for whom" of other Dasein). Essentially, Dasein goes into hiding by interacting with the *being-with* of others as if it were an innerworldly object. It does this by projecting the mode of *Dasein-with* on the *being-with* of others allowing them to function as the conscious subject of its own *being*. This is how it uses social spatiality to conceal from itself its own authentic mode of *being*. The result is that, in its encounters with others, Dasein imagines itself as an innerworldly object whose *being* is "kept company" by the

---

13. Ibid.

Dasein-with of others. In other words, Dasein conceals itself from itself by fleeing from its subjectivity to the pole of the object. In effect, this description is the nucleus of how epistemology has concealed ontology throughout the history of philosophy. The self is instrumentalized and objectified as the inauthentic subject that we refer to as "I."

Dasein is capable of fleeing only because its encounters with others are qualitatively different from its encounters with innerworldly objects. Dasein encounters innerworldly objects as existentially different from itself. Unlike Dasein, they show no *concern* for their *being* and leave Dasein with no choice but to be the subject (the *Dasein-with*) of their *being-in-the-world*. It is in this sense that they are described as *at hand, relevant,* or *useful* for Dasein. By contrast, Dasein's encounter with others is one in which Dasein existentially identifies with others as the "for whom" of its own *being*. In Heidegger's words, the encounter with others gives rise to the experience of them as "those from whom one mostly does *not* distinguish oneself, those among whom one also is."[14] Once the nature of this identification with others is clear we can catch our first glimpse not only of how, but also of why Dasein hides.

Heidegger points out that Dasein's "being-there-too with them does not have the ontological character of being objectively present 'with' them within a world."[15] Rather, since Dasein is not actually an innerworldly object, the sameness of *being* is an existential condition that causes Dasein to experience the world as the "one that I always already share with others."[16] For Dasein, this is an identity crisis. If we look at this identity crisis from a perspective that is grounded in anticipation, i.e., in Dasein's *always already* knowing its authentic self, the feeling that "I" have of "myself" as "the being that I always am" is powerfully threatened by my feeling of identification with the Dasein of others. This is because identification leads me to experience my own Dasein as being relentlessly bombarded and invaded by the Dasein of all those others with whom I am automatically connected. As a result of this existential experience, the authentic idea of the individual is dissolved by Dasein's perpetual

---

14. Ibid.
15. Ibid.
16. Ibid.

experience of the "world" that it shares with others as a "*with-world.*"[17] Thus, the category of *being-in* emerges as constantly saturated with the concurrent experience of *being-with* the others who are *always already* there,[18] accompanying and shaping even Dasein's encounters with inanimate innerworldly beings. *Being-in* the world of Dasein therefore assumes the form of *always already being-with* others, while the *being-in-itself* of innerworldly objects assumes the reverse form of *Dasein-with* with all the others too.[19]

This portrayal of Dasein's social identity as saturated in the *being-with* of others is an inevitable feature of all aspects of Dasein's *being-in-the-world*. If Dasein's encounters with the Dasein of others are inherent to its *being* in the context of *being-in-the-world*, it must be clear that all of Dasein's interactions (even those between Dasein and completely inanimate innerworldly beings) involve the *Dasein-with* of others who are also Dasein. Moreover, much in the same way as Heidegger portrayed both the *relevance* and the *usefulness* of innerworldly objects as modes of being *useful* and *not useful* – *relevant* and *not relevant* – for Dasein, Dasein's *being-with* the Dasein of others simultaneously assumes both the form of *being-together-with* and the form of *being-away-from* others. As such, even the "being-alone of Dasein too is being-with in the world."[20] In this sense, "being-alone is a deficient form of being-with; its possibility is a proof of the latter."[21] Consequently, in the same way that Dasein *is* never in isolation before it encounters innerworldly objects, all of Dasein's encounters with itself are ones in which Dasein's self is to be understood as *always already* "among" others. Heidegger calls this orientation toward the others with whom Dasein identifies "*taking-care.*" In the ontological sense in which the term is used here, *care* does not refer to kindness or to the ways in which people look after each other. Rather, *care* refers more specifically to the essential attentive experience of *being-together-with* that occurs between

---

17. Ibid., 116.

18. As we shall see, the subject of what it means for them to be "there" is one that requires further explanation. This question is dealt with in chapter 5 of *BT* and we will return to it below.

19. Heidegger, *BT*, 116.

20. Ibid., 117.

21. Ibid.

my Dasein and the Dasein of others all the time. This is an overwhelming experience from which Dasein can never truly escape.

We can now form a clear picture of both how and why Dasein hides. In sum, it is Dasein's natural desire to avoid the saturation of its identity by the Dasein of others that explains why Dasein uses the form of *Dasein-with* in order to conceal from itself the true nature of its subjectivity and go into hiding as if it were an object – a "for whom" – of others.

Dasein's Hiding Place in the *They* as "I"

Given this analysis, we can now begin to see not only how and why Dasein hides but also where. Dasein's hiding place is in the inauthentic object of its subjectivity that it projects upon the world and calls "I." The way in which this happens becomes visible when we portray the social world of Dasein according to the structure of Dasein. The notion of the individual subject or the "self that I myself am" is always most readily adopted by Dasein in its inauthentic form, because the inauthentic illusion of the individual "I" that is "me" is comforting for Dasein in its state of saturation. The illusion of the "I" allows me to feel like an individual without forcing me to face the responsibility of what true individuality means. The illusion of the "I" comes to compensate for the deeper or more primordial loss of authenticity that takes place when Dasein experiences itself as *always already together-with* the Dasein of others. This primordial merging of Dasein with the Dasein of others is what Heidegger refers to as the submersion of Dasein in the *with-world* of the "*they*."

The answer to the question of who everyday Dasein *is* must therefore be addressed in the context of its absorption in the Dasein of the others from whom Dasein's "concernful taking care" is never separated. Thus, "being-with existentially determines Dasein even when an "other" is not factically present and perceived."[22] When the full extent of Dasein's inevitable participation in the collective identity of the *they* is appreciated, it becomes clear why "it is only because Dasein has the essential structure of being-with that one's own Dasein is encounterable by others as Dasein-with."[23] Put differently, *care* is

---

22. Ibid.
23. Ibid., 118.

a concept that we can understand as parallel to the *concern* that Dasein has for its own *being*. While up until now we have described *concern* as directed at innerworldly beings, we must now understand that Dasein's capacity for showing *concern* about its own *being* is *always already* mingled together with *taking care* of its *Dasein-with* other beings who are also Dasein. Thus, *concern* is always absorbed in *taking care*. This analysis allows Heidegger to assert that

> being-with with others [Mitsein mit Anderen] belongs to the being of Dasein, with which it is concerned in its very being. As being-with, Dasein "is" essentially for the sake of others. This must be understood as an existential statement as to its essence. But even when actual, factical Dasein does *not* turn to others and thinks that it does not need them, or does without them, it *is* in the mode of being-with. In being-with as the existential for-the-sake-of-others, these others are already disclosed in their Dasein…. The disclosedness of the Dasein-with of others which belongs to being-with means that the understanding of others already lies in the understanding of being of Dasein because its being is being-with. This understanding, like all understanding, is not a knowledge derived from cognition but a primordially existential kind of being which first makes knowledge and cognition possible. Knowing oneself is grounded in being-with which primordially understands…thus the other is initially disclosed in the taking care of concern.[24]

What this implies is that all Dasein's encounters with innerworldly beings already comprise Dasein's social identity. Thus, the most primordial forms of Dasein's self-knowledge and its knowledge of innerworldly objects cannot be accessed through "cognition." In this way, the epistemological analysis of the knowing "I" (that on its own "knows" things in the world) emerges as a hiding place that Dasein constructs to prevent itself from having to face the ontological truth about the complex constitution of its own self. Since one's own Dasein understands its own *being* as always related to the Dasein of others,

---

24. Ibid., 120.

one's own Dasein, like the Dasein-with of others, is encountered
initially and for the most part in terms of the surrounding world
taken care of that is shared. In being absorbed in the world of taking care of things, that is, at the same time in being-with toward
others, Dasein is not itself.[25]

This is Heidegger's account of how and why Dasein assumes an identity that
is not itself. What he is saying is that the "I" is first formed in the image of
how Dasein sees others while viewing itself as an innerworldly object that
is with them in the mode of *Dasein-with*. Dasein then projects this image
back onto itself, producing its inauthentic sense of self in which its mode of
Dasein-with stands in for its mode of *being-with* others. Heidegger describes
Dasein's *Dasein-with* standing in for its mode of *being-with* as "empathy" that
actively suppresses and conceals from Dasein its own genuine understanding
of itself. In Heidegger's words,

Dasein stands in *subservience* to others. It itself *is* not; the others
have taken its being away from it. The everyday possibilities of
being of Dasein are at the disposal of the whims of others. These
others are not *definite* others. On the contrary any other can represent them. What is decisive is only the inconspicuous domination by others that Dasein as being-with has already taken over
unawares. One belongs to the others oneself and entrenches their
power. "The others," whom one designates as such in order to cover
over one's own essential belonging to them, are those who *are there*
initially and for the most part in everyday being-with-one-another.
The who is not this one and not that one, not oneself, not some
and not the sum of them all. The "who" is the neuter, *the they.*[26]

While, as we have already said, the "who" of authentic Dasein is the constancy
of Dasein's *being-with,* the inauthentic or everyday condition of who Dasein
is comes into view when one realizes that Dasein has *always already* used the

25. Ibid., 122.
26. Ibid., 122–23.

mode of *Dasein-with* to construct itself as an object. The result is that in its everyday form, when we encounter Dasein it has *always already* surrendered itself to be an illusory "I" who is "nobody in particular." This surrendering is a kind of social *de-distancing* that allows Dasein to latch on to the *Dasein-with* of the *they* in order to totally distract its own attention from its own *being*. It is this mechanism that ultimately describes how Dasein becomes absorbed in society. Methodologically speaking, it is important to be clear that the facticity of this absorption is not a lesser form of Dasein. Dasein here is not really nobody or nothing. Rather, the persona of the nobody is a condition of Dasein's *being* that has the character of Dasein's *being-with* which – from within the authenticity of its true character – assumes for itself an inauthentic *they-self* in which Dasein hides under the pseudonym of "I."

The Psychological and Macro-Historical Significance of Dasein's *They-Self*

Dasein is drawn to the illusion that it can surrender its individual *being* to the *they* because the public collective *they* (which is a kind of ontological group-think), makes life easier. Dasein wants to take comfort in surrogates because it wants to shirk the burden of having to disentangle itself from the highly complex structures that comprise its *being-in-the-world together-with* others. The *they* indulges this tendency, offering Dasein a new identity in which the primordial self-knowledge that it *always already* has is replaced with the much more easygoing sensation of average everydayness. By constructing a *they-self*, Dasein escapes from its real self into the persona of a "nobody" from whom no one can make complex individual demands.

This portrayal of Dasein's *they-self* is Heidegger's account of how everyday Dasein appears when considered from a perspective that is *always already* authentic. The *they-self* is an ontologically authentic account of who it is that Dasein refers to when it describes itself as "I." What is important to remember here is that this exilic state of being is also Dasein's most natural state of being. The *they-self* is who Dasein most naturally is; it is who Dasein will usually choose to be unless it explicitly sets out to discover its own authentic *being*. Since this is a demanding choice, it can be made only if Dasein applies itself (perhaps as we are now) to the challenge of "clearing away the coverings and obscurities, by breaking up the disguises with which Dasein cuts itself off from itself."[27]

Heidegger's analysis here is first and foremost an ontological one. However, we might gain a more explicit appreciation of its significance to us if we stop briefly to restate it in psychological terms. The methodological justification for transitioning between ontology and psychology in this way comes from Heidegger himself. As we will see in our discussion of *attunement*, the psychological states of mind in which Dasein becomes visible and available for ontological analysis are of great importance to the analysis that unfolds in chapter 5 of *BT*. But even before we discuss this in detail, we can already sense something of deep importance as we observe the interplay between psychology and ontology in Heidegger's description of Dasein's motives for and methods of hiding.

The reason that Dasein constructs an inauthentic "I" is psychological angst. This angst is generated by the primordial demands of managing an awareness of self that devours space and that is *always already* merged *together-with* the collective *they*. In simple psychological terms, what Heidegger is suggesting is that Dasein is in a perennial state of existential identity crisis. First, as we saw in the previous chapter, it experiences a crisis of angst about the self-destructive nature of its own spatiality. Second, the ontological fact of Dasein's inseparability from the *they* is so overwhelming that Dasein prefers being a nobody to assuming its own identity. Instead of facing up to the true nature of its complex condition of *being*, Dasein constructs for itself an inauthentic façade in much the same way as people daydream, fanaticize, or simply watch television in order to deflect the pain and avoid the effort of living in the real world. These behaviors, which are so characteristic of Western popular culture, are closely connected to the near-to-ubiquitous cluster of psychological phenomena that emanate from the widespread "denial of death" in humanist culture.[28]

Though we are not yet quite ready to develop this next point, it is worth hinting already at this stage that Heidegger's psycho-philosophical analysis of the *they* is tremendously important when considered in the historical context

---

27. Ibid., 125.

28. For a full and penetrating discussion of the centrality of death denial in the Western psychological tradition, see Ernst Becker, *The Denial of Death* (New York: Free Press, 1973).

of Nazi Germany. First, it is one of the keys to understanding what it was in National Socialism that appealed to Heidegger's (and more generally speaking, Dasein's) concerns about the crisis of inauthentic identity in Germany. As such, it is crucial to understanding Nazism's project for the redemption of Germany from its exilic condition of *being*. When viewed in this way, Heidegger's obvious dissatisfaction with the submerged and subservient state of everyday Dasein is, as Steiner suggested, a clear echo of the National Socialist program to rehabilitate the authentic national spirit of the German people. Second, the association of inauthenticity with the denial of death – which, as we shall see, is essential to the climax of *BT* – assumes a unique macro-historical significance when considered against the backdrop of the Nazi attempt to associate robustness of culture with the ideal of the combatant hero who is brave in the face of death. Third, Heidegger's depiction of "subservience to the *they*" is haunting when considered in the historical shadow of those many millions of Germans who became both passive and active "nobodies" complicit in the *they* that tortured and murdered millions. Insofar as it is broadly true of modern Western civilization, Heidegger's portrayal of the "nobody" and the "*they-self*" inadvertently provides us with a startlingly clear view of how the Holocaust was perpetrated within the borders of post-Enlightenment humanist civilization. This condition of Dasein's subservience to the *they* is a state of *being* that can be easily manipulated by anyone who promises to relieve Dasein of its burden. Dasein's latent desire for authenticity can be harnessed when a leader claiming to have seen the light offers vicarious authenticity to a *they* which in its totality is willing to be subservient to his deceit. Recognizing the centrality of this relationship between a *they* and its subservience to the Fuhrer principle[29] gives us a penetrating account of the detachment from "humanized humanity" that made the Holocaust possible. But, perhaps more urgently for our present concerns, noticing how this subservience of the *they* to the state underpins the suggestion of Derrida, Foucault, Adorno, Horkheimer, and Steiner that liberal humanist politics and Nazism – despite the immense differences between them – are tied at the hip.

---

29. For a full discussion of the Fuhrer principle and its role in Heidegger's theories about the function of the academy in the National Socialist regime, see Safranski, *Martin Heidegger* 252–59.

CHAPTER 13

Attunement and the Exilic Absorption of *Being* in the *"They"*

Dasein's Social Being in the *There*

Heidegger's portrayal of who everyday Dasein is – which we now know as the *they-self* – is followed by an investigation into the question of how everyday Dasein encounters innerworldly objects as part of its *being-in-the-world*. This is methodologically essential to Heidegger's project of seeing the analytic of Dasein "whole," i.e., without any part left out. Thus far, he has pointed out how Dasein relates to the world by exploring three primary dimensions of Dasein's *being-in-the-world*. These are *being-together-with* the world (*care*), *being-with* (*concern*), and *being-a-self* (*who*). From Heidegger's perspective, the demand that Dasein be seen in its entirety justifies his asking the simple question, "What more is there?"[1]

The path forward starts with the recognition that the *they-self*'s essential condition of *being* is one in which the *they* (*with-which* Dasein always and inescapably *is*) is somehow *there*. In other words, if we look out upon the *they* from the perspective of Dasein, we can understand it as something that is *always already* out *there*. To reach a full portrayal of Dasein's *they-self* we now need to develop an ontological analytic of the hermeneutic tools that give Dasein its primordial awareness of the *there*. Since what is out *there* is integral to Dasein's spatiality, giving an account of how Dasein knows the *there* is essential to explaining *where* the *they* ostensibly *is*. Chapter 5 of *BT*

---

1.   Heidegger, *BT*, 127.

is dedicated to answering this question within the context of what we have
already learned about the spatiality of Dasein's social world.

Ontological Hermeneutics and the analysis of the *There*

In the sense that both others and innerworldly objects populate Dasein's
with-world, the mechanisms that hold up their presence in that world (that
we might describe as their modes of interaction with Dasein) depend upon
their somehow being situated in a space that Dasein experiences as *there*. In
Heidegger's words,

> The being which is essentially constituted by being-in-the-world
> is itself always its "there".... The existential spatiality of Dasein
> which determines its "place"...is itself based upon being-in-the-
> world. The "over there" is the determinateness of something
> encountered within the *world*. "Here" and "over there" are possible
> only in a "there," that is, when there is a being which as the being
> of the "there" has disclosed spatiality.[2]

This first formulation of the *there*, not surprisingly, follows Heidegger's rule
that the entire analytic must keep to the ontological structure of Dasein.
Here he insists that any meaningful portrayal of the *there* must conform to
what we already know about the spatiality of Dasein. As such, the *there* exists
as something that is *in-the-world* of Dasein only because it is solely Dasein's
capacity for *care* – i.e., for attentive *being-together-with* – that discloses the
spatiality of the *there*. Since all spatiality is disclosed only in a form that is
relevant to Dasein's spatiality, any notion of place, whether it is a notion of
something as "here" or as "there," only *is*, *in-the-world*, *with-which*, Dasein
is. As such, all forms of here and there (which of course are not themselves
Dasein) are dependent for their *relevant being* on a notion of place that is
always "there" (and not "here") for Dasein. Consequently (unless there is no
being that has the character of Dasein in sight), *there* is an idea that refers to
both "here" and "there."

---

2.   Ibid., 129.

Ultimately, Heidegger's analysis of how everyday Dasein experiences the *there* is designed to uncover the mechanisms that generate for Dasein an inauthentic experience of its social *they-self.* His portrayals of this *they-self* are extended in this chapter to include three fundamental modes of social interaction with the world that is out *there.* Heidegger calls these "*idle talk,*"[3] "*curiosity,*"[4] and "*ambiguity.*"[5] Before we can begin the discussion of these three fundamental modes of social interaction, we must first prepare the ground by discussing how Heidegger uncovers the nature of Dasein's primordial knowledge of the *there.* He does this by offering an ontological analysis of four hermeneutic modes of *being.* These modes are like antennae that give Dasein its most primordial route of access to the world that is out *there* and allow it to experience the *there* as an integrated feature of its *being.* These four ontological antennae are "*attunement,*"[6] "*understanding,*"[7] "*interpretation,*"[8] and "*discourse*" (or "*language*").[9] In our analysis, for reasons that will soon become clear, we shall begin by paying separate attention to *attunement* and then move on to discuss *understanding, interpretation,* and *discourse* together.

Attunements as Ontological Moods

Attunement is the ontological parallel of what we know ontically as a mood. For Heidegger, an *attunement* gives us an indication, by way of our mood, about Dasein's condition of *being.* Significantly, the *attunements* that Heidegger discusses in this section are all ones that tell us something about how Dasein feels about its own mortality.

The ontic notion of a mood is perhaps most familiar to us in psychological terms. We all know what it is like to experience happiness, sadness, fear, and so on. We tend to think of these moods as coming and going. They are caused by what is happening to us either psychologically or physically. We can talk about moods as shifting because of something that happens to us or

---

3. Ibid., 161–64.
4. Ibid., 164–67.
5. Ibid., 167–69.
6. Ibid., 130–36.
7. Ibid., 138–44.
8. Ibid., 144–55.
9. Ibid., 155–61.

attribute them to chemical processes in our bodies. But all these portrayals of mood do not give us access to the meaning of *attunement* that Heidegger is interested in. The analysis in *BT* seeks to penetrate the ontological dimension of mood by looking past psychology and physiology at the inner dimension of *being*.

The aspect of mood in which Heidegger is interested is noticeable in the fact that our conscious understanding of ontic mood is always partial. Sometimes we pay no attention to our moods and think we do not even have one at all. Though we might often think that we understand the causes of our moods, we also know that we are quite frequently in a mood that we are completely unable to explain. Sometimes we experience our moods as a burden because we do not want them and do not know how to make them go away. All these ruminations about the experience of having or not having a mood suggest to Heidegger that there is no tabula rasa on which moods are inscribed and from which they can be erased. As such, "the possibilities of disclosure belonging to cognition fall far short of the primordial disclosure of moods in which Dasein is brought before its being as the there."[10] What Heidegger is saying is that having moods is one of the ways in which Dasein *is*. The primordial disclosure to Dasein of its state of *being* in the *there* is an ontological hermeneutic mechanism that suggests that all knowledge of the *there* is *always already attuned* by mood. Moods according to Heidegger are states of *being* in which Dasein's encounters with the *there* are disclosed to it. A psychological mood is like a measure of how Dasein is getting along with its ontological *being*. It tells Dasein how it "is doing" or "coming along."[11] To better understand what is meant by this, we must further clarify what is "coming along" in terms of "where from" and "where to."

The mood or *attunement* that Dasein most primordially experiences tells it something about the state of its *being-with* the *there* that always and inescapably surrounds it. Heidegger shows that *attunement* has three essential determinations. First, *attunement* allows Dasein to experience *throwness*. This is because what *attunement* essentially measures is how Dasein is getting along with its *being* as inevitably *given over to* or *thrown into* the *there*. Second, since

---

10. Ibid., 131.
11. Ibid.

Dasein's condition of *throwness* cannot but elicit a reaction to the "facticity of its being given over,"[12] Dasein discovers in this reaction not only what its condition of *being* is but also what or how it must *be*. In this sense, *attunements* have a direction, a "whither" or a "whence," that disclose for Dasein the gap that it feels between its authentic and inauthentic states of *being*. When authentic what its potentiality of *being* to Dasein, they measure its reaction to the *there*. But, more often than not, Dasein is puzzled by its moods or perhaps unaware of them because, in its inauthentic form, Dasein self-deceivingly experiences the *there* in a state of evasion. In Heidegger's words,

> In attunement, Dasein is always already brought before itself, it has always already found itself, not as perceiving oneself to be there, but as one finds one's self in attunement. As a being which is delivered over to its being, it is also delivered over to the fact that it must always already have found itself…in a finding which comes not from a direct seeking, but from a fleeing. Mood does not disclose in the mode of looking at throwness, but as a turning toward and away from it. For the most part, mood does not turn itself toward the burdensome character of Dasein manifest in it.[13]

Whether through an authentic or an inauthentic experience of the *there*, *attunement* is always a source of primordial information for Dasein. *Attunement* guides Dasein toward finding itself in the experience of its *throwness* that it has *always already* had. Thus, *attunement* "discloses Dasein in its *throwness* and, initially and for the most part, in the mode of an evasive turning away."[14]

If Dasein is capable of evasive tactics, this means that Dasein can generate for itself an inauthentic mood. The possibility of inauthentic mood is the key to uncovering the second essential determination of *attunement*. In Heidegger's words this is that

---

12. Ibid., 132.
13. Ibid.
14. Ibid., 133.

mood has always already disclosed *being-in-the-world* as a whole and first makes possible directing oneself toward something.[15]

We can understand this by clarifying the distinction between *attunement* in the ontological sense, and its ontic or psychological parallel. *Attunement* is not the same as the psychical condition of mood, because essentially it is an existential disclosure of Dasein's state of *being* in the *there*. This is the case even when that state is concealed, rather than revealed, by the emotional reaction that we know ontically or psychologically as a mood. Again, as we saw with *usefulness* and *relevance*, the ontological meaning of mood as *attunement* is one that discloses Dasein's state of *being* in the *there* even when the actual meaning of that disclosure is a concealment that closes Dasein off from itself. Heidegger's example of this is a bad mood: When we speak ontically or psychically, we know that bad moods have the effect of closing Dasein off from itself, because "the surrounding world is veiled" and the "circumspection of taking care is led astray."[16] Put simply, a bad mood often warps our view of others and even of inanimate objects. However, when we look at bad moods ontologically, we can see them as essential to Dasein's *being-in-the-world*. This is because a bad mood is not some inner experience that reaches out and assails a perception of a world that Dasein might know differently if it were happier. Rather, the mood is integral to the mode of *being-in-the-world* through which *world* is disclosed to Dasein. Thus, "mood has always already disclosed *being-in-the-world* as a whole."[17] Mood is an essential feature of how the world discloses itself to Dasein. Dasein itself does not know the world without *attunement*. *Attunement* is one of its primordial antennae in the sense that every encounter that Dasein has with its *being-in-the-world* is *always already attuned*. Thus, evasive mood swings disclose the condition of *being* in which Dasein steers itself one way or another, toward or away from, something that it *always already* knows in *attunement*. Therefore, even (and perhaps especially) inauthentic moods disclose for Dasein the direction of its *being* in the *there*.

---

15. Ibid.
16. Ibid.
17. Ibid.

Third, *attunement* gives Dasein access to the *there* in a mode that is *always already* colored by its existential sense of what it needs to know and why. In this sense, *attunement* discloses to Dasein why the world matters. Of course, the disclosure of what matters can also take the negative form of disclosing what does not matter. Similarly, the encounter with something that is threatening discloses the mode with which something that is not threatening is *de-distanced* and *given over* to Dasein's attention. Dasein becomes open to the world because it is interested (or not) or because it is threatened (or not) or because it is excited (or not), etc., by the *there*. In other words, it is only because the essential structure of Dasein's *being-in-the-world* is *always already attuned* that the senses can reach out to things in the *there* that are always disclosed to Dasein as either mattering or not to Dasein's *being*. This "moodedness of attunement therefore constitutes existentially the openness to world of Dasein."[18]

The *Attunement* of Fear as the First Keyhole Glimpse of Death

While, in the context of an ontological analysis, we must be careful to avoid the mistake of judging the distinction between good and bad moods in moralistic, ethical, societal, or psychological terms, there are still clear differences of value between moods. There are certain modes of *attunement* that Heidegger considers more valuable for ontological analysis than others. These are differences that must be measured in terms of what (and how much) they disclose about Dasein's state of *being*.

Since *attunement* is an equiprimordial and inescapable feature of *being-in-the-world*, paying attention to which moods are most valuable to Heidegger is crucial to understanding what the most primordial "whence" and "whither" (i.e., "where from" and "where to") of his analytic of *being* is. If *attunement* gauges for Dasein how it is "getting along," the moods that disclose the most are the ones that tell us most about what Dasein looks like "as a whole." They inform us most completely where Dasein is coming from and where it is headed. Given this, it is important to notice that immediately following his initial analysis of Dasein as *attunement*, Heidegger dedicates an entire section

---

18. Ibid., 134.

to "fear as a mode of *attunement*."[19] It is the only *attunement* that is singled out for this kind of special attention at this stage. Moreover, the scope of the conclusions that Heidegger draws from his analysis of fear is nothing short of striking. He clearly values fear as the widest keyhole through which the essential character of Dasein can ultimately be seen.

In this analysis of fear, Heidegger distinguishes between "what we are afraid of," "fearing itself," and "that about which we are afraid."[20] This three-fold combination, according to Heidegger, reveals the structure of *attunement* in general. This is already a surprisingly broad claim to pin onto a single mood. The first category, "what we are afraid of," points to innerworldly beings *at hand* or objectively present. What makes these objects fearsome is the threat that they pose to Dasein. These are objects that Dasein knows as potentially harmful. Harmfulness is a form of *relevance* that discloses the objects to Dasein as things that are coming near to it or toward it from afar. The second category, "fearing itself," frees threatening objects so that Dasein can be *concerned* with them. Fear is not a reaction to a threat that we notice and then become afraid of. Rather, Dasein discovers the threat in its fearsome-ness. What is fearsome or threatening is first discovered in the *attunement* of fear. Thus, fearing and fearfulness are a "dormant possibility of attuned being-in-the-world."[21] The breadth of the connection between fear and the overall structure of *being-in-the-world* is again striking. It is justified here by the argument that ultimately it is fearfulness that enables objects like a fearful thing to draw near to us because fear has the character of something com-ing toward us. Essentially, it is therefore the *attunement* of fear that operates the mechanism of *de-distancing,* which enables Dasein to encounter inner-worldly beings in the first place. The third category of "about which" focuses the *attunement* of fear on *being* itself, because "the about which fear is afraid is the fearful being itself, Dasein."[22] Fearing reveals Dasein in its vulnerabil-ity. Dasein is an essentially fearful being. The target of the threat that elicits fear exposes the "*with-what*" that defines Dasein's *being-with*. Since Dasein *is*

---

19. Ibid., 136.
20. Ibid.
21. Ibid., 137.
22. Ibid.

through its *taking care* of its own *being*, fear exposes the universe of Dasein's *with-world* with which it always *is*. In other words, Dasein knows itself in the world as the being that it fears for. This structure accounts for how Dasein can be afraid for others even when they are not afraid for themselves. As Heidegger says, "Fearing for is a mode of co-*attunement* with others" which, even if one does not experience their actual fear, is always fear for oneself. This is because "what is feared here is the being-with the other who could be snatched away from us."[23] In the sense that the "who" of Dasein is its *they-self*, its fear for all Dasein is essentially fear for itself.

Heidegger concludes this discussion by laying out the varieties of fear that can give us as full a sense as possible of the range of fear as an *attunement*. For example, he mentions that "alarm" is fear of something that comes upon us as a surprise. When what surprises us is entirely foreign to us, we will experience fear of it in the *attunement* of "horror." When alarm and horror are combined, the encounter takes the form of "terror." Other forms of this *attunement* can include timidity, shyness, nervousness, and misgiving. The contribution that this spread makes to the unfolding of Heidegger's portrayal of *attunement* in general is perhaps not clear. But when considered in light of the general importance that Heidegger attaches to fear, we can perhaps understand the excess. Fear is so important that Heidegger simply wants to familiarize his readers with all its varieties and possibilities.

This brings us to the overall conclusion of the analysis which, again, in terms of the scope and scale of the meaning that Heidegger attaches to fear, is extraordinary. He writes,

> All the modifications of fear as possibilities of attunement point to the fact that Dasein as being-in-the-world is "fearful." This "fearfulness" must not be understood in the ontic sense of a factical, "isolated" tendency, but rather as the existential possibility of the essential attunement of Dasein in general, which is, of course, not the only one.[24]

---

23. Ibid.
24. Ibid., 138.

Though Heidegger does say here that fear is not the only *attunement* with broad significance for Dasein, fear is the only *attunement* to which Heidegger dedicates so much attention at this stage. Moreover, the *attunements* he will continue to devote special attention to – anxiety,[25] conscience,[26] and guilt[27] – are ones that we can easily recognize as closely related to fear. The clear election of these specific *attunements* as the ones that have the highest ontological value is loaded with significance for our analysis. It points to the ultimate "whither" of Dasein and focuses the analysis of Dasein on what is clearly regarded as the most essential object of *care*. It tells us that Dasein is ultimately oriented in the direction of its most authentic form of *being* when it experiences that *being* as a cause for fear and anxiety. It knows itself most authentically when an indescribable urge (that Heidegger later goes on to call *conscience*) drives it to overcome the inauthentic tendency to avoid and evade the fear and anxiety that it feels about the ultimate culmination of its *being* as a being, and instead to break out for authenticity.

Heidegger's election of fear for special treatment gives us our first premonition of the notion that the ultimate culmination of Dasein's *being* can become visible only in Dasein's attitude toward death. It gives us our first taste of the claim that facing the fear inspired by death is the only way Dasein can completely encounter its ownmost *being* and truthfully see the world. It gives us our first keyhole glimpse of the ontological meaning of death itself as a deceit to which – from the perspective of Segulah – Heidegger himself has fallen prey.

Understanding, Interpretation, and Discourse

Understanding is always *attuned*, and *attunement*, though it might suppress it, always has its *understanding*. As such, *attunement* and *understanding* are equiprimordial constitutions of Dasein's *being*.[28] Phenomenally, *understanding* and *interpretation* correspond to the structure of *throwness*. Since Dasein

---

25. See, for example, Heidegger, *BT*, 178–84.
26. Heidegger, *BT*, 260–69 and 277–88.
27. Ibid., 269–77.
28. Ibid., 138.

is essentially thrown into its *being* in the *there*, its most primordial experience of that *there* has a circular structure that we have already noted.

To see the ontological dimension of *understanding* and *interpretation* clearly, it is necessary to appreciate the specific role that each one plays in the circle. The starting point of the circle is *throwness*. *Throwness* describes Dasein's consciousness of its own *being-in-the-world* as *being-thrown-into-the-world*. *Understanding* describes the way in which Dasein projects its consciousness onto that world as it shows *concern* for its *being*. Thus, the mode of *understanding* basically retraces the experience of *throwness*. It projects back, as it were, to the "from where" Dasein is thrown. In this looking back, Dasein *understands* what its potentiality of *being* is in the context of what is *there*.

The question here is what is it that *understanding* deals with or is concerned about. To do this, it is necessary to distinguish ontological *understanding* from the regular ontic meaning of the verb "to understand." Understanding in its ontic sense is the mechanism that brings knowledge to the detached subject that previously did not understand or know something. Ontologically speaking, the hermeneutic mechanism of *understanding* is best captured by one particular use of the verb that specifically refers to the ability to handle or to be up to something.[29] Only, as Heidegger says, "as an existential, the thing we are able to do is not a what, but being as existing."[30] Authentic Dasein does not understand things about the world in the same way that the "I" does. Rather, we should say that one of the ways in which Dasein *is* involves intuitive *understanding*. *Understanding* is part of the infrastructure of *being*. The act of *being* a being that actively and consciously *is*, involves *understanding* the fullest possible range of its own potentialities for *being-with*. Those potentialities are disclosed to Dasein by its ability to see, i.e., *understand*, the *there*. To *understand* is therefore to make a potentiality of *being* (defined by the *there* or by world) visible or accessible to Dasein.[31] The range and scope of this potentiality, as we shall see, are ultimately determined in terms of time and not only of space.

---

29. Ibid., 139.

30. Ibid.

31. Heidegger's discussion of the ontological connection between visibility or sight and *understanding* appears in *BT* at the end of page 142.

Since, according to Heidegger, Dasein actively *is* all the possibilities and all the potentialities of its own *being*,

> Dasein is in the way that in each case it understands (or alternatively, has not understood) to be in this way or that. As this understanding, it knows what is going on, that is, what its potentiality of being is.[32]

Dasein discloses to itself what its *being* is about, in the context of the full range of potentialities and possibilities that it can project itself toward in the *there*. This *projection* is not to be confused with ontic understanding, because Dasein's *projections* onto the *there* are equiprimordial with its *being* as *thrown*. *Understanding* is related to the full range of Dasein's possibilities and potentialities of *being*, because

> as a potentiality of being, understanding has possibilities which are prefigured by the scope of what can be essentially disclosed to it.[33]

The essential meaning of *understanding* is therefore a mode of Dasein's *being* that is an integral part of *being-in-the-world*:

> The disclosedness of the there in understanding is itself a mode of the potentiality-of-being of Dasein. In the projectedness of its being…lies the disclosedness of being in general…. Beings which have the kind of being of the essential project of being-in-the-world have as the constituent of their being the understanding of being.[34]

Following upon *understanding, interpretation* comes to fill in or recover the distance traveled in the process of *projection. Interpretation* is the third leg – along with *throwness* and *projection* – that completes the circular ontological

---

32. Ibid., 140.
33. Ibid., 141.
34. Ibid., 143.

infrastructure of Dasein's access to the *there*. Heidegger says, "In interpretation understanding does not become something different, but rather itself."[35] It is the development of *understanding*. *Interpretation* basically corresponds to what we have described above as the journey back to the spot where the arrow lands. The circle therefore appears as follows: *Thrownness* accounts for Dasein's position in the *there* when it becomes concerned about its *being*. *Understanding* is the reversal of that *thrownness*, which is accomplished by projecting consciousness of the potentialities of *being* into the *there*; and *interpretation* is the culmination of that *understanding* in the arrival of Dasein back at the spot in the *there* where the *projected* arrow of intuitive *understanding* lands.

Heidegger's primary purpose in this section is to distinguish authentic from inauthentic modes of interpretation. This is essential to bringing the discussion of *attunement* and *understanding* back to the challenge of portraying everyday Dasein. Heidegger wants to "pursue the phenomenon of interpretation in the understanding of the world, that is, an inauthentic understanding in the mode of its genuineness."[36] The circular genesis of inauthenticity in authenticity is a structure with which we are already familiar. Here, it steers us toward noticing how *interpretation* discloses to Dasein what it has *always already* known, while inauthentic interpretation comes from the authentic *understanding* that Dasein has *always already* reached. In this way, the meaning or the significance of something that becomes disclosed to Dasein through *understanding* and *interpretation* can be hidden under a Structure of Concealment that Dasein uses to hide from itself. This, according to Heidegger, is the case in scientific cognition.

When a scientist singles out an innerworldly object for analysis, he first notices its existence. This noticing is the first moment of discovery. It is the *projection* of his consciousness onto an object in the *there*. When that takes place, what happens is that the ontological meaning of the innerworldly object is disclosed to Dasein in the full range of its possibilities of *Dasein-with*. The discovery does not determine "this" meaning or "that." What it determines is the very condition of the innerworldly object as intelligible for Dasein.

---

35. Ibid., 144.
36. Ibid.

Meaning, in its most primordial form, is therefore the *upon-which* Dasein's projected attention falls. It discloses the innerworldly object to Dasein as an "intelligible something."[37] Meaning is therefore not the result of interpretation in the everyday or epistemological sense. Rather, "insofar as understanding and interpretation constitute the existential constitution of the being of the there, meaning must be conceived as the formal, existential framework of disclosedness belonging to understanding."[38] What Heidegger means by "meaning" is therefore not a property of the objects discovered by Dasein but of Dasein itself. "Meaning is an existential of Dasein" because it refers to the disclosing of innerworldly objects with the *being* of Dasein that might then be "appropriated in an understanding" or "confined to incomprehensibility."[39]

The ontological equivalence of these authentic and inauthentic outcomes of *understanding* is what allows cognition to go astray. "Every interpretation, which is to contribute some understanding, must already have understood what is to be interpreted."[40] This contradicts the notion that "scientific proof must not already presuppose what its task is to found."[41] If this is the case, science has no choice but to conceal or to hide from the circular structure of comprehension that it is *always already* engaged in. The construction of the "I" that comes in a detached way to "knowing" allows Dasein to hide from itself and criticize the circular structure of its own mode of understanding. This critique, which is a trademark of the Enlightenment, is a structure that conceals ontological *understanding* under the rubble of scientific rationalism. The result is that *understanding* goes astray in scientific cognition because the understanding of *understanding* itself is misrepresented. In Heidegger's words,

> But to see a vitiosum in this circle and to look for ways to avoid it, even to "feel" that it is an inevitable imperfection is to misunderstand understanding from the ground up.[42]

---

37. Ibid., 147.
38. Ibid.
39. Ibid.
40. Ibid.
41. Ibid.
42. Ibid., 148.

Rather, for Heidegger,

> The fulfillment of the fundamental conditions of possible inter-
> pretations lies in not failing to recognize beforehand the essential
> conditions of the task. What is decisive is not getting out of the cir-
> cle, but to get into it in the right way. The circle of understanding
> is not a circle in which any random kind of knowledge operates,
> but it is rather the expression of the existential *fore-structure* of
> Dasein itself.[43]

All correct *understanding*, as we have frequently commented with reference
to Heidegger's methodology in *BT*, is therefore dependent on a grounded
representation of Dasein. Since we are all Dasein, only by understanding how
understanding (in its most primordial form) works can it be possible to say
anything that is truly grounded.

For Heidegger, language and *discourse* are also equiprimordial with
attunement and *understanding*. In his words, "Discourse is the articulation of
intelligibility."[44] Articulation always lies at the basis of *interpretation*, because
intelligibility is *always already* articulated. As such, the first moments of *understanding* are already in language in the same way that *understanding* is *always
already attuned*. There is no prior understanding that is then transposed into
words. Language itself is a *de-distancing* mechanism that discloses intelligibility to Dasein. Thus, Heidegger understands discourse as an "existential
constitution of Dasein."[45] The mode of Dasein that discourse constitutes is
its communicative structure, which Heidegger calls "being-with-one-another
understandingly."[46] In this structure something significant is always given
over or passed between. This is not necessarily what is said. It is perhaps better described as what is "shared" when Dasein experiences *attunement-with*
and *understanding-with* another.

---

43. Ibid.
44. Ibid., 155.
45. Ibid., 156.
46. Ibid.

Through the act of communication Dasein once again discloses itself as something that is *always already* "outside" or above. There is no prelinguistic inner stage of understanding that originates within and which is then dispatched off to the outside in words. Rather, like Wittgenstein, Heidegger insists that what is expressed verbally is public or shared even before it is said.[47] Dasein *understands* in a way that *always already* involves *projection-onto* that which is *always already* disclosed as *attuned discourse*. Consider, for example how someone in a sudden state of shock with no time to meditate or formulate thoughts calls out "Help!!!" This scream is effortlessly articulate because the initial or most primordial perception of the threat has already taken place in words. Similarly, listening is primordially integrated into the processes of *understanding* and intelligibility. As such, not hearing the words clearly when someone speaks can override our sense of having heard anything at all. As Heidegger says, "It requires a very artificial and complicated attitude in order to hear a pure noise…. Essentially understanding, Dasein is initially together-with what is understood."[48] Similarly, he observes that "it is not a matter of chance that, when we have not heard 'rightly,' we say that we have not 'understood.'"[49] Listening is tied to discourse and language, and as such it is a mode of *understanding* that indicates Dasein's "existential being-open as being-with for the other."[50]

Since *discourse* and communication are equiprimordial with Dasein's *being-in-the-world*, we can now add to our portrayal of *world* the idea that Dasein's *with-world* is populated by things that are intelligible in language to Dasein. In this sense, Heidegger's analysis of language, discourse, listening, keeping silent, reticence, and idle talk, all of which are modes of language and communication,

> has the sole function of pointing out the ontological "place" for
> this phenomenon in the constitution of being of Dasein and above

---

47. Wittgenstein's argument against private language appears in Ludwig Wittgenstein, *Philosophical Investigations*, trans. G. E. M. Anscombe (New York: Macmillan, 1953), 89e–100e, especially paragraphs 243 and 256 and onward.

48. Heidegger, *BT*, 156.

49. Ibid., 157.

50. Ibid., 158.

all of preparing the way for the following analysis, in which, taking as our guideline a fundamental kind of being belonging to discourse, in connection with other phenomena, we shall try to bring everydayness into view in a way that is ontologically more primordial.[51]

Killing Time

Heidegger's analysis of everyday Dasein culminates in the key insight that the essential *being* of everyday Dasein is *taking care*. What this means is that everyday Dasein's primary preoccupation is to *take care* of its own *being* by actively engaging in activities that keep it hidden away from itself. This condition of *being hidden away from* itself is what Heidegger calls *falling prey*. The "to whom" that everyday Dasein *falls prey* is the *they* while the "in-whom" or the "where" "in-which" every Dasein *falls prey* is the *there*.

Again, this condition of *falling prey* is not to be misconstrued as a lesser condition of *being*. Dasein does not drop into it from a higher state. Rather, this is Dasein's most natural initial state of *being*. In Heidegger's words, this is not Dasein's "nocturnal side, it constitutes all of its days in their everydayness."[52]

The mechanisms with which Dasein *falls prey* are all equiprimordial with the structure of *being-in-the-world*, and they include, *throwness*, *understanding*, *interpretation*, and *discourse*. Likewise, each of these originates equiprimordially with *attunements* that disclose to Dasein the authentic and inauthentic states of its *being* through moods and evasiveness. But in its *falling prey*, everyday Dasein specifically applies these primordial modes of its *being* to everyday activities that distract it and allow it to experience a kind of *being* that when viewed from a perspective of authenticity appears like reluctance to get out of bed. It is a kind of self-tranquilizing *non-being*. However, the analogy with staying in bed falls away as soon as one considers the actual character that this mode of *being* assumes. In place of docility, everyday Dasein remains "entangled" in the *they* and the *there*, by keeping itself "busy" and turbulent." Busyness and turbulence keep everyday Dasein in a state of

---

51. Ibid., 161.
52. Ibid., 172.

entanglement-in-the- world in which Dasein does not allow itself to disclose to itself the authentic condition of its *being-in-the-world*.

Dasein's *falling prey* to "world" is not an element that comprises a part of *being-in the-world* like *being-in*, *being-with*, and *Dasein-with*. Rather, Heidegger states that *falling prey* is a general mode or a general characteristic that describes the overall character of everyday *being-in the-world* as a phenomenon. It is the characteristic gesture or signature of everyday Dasein's way of *being*. It is how everyday Dasein goes about *being*. Everyday Dasein *is* in the world, in the mode of *falling prey* that is characterized by busyness and turbulence.

Heidegger describes three specific ways in which Dasein distracts itself. These are *idle talk*, *curiosity*, and *ambiguity*. Each of these is an activity in which Dasein can direct its *understanding*, *interpretation*, and *discourse* away from its own *being*. In Heidegger's words, "Idle talk, curiosity, and ambiguity characterize the way in which Dasein is its "there," the disclosedness of being-in-the-world, in an everyday way."[53] These activities constitute Dasein's everyday *being* and generate its *entanglement*. They generate for Dasein a positive mode of *non-being*, a kind of bliss of self-imposed ontological ignorance, "in which Dasein mostly maintains itself."[54]

Idle talk is a way for Dasein to keep company while using its engagement with that company as a means for maintaining its everyday *entanglement* in the mode of *falling prey*. The whole purpose of *idle talk* is busyness. *Idle talk* plants Dasein's *being* in the *there* and effectively allows it to *be* its *they-self*. In *idle talk*, what is said is less significant than the act of speaking. The busyness of *idle talk* may perhaps be compared to what Adorno and Horkheimer (in a passage already quoted in chapter 5 above) called "industrial society." In their critique of Kant's a priori structures of objectivity, they comment,

> The true nature of the schematism which externally coordinates the universal and the particular, the concept and the individual case, finally turns out, in current science, to be the interest of industrial society. Being is apprehended in terms of manipulation

---

53. Ibid., 169.
54. Ibid.

and administration.... The senses are determined by the conceptual apparatus in advance of perception; the citizen sees the world as made *a priori* of the stuff from which he himself constructs it."[55]

Through manipulation and administration, industrial societies construct a view of the world that they then believe is truthful. This view of the world becomes true, not because it has in some way been grounded or verified in inner or authentic experience, but because it has been constructed and disseminated around society in such a vivid way that it is now embraced as truth. For Kuhn and Latour this is also part of how scientific theories and truth claims gain credence. But it is also how rumors are taken seriously. It is how elaborate advertising campaigns convince us that we "need" Coca-Cola and nothing else when we have a formidable thirst to quench. It is also how elaborate mechanisms of propaganda convince us that we are under attack by an enemy who lives among us, an enemy who is not as he appears, an enemy who is in fact a rodent and not a human being. Even if there is no evidence to corroborate the claim, the self-generative power of the rumor itself is enough to substantiate it. It becomes so because everybody says so. The "everybody that says so" is what Heidegger refers to as the *non-being* of the *they-self*. It is this *non-being* that maintains its everydayness through *idle talk*. *Idle talk* is how everyday Dasein discloses itself in the *there* and keeps itself sufficiently busy to distract itself from the ennui that would necessarily set in were life any less turbulent. In Heidegger's words,

> Discourse, which belongs to the essential constitution of the being of Dasein, and also constitutes its disclosedness, has the possibility of becoming idle talk and as such of not really keeping being-in-the-world open in an articulated understanding but of closing it *off* and covering over innerworldly beings. To do this, one need not aim to deceive. Idle talk does not have the kind of being of *consciously passing off* something as something else. The fact that one has said something groundlessly and then passes it along in further

---

55. Horkheimer and Adorno, *Dialectic of Enlightenment*, 65.

retelling is sufficient to turn disclosing around into a closing off.…
Thus, by its very nature, idle talk is a closing off since it *omits*
going back to the foundation of what is being talked about.[56]

Like *idle talk*, *curiosity* is a mechanism that prevents everyday Dasein from
falling into a state of ennui. *Curiosity*, in the sense that Heidegger means here,
is not interest in the discovery of new truths. It is the incessant, turbulent and
busy quest for new distractions. This is the kind of curiosity that kills cats.

> When curiosity has become free, it takes care to see not in order to
> understand what it sees, that is, to come to a being toward it, but
> *only* in order to see. It seeks novelty only to leap from it again to
> another novelty. The care of seeing is not connected with compre-
> hending and knowingly being in the truth, but with possibilities of
> abandoning itself to the world. Thus curiosity is characterized by a
> specific *not-staying* with what is nearest. Consequently, it also does
> not seek the leisure of reflective staying, rather it seeks restlessness
> and excitement from continual novelty and changing encounters.
> In not-staying, curiosity makes sure of the constant possibility of
> distraction.

Idle talk is the mode of discourse that prevents *curiosity* from reaching a terminus. *Idle talk* keeps *curiosities* in circulation by spreading and repeating the
novelties that are incessantly talked about. It makes sure that there are always
new distractions to be discovered. *Idle talk* facilitates the recycling of old
curiosities by keeping them in play as they pass from person to person. What
was said about so-and-so last week remains interesting because this week the
same thing is said of someone else.

The danger of *idle talk* turning stale is fended off by *ambiguity*. When
everyday *being-with-one-another* generates a powerful *they-self*, the collective
groupthink makes every reaction of every so-called individual to every situation predictable and repetitive. This is threatening for everyday Dasein
because it is here that ennui might slip in and cause the distraction to lose its

---

56. Ibid., 163.

power. When everyone can guess what everyone else is going to say and think, a monotonous consensus or general agreement threatens *curiosity*'s capacity to prevent *idle talk* from running dry. If this happens, shared opinions and beliefs are in danger of being translated into deeds. Action of this sort is against the deepest interest of inauthentic Dasein. Dasein guards against this threat by ensuring that *ambiguity* and uncertainty close off the path to action and ensure a new cycle of *idle talk*. *Idle talk* then absorbs whatever course of action it is that has been proposed and introduces it back into the endlessly repetitive cycle of idle discussion. In Heidegger's words,

> Even supposing that what *they* guessed and felt should one day be actually translated into deeds, ambiguity has already seen to it that the interest for what has been realized will immediately die away. This interest persists only, after all, in a kind of curiosity and idle talk, only as long as there is a possibility of a non-committal just-guessing-with-someone.[57]

Were this non-committal guessing to dissipate, *idle talk* and *curiosity* would lose their power. Faced with the threat of losing power, Heidegger tells us that "they are quick to take their revenge."[58] Heidegger continues,

> In light of the actualization of what they guessed, idle talk is quick to maintain that they could have done that, too, for, after all, they had guessed it, too. In the end idle talk is indignant that what it guessed and constantly demanded now *actually* happens. After all, the opportunity to keep guessing is thus snatched away from it.[59]

Ultimately, the use of *understanding*, *interpretation*, and *discourse* in *idle talk*, *curiosity*, and *ambiguity* in the mode of *falling prey* is how everyday Dasein hides in society. These busy, turbulent social activities disclose for us the primary concern that everyday Dasein *takes care* of. This concern is its inability

---

57. Ibid., 167.
58. Ibid.
59. Ibid.

to face time. The fear of ennui is in fact the fear of facing the expenditure of time. For Heidegger, as we shall see, the devouring expenditure of time is the heart of *being*, and as such, the avoidance of temporality is the quintessential feature of inauthentic *being*. Everyday Dasein's mode of *taking care* of its own *being* is to fill its time with busyness and turbulence so that it can hide from the nagging awareness that its mode of spending time is in fact a distraction from everyday Dasein's need to waste or kill time.

Heidegger's fundamental distinction between everyday Dasein and authentic Dasein, as we will learn, is determined by the resolve that Dasein can muster to face the inevitability of its own demise. More specifically, Heidegger insists that a complete picture of *being* must include the full scope or the ultimate horizon of being's *being*. This is something that Heidegger finds in Dasein's capacity to confront its own future *non-being*. Heidegger refers to this as *being-toward-death*. Though authentic Dasein's capacity of *being-toward-death* will be the focus of our discussion in the next chapter, we mention it here in order to contextualize the conclusions that we can now draw from our discussion of Dasein's social spatiality. These conclusions concern the meaning of everyday Dasein's need to waste or kill time.

Caritas and Self-Sacrifice

Dasein's obsession with the finite limits of *being-in-time* is ultimately predicated on Dasein's experience of time as a limited resource. Due to the limit that death imposes on Dasein's supply of time, the essence of Dasein's *being* in both its forms is basically the same *concern* for its own *being* in mortal time. This is what Heidegger means when he says that the essential *being* of Dasein is *care* and that the essence of *being* is time.[60] As such, Dasein cannot imagine being generous with time. It is this selfishness with time that corners Dasein in egoism and forces it to choose between only two notions of temporality: *being-toward-death* and killing time. From Heidegger's perspective, the distinction between these is, of course, of crucial importance. However, from the perspective of Segulah, Heidegger's understanding of this distinction is

---

60. This is essentially the theme of *BT*, section I, chapter 6, which is entitled "Care as the Being of Dasein," 175–220.

flawed, since both authentic and inauthentic Dasein are tied to and limited by an erroneous association of time with death.

There are still preparatory arguments that need to be made before we begin to replace Dasein's angst about the expenditure of time with an alternative onto-theology. All the same, we can reflect on Dasein's belief that *idle talk, curiosity*, and *ambiguity* can help it evade death. While Dasein can of course show *concern* for others in the sense of its "existential being-open as being-with for the other,"[61] this is a condition of *being* which, as we have already seen, finds its source in Dasein's *concern* for itself. This ontological selfishness of *being* finds its ontic expression in the instrumentalization of "social life." Even when Dasein is engaged in acts of tremendous charity and kindness, the ontological social life of Dasein is always *entangled* in Dasein's inevitable instrumentalization of the others who are *always already* complicit in the construction of its *they-self*. Moreover, though Dasein is capable of fathoming for itself the value of charity and kindness, etc., the time "spent" on them is *always already attuned* in terms of angst, fear, and selfish guilt that must be overcome and suppressed. In this sense, in Western thought Caritas is inextricably and perhaps irredeemably tied to Self-Sacrifice.[62]

---

61. Heidegger, *BT*, 158.

62. The idea that the value of giving to others is connected to sacrifice is central to Western theology and is perhaps epitomized by the image of Christ dying on the cross for the sins of others. The extension of this image into the broader understanding of giving as sacrifice finds its philosophical grounding in Heidegger's analysis of Dasein's existential selfishness. See Christopher Elson and Garry Sherbert, "A Religion of the Event," in *In the Name of Friendship: Deguy, Derrida and Salut* (Leiden: Brill-Rudopi, 2017), 405–6.

CHAPTER 14

~

The Temporal Analysis of Dasein as Churban

Klippat Yavan and Self-Deception

In this chapter we shall discuss the sequence of *BT* that begins with the analysis of truth at the end of division 1 and culminates in Heidegger's climactic understanding of *resoluteness* in division 2. Reading this sequence, we shall reach the climax of our analysis of Churban and bring our linear reading of Heidegger's *BT* to a close.[1]

At the outset we introduced *BT* as a psycho-philosophical exploration of Dasein's capacity for self-deception. By underlining the significance of Greek thinking to Heidegger's philosophical system, we connected Heidegger's thought to the kabbalistic concept of Klippat Yavan (the Hellenistic shell) underlining the connection between the human experience of *being* that *BT* describes and the self-deceptive self-absorption that characterizes Klippat Yavan. Until now, the nature of this egoism has been demonstrated exclusively in terms of Dasein's spatiality. We have shown how Dasein's *concern* or *care* for its own *being* reflects an existential ontological crisis that pushes Dasein into hiding. It also presents in the form of self-absorbed *attunements* such as fear and angst. It is these that most starkly express everyday Dasein's sense of crisis about the inauthenticity of its identity in the *they-self* and the devouring spatiality of its own *being-there*.

Now that Dasein has been found and discussed in its place of hiding, what remains is to see how Heidegger proposes to remedy the situation. Conventionally, Heidegger's discussion of time in division 2 of *BT* is

---

1. We will deal only briefly with Heidegger's discussions of history and historical destiny that follow the analysis of resoluteness in the final sections of *BT* without offering a systematic or detailed reading of these chapters.

understood as a journey from inauthentic to authentic *being* that puts an end to Dasein's self-deception and pulls it out of hiding.[2] What we shall propose in our reading is an alternative understanding of authenticity, arguing that in both its authentic and inauthentic forms, Dasein is characterized primarily by its capacity for self-deception.

Heidegger's Kampf

Heidegger begins his portrayal of authentic Dasein with the idea that the path to authenticity is followed by removing the concealment that inauthentic Dasein imposes on time. As we have already seen, Heidegger writes in the introduction to *BT*,

> Time must be brought to light and genuinely grasped as the horizon of every understanding and interpretation of being. For this to become clear we need an *original explication of time as the horizon of the understanding of being, in terms of temporality as the being of Dasein which understands being.*[3]

In division 2 of *BT* Heidegger sets about this task of understanding time as the horizon of *being*. His portrayal of time as an aspect of Dasein's *being* comes to disabuse us of the notion that time is an endlessly flowing river – as eternal as the God who created it. Heidegger dismisses this idea of time as inauthentic to the structure of Dasein's *being-in-the-world*.

As we mentioned in our discussion of Steiner's monograph, what interests us here is how Heidegger's presentation of Dasein's temporality can be understood as a strategy for prizing Dasein's *being* from the clutches of an onto-theology that predicates human *being* on the immortality of God. In our reading of *BT*, the climax of authentic Dasein's *care* or *concern* for its own *being* is buried in the power it discovers to reject the plausibility of divine *being*. We shall argue that this answer is found not when Dasein faces the totality of its own *being* in its ownmost experience of death (as Heidegger himself claims). Rather, it is disclosed to Dasein in its ability to embrace the

---

2.   See, for example, Safranski, *Martin Heidegger,* 163–70.

3.   Heidegger, *BT,* 17; italics are in the original.

inevitability of its own death as a totality even when its most natural inclinations lead it to suspect that other possibilities exist. In this sense, as Safranski put it, Dasein fears life, not death.[4]

This reading of Heidegger is one that might be called a violent one, because it forces a worldview on Heidegger that does not take him at his own word. What we propose is that this is the only legitimate way to read him. This is justified by Heidegger's own admission that "the existential analytic constantly has the character of *doing violence*."[5] For Heidegger, violence and destruction are essential to the philosophical effort to wean human thought off its predilections with ordinary or everyday concealments. This is a claim that we have already encountered in our discussion of Heidegger's Kant lectures at Davos, where he sought to destroy Kant's "self-deceptive tradition of metaphysical rationalism." As Peter Gordon's writes,

> Accordingly, a suspicious and necessarily "violent" reinterpretation of Kant's philosophical legacy was crucial, although it was to be only one step in what Heidegger promised would be a wholesale "destruction" of the "former foundation of Western metaphysics."[6]

Moreover, our violent reading of authentic Dasein is supported by Heidegger's own feeling that he never really found the clearing that he sought. He was always "on the way" or "under-way"[7] and never really believed he had freed *being* from what Steiner called "the drive toward objective contemplation, logical analysis, scientific classification which ... presses on the Western intellect."[8] Ultimately, what this implies is that, since we are all Dasein, we must recognize that violently destroying Structures of Concealment is essential to all ontological analysis. So, methodologically speaking, Heidegger's *BT* is fair game.

---

4. Safranski, *Martin Heidegger*, 163: "Heidegger's analysis...expressly does not have fear of death as its subject. It would be more correct to say that its subject is fear of life."
5. Heidegger, *BT*, 298.
6. Gordon, *Continental Divide*, 132.
7. Steiner, *Martin Heidegger*, 80; Heidegger, *BT*, 414.
8. Steiner, *Martin Heidegger*, 79.

Our analysis of the self-deceptive inauthenticity of authentic Dasein will also allow us to explain authentic Dasein's attachment to power and historical destiny. According to our reading, authentic Dasein believes in power, fate, and historical destiny because it has found a way of seizing the foundational experience of *being* from the hands of an ontological aliveness that it suspects permeates all *being-in-the-world*. Authentic Dasein as we understand it is not the alternative to this point of view so much as it is its enemy. If we can show that Heidegger glimpsed this, then *BT* can be read as Dasein's struggles (Kampf) to assert the power of mortality over eternity, of death over life, and of humankind over God. These struggles are what ultimately make *BT* the philosophical parallel of Nazism's Kampf to incinerate the eternity of Jewish history in Auschwitz, Majdanek, Bergen-Belsen, and Buchenwald.

The Role of Truth in the Transition from Everyday to Authentic Dasein

We shall take up the line of argument from Heidegger's discussion of truth which appears in chapter 6, at the end of division 1 of *BT*.

Heidegger understands truth as the disclosedness (Aletheia) of Dasein. This disclosedness, like Dasein itself, has both an authentic and an inauthentic form. Because of these two forms, what he calls "the primordial phenomenon of truth" must be laid bare by placing the traditional or inauthentic understanding of truth in the context of its authentic ontological foundations. The traditional understanding to which Heidegger relates is the classical Greek definition of truth as an "agreement" between a proposition and its object. As an agreement, truth is essentially a relation between two things that might otherwise be seen to stand apart or separately from each other. The first something is the "proposition" that is generated by the intellect of a subject, while the second is the object that lies beyond the subject and agrees with it. While not all relations are equivalent, a relational definition of truth that is founded on agreement must assume that equivalence. Where it is absent one discovers untruth. In this sense, the statement that "the number 6 agrees with 16 minus 10" is truthful because "these numbers agree; they are equal with regard to the question of how much."[9] Were the statement to suggest that the number 6 agrees with 16 minus 9, applying the traditional understanding of untruth as a lack of agreement, we would be obliged to define the statement as false.

Heidegger brings the limitations of this definition into view by examining the ontological distinction between the *being* of a proposition and its object. From a phenomenological point of view, the intellect of the subject and an object in the world cannot be in total agreement unless the two are beings of the same order. Since a totality of agreement between these two cannot be assumed, Heidegger insists that understanding the nature of conventional truth requires us to consider the context in which the total equivalence between subject and object can be made possible.

To explain this a little more, we can draw a parallel with Heidegger's earlier portrayal of the relationship between the subject and the verb in the sentence "I am." Consider the "I" that is a presumed freestanding, detached subject (i.e., that in theory only enters *being* when it performs the action of the verb). As we have already seen, Heidegger insists that no theoretical detachment of the "I" from *being* exists and therefore characterizes the "I" as a pseudonym or inauthentic expression of Dasein's *they-self*. Similarly, he sees the free-hanging detached propositional truth statement that awaits confirmation as inauthentic. For example, he postulates,

> Let someone make the true statement with his back to the wall: "The picture on the wall is hanging crookedly." This statement demonstrates itself when the speaker turns around and perceives the picture hanging crookedly on the wall.[10]

Heidegger then asks the question "What is shown in this demonstration?"[11] What is in fact confirmed by looking at the picture, and how does this confirmation take place? In this example, the confirmation that seemingly takes place at the pole of the object (which in this case is a crookedly hanging

---

9.   Heidegger, *BT*, 207.

10. Ibid., 209.

11. Ibid.

picture) is an inauthentic expression of a relational agreement that *always already* exists between the intellect of Dasein and the object that its *being-with* is *always already* with when the propositional truth claim is articulated. What is confirmed is not exactly the agreement between the statement and the crooked picture, but "*that* this being *is* the very being that was meant in the statement."[12] Thus, conventional truth is an inauthentic expression of a condition of *being* whose authentic form is disclosed by the statement itself that *is,* because it possesses the character of what Heidegger calls "a *being-toward* the existent thing itself." In his words,

> Making statements is a being toward the existent thing itself. And what is demonstrated by perception? Nothing else than *that* this being *is* the very being that was meant in the statement. What comes to be demonstrated is that the expressive being toward that which has been spoken about is a pointing out of the being; *that* it is the being-revealing of the statement. What is to be confirmed is *that* it *discovers* the being toward which it is. What is demonstrated is the discovering-being of the statement.[13]

The *discovering-being* (or pointing capacity) of the statement is *always already* relational in that its *being* has the structure of Dasein. In substantiate our claim terms, we might say that the *discovering-being* is Dasein in the sense that discovering is a form of *being-with*. Thus, the statement has the capacity to point only because it has the structure of Dasein. This is the circular structure of *throwness* that must *always already be-with* something so that whatever the statement describes can *be* at all. In this sense, the *being* of the statement is *always already* true before it is confirmed. Since in its formulation it is *always already* an expression of its *being-toward* the extant object it described, its truthfulness is a quality of its *being*. Without this truthfulness, the statement could not *be* at all. The very *being* of the statement is therefore its truthfulness and its truthfulness is its *being*. The statement *is* as something true. Heidegger continues,

---

12. Ibid.
13. Ibid.

Here knowing remains related solely to the being itself in the act of demonstration. It is in this being that the confirmation takes place. The being that one has in mind shows itself *as* it is in itself, that is, it shows that *it*, in its self-sameness, is just as *it* is discovered or pointed out in the statement. Representations are not compared neither among themselves nor in *relation* to the real thing.... What is to be demonstrated is solely the being-discovered of the being itself, *that being* in the "How" of its discoveredness.[14]

Heidegger insists that his definition of truth is one that does not "shake off the tradition."[15] Rather, it allows us to see the tradition (i.e., that truth involves an agreement between the intellectual proposition and an object) as an "appropriation" of the primordial agreement between the *being-discovered* of *being* itself and the statement that, in the very nature of its *being* as *being-toward* the existent thing, points something out. In other words, the statement is an expression of the essence of Dasein's consciousness of *being* which Heidegger calls *care*. The circular structure of *care*, which is always "care about the disclosure of something to Dasein" and which is therefore always *ahead of itself* (or *always already being-in-the-world*) is the structure that allows Dasein to *be-together-with* innerworldly beings. It is this structure that allows the equiprimordial disclosure of Dasein's *being* with the *worldliness* of the *world* to generate the inauthentic notion of truth as "an objectively present relation between objectively present things." This occurs because "the disclosedness of Dasein becomes an objectively present property" (or "I") that can be either in agreement or in disagreement with "innerworldly things as objectively present."[16] The only meaningful way in which we can talk about authentic truth is therefore to see Dasein as self-disclosure or Aletheia. Dasein discloses itself and the world equiprimordially. In disclosing itself, it discloses the world in which it *always already is* truthfully.

This is the insight that leads Heidegger to say that Dasein *is* "in the truth." What he means by this is perhaps best summed up by the formulation

---

14. Ibid.
15. Ibid.
16. Ibid., 215–16.

that "Dasein essentially is its disclosedness, and, as disclosed, it discloses and discovers."[17] Thus, Dasein is truth because it discloses, and all truth is disclosure that takes place through Dasein. Truth is itself a testimonial to Dasein's being a conscious witness to the world as conscious *being-in-the-world*.

Eternity as the Temporal Locus of Eternal Truth

As we have already seen with *relevance* and *irrelevance* (as well as *usefulness* and *uselessness*, etc.), Heidegger's ontological understanding of truth is not limited to the conventional notion of agreement alone, since truth also discloses the ontological structure of untruth or disagreement. Heidegger insists here, as he has in similar cases elsewhere, that negative value judgments of untruth must be avoided, since being-in-untruth "constitutes an essential determination of being-in-the-world."[18] Put differently, since Dasein essentially *falls prey* to the world, its condition of untruth must be seen in accordance with its constitution of *being*, since "being closed off and covered over belong to the *facticity* of Dasein."[19] "Untruth" is therefore a form of Dasein's *being-in-truth* in which agreement and truth take the counter form of disagreement and untruth.

From the perspective of Segulah, Heidegger's unification of truth and untruth is crucial for two reasons. First, it identifies truth as having a locus in *being*. In Heidegger's words,

> The most primordial "truth" is the "locus" of the statement, and this primordial truth is the ontological condition of the possibility that statements can be true or false (discovering or covering over).[20]

Heidegger's identification of the locus of truth in *being* tells us that truth is uncovered or revealed in *being-in-the-world* and not deduced or proven by a detached intellect that peers into the world as if from the outside. This is helpful to us, because it exposes the flaw in Survival and System's reliance

17. Ibid., 212.
18. Ibid., 213.
19. Ibid.
20. Ibid., 217.

on and trust in verifiable truth as a humanist principle.[21] Second, removing the claim that truth depends on an agreement between a proposition and a reality expands the limits that confine the conventional idea of truth. It now becomes plausible to imagine an ontological truth that is not predicated on either the subject-object relationship or Dasein but on the possibility of an unlimited total unity of *being and non-being* that Jewish thought refers to as Havayah.

Truth and the Totality of Dasein in Time

But this is not Heidegger's position. For Heidegger, the totality of truth is the totality of Dasein in time. To understand this, we need to begin with Heidegger's conception of the future. For Heidegger, the totality of truth indeed includes those forms of untruth that are temporally untrue in the sense that they have *not yet* been discovered as true. In Heidegger's words,

> The fact that before Newton his laws were neither true nor false cannot mean that the beings which they point out in a discovering way did not previously exist. The laws became true through Newton, through them beings in themselves became accessible for Dasein. With the discoveredness of beings, they show themselves precisely as the beings that previously already were. To discover in this way is the kind of being of "truth."[22]

Because Heidegger insists that authenticity requires Dasein to grasp the truth as a totality that reaches into the future, the temporality of what Heidegger calls the *potentiality-of-being* or the *not-yet* of *being* must be made accessible. To see this more clearly, we need to pay closer attention to the temporal dimension of *projection*. Heidegger dedicates much of chapter 4 of the second division of *BT* to the elucidation of this point. Essentially, what he shows

---

21.   It is highly significant to our argument that this formulation of truth is in crisis in today's world. Subjectivism and relativism have resulted in its blurring, with profound and far-reaching social and political effects. When every individual has his or her own facts and fake news to believe, societies become divided in alarming ways and the type of social cohesion that Survival and System depends upon becomes hard to achieve.

22.   Heidegger, *BT*, 217.

there is that *projection* – which is composed of: *understanding, attunement, falling prey, interpretation,* and *discourse* – has a temporal dimension that is internal to the *being* of Dasein. Since, as we have already seen, each of these modes of *being* is an essential constituent of Dasein's spatiality which can only take place within the *being-with* or *being-in* of Dasein, their temporality can be measured only against what Heidegger refers to as Dasein's own *being-in-time.* Thus, for example, all *understanding,* which, when formulated primordially or existentially, refers to the disclosure of *world* to Dasein, has a temporal dimension. Adding this dimension to what we have already learned, *understanding* now means

> *to be projecting toward a potentiality-of-being for the sake of which Dasein always exists.* Understanding discloses one's own potentiality-of-being in such a way that Dasein always somehow knows understandingly what is going on with itself.... When one understands oneself projectively in an existential possibility, the future underlies this understanding, and it does so as a coming-toward-oneself from the actual possibility as which Dasein in each instance exists. The future makes ontologically possible a being that is in such a way that it exists understandingly in its potentiality-of-being.[23]

Heidegger insists that the *potentiality-of-being* that is disclosed to Dasein is not to be confused with an inkling of an objective future that takes place outside Dasein's *being-in-time.* Rather, it is a condition in which Dasein in its *being* is directed toward a future possibility of its own *being.* To know or to *understand* is therefore to move toward something that is *not-yet* known. When that *understanding* remains unrealized, what it *is,* is a potentiality of Dasein's *being-with* that is in Dasein's future. Similarly, *ignorance,* the opposite of *understanding,* represents a deficient form of this *projectedness.*[24] Either way, while Dasein engages in either *understanding* or *ignorance* it is "expecting to understand" or "anticipating an understanding" that belongs *in the present* to the potentialities of Dasein's own inner future. The internality of

---

23. Ibid., 321.
24. Ibid.

this future is perhaps best captured when we consider how this condition of expectation or *anticipation* is always *attuned* and, as such, is always an inner measure (like a mood) of what the disclosure of *world* to Dasein can tell us about how Dasein is "coming along" with its own *being*. The expectation, which is future oriented and *attuned*, is therefore part of Dasein's ownmost *being*. When *attuned understanding* is *anticipated*, its *being* is oriented toward a future that we can only know as a future of Dasein's *being* in which the *anticipated understanding* will either be accomplished or not. Dasein experiences this *anticipation* in time as something that it *makes present*. *Making present* is the temporal equivalent of *de-distancing*. *Making present* the potential to *be-with* an *understanding* allows Dasein to experience the potential disclosure of *world* as temporally *at hand*.

In order to *be* in truth, Dasein engages in the equiprimordial disclosure of itself and of the innerworldly objects *with-which* it *is* in time. But this disclosure does not open a door toward eternal time and unlimited possibility. On the contrary, *making present* expends time in the same way as *de-distancing* expends space. "Being" – which is a present continuous verb – expends time. The time that is expended when the *making present* of objects *at hand* takes place is the time that *being* takes to *be*. This idea is a temporal equivalent of our arrow shot in the dark. If we think of Dasein expending time finding its way back to the place where the arrow has taken time to land, we can perhaps see the temporal dimension of *understanding* more clearly. We may conceivably think of this as a vertical axis of time that accompanies the horizontal axis of distance in any measuring of speed (such as miles per hour or meters per second). In Heidegger's words, "in the literal sense, Dasein takes space in."[25] But, he continues, this taking in involves a "unit of temporality."[26]

Heidegger understands both truth and untruth as total, because the characteristic of *truthfulness* is descriptive of everything that *is*. But authenticity depends on the discovery of *projection* as a mode of Dasein's *being-in-the-truth* that is totality built into its temporal dimension. This can be discovered primordially only if the temporal constitution of Dasein is seen to belong to

---

25. Ibid., 350.
26. Ibid., 351.

its inner *being* alone. "It is," in Heidegger's words, "disclosive being toward its own potentiality-of-being."[27] He continues,

> Dasein *can*, as an understanding being, understand *itself* in terms of the "world" and others, or else in terms of its ownmost potentiality-of-being. This possibility means that Dasein discloses itself to itself in and as its ownmost potentiality-of-being. This *authentic* disclosedness shows the phenomenon of the most primordial truth in the mode of authenticity. The most primordial and authentic disclosedness in which Dasein can be as a potentiality-of-being is the *truth of existence*. Only in the context of an analysis of the authenticity of Dasein does it receive its existential ontological definiteness.[28]

The importance of this passage is in the connection that Heidegger makes here between time and authenticity. As we shall see, time, which is implicit in his references to potentiality, represents authentic *being* only when it can be seen to cover the full scale that begins when we begin to *be* and ends in totality which, for Heidegger is defined by the moment when we cease to *be*. The key to understanding the significance of this is the connection between the totality of *being* and what Heidegger considers the frontier of *non-being*. This totality suggests that time has a devouring quality which is like the devouring quality of Dasein's spatiality. This is what Heidegger refers to as Dasein's "spatio-temporality."[29] Since expending the time that it takes to *be* is existentially connected to the incoming of *non-being,* the totality of Dasein's *being* is something that is disclosed to Dasein by the *attunement* of anxiety. This is a highly significant feature of Heidegger's argument to which we will presently return. For now, however, our point is to underline the connection between Heidegger's notion of temporality and authentic truth.

The meaning of authentic truth is the total or full disclosure of Dasein in the fullness of Dasein's time. The meaning of totality or fullness here is

---

27. Ibid., 212.
28. Ibid., 212–13.
29. Ibid., 349.

not so much a culmination or climax of *being* as it is its completion. This is something that comes into view only when all the *being* that a being can *be* already *is* (or already *has been*). As a result, the full truth about Dasein's *being* is disclosed only when Dasein's *being* has run its full course into *non-being*. Since this *being is* in time, truth is fully disclosed only when Dasein's *being* stretches to the full extent of its time. Dasein's autobiography must have ceased to *be*, as the total tale of a being's *being*, for it to be authentically true. Otherwise, the full disclosure of Dasein's *being-in-time* will remain deficient. This is what Heidegger means when he says, "The most primordial and authentic disclosedness in which Dasein can be as a potentiality-of-being is the *truth of existence*." In other words, if authentic time is accessible only inside Dasein's ownmost experience of it, the totality of truth must be seen to run out at the frontier where Dasein's *being* encounters the fullness of its *potentiality-of-being* in time.

Our purpose in the remainder of this chapter is to demonstrate that this notion of temporality is fatally flawed (again, pun intended!). Heidegger's notion of authentic truth insists that *being* itself cannot transcend the frontier of *non-being*. This discounts not only the possibility of life after death (which Western civilization sees as a matter of faith) but also (counterintuitively) rejects the possibility of the *world's* continued existence after Dasein's death. This claim is organically connected to the idea that Dasein cannot *be* authentically in the *they*. But, as we shall see, this claim generates a serious philosophical challenge that Heidegger ultimately overcomes with self-deceit.

This is only an outline. Before we can turn to a further elucidation of its precise meaning we must first clarify the meaning of our suggestion that authentic Dasein is best apprehended as self-deception in the face of eternal time. In order to do this, we will begin with a description of authentic Dasein.

Wholeness and Singularity in Heidegger's Understanding of Authentic Dasein

At the outset of the second division of *BT* Heidegger states that the "totality of the structural whole" reveals itself as *care*.[30] Authentic *care* represents the totality of Dasein's *concern* for its own *being*. This, in Heidegger's view, is the

---

30. Ibid., 221.

key to unlocking the unity of all *being*, since "all *being* is disclosed through Dasein's *care* for its own *being*." He continues,

> We must see it with respect to the *unity* of the possible factors related to it. Only then can the question of the meaning of the unity that belongs to the totality of being of all beings be asked and answered with phenomenal certainty.[31]

What makes the totality of Dasein's *care* authentic is the fact that it is singularly concerned with Dasein as an individual self. This singularity untangles the individual self from the *they-self*. The more primordial and hence more authentic experience of self can be grasped only when the individual self of Dasein (which is lost in the *they*) is recovered. According to Heidegger's method, the recovery of Dasein's singular individuality and the totality of Dasein coincide in death. Death is the absolute frontier of Dasein's *being-in-the-world* (as opposed to *non-being*), and it is also the definitive event that Dasein experiences alone. Death is experienced authentically only when it happens to you. In Heidegger's words,

> With death, Dasein stands before itself in its *ownmost* potentiality-of-being. In this possibility, Dasein is concerned about its being-in-the-world absolutely.[32]

> Death is the *ownmost* possibility of Dasein. Being toward it discloses to Dasein its *ownmost* potentiality-of-being in which it is concerned about the being of Dasein absolutely.[33]

The idea that an authentic understanding of death refers to the death that happens to you, while central to Heidegger, also presents a significant philosophical problem. This problem concerns what Heidegger refers to as "the seeming impossibility of ontologically grasping and determining Dasein as a

---

31. Ibid., 222.
32. Ibid., 241.
33. Ibid., 252.

whole."[34] This impossibility, while not psychological, might be portrayed as the ontological dimension of what Heidegger describes as the psychological impossibility of imagining one's own death. According to Heidegger, people cannot imagine their own death because they cannot imagine themselves without a future. People live into their futures. As entities who perennially live with a sense of a future, it is impossible for us to project ourselves into a condition of *being* which none of our experiences of life have equipped us to envisage. Ontologically speaking, the problem of our inability to deny the possibility of a future and face death is caused by the very structure of *care*'s temporality. Since *care,* which has the structure of *throwness,* is always in *anticipation* outside or ahead of itself, the essential constitution of *being* as *care* requires us to think of Dasein as incomplete. In Heidegger's words, "This structural factor of care tells us unambiguously that something is always *outstanding* in Dasein which has not yet become "real" as a potentiality-of-being."[35] If this is so, then the totality of *being* as death cannot coincide with the essential structure of *being* as *care.* In other words, the singularity of my *care* for my own *being* (which always leaves something *outstanding*) cannot coincide with the totality of my own *being* after which there is only my *non-being.*

Before introducing his solution to this problem, Heidegger dedicates a significant passage to the challenge of discounting the "the death of others" as presenting the "possibility of grasping Dasein as a whole."[36] In this mysterious and surprising passage he delineates the boundary between *being-in-the-world* and the *being-there* of the deceased. Rather than insisting, as one might expect, that, after dying, the body of the deceased simply becomes an innerworldly object that is no longer Dasein, Heidegger feels compelled to somehow explain why the *being* that *is* beyond death cannot supply *care* with a locus in which wholeness and *being-ahead-of-itself* can coincide. What he in fact says here is that "the deceased himself is no longer factically 'there' [because] being-with always means being-with-one-another in the same world."[37] Therefore, even though the deceased might be said to have "aban-

---

34. Ibid., 227.
35. Ibid.
36. Ibid., 229.
37. Ibid., 231.

doned our 'world' and left it behind," it is only "*in terms of this world* that those remaining can still *be with him*."[38]

The shifty complexity of this formulation invites a "violent" reading that questions the integrity of Heidegger's decision to disqualify the death of others as the frontier between *being* and *non-being*. Heidegger seems to be contemplating and rejecting the plausibility of there being such an ontological category as *being-beyond-death*. This is not the only passage in *BT* in which Heidegger grapples with the possibility that there is *being* beyond death – and we will indeed return to this passage (along with some of the other similar ones) when we come to substantiate our claim that the idea of eternal time is known to authentic Dasein. All the same, for now we shall take what Heidegger says here at face value and accept his conclusion that "the going-out-of-the-world of *Dasein* must be distinguished from a going-out-of-the-world of what is only living."[39] While "what is only living" represents the Dasein of others, the going-out-of-the-world of *Dasein* "implies a mode of being in which each and every actual Dasein simply cannot be represented by someone else."[40] It is this that drives Heidegger to formulate *being-toward-death* as the category that allows for the singularity of Dasein and its totality to coexist. His solution to the problem of Dasein's future is to describe *being-toward-death* as a possibility of Dasein that can *be* in the mode of *not-yet*. In this, *being-toward-death* is distinguished from the actuality of a death. What remains is to explain why *being-toward-death* and not death itself represents the totality of Dasein's *being-in-the-world*.

Being-Toward-Death as the Totality of Dasein's Being-in-the-World

Death is the point at which Dasein admittedly comes to its end, but not in a way that captures the totality of Dasein's *being-in-time* any more than any other single moment or event in everyday life. The chronological positioning of death at the end of life is therefore not the characteristic of death that Heidegger associates with the wholeness of Dasein's *being*. This is the idea

---

38. Ibid.
39. Ibid., 232.
40. Ibid., 233.

that he captured in his infamous and somewhat macabre phrase "as soon as a human being comes into life, he is old enough to die."[41] Despite what sounds like insensitivity to the tragedy of infant mortality, Heidegger's main point is that *being-toward-death* is not especially connected to the phenomena that we conventionally associate with the end of life. It therefore does not imply a condition of *being* in which a person contemplates suicide or becomes bogged down in depression while preparing to leave the world.[42] It is an experience that is no more authentic for the fatally ill or the elderly than it is for a child who has just been born. *Being-toward-death* is not proximity to death. It is an ontological possibility of *being* that is present in Dasein's temporality all the time.

As we have already said, the phenomenology of Dasein's temporality refers to the constitution of *being* of Dasein from inside the temporality of every moment of Dasein's *being-in-time*. This temporality, which has the capacity of *making present*, has a structure that Heidegger refers to as *being-toward*. *Being-toward* is a temporal orientation that discloses to Dasein its ownmost experience of the potentialities of its *being*. Since death is a potentiality of Dasein's *being* that always lays ahead in time, Dasein experiences living as *being-toward* that potentiality. When the entire scope of Dasein's *being-in-time* from birth to death is considered, the totality of Dasein's *being* is something that Dasein can capture in every moment of life in the mode of *being-toward-death*. In terms of the entire span of Dasein's lifetime, *being-toward-death* represents the totality of Dasein's *being* all the time. On a micro-timescale, *being-toward-death* is the fundamental experience of Dasein's *being-inside* every moment *in-time*. This is because the very act of *being* is one of *making present* the dying of every moment. Dasein's experience of time is therefore its expending of time. *Making present* is an experience that places Dasein, at every moment, at its end. In Heidegger's words,

> Just as Dasein already *is* its not-yet as long as it is, it also *always already is* its end. The ending that we have in view when we speak

---

41. Ibid., 236.

42. Similarly, *being-toward* does not fall under the regular meaning of *care*, whereby one engages in the actualization of *useful* things by getting them ready or thinking about them in the sense of "dwelling upon" them. See Heidegger, *BT*, 250.

of death does not signify a being-at-an-end of Dasein, but rather a *being toward the end* of this being. Death is a way to be that Dasein takes over as soon as it is.[43]

The wholeness of Dasein and its singularity can coincide in this formulation because the wholeness of Dasein is the *making present* of death which in turn "is possible in Dasein itself in accordance with its structure of being.[44] Because of its temporal structure of *being-with* all innerworldly possibilities in time, its ownmost experience of time is one that Dasein encounters as a totality when it brings its *being* into focus all the time as something that runs out at the frontier of its *non-being*. "This is a possibility of *being* that Dasein always has to take upon itself."[45] Heidegger continues,

> With death, Dasein stands before itself in its *ownmost* poten-
> tiality-of-being. In this possibility, Dasein is concerned about
> its being-in-the-world absolutely. Its death is the possibility of
> no-longer-being-able-to-be-there. When Dasein is imminent to
> itself as this possibility, it is *completely*, thrown back upon its own-
> most potentiality-of-being. Thus, imminent to itself, all relations
> to other Dasein are dissolved in it.... Thus, death reveals itself as
> one's *ownmost, nonrelational,* and *insuperable possibility*.[46]

Given the perennial presence of death as the absolute frontier of being *with-which* Dasein *always already is* in its *being*, the authentic form of Dasein's *care* for its own *being* is always focused on that point of consciousness in which its *being* can discover its most complete form. This complete form is *being* at its highest pitch. It is absolute, complete, and insuperable. It is a mode of *being* that authentically delivers to Dasein's consciousness of *being* the fullness of that consciousness in the sense that it includes death.

---

43. Heidegger, *BT*, 250.
44. Ibid., 240.
45. Ibid., 241.
46. Ibid.

Inauthentic Dasein from a Temporal Perspective

In order to offer a complete existential portrayal of Dasein's temporal *being*, Heidegger must give an account of *being-toward-death* not only in its authentic, but also in its inauthentic, form.[47] He therefore presents a phenomenologically appropriate understanding of everyday Dasein's evasion of death. The mode of this evasion becomes accessible when we consider that Dasein's consciousness of *being-toward-death* is delivered through the *attunement* of absolute anxiety. Heidegger distinguishes this anxiety from regular or everyday fear. This is not anxiety about this thing or that. It is the absolute anxiety about *being* that expresses the most focused, complete form of Dasein's *care* about its own *being*:

> Anxiety in the face of death is anxiety "in the face of" the ownmost, non-relational, insuperable potentiality-of-being. What anxiety is about is being-in-the-world itself.... Anxiety about death must not be confused with a fear of one's own demise. It is not an arbitrary and chance "weak" mood of an individual, but, as a fundamental attunement of Dasein, it is the disclosedness of the fact that Dasein exists as thrown being-*toward*-its-end.[48]

From a perspective that is rooted in Heidegger's formulation of authentic *being-toward-death*, everyday Dasein's evasion of death can be disclosed to us ontologically as connected to Dasein's eminently understandable desire to evade this very unpleasant form of existential anxiety. As we saw when we discussed everyday Dasein's spatiality, this is accomplished through *busyness*, *idle talk*, and other such distractions that waste or conceal the passage of time. However, according to Heidegger, what uniquely characterizes Dasein's temporal evasion is its focus not on death itself but the evasion of death's certainty.

For authentic Dasein, *being-toward-death* is certain because that *being* "which is essentially and irreplaceably mine"[49] is both certain and indefi-

---

47. Ibid., 245.
48. Ibid.
49. Ibid., 243.

nite. What this means is that death is something that must happen to me, and which can happen to me at any time. It is therefore a potentiality of my ownmost *being* all the time. It permanently invades my experience of *being-in-time*. However, since everyday Dasein experiences its own *being* in the *they*, it can cover over the certainty of its own death by projecting its factual knowledge that death is a certainty onto what Heidegger calls the "empirical" meaning of certainty. For everyday Dasein, death is a certainty simply and only because all others experience it. Death is therefore something that I understand will happen to me in the same way as it happens to others. But, as Heidegger insists, this kind of certainty is deniable. For everyday Dasein, since this kind of certainty is applicable to me only in the context of my *they-self*, it is not experienced as an unconditional certainty about me. So long as death remains outside of my ownmost experience of *being*, the certainty of what others experience is diminished with regards to me.

If we restate this using the terms that we relied on in our discussion of spatiality, we can say that everyday Dasein faces death through its mode of *Dasein-with*, in the *they-self*. Dasein projects onto its own *being-toward-death* a presumed and inauthentic "being-toward-death" that is actually the "being-toward-death" that the Dasein of others projects onto me as an instrumentalized innerworldly object. The point here is that the moment that awaits us at the end of life (a moment that we know is there but care not to think of) is not the object of everyday Dasein's denial of death. To deny that we are all going to die would not be plausible enough a proposal. Inauthentic Dasein's power of self-deception would not be up to the task of selling such an easily refutable lie to itself. Rather, the object of denial is certainty about the individual *being* of the self. By projecting authentic *being-toward-death* onto the inauthentic being-toward-death of the *they*, Dasein can delude itself into thinking that the death of others, while no less final for them, is uncertain. Dasein deceives itself by allowing itself to construct for itself an imaginary sense of its ownmost *being* that is nothing more than an inner projection of the *they*. It is this "image" of *being* that can acknowledge the factual inevitability of death while at the same time covering over Dasein's ownmost certainty about its own future *non-being*. In Heidegger's words,

> Everyday taking care of things makes definite for itself the indef-
> initeness of certain death by interposing before it those manage-
> able urgencies and possibilities of the everyday matters nearest to
> us. But covering over this indefiniteness also covers over certainty.
> Thus, the ownmost character of the possibility of death gets cov-
> ered over.[50]

In sum, we can say that Dasein flees not only from its own death but from
the invasion of its very experience of time as dying. It does this by evading
both singularity and certainty. From Heidegger's perspective, if the totality
and the singularity of Dasein's *being* are to be reawakened, Dasein must be
summoned away from the *they-self* in which it hides.

The problem here is that people are not naturally predisposed to authentic singularity. In Heidegger's words,

> Factically, Dasein maintains itself initially and for the most part in
> an inauthentic being-toward-death.[51]

When left to its own devices, Dasein prefers the evasion of death's certainty
to anxiety. People prefer the kind of optimism that an inauthentic sense of
being-toward-death can supply. This preference is the first hurdle that any
effort to attain an authentic sense of *being* must overcome. Whether authenticity is more primordial or not, it seems more natural to almost all people
to delineate the boundaries of their individuality within the network of their
inextricable ties to the *they*.

In order to establish the priority of authentic *being* Heidegger must therefore do battle with Dasein's natural inclination, prizing it from the grip of its
attraction to everydayness. Though, as we shall see, this is primarily a philosophical problem for him, it is important to mention how Heidegger's philosophical battle discloses what the macrohistorical, social-political struggle of
National Socialism with the German public was ontologically about. Hitler's
social, political, military, economic, and educational efforts to reawaken

---

50. Ibid., 248.
51. Ibid., 249.

the authentic spirit in a depleted and deflated German public could read-ily be taken as a struggle against the dormant masses. If authenticity means full access to the power embedded in imminent metaphysical experience, National Socialism and its implementation of the notorious Fuhrer princi-ple can be described as a social-political effort to disseminate this power in mass production. Troubling as this principle undoubtedly is, its failure to transform the German public "from within" yielded a very special kind of inauthenticity that is no less disturbing. It is the ominous features of this inauthenticity that are captured in Arendt's infamous notion of "banal evil."[52] Banal evil is completely integral to the self-deceit that conceals "authentic Dasein's" underlying inauthenticity.

Eternal Time and the Potential Authenticity of the *They-Self*

To establish the priority of Dasein's authentic form, Heidegger must under-mine the plausibility of eternal time and the possibility that Dasein can expe-rience the fullness of its own *being* in the *they*. This is hard to do, because Dasein is naturally drawn to both. They pull Dasein in the direction of its more natural yearnings, i.e., not to be alone and not live in angst about the finality of death. Heidegger forces Dasein to charge against these yearnings with all the power it can muster. He insists that Dasein must struggle against its nature in order to break itself free for its ownmost state of singular *being-toward-death*. What we wish to argue is that the signs of this struggle give away our claim that "authentic" Dasein, like inauthentic Dasein, is charac-terized primarily by self-deception.

We can begin with the fact that Heidegger admits that the path Dasein must follow from its *they-self* to *being-a-self* is methodologically problematic. From a phenomenological point of view, Dasein's natural preference for its everyday form calls into question his most basic assumption that authentic Dasein is in fact the more primordial. The problem is not one that can be

---

52. This is of course a reference to the infamous subtitle of Hannah Arendt's book on the Eichmann trial held in Jerusalem in 1961. This term stands in stark and intriguing contrast to the notion of "radical evil" that she develops in her analysis of totalitarianism, but, interestingly, beyond the subtitle, the phrase does not appear elsewhere in the book itself. See Hannah Arendt, *Eichmann in Jerusalem: A Report on the Banality of Evil* (Penguin Classics, 1963).

seen from the outside, i.e., it is not concerned with whether the traits and characteristics of authentic Dasein appear to be more primordial. Rather, it is one that must be accessed from within the sequence of Heidegger's philosophical journey. The difficulty is inherent in the order in which Dasein naturally encounters its everyday and its authentic self. If Heidegger's methodology is rooted in the assumption that we are all Dasein, then as Dasein, it is problematic that we must discount the validity of our first and most natural experiences of *being* in our quest for authenticity. Given a starting point in inauthenticity, how can Dasein access the primordial experiences that draw authentic *being* out of hiding when these are the very experiences concealed by everyday *being*? Put slightly differently, if we assume that everyday Dasein can be viewed (authentically) only from a vantage point of authenticity, how can it first reach the point from which the analytic must begin? Considering this methodological problem, it becomes extremely difficult to ground the claim that authentic Dasein is in fact the more primordial form. This is the primary problem with which Heidegger is concerned in chapters 2 and 3 of the second division of *BT*.

For Heidegger, authenticity is a calling that summons Dasein back from its condition of being lost in its *they-self*. Death gives this calling its focus, because *anticipation* brings Dasein, "face to face with the possibility to be itself…in a passionate, anxious freedom toward death which is free of the illusions of the *they*, factical and certain of itself."[53]

What Heidegger essentially wants to show is that *being-toward-death* discloses to Dasein an *anticipatory* encounter with its authentic state of *being* in which it can be free toward death. This freedom does not involve gaining any relief from anxiety. Rather, it suggests an ability to use what is disclosed by that anxiety in order to encounter the authentic *being* of the self freely. Freedom in this context is the absolute individuality and singularity of the self that becomes uniquely and singularly responsible for its own path in time. This is its fate or its historical destiny. Dasein can truly embrace this destiny only when its potentiality for *being-a-self* catches up to the future and discloses itself to Dasein in its actual present *being*. This condition is what Heidegger calls "an existentiell," by which he means a state of ontological

---

53. Ibid., 255.

being in which ontological primordiality comes to the surface. In Heidegger's words,

> The existential project, in which anticipation has been delimited, has made visible the *ontological* possibility of an existentiell, authentic being-toward-death. But with this, the possibility then appears of an authentic potentiality-for-being-whole – *but only as an ontological possibility.…* We are looking for an authentic potentiality-of-being of Dasein that is attested by Dasein itself in its existentiell possibility.[54]

The precondition for the fulfillment of Dasein's historical destiny is its discovery of itself and its extraction of that self from the *they*. Since I myself am not for the most part the who of Dasein, rather the *they-self* is, the singularity of the self must be discovered from a starting point of everydayness. This presents a philosophical problem that Heidegger believed he could overcome, because "authentic being-a-self shows itself to be a modification of the They, which is to be defined existentially."[55]

Five Landmarks of Self-Deception in the Journey to Authenticity

The "violent" reading that we now wish to develop is based on the claim that the path to authenticity that Heidegger presents from this point onward is fraught with self-deception. In this sense, there is nothing "authentic" about authentic Dasein at all. In order to support this claim, we shall focus on five fundamental landmarks along Heidegger's route from everydayness to authenticity in these chapters, each of which bears the signs of an overt uphill struggle to overcome the problem that authenticity is not Dasein's most natural state. These are:

- The methodological irregularity of Heidegger's claim about the primordiality of choice
- The inescapability of conscience, guilt, and anxiety

---

54. Ibid., 255, 266.
55. Ibid., 257.

- The need for *resoluteness*
- The need for repeated methodological interrogation of Dasein's perennial relapses into inauthenticity
- The need to cover over the tracks of Dasein's suspicion that its authentic state is to be found in the *they*.

In our analysis, we shall home in on the philosophical problem that each of these is designed to tackle in order to understand how and why Heidegger uses each one in his attempt to resolve it. Our focus here will not simply be on understanding Heidegger's position but on discovering, in what he covers over, the foundations of an onto-theology in which eternal time is plausible and Dasein can experience the fullness of its own *being* in the *they*.

Heidegger's Methodological Irregularity

The first landmark in the path along which Heidegger tries to extricate the self from the *they* is his discussion of "choice."[56] In Western thought, "choice" is the pivotal characteristic of liberty and freedom. For Heidegger, choice is also connected to freedom but in a different way. Heidegger defines authentic freedom of choice as the freedom to choose death in the face of death.

Heidegger finds authenticity in the ability of the individual to embrace the historical destiny that one has chosen. Though arguably, inaction is also a choice, Heidegger insists that Dasein lapses into inauthenticity when it does not make the choice to *be* authentically. In this sense, everyday Dasein is no one because it has been lost and led on "without choice."[57] In order to bring itself back, "the bringing-back must have the kind of being *by the neglect of which* Dasein has lost its authenticity.... This must be accomplished by making up for not choosing."[58]

This is a crucial turning point in Heidegger's argument. While up until now every ontological possibility has been presented as equiprimordial with its deficient form, in this analysis, "choice" and "not choice" are presented as qualitatively different from one another. This attitude to choice recalls the

---

56. Ibid., 258.
57. Ibid.
58. Ibid.

adoration of decisionism that characterizes Schmitt's portrayal of sovereignty and which is characteristic of totalitarian regimes.[59] For Heidegger, to make a choice about authentic *being* is primordial; to make a choice about everydayness is not. Authenticity is self-propelled destiny and control. To choose to be in power over one's own *being* is to be authentic. To lose one's *being* in the *they* is not.

By drawing an ontological distinction between choice and neglect, Heidegger establishes the methodological baseline from which he can move forward from everydayness to authentic *being*. Since everydayness as a choice that has not been made is seen as a less primordial state of *being*, the potentiality of making an authentic choice is a possibility that always precedes Dasein's neglectful lapsing into its inauthentic state. Fundamentally, this is an assault on the right to claim that a "choice not made" is an equiprimordially authentic expression of Dasein's *being*.

This principle exposes how the very notion of sovereignty is oppressive. In order to surrender oneself to the concerns of others, it must be possible and reasonable not to make every choice. To live together in peace, people must be able to shun their obligation to choose and consider the act of not choosing a choice too. Heidegger's distinction between choice and neglect is a sign of his struggle against the equiprimordiality of acquiescence. The need to struggle against "neglect to choose" discloses Dasein's

---

59. Carl Schmitt, "The Führer Upholds the Law," in *Political Theology: Four Chapters on the Concept of Sovereignty*, trans. George Schwab (Chicago: University of Chicago Press, 2005), 35. See Karl Löwith, "Heidegger's Existentialism: Political Implications," http://www.lacan.com/symptom/?p=55. See also Avinoam Rosenak, Alick Isaacs, and Sharon Leshem-Zinger, "Human Rights: On the Political, the Dynamic, and the Doctrine of Unity of Opposites," in Hanoch Dagan, Shahar Lifshitz, and Yedidia Z. Stern, eds, *Religion and the Discourse of Human Rights* (Israel Democracy Institute, 2014), 19–20: "According to Löwith, there is a link between the notion of 'authenticity' expressed in Heidegger's 'resoluteness' and Schmitt's concept of 'decisiveness.' The sovereign must be one who knows how to decide. According to Heidegger, the sovereign's firm decision is not the product of rational deliberation; rather, it grows out of the unique moment, the here and now. That idea, Löwith says, is the basis for understanding what takes place when a judge issues a ruling. Judicial decisions are arbitrary; passing judgment is a constant function of human life; hence human life is arbitrary. The sovereign is called upon to exercise firm and arbitrary power. Indeed, anything less (even in liberal societies) is considered a shirking of the responsibility to govern."

natural propensity to defer its entitlement to choose and freely give itself over to the *they*.[60]

The inescapability of conscience, guilt, and anxiety

Continuing his assault on Dasein's nature, Heidegger insists that Dasein cannot remain indifferent to its neglect of choice. He insists that inauthentic Dasein finds no peace in its everydayness. By not making a choice, everyday Dasein has neglected its *being*, and for this it is plagued by the "voice of conscience."[61] This voice of conscience (which, when we speak of it here, must not be confused with an ethical voice of good or bad conscience) has a purely ontological purpose. It summons the self back from the *they-self*. "The call of conscience has the character of summoning Dasein to its ownmost potentiality of being-a-self by summoning it to its ownmost being-guilty."[62] In Heidegger's view, when the choice of *being-a-self* is neglected there is cause for ontological guilt.

However, and this is crucial, the call of conscience is not one that can alleviate the guilt that everyday Dasein experiences. Rather it allows it to experience that guilt authentically. The call of conscience is Dasein's call to its authentic *being-guilty*. It calls Dasein to understand itself as inescapably guilty which, in its calling, discloses itself *in-guilt* to Dasein. But this understanding is not understanding of any "particular" thing. It does not point at this or that about which a person feels guilt. "The call passes over all this and disperses it, so as to summon solely the self which is in no other way than being-in-the-world."[63] In this sense, the call is indefinite. It is a *potentiality-of-being* that discloses to Dasein that it is a self. "Conscience calls the self of Dasein forth from its lostness in the They…. The self summoned remains indifferent and empty in its what."[64] The summons is a call "to the ownmost

---

60. Heidegger is critical of this for his own reasons, but so are most liberal societies in which non-participation is seen as non-democratic behavior. This is an expression of the idea that everyday Dasein is not comfortable with neglecting to choose, as we shall see in Heidegger's discussion of conscience in *BT*, 258–259.

61. Heidegger, *BT*, 258.

62. Ibid., 259.

63. Ibid., 263.

64. Ibid., 264.

potentiality-of-being-a-self, it calls Dasein forth (ahead-of-itself) to its most unique possibilities."[65] In this call of Dasein to itself, "conscience reveals itself as the call of care."[66] As the essential mode of Dasein's *being*, Dasein's *concern* for itself is the source of its conscience. The substantive meaning of Dasein's guilt has no bearing on the *being* of any other being. Guilt, conscience, and *care* underline the quintessential and pure egoism of authentic Dasein's ultimate *concern* for the authenticity of its own *being*.

The authentic experience of guilt takes a form that Heidegger refers to as "wanting to have a conscience."[67] This twist against nature, in which Dasein must come to want something that is ultimately undesirable, is the second landmark along the path of our topology. To see the meaning of this, we need to understand that the call of conscience is not a call to correct anything. The conventional notion of having a bad conscience is one that leads Dasein to believe that it owes a debt that must somehow be repaid. This sense of debt and repayment covers over the primordial call of conscience and serves everyday Dasein's need to be well adjusted in the *they*. Hence, when conscience calls, everyday Dasein seeks to rectify its condition of *being* in the *they* by turning to courses of action that allow "human beings to say of themselves:

> "I am good." Who else can say this, and who would be less willing to affirm it, than one who is good? But from this impossible consequence of the idea of good conscience, that fact only becomes apparent that being-guilty is what conscience calls.[68]

For Heidegger, guilt is not a call that enables Dasein to act or to do something that will relieve its anxiety. As such, the authentic call to conscience is not one that people can be easily convinced to want (in the same way perhaps as one might be convinced to endure the sting of a syringe) in order to feel better. Rather, it calls Dasein to the very painful heart of its ownmost anxiety. This is the more primordial meaning of conscience for Heidegger, because if

---

65. Ibid., 263.
66. Ibid., 267.
67. Ibid., 276.
68. Ibid., 279.

it were otherwise, we would not be able to characterize "the good conscience" as anything other than "an experience of that call not turning up." The self's conclusion "that I have nothing to reproach myself"[69] does not represent an act of conscience. Or, in Heidegger's words, "Becoming certain of not having done something does not have the character of a phenomenon of conscience at all."[70] Thus, the actual message of the call of conscience must be heard underneath the level in which everyday Dasein acts in the *they*; it must be seen to summon Dasein to a *potentiality-of-being* that propels Dasein against its nature to face its "*ownmost* potentiality for becoming guilty."[71]

If the call of conscience is nothing other than a call to feel guilt, the state of *being* to which conscience calls is the state of *being-guilty*. Dasein must bring itself to embrace this guilt as the fulfillment of its potentiality for *being-guilty* and in this sense disclose what Heidegger calls "a willingness for conscience." As a result, we can see that

> being-guilty does not result from indebtedness, but rather the other way round: indebtedness is possible only on the basis of a primordial being guilty.[72]

If we can understand the summons of conscience itself as a mode of *being* of Dasein, then an existentiell experience of conscience and guilt are states of mind that must be experienced for the modes of *being* that they disclose to be realized. Without these experiences, Dasein's range of *being-with* remains incomplete. In its inauthentic form guilt is a kind of indebtedness. This sense of debt stimulates everyday Dasein to seek out why and how it must serve its *they-self* by placating its concerns about others. On the other hand, authentic *being-guilty* is an existentiell mode of *being* which "is understood only by existing in this possibility."[73] *Being-guilty* is the very purpose and meaning of guilt. The call of conscience is a call to feel guilty about the very fact that

---

69. Ibid.
70. Ibid.
71. Ibid., 275.
72. Ibid., 272.
73. Ibid., 283.

we *are*. From this Heidegger deduces that "wanting to have a conscience becomes a readiness for anxiety."[74] According to Heidegger, it is the ability to embrace the *attunement* of anxiety that leads Dasein on its journey toward authenticity. Thanks to its anxiety, Dasein begins to feel un-at-home in the world. This condition of *unheimlichkeit*, (usually translated as "uncanniness") leaves Dasein in a perpetual state of discomfort in the *they*. In Heidegger's words, "The call introduces the fact of constantly being-guilty and thus brings the self back from the loud idle chatter of the they's common sense."[75] Again, since the extraction of Dasein from the *they* is not one that relieves its anxious sense of not being at home in the world, pushing forward toward understanding the meaning of guilt and anxiety will bring no relief of any kind. This uphill struggle against Dasein's simple human desire to be fulfilled and "at-home" needs to be propelled on by a force that resists Dasein's natural yearning. This force is *resoluteness*.

The need for resoluteness

Resoluteness is the third landmark on Heidegger's uphill path away from everydayness and into authenticity. As he brings his analysis of *being-in-guilt* to a close, Heidegger writes,

> The disclosedness of Dasein in wanting-to-have-a-conscience is thus constituted in the attunement of anxiety, by understanding as projecting oneself upon one's ownmost being-guilty.... The eminent, authentic disclosedness attested in Dasein itself by its conscience – *the reticent projecting oneself upon one's ownmost being-guilty which is ready for* anxiety – we call *resoluteness*.[76]

Resoluteness is required because Dasein's experience of uncanniness in the *they* is hard to maintain. The forces that seek to dispel the *attunements* of anxiety and guilt need to be overwhelmed so that Dasein can hold itself in a state of authenticity. *Resoluteness* holds Dasein in the slipstream of its authentic

---

74. Ibid.
75. Ibid.
76. Ibid., 284.

potentiality-of-being, keeping it on course despite all the forces that suck it back into its *they-self*. Moreover, beyond its holding Dasein on the path to authenticity, examining what the capacity of Dasein to be *resolute* discloses to Dasein about its *being* emerges as the key to authenticity.

Before we consider how *resoluteness* must focus its resolve in order to unlock authenticity, we need to take a moment to underline just how significant it is to Heidegger that Dasein is capable of being *resolute* about its *being*. In a passage that follows his first mention of *resoluteness* and precedes his explication of its meaning, Heidegger reconstructs the entire analytic of Dasein, in order to demonstrate how *resoluteness* is the very foundation of the potentiality for authentic *being* on which the whole of *BT* basically rests.[77] Though the meaning of the term is not yet clear, we are told that *resoluteness* is the most primordial truth, simply because it is the meaning of authenticity. As we know, Dasein is in the truth in the sense that it discloses the primordial truth about *being*. Dasein and truth equiprimordially disclose the whole of *being-in-the-world*. Innerworldly beings are disclosed for Dasein as *at hand*, *relevant*, and *objectively present* by *care* and *significance*. *Significance* is disclosed by understanding the structure of *for-the-sake-of-which* to which discovering the totality of *relevance* goes back. Now, when we see Dasein as *thrown* into its *there* we can understand that Dasein is always factically dependent on "world" (by which we are referring of course to Dasein's *with-world*) in which Dasein becomes lost as its *they-self*. Finally,

> this lostness can be summoned by one's own Dasein; the summons can be understood as *resoluteness*.... As *authentic being a self, resoluteness* does not detach Dasein from its world, nor does it isolate it as a free floating ego.... *Resoluteness* brings the self right into its being together with things at hand actually taking care of them, and pushes it toward concerned being-with with the others.[78]

In other words, the entire disclosure of both inauthentic being in the *they* and authentic *being-a-self* depends upon *resoluteness*. It is *resoluteness* that

---

77. Ibid., 284–85.
78. Ibid., 285.

discloses Dasein's primordially authentic ownmost *potentiality-of-being* a *self*, and hence it is *resoluteness* that discloses to Dasein the entire structure of its *with-world* in both its authentic and inauthentic forms. One might say that since Heidegger, like us all, is Dasein, it is only on account of his discovery of *resoluteness* that the whole possibility of composing *BT* came into view. In this sense, *BT* is the autobiography of Heidegger's Dasein composed from the vantage point of *resoluteness*.

So what is the power of *resoluteness* that discloses all of this? Why is it the foundation of Dasein's authentic consciousness? In what sense does *resoluteness* allow Dasein to open its eyes and bare testimony to a world of *being* that must otherwise remain unexamined?

Heidegger's answer is protracted and circular. All the same, from the perspective of Segulah, it is the crucial climax of *BT*. *Resoluteness* is qualitatively different from the other conditions of *being* that we have encountered thus far, because in *resoluteness* the existential and the existentiell *being* of Dasein coincide. Put succinctly, *resoluteness* is authentic *being*. In its throwness, Dasein discovers that *resoluteness* can bring it back through time to the point from which its most authentic sense of *self* is/was thrown. Despite the circularity of this argument, Heidegger insists on its methodological validity, because "Dasein itself summons this possibility right out of the ground of its existence."[79] What this means is that *resoluteness* is the vehicle that brings the *projection* of Dasein's *being-toward-death* back to itself in Dasein. *Resoluteness* summons the self out of its lostness in the *they* but not by dangling an empty idea of existence before it. It realizes the call of conscience by *being* the practical expression of *being-toward-death*. In *resoluteness*, Dasein brings the possibility of total existence into facticity. *Resoluteness* is the missing piece that allows Dasein to be whole, because it realizes or fulfills the very potentiality of Dasein's *being* that lacks attestation.[80] As such, we might say that it brings Dasein's *being-toward-death* face-to-face with itself. In *resoluteness*, Dasein catches up with its *throwness* into death. How does this happen?

In order to bring Dasein face-to-face with the attestation of death, *resoluteness* needs to fill in the temporal gap that the structure of *being-toward*

---

79. Ibid., 297.
80. Ibid., 287.

leaves between *being-toward-death* and death itself. This is because the temporal structure of *anticipation* allows Dasein's *being-toward-death* to evade what Heidegger refers to as "the nearest nearness of death."[81] Insofar as death is a possibility of Dasein, its *anticipation* is only a way of approaching it. It is not an encounter with the thing itself. On the other hand, death itself does not give Dasein anything to be actualized, because it does not present Dasein with anything real that it could itself actually *be*. Coming to this nearest nearness of death is therefore an understanding of the whole potentiality of Dasein's *being* that is not the same as dying. Rather, it is captured by *anticipation* in a mode of *being* that Heidegger refers to as *anticipatory resoluteness*.

Anticipatory resoluteness is expressed in all the characteristics of authentic Dasein that we have seen thus far. It is why authentic Dasein *is* in time. It is why it wants to have a conscience. It is why authentic Dasein embraces the anxiety of *being-in-guilt*. It is the underlying primordial experience of *being* that is the true source of Dasein's anxiety. *Anticipatory resoluteness* has what Heidegger refers to as a "relentless severity with which Dasein is essentially individualized down to its ownmost potentiality-of-being."[82] This is because it completely drives the non-relational possibility of death into Dasein's conscience by boring into Dasein's consciousness a sense of guilt about its *being-toward-death*. In other words, because Dasein is *being*, the overwhelming extent to which that *being* is *toward-death* is experienced by Dasein as acquiescence to the inevitability of *non-being*. *Anticipation* forces authentic Dasein, whose *care* and *concern* are solely focused on *being*, to acquiesce to the inevitability of future *non-being* (or *being-toward-death*). This is something that pervades Dasein's sense of self and from which Dasein suffers. Immersion in the *anticipation* of *non-being* is a betrayal of Dasein's commitment to *being*. *Resoluteness* is required because Dasein cannot authentically evade this betrayal; it can only remain defiant as it gives itself over to it. Thus, *being* in its authentic form feels guilt, anxiety, and the call of conscience when it discloses to itself the fact that the wholeness of its *being is* and always *has been* oriented *toward* a betrayal of its ownmost *being* to *non-being*. In Heidegger's words,

---

81. Ibid., 251.
82. Ibid., 294.

The indefiniteness of death discloses itself primordially in anxiety. But this primordial anxiety strives to expect *resoluteness* of itself. It clears away every covering over of the fact that Dasein is itself left to itself. The nothingness before which anxiety brings us reveals the nullity that determines Dasein in its *ground*, which itself is throwness into death.[83]

The power of *anticipatory resoluteness* is that its very *resoluteness* (i.e., its resolute ability to remain resolute when facing its ownmost *throwness* into death) is what attests to the fact that Dasein has the power to negate itself. Dasein discovers in *anticipatory resoluteness* its power to act, as it were, within the sphere that is controlled by *non-being*. (Heidegger is reluctant to use the word "act" because it might be misleading since it refers here solely to the "act" of existing.)[84] It discovers that it can take hold of its *being* in the sphere of death (which one might think of as a kind of ontological killing, suicide, dying, destroying, and annihilating) in that it can *be* right into death. It is *resoluteness* itself that gives it this power. *Resoluteness* gives Dasein the strength to "break the news" to itself that *non-being* awaits it in time all the time. This is what Heidegger means when he says that *resoluteness* gives Dasein transparent access to the nature of its own *being*. In Heidegger's words,

> Anticipation is not some kind of free-floating behavior but must rather be conceived of as the possibility of the authenticity of that *resoluteness* existentielly attested to in such *resoluteness* – a possibility concealed and thus also attested. Authentic thinking about death is, wanting to have a conscience, which has become existentially transparent to itself.[85]

In *being-toward-death* Dasein must embrace its conscience about its *being* which knows it has betrayed and been betrayed. In every moment in which Dasein *makes present* its death in time, Dasein knows that it has *always already*

---

83. Ibid., 295.
84. Ibid., 287.
85. Ibid., 295–96.

surrendered to death's capacity to take back its *being* from it. Only in a free act of resolve that resolutely holds Dasein to the truth of that, can Dasein freely take itself back or freely betray its *being* by being free for death.

> The holding-for-true that belongs to *resoluteness* tends, in accordance with its meaning, toward constantly keeping oneself free, that is, to keep itself free for the *whole* potentiality-of-being of Dasein.... In its death, Dasein must absolutely take itself back. Constantly certain of this, that is, *anticipating*, *resoluteness* gains its authentic and whole certainty.[86]

It is this certainty in the face of Dasein's innermost betrayal of its own *being* that ultimately enables Dasein to affirm the fullest meaning of its *being-a-whole* in the face of death. This is the exact opposite of everyday Dasein's denial of death. It does not suggest any pretensions about overcoming death or steering consciousness away from the fear of death. Deep inside the anxiety of the betrayal, living in a call of conscience about the betrayal, Dasein resolutely *is* in anticipation of death and, as such, becomes completely free for death. It takes control of its *being* in death. Dasein most wholly and singularly exists "in the understanding that follows the call of conscience and that frees for death the possibility of *gaining power over* the *existence* of Dasein and of fundamentally dispersing every fugitive self-covering over."[87] In the fullest sense, authentic Dasein is the total surrender of all the power of *being* and existence to death. *Being*, when faced resolutely, can be discovered as existing inside the realm of *non-being*. It is this discovery that discloses to Dasein the ultimate meaning of the human power to both kill and self-destruct.

From the perspective of Segulah, Dasein's ability to embrace its ownmost betrayal of *being* to *non-being* is the greatest self-deception of which human beings are capable. To perform this act of self-deception, Dasein must struggle to completely isolate itself from the *they*. It must recruit extraordinary powers of resolve in order to hold itself lined up for the experience of being deceived by that same resolve. In this deception, Dasein actively believes that

---

86. Ibid., 295.
87. Ibid., 296.

its illusory power to dominate its ownmost alive *being* by *making present* its *throwness into death* – an illusion that is seemingly confirmed by the human power to kill and destroy life on one's own – is an ultimate resource for its struggle for power in life. By dispersing the indebtedness generated by the call of conscience to *be* – by embracing guilt and anxiety and by resolutely facing the nearest nearness of death – Dasein silences the life that courses through its *being* and defiantly betrays its very *being*. It does this because it can, but not necessarily because it has no choice. *Resoluteness* gives Dasein the power to condense time into the supremely egotistical time of its own *with-world* alone. It is in this time and this time alone that it can persuade itself to imagine its own death as the end of *being-in-the-world*. Thus, Dasein in an extreme act of resolute egoism gives over the power and the essence of its *being-in-the-they* to the absolute wholeness and self-absorbed singularity of its own death. It finds the ultimate source of the world's *being* inside itself and remains steadfast in this conviction through its own efforts to focus its consciousness of *being* on the definitive moment of *being* that is wholly its own.

It is here, at this point, where so much force must be used to hold Dasein firm in its resolve to *be into death,* that Heidegger discloses the human possibility of Auschwitz and the point of Churban. This analytic of Dasein tells us, from the inside, what Nazism felt like for Dasein. Nazism was an expression of the manipulative dominance of the "lost" by the "resolute." The *resoluteness* of the Führer and those who followed dangled the self-deception of authenticity and fear of inauthenticity before the eyes of the lost, forcing upon them the deceit that they can face death by embracing their innate guilt and anxiety. This deceit and the flooding awareness of death's power to extinguish life, drowns out the inner call of conscience that whispers into their hearts confirming their suspicion that the life of the *they* to which they are drawn is enduring. This drowning out of Dasein's natural attraction to the *they* in its willingness to betray life in favor of self – to give itself over to the totality of its own mortal *being* – is the meaning of Churban. The self-destructiveness implied by this willingness to give over the totality of *being* to my own death spurs even everyday Dasein to seek the rush of *resoluteness* in compliance with a plot to annihilate *eternal being* from humanity. From within, the possibility of *resolute* self-deceit silences the whisper of Dasein's being transcended by *concern* for the *they* that echoes inside the self-conscious *being* of Dasein.

From without, as Dasein seeks to implement its politics of Churban in the world, Dasein applies the brute power of its *resoluteness* to the task of eradicating the people whose sense of self is defined by their enduring collective *being* in the *they*. Dasein must kill them all to justify its self-deceitful "choice" and prove them wrong.

The need for repeated methodological interrogation of Dasein's perennial relapses into inauthenticity

Heidegger's discussion of *resoluteness* is interrupted in full swing by a methodological reflection. In this section he basically deals with what he calls "the methodological character of the existential analytic in general."[88] In essence, the problem that Heidegger is worried about is the discrepancy between the presumed power of *anticipatory resoluteness* and Dasein's own tendency to relapse into the *they*. These relapses, which for Heidegger are frustrating if not infuriating, disclose a tendency of Dasein's which seems to call into question the validity of the claim that choice, guilt, willingness for conscience, anxiety, freedom for death, and finally *anticipatory resoluteness* of death can bring Dasein back to its ownmost authentic state of *care* for its ownmost mortal *being* alone. Heidegger is forced to admit that the instability or inconstancy of Dasein's grip on authentic *being* truly is a problem for which he has no definitive answer. There seems to be an elastic cord that pulls Dasein back into its everydayness that he cannot sever. Dasein is attracted by a gravitational force that is no less strong than *anticipatory resoluteness*'s power to pull itself away.

Heidegger's method is grounded, as is to be expected, in the fundamental temporality of life that always moves toward death. Since, intuitively speaking, death cancels *being*, it is only natural that *being* itself will resist by fleeing into everydayness. Since anxiety and guilt are unpleasant, it is only natural that *being* will seek to avoid them by *falling prey* to *idle talk* and *busyness*. But, since *being* is always already thrown toward death, its avoidance cannot express the nature of *being* authentically.

If we look closely at these arguments, there is little here that Heidegger has not already said. As such, their repetition reveals a degree of insecurity

---

88. Ibid., 297–302.

that is uncommon to the style and tone of *BT*. So, what is interesting about this section is not really the arguments themselves but what this insecurity can tell us. More specifically (though Heidegger does seem to conclude at the end of this section that he has managed to ground his method to his own satisfaction), there are glimpses of self-doubt here that he does not conceal. For example, he writes,

> But does not a definite ontic interpretation of authentic existence, a factical ideal of Dasein, underlie our ontological interpretation of the existence of Dasein? Indeed. But not only is this fact one that must not be denied and that we are forced to concede, it must be understood in its *positive necessity*, in terms of the thematic object of our inquiry. Philosophy will never seek to deny its "presuppositions," but neither may it merely admit them. It conceives them and develops with more and more penetration both the presuppositions themselves and that for which they are presuppositions. This is the function that the methodological considerations now demanded of us have.[89]

This passage essentially lays open both the ultimate strength and the Achilles heel of Heidegger's ontology. This passage basically protests any attempt to evaluate the truth or untruth of his philosophy in epistemological terms. The circularity of Heidegger's method is obviously a problem for any conventional philosopher. This is his Achilles' heel, and Heidegger admits it. But it is laid out in the open here because he believes that, on a fundamental level, this is not really a problem. This is because in his mind, circularity gives credence to any experience of *being* that, through proactive thinking, Dasein can be brought into. Forced thought is disclosure or Aletheia which means that it is also authentically true even if in conventional terms it is not. If one can think oneself into a state of authenticity, even if this is a task that requires enormous resolve, the discovery of what that resolve can disclose is the disclosure of that resolve's authenticity. In Heidegger's words, "Every ontologically explicit questioning about the being of Dasein has already had the way prepared for it

---

89. Ibid., 297.

by the kind of being of Dasein."[90] In other words, if one can discover a power of self-convincing that is strong enough to authentically deceive the self, the mere ability to deceive demonstrates that self-deception is a mode of thinking about *being* that is authentic to the structure of Dasein. Heidegger then asks, "How are we to find out what constitutes the 'authentic' existence of Dasein?" His answer is simple, and it has two conditions. First, self-convincing and self-deception must enter Dasein's existentiell (or actual present) experience of its own *being*, and second, it must bring that *being* face-to-face with death. If it fulfills both, it can claim authenticity. Heidegger's brutal honesty about his method in this passage is a primary source for our claim that in *BT* both inauthentic and authentic Dasein are characterized by self-deception.

A second methodological interrogation concerns *resoluteness* itself. Since *resolute* self-deception is the core of what Heidegger means by authenticity, he wants to show that it is a natural human possibility that is neither mysterious nor unfamiliar. It is composed of *willfulness, egoism,* and *self-deception*. It is a function of the mind that we saw above as System 2's (or the rider's) capacity to take over our consciousness when it intends to. Though it is not a rational force per se, authentic Dasein manipulates the association that many of us make between rational scrutiny and verifiable truth to convince us that we act rationally when we succumb to self-deception. It is the formidable force within us that can *make true* anything that the self can be convinced into accepting. At the same time, in the same way as the rider covers over the elephant's tracks, authentic Dasein covers over the tracks of its self-deception. It overwhelms intuition by using such willful tools as intimidation, persistence, cumulative evidence, priming, and selectivity in order to manipulate and convince. At its core, it works through *resoluteness* and violence and Heidegger openly admits it.

> Thus, the *kind* of being of Dasein *requires* of an ontological interpretation that has set as its goal the primordiality of the phenomenal demonstration *that it overcome the being of this being in spite*

---

90. Ibid., 298.

of this being's own tendency to cover things over. Thus, the existential analytic constantly has the character of *doing violence.*[91]

This violence is directed against everyday Dasein. But more challenging for Heidegger from a methodological point of view is the recognition that this is also an assault on the essence of Dasein itself:

> The path of the analytic of Dasein which we have traversed so far has led us to a concrete demonstration of the thesis only suggested at the beginning: *The being that we ourselves in each instance are is ontologically farthest from us.* The reason for this lies in care itself. Entangled being together with those things in the "world" that are taken care of guides the everyday interpretation of Dasein and covers over ontically the authentic being of Dasein, thus denying the appropriate basis for an ontology oriented toward this being.* Thus, the primordial phenomenal parameters of this being are not at all self-evident, even if ontology initially follows the course of the everyday interpretation of Dasein. Rather, freeing the primordial being of Dasein must be wrested from Dasein by moving in the *opposite direction* from the entangled, ontic, and ontological tendency of interpretation.[92]

Care, which is the essence of Dasein's *being,* is entangled. Therefore, Heidegger must use violence to wrest Dasein from its gravitational attraction to entanglement. To do so, the analytic must struggle against Dasein's own way of thinking about its own *being.* Though, as we have said, Heidegger shows that Dasein can do this "authentically," since the reason for the difficulty in the first place emanates from the structure of *care* itself, he remains troubled. The confessional aspect of this passage is underlined by a note that corresponds to the asterisk in the text above. This note is a comment that Heidegger wrote in his own hand in the margins of his copy of *BT,*

---

91. Ibid., 298.
92. Ibid., 297–98.

Wrong! As if ontology could be taken from genuinely ontic investigation. For what is a genuinely ontic account if it is not genuinely
taken from a pre-ontological project.[93]

The struggle of authentic Dasein therefore faces a formidable enemy when it
must confront *care's* natural way of *being*.

Not only the demonstration of the most elemental structures of
being-in-the-world ... but above all the analysis of care, death,
conscience, and guilt show *how,* in Dasein itself , the common-
sense way of taking care has taken over the potentiality-of-being of
Dasein and of its disclosure, which amounts to its closure.[94]

This *potentiality-of-being*, which is ultimately *care's* entanglement in everydayness, has the power to take over. Though Heidegger has demonstrated
how, through violence of thought, Dasein attains the power to break free, he
is never fully satisfied that the ontological possibilities that he demonstrates
both existentially and existentielly are in fact "necessary and binding,"[95]

The need to cover over the tracks of Dasein's suspicion that its authentic state is to be found in the they

The fifth and final landmark along Heidegger's route from everydayness to
authenticity once again bares signs of his overt uphill struggle. This struggle
is attested to by acts of concealment which repeatedly close off a path that
Heidegger seems to know is there. The characteristic of this path is that it
leads toward the possibility of Dasein's attaining an authentic state of *being-
beyond-death* which it can know only by remaining absorbed in its *they-self.*
Heidegger's suspicions about this possibility are only implicit in his argument. He is never particularly troubled by them because the tools of willful
choice, ontological egoism and self-deception seem to him to be more than

---

93. Ibid.
94. Ibid.
95. Heidegger asks, "Is this possibility an arbitrary one?" and again in a note comments,
    "Probably not; but "not arbitrary" does not yet mean "necessary and binding." See *BT,*
    299.

equal to the task of 'reasonably' (and authentically) discounting them to his own satisfaction. All the same, the signs of the struggle are there. For example, Heidegger suggests that the temporality of Dasein "is the meaning of being of care…regardless of whether this being occurs "in time" or not."[96] Similarly, he speaks of Dasein as a spiritual being that transcends the limits of its corporeality. In his words,

> The spatiality of Dasein [may not be] interpreted as a kind of imperfection that adheres to existence on account of the fatal connection of the spirit with a body. Rather because Dasein is spiritual *and only because it is spiritual,* can it be spatial in a way that essentially remains impossible for an extended corporeal thing.[97]

While the direct purpose of this observation is to give an account of the possibility that spiritual being can take place within the confines of authentic Dasein's phenomenology, this passage serves a more fundamental purpose. Heidegger defines Dasein as spiritual in order to tie spirituality itself to Dasein's ownmost self-absorbed mode of *being.* By doing this, he ties spirituality to the certainty of Dasein's ownmost *being-toward-death* and covers over the association of spirituality with *being-beyond-death.* By doing this, he actively blocks a path that might lead from Dasein's propensity for extension beyond its corporeal limits to a kind of transcendental absorption of *being* in the *they.* Essentially our point is that what Heidegger is doing here is to deliberately not follow a path that he all the same suspects is there. The path he rejects is one that allows us to uncover an authentic notion of temporality that does not end in death. This is the onto-theological temporality in which time is eternal. The significance of the challenge that this poses to Heidegger is perhaps best observed if we return to his discussion of the "death of others" already mentioned above.

As we have already seen, Heidegger includes in his analysis of *being-toward-death* a highly significant discussion in which he disqualifies "the death

---

96. Heidegger, *BT,* 349.
97. Ibid., 350.

of others" as presenting the "possibility of grasping Dasein as a whole."[98] In this mysterious and surprising passage he introduces a unique category that does not return elsewhere in *BT* which he terms "the *being-there* of the deceased".[99] Again, as we already stated above, what is important about the *being-there* of the deceased is that it is very obviously not the same kind of *being* as the *being-there* of an innerworldly object. It is true that neither one represents a totality of Dasein. Similarly, neither one undermines the necessity of *being-toward-death* as the source of that totality. All the same, the careful distinction that Heidegger draws between the *being-there* of an innerworldly object and the *being-there* of the deceased suggests that he is in fact troubled by what everyday Dasein's attitude to the death of others might mean.

According to Heidegger, the *being-there* of an innerworldly object which is *at hand* for Dasein does not represent a totality of *being* because the time that Dasein expends *being-with* it does not bring Dasein face to face with the limit of its own *being-in-time*. On the other hand, the *being-there* of the deceased does not represent for Heidegger a totality of Dasein's *being* because "being-with always means being-with-one-another in the same world."[100] The significance of this distinction is that, in order to hold it up, Heidegger must go to the trouble of narrowing down or constraining the meaning of totality. He does this by confining the category of *being-in-the-world* to include only those modes of *being* that can be defined "in terms of this world" alone.[101] This active constraint reveals the possibility of a kind of *being* beyond *non-being* which Heidegger is intent on rejecting.

It is important at this point to clarify that what matters here is not the question of whether Heidegger believed in an afterlife. It is not the possibility of this belief that singles out the death of others as a challenge to his equation of *being-toward-death* with the totality of Dasein's *being*. Rather, what Heidegger must dispel is the suspicion that everyday Dasein, in the context of its *they-self*, can experience the death of another as an authentic face to face encounter with the nearest nearness of *non-being*. If Dasein's awareness

---

98. Ibid., 229.

99. Ibid.

100. Ibid., 231.

101. Ibid.

of its own *being* is essentially *care*; and if *care* is essentially entangled in the *they*, then it follows that Dasein might experience a death 'in the family of *being*' in which its *they-self* is entangled, as an authentic encounter with its ownmost *non-being*. This experience, which would be beyond the reach of an isolated 'authentic' self-absorbed, singular Dasein, suggests that it is possible for Dasein to face death and survive. If this is so, then it follows that mourning is more than just a yearning for another *being* who is no longer nearby. (Anyone who has genuinely mourned the loss of a loved one knows that it is much more powerful than that). Mourning is *care* about the diminution of *being* itself. It is the ontological *attunement* that discloses the possibility of facing death without betraying *being*. *Care* about the death of others discloses to Dasein the authentic nature of its entanglement in its *they-self* by sensitizing it to the meaning of life and its loss. Thus, Dasein mourns because it is existentially and empathetically implicated by the death of another. *Being* itself mourns because it has suffered a 'loss in the family' of its *being-with*.

Ultimately, the path that Heidegger's analytic seeks to conceal is one that can enable Dasein to trace the ontological source of mourning to the point in which it discovers authentic *being* in the *they*. At this point, Dasein may reach the conclusion that after its own death, 'the family' of beings in which its *being* is entangled will both mourn and continue to *be*. If death is a death in the family of its *being*, Dasein can know from its ownmost experience of mourning that after its death, the *they* in which it was always inextricably entangled will survive. Such a notion completely undermines Heidegger's understanding of authenticity and as such he cannot allow for it. To cover over this path Heidegger tellingly does not simply discount the possibility that the deceased who has "abandoned our 'world' and left it behind" is still a kind of *being* that has the same structure as *being-in-the-world*. Rather he insists that "We do not experience the dying of others in a genuine sense; we are at best always just nearby."[102] He writes,

> Even if it were possible and feasible to clarify "psychologically" the dying of others in this being nearby, this would by no

---

102. Ibid., 230.

means let us grasp the way of being we have in mind, namely coming-to-an-end.[103]

Why can we not experience the death of others as more than just being nearby? Contrary to the human experience of bereavement, Heidegger simply insists that this is so because the death of another is not my own. This argument — which can only claim to be authentic by relying on Dasein's capacity for *resolute* self-absorption and self-deceit — does nothing to dispel the authenticity with which the *they-self* mourns the death of another as a loss of *being* in its *with-world*. It is only because of Heidegger's violent association of ontological self-absorption with authenticity that he can confine his interest in death to the kind of death which is essentially singular.

Though Heidegger believed otherwise, this is a state of mind so unnatural to Dasein that it cannot be maintained over time. Indeed, one must go to extreme ends in order to disseminate it. How might this be done? Perhaps, if mass murder were made so ubiquitous that the *they-self* is led to indifference about the *being* of others. Maybe then ordinary people might become sufficiently self-absorbed by angst and fear that they may attain and hold on to an "authentic state of guilt-ridden anxious being" at least for a while. The total political dominance that would be required for the implementation of this scheme, though it would be a hard thing to sustain over time, would once and for all prove how the incredible powers of ego, resolve, and self-deception are equal to the task of erasing the image of God from humanity.

As such, our fifth landmark, which uncovers once again the ontological heart of Nazism, discloses how Heidegger conceals the possibility that my *being* may transcend death by *being-in-the-they*. In this act of concealment, the *resolute* audacity of authentic Dasein looks God in the face and declares war against the eternity of time that His *being* represents. Dasein's notion of self-redemptive authenticity emerges into view as the psycho-philosophical underpinning of Nazi politics. The ultimate project of this politics was the Churban of the divine spark of eternal life in humanity. The Jews of Europe faced a machine that was intent upon the destruction of eternal life itself. Our enduring mourning for their deaths insists that we turn away from a

---

103. Ibid.

civilization that idealizes the rights and morals of the atomic individual and follow Dasein's natural attraction to its *they-self* to a place where it can discover that its ownmost *being* is only a true self when that self is tied inextricably to the *being* of others and not by an extremely violable social contract.

Heidegger follows human anxiety, guilt, resoluteness, and the immense power of self-deceit to the conclusion that authenticity is grounded in death. His sneaking doubts about the egoism of authenticity led Heidegger to misunderstand the meaning of conscience and to read it as a signpost that summons us nowhere other than death itself. Here in this place, in the depths of the dark, the meaning of Churban can come more fully into view.

The Meaning of Churban

Churban is the power of self-absorption and self-deception to convince us that the climax of *being* is death and self-destruction. The power of self-destruction is not only suicidal; it is murderous, since destroying others is one way to dismantle one's entanglement in the *they*. Acts of destruction are singular in that they require no partners and no accomplices. Human beings can kill on their own. They kill when they believe they are not being watched. Genocide, murder, war, death, suicide and destruction are the fullest ownmost expressions of the power over life that an individual can wield in his or her solitude. This power is intoxicating. It frees the individual from dependence and expresses most fully the desire of the inner ego to *be* in the fullest sense of its ownmost *being*. It *is*, in the sense that it is the epicenter of its own universe of consciousness. Thus, it becomes an independent, free-standing, outstanding, self-serving, self-aggrandizing, self-worshipping, self-sacrificing and self-sufficient *being*. Though it brings destruction and chaos into the world, in this state, Dasein believes it is redeemed. It believes it has extracted itself from an exilic existence and that it has stood itself up on its own two feet to face anything and everything that the world can throw at it.

But, despite the colossal power it wields and the catastrophic destruction that it causes, free-standing and authentic Dasein is in fact pathetic. Ironically, it knows that it can only *be*, when it is *with* the very *with-world* that its *being* consumes. Overwhelmed by anxiety and conscience, Dasein deceives itself into accepting that the kernel of its *with-world* is its *being-with* itself alone. The meaning of Churban is both the destruction that authentic

Dasein causes and the self-destruction that it brings upon itself when its inner destructiveness is made known. By coming out of its hiding place or Galut, Dasein makes itself vulnerable to Churban. After 1945, even the most carefully concealed lair in which Dasein operates under layers of unstable altruistic virtues such as liberty, free choice, free market, truth and social justice can no longer conceal from view the existential self-deceiving, egotistical self-absorption that lurks within.

All these traits attest to the mechanism, which Heidegger calls "fate" that enables and indeed requires Dasein to acknowledge its need to *be* in community. The tone, the passion, and the power of *BT* are not maintained in the books' final sections in which Heidegger discusses fate, destiny, and history. In the closing chapters, the extreme individuation of Dasein comes circling back to an all-important though anti-climactic conclusion. "Only authentic temporality, which is at the same time finite makes possible something like fate, that is to say, authentic historicality."[104] The individual finite experience of Dasein can poison collectivism because even authentic Dasein can embrace fate, destiny, and history and be authentic within a collective that assists the apprehension of or *care* for its ownmost *being*. This is how Heidegger describes this collective expression of utter individuality,

> Dasein is not just an isolated unit; its ontological structure includes a with-being with others. Hence the coming-to-pass, structured by historicity, is achieved with other There-beings, all of which constitute a community or people.[105]

Safranski comments, "In actual fact Heidegger's authentic Being-with-one-another is not co-extensive with the concept of community. For surely, the concept of community includes the individual's wish to rid himself of his burdens of distance, his loneliness, his individuality."[106] In Steiner's words, "an exceedingly important political consequence" follows this principle. It suggests that Heidegger believed it to be the destiny of the German people to

---

104. See Steiner, *Martin Heidegger,* 112.

105. Ibid.

106. Safranski, *Martin Heidegger,* 168.

attain this form of non-communitarian authentic collective *being* in history by designing the political regime in which the utter individuality of authentic Dasein is the experience of the collective. In Heidegger's words,

> The historical There-being cannot achieve its own individual authenticity apart from the community. The heritage which There-being assumes in authenticity, then, is not simply its individual history but somehow the heritage of the entire people *with* which it *is*."[107]

Steiner concludes, "To accept one's Dasein in the full sense is to …accept actively one's individual finitude and the need to choose among finite options, but options that involve the community and the individual's afterlife in the destiny of the group."[108] Heidegger remains torn and tempted by the afterlife and the possibility of authenticity in the *they*. History as destiny requires the advent of an authentic collective in which even the concern for others is usurped and absorbed in the total finiteness of the self.

Here we bring our reading of *BT* to a close. We have offered an analysis that we believe adds greatly to our ability to understand the psychological and philosophical depths of National Socialism and the human possibility of the Holocaust. Moreover, we have gained fresh insight into the bearing of these on Western civilization in general which, one way or another, is steeped in the discourse of the self as "I" that Heidegger lays bare in *BT*. What we wish to show in the final section of this book is that Heidegger's portrayal of the inner self, the collective, space, time, life and death is the precise 'mirror' opposite of the structure of the self and its relationship to collective *being* modeled by the concept of Segulah. The next and final section of our discussion will try to move from Churban to Tikkun by inverting the ontological landscape that Heidegger paints in *BT* in order to retrieve the onto-theological system of the Torah that post-Enlightenment humanism has submerged underwater.

---

107. Steiner, *Martin Heidegger*, 113.
108. Ibid.

PART IV

TIKKUN

CHAPTER 15

~

Negating Heidegger from the Perspective of Segulah

The Onto-theology of Inner Torah

We have now reached the stage of Rehabilitation, to which the remaining chapters of this book will be dedicated. What we will attempt to show in these chapters is that some of the more abstract or mystical concepts of the Jewish tradition (which we shall call "inner Torah")[1] can be understood more

---

1. The totality of Heidegger's argument in *BT* leads us toward what might be considered the "danger" of proposing a "theory of everything" here that somehow covers all of Judaism and applies to every Jewish text or idea. This of course is not possible, since many of the texts that we shall be discussing in this section do not agree with each other. The honest way to proceed is to acknowledge that this tendency is indeed true of both Heidegger and many of the texts we will be reviewing in this section. The way forward is to suggest that we shall focus our comparisons on this "theory of everything-ness" itself. Pointing out this quality is one way of explaining how the specific texts discussed in the following chapters were chosen. In this sense, for example, Hasidic exegesis operates on the assumption that the Torah as seen in Hasidic commentaries is "a theory of everything" in the spirit of the famous rabbinic statement by Ben Bag in the Mishnah: "Turn it over and over, for everything is therein" (*Avot* 5:22). While it might also be appropriate to admit that we are implicated in this tendency ourselves, it is nonetheless reasonable to say that the Jewish texts we have chosen to analyze in the following chapters are compatible with Heidegger precisely because they claim to speak for Judaism in the same way that Heidegger claimed to speak for the entire Western philosophical tradition. The key difference is that he achieved this through hermeneutic violence, while the Jewish sources adopt a much more attentive and deferential attitude toward the canonical texts whose authority they revere.

    In practice, the texts that we have chosen and which display this tendency are connected to the modern mystical or kabbalistic revival that is found, for example, among the disciples of the Gaon of Vilna, the Hasidic masters, and the writings of Rabbi Kook. Due to the complexity of the relations between these different traditions,

tangibly when we consider them in phenomenological/ontological rather than ontic terms.[2] We wish to suggest that seeing the referents of inner Torah in a more concrete way is essential to their plausibility, and as such is a key element of the shift from Survival and System to Segulah.[3]

In many ways, the idea that the language of inner Torah must be seen in ontological rather than epistemological terms echoes the opening premise of *BT*. However, unlike Heidegger's claims about philosophy, we do not mean to suggest that the dimension of *being* or Havayah had ever been forgotten in Jewish thought. It would be more accurate to say that access to this domain of Torah was consciously restricted. For example, the masters of the kabbalah feared that if the inner Torah was studied without the necessary preparation, the unusual language that it uses would seem nonsensical and thus be subject to ridicule. Worse still, they feared that the metaphysical and seemingly fantastical terms used in kabbalistic texts would be taken at face value and that this would lead to fundamental misunderstandings and abuses.[4] As a result,

---

it is difficult to group them together under a single generic term. For our purposes, we have adopted the Hasidic term "inner Torah," which is used by many, including Rabbi Kook. What unites them for our purposes (despite the many differences between them) is the way in which they refer to faith in God using onto-theological language.

2. We shall suggest that this distinction is very helpful in trying to understand the relationship between literalist and inner approaches to the exegesis of the Torah. We shall argue that the layering of these two hermeneutic dimensions is compatible with Heidegger's presentation of authentic Dasein's deliberate hiding, which he holds responsible for generating everyday Dasein's experience of *being-in-the-world*. We shall discuss this below in our references to the difference between *peshat* (literal reading of the Torah) and *sod* (mystical reading of the Torah), which we will understand in Heideggerian terms as a distinction between ontic and ontological forms of *care* for *being*.

3. Rabbi Kook refers to the ontological or onto-theological dimension of his writing, which we have included in the concept of inner Torah, as the "Torah of the land of Israel." We shall return to discuss this term in more detail in the conclusion. For now, it is important to mention this as it underlines the connection between the ontological copula that we are establishing between Heidegger's analytic of Dasein and the inner Torah on the one hand and the Holocaust and the return of Jews to the land of Israel on the other. Thus, the inner dimension is connected to the social and political implications of the paradigm shift from Survival and System to Segulah.

4. The most famous source for this injunction appears in the masterful halachic work of Maimonides, the *Mishneh Torah* (*Hilchot Yesodei HaTorah* 4:13). Maimonides discusses the four chapters in the Bible that provide the mystical foundation of the Torah calling these, after the Rabbis, the *pardes*, a word that literally means a fruit orchard but which

these teachings were taught only to a select few, and even they were considered worthy of initiation only after long years of Bible and Talmud study.[5]

Significantly (and not uncontroversially), modern Jewish history has brought about a striking departure from this norm. The Hasidic movement, for example, played an important role in the popularization of kabbalistic psycho-philosophical ideas. The founder of Hasidism, Rabbi Israel Ba'al Shem Tov[6] and his disciples regarded kabbalah as crucial to basic spiritual development, and as a result, kabbalistic ideas were introduced into popular Hasidic teachings and commentaries. Similarly, a number of twentieth-century kabbalistic masters – one notable example being Rabbi Yehuda Ashlag – composed modern commentaries on classic works which for the first time made this literature far more accessible to uninitiated readers.[7] Largely due to

---

the Rabbis constructed as an acronym for the four key hermeneutical dimensions of the Torah. The Rabbis of the Talmud warn against entering the *pardes* without the proper preparation, and in Maimonides' words, "Even though they [the Rabbis of the Talmud who entered the *pardes*] were great men of Israel, not all of them had the potential to know and understand all these matters fully. I therefore maintain that it is not fitting for a person to enter in the *pardes* unless he has filled his belly with bread and meat. Bread and meat refer to the knowledge of what is permitted and what is forbidden and the like concerning the observance of the mitzvot."

5. In Jeremiah (3:14) God says, "I will take you one of a city two of a family." This biblical image, which describes the redemption as something that will happen only to a small number, was understood by kabbalists to refer to the small elite capable of achieving redemption through the study of mysticism. As such, metaphorically speaking, only one person in each city and two people from each extended family were deemed suitable to study the kabbalistic dimension of inner Torah.

6. Israel Ben Eliezer, or the Ba'al Shem Tov (1698– or 1700–1760), was the founder of the Hasidic movement. He has been the subject of many well-known books and studies. For a popular collection of tales and stories organized according to the chronology of the Ba'al Shem Tov's life span, see Yitzchak Buxbaum, *The Light and the Fire of the Baal Shem Tov* (Bloomsbury, 2006). For a more critical historical study, see Moshe Rosman, *Founder of Hasidism: A Quest for the Historical Ba'al Shem Tov*, Littman Library of Jewish Civilization (2013).

7. Rabbi Yehuda Ashlag (1885–1954) was one of the greatest kabbalists of the twentieth century. He is most notable for his extensive commentaries on the *Zohar* known as *HaSulam* (the ladder), which made the reading of the *Zohar* much more accessible to a public that extended beyond those who were specifically chosen as initiates by the teachers. For an extensive analysis of the *HaSulam* commentary in English, see Michael Laitman, *The Zohar: Annotations to the Ashlag Commentary* (Laitman Kabbalah Publishers, 2007).

the impact of Gershom Scholem, the academic study of kabbalah has grown into a large and popular field and is now taught to complete novices in "101" courses all around the world.[8]

Arguably, Scholem's agenda was closely connected to both the trauma of the Holocaust and his understanding of Zionism.[9] Likewise Rabbi Kook, though he was perhaps more cautious than others, certainly saw the carefully gradated introduction of kabbalah into the curriculum of Torah study as vital to the reawakening of the collective consciousness that he believed the national revival and return to the land of Israel required.[10] Something similar may be said about Buber's enthusiasm for the community structures of the Hasidic courts, which he saw as a harbinger of the unique brand of spiritual collectivism that he hoped the new Jewish nationalism would realize.[11]

---

8. Gershom Scholem is broadly considered the father of the modern academic study of kabbalah. His influence and impact remain central to the field, which in many ways is still dominated by the wide range of reactions to and refinements of his foundational theses published in his broad and varied oeuvre of scholarship. For a general introduction to Scholem's life and work, see David Biale, *Gershom Scholem: Master of the Kabbalah* (Yale University Press, 2018).

9. See Biale, *Gershom Scholem,* chapter 7, 130–55.

10. Rabbi Kook outlines the essential components of Jewish contemplative study in the introduction to his work, *Musar Avicha.* He lists five essentials, the last of which is contemplating the great truth of the kabbalah which, in his words is, "an essential reality." See Rabbi Kook, "A Sort of Introduction to the Moral Principle," in *Musar Avicha and Middot Raayah,* Mossad HaRav Kook, Jerusalem (1985) 13–14 [Hebrew]. See also the letters in which Rabbi Kook argued that the study of the Kabbalah should be part of the yeshiva curriculum, for example, *Iggerot ha-Raayah,* vol. 1, Letter 43. As Jonathan Garb shows, he also saw the dissemination of the Kabalah as a necessity mandated by the onset of the messianic era, the primary expression of which was the return of the Jewish people to the land of Israel. See Jonathan Garb, *The Chosen Will Become Herds: Studies in Twentieth-Century Kabalah* (Yale University Press, 2009), 23–29. Moreover, according to Joel Bakst, the revelation of Kabala was key to the Gaon of Vilna's understanding of the end days and the time that he referred to as Mashiach Ben Yoseph (The Messiah the son of Joseph). This theme, which later emerged as an important element in Rabbi Kook's Zionism, portrayed the end times as days in which the Torah and science would become aligned. This is accomplished through the widespread study of Kabalah. For an extensive discussion of this see Joel David Bakst, *The Secret Doctrine of the Gaon of Vilna: Mashiach ben Yoseph and the Messianic Role of Torah, Kabalah and Science,* vol. I (City of Luz Publications, 2008).

11. Buber famously saw the Hasidic movement as an important precedent for the brand of spiritual Zionism that he proposed. As he writes, for example, in his essay, "The Spirit of Israel and the World of Today," "Only one great attempt was made to create, under the

Our discussion of Tikkun is essentially an attempt to try to help this effort along by reading texts in a way that will allow us to rehabilitate the inner substance of this idea of spiritual collectivism and uncover the potential that Zionism has created for its realization as a form of politics. We do this with the conviction that passing the test of realism is essential to the politicization of spiritual collectivism in a public realm that defies the boundaries imposed by post-Enlightenment thought on the scope of religious thinking. In short, what we mean by Tikkun after Churban is the potential of bringing spiritual collectivism into the open by connecting the negation of Nazism by Zionism to the negation of Heidegger's ontology to the onto-theological phenomenology of inner Torah.

The Macro-/Micro- History of Rehabilitation

The central argument of this book is essentially built upon a reframing of the relationship between the Holocaust and the establishment of the State of Israel as a macro-historical relationship between Churban and Tikkun, which has a micro-historical parallel in the relationship between Heidegger's ontology and the modern development of the inner Torah. In this reframing, the idea of Churban is represented by the portrayal of inner human *being* that we encountered in our reading of *BT*. For our psycho-philosophical understanding of Tikkun, we will turn to a reading of Jewish texts that is based upon Heidegger's philosophical method. We shall interpret Jewish texts that take faith in God, totality as eternity, eternal time, eternal life, "non-devouring" spatiality, and organic collectivity seriously, trying to ground the meanings of these ideas in onto-theological terms crafted from the terminology that Heidegger uses in *BT*. In this way, we hope to take a significant step toward pulling these ideas out of the water in which they are submerged when they are considered in the context of post-Enlightenment humanism or Survival and System.

In and of itself, the idea that the language of inner Torah addresses a manifest realm of worldly reality is not at all new. The classical Hasidic text

---

restricted and restrictive conditions of the exile, a concrete social life, the fraternal life of sons of the One God living together. This was the attempt of Hasidism, and even it did not pierce to the vital, essential problem but crumbles away after time." See Martin Buber, *Israel and the World: Essays in a Time of Crisis* (Schocken Books, 1948), 187.

Tanya, for example, is insistent that the esoteric or concealed truth of the Torah is always very close to us if only we can train ourselves to see it.[12] Many others made similar claims. In our discussion we will try to "break out" the language of inner Torah from what appears to be a closed system of self-affirming and cross-fertilizing assumptions. Without denying the metaphorical nature of the language used in these texts, we suggest that putting Heidegger's ontology into an inverted form can attach to it a kind of concrete literalness that adds to its plausibility as a description of how humans *care* for their ownmost *being.* Unfortunately, this does not really simplify things any more than Heidegger simplified them. But this method does help us think concretely and practically about the public or political meaning of Jewish spirituality. Our suggestion is that in order to fully appreciate in practical terms the potential of the vision of Segulah that we first introduced as a statement of personal faith, we need to shift our description of it from an ontic/abstract faith system to a spiritual onto-theology.

The Juxtaposition of *BT* and the Inner Torah

The first grounding of our analysis is very similar to Heidegger's in *BT*: It is essential to retrieve the question of *being* in order to understand the *being-in-the-world* of the being, Dasein, that knows itself in its own *being.*[13] What this

12. The *Tanya* is the shortened name commonly used for the classic Hasidic treatise *Likkutei Amarim, Tanya* or "collection of statements." The *Tanya* was written by Rabbi Shneur Zalman of Liadi, the founder of Chabad Hasidism and was first published in 1797. In chapter 17, the *Tanya* expounds upon the biblical verse "And this matter is very near to you in your mouth and in your heart that you may do it" (Deuteronomy 30:14). In his analysis, he emphasizes the idea that even though the love and fear of God are tremendously difficult states of mind to attain, they are also the most natural state of a person's being and are hence very near. See Shneur Zalman of Liadi, *Likkutei Amarim, Tanya*, Hebrew with English translation (Kehot Publication Society, 770 Eastern Parkway Brooklyn, 1981).

13. In Hasidic texts the juxtaposition between Moses and Balaam is founded on their shared ability to penetrate the depths of what it means to cleave to God. While it was Moses' special gift to cleave to God and bring others closer to Him through the prophetic revelation of the Torah, Balaam's special gift was an evil power. According to the commentary of Rabbi Shalom Noah Berezovsky, *Netivot Shalom* (Jerusalem: Slonim, 1982) [Hebrew] on Numbers, chapter 22, the Moabite king Balak realized that he could not attack the children of Israel unless their bond with God was broken. It is for this reason that he enlisted the help of Balaam, whose gift was his ability to penetrate this cleaving and disrupt it. In a fascinating study entitled *The Duplicity of Philosophy's*

means is that the idea of the "subject" or the "self" as it is portrayed in Western philosophy is not helpful, and adopting it is the source of both identity conflicts and identity crises. Hence, any understanding of Torah that is based upon an ontic interaction between a "subject" or transcendental "I" encountering an "external world" filled with other "subjects" and "objects" will submerge significant elements of the Torah underwater. Rather, we must begin with the assumption that the self is a *being* that has the structure of Dasein, and which encounters itself through *concern* for its own *being-in-the-world*.

Second, in the same way that the portrayal of Dasein in *BT* begins with everyday or inauthentic Dasein, the understanding of the Torah begins with the realization that the self, who we are, is *always already* in exile or Galut. Pursuant to early examples of human failure and sinfulness, the Torah says,

---

Shadow: Heidegger, Nazism and the Jewish Other (New York: Columbia University Press, 2018), Elliot Wolfson dedicates a thought-provoking chapter entitled "Heidegger, Balaam and the Duplicity of Philosophy's Shadow" to the analogy of Balaam with Heidegger. Drawing richly on kabbalistic sources, Wolfson traces the tradition that accords to Balaam prophetic powers that are equal to those of Moses. Against this backdrop he suggests "a more complex approach to assess Heidegger's commitment to National Socialism and his relation to Judaism" (p. 194). Wolfson goes on to develop this juxtaposition in a way that is very different from ours and which is not confined in the same way as ours to the analysis of *BT* alone. Despite the many differences, his work sets an important precedent for our methodology that rests on the assumption that the penetrating analysis of *BT* yields Balaam-like insights of prophetic importance that can be inverted and applied to our understanding of Torah. The overall thrust of Wolfson's framing of this relationship is perhaps made more explicit in a second and far more expansive study entitled *Heidegger and Kabbalah: Hidden Gnosis and the Path of Poiesis* (Bloomington, Indiana University Press, 2019). In this much larger work, Wolfson's discussion deals more with the underlying currents that connect the mystical dimensions of Heidegger's thought with kabbalah, and while the two are juxtaposed and the author remains sensitive throughout to the complexity of this comparison, the primal tendency of his reading is perhaps captured in the closing paragraph of his introduction, where he writes, "However, it is my hope, that the juxtaposition of the ostensibly incongruent fields of discourse, the belonging together of what is foreign, Heidegger and kabbalah, will not only enhance our understanding of both, but, in an even more profound sense, will serve as an ethical corrective of their respective ethnocentrisms, thereby illustrating the redemptive capacity of thought to yield new configurations of unthought colluding on disparate paths of contemplative thinking" (p. 13). Wolfson's mastery of both the Western philosophical and the kabbalistic canon is breathtaking. But his basic intuition about the compatibility of Jewish and Western racist ethnocentrism belongs to the paradigm of Survival and System from which we are trying, in this and the following chapters, to break free.

"The inclination (or constriction) of man's heart is evil from his youth" (Genesis 8:21). This phrase, which is echoed ominously in Heidegger's idea that "as soon as a human being comes into life; he is old enough to die,"[14] is understood in the inner Torah as describing the mortal self-absorption of the ego in which we are all entangled from birth. Like Heidegger in *BT*, the inner Torah seeks to take us on a journey that begins with this sense of the self who we most naturally *are*.

Third, parallel to Heidegger's idea that inauthentic Dasein is an expression of Dasein in its authentic form, the inner Torah assumes that the self in Galut has *always already* experienced Tikkun and hence the journey of the Torah is one of "return" to *being* the being that we *always already are*. However, the inner Torah sees the covenant between God and the Jewish people as an antidote for the hardness of heart that conceals this possibility of Tikkun from us. To understand this, we need to invert our use of *BT* and say that the purpose of inner Torah is to negate the diverse effects of self-absorbed, human existential anxiety about *being-toward-death*. This is possible because the portrayal of the inner self that the Torah proposes contains possibilities of *being-a-self* that lie beyond those outlined in *BT*. These include the possibility of Dasein's *care* for its ownmost *being* as *being-toward* an infinite totality of *being*. This expanded capacity for *being* does not replace our natural understanding of the self. On the contrary, it relies upon it to find expression in the world.[15] It is a broader expression of a totality or macrocosm of which the constricted self is *always already* a microcosm.

---

14. Heidegger, *BT*, 236.

15. This idea is referred to in Hasidic texts as "God's desire for a dwelling in the world below." See, for example, Shneur Zalman of Liadi, *Likkutei Amarim, Tanya*, section 1 chapter 36. This idea is based upon Midrash Tanchuma, Numbers, *Naso*, 16: "Rabbi Shmuel Bar Nachman said, When the Holy One, blessed be He, created the world He longed to have a place of dwelling below just as He had above. After He created Adam, He commanded him, saying, 'You may eat freely of any tree in the garden, but you may not eat from the Tree of Knowledge of Good and Evil.' Then he sinned against this commandment. The Holy One, blessed be He, said to him, 'This is what I longed for, that just as I have a dwelling on high, I would like to have one below. Now when I have given you one commandment you have not observed it.' Immediately, the Holy One, blessed be He, withdrew His presence up to the first level of heaven."

In this structure, Dasein's *care* is the dwelling that God desires in the lower world. The divine withdrawal to the heavens is understood as referring to God's withdrawal to a dimension of *being* in which *care* for the totality of divine *being* is still accessible to

Finally, the onto-theology of the inner Torah includes a middle ground between the individual self and totality of *being*. This middle ground is compatible with Heidegger's impersonal concept of the *they*, which he rejects as inherently inauthentic. In the inner Torah's portrayal of this middle ground, every individual Jewish person is *always already* an expression of the totality of the Jewish collective (and thereafter of all humanity) across time. The possibility of seeing *care* for the self as a microcosm of *care* for the collective comes to ease the journey from absorption in selfness to absorption or *care* for the totality of eternal *being* or Havayah.

In sum, the expansion of Dasein's *being-toward-death* in the direction of both collective and eternal *being* is what the biblical prophets in various places described as "the circumcision of the heart" or the "conversion of the heart from stone to flesh."[16] By taking *BT*'s portrayal of Dasein as a close analysis of what is meant by this hardness of heart, we will try to understand the meaning of the antidote to it, which the prophet refers to as Da'at Hashem.[17]

Our purpose in the following chapters is to tackle the ontological interpretation of concepts whose meanings seem implausible when they are considered in terms of the self as an "I." We will build a lexicon of ontological interpretations based on a comparison between the network of categories that we learned from Heidegger's analysis of Dasein in *BT* and either their parallels or their inversions as these appear in the language of Torah. Our account of this lexicon is by no means complete, but we will try in this chapter to elucidate several key terms: Tzelem Elohim, Nefesh, Neshamah, Chochmah, Binah, Da'at, Middot, Ahavah, Yirah, and Kavanah.[18] In the chapters that

---

additional possibilities for *care* that have no place in *BT*'s ontological system. However, the purpose of these additional possibilities is not to transcend the boundaries of this world; neither is it to replace an inauthentic self with an authentic one. Rather, it is the indwelling of *care* for the totality of *being* in the concrete *being* of Dasein's *being-in-the-world*.

16. See, for example, Ezekiel 36:26, "And I will take away the heart of stone from your flesh and replace it with a heart of flesh."

17. This concept appears in Isaiah 11:9 and it literally means "the knowledge of God." In the inner Torah, as we shall see, it refers to a kind of cleaving of consciousness or *care* to God that Hasidic texts – based on biblical passages in Deuteronomy (10:20, 11:22, 13:5) – refer to as *devekut*.

18. The meanings of all these Hebrew terms will be explained in the discussion below. All translations of Hebrew sources henceforth until the end of the book are ours unless

follow, we will examine how this portrayal of the self can be applied to our understanding of time, space, and collective identity.

Tzelem Elohim – The Image of God and the Structure of Dasein

In our discussion we are going to use the concept of Tzelem Elohim as a general term that is parallel to Heidegger's use of "the overall structure of Dasein" in *BT*. We will begin by elucidating the meaning of this term and then go on to divide it up into component parts. Tzelem Elohim is a biblical phrase which is generally taken to denote a broad range of qualities which single out human beings as uniquely created "in the image of God." Scholars have variously interpreted it as referring to speech, abstract thought, upright stance, freedom of choice, the ability to use tools, moral judgment, creativity, and more.[19] We will not discuss any of these and will not try to decide between them. Rather, we want to try to discover the underlying principle of what all these characteristics of Tzelem Elohim mean. We will do this by using the terms that Heidegger gives us in *BT* to transpose the entire discussion of all these options from an ontic to an onto-theological plane. What we would like to show in this analysis is that Tzelem Elohim is the basic category that the Torah uses to describe human *being*. While this is a broad topic that is discussed in many sources, we shall focus our analysis on one illustrative example.

---

otherwise stated.

19. The emphasis on the unique human ability to speak features famously in the biblical translation Targum Onkelos, who translates the biblical description of the spirit of man as created by God in Genesis 2:7 as *ruach memalala*, literally meaning "a speaking spirit." The idea that abstract thought captures the essence of Tzelem Elohim is most famously attributed to Maimonides, who dedicates the first chapter of his philosophical masterpiece, *The Guide for the Perplexed*, to this theme. He writes, "The term Tzelem… signifies the specific form, that which constitutes the essence of a thing, whereby the thing is what it is; the reality of a thing insofar as it is that particular being. In man the "form" is that constituent which gives him human perception, and on account of this intellectual perception the term Tzelem is employed in the sentence 'In the Tzelem of God He created him' (Gen. 1:27)." See Maimonides, *The Guide for the Perplexed*, 4th ed., trans. M. Friedlander (New York: E. Dutton), part 1, chapter 1. For a comprehensive summary of the various interpretations that appear in both classical and modern scholarship, see Yair Lorberbaum, *In God's Image: Myth, Theology, and Law in Classical Judaism* (Cambridge University Press, 2015).

Rabbi Chayyim lckovits of Volozhin (Rabbi Chayyim) dedicated the first section of his master work, *The Soul of Life*,[20] to the explication of Tzelem Elohim. He begins by dividing up the two-word phrase into its component parts. Through a series of philological comparisons, he reaches an initial working assumption that "per the plain-text commentators," what is meant by the word *tzelem* is "that the one resembles the other in some fashion."[21] Rabbi Chayyim goes on to say that this similarity or resemblance between God and humankind is what allows interaction between them. This interaction takes the form of prayer from man to God and revelation of Torah from God to man. The substance of this resemblance or interface between God and man is the overall theme of the aptly named *Soul of Life*.[22] Thus, the first "gate" of the book, which is dedicated to Tzelem Elohim, is followed by two further gates which deal with prayer and Torah study, respectively.

Rabbi Chayyim insists that in order to understand the concept of Tzelem Elohim, we need to uncover an appreciable insight into what it is that makes human beings "like" God. Given how little we can know of God, this is not a simple task. He tries to move beyond a conventional religious definition of Tzelem Elohim by accessing a more concrete (though perhaps more esoteric) meaning of human *being* in God's image. In order to appreciate this, we need to uncover the interplay between the levels of *peshat* (plain meaning) and *sod* (hidden or mystical meaning) in Rabbi Chayyim's discussion.

At the beginning of the first chapter, while commenting on Genesis (9:6), Rabbi Chayyim says,

> This is a reference to the deep inner meaning of Tzelem, it being one of the loftiest concepts in creation, containing within it most of the Zohar's innermost secrets. That said, herein we will address the term *Tzelem* in the manner of the early plain-text

---

20. Rabbi Chayyim lckovits of Volozhin (1749–1821), *The Soul of Life: The Complete Nefesh Ha-Chayyim*, trans. Eliezer Lipa (Leonard) Moskowitz (Teaneck, NJ: New Davar Publications, 2014).

21. Ibid., 43–44.

22. The title of this work, which in the Hebrew original echoes the name of the author, "Chayyim," is particularly significant to our analysis, which is ultimately geared toward the argument that Jewish thought predicates the soul or Dasein's awareness of *being* in terms of life and not death.

commentators on the verse "Lets us make man with our *Tzelem*" (Genesis 1:26).[23]

The allusion here to the mysticism that he is *not* writing about gives this entire section of the book an apophatic tone. The key principle that is elucidated in this passage (as well as in many other examples throughout the section) is that the plain meaning, or *peshat*, of Tzelem is only the outer covering of another level that resides within. Rabbi Chayyim wants to focus upon "plain meaning," but he says so in a way that calls our attention to the level of *sod* that he says he will not speak about directly. What we propose is that his pointing away from *sod* in this manner, apophatically draws us toward it, implying that the point of contact between God and man is parallel to the hermeneutical connection between *sod* and *peshat*. In other words, the image of man is a revealed form of a hidden dimension that lies within. This parallel is what gives the study of Torah its meaning; to study the different levels of the Torah is to uncover the levels of *being* that ultimately unite *care* for mortal human *being* with eternal divine *being*. Thus, clarifying the precise nature of the interface between *peshat* and *sod* is intrinsic to lining up the concealed aspects of *care* for Havayah that everyday concern for *being-a-self* apophatically alludes to.

The tendency to focus explicitly on the plain-text commentators implies that the plain meanings of the Torah are always surface expressions of something immensely deep and concealed. This principle establishes a relationship between *peshat* and *sod* that runs in two directions. In the first direction, the *peshat* is the surface or revealed meaning of the text, while *sod* is esoteric, hidden, and mystical. Conversely, since the *peshat* is always the *peshat* of the *sod* and the *sod* is always the *sod* of the *peshat*, it turns out that both are equally mysterious, while "in truth" *sod* is the more explicit. In this sense, *sod* is an explicit account of what the *peshat* conceals. Since the *peshat* conceals *sod*, the true meaning of the *peshat* is even more concealed.[24] In this sense, the

---

23. Rabbi Chayyim of Volozhin, *Soul of Life*, 43.

24. This inversion reflects a similar one that appears with reference to the names of God. See, for example, the commentary of the Ba'al HaTanya in *Likkutei Torah* in which he refers to the name YHVH as being the most esoteric name of God that refers to the totally abstract eternal being of the divine, which the kabbalistic literature refers to as

ultimate object of Torah study is the *peshat*, not the *sod*, because the journey from *peshat* to *sod* and back extends the dimension of *sod* into the concrete reality of life in this world. This is what Rabbi Chayyim means when he says that Tzelem is "one of the loftiest concepts in creation that contains most of the *Zohar's* inner secrets."[25]

Given this, we might say that as an adherent of the (anti-Hasidic) Lithuanian convention of keeping mysticism secret, Rabbi Chayyim admittedly does not enter detailed discussion of the *Zohar*. This is consistent with his being a disciple of the Hasidic movement's most famous opponent, Rabbi Elijah the Gaon of Vilna.[26] However, Rabbi Chayyim's recurring allusions to the hidden meanings of Tzelem also make it clear that he is telling us openly not to be deceived by the apparent simplicity of literalist interpretations of Tzelem Elohim, which, when taken at face value, are blatantly inadequate to the task of guiding us toward a satisfactory understanding of the human capacity to *care* for divine *being*.

Rabbi Chayyim's allusion to the *Zohar* is there to prevent our overlooking the implicit mystery concealed in the plain text of the entire Torah. Since exoteric being or "everydayness" is grounded in the esoteric *being* of being (that *sod* addresses), it is necessary when turning to the Torah to acknowledge that the basic structure of Tzelem Elohim includes an esoteric dimension. Otherwise, you run the risk of getting stuck or stopped at the seemingly self-explanatory or plain everyday level of meaning that first presents itself as *peshat*. The challenge here is especially pronounced because of the relative ease with which the plain meaning can be read. Our propensity for ignoring

---

the "Ein Sof," while Elohim refers to the more accessible God of creation. However, following this, YHVH comes to allude to God's imminence and thus His accessibility to human experience. In his words, "Elohim is the lower name of the two, which is also the higher." Similarly, light refers to clarity, while darkness is obscure. "However, if light is dazzling then it is only in the dark that one can see." See Rabbi Shneur Zalman of Liadi, *Likkutei Torah*, "*Drushim* for Shabbat Shuva," *Otzar HaHasidim*, 128 [Hebrew].

25. Rabbi Chayyim of Volozhin, *Soul of Life*, 43.

26. The mystical writings of Rabbi Eljah the Gaon of Vilna have generated quite significant scholarly debate, particularly concerning his doctrine of the twin Messiahs and its impact on Zionism. For some examples of the extensive scholarship in this field, see Arie Morgenstern, *The Gaon of Vilna and His Messianic Vision* (Jerusalem: Gefen Publishing House, 2012); Immanuel Etkes, *The Gaon of Vilna: The Man and His Image* (University of California Press, 2002).

the underlying mystery of the Torah blocks our curiosity about the onto-the-ology that hides behind natural phenomena which we take for granted. So we might say that pointing apophatically at *sod* is Rabbi Chayyim's way of retrieving the question of *being*.

In our understanding, the relationship between *peshat* and *sod* is a herme-neutic principle that not only alludes to but *is* the onto-theological structure of Tzelem Elohim. Tzelem Elohim is dependent upon the interrelation of *peshat* and *sod* which, bound together, describe the unity of human *concern* for the self and *care* for the *being* of Havayah. In the same way that "every-dayness" is a layer of authentic Dasein's *being-in-the-world*, everything that appears plain or simple also contains a concealed but more explicit inner dimension that is its point of interface with Havayah. This inner dimension is like the engine under the hood of a car that, though it is not in plain view and is generally not understood by most drivers, gives us a grounded account of why the seemingly random act of pressing down a pedal propels a vehicle forward. Following this analogy, Tzelem is the point of contact between the engine and the plates that turn the car's wheels, while Elohim is the engine of human *being*. It is what makes us enduringly alive.

Thus, what appears revealed – what appears to be part of everyday reli-gious language or normal life – must always be the outside of an inner or more concealed level at which revelation is made more explicit. In reverse, what is seemingly hidden must always be the inside of a phenomenon that has to also have an outer expression in the world. When aligned, these two aspects of consciousness serve as the inside and the outside of a unified whole in which everything has both revealed and concealed dimensions. This is a structure that applies to the world and to the Torah, and it has a significant impact on how we understand the purpose of Torah study. One does not study the onto-theological dimension of inner Torah in order to replace the superficial *peshat* with a deeper insight that we call *sod*. Rather, the objective is the unifying alignment of *peshat* and *sod*. Rabbi Chayyim's allusions to inner meanings coupled with his reticence about dealing with them explicitly point toward a hermeneutic structure that duplicates the structure of Tzelem, which, as he says quite clearly, points to a "likeness" or a "similarity" between different levels of *being* that, because they depend upon one another, must all *always already be-there* whenever any one of them *is*.

This point becomes a little clearer in Rabbi Chayyim's discussion of why the word Tzelem is attached specifically to the divine name of Elohim. This name, he explains, "implies that He (blessed be His name) is the master of all powers."[27] He continues,

> However, to understand why He specifically stated "in the image of God-Elohim" and not some other name, it is because the meaning of the name Elohim is well understood, that it implies that He (blessed be His name) is the Master of All Powers.[28]

Again, this is a concept that has a *peshat*. The idea that God is the master of all powers is a conventional matter of religious faith. But here, Rabbi Chayyim is pointing to something more concrete. Tzelem Elohim depends on the fact that human beings, more than any other creature, are also masters of the world. He suggests that this likeness is a clue to something that lies beyond. In his words,

> The matter of why He (blessed be He) is called "Master of All Powers" is because the attributes of the Holy One (blessed be He) are not like those of flesh and blood. For man, when he builds a structure (for example: of wood), the builder doesn't create and materialize the wood from his own powers; rather, he takes pre-existing lumber and organizes it into a structure. After he completes arranging it according to his will, if he ceases his efforts and departs, the structure still persists. In contrast, He (blessed be His name), as during the time when all of the worlds[29] were created,

---

27. Rabbi Chayyim of Volozhin, *Soul of Life*, 44.

28. Ibid.

29. What is meant here by "worlds" is explained in note 90 on page 45 of Moskowitz's translation of *The Soul of Life*. He writes there, "When the author speaks of worlds, he uses the context described by Rabbi Yitzchak Luria who…describes four accessible worlds, one above (so to speak) the other, through which God's influence flows. This lowest world is referred to as the world of action, above this is the world of formation. Above that the world of creation and above that is the world of emanation. What is above the world of emanation is generally inaccessible." We will return to discuss this fivefold structure in greater detail below.

created and materialized them ex-nihilo, with His infinite powers.
So it continues since then, every day and truly every moment; all
of the powers that make them exist, structure them and sustain
them are dependent only on what He (blessed be He) impresses
upon them via His will at each moment via the power and the
influence of the newly created light. And if He (blessed be He)
removed the power of his influence for even one moment, in that
moment everything would revert to nothingness and chaos.[30]

God and humans are similar in that they can both make things. However,
while a carpenter can build a chair and leave it, were God to leave behind
His creation it would cease to exist. Thus, despite the similarity between
them, "God-made" and "man-made" are not exactly alike. They are only similar. God's creation, which is ex nihilo (*yesh me'ayin*), depends forever on His
influence, while human "creations" – made of preexisting source materials
(*yesh meyesh*) – also depend forever on God's perpetual creation and not on
the human being who crafted them. This is a temporal distinction. To the
extent that a humanly crafted object is *yesh meyesh* its *being* is finite. People
can make chairs and tables out of wood, but they can't make them continue
to *be*. Their ability to make the chairs is therefore a clue that points toward
God's role in perpetuating their *being*. Persistence of *being* across time is the
quality or the aspect denoted by the name Elohim that is attached to Tzelem.
Human creative power, or Tzelem, is the *peshat* of which Elohim is the *sod*.
This idea is reinforced and developed in an annotation to the text which
reads as follows:

> Even if the renewal is not apparent to the eye, truly the four super-
> nal elements, they who are the ancient roots, the precursors of all –
> as it is written in the Zohar (Va-eira 23b) that they are the root
> of all the events associated with creation and their inner aspect –
> and they are the four letters of YHV"H (Blessed be He). Their

---

30. Rabbi Chayyim of Volozhin, *Soul of Life*, 44–46. The word "light" that appears in this
    passage is also a term that is used with specific metaphorical meanings in kabbalistic
    literature. One explanation of this appears in note 91. We shall return to discuss this in
    greater detail below.

combining and assembling at every moment and instant in their root of roots is not perceived at all, and He (blessed be His name) renews them in every instant according to His will. And the matter of their combining in every instant, they are the one thousand and eighty permutations of the Name (blessed be He), according to the variation in their punctuation during the one thousand and eighty divisions of the hour. And they vary even more so each hour to still other permutations, and also that the quality of the day is not equivalent to the quality of the night, no day resembles the one before or after it in any way. That is why it is specifically written, "who actualizes…the event of creation."[31]

To understand the onto-theology that Rabbi Chayyim is developing here, we need to look at how he interprets the name God-Elohim, which in the Hebrew combines the name Elohim with the four-letter name YHVH in the second chapter of Genesis.[32] Rabbi Chayyim emphasizes the permutations of the four letters of Havayah,[33] each of which represents a different dimension of inner *being*. Through each one, *being* extends itself toward us; starting out or emanating from an absolute totality of infinite abstraction and ending up in the innerworldly objects (such as ourselves) that are the totality of *being's* exterior or surface forms. Each of these forms – that together comprise the entirety of things that *are in-the-world* - is a different way of Havayah's *being-in-the-world* ordered along a scale of varying degrees that starts with total abstraction moving toward concretization. The permutations of these forms or degrees into the one thousand and eighty divisions of the hour that form and re-form hour after hour, are the infrastructure of how *being* extends itself into finite or mortal time at every moment. Every moment in which things *are* is thus an expression of the totality of abstract and infinite *being's* entry into finite *being* at every moment in the infinite process through which *being* continually makes itself present in the form of everything that *is* at any and every moment in time. Rabbi Chayyim continues,

---

31. Ibid., 47.

32. See Genesis 2:4: "These are the generations of the heaven and the earth when they were created on the day that YHVH (Elohim) made heaven and earth."

33. In Hebrew the four root letters of Havayah are *yud*, *heh*, *vav*, and *heh*.

And this is why He (blessed be His name) is called God-*Elohim,*
Master of all powers. All powers found in any of the worlds – every
one of them – He (blessed be His name) is Master over their power.
He impresses within them the power and constrained strength
during every moment, and they are constantly dependent upon
Him to change and organize them according to His will.[34]

Rabbi Chayyim's emphasis here on divine will is also worthy of comment.
There is a willfulness to *being* that applies to the *being* of all beings in a similar
way that Heidegger's Dasein is willful. Through this structural similarity, we
can see how the onto-theology of inner Torah negates Heidegger's premise
that *concern* for *being* is what makes Dasein unique. From the perspective
of the inner Torah, what makes Dasein unique is the "degree" to which it
draws upon the consciousness *being* of Havayah. The willful consciousness of
Dasein *is* only in the sense that its *being is-toward* the willful consciousness
of YHVH at any and every moment. This idea is expressed in the rabbinic
instruction "Make His will your will so that He will carry out your will as
though it were His. Set aside your will in the face of His will" (*Avot* 2:4).
In this sense, the alignment of human will with God's will is understood
as an extension of divine willful *being* into the human form that it takes in
this world. But this concept, which reaches its greatest expression in human
consciousness, is characteristic of everything else as well – only to a lesser
degree. Thus, human *care* for *being-a-self* is an expression of divine *care* for
the perpetual *being-across-time* of everything that *is*. Dasein's care for its own
being is not its source and – crucially – must not be its sole *concern*. It follows
that from the perspective of the Torah, Dasein must learn to *care* primarily
for the *being* of *Elohim* in order to gain access to the source of its ownmost
being-a-self. This redirection of Dasein's *care* is the feature of Tzelem Elohim
that most acutely negates the ontology of *BT*, and it is the heart of the inner
Torah. As Rabbi Yehuda Ashlag emphasized, the Torah focuses on countering
egoism with selfless altruism.[35]

---

34. Ibid., 47.

35. This is the central principle of Rabbi Yehuda Ashlag's teachings. It is succinctly outlined
    in his essay on world peace originally published in Hebrew as "Hashalom." See *On*

Nefesh (Everyday Dasein)

We are going to use the term Nefesh to denote a component of the overall structure of Tzelem Elohim that is parallel to Heidegger's use of "everyday Dasein" in *BT*. Nefesh is generally used to refer to the "soul" that living beings are said to possess. In our discussion we shall try to avoid the vagueness of this term "soul" by looking more precisely at the meaning of the Hebrew word and its specific function.

In its first biblical use (Genesis, chapter 2), the Nefesh is not actually something that human beings are said to possess, but rather it refers to the sense of self as "*being* alive" that we most naturally have. In Genesis, chapter 2, God's creation of Adam is described as His "breathing life into the dust on the ground." This combination of God's breath and the dust is the "living soul" or "Nefesh *chayah*" (Genesis 2:7). In the inner Torah, the Nefesh is understood more specifically as the lowest level of consciousness, and it is described as close to the physical body. In one commonly used analogy, it is like air that has been blown into molten glass by a glassblower.[36] On account of this closeness to the physical body, the Nefesh is often referred to as the lower Nefesh or the animal Nefesh, which distinguishes it from a higher or still more abstract divine Nefesh that we will return to below.

In several places in the Bible, the Nefesh is both literally and metaphorically associated with blood. When the Bible speaks against spilling human blood and consuming animal blood,[37] the prohibition is justified by the assertion that "the blood is the Nefesh" and it is the Nefesh that must not be killed.[38] When the inner Torah speaks in more metaphorical terms about the Nefesh as the lifeblood that flows within us, it represents the point of contact between the physical body and an inner life force which "comes to rest" as the Nefesh in its closest to physical form. This closest to physical form is the lowest dimension of Tzelem Elohim which is responsible for infusing the body

---

World Peace: Two Essays by the Holy Kabbalist Rabbi Yehuda Ashlag, ed. Michael Berg (Kabballah Publishing, 2013).

36. See, for example, *Zohar* III, 25a. We will return to discuss this analogy in more detail below.

37. See Genesis 9:6; Leviticus 17:14; Deuteronomy 12:23.

38. "Be strong, not to eat the blood, for the blood is the life (Nefesh) and you shall not eat the Nefesh with the flesh" (Deuteronomy 12:23).

with life.[39] This idea is developed considerably in mystical and Hasidic writings. For example, in his book *Derech Hashem,* Rabbi Moshe Chaim Luzzatto (the Ramchal) distinguishes between the lower and the higher Nefesh, identifying the lower Nefesh as

> one type of Nefesh that man has [which] is the same that exists in all living creatures. It is this [animal] Nefesh that is responsible for man's natural feelings and intelligence that are ingrained in his nature.[40]

The Ramchal identifies blood and semen as the physical carriers of the lower Nefesh. This lower Nefesh is said to determine the characteristics of each creature according to the traits of its species in much the same way as DNA does. In humans, the Ramchal explains, the Nefesh is responsible for "imagination, memory, intelligence, and will."[41] In its lower form, these potentialities of the Nefesh are said to express themselves "within boundaries" that he goes on to describe as "limited by private concerns."[42] The Nefesh's *concern* for itself, according to the Ramchal, is caused by its intrinsic anchoring in the body. This limits it, as it were, from below.[43]

---

39. This association is attested to by the verse (Genesis 9:6 mentioned above) "Whoso sheddeth man's blood, by man shall his blood be shed; for in the image of God (Tzelem Elohim) made He man." Note also that the Hebrew word *vayinafash*, which has the same root as the word Nefesh, appears with reference to God's resting on Shabbat in Exodus (31:17). This resting is understood as God's "coming to rest" in the world. The Nefesh therefore represents the idea that the spiritual 'comes to rest' in the physical. This relationship is echoed in the idea that the life blood of the Nefesh comes to rest in the body and is thus the dimension of consciousness that is closest to physicality.

40. Rabbi Moshe Chaim Luzzatto, *Derech Hashem* (c. 1730), 3:1 [Hebrew].

41. Ibid.

42. Ibid., 3:3.

43. Ibid. Our use here of the term below is consistent with much of the literature in this field. However, this vertical terminology of higher and lower might be more appropriately rendered for the modern reader in different terms. Arthur Green suggests that rather than thinking of God and the giving of the Torah as a vertical event, we might think of this as an ancient metaphor that is better described today in terms of inwardness. In his words, "Spiritual growth, in this metaphor, is a matter of uncovering new *depths* rather than attaining new *heights*." See Arthur Green, "God Above, God Within," in *Seek My Face: A Jewish Mystical Theology* (Jewish Lights Publishing, 2003), 8–10.

Given all of this, it seems reasonable to identify the Nefesh with what we would call today the human psyche or the *res cogitans* (knowing self) in all its conscious and subconscious forms. It is the "subject" of our mortal being, and hence it is the object of the Torah's prohibition against murder (the spilling of blood). But it is also a "subject" that is characterized by its *concern* for its *being*, and in this sense it is equivalent to Dasein. However, in our lexicon the lower Nefesh is distinguished from Dasein by the fact that it is part of the larger structure of Tzelem Elohim. The Nefesh represents the modes of *being* that are connected to and concerned with the *being* of the body and bodily consciousness of the self. Hence, as the Ramchal said, they are "limited with private concerns."[44] Since it is anchored in the body, it *falls prey* to the concerns of the body and is distracted from the higher or deeper *concerns* that according to the Ramchal it can know only as an aligned aspect of the overall structure of Tzelem Elohim.[45]

This lower aspect of the Nefesh is referred to by Rabbi Shneur Zalman of Liadi in the *Tanya* as the Nefesh *behemit*, or animal Nefesh, which he understands as a lower or outer expression of a higher consciousness that he refers to as the divine Nefesh (Nefesh Elohit or Neshamah).[46] Rabbi Samson Raphael Hirsch elucidates the animalistic nature of this lower Nefesh in his commentary on the Garden of Eden story. For Rabbi Hirsch, the fruit of the Tree of Knowledge is enticing to the body because it satisfies its curiosity and demystifies what is concealed from it.[47] It represents the illusive lure of the idea that access to concealed knowledge is a source of power. According to Rabbi Hirsch, the genuine secret of the tree – the knowledge that truly enables

---

44. Rabbi Luzzatto, *Derech Hashem*, 3:3.

45. Ibid.

46. In the *Tanya*, Shneur Zalman of Liadi identifies the ability of a higher Nefesh to dictate the thoughts, speech, and actions of the lower one as the special trait of the Tzaddik. However, recognizing that few people are capable of this, the *Tanya* famously champions the objective of becoming a Benoni (intermediate), i.e., one who, though he is not capable of totally aligning the lower with the higher Nefesh, is able to cultivate the strength of the higher one sufficiently to gain the freedom of choice and the strength to act consistently according to the will of God as expressed in the Torah.

47. See Genesis 3:6, where the tree is described as a delight (more literally, a source of lust) for the eyes. This phrase underlines the basic trait of the fruit of this tree, which is its appeal to the animal soul.

mankind to distinguish good from evil – was offered to Adam and Eve by the
commandment not to eat from the tree. This negative commandment brings
them face-to-face with their free choice. On the one hand, they can either
obey the inner voice that represents their higher or better selves as beings
created in Tzelem Elohim or, on the other, they can heed the voice of the
serpent. But the voice of the serpent is not evil per se; it is simply the natural
and healthy "animal" voice which animals are instinctively geared to obey but
which human beings should transcend. When Eve listened to the serpent, she

> followed her impulses, ate, and also gave her man to eat and their
> eyes were opened, and they saw – not that they were God but that
> they were naked and ashamed of their bodies, for they had sunk
> to the level of the animal! For if man lets himself be dominated by
> his body, his senses and desires, instead of being governed by the
> divine will; he has forfeited his human dignity.[48]

In ideal terms, the lower Nefesh is most naturally drawn to a higher willfulness. This is how the *Tanya* understands the meaning of the key verse "It is
not in heaven…but very close to you" (Deuteronomy 30: 12–14). But as a
result of the lower Nefesh's proximity to the body, this is a very hard choice
to make.

The problem the inner Torah targets here is therefore the giving over of
the entire self to the urges and desires of the lower Nefesh. This is what we
might refer to as the entanglement of the lower Nefesh in its *with-world*. This
entanglement creates the illusion of *being-a-self* which is separate from (or in
denial of) the higher Nefesh. When we compare this with the problem of inauthenticity that Heidegger tackles in *BT*, we can see the contrast. According to
Heidegger, inauthenticity is connected to Dasein's difficulty freeing itself to
face its ownmost *being-toward-death*. In the inner Torah, the challenge that
the animal Nefesh faces is to maintain its connectivity with the totality of
being. The inner Torah seeks the freedom to bind the concerns of the lower
Nefesh with boundless *care* about the *being* of everything – Havayah.

---

48. Rabbi S. R Hirsch, commentary on Genesis, chapters 2–3, from the Isaac Breuer
Institute Edition (Jerusalem, 1989) [Hebrew].

We will return to consider this as we look at the way in which the *Tanya* sets up the contrast between the lower and higher forms of Nefesh. However, first we would like to offer a brief analysis of a passage that appears in the introduction to the *Tanya* and which alludes to the importance of connectivity in an interesting way:

In his introduction to the *Tanya*, the author explains his reasons for writing the book. He is overwhelmed by the number of disciples who seek his counsel. In order to ease his burden, he has written a book that he believes can be of help to those who have already spent hours and hours with him receiving spiritual guidance. But he is reticent about writing because the spiritual advice that he wants to give can only ever be fully appreciated by those who come into personal contact with a teacher. He comments that spiritual guidance is hard to get from books, "because the reader reads after his own manner and mind, and according to his mental grasp and comprehension at that particular time."[49] He continues,

> Apart from this, the books on piety which stem from human intelligence certainly have not the same appeal for all people, for not all intellects and minds are alike, and the intellect of one man is not affected and excited by what affects and excites the intellect of another.[50]

The difficulty here can perhaps be compared to one of the central philosophical problems that we addressed in our reading of *BT*. Heidegger is troubled by the challenge of beginning his analytic of authentic Dasein, since the starting point is always one in which Dasein only knows itself in its everydayness. Since most of us, in our natural state, know ourselves as the lower Nefesh, it is hard for us to refine our actions, thoughts, and will to a level of purity in which the eternal truth of the Torah can be grasped. The "human intelligence" of the lower Nefesh, which is anchored in the body of the individual, blocks us from communicating the eternal higher truths of inner Torah to one another. The *Tanya* goes on to say that this problem applies even when

---

49. *Tanya*, introduction, xiv.
50. Ibid.

individuals study the most precious books, "whose basis is in the peaks of holiness such as those written by the Sages of the Midrash…[who] possessed the spirit of God."[51] The point by implication is that even when the book itself shares the insights of the higher Nefesh, the lower Nefesh is not capable of learning from it.

The solution that the *Tanya* proposes is to instruct his readers to study his book together or in classes with a teacher where they can ask questions. This classic Jewish emphasis on studying together – coupled with a general preference for the reliability of what is learned in face-to-face, orally transmitted study from a teacher – is perhaps not unusual. It makes simple sense to claim that misunderstandings can be avoided by studying with a more knowledgeable teacher. However, it is possible that there is something more here. Since the *Tanya* is dedicated to the overall struggle against the limitations of the lower Nefesh, whose individualistic concerns must be overcome in order for the true meaning of the Torah to be grasped, it seems that studying together serves that purpose of connecting the individual lower Nefesh to its higher potential by ensuring that it remains connected to the collective.

By making this suggestion, we are laying the foundations for the claim that the individualistic and self-oriented traits of the lower Nefesh are not equal to the task of seeing the higher totality that only a spiritual collective can attain. The individual lower Nefesh is confined by the boundaries of the self-oriented "mind, intelligence, imagination, memory and will" that the Ramchal referred to in the passage above. As we saw in Rabbi Hirsch's commentary, the higher mind is blocked and concealed from the lower one by bodily desire. In this state, when the lower Nefesh yearns to be a self, it is susceptible to the corrupting and destructive forces that suck it down into the darkest depths of Churban Olam.

The Higher Nefesh or Neshamah

The concept of the Neshamah refers to a higher soul, or a divine soul that is conventionally understood in metaphysical terms. It is genuinely hard to know whether this metaphysical tendency accurately reflects classical Jewish thought or not. What we can know is that metaphysics is so natural to Greek

---

51. Ibid.

and Western thought that in our effort to break free from Klippat Yavan it makes sense to avoid what – as we have already seen – Wittgenstein referred to as hopelessly running against the walls of a cage.[52] For this reason, our presentation of the Neshamah will try to connect it meaningfully with something that human beings do in this world. In this spirit, our understanding is that the Neshamah is part of the onto-theological structure of Tzelem Elohim and what it does is to *care* absolutely for the totality of *being* or Havayah.

In his discussion of the Nefesh Elohit, the *Tanya* cites the teaching of Rabbi Chayyim Vital, who wrote,

> In every Jew, whether righteous or wicked, there are two souls. There is one which originates in the Klippah and Sitra Achra, and which is clothed in the blood of the human being giving life to the body.[53]

The first Nefesh is responsible for "all kinds of enjoyment; frivolity and scoffing, boasting and idle talk."[54] The second soul is "truly a part of God above."[55] To understand this in non-metaphysical terms, we need to focus on the ideal relationship between the lower and higher aspects of the Nefesh. Though this lower Nefesh has bodily functions and concerns (it is responsible for appetite, temptation, and self-serving sinfulness), according to the *Tanya*, it – like the body that it animates and which is lower still – is rooted in and derived from "the highest ranks of the Supernal Mind."[56]

It is interesting that the lower Nefesh is characterized by idle talk and frivolity. These forms of negative speech are censured in biblical law and are the object of severe criticism in the *Tanya* as in many other works (notable among

---

52. Ludwig Wittgenstein, "Lecture on Ethics" (1929), first published in *Philosophical Review* 74, no. 1 (1965) 3–12.

53. Ibid., 3. The Sitra Achra refers to the "other side," or the side of evil that the kabbalah associates with the isolated Nefesh.

54. Ibid.

55. Ibid., 5.

56. Ibid., 7.

them the *Chafetz Chaim* and *Shemirat Halashon*).[57] As we saw in Heidegger's analysis of idle talk, the endless cycle of busyness and turbulence that Dasein generates as it gives itself over to the *they* function as a powerful distraction from the call of conscience to *be a self*. Similarly, though conversely, in the *Tanya*, the effort dedicated by the lower Nefesh to frivolity and idle talk distracts and conceals from the lower Nefesh its possibility of discovering a deeper alignment with the higher or inner dimensions of the self that are oriented toward the *concerns* of the "Supernal Mind."

To understand what the *Tanya* means by the "Supernal Mind" in non-metaphysical terms, we must assume that what we are talking about – however abstract – is something that human beings have access to. This means that the thoughts and feelings of the Supernal Mind or the higher Nefesh are disclosed as feeling, thought, speech, and actions of the lower Nefesh and the body. In chapter 9 of the *Tanya* these functions are portrayed in strikingly corporeal terms:

> The abode of the divine soul is in the brains that are in the head, and from there it extends to all the limbs; and also in the heart in the right ventricle...as it is written "The heart of the wise man is on his right" (Ecclesiastes 10, 2). It is [the source of] man's fervent love toward God which, like flaming coals, flares up in the heart of discerning men who understand and reflect, with the [faculty of] knowledge of their brain, on matters that arouse this love; also [of] the gladness of the heart in the beauty of God and the majesty of His glory [which is aroused] when the eyes of the wise man, that are in his head i.e., in the brain harboring his wisdom and understanding, gaze at the glory of the King and beauty of His greatness that are unfathomable and without end or limit...

---

57. Rabbi Israel Meir Kagan (b. Poland 1838) is generally referred to as the "Chafetz Chaim" after a work of this name which he dedicated to the laws concerning the biblical and rabbinic prohibitions against all forms of malicious speech and gossip. A second work of his on the same theme, *Shemirat HaLashon* (literally "guarding the tongue"), deals with the more ethical aspect of these laws.

The brain, which is described here, is clearly associated with the capacities of the higher Nefesh. But the *Tanya* is also clearly referring to the physical organ, which has both left- and right-side functions. So this physical brain is an organ but is also a lower embodiment of something higher. The more abstract "brain" or "Supernal Mind" is not a different organ or even an abstraction of one. It is a higher level of abstract thought that transcends the *concerns* of the lower Nefesh. This higher thought is not metaphysical. Rather, it is a different order of *care* for *being* which, like the lower brain, has both left and right brain functions. The functions of these left and right sides are mapped onto the top row of Keter in the chart of spheres.[58] This row comprises the faculties of Chochmah (usually translated as "wisdom") and Binah (usually translated as "understanding"), which together yield Da'at (usually translated as "knowledge") and which are positioned at the left, the right, and the center of the chart, respectively.

The *Tanya*'s celebrated "Hasidic rationalism" is connected to its emphasis on intellectually rigorous study of Torah. This practice achieves an alignment of the lower Nefesh with the higher one so that lower *concerns* are expanded by, and hence nourished by, higher ones. More specifically, the application of Chochmah, Binah, and Da'at to the study of Torah opens a higher level of inner awareness to the idea that the deepest *concern* of human *being* is the *being* of Havayah. This form of *care* or *concern*, which the *Tanya* describes here as a "gaze," is essentially the direct opposite of Heidegger's *being-toward-death*, since it discloses to the lower Nefesh a sense of itself *being-toward* or gazing at "the greatness of God that is unfathomable and without end or limit." Though not metaphysical, this *care* is how we propose to understand the precise meaning of Neshamah. To understand how it is "truly a part of God above," we need to look more closely at the interaction between the components of the Neshamah which are Chochmah, Binah, and Da'at.

---

58. The ten spheres or *sefirot* are the different emanations of the divine in kabbalistic thought which appear, for example, in the early kabbalistic tract *Sefer Yetzirah*, which is presumed to have been composed between the second century BCE and the second century CE. These spheres are mapped out as the "Tree of Life" that corresponds in its shape to the human body. The level of Keter, or "crown," corresponds to the head, where Chochmah and Binah appear on the right and left sides, respectively. For a useful introduction to the history and themes of this book, see Aryeh Kaplan, *Sefer Yetzirah: The Book of Creation in Theory and Practice* (Weiser Books, 1997).

Chochmah and Binah (Understanding and Interpretation)

Heidegger's portrayal of *understanding* and *interpretation* in *BT* can provide us with extremely useful language for explaining how this triad that the *Tanya* famously abbreviates as "Chabad" is truly a part of God above and what it is about the workings of this mechanism that accomplishes this state of "gazing" in the brain/Keter. We will begin with Chochmah and Binah and then move on to discuss Da'at in a separate section.

. The *Tanya* states as follows:

> The intellect of the rational soul, which is the faculty that conceives anything, is given the appellation of Chochmah – the potentiality of what is....[59] When one brings forth this power from the potential into the actual, that is, when a person cogitates with his intellect in order to understand a thing truly and profoundly as it evolves from the concept which he has conceived in his intellect, this is called Binah.[60]

Chochmah is to conceive the potentiality of *what is*. The *Tanya* explains that the meaning of the term is ostensibly derived from a dissection of the Hebrew word – into *choch* (read *ko'ach*, which means "potentiality") and *mah* (meaning "what-ness," "is-ness," and "from God"). This is clearly ontological language.

As we explained in our linear reading of *BT*, *understanding* is one of the hermeneutic antennae with which Dasein *is-there*. Since Dasein is essentially *thrown* into its *being-there*, its most primordial experience of that *there* has a circular structure, the starting point of which is *throwness*. *Throwness* describes Dasein's consciousness of its own *being-in-the-world* as *being-thrown-into-the-world*. *Understanding* describes the way in which Dasein projects its consciousness onto that *world* as it shows its first or initial *concern* for its *being*. Thus, the mode of *understanding* basically retraces the experience of *throwness* by projecting back, as it were, to the "from where" Dasein is *thrown*. In

---

59. This is extrapolated from the reorganization of the letters of the Hebrew word חכמה, which are read as כח מה – denoting the power over what *is*.

60. *Tanya*, chapter 3, 10–11.

this looking back, Dasein *understands* what its potentiality of *being* is in the context of what is *there*.

Chochmah, which, as we have seen, refers explicitly to the discovery of a potentiality of *being*, corresponds still more closely to Heidegger's definition of *understanding* if we first consider the biblical context from which the *Tanya's* use of the term is derived. In the Bible, Chochmah (or more specifically *chochmat lev*, i.e., of the heart) refers to a kind of know-how or creative ability that was bestowed upon Bezalel and the other artisans who built the Mishkan (Tabernacle) in the wilderness.[61] In this biblical context, a *chacham lev* is someone with the architectural know-how to imaginatively glimpse a blueprint that will guide them in the task of building. The inner Torah understands the Mishkan as a place whose architectural features and accompanying rituals function as a spatial mirror of the inner structure of Tzelem Elohim.[62] It is a space that embodies an idea of the self with a layout that corresponds not only to the human form but to the chart of the spheres.[63] Phenomenologically speaking, the experience of being inside the Mishkan brings the lower Nefesh face-to-face with an external image of its ownmost higher Nefesh-*self* with the purpose of having a transformative impact upon it. In this sense, the Chochmah required to glimpse the blueprint of this structure relates less to the external architecture of the building and more to the inner architecture of the self to which it corresponds.

Chochmah generally refers to the human capacity to think creatively and, as in a moment of creative inspiration, to intuitively grasp the germ of an idea. This is like Rabbi Chayyim's idea in the *Soul of Life* that human creativity is a shadow of and therefore a clue to divine creativity. Chochmah is the experience of creativity in the sense that the capacity for creativity possessed by the lower Nefesh is informed by an experience of *createdness* that the higher Nefesh *always already* knows. Considered within the structure of Tzelem Elohim, the function that Chochmah performs in Keter (the Supernal Mind) is to provide the lower Nefesh with an inspirational glimpsing of the

---

61. Exodus 31:1–11.

62. See, for example, J. Zohara Meyerhoff Hieronmus, *Sanctuary of the Divine Presence: Hebraic Teachings on Initiation and Illumination* (Vermont: Inner Traditions Press, 2012), 36–67.

63. Ibid.

"*from where*" of human *being*. This idea is found, for example, in the prophetic words "You that seek the Lord, look unto the rock whence you were hewn" (Isaiah 51:1).

When we compare this to the meaning of *understanding* as a first glimpse of *thrownness*, the juxtaposition of the two becomes clear. *Thrownness* is a form of Dasein's *concern* about itself. Chochmah raises the level of this to a higher realization of *createdness*. Chochmah gives the lower Nefesh a glimpse of its ownmost self as *being* within a unified totality of *created-being*. *By* glimpsing the "*from where*" it is *thrown* in terms of *createdness*, Chochmah is a form of *care*. Chochmah is the flash of inspiration that redirects Dasein's *concern* for itself past itself, as it were, and further inward toward the potentiality for *being* a *self* that is perpetually *from* the totality of Havayah.

The meaning of Binah is similarly elucidated by comparing it with the hermeneutic antenna that Heidegger calls *interpretation* in *BT*. It refers to the process of integration and detailed comprehension that follows an intuitive insight. As the *Tanya* says in the passage cited above, "When a person cogitates with his intellect in order to understand a thing truly and profoundly as it evolves from the concept which he has conceived in his intellect, this is called Binah." Binah is comparison and deduction that processes the *care* for *being* that Chochmah has initially and sometimes instantaneously – as in a flash of initial inspiration – glimpsed. In *BT*, *interpretation*, as we saw, comes to fill in or recover the distance traveled when Dasein becomes aware of itself as *being-thrown*. *Interpretation* brings back to Dasein what has been *understood*, thus fulfilling its potential to *care* for *being-with* innerworldly objects and thus disclose more and more modes of its own *being-with* to itself. Like *understanding* and *interpretation,* the interaction between Chochmah and Binah follows a circular structure that involves both spontaneous discovery and *interpretation*. These enable the self to come face-to-face with itself in terms of coming to know what it *cares* most about.[64] While Dasein discovers its ownmost *care* for *being-a-self,* in the structure of Tzelem Elohim, Binah discloses to the lower Nefesh that its ownmost *care* is for Havayah.

---

64. The collaboration between these two is perhaps similar to the correct functioning of Systems 1 and 2 in Daniel Kahneman's *Thinking, Fast and Slow* as discussed in chapter 3.

The Meaning of Da'at as the Opposite of *Discourse*

In *BT* Heidegger describes *discourse* as a kind of knowledge that can be conveyed in language. The *Tanya* describes Da'at as "gazing at the fathomless glory of the King." Da'at refers to the human capacity to become totally absorbed – and hence "truly a part of" – the infinity of the "*from where*" it is *thrown*. In this sense, Da'at is the opposite of *discourse*. It does not condense; it is expansive *care* for infinite *being* through the encounter with the limitless potentiality of *being* that Chochmah and Binah disclose.[65]

The *Tanya* interprets the verse "The heart of the wise man is on the right," saying,

> It is the source of man's fervent love toward God which, like flaming coals, flares up in the heart of discerning men who understand and reflect with the faculty of Da'at.[66]

Da'at is the reception and saturation of the inner dimension of my ownmost *being* with God's *being* and as such, within the structure of Tzelem Elohim, it is an intimate experience. However, the concept of Da'at cannot be understood in cognitive terms alone. As an intimate state of *being* it is *always already attuned*. In this passage, the centrality of *attunement* is represented by the *Tanya's* reference to fervent love.

Middot Neshamah – Higher *Attunements*

In *BT*, Heidegger describes *understanding, interpretation*, and *discourse* as *always already attuned. Attunement* and cognition are equiprimordial constitutions of Dasein's *being*.[67] According to Heidegger, fear and anxiety disclose to Dasein its authentic mode of *being-a-self*. By way of contrast, in the *Tanya* fear and awe play a fundamental but opposite role. The *Tanya* states,

> Chochmah and Binah are the father and the mother that give
> birth to love of God and awe and dread of Him. For when the

---

65. In many ways, this formulation echoes the principle of infinity as Levinas describes it in his *Totality and Infinity: An Essay on Exteriority* (Kluwer Academic, 1991), chapter 5.
66. *Tanya*, 38–39.
67. Ibid., 138.

intellect in the rational soul deeply contemplates and immerses itself exceedingly in the greatness of God – how He fills all worlds and encompasses all worlds and in the presence of Whom everything is considered as nothing – there will be born and aroused in his mind and thought the emotion of awe for the Divine Majesty, to fear and to be humble before His blessed greatness, which is without end or limit, and to have the dread of God in his heart. Next his heart will glow with an intense love like burning coals with a passion, desire and longing, and a yearning soul toward the greatness of Ein Sof (eternity). This constitutes the culminating passion of the soul.[68]

This passage (and many others like it), describes the precise nature of how Dasein's *attuned being-a-self* is negated by the inner Torah. The point here is not the denial of what Dasein's *attunements* disclose about its *being*, but the healing or correction (Tikkun) of this through alignment with the *attunements* that comprise cognition in the higher Nefesh. Chochmah and Binah bring about alignment between the *concerns* of the lower and higher Nefesh in terms that can be measured through attention to *attunement*. Chochmah and Binah are said to "give birth" to love of God through "awe and dread of Him." What the *Tanya* is describing here is a higher form of *attuned* cognition that emerges from within a lower one. As we add more and more terms to our lexicon, we shall refer to the higher cognition as Mochin deGadlut (or simply Gadlut) and to the lower one as Mochin deKatnut (or Katnut).[69]

The *Tanya* says,

In the case of a person who is intelligent enough to know God and to reflect on His blessed greatness and to beget out of his understanding a lofty fear in his brain and a love of God in the right part of his heart...his soul will thirst for God, seeking to

---

68. Ibid.

69. This is a distinction that is repeated widely in both kabbalistic and Hasidic literature. It appears expressly in Rabbi Chayyim Vital's masterful rendition of Lurianic kabbalah, *Etz HaChayyim*, gate 40, *derush* 9 [Hebrew]. Gadlut refers to expansiveness or largesse, while Katnut connotes small-mindedness and constriction.

cleave unto Him through the fulfillment of the Torah and its commandments.[70]

In this passage, the *Tanya* is saying that when the readily accessible capacities of the lower mind are focused on the study of Torah and the fulfillment of its commandments, they yield a higher love and fear that generate cleaving to God. This cleaving is a higher Da'at which emerges equiprimordially with the higher *attunement* of passionate love for God. Here, as in *BT*, cognition and *attunement* are equiprimordial. Knowledge and love of God are never separate. One does not lead to the other. They are contained within each other, and hence passionate love of God is the *attunement* that discloses to us cognition in Gadlut.

We can see the idea of lower and higher forms of Da'at in chapter 3, where the *Tanya* interprets the verse "Adam knew Eve" (the word *yada*, meaning "knew," is from the same etymological root as Da'at). In the biblical verse this clearly refers to sexual love. However, in higher Da'at,

> one binds the mind with a very firm and strong bond to, and firmly fixes his thought on, the greatness of the blessed Ein Sof (eternity of God) without diverting his mind. For even one who is wise and understanding of the greatness of the blessed Ein Sof, will not – unless he binds his knowledge and fixes his thought and perseverance – produce in his soul true love and fear but only vain fancies. Therefore, Da'at is the basis of the *middot* and the source of their vitality.[71]

What the *Tanya* is describing here is how Chochmah and Binah can accomplish the transposition of Da'at in Katnut – which refers to physical sexual intimacy – into Da'at in Gadlut, which is total intercourse of the mind – total absorption in *care* for the *being* of God. Again, the distinction between these two states of mind is discernible through *attunement*. The lower *attunements* or Middot Nefesh are referred to in the passage as "vain fancies." The

---

70. *Tanya*, chapter 38.
71. Ibid., chapter 3.

sequential language explains the nature of the transposition of these into their higher form. Higher Da'at is identified by the extent to which the interaction of Chochmah and Binah generates true Yirah and Ahavah. One might surmise that the lesser *attunements* here are forms of fear, anxiety, and love that are driven by the self-absorbed feelings and *concerns* of the ego. But these are clues, like sexual attraction, to potentialities that lie beyond.

Similarly, in his *Middot Raayah*, Rabbi Kook offers a systematic portrayal of Middot Nefesh and Middot Neshamah working through a range of *middot* which includes Ahavah (love), Emunah (faith), Brit (covenant), Gaavah (pride), Devekut (literally "cleaving" but in the Heideggerian sense we refer to this as *care*), Yirah (fear), Ratzon (will), and others.[72] Again, our key contention is that this portrayal can and should be read onto-theologically. What this means is that each of these qualities describes a permanent or stable state of *being* on the level of the Neshamah that has ontic expressions on the level of Nefesh. These *middot* are *attuned* modes of the Neshamah's *care*. They are the measure against which the *middot* of the Nefesh are to be aligned. Hence, each *attunement* has both a full and a deficient state as Rabbi Kook writes, "Every good *middah* has deficiencies that come with it and the complete service/work (*avodah shelemah*) is to bring to the light of the world the good form of the *middot* cleansed of all remnants of their deficient forms."[73] This bringing into the light of the world is the extension from the concealed level of the Neshamah into the Nefesh through alignment. The pleasure that this alignment yields is also a form of *attunement*, but it is one that the Nefesh or everyday Dasein denies itself by hiding from itself:

> The holy fire of the love of God, is it not always burning in the Neshamah, warming the Ruach, enlightening the life and its endless pleasure...and how cruel is man to himself that he is immersed in the darkness of life, absorbing himself in his own many inventions,[74] but the life of life, the pleasure drawn from

---

72. See "Middot HaRaayah" in Rabbi Kook's *Musar Avicha U'Middot HaRaayah* (Jerusalem: Mossad HaRav Kook, 1971) [Hebrew].

73. "Toward the Middot," introduction to *Middot HaRaayah*, 91.

74. The Hebrew phrase *cheshbonot rabbim* is taken from Ecclesiastes 7:29. This translation of the phrase as "many inventions" is taken from the Mechon Mamre Hebrew/English

the foundation of life he conceals from his heart and as a result he
has no part in it.[75]

The love that Rabbi Kook is describing here is disclosed in the *attunements* of
the heart, which is equivalent to the supernal mind or the Neshamah. This
care that this aspect of the self gives is *attuned* as pleasure from the "life of
life." The life of life is the inner Torah's equivalent of the *being* of being; it is
the foundation of the aliveness of *being*, which is disclosed *attuned* in love as
the knowledge of its ownmost *being* as Da'at Hashem. Similarly, Rabbi Kook's
portrayal of Emunah takes a lower and a higher form. In its lower form it
is faith; however, in its higher form it is an *attuned* mode of the Neshamah's
care for its ownmost *being* that first experiences itself as aware of its own *being*
as *from* Havayah. Emunah is the *attuned* content of that awareness. Finally,
Yirah is the inner experience of Chochmah. It is the deepest initial glimpse
of *createdness* that discloses in the lower Nefesh a sense of awe stimulated
by a paradox that Rabbi Kook describes as comprised of two opposite but
united poles: on the one hand, "total lack of knowledge about the essence
of the divine" and, on the other, "total certainty about the createdness of all
that is."[76] Given the similarity of this awe to existential angst, its role in the
negation of Heidegger's ontology requires some further explanation.

The Replacement of Fear and Anxiety with Awe (Yirah) and Love (Ahavah)

As we have suggested, Yirah and Ahavah are not simply emotions, feelings,
or even moods, but *attunements.* As such, they are not opposites but may
be aligned on a continuum according to which the insight that is disclosed
through Yirah culminates in a higher or more inward insight that is disclosed
in the form of Ahavah. We will now try to unpack the mechanism that establishes a continuum between Yirah and Ahavah and allows for the journey
inward to ensue. We will do this, as before, by analyzing this progression as a
negation of the role that fear and anxiety play in *BT*.

---

online bible https://www.mechon-mamre.org/p/pt/pt3107.htm

75. Rabbi Kook, *Middot HaRaayah*, 93.
76. Ibid., 124.

For Heidegger, fear and anxiety are especially telling because they disclose to Dasein the inescapability of its own *being-toward-death* and propel it forward toward the totality of its own *being-in-time*. Anxiety, as we have seen, is the *attunement* that discloses resolute *being-toward-death* as freedom from the *they*. There is no escape from it. Indeed, inauthentic being is its evasion. In the *Tanya*, Yirah has precisely the opposite effect. Yirah is indeed imposing, but the source of this imposition is not the inescapable animal fear of death.

Yirah breeds Ahavah in the following way: The lower Nefesh is self-absorbed in its *concern* for its own being. In the cyclical interaction of Keter, Chochmah gives the lower Nefesh a first glimpse of the *from-where* of its own mortal *being* that transposes its *concern* for itself into awe of its *being* as *being-created*. This *attuned* glimpse evolves through Binah into an integrated and detailed comprehension that the lower Nefesh's concern for itself is a problem. As cognition progresses inward or upward in the leveled structure of Tzelem Elohim, the self, experiences its *concern* for its mortal self as a form of *being* that *is from* the infinity of all *being*-Havayah. It becomes aware that the fact of its self-absorption is grounds for fear, and thus the lower Nefesh's sense of itself is disclosed to it as *attuned* fear of the overwhelming limitless-ness of all *created-being*. In the next step, the interaction of Chochmah and Binah points out to the lower Nefesh that its ownmost *being-a-self* is a microcosm of all created *being*. It is the *peshat* of the *sod*. This insight then allows the transposition of its fear and anxiety about its embarrassing *concern* for itself into love. The lower Nefesh learns to feel its initial *concern*, i.e., its love of self (which in its lower form is a vain fancy that breeds fear for self) as love for *being* itself, of which its ownmost *being* is always a part. Thus, the *middah* of Ahavah is essentially self-love as the *peshat* or the microcosm of the *sod* or macrocosm which is love for Havayah. Thus, in the structure of Tzelem Elohim, love of self is unified with the love of everything, just as the lower Nefesh is unified with the Neshamah in Da'at. Ahavah is therefore the innermost *attunement*, which is why the *Tanya* concludes that "Da'at is the basis of the *middot* and the source of their vitality."[77]

---

77. *Tanya*, chapter 3.

Ahavah and Social Spatiality of Dasein

In this microcosmic/macrocosmic manner of *peshat* and *sod*, the three levels of self-love, love of others, and love of God are united through the transformation of *throwness* into the experience of *being-created*. Through the structure of Tzelem Elohim, the *from-where* of other beings extends Dasein's *care* for its own *being-created* to the *being* of all *created-beings* and to the *being* of God. This complex analysis of where Ahavah comes from is captured famously and succinctly in the verse "Love thy neighbor as thyself [for] I am God." [78] This is a striking and perhaps puzzling idea. On the one hand, *concern* for others seems grounded in selfishness, while on the other hand, the idea that one can be commanded to love another seems ill-suited to what we know about the fickle nature of human emotions.

An onto-theological reading of this verse based on our analysis of the structure of Tzelem Elohim sees it as establishing the principle that the love of self, love of others, and love of God are all part of the same continuum. Specifically, when read in context, this biblical passage underlines the special role that the social collective of Israel has in disclosing to the world this kind of "self-love as love of others and God." The passage sees the collective of Israel as a middle ground; it is a nation-sized microcosm that stands between the individual and totality. Since love is a uniting force, love between the people is an echo or a microcosm of the greater macrocosmic dimension, which Rabbi Chayyim Ben Attar in his commentary on this passage describes as the infinite unified *being* of God.[79]

Seeing the individual, the Jewish collective, and the totality of human-*being* as microcosms and macrocosms of each other that culminate in the ultimate macrocosm; the totality of Havayah – allows us to point out the onto-theological meaning of the interpersonal commandments of the Torah or *mitzvot bein adam lechavero*.[80] What makes the interpersonal aspects of the Torah so important is that they are "commandments" in the sense that they are clues *from* Havayah. This idea grounds the Jewish notion of collectivity in

---

78. Leviticus 19:18.

79. See Chayyim Ben Attar, *The Light of Life* (Venice, 1742) Deuteronomy 32:9 [Hebrew].

80. This is a reference to the famous teaching that appears in the Jerusalem Talmud, *Nedarim* 9:4, where Rabbi Akiva teaches that the basic principle of these mitzvot and indeed of all the Torah is embedded in this verse.

an ontological principle that fundamentally negates Heidegger's idea in *BT* of Dasein's "existential being-open as being-with for the other."[81] This is a condition of *being* which, as we have already seen, finds the source of collective destiny in Dasein's *concern* for itself alone.

Mitzvot bein adam lechavero frame the meaning of collectivity in the context of a continuum in which love of self extends to love of others and love of Havayah. The fact that they are "commanded" rather than intuitive, ethical, or moral is what makes them clues to the intrinsic value of all *being* as *created-being*. Hence, the obligation to 'love thy neighbor as thyself' is grounded in the statement "For I am God." This argument leads us to a clearer understanding of the negation (to which we will return in the next chapter) of individual mortal time by the temporality of the collective. Though the individual Nefesh in a state of Katnut is capable of fathoming for itself how it can profit from charity and kindness, etc., the existentially selfish meaning of these acts can be tolerated only when they are experienced as clues that include Dasein's ownmost *concern* for its mortal self in a totality of eternal *being*. This approach allows us to dispense with the idea that values need to be selfless in order to be moral or pure. They can be selfish when they are in a state of Katnut since the self is understood as a clue to the collective and the collective as a clue to the totality. This is the function of mitzvah (commandment). It allows for Gadlut, which means the transposition of fear for love, of existential selfishness for a sense of self that is the *peshat* of a *sod*. When performed as covenantal commandments, acts of loving-kindness give the Nefesh access to the Neshamah's experience of *being* as Havayah. Ultimately, when applied to *mitzvot bein adam lechavero*, Gadlut is the meaning of Rabbi Chaninah's counterintuitive teaching: *Gadol hametzuveh ve'oseh* – "It is greater (*gadol* is from the same root as Gadlut) to perform an act of kindness as one who is commanded than as one who volunteers."[82]

---

81. Heidegger, *BT*, 158.

82. This principle appears in the Talmud (*Eiruvin* 3a). See also the commentary of the Tosafot on this page, where they explain that the reason for this is that someone who acts because he is commanded overcomes his evil inclination and focuses his concern on the will of God.

Kavanah – The Meaning of Intention as Direction

The last concept that we will discuss in this chapter is Kavanah. This term generally refers to the mental effort of concentrating on the meaning of the prescribed words uttered in prayer. More broadly, Kavanah also means the concentration and intentionality that accompanies the performance of any mitzvah. Indeed, the requirement of Kavanah is always discussed apropos mitzvot. While there is unanimous agreement in rabbinic literature that Kavanah is always desirable, there is some debate about whether the obligation to perform a mitzvah can be fulfilled without Kavanah. The discussion of this question originates in the Talmud with the conflicting opinions of Rabba and Rabbi Zeira, the former stating that mitzvot require Kavanah and the latter stating that they do not. [83] However, as the discussion unfolds in Talmudic and halachic literature, a distinction emerges between commandments that involve a physical action and those that do not. For example, Maimonides and Rabbi Yosef Karo rule that mitzvot that involve a physical action (such as eating matzah on Passover[84]) can be performed without Kavanah, while those that are performed as acts of pure thought or paying attention but without a specific action (such as hearing the sound of the shofar[85]) cannot be fulfilled without Kavanah. In addition, the halachic debate about Kavanah distinguishes between different types of Kavanah, saying that certain mitzvot require focused intentionality while others require only latent or contextual intentionality. This is the case, for example, when a person attends the prayers in the synagogue without focusing his intention on the words. Since the act of coming to the synagogue indicates his overall intention to pray, his showing up is considered latent intentionality. In this case, the fact that he is in attendance is proof enough of Kavanah for the obligation of prayer to be fulfilled.[86]

---

83. See *Berachot* 2a and *Rosh HaShanah* 28a.

84. Matzah is the unleavened bread that Jews are obliged by biblical command to eat for seven days on the festival of Pesach (Passover) according to the verse "For seven days you shall eat matzot" (Exodus 12:15).

85. It is one of the obligations of the festival of Rosh HaShanah (the new year) to hear the shofar being blown. The precise emphasis on "hearing" that this injunction requires is elucidated by Maimonides in his *Mishneh Torah, Hilchot Shofar VeSukkah VeLulav* 2:1.

86. For a clear summary of the laws concerning this matter, see Rabbi Eliezer Melamed, *Peninei Halachah*, "The Laws of Prayer," chapter 15, section 8 [Hebrew], also available in English translation at https://ph.yhb.org.il/en/category/tefila/.

This illustrates the principle that the obligation to perform a mitzvah is first and foremost connected to the body. The mitzvah is performed by the body and the action itself is the body of the mitzvah. Next to this body, Kavanah is the soul of the mitzvah, which in turn is said to be performed by the soul.[87] Thus, only when the mitzvah in question has no body is Kavanah indispensable. We can therefore say that Kavanah is as an intrinsic or inner element of any mitzvah but not one that is required for the performance of a mitzvah with a body.

Kavanah is the inner dimension of the mitzvot, and as such, it is essential to understanding the overall structure of inner Torah. Similarly, the need for Kavanah shows how the inner Torah corresponds to the structure of Tzelem Elohim. Like the body, the Nefesh, and the Neshamah, the mitzvot have a body and an inner dimension. Our suggestion is that something very general and significant about the relationship of *sod* and *peshat* is disclosed by the way in which the role of Kavanah in the performance of mitzvot is understood. This is because the soul of the mitzvot (or the *sod* of the mitzvot) is a concept that – rather than focusing on meaning, symbolism, or purpose – is concerned with directionality. In order to understand this more fully, we need to move beyond the general meaning of soul and explore how Kavanah fits in with the more precise system of terms that we have discussed so far. As before, we shall compare the meaning of Kavanah with *BT,* this time focusing on the principle of *directionality*, which Heidegger sums up as Dasein's *taking care of being as being-toward.*

Kavanah is integrally connected to *attuned* cognitive functions that disclose the cognition of the higher Nefesh in the lower one within the overall structure of Tzelem Elohim. We can see this already in the first words of the second gate of Rabbi Chayyim's *Soul of Life*:

> It is written to love God and serve Him with all your hearts/minds and all your souls (plural). And the Rabbis stated…what is service using the hearts/minds? …This is prayer…. Now the meaning of what is stated regarding the context of prayer with all your hearts/minds is plain and describes the intention of the text in two

---

87. Ibid.

contexts. The first, specifically is to empty his heart/mind from the burden of thoughts and to divert it to the direction (Kavanah) of attending completely to the words of the prayer...as they stated, "one who prays must adjust the direction of his heart/mind toward the heavens".... And the second is to eradicate from his mind all worldly pleasures and their delights from all sources during the service of prayer and to exclusively gaze heavenward towards the majesty of the Creator. As was stated, one who prays must transfer his heart/mind upwards.... And...the early pious ones...would settle down the mind for an hour so that they could adjust the direction (Kavanah) of their hearts/minds toward God.[88]

As we mentioned above, *Soul of Life* discusses prayer after Tzelem Elohim, because prayer depends upon the similarity between man and God. What we can see in this passage is the more specific idea that prayer is an activity with the particular purpose of accomplishing the alignment that connects the body and the lower Nefesh with the higher one. The terminology used here rests upon the semantic cluster that connects the flow of blood in the heart, the flow of lifeblood in the Nefesh, and the flow "upwards" (which in Art Green's words is "a vertical metaphor for an inward event")[89] of consciousness into the realm of the higher Nefesh or mind, which is disclosed by the *attunement* of Ahavah. These are precisely the elements of Tzelem Elohim that must be aligned to nurture the point of contact that worship seeks to cultivate. "Service" in the passage above is the translation of the word Avodah, which is a term that pertains to the work or service of the heart in prayer as a replacement for the Avodah – also meaning sacrificial ritual – of the Mishkan. As we saw above, the references to the heart in the context of the Mishkan also connote Chochmah, which in turn is connected to the mechanism that generates Ahavah. What we want to understand here is the role that Kavanah plays in the interaction of all these.

Prayer is described here as a mental act that depends on appropriate directionality. Its impact is described as an event that takes place in the Nefesh/

---

88. Rabbi Chayyim of Volozhin, *Soul of Life*, 197–99.
89. Arthur Green, *Seek My Face*, 9.

mind/heart. Here Kavanah has a very specific purpose. It meditatively reverses the directionality of the lower Nefesh away from Dasein's *with-world* and toward the "from where" *being* – as *being-created* - is *thrown*. Kavanah enables Avodah of the heart to redirect the flow of *taking-care* of *being* away from the self (described in the passage as "eradicating from the mind all worldly pleasures") and toward the *from where* of *created-being* (described in the passage as "gazing heavenward toward the majesty of the Creator"). In this sense, prayer is Kavanah because it aligns or extends consciousness from the body all the way inward or upward to a place *from where* the entire self can intimately gaze upon and address God.

A particularly fascinating breakdown of this process appears in chapter 38 of the *Tanya*. The discussion begins with a mention of the Talmudic question about whether the performance of a mitzvah requires Kavanah. This question leads to a more specific question about why certain types of prayer when meditated upon without articulation require Kavanah but when uttered out loud do not. The *Tanya's* lengthy answer to this concerns the distinction between body and soul (*peshat* and *sod*) that we mentioned above. It offers an especially rich portrayal of the elements of this distinction and is therefore worth quoting almost in full. The *Tanya* answers its own question as follows:

> The reason is that the *neshamah* needs no *Tikkun* for herself by means of the commandments but has only to draw forth light to perfect the vivifying soul and body by means of the letters of speech which the *nefesh* pronounces with the aid of the five organs of verbal articulation. This is similar to the active commandments which the *nefesh* performs with the aid of the other bodily organs. Nevertheless, it has been said that prayer (or other benedictions) recited without *Kavanah* is like a body without a *neshamah*. This means that, just as in all creatures in this world, possessing a body and a soul, namely the *nefesh* of all living, and the *ruach* of all human flesh, and the *neshamah* of all that has the spirit of life in its nostrils among all living creatures, all of which God animates and brings into existence *ex nihilo,* constantly, by the light and vitality which He imbues into them, for also the material body, and even the very inanimate stones and earth, have within them light and

vitality from His blessed self, so that they do not revert to naught and nothingness as they were before – there is, nevertheless, no comparison or similarity whatever between the quality of the light and vitality that illumine the body, and the quality of the light and vitality that illumine the *neshamah* which is the soul of all living…. And just as the illumination and flow of the vitality in the inanimate and vegetable bear no comparison or parallel with the illumination and flow of vitality which is clothed in animals and man… likewise in the case of precepts that depend on verbal articulation, and utterance of the lips without *Kavanah,* by comparison with the illumination and flow of the light of the blessed *Ein Sof* which irradiates and pervades the *Kavanah* of the active precepts that a person intends, while engaging in them, to cleave to Him, blessed be He…it is comparable to the superiority of the light of the soul over the body, which is a vessel and garb for the soul, as the body of the commandment itself is a vessel and garb for its *Kavanah.*

And although in both of them, in the commandment and in its *Kavanah*, there is the same Will…which is perfectly simple without change or multiplicity…which is united with his blessed Essence and Being, in perfect unity, nevertheless the illumination is not the same in respect of contraction and extension and it, too, is differentiated into four grades. For the "body" of the commandments themselves constitute two grades, namely the commandments involving real action and those which are performed verbally and mentally, such as the study of Torah, reciting the Shema, praying, saying Grace after meals, and other benedictions. The *Kavanah* of the commandments i.e., the intention to cleave to His blessed self, being like the soul to the body [of the commandments] is likewise subdivided into two grades, corresponding to the two categories of soul which are present in corporeal bodies, namely in animals and in man [respectively].

In the case of a person who is intelligent enough to know God and to reflect on His blessed greatness, and to beget out of his understanding a lofty fear in his brain and love of God in the right part of his heart, so that this soul will thirst for God, [seeking] to cleave to Him through the fulfillment of the Torah and commandments, which are an extension and reflection of the light of blessed *Ein Sof*, onto his soul thereby cleave to Him; and with this intention he studies Torah and performs the commandments, and likewise with this intention he prays and recites the blessings - then this *Kavanah* is, by way of a simile, like the soul of a human being, who possesses intelligence and freedom of choice and speaks from knowledge.

But he whose intelligence is too limited to know and reflect on the greatness of the blessed *Ein Sof* and to beget out of his understanding a conscious love in his heart and also awe in his mind and dread of God in his heart…yet he recalls and awakens the natural love that is hidden in his heart, bringing it out of the hidden recesses of the heart and into the conscious mind…and in this love is also contained fear to accept his rule and not rebel against Him…and with this *Kavanah* he turns away from evil and does good and studies and prays and recites benedictions…this *Kavanah* is by way of a simile like the soul of a living creature that has no intelligence and freedom of will whose midot, namely its fear of harmful things, are only instincts and do not originate in its understanding and knowledge.[90]

There are several parallel systems in play in this passage. Each of them is constructed on five levels that Aryeh Kaplan calls the structure of "inner space." In his words,

The Kabbalists refer to the five levels of the soul. The highest level, corresponding to *Adam Kadmon* and the apex of the *Yod*, is *Yechidah*-Unique Essence. The next corresponding to the letter *Yod* itself is *Chaya*-Living Essence. The next three, corresponding to the last three letters of the Name are Neshamah-Breath, *Ruach*-Spirit and finally Nefesh-Soul.[91]

---

90. Shneur Zalman of Liadi, *Likkutei Amarim, Tanya,* 38: 180–86.

91. Aryeh Kaplan, *Inner Space* (Moznaim, 1990), 16. See also note 40 and the references to *Bereishit Rabbah* 14:9; *Devarim Rabbah* 2:9; *Derech Hashem* 3:1:4.

These in turn correspond to five levels of existence which – translating the word *olam* – Kaplan calls "universes." These are *Adam Kadmon*-Primordial Man, *Atzilut*-Nearness, *Beriya*-Creation, *Yetzira*-Formation, and *Assiya*-Action or Completion.[92] Kaplan continues,

> Looking at the etymology of these terms, we see that the word *Yechidah* comes from *Echad* and *Yichud* meaning "oneness" and "unity." The word *Chayah* derives from *Chai* which means "life" and *Chayut* "life force." The word Neshamah stems from *Neshimah* meaning "breath." The word *Ruach* is often translated as "spirit," but it is also found with connotations of wind, air or direction. The word Nefesh comes from the root *Nafash* meaning to rest.[93]

This five-leveled structure also parallels the five stages through which, according to kabbalistic texts, *being* itself emerges from the pure will of God and reaches the consciousness of man. This structure, which the *Zohar* illustrates using the analogy of the glassblower (mentioned briefly above) sees the *being* of the world as emerging in the will of God (apex of the Yud/Adam Kadmon/Yechidah). This is compared to the will or decision of a glassblower to create a glass vessel. Once made, the decision which originates as pure unified and singular energy takes the form of a life force or source of *being* (*yod*/Atzilut/Chayah), which is compared to the glassblower who holds air in his lungs. The breath itself, still held in the lungs of the glassblower, is the higher Nefesh (*heh*/Beriyah/Neshamah). When it is breathed into the glassblower's tube it becomes spirit, wind, or direction (*vav*/Yetzirah/Ruach) and when it forms the physical vessel the breath that began its journey in the lungs of the glassblower comes to rest in the lower Nefesh (*heh*/Assiyah/Nefesh) in close proximity to the body.[94]

This analogy parallels the way in which the inner Torah understands the different sounds made by the letters of the Hebrew alphabet. Open vowel sounds (such as *alef*) are sounds in which the breath flows uninterrupted

---

92. Kaplan, *Inner Space*, 16.
93. Ibid.
94. Ibid., 17.

from the lungs. Next are guttural consonants in which the breath is blocked at the back of the throat (as in *ayin, gimmel,* and *chet*). Soft consonants are produced by the blocking of the breath by the tongue (as in *lamed* and *nun*) and hard consonants are formed when the breath is blocked either by the teeth (as in *tet, tav, shin, and samach*) or by the lips (as in *bet, mem,* and *peh*). This five-level structure is essentially the overall makeup of both the macrocosm of creation and the microcosm of Tzelem Elohim.

Now let us return to the *Tanya*. The focus of this passage is Kavanah. The passage begins by stating that the level of Neshamah or the higher Nefesh is one in which no Kavanah is required. Insofar as a person's active consciousness or *care* for his ownmost *being* is *always already toward created-being*, there is no need for the alignment of that consciousness at the level of Neshamah. This level represents the consciousness of *being* that is analogous to the breath that the glassblower still holds in his lungs. At this level of *being* the five levels of verbal enunciation used in prayer are *always already* aligned. In other words, if we consider prayer as an act of alignment that works on the heart, the highest form of alignment is described here as the Neshamah in a state of perpetual silent prayer. In the inner Torah, aligned *being* is itself this perpetual prayer. Prayer in its lower forms is the conscious act that aligns the lower concerns of the Nefesh with the perpetual prayer/*being* of the Neshamah. Alignment of the lower Nefesh with the perpetual prayer of the Neshamah is therefore both the purpose of prayer and the action. Kavanah is the directionality of this alignment.

What the *Tanya* says here is, if Kavanah is not simply paying attention to the words, but is actually the directionality of all *being*, it must then apply to the totality of *being* which, in its lower forms, includes "animals, vegetation and even the very inanimate stones and earth," all of which "have within them light and vitality from His blessed self." The fact that these inanimate beings *are* without conscious *being* of any sort illustrates for the *Tanya* how certain lower forms of prayer can fulfill the obligation to pray without Kavanah. In all forms of *being* there is an "identical light," but just as it is not manifest in the same way on all levels of Tzelem Elohim, it manifests itself by varying degrees in the rest of creation. It is this variation in degree that distinguishes stones from flowers, flowers from lower life forms; lower life forms from more complex ones, and so on. In stones, the concealment and constriction of the aliveness or light of conscious *being* is so intense that they do not even have the power of vegetation. In flowers, the flow of the aliveness or light of conscious *being* is greater, but it is still constricted in such a way as to conceal from flowers the powers that are accessible to animals and so on. Thus, the onto-theological structure represented by the letters YHVH is duplicated in different registers; the lowest of which is the body-ness or corporality of "mineral, vegetable, animal and man"; and the highest of which is the tip of the Neshamah.

In this portrayal, all *being* is alive *being*. Nothing is completely dead or inanimate. With different degrees of constriction and concealment, the *is-ness* of all beings discloses the infinite aliveness of *being* itself as perpetual prayer. The world is a prayer to God. This is the reason why the *Tanya* says that it is still possible to fulfill the formal obligation of a mitzvah, i.e., the seemingly inanimate body of that mitzvah, without Kavanah. The body of every mitzvah, like the physicality of everything, is already a prayer. Hence, the body of prayer – words that are uttered out loud – requires no Kavanah.

In the next stage, the *Tanya* moves on to the higher forms of *being-as-prayer*. In certain elements of the liturgy, such as the reciting of the Shema, in which the unity of God is declared, the fulfilling of the mitzvah is an act of *caring* for the *being* of Havayah that takes place in the Nefesh. In this case, the Kavanah or *care* is the act of the mitzvah, and so without Kavanah the mitzvah is not fulfilled. Here Kavanah means directionality that requires "intelligence," i.e., the interaction of Chochmah and Binah that generates *attuned* Da'at disclosed "in the heart and the souls" as Ahavah. And, as we have already seen, the *Tanya* distinguishes here between lower and higher forms of cognition accompanied by lower and higher forms of *attunement*. Hence, "in the case of a person who is intelligent enough to know God," the *Tanya* describes Kavanah "by way of a simile as the soul of a human being who possesses intelligence and freedom of choice and speaks from knowledge." But in the case of a person who lacks this intelligence, Kavanah "is like the soul of a living creature that has no intelligence and freedom of will whose midot, namely its fear of harmful things, are only instincts and do not originate in its understanding and knowledge."

If we look broadly at this passage in the *Tanya*, its underlying theme is that Kavanah is the lifeblood that animates the entire structure of Tzelem Elohim. It is the directionality in which the fear-ridden, self-centered, constricted *prayer-being* of the lower Nefesh must move in order to align itself with the perpetually conscious loving *prayer-being* of the Neshamah. As we mentioned in our discussion of Rabbi Chayyim and *The Soul of Life,* prayer is the reverse of Torah study in the structure of Tzelem Elohim. Kavanah in prayer is the reversed directionality of *Ruach* flowing inward and upward back into the lungs of the glassblower.

The significance of Kavanah transcends the formal act of prayer itself. It discloses the unity of *care* for *being* as *care* for *created-being* and as such is the soul of all mitzvot. Kavanah in prayer works on the heart; it aligns the directionality of *taking care* in the lower Nefesh with the perpetual prayer of the higher one. It is the *directionality* that points the cognition of the lower Nefesh, the body and all corporeality toward the awareness that *being* itself is grounded in the aliveness that flows outward from *Atzilut* to *Assiyah*. The totality of the limitless unity of *being* that emerges from the unity of *being* and *non-being* extends all the way to the *createdness* of animals, trees, rivers, and rocks. The non-human world is complicit in the prayer of *being* or, in the words of the psalmist, "Let the rivers clap their hands; let the mountains sing for joy together before the Lord for He has come" (Psalms 98:8–9). Kavanah is the directionality or the flow between *peshat* and *sod*, Yirah and Ahavah. It connects us to the awareness that all the world and everything in it, by varying degrees, is the *peshat* of which the indwelling, united *being* of Elohim and Havayah is by varying degrees *always already* the *sod*.

BT and the Lexicon of Inner Torah

The lexicon that we have offered here is by no means complete. But it is enough to see how the negation of *BT* can help us to uncover a system in which life and love are the grounding for anxiety and death and not the other way around. Having dispensed with the transcendental "I," as Heidegger did, our efforts now must be directed toward further disentangling the self from Western thought by dispensing with the analytic of Dasein in *BT*. We can begin to do this by looking at *BT* and Heidegger's Nazism from a perspective that is grounded in the onto-theology of Tzelem Elohim.

Essentially, *BT* is an exploration of the Nefesh and its capacity to constrict the depths of its ownmost being to the confines its own *being-in-the-world*. Significantly, this is an exploration that Heidegger chose to conduct very

consciously within the discourse of the classical Greek philosophical tradition –
the same tradition that the inner Torah refers to as Klippat Yavan.[95] In *BT* as we
understand it from the perspective of Segulah, Heidegger maps the topology
of Dasein, sealing off the possibility that the question of *being* with which he
begins *always already* contains additional levels that are disclosed by the formulation of the tautological question of Emunah within the structure of Tzelem
Elohim. The analytic of Dasein is conducted with the willfully destructive purpose of seizing the foundational experience of *being* from the hands of aliveness. *BT* is thus a struggle for the independence of the "detached or unaligned
Nefesh" founded on its own capacity to obscure, deny, and dominate the level
of Neshamah. It offers an analysis of the mortal Nefesh that seeks to violently
obscure the unassailable freedom of the Nefesh to choose *care* for the perpetual
aliveness of the Neshamah. Face-to-face with this choice, Heidegger discovered
and celebrated Dasein's ability to resolutely choose death.

The stages and details of Heidegger's analysis correspond closely with the
parallel but opposite explorations into the depths of the Nefesh conducted
by scholars of inner Torah – a small selection of whose texts we have considered in this chapter. The alternative to Heidegger's ontology offered by the
onto-theology of inner Torah is one that seeks to resist the self-vindicating
destructiveness of authentic Dasein's choice. It replaces it with the conviction
that the freedom to choose death does not absolve us of our responsibility
to go further inward and choose life. The Torah explains that this freedom
of choice is what enables cognitively gained, *attuned* knowledge of Havayah.
This knowledge or Da'at Hashem is the pleasure of love that delights the
Nefesh when it becomes the extension of the perpetual gazing prayer of the
Neshamah. In the next chapter we will explore the meaning of this in the
context of Dasein's collective eternal *they*-self and try to disclose the dimension of Netzach that negates the very concept of death itself.

---

95. This is significant because of the historical relationship or opposition between Judaism
and Hellenism. As we saw in our reading of Heidegger's analytic of Dasein, this is
a relationship of negation that is founded in the very close and similar purposes of
Judaism and Greek philosophy. As such, our analysis of Tikkun endorses much of
Heidegger's analytic identifying the one chromosome of difference that creates the
stark negation. Similarly, as many scholars (most notably Maimonides) pointed out,
Hellenism is closer to Judaism in its overall orientation than any other of the classical
cultures.

CHAPTER 16

*Being-toward-*Netzach

Beyond Authenticity

In this chapter we shall approach the hardest question that the ontological system presented by Heidegger in *BT* poses to the perspective of Segulah. The foundational principle of Heidegger's analysis is that the horizon of *being* is time. *Being* is an event and an activity that occurs in Dasein's ownmost individual experience of time, the totality of which defines Dasein's *being-in-time* as its *being-toward-death*. Any ontological system that seeks to negate Heidegger's portrayal of Dasein's individual ownmost mode of *being* can do so only if it can offer a plausible alternative to the finality and totality of death as the ultimate ontological event. Such an alternative cannot simply revert to evasion or denial of death. Similarly, religious faith in God's eternal being, the endurance of the soul, reincarnation, life after death or even the commonplace idea that the world objectively continues to exist after my death is not equal to the task of providing us with a grounded onto-theological negation. Death, in Heidegger's portrayal of it, is too stubborn an obstacle for such things to simply brush aside.

We shall begin this daunting task with the premise that, from the perspective of the inner Torah, Heidegger fundamentally misdiagnosed the causes of everyday Dasein's inauthenticity. As we stated in our analysis of the sections in *BT* that deal with authentic Dasein, the ontological behaviors or modes of *being* that characterize the spatiality (and the social spatiality) of everyday Dasein are only amplified and exacerbated – taken to their most far-flung and least authentic form – by the temporal path to "authenticity" that Heidegger plots. Both inauthentic and authentic Dasein share the same characteristic of self-deception. So our sense of the flaw need not actually question the finality of death per se, but rather we shall focus on his more preliminary methodological assumption that authentic Dasein experiences death as a finality because its primordial state of *being* is *being-a-self*. Hence, we propose that the negation of Heidegger's idea that inauthenticity is caused by Dasein's desire to evade anxiety, fear, and ownmost selfness must start with the suggestion that inauthenticity is a state of *being* in which the self is distracted by – rather than evasive of – the illusion that the totality of its ownmost potentiality for *being* originates in the inevitability of its own death. In our reading, we shall suggest that Dasein gives ontological priority to fear, anxiety, and self-*concern* over joy, love and *concern* for others because it is deluded by the illusion of its selfness. The alternative to this must consider the total aliveness of infinite *being* (despite human mortality) as a totality instead.

Building upon the lexicon constructed in the previous chapter, we will show that Heidegger was ostensibly correct in his observation that everyday Dasein or the lower Nefesh in its unaligned state is indeed blind to that totality of *being* of which its *being* is an extension. But from the perspective of the inner Torah we suggest that the unaligned Nefesh is perpetually looking (admittedly in the wrong places) for its ownmost self and not fleeing from it; it is essentially moving appropriately away from *being-a-self* – when it seeks comfort in society, in busy-ness and in empathy with the death of others. As Heidegger correctly shows, Dasein fabricates for itself an inauthentic *they-self*. However, in our analysis, this fabrication of the *they-self* is a step in the right direction, because the desires that this self seeks to satisfy are unrealized shadows of the general *being* that is disclosed through alignment of the lower Nefesh with the Neshamah.

We shall apply this specific negation of Heidegger as a template to the interpretation of identity, time, and mortality in Jewish thought. As we said in the previous chapter, the reading that we propose will not make things any simpler. However, it can provide us with a method for grounding the ineffable experiences of *being,* of which the texts we shall discuss here are a report, in a more concretely plausible onto-theological system. This system will also enable us to understand more clearly what the inner Torah teaches us to do in order to achieve a state of alignment.

Rabbi Kook's Lights of Holiness

In the discussion that follows we will focus our efforts on trying to face down the ontological totality of death by extracting an alternative to it found in certain passages that appear in the second and third volumes of Rabbi Kook's *Lights of Holiness*.[1] Specifically, we will look at excerpts from the sections entitled "The Foundation of Generality" and "The Tendency of Eden."[2] We shall try to tease out the meaning of these passages by drawing upon our lexicon of inner Torah terms according to the template of negation outlined above.

In chapter 1, we lamented the fact that Rabbi Kook is often misappropriated and distorted when he is read from a humanist perspective. When one encounters the principles that organize his thought, treating them as religious assumptions – as ontic expressions of faith – his writing is hard to decipher and even harder to read as grounded in human experience. In this sense it demands a "leap" that leaves behind those who will not make it and those who do make it in danger of remaining seemingly out of touch with the ground. In our reading, we shall try to overcome this as we explore his position on key questions that concern the genus of the Jewish individual, mortality, and the Jewish collective from an onto-theological perspective.

The General Foundation

The chapter entitled "The Foundation of Generality" deals with the relationship between the individual and the collective in Jewish identity. The first subsection in this chapter is called "The General Foundation," which begins as follows:

> A person must liberate himself from confinement within his private concerns. This pervades his whole being so that all his thoughts focus only on his own destiny. It reduces him to the worst kind

---

1. See Rabbi Abraham Kook, *Lights of Holiness*, 4 vols. (Mossad HaRav Kook, 1985) [Hebrew].

2. The term *klaliut* is translated here as "generality," though it is often rendered into English as "universality." See, for example, the translation of Ben Zion Bokser in *Abraham Isaac Kook: The Lights of Penitence, the Moral Principles, Lights of Holiness, Essays, Letters, and Poems* (Paulist Press, 1978), 201, 232.

of smallness and brings upon him endless physical and spiritual distress. It is necessary to raise a person's thoughts and will and his basic preoccupations toward universality, to the inclusion of all, on the whole world, to man, to the Jewish people, to all of existence. This will result in establishing even his private self on a proper basis.[3]

The language here closely echoes that of Rabbi Moshe Chaim Luzzatto in *Derech Hashem* that we discussed in the previous chapter. The path that it plots begins with the private and limiting concerns of the lower Nefesh. Rabbi Kook describes a kind of total *concern* for *being-a-self* that defines the total possibilities of *being* in terms of one's own destiny. The "kind of smallness" mentioned here is Katnut. By way of contrast, the key theme of this passage and of these sections in general is the idea that the redirection of *concern*, of will, and of basic human preoccupations toward a category that Rabbi Kook calls "generality," or *klaliut*, cultivates *concern* for *being* in a state of Gadlut. Therefore, Gadlut is not only about a higher, deeper, or more abstract inner state of mind; it also has a horizontal dimension that we referred to above as the middle ground between the individual and the totality of Havayah.

In the same way that every force has its equal opposite, Rabbi Kook is saying that the contemplative deepening of inner awareness is intrinsically tied to the broadening of external collective horizons. Hence, Rabbi Kook writes that the state in which *care* is aligned with Gadlut includes "all, the whole world, man, the Jewish people and all existence." These are all part of *klaliut* (translated by Bokser as "universality"[4]) and, as we shall see, this is a complex concept that has additional dimensions and meanings.

The second key point that Rabbi Kook makes here is that the transition caused by the redirection of *care* toward generality is not a replacement of the lower Nefesh with a higher one. Rather, the new state extends the Neshamah into the Nefesh by energizing it, as it were, from beyond its narrow self. Elsewhere, he refers to this as cultivating a "Nefesh Havayah which

---

3.   Bokser, *Lights of Penitence*, 232.
4.   Ibid.

transcends psychological awareness and gazes at the song of…inner light."[5] This, Rabbi Kook writes, "will result in establishing even his private self on a proper basis." The passage continues,

> The firmer a person's vision of universality (generality), the greater the joy he will experience and the more he will merit the grace of divine illumination. The reality of God's providence is seen when the world is viewed in its totality. For the divine presence cannot rest in a place that is lacking or deficient, in a place where there is only a weak point that is constricted and built on nothingness, which is individuality and selfness alone.[6]

Rabbi Kook gives precedence here to what is disclosed by joy. The establishment of the private self on a proper basis is disclosed by joy and, in reverse, suffering and anxiety are signals of inner misdirection. In this framing, Dasein's desire to avoid suffering, take comfort, and seek pleasure is therefore appropriate. Life indeed values joy and pleasure. However, the joy that Dasein needs to seek cannot emanate from its desire to *be a self*. For Rabbi Kook the unhealthy quest of the Nefesh for joy and happiness in a state of Katnut is healed (Tikkun) when they are sought in a vision of generality. In the words of Bokser's translation, this is accomplished by "seeing the reality of God's providence."

This ontically conventional religious formulation is not actually what Rabbi Kook offers us here. Unfortunately, the deeper meaning of what he says is completely lost in this translation. Bokser adds in a note that the phrase might be rendered more literally as "God's full name,"[7] and this is definitely better. However, we propose a different translation of the whole sentence, which should read, "The full name of God applies (or corresponds) to the full world." This catches Rabbi Kook's explicit reference to the five-level structure of Tzelem Elohim described in the *Zohar*'s glassblower analogy. The five-leveled structure that emanates from the apex of the *yud* and then

---

5.   Rabbi Kook, *Lights of Holiness*, vol. 2, 348.

6.   Ibid.

7.   Bokser, *Lights of Penitence*, 232, note 12.

yud, heh, vav, and *heh* (YHVH) is the full name of God that corresponds to the multilayered fullness of the world that emanates from Adam Kadmon/Yechidah, through Chayah/Atzilut, Neshamah/Beriyah, Ruach/Yetzirah, *and* Nefesh/Assiyah. Seeing this is seeing the world in generality from a perspective of Gadlut.

Put into the terminology of our lexicon, what Rabbi Kook is saying is that the *from-where* of *being* is visible when the world is seen from within a total consciousness that is *concerned* with generality. The experience of *being* that is disclosed in the higher Nefesh or Nefesh Havayah is *attuned*, and hence it is significant that it is described as a source of joy. More precisely perhaps, when the *care* of the higher Nefesh is disclosed in the lower one, it is disclosed as joy or *oneg*, because joy is the Middat Nefesh that discloses truthful *care* for generality. This is the joy that the Nefesh truly seeks but cannot find without alignment. The totality of this generality is what Rabbi Kook means here by "divine illumination," which is akin to the "gaze" of Da'at Hashem that we saw in the *Tanya* and elsewhere. It is the fullness of human *being* that is equal to or corresponds with – and is hence able to interface with – the fullness of the world. When there is no interface between the lower Nefesh and the higher one, Dasein's *being* comes face-to-face with itself as *care* for *being-a-self.* In this deficient – and hence sad and constricted – state (which Rabbi Kook describes as "individuality and selfness alone"), the divine presence cannot rest. Accordingly, in this state of *being*, alignment between the *concerns* of the lower and higher Nefesh is not possible.

The passage closes saying that the demand to maintain a consciousness of Gadlut is incumbent upon Tzaddikim (righteous people). "For this is the foundation of the Neshamah of the righteous who walk before Elohim and find joy in Hashem (God), and they must fortify themselves to *know* (Da'at) their ownmost will and not allow any force in the world to prevent this."[8] The precise meaning of Tzaddikim and their role is a theme to which we will return below. But first, what we want to show is that everyday Dasein's alleged evasion of itself and its presumed hiding in society can be seen from the perspective of inner Torah as deficient attempts to find joy by showing *concern* for others. While not an ideal by any means (on the contrary, when

---

8. Rabbi Kook, *Lights of Holiness*, 148.

anxiously *concerned* about *being-a-self*, this search can be the very meaning of *falling prey* in a state of Galut to the Sitra Achra), hiding in society is better than total self-absorption (Churban). It is a deficient form of an appropriate desire to find ultimate joy in generality (Tikkun).

Tikkun Klali – General Healing

The next section connects the concept of *klaliut* with Torah, suggesting that the transformative power of Torah is found in the way it cultivates general *concern*. In Rabbi Kook's words,

> The way one studies [Torah], the way one prays and the way one shows concern for the rest of the world (settlement of the world), whether one is concerned with matters that are essential to the narrow existence of man and creations or whether one is concerned with matters that may expand his knowledge (Da'at) and improve his life, everything is assembled and held together in one unity to complete the general healing of the entire world (Tikkun Klali) and to bring it closer and closer to the sought-after ideal, to make life good and fair and gradually more and more prepared to connect eternally and be bonded with holiness in a bond of eternal happiness; in a bond of gentle pleasure, bonded to the supernal light, the light of eternal aliveness. "He knows what is in the darkness and light dwells with him."[9]

Again, the key elements of the *attuned being* of the Neshamah are central to this passage. However, three additional features appear here that we need to unpack in order to understand them more deeply.

The first concerns the meaning of the term *yishuvo shel olam*, which we translated as both "concern for the rest of the world" and "settlement of the world." Broadly speaking, this term refers to the practice of *mitzvot bein adam lechavero* and to the *care* for others that cultivates Gadlut. However, it has additional meanings which made the double translation necessary even

---

9.   Ibid. Note that the final line of this passage is a quote from the book of Daniel (2:22). The entire verse reads, "He reveals the deep and secret things, He knows what is in the darkness and the light dwells with Him."

though it still does not quite capture the idea in full. *Yishuvo shel olam* indeed refers to looking after others in the world – i.e., the rest of the world. It refers to settlement in the sense of populating, building, and developing the world. But this is a phrase that also has spiritual connotations. In the English idiom it is helpful that both "rest" and "settlement" carry connotations which are found in the expressions "coming to rest in the world" and "settling down in the world." These both help to underscore the connection between *yishuv* and the *throwness* of the Nefesh. The root source of *yishuv* is grammatically connected to the word Shabbat. Shabbat is when the totality of *being* "comes to rest" in the world as in the biblical phrase *Shavat vayinafash*, "He rested, and He came to rest" (Exodus 31:16). The aligned Nefesh that is extended into the *being* of the world is Shabbat. Shabbat is not only God's day of rest in the sense that we think of a holiday as a day off work. It is a day of coming to rest in (i.e., being present in) the world as a facet of creation. Finally, the same root, *shav,* connotes a kind of culmination of history with the world returning to its source, which Rabbi Kook associates with the mitzvah of repentance (Teshuvah) in his *Lights of Repentance.*"[10] *Yishuvo shel olam* is therefore rich in meanings that connote the furthest extensions or "comings to rest" of the Neshamah in the lower Nefesh's aligned *being*, which in this context means the human capacity to view the alignment of the entire world with the Neshamah and hence to bear witness, as the very idea of Shabbat suggests, to the *created-ness* of all *being*.[11] This is what is meant by the correspondence between YHVH and the full five-leveled emanation of *being* into the whole world.

Rabbi Kook's use of this phrase points toward the phenomenological importance of generality or *klaliut*. Generality is indispensable to the human discovery of Tzelem Elohim, because in order to see the inner dimensions of the self, the totality of the five-leveled structure of Tzelem Elohim must also be recognized in the total *being* of the entire world. Thus, there is a

---

10. Rabbi Kook, *Lights of Repentance* (Yeshivot Bnei Akiva, Or Etzion, and Merkaz Shapiro, 1966) [Hebrew]. For a different translation, see Bokser, *Lights of Penitence.*

11. This is an idea that is central to the Shabbat liturgy (for example, the Kiddush and Friday night services) in which Shabbat is described as *zecher lema'aseh bereishit* (i.e., in remembrance of the act of creation).

correspondence between *concern* that takes the form of Gadlut and *concern* whose object is *klaliut*.

Second, in this description of Torah study, prayer, and *yishuv olam*, Rabbi Kook gives us a clear sense that the structure of alignment is one that reaches down into the smaller concerns of the Nefesh as well as connecting them to general ones. As we saw above, alignment with the higher Nefesh does not do away with the lower needs of the individual. It doesn't even transcend them; rather, it rehabilitates them where they are in the same way as self-love becomes love of Havayah. With the appropriate Kavanah or directionality of *being-toward* generality, narrow concerns of the individual become part of the general healing of the world. In this sense, the narrow individual is a microcosm whose *concerns* are not canceled or saturated by alignment with the macrocosm. They are deepened or extended and thus "corrected" by it. Put differently, the higher Nefesh does not seek to invade or replace the lower one. When the two are connected, the individualistic narrow concerns of the lower one and the general concerns of the higher one align.

Third, in this passage we are given a taste of the temporality that Rabbi Kook will continue to develop in his portrayal of generality. The *care* of the higher Nefesh has a temporality of eternity. Naturally the individual *care* of the lower Nefesh is narrow and mortal. Generality transcends this temporality, assigning to the individual the lifespan of the collective. This is a very significant and perhaps radical theme in Rabbi Kook's writing, and it must be understood precisely. Rabbi Kook is not saying that we can ignore or overcome death by ontically subsuming the death of the individual in the ongoing life of the collective. Rather, the point here is that the alignment of lower *concerns* with higher ones extends the temporality of eternity in a downward or outward direction. In this process, the life span of the Neshamah becomes the life span of the Nefesh. The implication of this as we will see later is that for Rabbi Kook eternal life is a concrete or tangible matter for this world and not a fantasy. This this-worldliness is the unique quality that characterizes the inner Torah's temporality of *being-toward*-Netzach and it is found in Isaiah (25:8), where the prophet envisions an age in which "God will swallow up death forever" or in our terms, an age in which the *being-toward-death* of the Nefesh will be combined with the *being-toward*-Netzach of the Neshamah. Again, this is a theme to which we will return.

Fourth and finally, this describes the role of Jewish law (i.e., Torah and mitzvot) in attaining Gadlut. As we mentioned in our discussion of the *Tanya*, Torah and mitzvot are central to all the texts of the inner Torah. This leads us to the meaning of the service of God through Torah and mitzvot, which Rabbi Kook refers to as General Avodah.

General Avodah

In this section Rabbi Kook begins to explain what is specifically required for *care* to be directed toward generality. In particular, he identifies Avodah as the practice and the substance of general *concern*. He writes,

> The holy feeling that is connected to higher Binah connects the service of God in all its purity with all *created-being*. It sings together with all singers of songs, with all humanity, the song of longing toward the God who created everything. And this generality, which is free and broad, will never cease to be the foundation of faith (Emunah) that is filled with love of God, love of man, and love of all creation. And a man of Israel can make this foundation stand out in accordance with the special imprint of the divine law which exists in the light of Israel as a Torah and a mitzvah, the inheritance of Jacob that will never tire, oppress, or constrict the foundation, which is broad and free; rather, it will widen it and cast its shining light upon it.[12]

In this passage Rabbi Kook begins to explain how Avodah, meaning the purposeful practice of Jewish law, accomplishes alignment. He seeks to explain why the observance of this law, rather than constricting and repressing the self, is the self's soteriological hope for freedom.

The passage begins with Binah that discloses to the lower Nefesh an internalized *interpretation* of what Chochmah has glimpsed about the *from-where* of its *being*. Binah is the journey back to the self whose *being* we *always already are*. We are not objects, and not subjects. We are the verb – the doing of that *always already being* – which Rabbi Kook refers to in that passage

---

12. Rabbi Kook, *Lights of Holiness*, 149.

as Emunah. As we suggested in our analysis of Heidegger's circular argumentation, Emunah is the circular hypothesis of our *being*'s concern for its Neshamah-*self*. It is the idea that is *always already* known when the question of *being* is retrieved, and as such in the higher Nefesh it is very specifically *attuned*, i.e., "filled with love of God, love of man, and love of all creation."

The next metaphor here is song. The language of the passage connotes prayer, and the term "chapters of song" in particular indicates biblical passages such as the praise found in the book of Psalms, the Song of Songs, the Song of the Sea, and others. "Song" here means alignment or *being-in-harmony* with the *being* of all creation. This is song that gives praise as an expression of *createdness*, as in Psalms 146 (verses 1–2), "My soul will praise the Lord; I will praise the Lord with my life, I will sing to God with my being." It has the same onto-theological meaning as the mode of *being-in-prayer* that we saw in our discussion of Kavanah in the *Tanya*. It is the form of song that, in the words of the *Sefat Emet*,[13] emanates from the "inner point" that is concealed within all creation,

> For in every created being there is an inner point…and this is the meaning of chapters of song: that every created-being has/is a song of praise to God. "And then Moses and the people of Israel sang" means the song that is already known, and which emanates from all creation.[14]

In alignment with our very *being* is a song that resonates of its own in the same way that the strings of a guitar resonate and play when they are next to a loudspeaker playing music. This song is a metaphor of sound that runs

---

13. *Sefat Emet* is a Hasidic commentary on the Torah written by Rabbi Yehuda Leib Alter of Gur (1847–1905). Sections of it have been translated into English by Arthur Green, *The Language of Truth: The Torah Commentary of the Sefat Emet* (JPS, 1998). The teachings of the Sefat Emet are organized according to the years in the Hebrew calendar in which they were delivered.

14. Rabbi Yehuda Aryeh Leib Alter of Gur (known as the Sefat Emet after the name of his commentaries on the five books of the Torah and the festivals), *Sefat Emet* (Language of Truth), Parashat Beshalach (5631). The concept of the "inner point" is central to the writings of the Sefat Emet, and we shall return to discuss this in the next chapter. All translations of the text are my own.

parallel to the more common visual metaphor of light. The self is the resonating box of that sound in the same way that the consciousness is often referred to as a vessel for containing divine light.

If we translate this analogy back into our passage from Rabbi Kook, the idea here is that this song of *being* is an expression of Emunah elicited from the depths of the soul, i.e., from the more abstract or inner levels of Tzelem Elohim, through the observance of the law. Thus, the song of the world is the loudspeaker that sounds the ownmost *being* of all *being*. What places the guitar next to this loudspeaker — what prepares the strings to vibrate — is the unique obligation of Am Segulah to observe Jewish law. The Hebrew word *chakukah* used in that passage for the law stems from the word *chok*. This word, which formally describes statutory laws for which the Torah provides no rationale, literally means "legislated" or "mandated" but can also be translated as "engraved" or "imprinted." In this sense, the legislated law is an image or a mold taken from a form that is imprinted on the heart or higher Nefesh. What Rabbi Kook means by this is that the strict observance of the law is the most natural and free behavior of the higher Nefesh and the most natural and complete expression of its most intuitive *concerns*. Observing the law, or Avodah, is following the path that leads us back to our ownmost selves with *concerns* that are aligned in Gadlut with the totality of all *being*. When the lower Nefesh feels constricted and confined by the mold of the law, this is an expression of its distraction from itself. It is missing the point or the call of conscience, because this seemingly inhibiting mold has the shape of its ownmost free and general self. To follow the law, to take upon oneself the shape or the form of the law, to adjust one's *being* to its mold, is to align the lower self with the higher one and assume the form that finally allows it to slip free of constriction. Rabbi Kook continues,

> At first one discovers the full content of the entire Torah in all its breadth within the private Nefesh in its healings and deficiencies, its ups and its downs, and after this one discovers the private Nefesh as it is intertwined with all generality. Next one discovers the content of generality in the entire world, and the Havayah (being of being) is left dependent on the completeness of the morality and the Torah of each individual. Every man must say, The world was

created for me and when will my actions equal those of Abraham, Isaac, and Jacob our forefathers.[15]

When the lower Nefesh takes the law upon itself, it discovers that the law is its release from confinement. The law is the aligner that extends *care* for *being* from the confinement of the narrow self and releases it into a state of *being-free-toward* its most general self. This is Gadlut, and it is the state of mind in which the law was received. Hence, any constriction that the lower Nefesh feels when it pushes itself to observe the law is really a release. It is perhaps like the pressure that a fetus feels when the birth canal contracts to prepare it for birth. Similarly, the lower Nefesh must squeeze through the law in order to emerge into the joyful generality that it experiences when it is given access to the innermost natural state of alignment with the Neshamah that the Bible describes as *panim el panim* (the trait – which only Moses enjoyed – of gazing face-to-face with God).[16] Avodah, meaning observance of the law, is a term that, as we saw in the previous chapter, is directed at the heart (itself a metaphor for the higher Nefesh). Keeping the law molds the lower Nefesh into the shape that it must assume in order to resonate and vibrate with the song of life. Because the law makes demands of the body that require Kavanah, it has the power to align the body and the Nefesh and hold it, as it were, in the required position for the Neshamah to extend fully into it and through it to touch the concrete world.

As we saw in the passages above, Rabbi Kook describes this state of alignment as one that allows for movement in more than one direction. The extension of the *concerns* of the lower Nefesh upward or inward is coupled by an extension of the *concerns* of generality into the individual. This is a key principle in his thought that captures the essence of what is special about the framing of the individual and the collective in the perspective of Segulah. This passage offers a way out of the endless struggle between socialism and capitalism, equality and equal opportunity, individuation and collectivism,

---

15. Rabbi Kook *Lights of Holiness*, 149.

16. Moses is described in the Torah as the only prophet with whom God converses "face-to-face"; see Numbers 12:8, Exodus 33:11. The uniqueness of Moses's prophecy is famously listed by Maimonides as one of the foundational principles of Jewish thought. See Maimonides, *Mishneh Torah, Hilchot Yesodei HaTorah* 7:6.

the freedom of the citizen and the coercion of the state. In this model, the general significance of the individual's *concerns* is not subsumed into the *concerns* of the collective. The individual that fails to align is not at fault for "letting the team down" or being in violation of the general will or law. The individual is not compressed into the collective in any way. Rather, general *concerns* and individual ones are correspondingly interconnected in a way that follows the structure of *peshat* and *sod* – microcosm and macrocosm. Hence the total breadth of the entire Torah is discovered within the private Nefesh, with its healings and deficiencies, while conversely, the content of generality in the entire world is dependent on the private individual.[17]

The idea that the expansion of universal space corresponds with the expansion of inner space is also the key to understanding the two rabbinic injunctions that Rabbi Kook quotes at the end of the passage: "Every individual is obliged to say, 'The world was created for me'" (Mishnah *Sanhedrin* 4:5) but must also ask, 'When will my actions equal those of Abraham, Isaac, and Jacob?'" (*Tanna Devei Eliyahu*, chapter 25). On the one hand, the world is created for me because my inner *being* reflects the generality of all *being*. On

---

17. This structure is essential to Rabbi Kook's enthusiasm for the Zionist idea and the establishment of a Jewish state. The Jewish state is for him an ideal in the sense that it is understood in ontological terms as an institution that brings the lower and higher – individual and collective – Jewish self into a state of alignment. Life as lived and experienced ideally in this Jewish state is envisaged by Rabbi Kook as one of attuned ontological experience which is disclosed as joy. Rabbi Kook dedicates a section of his *Lights of Holiness* to the idea of the state which is called "The Joy of the ideal state." Here he writes, "The state is not the highest joy of man. This is something that we can say about a regular state which does not aspire to be of higher value than other states; where the ideas which crown the aliveness of humanity float above but remain out of reach. However, this is not the case with the state that is, at its foundation, an ideal, which has the highest ideal imprinted on its being, which is indeed the true joy of the individual. This state is the highest form of joy and it is our state, the State of Israel, the foundation of the seat of God on earth whose sole desire is for God to be One and for His name to be One." The themes that appear here with reference to the ideal state echo what Rabbi Kook said about the life of Torah and prayer in the passage above. Hence there is a parallelism between Torah and the state. The law of the ideal state is therefore described as *chakukah*, i.e., it is an expression of an *attuned* ontological consciousness that is imprinted on the *being* of the individual and on the *being* of the state. The state is an expression of generality that releases the individual into a state of joy. This is the joy that is disclosed by alignment, which here is expressed as elsewhere in the unification of God's *being*, which is One with His name, which is One. Hence, Rabbi Kook's idea of nationalism is not a political one per se, but a Torah-infused, spiritual one.

the other, one still feels deficient when the unaligned Nefesh is not resonating with the song of the Neshamah (represented here by the patriarchs).[18]

Individual and General Perception/Consciousness

> Everything that happens to the individual and his Nefesh, the events from the day that his creation/formation begins until it is completed, his ascensions, changes, and developments, is all of the same magnitude as what has happened to and happens in the great creation and in all the worlds, and what happened in all of the worlds happens in every man.
>
> Admittedly, there are things that are perceived first in generality from the shining that emanates from universal creation; from the act of creation, they reach the private soul's awareness. And there are things which are perceived first in the private soul, and from there the light of knowledge spreads out to the wisdom (Chochmah) of the worlds. And there are many matters that flow in both directions that meet and fulfill each other, completing and clarifying each other.[19]

What stands out in this passage is the extraordinary equivalence with which Rabbi Kook describes the relationship between the *being* of the individual and the *being* of the world. He explicitly equates the magnitude of individual life with the history of the world. Similarly, he says that the great processes of history have the same magnitude as the twists and turns that take place in the life story of every individual. From an ontic perspective this is hard to

---

18. The Midrash (*Bereishit Rabbah* 47:6) describes the patriarchs as the *merkavah* (chariot) that is the platform or pedestal of divine presence in the world. It is the patriarchs who enable God's accessibility in the world, since their collective Neshamah is the foundation for the *being* of the divine spirit (Shechinah) in the physical world. Rabbi Kook explains this Midrashic theme: "The patriarchs establish the whole world on its foundation, with the full height (standing) of the Neshamah as a chariot for He who forms all eternity (Tzur Ha'olamim) by virtue of their total purification of self and ideas, the freedom of their spirit, and their cleaving to (total *concern* for) God" (Rabbi Kook, *Lights of Holiness*, vol.1, 215).

19. Rabbi Kook, *Lights of Holiness*, vol. 3, 150.

understand, to say the least. However, if we read this ontologically, focusing our attention on what Rabbi Kook is saying about *being*, the meaning of this passage becomes easier to decipher in concrete terms.

This notion of equivalence is based on the idea that, in Gadlut, the *being* of everything is unified. There is no being that is less or more in its *being* than any other. The difference (as we saw in the *Tanya* when we discussed the aliveness of stones, trees, and animals) is in the degrees of aliveness. But the aliveness in everything that is, *is*, as it were, of the same substance. Thus, the *created-ness* of all beings is equal; the *from-where* is the same. It is only in quantity of aliveness that inanimate and animate beings are distinguished from one another. What Rabbi Kook does here is to supplement this unified structure of *being* with an additional dimension – namely, generality. In generality, the individual is an extension of the collective in the same way as the Nefesh is an extension of the Neshamah. In reverse, the collective is also an extension of the individual. Metaphorically speaking, individuals are not pieces of a puzzle that comprise a greater whole. Neither is the whole an indiscriminate blur that is only decipherable when it is broken down into its parts. Rather, the pieces and the whole are equal reflections of what Heidegger would refer to as the puzzle's *usefulness*. The puzzle is the same in terms of its *being at hand* as a puzzle. In both its dismantled and assembled forms the ontological *usefulness* of the puzzle for Dasein is equally fulfilled. Moreover, the pieces are only ever pieces of the whole and the whole is only ever the pieces assembled. On this plane there is no struggle between the individual and the collective and no clash of interests between them, because in both forms the *createdness* of their *being* is the same.

Rabbi Kook begins the second paragraph by saying that the narrow *concerns* of the individual about *being* can be of general importance. In this the *relevance* of inner space and outer space to the generality of *being* is equalized. Thus, the deeper dimensions of individual inner space are potentially general in nature. This is one of the reasons why *concern* for the collective is a dimension of generality that aligns the Nefesh and the Neshamah.

However, this is not the whole idea. Rabbi Kook refines it by clarifying how the total equivalence between the individual and the collective – in terms of their *being* – establishes a principle of reciprocity between them. He "admits" that certain general concerns are disclosed first by *concern* for the *being* of the collective which points upward toward the *from-where* of the vastness of the universe. But there are also matters that are *relevant* to general and universal *care* for *being* that are first disclosed in the individual's *concern* for the inner *being* of itself. Since this inner self is no less grounded in *created-ness,* generality is not lost in or restricted by the individual's *concern* for its deeper self. Rabbi Kook says "admittedly" because the point he is making is perhaps counterintuitive and especially so in his time, when the ethos of collectivism was so pronounced. But generality is neither collectivism nor individualism. In this model, individual *concerns* can disclose generality to the collective in the same way as this happens the other way around. Since both individual and collective *concerns* in their *being* are no more or less extensions of the totality of *being,* there are general *concerns* that first germinate in individual *concern* for the inner self, and there are others that reach the individual only through his *care* for the *being* of the collective. Finally, there are modes of showing *concern* for the totality of *being* that emanate in both and meet in the middle.

This clarification shows how Rabbi Kook's concept of generality challenges both individualism and collectivism, offering an alternative to each and to any combination of the two. The flaw of collectivism is not healed by the prioritization of the individual, and the flaw of individualism is not healed by expecting every individual to sacrifice his or her individuality to the demands of the collective. More specifically, the danger that individual ego will block *concern* for all *being* is not healed by the collective, because collective ego can block *concern* for all *being* in the same way. Thus, the presumed ontological priority of the collective is a flaw that we can see in such ideologies as communism and socialism. This is the flaw that Orwell parodied in his famous quip that "some animals are more equal than others."[20] Put differently, since equality is unnatural to Dasein in its anxiety about *being-a-self,* collectivism in all its forms requires certain people to have greater powers that ironically entitle them to enforce equality on others. The reverse is the flaw of capitalism, which blurs the value of equality by predicating the value of the collective on its service to the individual. In such societies the enhancement of ego runs rampant and the replacement of an ethos of equality with one

---

20. George Orwell, *Animal Farm: A Fairy Story* (London: Secker and Warburg, 1945).

of equal opportunity soon erodes away as the elite presents insurmountable obstacles to the social advancement of those less privileged.

Rabbi Kook imagines a healed society in which there is an ontological unity of *createdness* with a dialogic structure that enables both individual and collective concerns "to meet and clarify each other." In this model, the collective and the individual are both extensions of the same generality, each of which has its own didactic advantages and disadvantages for getting the message that all *being* is equivalent in its *created-ness*. Some parts of this message are better disclosed as collective concerns. Others are best disclosed first to the individual. But all emanate from and point to the same totality.

If we bring this to the negation of Heidegger, this insight suggests that the *they-self* is inauthentic only in so far as its *they-ness* is too limited and narrow for it to reflect the ownmost *care* for the totality of *being* that is the *being* of both the individual self and the collective self. Thus, potentially there is equal potential for finding either authenticity or everydayness in both the *they-self* and in *being-a-self*. As we shall see later, this equivalence of the individual and the collective is the source of their shared role in reflecting the general *being* that animates them both (and the rest of all *being*) and which has a temporality of Netzach. When the temporality of Netzach is disclosed in the individual it is of the same order as the temporality of Netzach that applies to the collective. The presumed eternal life of the collective (that lives on after my death) is not its source. This is the crucial principle that distinguishes Rabbi Kook's notion of eternity from the delusional Dasein that hides in society seeking comfort from ontological anxiety by absorbing itself in idle talk with others.

Alignment with Eternal Life[21]

The next passage takes our understanding of the relationship between the individual and the collective toward the temporality of Netzach. This and the following sections focus specifically on the role of the Tzaddik. We shall read

---

21. Rabbi Kook, *Lights of Holiness*, 151–52. Our translation here of the title of this section deliberately echoes the theme of alignment which we have been discussing. Arguably this title (which in the Hebrew original is *Ha-Hishtavut LeChayyei Olamim*) could be translated differently depending on how the word *hishtavut* is understood. Possible alternatives include "similarity," "resemblance," and "equalization."

Rabbi Kook's portrayal of the Tzaddik as a negation of Heidegger's claim that authenticity is contradicted by a *they-self* and by the denial of death. Rabbi Kook writes,

> All of the thoughts and ideas, the great passions and immense trials that must pass through the individual Nefesh of the Tzaddik all pass through the generality of the nation and universally over the generality of man and in still broader terms over the generality of the world and of all the worlds.[22]

The title of this section, which we translated as "alignment with eternal life" might perhaps be translated more literally as "Being equal to the life of all the worlds" or "attaining equivalence to life of all the concealed worlds." These translations are attempts to reflect the complex and subtle meanings that resonate in Rabbi Kook's word choice. In this passage he describes the Tzaddik as an individual who has achieved such a high degree of alignment that the fullness of human *being* is equal to or corresponds with – and is hence able to interface with – the fullness of the world/s. The Tzaddik is someone who has cultivated *concern* in his Nefesh for all the dimensions of generality, which include the collective life of the nation, of humanity, of the world as we know it in emanation, and of the various hidden levels of *being* from which it emanates through the five levels that run from Atzilut to Assiyah. What Rabbi Kook is emphasizing here is that the Tzaddik's private individuality at the level of the Nefesh is totally *concerned* with the various levels of generality that start with the Jewish nation and fan out to include the generality of humanity, of the world and all the worlds. The Tzaddik is therefore a general individual whose individual *care* for the *being* of the Jewish nation, humanity, the world, and all the worlds is genuinely an ownmost *concern* of his *being* that is the same as his *care* for the *being* of his self.

In many places, Rabbi Kook describes this alignment as the joyful path of holiness that is achieved through Avodah (i.e., Torah study, prayer, and the practice of mitzvot).[23] However, in the next section, Rabbi Kook

---

22. Ibid.
23. See, for example, ibid., vol 3, 151.

describes the attainment of this degree of alignment as the near death of the Nefesh. Near death is accomplished by restraint through which the Tzaddik divests his lower Nefesh of all hope that it might find pleasure in its *with-world*. In this state of desperation, it pins all its attention upon the Neshamah and on the hope of delighting in the gaze or the song that we discussed above. In this state the Nefesh is deprived of all its lower appetites, and hence it experiences a kind of death from which it is revived by the power of the Neshamah. Because it despairs of the life that it knows, it learns to despair of its detached self and to see the Neshamah as its only hope for salvation:

> And the more the inner and surrounding light/space is demanded and imprinted in great truth in the Neshamah of man, then, as he passes through the world suffering from a thirst due to the needs of his Nefesh for higher refreshment, until the misery of it brings his Nefesh to a state of total gloom and dejection and he is literally nauseated by life and depleted in his strength…he still does not turn to conceit and is not tempted to intoxicate himself with the external poisons of the world, not with physical lusts nor with spiritual or imaginary ones either, and not with what they call intellectualism, but he stands guard over himself, holding out for the higher truth and total good in his Neshamah as his only hope and desire. With the strength to overcome and restrain himself, he becomes equal to the Ruach of all the worlds and can see everything from within his inner space and by the light that comes to him in his darkness until he can see faithfully from the end of the world to its other end, seeing every individual detail in its proper standing with the *yirah* of the majesty of God, which is strength and delight. And the path of Tzaddikim is like the light of the moon brightening until the day is ready.[24]

In many ways, this remarkable passage might be a description of the realization that Adam was supposed to have reached in the Garden of Eden. Total

---

24. Ibid., 151–52.

despair of the pleasures that can be taken by the detached Nefesh from the fruit of the Tree of Knowledge would have empowered him to restrain himself and to hold out for the total pleasure of the gaze represented by the Tree of Life. The passage ends with a mention of the Tzaddik's capacity to see the world from one end to the other (*misof ha'olam ve'ad sofo*). This is an ability that Adam is said to have lost when he failed to resist temptation and was plunged into the temporality of mortality.[25] This vision (that sees all of *being* across all of time) is given by the primordial light, which as we understand it represents the ontological consciousness of the Neshamah that is normally concealed from the unaligned Nefesh. The Tzaddik is thus someone whose restraint heals and reverses Adam's lack of it and who, like Adam before the sin, represents in his inner *being* the potentiality of *being* of all humanity.[26]

The idea that the Tzaddik regains access to this general consciousness recurs in the passage in Rabbi Kook's reference to the strengthening of the moon. This connotes the rabbinic idea that the light of the moon had once been an independent light that burned as brightly as the sun. However, the Talmud says that the moon itself recognized that "a sovereign cannot wear two crowns" and so it diminished its own radiance.[27] In the metaphor of the inner Torah, the loss of primordial light and the diminishing of the moon are the Structures of Concealment that leave the Nefesh with the misaligned

---

25. *Chagigah* 12a.

26. This is a capacity that the rabbinic tradition attributes to Joseph, who leaves his coat behind in the hand of Potiphar's wife and thus at the same time resists both sexual and materialistic temptation. He strips himself of the bodily desires of the Nefesh and emerges as a Tzaddik. The Rabbis expound in what may seem like hyperbolic terms about the importance of this incident and about the tremendous hidden temptations that Joseph overcame as well as the supernatural assistance with which he resisted them. See, for example, *Sotah* 36b. Great importance is attached to this scene in kabbalistic and Hasidic literature since the character of Joseph represents the sphere of Yesod, which is the gateway to redemption. Yesod, which is also connected to the reproductive organs of the body, is the sphere of sexual temptation, and thus Joseph's overcoming this temptation is seen as the gateway to the redemption from Egypt. This theme is widely discussed and developed in Zoharic, Hasidic, and other texts. For one clear and accessible example of a full and relatively modern explication of this theme, see Rabbi Sholom Noach Berezovsky, *Netivot Shalom*, Parashat Vayeshev (Jerusalem: Slonim, 1985–95), 253–58 [Hebrew].

27. See *Chullin* 60b.

anxious desire to *be a self.* The moon reflecting the light of the sun represents the Nefesh that relies on the Neshamah for its alive-consciousness or *being.* But the desire or willfulness of the self is also the condition that makes free choice possible, and in this sense it reflects the concept of *tzimtzum* or constriction without which God's total dominance over creation would leave no room for the freedom of beings to act according to their own will. It is this constriction that gives meaning to the power of restraint, because restraint is essentially an exercise of free choice. It is the choice of the Nefesh not to align with the body, not to eat the fruit of the tree, not to *know* by assertively taking knowledge for oneself but instead to hold out for the Tree of Life. Freedom is the power to choose to deprive the Nefesh of all the physical, intellectual, and psychological nourishment that it seeks for itself until it despairs of everything other than the deeper pleasure that comes from alignment with the Neshamah. The refreshment that quenches its thirst, satisfying all its tastes and needs, is disclosed to the Nefesh and in the Nefesh by the sweetness and wonder of fulfilling its innermost desires. Only at this level, those innermost desires – desires that have always been there hiding behind the misdirected and insatiable appetites of the detached Nefesh – reveal the desires of the Neshamah to *be* the song and the gaze.

What Rabbi Kook is saying here is that *care* for the *being* of all beings (Havayah) is the only *care* that gives true satisfaction, and hence it is the deeper root of desire itself. It is the key to, the way to partake in, true pleasure in the most direct and literal sense. Satisfaction is found by looking more deeply into – i.e., beyond the limited self's – desire. Instead of fighting against it, it must be explored and deepened – cultivated and refined rather than superficially indulged – until its source can be felt and grasped. This is the secret of the true nature and purpose of restraint that Rabbi Kook calls Sod HaGevurah. The door to true pleasure cannot be unlocked until the Nefesh sees its narrow *with-world* as total darkness and hence embraces restraint as a means of expressing its anticipation of light. Restraint is the same as resisting our first object of desire and looking beyond it in order to discover a deeper or higher purpose for it. To achieve this is to transpose desire from the lower physical to its higher spiritual object. This is what it means to become a Tzaddik who aligns with generality and gradually intensifies the light of the moon. Rabbi Kook continues,

All the worlds in their generality are the aliveness of the Ruach of God. And their power (their is-ness) is full of life…and man, through his choices, must set the content of his life in such a way that it fits the life of all the worlds. And this is the secret of restraint that is in fear of Heaven, that all the vitality of all the worlds assists whosoever sets his path in the ways of God. And the more a person purifies his Nefesh, the more the demand to align with the light of all eternal life becomes stronger within him and spreads through all his actions…until he cannot be hindered even by his own animal [lower Nefesh].[28]

This passage goes on to explain in more detail what restraint is. Any translation of this language runs the risk of obscuring how precise the onto-theological terminology is. But what Rabbi Kook is clearly saying is that restraint, which literally means the strict observation of the negative commandments in the Torah, is a mode of *being* that is *attuned* as Yirah. The "Ruach of God" and "the ways of God," as before, are clearly references to the five layers of emanation from which the total simple and abstract unity of God congeals and hardens into the multiplicity and physicality of the body-world. Alignment of our *concern* for this concrete physicality with the more abstract unity of *being* from which it emanates is accomplished by the "choices that set the content of life." Choice attuned as Yirah moves the gaze of the Nefesh into alignment with the gaze of the Neshamah. The choice of restraint is a form of Avodah, and hence it works on the heart. The outcome is the purification (meaning total alignment of *concern*) of the Nefesh to such a degree that its *care* for the aliveness of all *being* is no longer hindered or dragged back toward the temptations of its *with-world* by its animal physicality.

Most importantly for our purposes, Rabbi Kook is plainly describing aliveness in this passage as the mode of all *being* in the sense that all *is-ness* is *aliveness* and therefore *aliveness* is the central characteristic of *being* itself. He also makes it quite clear that *is-ness* is a quality that actively *is* in all things by various degrees. In the same way as a stone is less alive with *being* than a tree and a tree than an animal, Rabbi Kook is saying here that the unaligned

---

28. Ibid., 152.

Nefesh is quantitatively less alive with *being* than the aligned one. Thus, mortality is a matter of degree that can shift with alignment.[29] What this means is that the alignment of the Nefesh with the Neshamah transforms the degree to which Dasein as the *being* that we all *are* is alive. It follows then that the equalization of the Nefesh with the eternal *being* of being enhances the very aliveness of its *being* in the direction of Netzach, in much the same way as a knob on a dimmer switch can intensify the light of a bulb from near darkness to full brightness. This intensification of aliveness has both quantitative and qualitative implications. Qualitatively speaking, to align one's *care* with generality is a way to *be-alive* with greater intensity. To live "more" therefore means to endow the life of the individual with the general aliveness of the collective. This intensification of aliveness pushes back against Heidegger's concepts of *being-a-self* and *being-toward-death*. Since all *being* is eternally alive with its *being*, the more one is aligned with the *being* of all being (the more one's being participates in eternal aliveness; the more eternal aliveness "becomes stronger within" one's *being*); the more one's enduring *being-in-the-world* and *being-in-time* is nourished by nothing other than infinite *living-being* itself.

Quantitatively speaking, this notion of general aliveness may refer to the eternal life of the collective (Netzach Yisrael).[30] However, in a series of passages that appear in the second volume of the *Lights of Holiness*, Rabbi Kook brings the quantitative enhancement of aliveness even more directly to bear on the life of the individual. Rabbi Kook discusses the nature of individual identity and the reason for the illusion that Heideggerian ontology *falls prey* to when it describes Dasein's ownmost being as *being-toward-death*. Rabbi

---

29. This passage in Rabbi Kook might be seen as a comment on the Genesis narrative that describes the declining life spans of the generations that followed the expulsion of Adam and Eve from the Garden of Eden. According to this structure of thought, the biblical narrative is showing how, after the sin, the power of death gradually imposes itself upon the power of life by degrees. The lifespans of Adam, Jared, Mahalalel and Methuselah are all around nine hundred years. In the following chapter we encounter people who live no longer than 120 years. See Genesis, chapter 5, and compare with Genesis 6:1–3.

30. The idea that the Jewish people will endure forever is generally founded on the verse in I Samuel 15:28–29: "The glory of the eternal Israel will not lie."

Kook's first premise, like Heidegger's, is that the true inner nature of the individual has been lost and as such is in a state of exile or Galut. He writes,

> And the "I" (the self) is in exile. The "I," the inner, ownmost self of the individual and the collective, cannot be revealed apart from the innermost content of its sanctity and purity, according to the value of its higher Gevurah (restraint and strength), which is saturated in the pure light of higher splendor that excites (like a flame) from within. Our sin along with that of our forefathers, the first sin of Adam, is that he was alienated from the self; he turned away and embraced the consciousness of the snake and lost himself. He could not give a clear answer to the question "Where are you?" because he did not know his self, because the true I-ness (the true nature of the I) was lost to him in the sin of worshipping a false god. Israel sinned, lusted after foreign gods; it cast its true self aside, abandoned the good of Israel. The land has sinned, denied its true self, constricted its valor, followed after tendencies and purposes; it has not given its true hidden valor to allow the taste of the tree to be the taste of the fruit...the moon has recused; its inner circumference, the joy of its part, has been lost ...and thus the world dives into the abyss in which the self of every individual and of generality is lost.[31]

This passage offers the quintessential account of the state of Galut in Rabbi Kook's writing. He describes the condition of Dasein's entanglement in its *with-world* as a state of sin caused by the choice that Adam, the first and primordial man, made between his Neshamah-self and alignment with the snake. Man alienated himself from his true inner self by choosing his body-self, the snake, the anxious being that is limited by its *concern* for its own narrow *being*. Not knowing the self through the betrayal of the self is the source of idolatry, of exile, and of the inner inconsistency, gap, conflict, or lack of alignment that is symbolized by the difference between the taste of

---

31. Ibid., 140.

fruit and the taste of the tree.[32] The taste of the fruit represents the ability to control those aspects of the self that are given over to the lower Nefesh, while the taste of the tree represents those attributes of human *being* that, since they are given over to the control of the higher Neshamah alone, are submerged in our deeper consciousness and out of our reach. In this condition, the fruit is sweet but temporary; destined to fall off the tree and die. Thus, the choice to eat willfully of the fruit is the choice to be severed from the tree. The multiplying of individuality after this fashion is the source of mortality and the beginning of Dasein's long history of *being-toward-death.*

In the next passages, Rabbi Kook writes explicitly about the temporality of Netzach and about the nature of general life that transcends the constriction of individual death. In a section entitled "The Aspiration of Netzach," he writes,

> Our temporal *being* is a single spark in the temporality of Netzach, in the glory of the eternity of eternities. And the hidden treasure of temporal life cannot become visible in the world unless it is aligned with the temporality of eternal life.
>
> And this is the inner awareness that is immersed in the spirit of the entire totality of being (universe/creation)…and even that which opposes it, in the depths of its truth, is in support of it.
>
> Netzach (eternity) is the firm foundation of all civilized life in its full meaning. The aspiration of Netzach in all its glory conquers death and wipes a tear from every face.
>
> Great people come to even the smallest matters and desires in the ways of Gadlut.[33]

This passage is one of a sequence that is remarkable in its bold explicitness about the possibility of *being-toward-*Netzach as a state of *being* in which

---

32. Rabbi Kook states, "The land sinned such that the taste of the tree and the taste of the fruit are not equal. This is the cause of the misalignment of all the levels that now oppose each other. And in the world of ethics and society this is the source of the strife between people whose roles in life are spirituality, science, faith, Torah, and higher ethics on the one hand and those people whose fate is government and leadership" (ibid., 294).

33. Ibid., vol. 2, 377.

death is overcome. In these passages, life prevails over death through the total alignment of the innermost self with an inner awareness that is *always already* in the general inner self and pervasive in its interactions with all things great and small. Accessing this awareness and fusing it to the physical concerns and desires of everyday life is what great people do in a state of Gadlut. See, for example, the following section, which is entitled "The Illusion of Death":

> Death is an illusion. Its impurity is its lie. What people call death is only the reinforcement and the strengthening of life. From the endless descent into Katnut which the inclinations of man have immersed itself in, he comes to imagine this reinforcement in a dark and harmful way, which he calls death.
>
> In their holiness, the priests rise above listening to this lie, which can be escaped only while the governance of lies rules the world by looking away from the sights that leave this deceitful impression on the Nefesh.[34]

Even though our translation of this text quite deliberately connotes the specific terms that we have already defined in our discussion, the ontological language here is unmistakable in the original Hebrew as well. Built upon a logical foundation that emanates from the eternity of *being* itself and from the notion of the individual as a constriction of that *being* through unaligned concern for *being-a-self*, Rabbi Kook concludes that death is an illusion to which we all *fall prey* in our selfness. This passage challenges this illusion, stating that it is held in place by a politics or governance that is motivated by the fear of death and anxiety. When we think about what this means, it is important not to confine ourselves to obvious associations with totalitarian regimes – with their perverse rituals of death and the totality of their terrorization – alone. In this passage Rabbi Kook speaks widely and broadly to even the most benevolent forms of government that Dasein is prone to design. The fear of death plagues them all. By contrast, the politics of Tikkun Olam in this passage is cocooned in and confined to the world of the Temple and the priests. This is a place that is distanced from impurity (in biblical law

---

34. Ibid., 380.

impurity is inherently connected to contact with death) and hence from the
negative effects that the Nefesh – meaning Dasein's obsession with its own
death – has on the whole self. Rabbi Kook continues in the next passage,
entitled "Release from the Fear of Death":

> The fear of death is the sickness of mankind in general, which
> comes from the sin. The sin created death, and Teshuvah (repen-
> tance/return to alignment) is the only cure that can purge the
> world of it.
>
> All of man's efforts go round and round in the effort to be
> saved from death. And he will not reach his goal in any way other
> than through the expansion of his Neshamah from its inner source.
> Immersion in the earth of physicality and the enthusiasm of the
> Nefesh for all its values only enlarges death and adds to the fear
> of it.[35]

The basic point here is clear. Adam indulged his desire to *be a self* when he
failed to restrain himself in the Garden of Eden and in so doing determined
that mortality – which is a sickness of the soul or a weakening of its presence
in our consciousness – would plague humankind in general. Henceforth,
humankind is obsessed with death, and life is taken over by futile attempts
to keep our distance from it. What Rabbi Kook says here is that, from the
perspective of an anthropology that sees the foundation of humanism in the
structure of Dasein or the Nefesh, Heidegger is right. There is no way out. All
that can be done with the Nefesh in its state of *being-in-the-world* is to enlarge
death and add to the fear of it. The way out cannot begin with the *being* of
the Nefesh; it requires the extension of the Neshamah. The implication of
this is that the expansion or extension of the Neshamah is the reversal of the
sin and the path to the tree of eternal life.

The challenge here is to try to evaluate to what extent an ontological reading of this proposition can help us think about its mystical claim in seriously
plausible terms. As it stands, it seems entirely out of touch with the history
of the human condition as we experience it. However, when considered from

---

35. Ibid., 381.

within an onto-theological perspective that identifies the source of death in the confinement of *care* to the concerns of the body-self, and which sees this confinement of *care* as the condition of humanity in Galut, and hence as a permanent feature of human history as we know it but not as an inevitable necessity of *being*, associating the ontological negation of this with eternal life begins to make sense. If there is such a thing as redemption from the misalignment of the Nefesh and the Neshamah (Galut), then it will necessarily involve the negation of *being-toward-death* and its replacement with *being-toward*-Netzach. Were Dasein's *care* redirected in this way, it follows that death would not plague us as it does. One might even suggest that the denial of death is not in fact an expression of inauthenticity but rather an awareness of something that the Nefesh *always already* knows at the level of Emunah – the level at which it experiences the source of its aliveness in the Neshamah self.

Logical as this is, it is still too far from human experience to be adopted lightly, which is why the theme developed in the next paragraphs is so thought provoking. In the sequence that follows, Rabbi Kook tries to ground his utopian ontology of Netzach in Dasein's mortal temporality by connecting the temporality of Netzach with a comment on the meaning of long life. In our modern era, in which life expectancy has been extended significantly, this is a matter of great interest. Rabbi Kook writes,

> The real cures that enable the world to release itself from its enslavement to death are embedded in the treasure of life itself, in the Neshamah of Torah, which is disclosed in its fully revealed form and which is very well hidden. The first of all cures is long life, life that is long enough for the spiritual and physical, personal, familial, universal, and political nature of mankind. When this blessing spreads in the world, the form of death that casts its terror begins to disappear, and in its place the vision of Havayah, which will be evaluated according to its true value and will no longer confuse [misalign] Da'at and Binah, will return, and we will realize that there is no death at all and that this depressing and illusory image is trapped in the heart to suppress life, and we will look at the day of death and sing a song: "Lord my God, You are very great. You are clothed with glory and majesty."

Length of life comes through the Tikkun of life in all its meanings, and in particular in its ever-expanding moral meaning…the
spirit of the highest morality, which distills life in all its measures,
is alive and dwells in the Nefesh according to the degree to which
the lights of life can be seen to shine in it, and the lights of life can
be seen to shine in their full brightness only when the Nefesh is
filled with the Da'at of the living God, the source of Chochmah,
Chesed, and Gevurah united.[36]

The idea here is that long life is the product of an intensified aliveness in our
experience of the aliveness of *being*. Partial realignment of the Nefesh and the
Neshamah is enough for the experience of aliveness to be rooted in the temporality of Netzach, and this expresses itself not in immortality but in an intensification of Dasein's experience of *being* as life. This is made accessible to the Nefesh
when it is infused with the Binah and Da'at of Havayah through Torah. The
lengthening of life is therefore part of the process of redemption and an indication that the internal shift in Dasein's *care* for *being* is underway. This shift toward
what Rabbi Kook refers to as a higher morality (and which we suggest is equivalent to the *Tanya's* sense of appropriately directed Kavanah) fills the Nefesh's
interactions with the world (Dasein's *being-in-the-world*) with the light of Da'at
Hashem. The more this defines Dasein's experience of *being*, the more the shift
toward a temporality of Netzach expresses itself in the length of life as we know it.

A society that is oriented toward Netzach is one that venerates the elderly.
Rabbi Kook sees this respect for age as something that stands in contrast to
Greek culture, or Klippat Yavan, "which looks at the old with contempt."[37]
The alternative to this is an attitude to the healing of society, the world, the
individual and the collective that is temporally oriented toward Netzach:

Higher thought can become complete in man only when he elevates
himself to imagine the general good – making an effort to desire
it for himself and for the entire world – only if he seeks a form of
life…that will distinguish between good and evil in the private

---

36. Rabbi Kook, *Lights of Holiness,* vol. 2, 382–84.
37. Ibid., vol. 3, 180.

life of the individual internally and externally and which builds its foundation for life in general as eternal life (Netzach), which is tied to the purification of the Neshamot…is what is drawn forth from the healing and ordering of the individual and society.

Here we can see a convergence of several themes: there is a clear correlation between the healing of the individual and the collective, which is accomplished through a form of action that is accompanied by a higher form of thought. This thought aligns *concern* for the individual with the collective, the external with the internal, and the temporal with eternal time. By aligning the inner with the outer, the higher with the lower, the general with the individual, and, ultimately, the emanation with the source, the efforts that we make in practical terms to heal the world can succeed. Without this alignment that connects both poles, both spiritual efforts and physical efforts are deemed to perish "because of Katnut and because of the contamination and stench that physical life is naturally diminished by when it is detached from the source of *being-toward eternal life*."[38] Hence, for Rabbi Kook, eternal life is a potentiality of *being* whose plausibility is brought closer to human experience by long life and respect for the old.

The General Neshamot

Returning to our sequence in the third section, Rabbi Kook now moves on to describe in more detail how the individual Nefesh of the Tzaddik is endowed with generality,

> The large Neshamot are prepared so that the vision of entirety will shine from within them because of their higher and purer desire in its most general form, which progresses downward like links in a chain all the way to the smallest, furthest away, and most private actions…. The Neshamot of the great Tzaddikim include everything, and they have in them all the good of everything and all the evil of everything, and they suffer for everything and gain pleasure from everything and turn all evil into good. And through

---

38. Ibid.

their suffering everything is sweetened, because the root of their Neshamah is empowered by the branches of all the souls, and they are very numerous indeed. The Tzaddikim are their foundation.[39]

Again, reading this from a perspective that is grounded in the negation of Heidegger, we suggest that this portrayal offers a description of what it means to find the self in the *they-self*. The condition of Gadlut as described here is characterized by the penetration of generality into the *care* of the individual for its own *being*. As we have already seen, the idea here is not that the individual somehow gives himself over to the collective or that he represses the everyday sense of individuality in order to hide in a collective identity. Rather, the alignment of the Nefesh with the Neshamah creates a condition of *being* in which the Nefesh becomes aware of the general concerns that were *always already* its ownmost *concerns*. In this sense, individuality is only ever an extension or an emanation of a totality in which both the individual and the collective are always implicit. This is what Rabbi Kook means when he says that general desires progress downward "all the way to the smallest, furthest away, and most private actions."

Individuality is thus an episode in generality that comes to know its ownmost self only when, in its individuality, its inner form resembles generality in microcosm. This is why this passage places such a significant emphasis on the evil and the suffering that the Tzaddik must endure. The totality that is condensed as generality into the individual Nefesh of the Tzaddik contains in microcosm all the evils of the world in the same way that generality contains both the animalism of unaligned Nefashot (i.e., Nefesh in the plural form) and all the non-conscious physicality of inanimate objects that are impervious to the nature of their *alive-being*. But here the Tzaddik has a special function. The inner *being* of the Tzaddik consumes his *with-world* in the same way that Dasein's *being-with* devours space and time. Only here the meaning and the direction of this devouring are reversed. Through Kavanah, the Tzaddik's concern for his *with-world* animates everything in it by passing it through his consciousness in the direction of Neshamah. *Care* passes innerworldly beings through the consciousness of the Tzaddik in the same

---

39. Ibid., 153.

way that a blade of grass can become life-energy when it is consumed by an animal. On a higher level, the consumption of food by people drives not only physical movement but active consciousness when the digested food becomes the fuel that energizes a conscious human being. Similarly, the *care* for the *being* of all beings in the individual consciousness of the Tzaddik fuels the consciousness of the Tzaddik "sweetening the root of evil" and "empowering the Neshamah." This principle, elucidated here by Rabbi Kook, is at the heart of Jewish practice concerning blessings over food, smells, beautiful sights, and, most explicitly, sacrificial ritual. The purpose is the Kavanah that directs the human consumption of these up the ladder of Tzelem Elohim from *peshat* to *sod*, from body and Nefesh in Katnut all the way to the point of contact between Neshamah in Gadlut and Yechidah.

The Central Neshamah

In the next passage Rabbi Kook continues this theme, maintaining that nature, which is constructed according to rising or descending degrees of consciousness, is constantly pushing upward, vying, as it were, to feel the ultimately refined consciousness of a human being whose Neshamah discloses the fullness and the unity of Havayah, strengthening the aliveness of the world for those whose conscious aliveness of *being* is deficient.

> Creation (Yetzirah) is following its path, creating (Beriyah) its degrees, aspiring to a higher and more refined form in which the entire essence of Havayah (the totality of being) will be reflected. All of its strength and resilience, all of its beauty, its virtue, and its wisdom (Chochmah) – this is the complete and perfect Neshamah of mankind, the chosen among whom has perfected the chosenness that is within him, the one who has refined with his will his inner being next to [or aligned with] the highest good until he discovers inner creativeness, which contains the essence of absolutely good action.
>
> The highest level of the Neshamah finds its strength and resilience within and needs nothing other than itself. It is content with the general strength that it embodies, and because of this it draws

life to the being of everything and delivers grace [kindness and benefit] to all forms of deficiency.[40]

The degrees of consciousness here make a subtle yet unabashed reference to the special role for which the Jewish people were chosen. The passage describes an internal gradation that culminates in an abstract messianic quality characterized here as the total expression of the highest Neshamah. It is hard to discern if this quality refers specifically to the person who is endowed with it or if it is a general feature of creation that always remains permanently accessible and present in the totality of all *being*. This blurring is integral to the actual concept of generality, since generality arises equiprimordially in the *being* of all individual beings and in all *being*. The totality of *being* is scaled down to the chosen nature of Jewish collectivity and from there to the individual who chooses to identify completely with chosenness. But the meaning of this chosenness is always directed toward generality, and as such it is attained by the individual or the collective only for the scale to then slide upward and outward. The general individual and the general collective by necessity disclose in their individuality and collectivity the same generality of everything. In this sense, their identity is not about themselves, and this is how the ideal individual or collective elevates the world. The creativeness that is discovered within is disclosed by Chochmah, and as such this passage reaffirms our analysis in the previous chapter in which we presented the connection between Chochmah, i.e., human creativity or creative inspiration, and *created-ness* as *concern* for *being-created*. But here, in the quality of chosenness, creativity and the general consciousness of *createdness* are not only glimpses. They pull aliveness down, as it were, in order to bestow vigor on a deficient world which through the agency of the general Neshamah fulfills its aspiration for total joy and refinement.

And the many, who hold pieces of the Yetzirah, cannot find relief for the deficiency in their inner beings. They require a great deal to fulfill their need to heal what is damaged in their inner *self*, which

---

40. Ibid., 154.

after all cannot be healed other than by the higher Tzaddik, who possesses the central Neshamah.[41]

Again, the possession of "the central Neshamah" suggests a kind of ambiguity between the particularist and the universal dimensions of identity. It simultaneously refers to something that an individual seems to possess and to something that defies all ownership and boundary. The whole world depends on the individual who has discovered the central Neshamah within him- or herself, because it is the Neshamah of the whole world. Echoing the couplet that was mentioned above (when Rabbi Kook quoted the saying that "Every man must say the world was created for me, and when will my actions equal those of Abraham, Isaac, and Jacob our forefathers"), Rabbi Kook concludes this passage citing the Talmud (*Berachot* 17b),

> And a heavenly voice will sound from Mount Horev saying, The whole world draws sustenance from Chaninah My son, and Chaninah My son needs no more than a *kav* of carobs from Shabbat Eve to Shabbat Eve.[42]

Generality, Netzach and Avodah

The close readings of these passages from *Lights of Holiness* offered in this chapter are but a small illustration of a wider methodological claim, namely, that the negation of Heidegger's ontology and the construction of our lexicon of inner Torah is a powerful interpretive tool for eliciting the concrete meanings and frames of reference in Rabbi Kook's mystical writing. The process of writing this chapter has been one of selection and restraint, since so many familiar yet elusively aloof passages seem to give up their meanings when subjected to this kind of reading. It is our hope that these illustrations will suffice for those who wish to continue applying the method to other bodies of Rabbi Kook's masterful writing and teaching.

Returning more specifically to the challenge that we outlined at the beginning of the chapter, our analysis of these particular passages has yielded

41. Ibid.
42. Ibid.

crucial insights into what the alternative provided by the onto-theology of inner Torah to the prevalence of *being-toward-death* actually looks like when it emerges as a plausible analysis of Dasein's *being-in-the-world*. Our claim in this chapter is not that we no longer need to take death seriously or that we have found the elixir to eternal life. The point is that death, which is the inevitable fate of the Nefesh, is not the ownmost *concern* of the self or Tzelem Elohim. In Rabbi Kooks' own words, as translated by Bokser,

> To be attached to God is the most natural aspiration of a person. What is throughout all existence in a state of dumbness and deafness, in a form of potentiality, is developed in man in a conceptual and experiential form. There can be no substitute in existence for the longing to be absolutely linked with the living God, with the infinite light. As we are under a compulsion to live, to be nourished to grow, so are we under a compulsion to cleave to God.[43]

What we have tried to show in this chapter is that the idea of building human consciousness upon this potentiality of cleaving to eternal aliveness is a plausible one. Our argument is that *being-toward-death* comes from the absence of alignment and that in a state of alignment the total aliveness of Tzelem Elohim can be plausibly presented as Dasein's ownmost total *concern*. Given this, texts that speak of the concept of the Neshamah in the temporality of Netzach can be taken seriously enough to provide the plausibility required for a paradigm shift from a politics of Survival and System to one of Segulah.

Through our specifically chosen readings in this chapter we uncovered three key principles of what we have been referring to throughout as the perspective of Segulah. The first is that, despite human mortality, Dasein's ownmost mode of *being-toward* is plausibly describable as an ownmost state of human *being* in the temporality of Netzach. This mode of *being* requires total absorption in the totality of *being* as Havayah (i.e., Da'at Hashem in Gadlut), and it is characterized by total *care* for an interminable aliveness that plays more powerfully on the unique human capacity for reflexive *care* for *being* than Heidegger's conscience-ridden, anxious, *being-toward-death*.

---

43. Bokser, *Lights of Penitence*, 282.

In this state of *being*, fear of death is allayed, life expectancy is extended, and redemption from death is something to be reasonably anticipated and non-egotistically prayed for.

Second, this attitude toward the totality of alive *being* is made accessible to individuals through their inextricable membership in or belonging to collectives. It is in this regard that the *they-self* identity of Israel as Am Segulah attains its meaning. The idea that the purpose of Israel as a collective is to be a "light unto the nations" can now be understood here in the sense that the specific structure of Israel's ideal of collectivity provides an example of how collective identity can be built on the principle of *klaliut* or generality. This generality is distinguished from regular collectiveness by the fact that it serves to disclose to the individual the totality of *being* as Havayah rather than itself being an expansion of the individual ego. It is not a social contract that the individual negotiates with the collective which he or she assumes membership in. Am Segulah is a collective identity that, through its middle-ground particularism, aspires to universal *care* for the totality of eternal *being*. It is an expanding structure that directs individual *concern* toward the enduring *being* of the collective rather than an expanded mortal ego to which Dasein clings in its desperate struggle to distract itself from its anxious concerns about death.

Third, the concept of Avodah or the performance of Torah and mitzvot can now be described as the mechanism that gives access to the inner dimension of ontological *being* by generating the required alignment between the Nefesh and the Neshamah. This is accomplished by the directionality of *concern* or Kavanah that is pointed toward generality specifically through the study of Torah and the practice of its commandments in covenantal relationship with Havayah.

In the next two chapters we will look at how Avodah discloses the temporality of Netzach in what we shall refer to as the "architecture of Segulah." Drawing upon the Maharal of Prague and Hasidic sources, we will try to grasp the meaning of space and time in the inner Torah.

CHAPTER 17

The Space/Time of Inner Torah and the
Gateways to Netzach

Mortality and the Temporality of Netzach

In the previous chapter we used our method of negating Heidegger's ontology in order to construct an analysis of the temporality of Netzach particularly as it appears in Rabbi Kook's *Lights of Holiness*. Following the process of Churban and the conclusions we drew from *BT*, our methodological premise was that Heidegger's analysis was flawed and that Dasein's ownmost concern for its own *being* need not be confined to the death-obsessed individual self. We suggested an alternative in which the care of Dasein's ownmost self is directed at a totality of *alive-being* or Havayah, which, though not accessible to the unaligned Nefesh (Heidegger's Dasein in both its everyday and authentic forms), is the primary concern of the Neshamah and hence of the Nefesh too. In the specific context of Rabbi Kook's *Lights of Holiness*, this led to the suggestion that a principle of causality can be traced between the aligned Nefesh's total *concern* for the "aliveness" of *being* and the plausibility of eternal life.

In our conclusion we argued that despite human mortality, Dasein's ownmost mode of *being-toward* is plausibly describable as an authentic state of human *being* in the temporality of Netzach. This mode of *being* requires total absorption in the totality of *being* as Havayah (i.e., Da'at Hashem in Gadlut) and it is characterized by total *care* for an interminable aliveness that sits more naturally with the uniquely human capacity of reflexive *care* for *being* than Heidegger's conscience-ridden, anxious, *being-toward-death*. However, despite this emphasis on eternity, this state of *being* does not depend on the

445

immortality of the body, and as such it is a this-worldly or non-metaphysical experience.

In this chapter we shall try to understand in more detail how and why the Nefesh's experience of Netzach is not contradicted by the mortality of the body. In order to do this, we shall use our method to offer an onto-theological analysis of Jewish texts that make the connection between the temporality of Netzach and the concept of Avodah which, in our lexicon, refers to this-worldly practice of Torah and mitzvot. We will begin by looking in temporal terms at the effect of Avodah on the relationship between the Neshamah and the mortal body. We will see how Tzelem Elohim's experience of Netzach is characterized by a kind of correlation between space and time that we will refer to as the space/time of inner Torah. In the second half of the chapter our focus will be on the Avodah of Shabbat. In the next chapter we will take this forward and apply our understanding of the correlation between space and time to the Mishkan, Mount Moriah in Jerusalem, and more generally, the land of Israel.

Avodah and the Alignment of Body

The Talmud in *Yoma* 28b states in a discussion about the Patriarchs that Abraham performed all the commandments of the Torah. This is the opinion of Rav, who says,

> Abraham our patriarch fulfilled the entire Torah before it was given, as it is stated, "Because Abraham hearkened to My voice and kept My charge, My mitzvot, My statutes and My Torahs" (Genesis 26:5).[1]

At first glance the temporal premise of this passage is strange, because it makes no sense to assume that the patriarchs observed the commandments prior to the giving of the Torah at Mount Sinai. Indeed, this is perhaps the rationale behind Rabbi Shimi Bar Chiyya's suggestion that Abraham observed only the Noahide laws,

---

1.   *Yoma* 28b, English translation, https://www.sefaria.org.il/Yoma.28b.9.

Rabbi Shimi bar Chiyya said to Rav, "That verse means he fulfilled only the seven Noahide mitzvot and not the entire Torah."[2]

The next section of the passage might also be considered suspect because of the exegetical effort required to rebut Rabbi Shimi bar Chiyya's suggestion and establish the principle of Abraham's prior adherence to the precepts of the entire written law.

The Gemara asks, But isn't there also circumcision that Abraham clearly observed, which is not one of the Noahide laws? Apparently, Abraham fulfilled more than just those seven. The Gemara asks: And say he fulfilled only the seven mitzvot and circumcision. Rabbi said to him, "If so, why do I need the continuation of the verse that Abraham kept My mitzvot and My Torah? That is a clear indication that he fulfilled mitzvot beyond the seven Noahide mitzvot and apparently fulfilled the entire Torah."[3]

Finally, the text seems to protest too much, as it permutates itself into making the claim that Abraham observed not only the entire written law but even rabbinic injunctions that postdate the biblical period by hundreds of years.

Rabbi said in the name of Rabbi Ashi, "Abraham our forefather fulfilled the entire Torah, even the mitzvah of *eruv tavshilin*, a rabbinic ordinance instituted later, as it is stated, My Torahs. Since the term is in the plural, it indicated that Abraham kept two Torahs: one the written Torah, and one the oral Torah. In the course of fulfilling the oral Torah, he fulfilled the details and the parameters included therein.[4]

The "natural" reaction to this is perhaps to accuse the Rabbis of seeking ex post facto, pseudo-epigraphic justifications for their later rulings. Indeed,

---

2. Ibid.
3. Ibid.
4. Ibid.

this is the rational position that might also be applied to many other cases in which rabbinic literature speaks retrojectively about the origins of its authority.[5] The basic premise that guides this attitude is that the chronological logic of the biblical text requires rabbinic interpreters to ascribe to Abraham only knowledge that was available to him during his lifetime. Skepticism about some of the more fantastical truth claims of the Torah might perhaps lead us to insist that rabbinic interpretation must at the very least confine what is said about Abraham to what he could have known according to the chronology of the book in which he appears as a character. Whether rabbinic interpretation makes the Torah's truth claims seem more plausible or not, the perception of time here necessitates that at the very least we avoid making claims that contradict the reader's common sense.

Based on what we have already said about post-Enlightenment Jewish humanism, we might conclude that this insistence upon the reasonableness of the sequential temporality in exegesis – which arguably conceals a basic skepticism about the truth claims of the Torah itself – is symptomatic of what we referred to above as the strategy of Survival and System. From the perspective of Segulah, this strategy salvages nothing worth keeping in this case. The corrosive effects of this epistemology upon our ability to even begin to understand what the Torah's truth claims are, as well as those of rabbinic interpretations, are devastating. This is perhaps a perfect example of how Survival and System's reasonable resolution of an interpretive dilemma can prove counterproductive and even harmful to the perpetuation of Jewish identity.

By contrast, Hasidic and kabbalistic readings seem to take the temporality implied in this Talmudic passage much more seriously. This may indeed be accredited to a kind of prima facie religious loyalty to the truth claims of

---

5.   An interesting example of this is the case recounted in the Talmud (*Menachot* 29b). The Talmud describes how Moses is transported to a session of Torah study in the future where he hears Rabbi Akiva teaching laws that he does not recognize or comprehend. He is shocked to the brink of death by the thought that the Torah he is going to receive from Sinai will one day be lost and unrecognizable to him. He recovers when one of the students asks Rabbi Akiva where one of his teachings is derived from in the Torah and Rabbi Akiva answers that it is a law handed down expressly by Moses (*halachah leMoshe miSinai*). For a discussion of this story and its implications for our understanding of the traditionalist and antitraditionalist tensions in rabbinic literature, see Menachem Fisch, *Rational Rabbis: Science and Talmudic Culture* (Indiana, 1997), 192–96.

authoritative texts. But our contention is that the reasons for this are much deeper. We propose that a different experience of time is in play and that by negating Heidegger's ontology and replacing it with the structure of Tzelem Elohim we can uncover the content of a rich temporal phenomenology of *being* that is quite simply not known to the perspective of Survival and System.

In this phenomenology, an active interaction or relationship between the knowing self and the Torah is plausibly understood as changing Dasein's experience of time. In this context, Rabbi's statement about Abraham's observance of the mitzvot depends more on *attunement*, i.e., on how he is coming along with the alignment of his Nefesh and Neshamah, than it does on the chronology of either the biblical narrative or historical time. Hence, Rabbi's reading of the verse "Abraham hearkened to My voice" does not project upon Abraham an anachronistic rabbinic definition of the patriarch's religiosity. Rather, Abraham's hearkening refers to his Kavanah and its impact on his experience of time.

Correlation between Kavanah and time is common in Hasidic texts. For example, Rabbi Haim Ben Solomon Tyrer writes in his biblical commentary *Be'er Mayim Chayim* (BMC),

> Indeed, it is known that a person whose limbs are purified and polished from head to toe in complete purity will achieve by himself the words of the Torah, like the patriarch Abraham, about whom the Rabbis said (*Yoma* 28): Abraham our Father observed the entire Torah before it was given.[6]

The focus here is on the outermost level of Abraham's *being*, i.e., his physical body. The key idea here, which is already made explicit in classical rabbinic texts,[7] can be found in the words of the sixteenth-century Lurianic kabbalist Chaim Vital:

---

6. Haim Ben Solomon Tyrer, *Be'er Mayim Chayim* (Jerusalem: Even Yisrael Institute), Exodus 19:1–8 [Hebrew].

7. See, for example, Mishnah *Ohalot* 1:8 and Talmud *Makkot* 23b.

It is understood by discerning people that a person's body is not the actual person. The body is simply the "flesh" of the person, as it is written, "You have clothed me with skin and flesh, and covered me with bones and tendons" (Job 10:11)…the actual person is the [soul]; the body is merely a garment the soul wears…. The same way that a tailor will make a physical garment in the shape of a body, God similarly made the body, which is the garment of the soul, in the shape of a soul, with 248 limbs and 365 tendons…[corresponding to] 248 spiritual limbs and 365 spiritual tendons…[so that] the 365 spiritual tendons of the soul "wear" the 365 physical tendons of the body.[8]

In this passage the correspondence between the human body and the mitzvot echoes the relationship between the levels of *peshat* and *sod*. In the same way that the *peshat* is always the *peshat* of the *sod* and the *sod* is always the *sod* of the *peshat*, the external body in a state of alignment, or "purity," is always the external expression of the inner dimension of the Neshamah and vice versa. What these have in common is their shape or form, which according to this passage corresponds to the "shape" of the mitzvot. It is this shared shape that allows them to align. This is what is meant by the numerical correspondence between the 613 mitzvot and the total number of limbs and tendons in the body, as the 248 limbs and 365 tendons correspond to the 248 positive and 365 negative mitzvot, respectively. This system of correspondence is even intricate enough to connect each mitzvah to a specific limb or tendon.[9] The text continues,

The food for the soul comes from fulfilling the Torah, which includes 613 mitzvot corresponding to the 613 spiritual parts. The Torah is called "bread," as is written, "Come, eat my bread"

---

8. Rabbi Chaim Vital, *Sha'arei Kedushah*, part 1 gate 1; see Rabbi Jack Abramowitz, https://www.ou.org/torah/mitzvot/taryag/limbs/.

9. This idea, which is repeatedly echoed in the language of inner Torah, associates the 248 positive commandments of the Torah with 248 bodily limbs and the 365 negative commandments with a corresponding number of tendons. See, for example, Mishnah *Ohalot* 1:8 and Talmud *Makkot* 23b.

(Proverbs 9:5). Each of the 248 spiritual limbs gets its nourishment from a particular mitzvah that corresponds to that limb. When a person fails to perform that particular mitzvah, the corresponding limb will lack its proper nourishment.[10]

This section adds to the principle of correspondence an idea of nourishment. Translated into our lexicon, what this means is that the extension of the totality of *being* or Havayah into the specific *being* of Dasein is made possible by the architecture or the body shape of the mitzvot. Due to the closeness of the Nefesh-self or animal soul to the body, each physical limb in the human body as well as each element of the Nefesh that corresponds to it, *is* in the sense that its *being* is an extension or emanation of the consciousness of Havayah that "nourishes" its *being* from the Neshamah. The meaning of the mitzvot in general and of each mitzvah and its corresponding "body parts" is therefore the extension of *being* from the Nefesh into the body. The mitzvah is thus a law of nature that enables the totality of *being* to become externalized, extended into worldliness, or precipitated into the concrete *being* of the corresponding limbs in the Nefesh and body. If we fill this in across the whole structure of Tzelem Elohim, we can say that the overall principle here is an intrinsic system of correspondence that allows *alive-being* to flow from the *care* of the Neshamah, through the *care* of the Nefesh and into the body. This is made possible by the alignment of *care* or a directionality that molds the body into the shape of the mitzvot.

If we return to the BMC, we can now understand that what Rabbi Tyrer is saying about Abraham is that in his exemplary case, a person who has "purified and polished his limbs from head to toe" through Avodah and Kavanah can discover the mitzvot. This is not because they were given to him before the revelation at Sinai, but rather because he has aligned his body with its most natural shape or architecture, and as such his most natural bodily desires and actions *are* the mitzvot, which correspond to and are the life source of each limb.

Though, as we saw in the previous chapter, what is required for this correspondence to be achieved is a combination of Avodah and Kavanah that

---

10. Vital, *Sha'arei Kedushah*, part 1, gate 1.

takes place on the level of the *attuned* Nefesh, what is implied here is that alignment takes place at the level of the body as well. In other words, it is indeed possible that the Avodah that was available to Abraham comprised only of the Noahide laws, but in the state of purification that he achieved in body and Nefesh, the body itself aligns with the Neshamah, in which it "knows" – in the sense that in its very *being* it takes the shape or the form of – the mitzvot. Thus, in the same way that the unaligned Nefesh *always already* "knows" its existential need for animal-bodily desires such as food, water, and air, the aligned body *always already* experiences its ownmost natural physical desires as the mitzvot that correspond to each limb and tendon.

An Episode in Eternity: The Temporality of Avodah

As we said, what is of special interest to us here is the temporal dimension of this structure. It suggests that alignment of the lower levels in the structure of Tzelem Elohim with the higher ones redefines the meaning of *being-in-time*. By extending the structure of *being* "out" to the body and inward, past the Nefesh to the Neshamah, this alignment of the body, according to a shape that is *always already* known, grounds our sense of time in an architecture in which finite temporality emanates from eternity in the same way that the *being* of the body emanates from the Neshamah. What emerges from this passage is a meaning of Netzach that is not contradicted by death. It is the possibility of the finite and mortal consciousness of the Nefesh gaining temporal access to a dimension of its own consciousness that in its *"always and already-ness" is* in the temporality of Netzach. In this sense the mortal self (the temporality of the body and the Nefesh) can live its mortal life as an episode in eternity (the temporality of the Neshamah).

Following what we said about longevity of life in our discussion of Rabbi Kook, it is indeed noticeable that Abraham and other prominently righteous characters in Genesis are described as having lived extraordinarily long lives. But the point here is closer to Rabbi Kook's comment about the qualitative vitality of life which does require length of life to be considered more of life. In this sense, the mitzvot are a gateway between mortal time and Netzach which mortal individuals can align with whether periodically or, in exceptional cases, throughout the duration of their (long or short) lifetimes. This is what is meant in Hasidic literature by Devekut (usually translated as cleaving to God). Thus, though Abraham lived the life of a mortal and died, the temporality of his body-consciousness as well as his *care* for his ownmost *being* gave him access to the mitzvot. Put differently, the experience of *being-toward*-Netzach is one in which the Torah and the mitzvot as they are revealed across time are *always already* accessible at all times in the ownmost desires of the body, the *concerns* of the Nefesh, and the architecture of the Neshamah. This is what made them accessible to Abraham before Sinai, and this is what observant Jews pray for every day when they utter the words "Open my heart with Your Torah" – i.e., give me access through Torah to my Neshamah – "and may my Nefesh then desire Your mitzvot."[11] The Torah and the mitzvot are both the ends and the means in this prayer. The most natural desire of the body is to assume the shape of the mitzvot, but it is through the observance of the mitzvot (Avodah) that this most natural of our ownmost desires is discovered. Thus, as we have said, the *peshat* is always the *peshat* of the *sod* and the *sod* is always the *sod* of the *peshat*.

The temporality of Netzach and its connection to the architecture of the mitzvot is also discussed in the work *Kedushat Levi* by Rabbi Levi Yitzchak of Berditchev.[12] In the first of his three homilies on the festival of Purim, he comments on the curious phrase that appears in Esther (9:27), "The Jews fulfilled and then took upon themselves." As in the case of Rabbi's teaching about Abraham, this verse seems to imply that the Jews observed the decrees issued by Mordecai and Esther before they knew what they were. The Kedushat Levi compares this with the passage in Exodus 19 in which the people accept the Torah before it is given and asks,

> And we must understand what is meant when it says that Israel
> acted before they heard. How can they do anything before they
> hear about it? It seems to me that we need to understand this

---

11. These words are recited three times daily at the end of the standing prayer (the Amidah). The final paragraph of this prayer is an addendum that was composed by Mar the son of Ravina as described in the Talmud (*Berachot* 16b–17a).

12. Rabbi Levi Yitzchak of Berditchev (1740–1809) was a Hasidic master and contemporary of Rabbi Shneur Zalman of Liadi. He is the author of a series of works on the Torah and *Pirkei Avot* called *Kedushat Levi*. Though this is the name of his book, we shall be using it here to refer to his person and henceforth will not italicize unless referring specifically to the book.

in the same way that we understand what it says in the Passover Haggadah that it would have been enough (*dayenu*) if God had brought us close to Sinai without giving us the Torah. And we must understand what value there is in coming close to Sinai without receiving the Torah.[13]

He goes on to suggest that the physical proximity of the people to the holy mount was enough for them to receive the Torah. As a proof text for this idea, he cites our Talmudic passage concerning Abraham's observance of the mitzvot and asks, like the BMC, How did Abraham know these laws?

> And we must understand that the 248 positive commandments correspond with the 248 spiritual limbs, while the 365 negative commandments correspond to the spiritual tendons, and whoever looks at the spiritual energy of his limbs and tendons will attain the 248 and the 365 positive and negative mitzvot. And in the same way that each of the limbs of the body requires its own nourishment from food, so too does each of the spiritual limbs require its nourishment from mitzvot. And in the same way that there is no need to teach the physical limbs what nourishment they need, so too, there is no need to teach the spiritual limbs about the mitzvot, because they know this naturally of themselves, and also because the mitzvot are their aliveness.... because the spirit is the refinement of the mind and the purification of thought which is only the mitzvot.[14]

The Kedushat Levi echoes the principles of correspondence and nourishment that we discussed above, suggesting that the closeness of the Nefesh to the body enables the Nefesh to disclose in the body its ownmost natural desires. As we already saw, these become accessible when the mind is refined and formed in the shape that allows the most natural desires of the Neshamah to appear in the Nefesh. In this structure, willfulness and the refinement of

---

13. Rabbi Levi Yitzchak of Berditchev, *Kedushat Levi, Kedushah Rishonah*, Purim, Mesamchei Lev edition, 462 [Hebrew].

14. Ibid., 463.

desire enable a free flow of the consciousness of *being* between the upper and lower levels of Tzelem Elohim. But this can also flow in reverse. Thus, the Kedushat Levi continues, the Talmud in *Shabbat* 146a states that the people of Israel were purified by standing at Mount Sinai and not by receiving the Torah,

> Because by standing at Sinai and preparing for the giving of the Torah they were purified, and because of this they were able to receive the Torah, since the Torah is comprised of 248 spiritual limbs and 365 spiritual tendons. Thus, the light of the intellect cleaved to the light of the mitzvot, because they are all one. And this is what is meant when the Haggadah says that if we had only come close to Mount Sinai it would have been enough.[15]

The unity and oneness that is emphasized in this passage is essentially the coming together of all the different levels of Tzelem Elohim in a state of alignment. Thus, as we already said, the Torah and the mitzvot are both the means and the ends; the mind and the body, the Nefesh and the Neshamah are all one in a state of cleaving, or Devekut, in which the revelation of the Torah from "above" and the effort to attain it from "below" (or within) are one and the same thing.

The Kedushat Levi then applies this idea to the story of Purim. He asks not only what the book of Esther means when it states that the Jews accepted the decrees of Mordecai and Esther before they were issued, but why the Talmudic commentary on this verse insists that it applies not only to the decrees of the time but in fact to the entire Torah and to the recognition that the whole world is a divine creation.[16]

> And [the passage in the Talmud] is difficult, for why should the people finally understand this in the time of Mordecai and Esther when the miracles of the Exodus such as the splitting of the sea and the halting of the sun and the moon in the time of Joshua

---

15. Ibid.
16. See Talmud *Megillah* 11a.

were so much greater? For as we have already explained, there are two types of miracles: the first is revealed and the second is concealed. Revealed miracles such as the Exodus and the splitting of the sea can be seen by all, and they depart from the laws of nature. Concealed miracles such as those that took place in the time of Mordecai and Esther take place within the laws of nature without altering them.[17]

The Kedushat Levi distinguishes here between two types of miracles. The first are called revealed miracles and the second concealed miracles. He then goes on to compare these with heaven and earth, respectively:

> The miracles that belong to the category of heaven are called Neshamah, and those that are in the category of earth are called body. And nature is the body…and the Rabbis of the Talmud teach us that the miracles that took place in the time of Mordecai and Esther were miracles within nature, and so the miracle is greater because it was concealed.[18]

The miracles of heaven are witnessed by the Neshamah and perhaps can be compared to the level of *sod*, while those of the earth can be compared to the body. We could say that the Kedushat Levi is making a conventional point of religious faith here, i.e., that a concealed miracle is greater because the act of believing in it is greater. Since God's intervention in the story of Esther is veiled, and the turn of events is explicable by other means, the insistence that it is indeed a miracle is a greater act of faith than the faith required by those who bore witness to supernatural events such as the ten plagues in Egypt and the splitting of the sea. This understanding, which requires us to choose faith over common sense, might point to a religious virtue but it is one that undervalues the importance of rational perception and further entrenches our sense that the perspective of Segulah, if this is what it demands, is not capable of withstanding rigorous interrogation. Our suggestion, once again,

---

17.　Rabbi Levi Yitzchak of Berditchev, *Kedushat Levi*, 463.
18.　Ibid.

is that an onto-theological analysis of what is being said here enables us to uncover something more compelling.

In an extensive discourse on the relative greatness of the miracles of the Exodus and Purim, the Kedushat Levi essentially offers a teaching that connects between three points. First, he states that the miracles that take place in nature without contradicting the laws of nature are like the body that has a concealed Neshamah. In this sense, the earth and nature are a revealed miracle. The earth is the emanation and revelation of what is mysterious about the created-*being* of the world in the same way that the body is the explicit extension of the mysterious *being* of the Neshamah. With this recognition, everything that is more concealed than nature along with nature itself is revealed as part of the same totality of *createdness*. This is the first reason why the miracle that takes place inside the laws of nature is the greater of the two.

Second, he explains that the miracle of Purim was recognized by virtue of the mitzvot performed on the festival of Purim: the reading of the Megillah, giving charity to the poor, exchanging gifts of food, and eating a festive meal. With the reading of the Megillah and the other rituals of Purim, the Kedushat Levi says, we have a microcosm of the entire structure of Torah and mitzvot. As with the miracle itself, the act of reading the Megillah and performing its mitzvot extends the revelation of Torah from the level of the Neshamah to the level of nature and the body. Thus, telling the story of the miracle and performing the mitzvot of Purim accomplish the greater goal of connecting the mystery of heavenly revelation with our natural experience of the world. This is his second and deeper reason for saying that the natural miracle is of greater value.

Third, the Kedushat Levi says that the revealed miracles that took place in the time of the Exodus inspire fear because of the overpowering presence of God's visibility. There is a kind of excitement of the heart that makes the individual receptive to the incoming revelation. But this fearful awe is temporary. No sooner was the revelation of Sinai over than the fear dissipated, and the people worshipped the Golden Calf. However, in the time of Esther and Mordecai, the recognition that took place within nature was less overpowering, and as such, rather than being *attuned* with fear, it was disclosed in the *attunement* of love. The Kedushat Levi says that it is love that opens the heart to acknowledge and receive the consciousness that emanates from the inner levels of heaven/Neshamah. Thus, the 248 limbs and the 365 tendons of the body are filled with love and life that then opens the heart and the mind to a consciousness that moves backward in time to the retrojective recognition of what is *always already* revealed about nature and the body in Torah. In his words,

> And so when the people of Israel read from the Megillah, the physicality of the reader is purified, and the combinations of names that become enlightened in the mind of the reader who reads from the scroll of the Megillah enlighten all physicality and its vitality. And this is the realization of Torah and mitzvot. Whoever reads with Kavanah is filled with the desire to observe all the mitzvot of the Torah and not to violate the 248 negative commandments. And all the natural world is healed (undergoes Tikkun), just as the reader is healed and restored to his natural state.[19]

This staggering passage connects the phenomenology of Avodah with the ontology of Havayah, because it links the experience of reading the Megillah with changes that take place in the reader's experience of his ownmost *being*. When we combine these three points, we are presented with a complex and multileveled matrix of interrelated parts. On the first level of Avodah, the dimension of the body, which is also referred to as the natural state of the world, corresponds with the reading of the Megillah and the practice of its mitzvot. By virtue of the love that *attunes* our understanding of natural miracles, the body and the Nefesh go on to desire the Torah and the mitzvot that were revealed through heavenly miracles at Sinai. Ultimately, this matrix of interactions comes to explain not only how the people knew the Torah at the mountain before it was given or why the people accepted the decrees of Mordecai and Esther before they were given, but in more general terms it explains how finite moments in time such as the natural story of Purim and the mitzvot that accompany it can be a natural window to the temporality of Netzach and the timeless revelation of Sinai.

---

19. Ibid.

Space and Time in the Architecture of Segulah

As we continue with our method of negating Heidegger, what we wish to show now is how the architecture of Segulah applies to both space and time. As we saw in the *Kedushat Levi*, Sinai, which is a place, represents the temporality of Netzach and so, as in the passage from the song "Dayenu," proximity to the mountain was enough for the Torah – that was given later – to become accessible before. In this sense, Abraham's body is also a category in space that, assuming the shape of the mitzvot, became a gateway to a different dimension in time.

This correspondence between the architecture of time and space negates one of the basic principles in Heidegger's ontology. In *BT*, Heidegger turned to the dimension of time in order to ground his philosophical inquiry in a principle of totality. In death, Heidegger found a temporal finality which gave him a ground in which to anchor his insistence on totality in time. By orienting the horizon of *being* toward that finality, he was able to bring ontological thought to its total limit.

As we have already begun to see, in the architecture of Segulah, the relationship between time and space is structured differently. On the lower levels of the structure of Tzelem Elohim, where Dasein's spatial possibilities of *being* are limitless, the horizon of time is limited by death. However, this lower level of the body and the Nefesh can be aligned with an upper level in which infinite space and infinite time correspond completely. Once this correspondence is discovered, it affects the way in which we see the unity of time and space in the lower or more external levels as well, since these are both emanations of a single unified spatial/temporal *being*.

We wish to illustrate this idea by looking very closely at an extraordinary passage that appears in the writings of the sixteenth-century Talmud scholar and mystic widely known as the Maharal of Prague.[20] As in the passages above, the theme of time and its relationship to space emerges in the context of a discussion about the relationship between Torah, mitzvot, and the structure of Tzelem Elohim. The practical question that lies on the surface of this passage is how we decide what to do when presented with a choice between

---

20. Rabbi Judah Loew Ben Bezalel of Prague (the Maharal of Prague), *Netivot Olam, Netiv HaTorah*, chapter 1:8–9 [Hebrew].

performing a mitzvah and studying Torah. The Maharal considers the study of Torah to be of "added" value to a person because it is a matter of the higher mind. However, since the mitzvot are a matter of the body and its sustenance, the fulfillment of a mitzvah must take preference over the study of Torah, unless it is a mitzvah that can be performed by someone else. He then applies this principle to the famous discussion between Rabbi Akiva, Rabbi Tarfon, and the Elders that is cited in the Talmud:

> Rabbi Tarfon and the Elders were reclining in the loft of the house of Nitza in Lod, when this question was asked of them: Is study greater or is action greater? Rabbi Tarfon answered and said: Action is greater. Rabbi Akiva answered and said: Study is greater. Everyone answered and said: Study is greater, but not as an independent value; rather, it is greater, as study leads to action.[21]

The emphasis on practice in this passage supports the Maharal's idea that the mitzvot must take preference because they sustain the body. However, it is to the opinion of Rabbi Yossi that he dedicates the most detailed commentary. In the continuation of this passage in the Talmud Rabbi Yossi says,

> It is taught...that Rabbi Yossi says: Torah study is greater, as it preceded the mitzvah of separating *challah* by forty years. The Torah was given to the Jewish people soon after they left Egypt, whereas the mitzvah of separating *challah* came into effect only after they entered Eretz Yisrael. And it preceded the mitzvah of *terumot* (donations) and tithes by fifty-four years, as the Jews became obligated in these mitzvot only fourteen years after they entered Eretz Yisrael, once they had conquered and divided the land. Furthermore, the Torah preceded the observance of Sabbatical Years by sixty-one years, as they began to count the seven-year cycle only once they had divided the land. Finally, it preceded the Jubilee years by 103 years, as the

---

21. *Kiddushin* 40b.

fifty-year count to the first Jubilee year began only after they had divided Eretz Yisrael.[22]

The Maharal's analysis of this is long and complex but extremely important in terms of what we can learn from it about the meaning of time in the Torah. Let's take it one piece at a time. He begins as follows:

> The study of Torah is greater because it came first…since the Torah was given in time before the mitzvot this proves that the Torah is greater. And this is what can be seen from the verse (Numbers 13:22) "Now Hebron was built seven years before Zoan in Egypt," meaning that when one place is of a higher value than another it is said that it came first in time. And thus, it is said that the Torah came two thousand years before the creation of the world, meaning that it has priority over mitzvot.[23]

This passage is astonishing in the way it weaves space and time together with reference to the concept of the double entendre implied (in Hebrew as in English) by the word "priority." Exegetically, the Maharal says that when priority in time or space is mentioned in the Torah it can be taken as referring to priority in terms of importance. He goes so far as to say that this applies to a seemingly explicit historical statement about the order in which two cities, Hebron and Zoan, were built.

Next, he begins to analyze the sequential relationship between *challah* (the separation of dough before baking bread), *terumot uma'asrot* (donations and tithes) and Yovalot (the Jubilee year). The Maharal writes as follows:

> These words of Rabbi Yossi have tremendous depth. And you need to understand the following three mitzvot, which have three types of holiness attached to them. The first is *challah*, which a person separates from the dough and is holy. The second is donations and tithes that are separated from the produce, and they are holy. And

---

22. Maharal, *Netivot Olam, Netiv HaTorah*, chapter 1: 8–9.
23. Ibid.

the third, the Jubilee year, which is holy, tells us that the Torah is above the world, and the world has three levels. The lowest level is complex, and it is made up of compounds and combinations of elemental things. And mankind, the highest thing, correlates to the mitzvah of *challah*. That is because this mitzvah applies when the dough is made and some of it is separated and made holy, and mankind is like *challah*, as it says, "And God made the man out of the earth." And mankind is separated from among all the other compounds.

The next level includes the elemental things that are not compounds or complex at all. This level corresponds to the donations made and tithes taken after creation is complete. In the same way that the produce [fruit and grain] can be spread out, the donations and tithes are set aside.

The third level is without physicality, and it is above time. It is like the fiftieth year that follows the forty ninth and is beyond the counting [i.e., it is beyond the counting of forty-nine years], just as we do not count the fiftieth day on the festival of Atzeret [Shavuot] because this is a separate world that is beyond time. And even so, this level has a special quality, in that it is in fact connected to time because it is the fiftieth in the cycle of forty-nine years that are counted in time.

And of these three levels the *challah* came first, because compounds are closest to human beings. And afterward came the donations and tithes and afterward the Jubilee, because whatever is closest to humans comes first.[24]

Let us begin our explanation of this passage by introducing each one of the three mitzvot. The first mitzvah, *challah*, appears in Numbers 15,

Of the first of your dough you shall set apart a cake for a gift; as that which is set apart of the threshing-floor, so shall you set it apart.[25]

---

24. Ibid.
25. Numbers 15:20.

The obligation here is to set aside a piece of dough when making bread. This piece of dough is then given to the priests. Similarly, the second mitzvah is to set aside tithes and donations for the priests and the Levites from the produce of fruits and crops. This is described in Numbers 18:

> All the heave-offerings of the holy things, which the children of Israel offer unto the Lord, have I given you, and your sons and your daughters with you, as a due forever; it is an everlasting covenant of salt before the Lord unto you and to your seed with you. And the Lord said unto Aaron: You shall have no inheritance in their land, neither shall you have any portion among them; I am your portion and your inheritance among the children of Israel. And unto the children of Levi, behold, I have given all the tithe in Israel for an inheritance, in return for their service which they serve, even the service of the tent of meeting.[26]

Third and finally, the laws pertaining to the Jubilee year appear in Leviticus 25:

> And you shall hallow the fiftieth year…it shall be a Jubilee unto you; and you shall return every man unto his possession, and you shall return every man unto his family. A Jubilee shall that fiftieth year be unto you.… For it is a Jubilee; it shall be holy unto you.[27]

According to the Maharal, the key to unpacking the meaning of Rabbi Yossi's words is buried in how we understand the continuum between these three mitzvot. On the first level, as Rabbi Yossi says, the temporal continuum corresponds to the order in which these mitzvot are encountered after the arrival of the people of Israel in the land of Israel. The mitzvah of *challah* comes first because it is performed every time the people bake bread. This is followed by donations and tithes, which are encountered or practiced for the first time fifty-four years later and only after the division of the land between the tribes is completed. Finally comes the Jubilee year, which is observed only after

---

26. Numbers 18:19–21.
27. Leviticus 25:7–13.

counting forty-nine more years. Since this count began only after the division of the land between the tribes was completed, the beginning of the first Jubilee year was the one hundred and third year after entering the land. On this level, the practical meaning of "priority" in the continuum is connected to the amount of time that the people spend in the land. We might say that the discovery of these mitzvot is a function of the journey in space and time, as life in the land yields the order of their relative importance next to the study of Torah.

However, the Maharal's analysis probes this further by taking this temporal structure to an entirely different level that ultimately yields the ontological meaning of the sequence. To see this, we need to unpack what the Maharal is saying about the continuum between the different types of sanctity that apply to every one of these mitzvot. Each of these mitzvot involves setting something aside for holy purposes. In the case of *challah*, the portion that is set aside is torn away from the rest of the dough. However, before the mitzvah is performed this dough is simply part of the mix. The donations and tithes are fruit and crops that are indeed set aside. But before their separation from the other produce, they were never joined together. Unlike the *challah*, which was inside the same single lump of dough, these fruits lay separately alongside the other fruit and crops. Finally, the Jubilee year is a year set aside from others, but it is described as more separate still than the donations and tithes were from the rest of the fruit, because this separate year lies outside of the counting. It is the fiftieth year in a cycle of forty-nine.

Using our lexicon, we believe that it is possible to make the meaning of this continuum clearer still. Our basic assumption, taken from the Maharal's hint about the depth of Rabbi Yossi's words in the opening phrase of the passage, is that each of these mitzvot represents a dimension of inner human consciousness. Each one corresponds to a level of *care* for *being* that operates upon a horizon of time. The first level is the level of the body and the unaligned Nefesh. At this level the Maharal compares the relationship between human beings and the rest of the physical world to the separateness of the *challah* from the dough. Humans are complex compounds in the complex, compound world but are holy because they are set aside inside the world to which they belong.

In this sense, what the Maharal says about the set-aside-ness of the *chal-lah* from the dough corresponds to Heidegger's methodological premise that the only being that can give us access to the meaning of *being* is Dasein, whose reflexive consciousness of *being* is inextricably stitched into the fabric of its *with-world*. The donations and tithes in this structure refer to the level of the aligned Nefesh, in which human consciousness in its *being* is close to or basically the same as the finite temporality of the world but separate from it, in the same way that the fruit and crops are separate from each other on the threshing floor. In this metaphor, the unaligned Nefesh is like all the other fruit, but the donations and tithes in their holiness and set-aside-ness represent the Nefesh when it takes the form or the shape of the mitzvah itself. The refined Nefesh therefore has a reflexive consciousness that *is* in the world but from a greater reflexive distance.

Finally, from this finite state of alignment that corresponds to the forty-nine years in which the counting continues, the aligned Nefesh bears self-conscious witness to the *being* of the Neshamah that is represented by the mitzvah of the Jubilee year. This year is outside of time and yet rests on time in the same way that the being of the Neshamah is connected by alignment to the Nefesh and the body but is also beyond them. The fiftieth year that is not counted after the seven cycles of seven years corresponds to the fiftieth day that follows the cycle of seven weeks that are counted after the Exodus. This is what the Maharal refers to as the festival of Atzeret, which means "stopping," or Shavuot, which literally means "weeks." This festival marks the fiftieth day when the counting of time stops and the Torah is given at Sinai. Again, the Jubilee is a temporal cycle that is connected to and defined by spatiality in the sense that it applies only in the land of Israel.

The fiftieth year – counted after seven cycles of seven years, as the fiftieth day that follows seven cycles of seven weeks corresponds to the eighth day of the week that exists beyond time – is also called "Shabbat." This Shabbat is not the seventh day of the week. Rather, it is an eternal seventh day; a number 8 in a cycle of 7 which is also a number 50 in a cycle of 7 times 7. It is this Shabbat that the seventh day of the week points to among the days of the week. It is also the referent of the seventh year in the cycle of years that comprise the counting of forty-nine. Finally, it is the Shabbat that the land of Israel points to among the lands of the seventy nations of the earth. Each of these mitzvot is thus a window or a gateway inside mortal time that points toward the temporality of Netzach. In the Jubilee year the shofar that declares God's Kingdom (Da'at Hashem), reboots all human transactions in the land.[28] On Shabbat all transactions and acts of human construction are suspended, and human society yields to the Kingdom of God (Da'at Hashem). Atzeret, the Shabbat that follows forty-nine weeks, is the time when the Torah is given (Da'at Hashem). In all three cases the transition from the seventh to the eighth day of days/weeks/years is the meeting place of *being-in-time* and Netzach.

In this structure, the mitzvah of *challah* represents Dasein's temporality as *being-in-time* in the mortal world. The tithes rise to a greater distance and look on from within the temporality of the world as an episode in eternity. The Jubilee/Shabbat, which represents the window to eternal time, is furthest away from the body. It represents the most internal or conversely the most cosmically distant dimension of the human experience of *being*. The Torah that transcends time is both first and last in the sequence (which is how in the Maharal's interpretation of sequential priority, this continuum does not contradict Rabbi Yossi's statement that the Torah comes first). It is first in line from above but last from below. The Jubilee, the donations and tithes, and then *challah*, which are respectively closer to the surface from within (or closer to earthly time from without), represent the mitzvot. Though the study of Torah is greater, the mitzvot take practical priority, because, in the words of the Maharal, "Whatever is closest to humans comes first." Thus, the order of priority which is determined by physical closeness to the human experience of time is the order of Avodah. In this way the Maharal draws support from Rabbi Yossi for the general principle with which we began, i.e., that despite the Torah being greater, the performance of a mitzvah takes preference over the study of Torah unless the mitzvah can be performed by someone else. In other words, at the same time that these three mitzvot are lined up in space and mortal time in one order, they line up in Netzach in reverse. In this two-way system, the directionality of Avodah, which flows from the body

---

28. As described in Leviticus 25:9–18, the shofar is blown to announce the beginning of the Jubilee year, in which the land rests, all transactions over the purchase and sale of land are annulled and tribally owned lands are returned to their original owners, debts are canceled, and slaves are freed.

to the Neshamah, swims upstream like Kavanah against the directionality of Havayah that flows from Netzach to the mortal time of *being-in-the-world*. The meeting of the two is the energy that allows the Nefesh-consciousness of the body to transcend its boundaries and accomplish the goal of Teshuvah (returning), as in the verse "Return unto Me and I will return unto you, said the Lord (Havayah) of hosts" (Malachi 3:7). On the lower end of this scale, time and space are set apart, while on the higher level they are one. The continuum itself, represented by the mitzvot and perhaps corresponding to the dimension of Ruach, is what enables mortal time in space to be experienced as an episode in Netzach.

Makom: The Space/Time of Inner Torah

So far we have seen how the general category of mitzvot provides the shape or the structure that allows the alignment of different levels that run from the body to the Neshamah and back. We have shown how in this structure there is a progression that can be described in temporal terms that enables us to explain the experience of time in the body as a finite episode of Netzach in the Neshamah. Thus, the alignment of Nefesh and Neshamah is an alignment of mortal and eternal *being-in-time*. What we would like to show now is that in the system of the inner Torah, this alignment of the body's time and eternal time is also an alignment of space and time, which is variously represented in multiple networks or matrices of concepts. Some of these are most naturally associated with space, others with time; but when they are considered together it becomes clear that the correlations between them merge the two categories to form a kind of space/time. This is captured, for example, in the dual meaning of the word *olam*, which means both "the universe" and "forever."

Another example of this is the biblical word *makom* or *hamakom*, which most simply means "place" or "the place." This word is specifically used to designate very special dimensions in space. In the biblical story of the binding of Isaac (Genesis 22), the word *makom* appears repeatedly, and even a little ominously, to denote the undetermined place to which Abraham must lead Isaac unknowingly to the slaughter. This place is the holiest of places, Moriah, where the Temple is ultimately to be built. The word returns in the same repetitive way in the story of Jacob's dream (Genesis 28), this time referring to a place that prima facie is somewhere else, Luz.[29] Here, when Jacob is leaving his father's home and journeying to the house of Laban he arrives at a *makom*, a special place where he feels a meaningful presence denoted by the phrase "and he lighted upon the place (*makom*)."[30] It is in the context of this encounter with a meaningful place that Jacob lies down for the night and sees the vision of the ladder. When he awakens, he seems surprised to discover that he is in a holy place, exclaiming, "God is indeed in this place (*makom*) and I did not know it!" From this recognition he then concludes, "How full of awe is this place (*makom*). This is none other than the House of God and this is a gateway to the heavens" (Genesis 28:16–17). Quoting from the Midrash, the medieval commentator Rashi writes on this verse,

> R. Eleazar said in the name of R. José the son of Zimra: "This ladder stood in Beersheba and [the middle of]) its slope reached opposite the Temple" (*Bereishit Rabbah* 69:7). For Beersheba is situated in the South of Judah, Jerusalem in the North of it on the boundary between Judah and Benjamin and Bethel in the North of Benjamin's territory, on the border between the land of Benjamin and that of the children of Joseph. It follows, therefore, that a ladder whose foot is in Beersheba and whose top is in Bethel has the middle of its slope reaching opposite Jerusalem. Now as regards what our Rabbis stated (*Chullin* 91b) that the Holy One, blessed be He, said, "This righteous man has came to the place where I dwell (i.e., the Temple at Jerusalem, whilst from here it is evident that he had come to Luz) and shall he depart without staying here over night?", and with regard to what they

---

29. The city of Luz mentioned here is interestingly described as the gateway to heaven and in kabbalistic literature it is seen as a place of total joy in which the human soul can bask in the glory of the divine presence. The theme of the city of Luz in the writing of the Gaon of Vilna and the possible association between Luz (which in Hebrew also means a pine nut) and the pine nut–shaped pineal gland in the brain which is responsible for altered states of consciousness is discussed by Joel David Bakst in his books *The Secret Doctrine of the Gaon of Vilna: Mashiach ben Yoseph and the Messianic Role of Torah, Kabbalah and Science*, vol. 1 (City of Luz Publications, 2008); *The Secret Doctrine of the Gaon of Vilna*, vol. 2; and *The Josephic Messiah, Leviathan, Metatron and the Sacred Serpent* (City of Luz Publications, 2009).

30. Genesis 28:11.

also said, (Talmud Pesachim 88a) "Jacob gave the name Bethel to Jerusalem", whereas this place which he called Bethel was Luz and not Jerusalem, whence did they learn to make this statement (which implies that Luz is identical with Jerusalem)? I say that Mount Moriah was forcibly removed from its locality and came hither (to Luz), and that this is what is meant by the "shrinking" of the ground that is mentioned in the tractate (Chullin 91b)— that the site of the Temple came toward him (Jacob) as far as Bethel and this too is what is meant by, "he lighted upon the place" (i.e., he "met" the place, as two people meet who are moving towards each other; cf. Rashi on Genesis 5:11). Now, since Jacob's route must have been from Beersheba to Jerusalem and thence to Luz and Haran, and consequently, when he reached Luz he had passed Jerusalem, if you should ask, "When Jacob passed the Temple, why did He not make him stop there?" — If it never entered his mind to pray at the spot where his fathers had prayed should Heaven force him to stop there to do so? Really he had reached as far as Haran as we say in the Chapter Gid Hanasheh (Talmud Chullin 91b), and Scripture itself proves this since it states, "And he went to Haran". When he arrived at Haran he said, "Is it possible that I have passed the place where my fathers prayed without myself praying there?" He decided to return and got as far as Bethel where the ground "shrank" for him. This Bethel is not the Bethel that is near Ai (cf. Genesis 12:8) but that which is near Jerusalem, and because he said of it, "It shall be the House of God", he called it Bethel. This, too, is Mount Moriah, where Abraham prayed. [31]

Beyond the significance of the positioning of the ladder in the dream, the Midrash describes how Mount Moriah moved and the land shrank in order to make the place of Abraham and Isaac's prayer (i.e., Moriah) accessible to Jacob from Luz. The dual directionality between Netzach and body time recurs here and is arguably echoed in the image of the angels going up and down the ladder as well. In the same way that the directionality of Avodah

---

31. Rashi, Genesis 28:11.

flows from the body to the Neshamah and from Netzach to mortal time, Mount Moriah comes toward Jacob as he comes toward it, "as two people meet who are moving toward each other."[32]

Since this passage contradicts our normal experience of space, it perhaps goes without saying that a post-Enlightenment humanist reading of it will not be able to take it literally and perhaps not even seriously; either seeking to circumvent its oddness by explaining it away metaphorically or by making paternalistic, historical, or anthropological allowances for it. In the worst-case scenario, it might become the object of ridicule, but one way or another the plausibility of its truth claim seems hard to defend. Given all that we have already explained in this chapter, it is perhaps possible to jump past these objections straight to the main thrust of our argument. Our point therefore is that this striking passage applies the same principles that we saw in our discussion of time to the ontology of space. In other words, this Midrash ascribes to Jacob the same kind of access to Jerusalem from Luz or Bethel as Abraham had to the mitzvot prior to the revelation of Sinai.

Time and space behave in the same way in the space/time of inner Torah. Space and time share a structure or a shape according to which a lower or outer potentiality of *being* that is readily accessible to the everydayness of the body and the Nefesh can become aligned with the Neshamah's ownmost *being-in-the-world*. In the higher register of consciousness (Da'at Hashem in Gadlut), the temporality of Netzach is parallel to Mount Moriah. Just as the mitzvot are *always already* accessible at any point in time, Mount Moriah is *always already* accessible from anywhere in space. Moreover, the two-way directionality of *being-toward* that characterized the gateway in time is also characteristic of the gateway in space. Thus, the word *makom* describes not only a holy place but a place where there is a two-way gateway to a higher or inner *care* for *being*. This is Jacob's realization at the end of the episode when he says, "This is the gateway to the heavens."

In the very specific sense in which *makom* means a special gateway to Moriah, the connection between the etymology of the word and the similarly sounding word *mekayem* becomes clear. *Mekayem* is a word with ontological

---

32. Ibid.

meaning that refers to the enduring of existence across time.[33] The connection between these two words brings us back to the Maharal of Prague, who pointed out the link which, in our terms, is found in the underlying *being* of Havayah common to both space and time. Thus, in the onto-theology of inner Torah, every moment in time is potentially a gateway to – or an episode in – Netzach; while every place in the world is potentially the gateway to – or an encounter with – the boundless spatial *being* of Havayah. In this sense, Mount Moriah is the underlying or inner spatiality of the *being* or Havayah of the whole world. This is ultimately why the word Hamakom (*hamekayem*) is simply and frequently used as a name of God.

The Meaning of Shabbat in the Space/Time of Inner Torah

We shall try to understand this space/time correlation in more depth and detail by looking at a more elaborate but nonetheless specific example of it. Our chosen topic is Shabbat (which is a category in time) and its connection to the Mishkan and the land of Israel (both categories in space). This topic is a crucially important example of how the general principle of alignment between the Nefesh and the Neshamah is accomplished through the practice of mitzvot. But it is specifically relevant to the overall thrust of our argument since, after being discussed at some length, it will bring us closer to understanding the difference between Zionism after the Holocaust as viewed from the perspective of Survival and System and its meaning from the perspective of Segulah. The rest of this chapter will be devoted to the temporality of Shabbat, and in the next chapter we will explore the connections between Shabbat and its spatial aspects.

The Shabbat of Survival and System and the Problem of Holiness in Ontic Time

Most simply and obviously, Shabbat refers to the seventh day of the week. It is the day on which God rested in the creation story and which Jews have observed as a day of rest throughout history. It is also the object of the first appearance of sanctity in the bible. God blessed the seventh day and

---

33. The Maharal of Prague makes explicit the ontological significance of the connection between the words *makom* and *mekayem* in his *Chiddushei Aggadot* 147.

sanctified it because it was on this day that He rested from all His work of creation.[34]

In everyday or ontic temporality, the specific meaning of this day is often considered in three different ways. In the first, the seventh day refers to a recurring marker that functions as a sort of placeholder in the endless sequence of linear time. In this framing, time moves forward from its beginning to its end. The recurring sequence of seven-day cycles enables us to manage our experience of time but does not reflect an actual occurrence of repetition. By giving names and numbers to the endless succession of days we can divide them up into units of weeks, months, and years that make the passage of time easier to monitor and handle. Consequently, in this structure, each Shabbat that seemingly recurs every seven days is an unprecedented event in the sense that the notion of the recurring day is no more than a construct.

Alternately, we might consider this same division of time in cyclical terms and say that by allocating certain routines and behaviors to the recurring cycles of names and numbers, we attribute to each one of the seven days characteristics that recur in a loop. This creates the impression that after the completion of a cycle we can somehow return to its beginning. This way we can believe that we like Sundays and not Mondays, though there is nothing that connects between the recurring days other than the conventions that we timetable into them. Again, this cyclical structure is only ever a construction, since the notion that time is a loop is never more than a metaphor that overlays our intuitive experience of linear lifetime (biological time) ticking away. Finally, we might combine the two, resolving the dilemma of linear and cyclical time, by creating a spiral in which forward-moving linear time is simultaneously experienced in cycles. In this spiral we have last week's Shabbat, this week's Shabbat, and next week's Shabbat. They are not the same day. They recur in weekly intervals. But a certain recurring routine connects our experience of them, tying them together in our minds and thus creating an illusion of something cyclical that takes place on a forward-moving, linear scale.

---

34. Genesis 2:1–3.

There is much debate and discussion about the relative virtues of each of these depictions.[35] But the specific point that we are interested in making cannot be seen by trying to choose between them since, from the perspective of Segulah, all three of these options belong to the world of Survival and System. Even if one chooses to "believe" (in the ontic sense) that one or all these conventions was somehow instigated and then revealed by God Himself, there is nothing in any of these framings of time that gives us access to an inner rationale of time's categorizations. Since there is nothing essential about the Monday-ness of Mondays or the Thursday-ness of Thursdays, there is nothing in this framing that can help us take seriously the Torah's truth claim about the specific sanctity of Shabbat. On the contrary, it is the prescribed behaviors, rituals, customs, and commandments that endow any day and the recurring cycles of that day in the forward moving spiral of time with either unique or recurring meanings. Working on these assumptions it is only natural to define the meaning of Shabbat as Mordechai Kaplan did, in terms of the day of rest that it provides for the weary worker or in terms of the family and community values that it serves.[36] Even the most devout religious observance of the day, when constructed ontically, can only prescribe religious adherence to the commandments of the Torah at the appointed times while making no serious claim to discover the sanctity of the day in the day itself. In this paradigm, the claims to eternal sanctity that the Jewish tradition attaches to the Shabbat are no match for Heidegger's insistence on the authenticity of Dasein's mortal *being-in-time*.

It is no surprise then that in the Judaism of Survival and System, the fastidiousness of halachic demands concerning the observance of the Shabbat is given to attrition. Shabbat is seen as a particularist feature of the humanist construction of time that can easily be transposed into the metaphor of other cultures, celebrated in different but equivalent ways ("turning on and off a light switch is not work") or transferred (as in the Christian celebration of Sunday as the Sabbath) to different days of the week. This was

---

35. See, for example, Mordechai Rotenberg, *Jewish Psychology and Hasidism: The Psychology behind the Theology* (Open University, Ministry of Defense Publications, 1997), 83–91 [Hebrew].

36. Mordechai Kaplan, *Judaism as a Civilization: Toward a Reconstruction of American Jewish Life* (New York: Schocken Books, 1981), 443–49.

perhaps captured by Ahad Ha'am, who quipped, "More than the Jews have kept Shabbat; Shabbat has kept the Jews." The commandment to "keep" the Shabbat "holy" is replaced by the more sociologically obvious task of keeping the Jews Jewish. This is a framing that ultimately devalues the intrinsic meaning of Shabbat while reconstructing its meaning as a tool of Survival. From the perspective of Segulah, the corrosive effect of this is so potent that Shabbat seems no more likely to go on keeping the Jews than they can be expected to go on keeping it.

Our point is that when considered ontically, none of these options – linear, cyclical, or spiral – negates the time that Dasein experiences as the horizon of *being*. The inevitable relegation of Shabbat to a normative social convention that this ontic perception of time engenders ultimately blocks our ability to access the meaning of time as something that can contain holiness. Drawing on our lexicon of ontological terms, we shall seek to rehabilitate this devaluation.

Heschel's Shabbat – a Palace in Time

In our first chapter we cited Byron Sherwin's argument that prevalent attitudes to Abraham Joshua Heschel's work are based upon a categorical error and that Heschel's writings, rather than trying to facilitate a synthesis between Judaism and liberal humanism, are in fact a fierce attempt to break them apart.[37] An example of this can be found in the prologue to his very popular short book, *The Sabbath*.[38] Though there are no explicit references to Heidegger, this prologue does feel like a reaction to *BT*. Elsewhere in his writing Heschel responded openly to Heidegger's ontology, arguing, for example, that Heidegger's attitude to *being* is passive and submissive while the life of Torah is dedicated to the transcendence of *being*.[39] In many ways this is the

---

37. Byron L. Sherwin, "The Assimilation of Judaism, Heschel and the 'Category Mistake,'" *Judaism* 53, no. 3 (June 2006), 40–50.

38. Heschel, *The Sabbath*, 2–10.

39. "Simply to 'surrender to being,' as Heidegger calls upon us to do, he would...reduce his living to being. To be is both passive and intransitive. In living, man relates himself actively to the world.... The decisive form of human being is human living...to bring into being, to come into meaning. We transcend being by bringing into being – thoughts, things, offspring, deeds." This passage suggests that Heschel understands Heidegger's portrayal of Dasein as passively submissive to being and as such unable to act in time.

thesis of *The Sabbath* as well and it therefore supplies us with an additional precedent for our methodology of negating Heidegger that is worthy of close attention.

From Heschel's perspective, the stark contrast between Judaism and Western civilization is the difference between their respective attitudes toward space and time. While Western or technical civilization primarily sanctifies space at the expense of time, Judaism and Jewish theology are grounded first and foremost in the dimension of time. He writes,

> Technical civilization is man's conquest of space. It is a triumph frequently achieved by sacrificing an essential ingredient of existence, namely, time. In technical civilization we expend time to gain space. To enhance our power in the world is our main objective. Yet to have more does not mean to be more. The power we attain in the world of space terminates abruptly at the borderline of time. But time is the heart of existence.[40]

This brief paragraph has all the components in it of a deliberate conversation with Heidegger. But not everything here is a point of disagreement. Heschel's critique of technical civilization is one that Heidegger shared. Again, like Heidegger, Heschel offers a way out that is focused on time. Preoccupation with space and with the idea that power comes from the conquest of space is characteristic of Heidegger's critique of inauthentic Dasein and its inability to face the ownmost horizon of its own *being* as *being-toward-death*.[41] The observation that time is the heart of existence also echoes the primary thesis of *BT* that the horizon of *being* is time.

The difference appears in Heschel's allusion to the possibility of grounding the human experience of time in the temporality of Netzach. This is hinted at in the wry observation that the power we attain in space is stripped

---

See Abraham Joshua Heschel, *Man Is Not Alone: A Philosophy of Religion* (New York: Farrar, Strauss and Giroux, 1951), 69.

40. Ibid.

41. This echoed in the prologue to *The Sabbath* when Heschel says, "We suffer from a deeply rooted dread of time and stand aghast when compelled to look in its face" (page 5).

away from us at the "borderline of time," i.e., death. To understand what Heschel is saying here, we need to see why he is critical of primitive religion and of the widespread belief that "God is perceived by most of us to be a thing,"[42]

> A deity that resides in space within particular localities like mountains, forests, trees or stones which are, therefore, singled out as holy places; the deity is bound to a particular land; holiness a quality associated with things of space and the primary question is: Where is the god?[43]

Heschel understands paganism's concept of time as subservient to space and insists that Jewish thought sees things the other way around. He continues,

> We are all infatuated with the splendor of space, with the grandeur of things of space. This is a category that lies heavy on our minds, tyrannizing all our thoughts. Our imagination tends to mould all concepts in its image. In our daily lives we attend primarily to that which the senses are spelling out for us; to what the eyes perceive, to what the fingers touch. Reality to us is thinghood.[44]

A phenomenological reading of this (translated slightly more explicitly into the terms we have been using) would suggest that from Heschel's point of view, Dasein's infatuation with space leads us (since we are all Dasein) to conceptualize everything in terms of our own spatial experience of *being*. This applies to the way in which Heidegger's Dasein (in both its authentic and inauthentic forms) conceptualizes the meaning of time as well. However, this is the case only because Dasein has no access to an experience of time that is grounded in the *being* of the Neshamah. Thus, even authentic Dasein's experience of time is spatial, which is why its horizon of *being* is limited to the enduring spatial *being* of the mortal body. From Heschel's point of view,

---

42. Ibid.
43. Ibid., 4.
44. Ibid., 5.

this phenomenological preoccupation with space is a central characteristic of paganism that is shared by Western technical civilization. It is why religion has degenerated and people are unable to find God.

That said, our argument is that the contrast between space and time in this prologue should not be overstated. Rather, there is a crucially important role for space in Heschel's thought that corresponds to the meaning of *chol* or *chullin* – a general term that denotes the unsanctified in Jewish thought. Spatiality for Heschel is the business of the "unsanctified" six days of the working week. The Torah therefore encourages the effort to construct things in space during the six days of the week. However, in ominous language that is heavily laced with the looming memory of the Holocaust, Heschel suggests that a culture of space, theistic or not, that lacks the intermittent dimension of attention to sacred time is likely to spin dangerously out of control. In his words,

> To gain control of the world of space is certainly one of our tasks.
> The danger begins when in gaining power in the realm of space we
> forfeit all aspirations in the realm of time. There is a realm of time
> where the goal is not to have but to be, not to own but to give,
> not to control but to share, not to subdue but to be in accord. Life
> goes wrong when the control of space, the acquisition of things of
> space, becomes our sole concern.[45]

For Heschel, space is therefore the dimension in which human beings can attain and wield their own power. When there is an imbalance between our attention to space and time, society is given over to human power alone, and that is where the danger lies. This concern runs parallel to what we referred to as Dasein's anxiety about its own devouring spatiality. As we suggested, this anxiety is a source of tyrannical behavior, and when placed in the context of Heschel's life story, it is understandable that his fear of spatial tyranny connects his critique of American liberal materialism to the same human impulses that led Germany to Nazism. This is how Galut becomes Churban.

---

45. Ibid.

If this reading is correct, it might explain the somewhat skewed emphasis that Heschel gives to the dominance of time in certain places. He indeed writes that

> the Bible is more concerned with time than with space. It sees the world in the dimension of time. It pays more attention to generations, to events, than to countries, to things; it is more concerned with history than with geography.[46]

Because of passages like this, Heschel has, with justification, been accused of overstating the centrality of time at the expense of such things as the land of Israel and the Temple.[47] One way of looking at this is to associate his position with the Maimonidean view that the sacrificial ritual of the Mishkan with all its spatial imagery is in fact a concession that God made to the children of Israel after the sin of the Golden Calf. In this sense, the land and ritual objects are remnants of a pagan past; a time of spiritual and physical impoverishment that the released slaves of Egypt were not yet able to move beyond.[48] We have already seen Heschel's rejection of holy sites and his resistance to the idea that the deity is bound to a holy land.[49] But our sense is that this reading of Heschel actually misses the most important point that he makes in this book, even if he is partially responsible for giving the wrong impression.

In our reading, Heschel does indeed overstate and exaggerate the centrality of time at the expense of space but does not altogether miss the significance that the Torah attaches to space. Rather his insistence on the centrality of time should be taken as an observation about the spatial purpose of sacred time in the inner Torah. Heschel argues that the biblical word *davar*, like the word *makom*, can mean both "thing" and "speech; word; decision; sentence;

---

46. Ibid., 6–7.

47. See, for example, Rabbi Re'em HaKohen, *To Water the Garden*, transcribed and edited by Rabbi Eliezer Goldstein (Otniel 2009), 38–50 [Hebrew].

48. In a similar vein ת the Rambam famously comments that the sacrificial rituals of the Temple were ordained in the Torah only after the sin of worshipping the Golden Calf and that in the end of days they will no longer be required. For his discussion of how the Torah weans the children of Israel off their dependence on paganism, see *The Guide for the Perplexed*, section 3, chapter 32.

49. Heschel, *The Sabbath*, 6–7.

theme…events."[50] Similarly, agricultural festivals, which for ancient peoples "were intimately linked with the seasons" and with the "things nature did or did not bring forth," in Judaism became overlaid with higher meanings in time,

> In Judaism, Passover, originally a spring festival, became a cele-bration of the exodus from Egypt; the Feast of Weeks, an old har-vest festival at the end of the wheat harvest (hag hakazir, Exodus 23:16; 34:22), became the celebration of the day in which the Torah was given at Sinai; the Feast of the Booths, an old festival of vintage (hag ha-asif, Ex, 23:16) commemorates the dwelling of the Israelites in booths…. To Israel the unique events of historic time were spiritually more significant than the repetitive processes in the cycle of nature even though physical sustenance depended on the latter.[51]

If we look at this closely, it becomes clear that the accusation that this involves a deprecation of the meaning of space in the Torah is an exaggeration. Heschel writes explicitly,

> Our intention here is not to deprecate the world of space. To dis-parage space and the blessing of things of space is to disparage the works of creation. Time and space are interrelated. To overlook either of them is to be partially blind. What we plead against is man's unconditional surrender to space, his enslavement to things.[52]

As we understand it, Heschel's idea is that the interrelation of time and space is the key to redemption. We remain unredeemed and enslaved when we surrender ourselves entirely to the space that we most naturally inhabit. This is the enslavement of ancient Egypt; it is the enslavement of Nazism and it is the enslavement of modern, technical materialism too. But Heschel's

---

50. Ibid., 7.
51. Ibid.
52. Ibid., 6.

answer to this enslavement is not to get rid of space and think only of time. What he is describing here is a particular structure of space/time in which the Nefesh that lives in space can find a gateway to the Neshamah through the transposition of things in space to their parallels in time. Heschel's seemingly overstated insistence on time is essentially a passionate plea for freedom and against enslavement to tyranny. It is a call that Judaism and life must be about more than physical survival. The sustenance of human life is crucial, but it is not enough. What is required is redemption of space by the transformation of spatiality into time, because it is in time that the divine can be encountered:

> While the deities of other peoples were associated with places or things, the God of Israel was the God of events; the Redeemer from slavery, the Revealer of the Torah, manifesting Himself in events of history rather than in things or places. Thus, the faith in the unembodied, in the unimaginable was born.[53]

For Heschel, the transposition of space into time is the way in which the Torah describes redemption. Humanity is liberated from the tyranny of its servitude to space by having access to God in sacred time. This is how Heschel understands the Exodus story and the three central festivals that are associated with it. They begin with enslavement and end in freedom. They begin with agricultural things in space and end as historical events in time. Servitude becomes freedom, because to serve God is to live in space without submitting oneself to its tyranny. Time is the dimension in which Havayah can *be* without being reduced to thinghood. Our freedom is our ability to find Him in the redemptive interludes that sacred time holds out to us in a world in which we are otherwise dominated by space. It is attentiveness to the undulating rhythm of *kodesh* and *chol* (sacred and unsacred time) that is our freedom to *be-toward-Netzach*. In Heschel's words,

> Judaism is a *religion of time* aiming at *the sanctification of time*. Unlike the space-minded man to whom time is unvaried...to whom all hours are alike, qualitiless, empty shells, the Bible senses

---

53. Ibid., 8.

the diversified character of time. Every hour is unique and…endlessly precious.[54]

This brings us to the most famous image in the prologue and indeed in the entire book:

> Judaism teaches us to be attached to holiness in time…to learn how to consecrate sanctuaries that emerge from the magnificent stream of the year. The Sabbaths are our great Cathedrals; and our Holy of Holies is a shrine that neither the Romans nor the Germans were able to burn; the Day of Atonement…Jewish ritual may be characterized as the art of significant forms in time, as *architecture of time.*[55]

Heschel's choice of imagery here suggests that he is not dispensing altogether with the idea of sacred space. He is suggesting that space can be sacred but only when that sanctity is (or perhaps, is also) a category of time. One way of reading this is to suggest that he cares less for the Mishkan than he does for Shabbat, less for the Holy of Holies than he does for Yom Kippur – less for space than he does for time. But if this were indeed the case, we suggest that there would have been no value in describing Shabbat as a cathedral or a palace, Yom Kippur as the Holy of Holies. Perhaps this bias can be accounted for by Heschel's fear for the vulnerability of space and by the reassuring thought that when holiness in space is redeemed by *being-toward*-Netzach, the eternal heartbeat of Jewish life is placed beyond the destructive capabilities of Romans, Germans, and anyone else.

Shabbat as Ontological *Care* for the Created-ness of *Being*

Though Heschel sets a precedent for our methodology of Rehabilitation after Churban, his emotive style makes it hard to formulate his portrayal of Shabbat in strictly ontological terms. Since Heschel draws quite richly on rabbinic and Hasidic metaphors, it makes sense to go to his sources, which

---

54. Ibid.
55. Ibid.

do indeed provide us with more ontologically accessible tools to work with. In his chapter entitled "A Palace in Time," Heschel writes,

> To observe the Sabbath is to celebrate the coronation of a day in the spiritual wonderland of time.... Call the Sabbath a delight: a delight to the soul and a delight to the body....To sanctify the seventh day does not mean: Thou shalt mortify thyself, but on the contrary: Thou shalt sanctify it with all thy heart, with all thy soul and with all thy senses. Sanctify the Sabbath by choice meals, by beautiful garments, delight your soul with pleasure and I will reward you for this very pleasure.[56]

What stands out in this passage is the idea that physical pleasure has spiritual meaning in sacred time. The Shabbat is a day in which the soul delights in the pleasures of the body, and Heschel's explanation of this is that the Shabbat is a day in which an entire person with all his or her faculties must share the blessing.[57] He adds that

> to observe Shabbat is to celebrate the creation of the world.[58]

Nothing could be further from Heidegger's cumbersome and wordy neologisms than the beautiful images that Heschel conjures up in order to inspire, refresh, and motivate the spiritual passions of his readers. All the same, it is the wordy negation of Heidegger that allows us to speak of such things as "palaces in time," "delight," and "the celebration of creation" in a more grounded and systematic way. Put into more explicitly Heideggerian terms, the two themes that Heschel addresses here are the temporality of our ownmost *care* for the *created-ness* of *being* and the *attunement* of that *care* as "delight." Both are central and recurring themes in Hasidic texts, the more precise meanings of which we will now try to unravel.

---

56. Ibid., 19.
57. Ibid.
58. Ibid., 20–21.

In his commentary on the seventh day of the creation story in Genesis, the Sefat Emet writes,

> The Midrash on the verse "And the heaven and the earth were finished" (Genesis 2:1) says that they became vessels etc. That in truth the Holy One, blessed be He, renews the act of creation every day; however, on the six days of the working week the working world was fixed as a vessel that receives this renewal all the time. And everything that God created He created in His own honor. And this honor becomes clarified through the entire act of creation, and every creation is part of the vessel, and it is according to the service (Avodah) of each person that he is able to draw forth from potential into reality the revelation of His blessed honor. And this is the potentiality that is given to the people of Israel, as it says (Isaiah 43:10, 12), "You are My witnesses," and it says all that God did is for Him and for the witnessing of Him, because in truth all the world in its entirety bears witness to the blessed God. However, it is for people to clarify this testimony...[59]

This somewhat complex passage begins with a midrash that connects the word *vayechulu*, -which literally means "and they [the heavens and the earth] were finished" (Genesis 2:1), with the Hebrew word *kli*, which means "container" or "vessel."[60] In the Midrashic reading, what the verse now means is that the act of finishing the creation of the heavens and the earth is also an act of turning the creation into a vessel. The inference is that at the threshold between the sixth and seventh days, a final act of creation rendered the heavens and the earth a vessel in which the Creator can be discovered. When the Sefat Emet says, "Everything that God created He created in His own honor," he means that God created the world for His self, i.e., with the potentiality of His self being discovered in its *being*. Since human beings are also part of creation, they are also a vessel, but unlike other vessels, they are uniquely conscious of their own *being*. The final act of creation therefore endows human

---

59. Rabbi Yehuda Leib Alter of Gur, *Sefat Emet*, Parashat Bereishit (5648) [Hebrew].

60. Both the words *kli* and *vayechulu* (meaning "vessel" and "they were finished," respectively) share the same two root letters (*kaf* and *lamed*).

beings with the unique potentiality to bear witness to the *being* of Havayah in the *being-itself* of everything that *is*. More precisely (and alas more cumbersomely), we might say that after the final act of creation, represented by the word *vayechulu*, every being (by virtue of its *being*) is a vessel for the discovery by human beings (by virtue of their reflexive awareness of their *being*) of the *being* of Havayah in everything that *is*.

This unfortunately inelegant formulation spells out in ontological terms an idea that is in fact central to the teachings of the Sefat Emet. More than any other theme, the Sefat Emet returns time and again to the idea that there is an "inner point" in everything in the world. Phenomenologically, this inner point lies just beyond the ownmost self of human *being*. But in contradistinction to Heidegger, the inner point belongs to a dimension just beyond the self, from which Havayah is disclosed. In the imagery that we used in our discussion of Rabbi Kook; it is the "to whom" that the song of the Neshamah is sung. Thus, for the Sefat Emet, this inner point is not a dimension of human consciousness and it is not unique to human beings. On the contrary, it exists in everything that *is,* and it therefore refers to the dimension of *being* that the Neshamah is sensitive to in the *createdness* of the world, and in that sense, the inner point is also Shabbat. If we wish to spell out this association more explicitly, we need to understand that the ontological meaning of Shabbat as the inner point actually functions simultaneously in the three dimensions known as *ashan*,[61] a Hebrew acronym that refers to a matrix where space, time, and human consciousness coincide. As we saw in Heidegger, beings that are not Dasein are disclosed in their *being* by Dasein. Similarly, though conversely, in the Sefat Emet Havayah can be discovered by the Neshamah in the self and hence in space (the spatial experience of the self) and time (the temporal experience of the self) as well. Thus, the inner point is the underlying

---

61. The word Ashan literally means "smoke," but it is used here in the context of the acronym for the words *olam, shanah,* and *nefesh,* which refer to the three basic categories of sanctity – place, time, and human being. The term is widely used in Hasidic and kabbalistic literature and it originates from the classic and highly esoteric work *Sefer Yetzirah* (6:1), where it says, "These are the three Mothers.... And from them emanated Three Fathers and they are air, water and fire and from the Fathers, descendants. And seven planets and their hosts. And twelve diagonal boundaries. A proof of this true witnesses in the Universe, Year, Soul" See Aryeh Kaplan, *Sefer Yetzirah: The Book of Creation in Theory and Practice* (Weiser Books, 1997), 231.

directionality according to which the ontological dimensions of time, space, and inner consciousness align. As we see here and elsewhere, access to this dimension of *being* requires Avodah, which must therefore be a category that refers to the aligning of *ashan* (i.e., the self, space, and time).

The three dimensions of this structure are central to this passage. In the dimension of spatiality, the discovery of Havayah is something that takes place in the spatial interactions between the human *being* and the *created-being-of-the-world*. In temporal terms, this spatiality is specifically attributed to the six days of the working week, which become vessels for the discovery of Havayah. However, when the Sefat Emet writes that "the six days of the working week are fixed as a vessel that receives this renewal all the time," he implies that the source of this renewal is received from elsewhere. This is a reference to Shabbat. Thus, what he is saying is that in this temporal structure, the alignment of the Nefesh and the Ruach with the Neshamah corresponds with the alignment of the six days of the week with Shabbat. This idea is developed in a different teaching on the same verse (Genesis 2:1). Once again, the Sefat Emet begins with a midrash,

> The Rabbis say a parable: There was a king who had a ring made for him but what was missing? A stamp! In the same way, what was the world missing? A stamp![62]

And he explains the meaning of this as follows:

> And God completed the world on the seventh day — the Midrash says that this is like a ring that is missing a stamp. This is what we say in the prayers, that Shabbat is the purpose of heaven and earth. As it says, everything He did, He did for His *self*, as a testimony, to bear witness to Him, as it says, Shabbat is a testimony. For in everything there is matter, action, and form. And the purpose of matter is the body that is made, of action, the maker, and of form, the deed and the purpose of the deed. And the Nefesh, Ruach, and Neshamah are three dimensions. They are the three days preceding

---

62. *Bereishit Rabbah* 10:9.

and following the Shabbat, and they shine in the Nefesh, which is matter. And the Ruach is the forming of shape, and the Neshamah is the force of action, but the Shabbat is the purpose. And it is the additional soul, as it says (Psalms 150:6), "All the Neshamah will praise." What this means is that when the Neshamah is whole, then it bears witness and gives praise to God, may He be blessed, and that is Shabbat, as it says (Psalms 92:2), "It is good to give thanks," and that is the purpose. And in truth, every creation has a part in Shabbat because it is the purpose...and this is revealed to the people of Israel.[63]

The basic metaphor of this passage is that the ring corresponds to the six days of the week, while the stamp, which is the "purpose" of the ring, corresponds to Shabbat. The use of the word "purpose" here is significant, since in Hebrew it is a variant of the same grammatical root that the Sefat Emet used above to connect the finishing of creation with the creation of vessels.[64] Interestingly, using the image of the ring, the Sefat Emet sets up the week with Shabbat in the middle of the six days in the same way that the stamp sits in the middle of the ring that is wrapped in both directions around the finger. This structure gives us a differentiated waxing and waning of days that draw their purpose from the Shabbat that precedes and follows them.

While in ontic terms this portrayal of sacred time is arbitrary, the Sefat Emet is careful to supply us with a mechanism for grounding this phenomenology of space and time in the ontological structure of Tzelem Elohim. Thus, in this portrayal, the structure of time that is defined by the testimony of Shabbat corresponds with the dimensions of the self that *is-in-time* and with the things that *are* in space. Each of these is divided into three. The week is divided into two sets of three days. Next, physical thingness is divided into matter, form, and action ("action," we suggest, should be understood as the "act" of *being*). Finally, the inner *being* of the human self is divided into the levels of Nefesh, Ruach, and Neshamah. If we unpack this matrix, what the Sefat Emet is saying is that the structure of Tzelem Elohim corresponds

---

63. Sefat Emet on Parashat Bereishit (5647) [Hebrew].

64. The shared root letters of *vayechulu* and *kli* (mentioned above) are also the root letters of the word *tachlit*, meaning "purpose."

to both the spatiality of the world and the temporality of the six (two sets of three) days of the working week, while the Avodah that aligns these units of three opens up an additional inner reality that the Sefat Emet refers to as the additional soul.[65] This additional soul – or Neshamah Yeteirah – is Shabbat; the final creation, the coming to rest of Havayah in the *being* of the world, the inner point, or, in our terms: the ultimate intentionality of alignment.

In multiple places, this intentionality, which is Shabbat, represents an additional dimension of consciousness that is *always already attuned*. This *attunement* is the state of the *being* of the aligned Nefesh, Ruach, and Neshamah when they gaze upon the window or the gateway to the temporality of Netzach. In this condition, the ownmost *being* of the aligned self is disclosed as "delight." In the words of the Kedushat Levi,

> And behold, God wanted to give the seed of Israel a taste of the rewards of the spiritual world to come, which is why He gave them Shabbat, which is a taste of the delight of the world to come. And on Shabbat anyone can notice the spiritual delight. But since there are no rewards for the mitzvot in this world, how can a person enjoy the delight of Shabbat? Thus, the Holy One in His wisdom gave them a gift…in this world, which is to grant those who do His will and keep His Shabbat a taste of the delight of the world to come. It will forever be a sign of the delight of the world to come…as it says, "And it (Shabbat) is a sign for you that I am God who makes you holy"; what this means is that through keeping Shabbat you will come to know that I am God who makes you holy for the eternal world (time) and for the eternal Shabbat.[66]

---

65. For the Talmudic origins of this concept, see *Beitzah* 16a: "Rabbi Shimon ben Lakish said: The Holy One, blessed be He, gives a person an additional soul on Shabbat eve and at the conclusion of Shabbat removes it from him, as it states: 'He ceased from work and was refreshed (*vayinafash*)' (Exodus 31:17)." Rabbi Shimon ben Lakish expounds the verse as follows: "He ceased from work, and Shabbat has concluded and his additional soul is removed from him; woe (*vai*) for the additional soul (Nefesh) that is lost."

66. Rabbi Levi Yitzchak of Berditchev, *Kedushat Levi*, Parashat Ki Tisa, 222.

If we return to ask what Heschel means when he says that Shabbat is a day in which the soul delights in the pleasures of the body and that Shabbat is a day in which we celebrate the creation of the world, we can now unpack this using the ontological language gleaned from our readings of the Maharal, the Sefat Emet, and the Kedushat Levi. From within the context of its ownmost experience of time, Dasein discovers through Avodah that the mortal Nefesh and the body can bathe momentarily in the delight that shines through a gateway that gazes upon the inner point. This is an experience in time in which Dasein *is* in the temporality of Shabbat as the gateway to witnessing the *created-being* of the self and its *with-world*.

In this sense, as we saw above, the idea that Shabbat is a day of the week that was somehow made holy has no ontological meaning. The sanctification of Shabbat as we saw in the Sefat Emet is something else entirely. It is an act of creation, of finishing or giving purpose to creation, after which all of time is Shabbat. This is what the Nefesh realizes when, through the Avodah of Shabbat, it aligns its temporality with that of the Neshamah. For the Neshamah, all of time is animated by the *alive-being-in-time* of Havayah which, in the words of the Lecha Dodi prayer, is "from the beginning, from antiquity she was anointed, last in deed, but first in thought,"[67] or in our Heideggerian terms, "*always already* anointed." This totality of eternal *being-in-time*, which is concealed by mundane time, is embedded in the week, like light concealed in a vessel. The Nefesh experiences the seventh day of the week in ontic time, but in a state of alignment this day is disclosed as a gateway to the ownmost *being* of all *being-in-time*. This disclosure is equiprimordially *attuned* as "delight" that the body and the Nefesh experience. Delight is what discloses the full alignment of *created-being* in space, time, and soul with the inner point.

The seventh day is the gateway through which the mortal self experiences the momentary delight of alignment – Neshamah Yeteirah – in which the pleasures of the body and the soul are united. Here Shabbat is not the seventh day of the week. Rather, as we saw in the Maharal, it is an eternal seventh day;

---

67. This phrase, which appears in the Lecha Dodi prayer, was analyzed by Adina Shine in an unpublished paper entitled "An Ontological Reading of Kabbalat Shabbat" (2019). The prayer Lecha Dodi was composed in the sixteenth century by Rabbi Shlomo HaLevi Alkabetz.

a number eight in a cycle of seven. It is the means and the end, the day in the week and the day beyond the week that the seventh day of the week points to. The mitzvah of Shabbat is thus the shape of the gateway inside mortal time that points toward the temporality of Netzach. It is here at this threshold that the mortal self bears witness to the eternal source of all *created-being-in-the-world*. Thus, when the gateway is opened, the seventh day and its mitzvot are experienced as mortal and transient time, but also as an episode in eternity. It is the continuum between Shabbat as a mitzvah and Shabbat as the inner point that enables mortal time in space to be experienced as an episode in Netzach. It is this continuum that makes each Shabbat "a taste of the delight of the world to come."[68]

---

68. Rabbi Levi Yitzchak of Berditchev, *Kedushat Levi*, Parashat Ki Tisa, 222.

CHAPTER 18

The Architecture of Segulah: Shabbat in *Olam*, *Shanah*, and *Nefesh* (*Ashan*)

The Sanctity of Life in Space and Objects

In the previous chapter we briefly mentioned the concept of *ashan* – a Hebrew word that literally means "smoke" but which kabbalistic literature, going back as far as *Sefer Yetzirah*, uses as an acronym for the three-dimensional matrix of space, time, and soul.[1] In our discussion we explained that what the Sefat Emet refers to as "the inner point" is the orientation toward which each of these dimensions (and all of them together) faces. Thus, the inner point is the unity or correspondence between them. The unified orientation of *ashan* toward the inner point is a holistic, multidimensional description of inner *being* in its directionality, which in this context discloses the ability of the self to bear witness to creation as the revealed dimension of divine *being* or Havayah in the self, and – through the phenomenological spatiality and temporality of the self – in the alive *being* of everything in space and time. As we saw, this is how the Sefat Emet and other texts understand the experience of Shabbat as the *always already* underlying *being* of all time (the eighth day), the awareness of which is known in the self through the mitzvot of the seventh day of every week. This is an encounter with a dimension of the self that is referred to as Neshamah Yeteirah.

The onto-theological framework that we have been developing to describe this rests very significantly on the structure of Tzelem Elohim and on the

---

1. See Aryeh Kaplan, *Sefer Yetzirah: The Book of Creation in Theory and Practice* (Weiser Books, 1997), 231.

duality of Nefesh and Neshamah. In this structure the *care* of the Nefesh or animal-soul is anchored to the body, and the *care* of the Neshamah or divine-soul is absorbed in the inner point. The holistic experience of Havayah (i.e., of all time as Shabbat) therefore requires an alignment through Avodah (i.e. performing the mitzvot of Shabbat) of these two poles. We spoke about this alignment in order to offer a middle ground between Heidegger's *being-toward-death* and eternal life. In so doing, we ultimately sought to articulate what it means for mortal people to have contact with the divine as a this-worldly experience that is philosophically grounded in the same kind of phenomenological or immanent metaphysics that we found in Heidegger. We suggested that mitzvot are "shaped gateways" that place us into situations of physical action that open up inner realizations, the content of which is the ultimate conclusion that space, time, and the different levels of *being-a-self* are all part of one totality of unified *being* or Havayah. This is how the perspective of Segulah becomes a philosophical methodology that allows us to talk about the entry of God into the public sphere of political life. Havayah — as the *being* of everything in space, time and the self — is thus visible to eyes of flesh in the sense that it is a way of looking at the world.

However, this idea of visibility is dependent upon there being such things as sacred space and tangible sacred objects that eyes can see. In the previous chapter we discussed Heschel's emphasis on the sanctity of invisible time alone. We tried to moderate more extreme renditions of his position by looking at the spatial metaphors that he uses to illustrate what he means by structured time. Whether or not Heschel would agree (and we suggested that he would), many Jewish thinkers clearly acknowledge the sanctity of space. However, it is similarly clear that this sanctity of space is also a category of both time and human consciousness.

In this chapter we will shift our emphasis away from time and apply our understanding of Shabbat to the spatial categories of Mishkan/Mikdash and Am Yisrael (the Tabernacle/Temple and the Jewish people). Having already illustrated the interrelation of space and time in what we referred to as the space/time of the inner Torah, our emphasis here will be different. Here we will try to make the case for the Jewish idea that space and visible things can be sacred in and of themselves but in terms that are significantly different from the pagan understandings of "thing-ness" that Heschel criticized so vehemently. Rather, we shall try to show that the Mishkan/Mikdash and Am Yisrael are all spatial equivalents of Shabbat that relate to non-sacred spatiality in the same way that Shabbat relates to the six days of the week.

Drawing on the principle of *ashan*, we will seek to ground the concept of sacred spatiality in the reflexive phenomenology of alive *being*. Methodologically speaking, the convergence of space and time in the reflexive *being* of the self is of central importance to our ability to understand the meaning of sacred space in non-pagan terms. In the structure of *ashan*, the only true vessel of sanctity is neither space nor time but *alive-being* (or *being* as aliveness, i.e., Havayah) itself. Put more concretely, everything is holy because of its potential to disclose its *being* as God's *being* to us.

Thus, in the structure of *ashan*, sanctity is the *alive-being* of the Nefesh and its capacity to recognize the *alive-being* of Havayah in everything that *is* in both space and time. As with the six days of the week, not all spaces are sacred. But, like the six days of the week, everything has an inner point and consequently has the potential of becoming sacred.

Though the possibility of the mortal Nefesh *being-toward-death* in a Godless world is always everywhere – even inside the Holy of Holies on Yom Kippur – the counter possibility of everything being sacred all the time is also equally prevalent. In the everyday sense in which the Nefesh as Dasein *is* in the world, sacred spaces and sacred times are essentially mitzvot that point the Nefesh toward the inner realization that the inner point of Havayah is everywhere and forever.[2] Achieving this realization is tantamount to the sanctification of the world.

In our conclusion we shall argue that the establishment of these pointers as the institutions of public and political life is what is meant, from the perspective of Segulah, by the politics of Tikkun Olam. But first, let's try our hand at gaining an understanding of some of the pointers themselves.

---

2.   This concept of "everywhere and forever" describes the name of God and appears frequently in the Hebrew liturgy in the form of the rabbinic phrase *le'olam va'ed*. This phrase was uttered by the High Priest in the Temple on Yom Kippur as described in the Mishnah (*Yoma* 3:8).

The Mishkan: Symbolism and Reality

The Mishkan is an institution to which this principle of pointing applies. The Mishkan was the temporary Tabernacle that God commanded the children of Israel to build in the desert so that He could "rest among them."[3] The design and building of the Mishkan along with the ornaments, instruments, and ritual objects that it contained, the clothes worn by the priests, and the sacrificial ritual performed within fill half of the book of Exodus, almost the entire book of Leviticus, and significant parts of both Numbers and Deuteronomy. Of the six books of the Mishnah, two entire books are dedicated to the laws pertaining to the Mishkan/Mikdash, while references to these laws appear frequently in the remaining four books as well. This is a vast and detailed topic that classical and modern religious scholarship as well as academic literature has covered in such tremendous detail that it is beyond the scope of our argument to even begin to offer a summary of it here.

Since the destruction of the Second Temple in 70 CE (and in certain aspects, since the destruction of the First Temple in 586 BCE), this central element of the Torah has been absent from the actual practice of Jewish life, so much so that of the six books of the Mishnah, only the four that are not explicitly dedicated to the ritual of the Temple are covered in the Babylonian Talmud.[4] The laws and practices of the Mishkan and the Temple are a subject of study, prayer, and memory that, as time goes on, is harder and harder to hold on to. The passage of time as well as modern alienation from such things as animal sacrifice makes this topic hard to talk about in anything other than

---

3. In the context of commanding the children of Israel to build the Tabernacle in the desert, the biblical passage says, "And they shall make for Me a sanctuary so that I may dwell among them" (Exodus 25:8). The emphasis on dwelling among them (i.e., the people) rather than in it (i.e., the sanctuary) stands out in the biblical Hebrew and is understood, as we shall see, as suggesting that the purpose of the Tabernacle is to enable God to dwell in the hearts of the people.

4. The Babylonian Talmud, as its name suggests, was compiled in Babylon outside the land of Israel and documents rabbinic discourse on matters of Jewish law and lore that post-date the destruction of the Temple in Jerusalem by four hundred years and more. In the context of Jewish life in this period, it is an albeit well-known but nonetheless striking fact that the Babylonian Talmud deals only with laws that were practiced outside the land of Israel after the destruction of the Temple. As such, three of the six books in the Mishnah that deal with the agricultural laws that apply exclusively to the land of Israel, as well as laws concerning purity, sanctity, and Temple ritual, are not dealt with at all.

theoretical, historical, or anthropological terms.[5] In modern liberal circles the rituals of the Mishkan may perhaps appear primitive, and as such the dream of their being reinstated easily loses its luster. Many of those who do stick to it are branded, with equal ease, as fanatics. Moreover, according to many classical and medieval commentators, the entire project of the Mishkan was only ever a concession to the pagan instincts of a recently liberated enslaved people, and as such, sacrificial ritual plays no role in the future-oriented ideal of Jewish life.[6]

Our analysis begins with the premise that the Mishkan and the laws that pertain to it are of central importance in the Torah and as such are crucial to the perspective of Segulah in the past, present, and future. The question here is how we should go about analyzing them. We can begin with the observation that in many rabbinic, kabbalistic, and Hasidic texts the meaning of the Mishkan and its rituals is translated into a kind of symbolism that apparently finds its substance not simply in the rituals themselves, but also in the values they seem to represent. The question of how such symbols relate to the ideas they represent presents a significant methodological challenge. The problem here is inherent in the way in which post-Enlightenment religious thought tends to devalue the intrinsic value of religious symbols in favor of the humanistic meanings that can be attributed to them. This kind of transference or slippage is characteristic of rational religion; the issue being that if the symbol means only the value that it symbolizes, it can be easily replaced by something else. This type of corrosive transference is typical of post-Enlightenment Judaism, which even in its earliest forms sometimes allowed itself to make extreme changes to the ritual by virtue of the idea that the Torah's commandments are only symbols of "humanist values."[7] Similarly,

---

5. A pioneering example of a modern anthropological analysis of Temple ritual and its laws of purity is Mary Douglas's classic work *Purity and Danger* (Oxford: Routledge Books, 1966).

6. For examples of this attitude in rabbinic literature, see *Sifrei, Devarim* 1 and the commentary of Rabbi Bahye ben Asher (Rabbeinu Bahye), Exodus 25:6. See also the famous passage in Maimonides' *Guide for the Perplexed*, section 3, chapter 32.

7. There is a famous example of this in the letter that Abraham (the son of Moses) Mendelssohn wrote to his daughter Fanny in which he explains his decision to raise her in the Christian faith. Here he says, "The outward form of religion...is historical, and changeable like all human ordinances. Some thousands of years ago the Jewish form

the liberalization of Tikkun Olam that we discussed in the first chapter has had the same kind of corrosive effect on modern Jewish identity despite the beauty of social justice as a human and indeed Jewish endeavor.[8]

As in previous cases, we shall try to rehabilitate the meaning of the Mishkan's symbolism from the perspective of Segulah. Once again, our approach will be to seek out the ontological meaning of this symbolism by negating Heidegger's analytic of Dasein. As we saw in the chapters dedicated to *BT* above, Heidegger addresses the theme of signs and symbols in detail in his efforts to clarify to his readers what he means by the *worldliness of world*. In his presentation of *worldliness*, Heidegger offers what he calls "a concrete analysis of the structures in whose context a phenomenological analysis of worldliness can be possible."[9] He calls the structures that he singles out for this concrete analysis *references*. Just like all innerworldly beings, *references* are known to Dasein as *useful* and *at hand*. However, their structure of *being* is special because *references* – in addition to being themselves – also have a pointing capacity as *signs*. As we saw, Heidegger defines *signs* as "initially useful things whose specific character as useful things consists of indicating."[10]

Heidegger's analysis of *signs* hinges on the way in which they function as *referents* that are *useful* to us because they indicate something to us. In this sense, the *sign* discloses a sense of world to Dasein[11] which – as we said above – is like Hotei the laughing Buddha who points at the moon. For

---

was the reigning one, then the heathen form, and now it is the Christian. We, your mother and I, were born and brought up by our parents as Jews, and without being obliged to change the form of our religion have been able to follow the divine instinct in us and in our conscience. We have educated you and your brothers and sister in the Christian faith, because it is the creed of most civilized people.… By pronouncing your confession of faith, you have fulfilled the claims of society on you and obtained the name of Christian. Now be what your duty as a human being demands of you." Abraham Mendelssohn to Fanny Mendelssohn ca. July 1820, in S. Hansel, *The Mendelssohn Family (1729–1847): From Letters and Journals*, vol. 1, trans. C Klingemann (New York, 1882), 79–80, cited in Mendes-Flohr and Reinharz, eds., *The Jew in the Modern World,* 222–23.

8.   See Levi Cooper, "The Assimilation of Tikkun Olam," *Jewish Political Studies Review* 35, nos. 3–4 (Fall 2013).

9.   Heidegger, *BT*, 75.

10.   Ibid., 76.

11.   Ibid., 78.

Heidegger, "The meaning of signs lets what is at hand be encountered."[12] Signs "let their context become accessible in such a way that heedful dealings get and secure for themselves an orientation."[13] In the same way that the disclosure of the moon discloses for us the man who points at the moon, "useful things explicitly bring a totality of useful things to circumspection so that the worldly character of what is at hand makes itself known at the same time."[14]

With this description of two things happening at the same time, inner-worldly beings are first known to Dasein as *useful* or as *at hand*. This insight is crucial because it acknowledges that they have value or a purpose of their own and are not simply empty or meaningless placeholders for something else. However, in this capacity they also function as *signs* which disclose the *usefulness* or the *handiness* of the world. Thus, "what is taken as a sign first becomes accessible through its handiness."[15] But ultimately, this handiness is itself a disclosure of the world that enables things to function as *at hand* within it. In this way, an object that assumes the character of *being useful*

> takes over the "work" of *letting* things at hand become conspicuous.... But even as conspicuous things, they are not taken as objectively present arbitrarily, rather they are "set up" in a definite way with a view toward easy accessibility.[16]

Using Heidegger's language, our argument is that the Mishkan itself and all its vessels are essentially *references* or *signs*. As such, they are physical objects which are *at hand* and therefore have intrinsic value. However, as physical *signs* that are *at hand,* they perform an additional function. After disclosing how objects that are *at hand* are *useful* to Dasein, they disclose how "initially useful things whose specific character as useful things consists of indicating"[17] point to Dasein's *with-world*. On the first level, Avodah – which most naturally refers quite specifically to the sacrificial rituals performed in the

---

12. Ibid.
13. Ibid.
14. Ibid.
15. Ibid., 79.
16. Ibid.
17. Ibid., 76.

Mishkan – involves the *use* of things that are *at hand*. In the most strictly narrow ontological sense of the word *handiness,* these vessels are *at hand* for the purposes of Avodah. On the second level, since they are *useful* to Dasein as *signs* or *references*, these objects perform an additional function of pointing or indicating that reflexively determines the meaning of their *handiness* in the broader context that Heidegger called *world*. They are *at hand* as *signs* in such a way that also tells us what their *being at hand* as *signs* signifies. What we wish to show is that their more abstract or symbolic meanings disclose to Dasein the *worldliness* of the Neshamah's *with-world*.

To return to our Hotei analogy, if by pointing to the moon we must *always already* know the moon so that we can know Hotei as a pointer who points to it, the same thing can be said of the *usefulness* of the Mishkan. Thus, what the Mishkan with its vessels and rituals point at is what discloses their *usefulness*. Just as a danger sign is useful only because it is ahead of itself in the sense that it discloses the *always already-ness* of dangers that lie ahead in the road, the Mishkan and the vessels point here and now to an inner point that lies ahead; orienting time, space, and the self to the *always already-ness* of Havayah. To paraphrase Heidegger, they take over the "work" (Avodah) of letting the *alive-being* of Havayah become conspicuous in the Torah. In this sense, they are meaningful because as innerworldly objects they are *signs* only in the sense that they disclose to us modes of *being* that are *always already* "there" in the *with-world* of Tzelem Elohim.

The idea that the mitzvot in general and the Mishkan are symbols is central to many of the texts that we have been discussing. What we want to show is that the nature of that symbolism as it is described in the texts of the inner Torah both echoes and negates the directionality of what Heidegger means by a *sign* or a *reference*. When considered in this way, the meaning of the *sign* is not arbitrary; rather, as Heidegger put it, "The sign is 'set up' in a definite way with a view toward easy accessibility." In other words, what Dasein recognizes in the *sign* is something about its own *being-in-the-world* while the *sign* itself is specifically made to make accessible the potentiality of *being* that Dasein discovers in it. Thus, the *sign* has a pointing capacity somewhat like that of a mirror in which Dasein sees a reflection of its *being* in the mode of *being* that the *sign* specifically discloses.

When interpreting the passages in the Torah that describe the Mishkan, the texts we shall look at treat both the text itself and the physical construction of the Mishkan that it prescribes as *signs* that are specifically set up to disclose in Dasein's awareness of itself that its ownmost *being* is the alive *being* of Havayah. This is an ontological state that is attained through the alignment of the Nefesh and the Neshamah by means of Avodah. Though we believe this methodology can be widely applied to the reading of Torah texts about the Mishkan, in the following discussion we shall offer a deep analysis of only a few examples taken from the biblical commentaries of Rabbi Samson Raphael Hirsch, the Kedushat Levi, and the Sefat Emet.

The Mishkan as a Sign of Havayah in Space

Though not conventionally associated with either the kabbalistic or Hasidic traditions, the commentary of Rabbi Samson Raphael Hirsch on the Torah addresses the nature of biblical symbolism in a way that is clearly illustrative of our point.[18] In his commentary on the verse "And they shall make Me a sanctuary and I will dwell among them" (Exodus 25:8), he writes:

> We have already shown at great length in our book, Jewish Symbolism, that the meaning and character of the Mishkan is symbolic in general and also symbolic in the specifics of the substances from which it was made.... In Leviticus 26 the laws of the priests (Torat Cohanim) come to an end and there are two things that emerge with absolute clarity from here: 1. The verse "And I will dwell among them" extends far beyond the indwelling of divine presence in the Mishkan alone and in actuality what it means is that closeness to God inside the self with the fulfillment of our covenant between Him and Israel reveals itself in His bestowing upon us His protection, blessing and prosperity in the life of the individual and the collective. 2. God does not dwell

18. The theme of symbolism in the Torah is one that Rabbi S. R. Hirsch dealt with in detail in a volume dedicated to the topic, but it is also a recurring theme in his biblical commentary. See Rabbi S. R. Hirsch, "Jewish Symbolism," in *The Collected Writings of Rabbi Samson Raphael Hirsch*, vol. 3 (Feldheim, 1984), and Rabbi Hirsch, *The Pentateuch with Translation and Commentary* (Judaica Press, 1962).

among us nor does he give us His protection or blessing by virtue of the building of the Mishkan and the observance of its detailed requirements alone. This depends on the sanctification of our private and public lives and their dedication to God's Mitzvot. This is attested to not only by the historical events such as the destruction of the Mishkan in Shiloh and the two destructions of the Temples in Jerusalem but also by the verses of the Torah that issue explicit warnings about this.[19]

This passage is only the beginning of an extensive and minutely detailed systematic exegesis that runs through every physical aspect of the Mishkan and the materials from which it and its vessels are made. This exegesis continues throughout the book of Leviticus, unpacking the specific meanings of the words employed to name the animals, vessels, agricultural produce, and fragrances used in the sacrificial ritual. Though Rabbi Hirsch does not discuss any of those details in the introductory comments that we have quoted here, our passage nonetheless contains a very significant methodological statement that underlines the three key elements in his understanding of the Mishkan's symbolism in general. First, he establishes the principle that the Mishkan serves a symbolic purpose. Second, he insists that this symbolic purpose, which is intrinsic to the significance of the Mishkan, draws its meaning by also pointing beyond the ritual of the Mishkan. Thus, for Rabbi Hirsch, the Mishkan is a *reference* that discloses the closeness of the people to God in the inner life of the individual and in the collective covenantal life of Israel. Third (and most importantly in terms of our comments above about the corrosive effects of symbolic transference), he insists that the symbolism of the Mishkan is "real" in the sense that the practices of the Mishkan have real historical consequences. When seen in this way, his understanding of the Mishkan is similar to a central theme that we discussed in the previous chapter, i.e., that the mitzvot provide the shape that enables the Neshamah to align with its outer expressions in the same way that clothing fits the human body. Following this structure, Rabbi Hirsch describes the Mishkan as an inner institution which correlates to the collective body-politic of Israel like

---

19. Hirsch, *Pentateuch* (Exodus 25:3–5).

the Neshamah correlates to the body. Thus, what happens in the Mishkan is visibly clothed in political reality and therefore has historical consequences. Consequently, the Mishkan is not simply an empty vessel or a convention whose meaning depends only on what it points to. Rather, as we saw in Heidegger, the *sign* is "set up" in a definite way with a view toward accessibility of disclosure. If you fail to appreciate what is disclosed within, this failure is inextricably tied to behavior that will have real-life historical consequences. In Rabbi Hirsch's words,

> On all accounts the text that says that "I will dwell among them" is a consequence of "And they shall build me a sanctuary." Therefore, the sanctuary is none other than the expression of its general function, the fulfillment of which is a condition for the promised indwelling of God's presence among the people of Israel. The announcement "And they shall make me a sanctuary and I will dwell among them" therefore includes two concepts that the entire building of the Mishkan and its vessels are their symbolic expression: 'Mikdash' and 'Mishkan'. 'Mikdash' expresses the entire range of functions that we must perform for God. 'Mishkan' expresses the purposes that are promised to us by fulfilling our function. 'Mikdash' means the sanctification of our individual and collective lives and our sacrificing them at the altar of God's Torah; 'Mishkan' means the indwelling of God's presence as promised to us, which is revealed in the blessing of God, his protection and the prosperity of our individual and collective lives.... This holiness and this closeness: the mutual covenant between God and Israel which is formed by the giving of the Torah and the receiving of the Torah, is the context in which we must seek to understand the Mishkan in general and the specifics of its details.[20]

If we take this analysis a little further, what Rabbi Hirsch is saying here – through his dual image of "Mishkan" (referring to the indwelling of God) and "Mikdash" (referring to the physical sanctuary) – is that the symbolic

---

20. Ibid.

idea of the Mishkan is as real as the concrete structure of the Mikdash, while the meaning of the concrete structure of the Mikdash is as symbolic as the idea of the Mishkan. Thus, they relate to each other like the soul and the body (the self and its clothing). Each is both a symbol and a reality that corresponds to both inner and outer expressions of the ritual conduct and historical fate of the people of Israel. In more rationalistic terms we might say that if the ritual of the Mishkan communicates something to the people who perform it and dedicate their lives to it, it does so in a way that is meaningful and impactful. But it is this selfsame meaningfulness that points back to the pointing ability of the Mishkan, because what happens within affects events that occur outside.

Rabbi Hirsch goes on to show in copious detail why the materials that the people must donate to the Mishkan are both actual and symbolic acts of dedication to God and why each type of wood, metal, or fabric used in the construction of the Mishkan and all its vessels represent an idea or a value. He continues this in his commentary on the book of Leviticus, now applying the same principle of symbolism to the sacrifices. He focuses not only on the rituals themselves but on the etymologies of the words used to describe them in the Torah, drawing symbolic distinctions between the Hebrew words for lambs, goats and sheep, blood, water, and every type of incense, stone, or cloth. This continues with reference to the halachic details that determine who performs which ritual in which place and at what time. In each detail another aspect of the covenantal relationship between God and the people that is the heart of the Torah is connoted. Thus, for Rabbi Hirsch, the Mishkan, the space that lies beyond it, and the people all point to the principle that unites them, which is the meaning that their *being* assumes in the Torah.

Following this structure, we can appreciate how the Mishkan is a condensed inner context or microcosm that represents how the people are coming along with the practice of Torah. This tells us the state of the connection between human *being* and Havayah, and it is the heart of the body-politic of the people of the Torah. Similarly, each specific symbol in the Mishkan points to the correlation between the heart of individual consciousness and the purpose of Avodah.

Though Rabbi Hirsch is deliberately less explicit than Hasidic writers about the mystical dimension of this correspondence between the general purpose of Torah and the Mishkan, we believe that his point of view closely conforms with the more explicitly kabbalistic formulations readily found in Hasidic texts. The following passage in the *Kedushat Levi* seems to capture the overall thrust of our argument:

> "The cloths shall be in the rings of the Ark; they shall not be removed from it" [Exodus 25:15]. The *Zohar* says that it is specifically because of the Ark that the cloths should not ever be removed...and to explain this we have to elaborate and say that it is already known that just as the human is a microcosm in which all the 248 physical limbs hint at the 248 spiritual limbs and the 248 positive mitzvot, and the 365 tendons are the 365 spiritual tendons that correspond to the 365 negative mitzvot, similarly the structure of the Mishkan and all its vessels hint at the spiritual meaning of the mitzvot, and each vessel hints at a different one. And we know that there are certain mitzvot that are essential, that humans remember at every moment, and these are the thoughts that a person must hold in his mind at all times, such as the existence of God and His unity and our obligation to love Him at all times.... and the Ark corresponds to these mitzvot, upon which the whole religion of Israel depends...and which are the essence of faith, and so because of this the cloths must never be removed, and this hints to the mitzvot that Israel [....][21]

The *Kedushat Levi* is concerned here with a specific symbol in the Mishkan rather than with the general principle. Like Rabbi Hirsch, in his understanding, the Mishkan – its vessels and mitzvot – correspond to the whole of the Torah in general. In this way the Mishkan points beyond itself and toward the rest of the mitzvot of the Torah. However, it does so by virtue of its own importance. In this sense it is a meaningful microcosm of the Torah, which,

---

21. Rabbi Levi Yitzchak of Berditchev, *Kedushat Levi*, Mesamchei Lev Edition, commentary on Parashat Terumah, 197 [Hebrew]. Note that the last few words of the passage are missing in the original.

by corresponding to all the mitzvot, takes on the same shape as the limbs and tendons of the human body. In turn, these also correspond to the Nefesh, the Neshamah, and the entire structure of Tzelem Elohim. Specifically, the commandment to maintain physical contact between the cloths and the Ark corresponds to the meaning of *care* for the *being* of God and His unity, which is *attuned* in the forms of love and fear.

Since we have already engaged at length in the explication of these metaphors, it is sufficient to say here in brief that this specific detail illustrates the realist nature of the correspondence between the Torah, mitzvot, the human body, human consciousness, and the structure, vessels, and rituals of the Mishkan. The insistence upon the specific action discloses its own meaning as a *sign* that is *always already* a self-referential expression of the aliveness-of-*being* that is found in the cloth, in the Ark, in the reflexive consciousness of the Nefesh's *being*, and in the *alive-being* of the Neshamah, all of which are oriented toward the inner point or the object of *care*. This object is the *sign* that discloses the *alive-being* of Havayah in everything that *is,* and which is disclosed to Tzelem Elohim in a state of Da'at Hashem in *Gadlut*. In this sense, the Mishkan in its entirety is a *sign* that points to the potential disclosure of the *alive-being* of Havayah which is hidden…. absolutely everywhere.

Shabbat as a Category in Sacred Space – Melachah and Menuchah

This disclosure, as we saw with the meaning of Shabbat in time, is an underlying potentiality in space that is made more accessible in the *sign* – which in this case is the Mishkan. But the link we are suggesting here between the Mishkan and Shabbat is not by any means an arbitrary comparison of our invention. Rather, it is built into the symbolism of the Mishkan in multiple ways.

Returning to the structure of *ashan*, the referential pointing function of the Mishkan, which discloses the *being* of Havayah in the Nefesh, in the Torah, and in the thingness of the Mishkan itself, also corresponds closely with the temporality of Shabbat. As Rabbi Hirsch points out in several places, the Mishkan is a Shabbat in space in the same way that Shabbat is the Mishkan in time. This idea underlines the intermingling of spatiality and temporality in the meaning of Shabbat in the same way that we saw it in Heschel.

What we want to discover now is the more precise meaning of this correlation between the Mishkan and Shabbat. A primary example of it is the association of the building of the Mishkan with the concept of Melachah. This word, used in the Bible to denote the building of the Mishkan, also defines the forms of creative work that are prohibited on Shabbat.[22] As a result of this correlation, the Mishnah determines the very specific list of prohibited activities on Shabbat according to the thirty-nine acts of creative work that the Rabbis determined were employed in the construction of the Mishkan.[23] Similarly, with reference to the first Shabbat, the word Melachah denotes the work of creating the world from which God rested. In all three cases, the idea of Melachah meaning "work" stands in contrast to the concept of Menuchah meaning "rest."[24] In this copula, God's resting on Shabbat from the creation of the world means His replacing Melachah with Menuchah. Similarly, Shabbat requires the replacement of Melachah with Menuchah, as in Heschel's words,

> The words: "On the *seventh* day God *finished* His work" (Genesis 2:2), seem to be a puzzle. Is it not said: "He rested on the *seventh* day"? "In *six* days, the Lord made the heaven and the earth" (Exodus 20:11)? We would surely expect the Bible to tell us that on the sixth day God finished His work. Obviously, ancient rabbis concluded, there was an act of creation on the seventh day. Just as heaven and earth were created in six days, *menuha* [i.e., Menuchah] was created on the Sabbath.[25]

---

22. The thirty-nine Melachot prohibited on Shabbat are outlined and defined in the Mishnah (*Shabbat* 7:2). According to the principles of rabbinic homiletics, the proximity between the biblical passages that describe the construction of the Mishkan and the prohibition of work on Shabbat (for example, see Exodus 31:13 and Leviticus 19:30) is interpreted as signifying the correlation between the two. See the Talmud, *Shabbat* 42b.

23. Mishnah, *Shabbat* 7:2.

24. Genesis 2:3.

25. Heschel, *The Sabbath*, 22.

But what is the meaning of Menuchah with reference to the Mishkan? It follows from Heschel that resting from work on Shabbat is compliance with a divine creation that requires precise abstinence from very specific activities. It also follows that this rest has positive content. However, it is not yet clear what this content is.

The precise nature of this correlation and its ontological analysis is of tremendous importance to our argument and we will have to consider it in stages. We will first try to unpack the meaning of the Mishkan as Shabbat in space and then consider the copula of Melachah and Menuchah in more detail.

The Mishkan as Shabbat in Space

In the Sefat Emet's commentary there are countless examples of the correlation between the temporality of Shabbat and the spatiality of the Mishkan that illustrate the general point we are trying to make. For instance, the Sefat Emet explicitly ties the structure of the week that we discussed in the previous chapter to the structure of the Menorah, the candelabra that stood in the Holy of Holies inside the Mishkan.[26] In his commentary on Numbers 8:1, he writes,

> "The face of the Menorah": My father of blessed memory taught that this refers to Shabbat that is preceded and followed by the six days of the working week. Because Shabbat is the inner dimension of the other six days.... the purpose of which is returning everything else to its source.[27]

In this short but highly significant passage the six days of the week correspond to the lights of the Menorah, while the light in the center corresponds to the seventh day. Following what we saw in the previous chapter, the Sefat Emet is applying the structure of the week as a stamp on a ring to the appearance of the Menorah. As opposed to the ring and the stamp found in the Midrash, this example applies to a physical object that the Torah explicitly commands

---

26. The Menorah is the seven-branched candelabra that burned in the Mishkan and the Temple inside the Holy of Holies. See Numbers 8:1–4).

27. Rabbi Yehuda Leib Alter of Gur, *Sefat Emet*, Parashat Beha'alotecha (5638).

the children of Israel to build and keep in the Mishkan. Returning to the biblical passage, the lights of the Menorah on either side of the center stem are described as shining "in the face of the Menorah." It is this phrase that the Sefat Emet is specifically concerned with. As he understands it, the idea here is that the purpose of the Menorah is to reveal the meaning of Shabbat as the inner dimension of the other six days. But when he says that this *sign* reminds us that everything returns to its source, he means that the leaning of the six outer candles toward the "Shabbat" in the center (denoted by the phrase "in the face of the Menorah") must be seen as a *sign* that discloses to us the culmination of the seven days of the week in the inner point. Here, the inner point refers to the eternal Shabbat that the Neshamah faces. The Menorah is therefore a spatial representation of the gateway between mortal and eternal time which, as a symbol, attains holiness as a "thing" because what it *is* points to the dimension of *alive-being* that it discloses. This disclosure is not specific to either/or time and space. Rather, the disclosure of the *being* of Havayah in the self discloses to the self the nature of all *being* in both space and time. Thus, when the Torah says that the candles combine to face the inner point, the Sefat Emet understands this as a spatial reference to the united dimension of space and time that we have referred to as the eighth day.

In order to understand what this means in spatial terms we will return to the Kedushat Levi and to a remarkable passage in which he describes the consecration of the Mishkan by Moses. As we have already seen, the Kedushat Levi traces the correspondence between the Mishkan, the mitzvot, and the physical/spiritual limbs and tendons of the body. In this description he distinguishes very clearly between how Bezalel, the artisan who built the Mishkan and its vessels, understood this and the level of understanding that was attained by Moses alone:

> And behold, Bezalel made the Mishkan and all its vessels, such as the Menorah, which refers to the Middah (*attunement*) of love, and the table, which refers to the Middah of fear, and similarly all the other Middot (*attunements*), which form the general principles of the Torah, and the Torah is the general principle for the creation of the world.... But Bezalel did not know which vessel refers to which mitzvah. And this is what Moses did: he showed him which

vessel refers to which mitzvah, such that this vessel, which refers to love, represents this mitzvah, which also refers to love, and so on with all the mitzvot and all the vessels...and this constitutes the establishment (*kiyyum*) of the Mishkan, a task which could be performed only by Moses.... And the Ba'al Shem Tov explained the meaning of the raising up of sparks. It occurs when you see a Middah in its lowest physical form or, God forbid, in the form of evil, and then you serve God with this Middah, whether it be fear or love or any other Middah, and through this service the Middah can be elevated...and after this love or fear is elevated it attains a state of stable existence (*kiyyum*).... And thus the Mishkan was established after every Middah was established by cleaving to its corresponding mitzvah so that its existence (*kiyyum*) will continue in a permanent state of holiness. And this was something that only Moses could do, to connect the Mishkan to the Torah.[28]

Methodologically speaking, our understanding of what the Kedushat Levi is saying here depends on the terms that can be interpreted ontologically in this passage. These are Middot, mitzvot, and *kiyyum*. As we saw in our lexicon, the term Middot refers to *attunements* which can appear on the levels of the Nefesh and the Neshamah. In their lower forms, these *attunements*, as in Heidegger, disclose to Dasein how it is coming along with its own *being*. Heidegger singles out certain *attunements* associated with fear and anxiety for special attention considering the anxiety they disclose about Dasein's own-most *being* to point towards the authentic temporality of *being-toward-death*. This portrayal is indeed one that we negated in our lexicon of inner Torah but not by the denial of what these *attunements* disclose to Dasein about its *being*. Rather, our negation was predicated upon the idea that what is disclosed at this level can undergo a process of healing or correction (Tikkun) through the alignment of Middot Nefesh with Middot Neshamah.

Citing the Ba'al Shem Tov,[29] the Kedushat Levi describes this process precisely in this passage. However, he ties his description of it very specifically

---

28. Rabbi Levi Yitzchak of Berditchev, *Kedushat Levi*, Parashat Pekudei, 237.

29. Rabbi Israel ben Eliezer, the Ba'al Shem Tov (d. 1760), was the founder of the Hasidic movement in Poland. So many legends surround this enigmatic character that

to the correlation between the mitzvot, their corresponding Middot, and the vessels of the Mishkan. Ultimately, the key principle of this passage is that the stable form of these Middot is their ownmost or highest purpose and that the alignment of their lower expressions with their highest ones is akin to their being grounded in their source. This purpose, or source, which is the state of Devekut or Da'at Hashem in Gadlut, is also the aspect of the Middot that is represented as an ideal in the correlation between the Torah, the mitzvot, and the vessels of the Mishkan.

What the Kedushat Levi is essentially saying here is that the highest state of this correlation, which Moses uniquely appreciated, is also the stable state in which this correlation can endure or enduringly *be*. The use of the word *kiyyum* (like *makom* and *mekayem*) that refers to both the final establishment or consecration of the Mishkan and the enduring spatial stability of the correlation between the mitzvot, the Middot. and the vessels, suggests the ontological significance of these together as an expression of the enduring *being* of Havayah in space. This is what the Kedushat Levi calls "a permanent state of holiness." Thus, to return to the beginning of the passage, the correlation between the Torah, the Mishkan, the vessels, and the Middot in their highest form, points to the general principle of the created-*being* of the world, which in its highest form can disclose the permanent state of holiness that underlies all space.

The Kedushat Levi continues, now introducing his understanding of the distinction between the Mishkan and the Mikdash. The special role that Moses played in connecting the Middot, the mitzvot, and the Mishkan produced only an episode of this "permanent state of holiness." In temporal terms, this episode is like the Shabbat that appears each week as the seventh day in the cycle. The cyclical nature of this is echoed in the frequent dismantling and rebuilding of the Mishkan as the children of Israel wandered through the desert.[30] The purpose of this journey, like the journey through

the historical details of his life are hard to verify. For a rich collection of anecdotes and legends ordered chronologically according to the sequence of his life story, see Yitzhak Buxbaum, *The Light and Fire of the Baal Shem Tov* (New York: Continuum International Publishing Group, 2006). For a critical study of the historical figure, see Moshe Rosman, *Founder of Hasidism: A Quest for the Historical Ba'al Shem Tov* (Berkeley: University of California Press, 1996).

30. Rabbi Levi Yitzchak of Berditchev, *Kedushat Levi*, Parashat Pekudei, 237.

mundane time, was, in the words of the Kedushat Levi, "to raise up the Middot that had fallen and could be found in the desert." By this he is perhaps referring to the negative or misplaced *attunements* that the challenges of life in the desert disclose to the self, whether through the tribulation of wandering or through the encounters with other nations such as the Amalekites, the Moabites, and the Midianites. One way or the other, the point is that these experiences stand in contrast to the permanent state of the Middot that is maintained within the Mishkan and which reaches additional heights when the vessels arrive at their final resting place on the Temple Mount in Jerusalem. In the words of the Kedushat Levi,

> And this is what is implied by the phrase "These are the amounts (*pekudei*) of the Mishkan, the Mishkan of the testimony," since the testimony is the Torah and the mitzvot. And the word *pakad* means a connection or an accounting in the sense that…the Mishkan is (connected to or gives an account of) the Torah…. And If the [Middot of] fear and love are not for the blessed Creator, God forbid, then they have no rest (Menuchah). But when these Middot of love and fear and all the other Middot are directed toward the Creator, then they are in a state of rest…and when the Middot are in a permanent state of connection, this means that the vessels of the Mikdash and the Mishkan attain a permanent state of connection to the mitzvot only in Jerusalem in the Beit HaMikdash. The Middot reach a permanent state of rest (Menuchah), that is to say that serving the Holy One, blessed be He, was something that happened in the Mishkan…and this mindfulness of God is the meaning of rest (Menuchah). But in Jerusalem, which is the place of the Mikdash, they are established in permanence, that is to say, in endless connection. And this is what is implied by the phrase "this is an inheritance."[31]

---

31. Ibid. The Kedushat Levi bases his distinction between Menuchah and Nachalah (i.e., "Rest" and "Inheritance") on Mishnah *Zevachim* (14:6, 8).

There are two crucial points to be made here. The first concerns the relationship between the Mishkan and Shabbat as a day of Menuchah. The spatial meaning of Menuchah is made very clear here. It refers to the highest level of permanent connection possible in the Mishkan between the Middot, the mitzvot, the vessels, and the Mishkan. Following the structure of *ashan*, the spatiality of the Mishkan, the mitzvot, and the vessels corresponds here to the *attunements* in the self. When these attain their highest state, i.e., when they are expressed as *care* for the total *alive-being* of Havayah, they come to rest in a state of Menuchah. In this sense, the work that went into the construction of the Mishkan, like the creation of the world, corresponds to the temporal dimension of the six days. All of these are connected to Melachah. By contrast, the enduring *being* of the Mishkan in its complete form corresponds to Menuchah and hence to Shabbat. The spatial Shabbat as it is described here refers to the Middot, the mitzvot, and the vessels reaching a state of Menuchah in the Mishkan. Comparing this to the Menorah as described in the *Sefat Emet*, we might say that after its completion, the enduring *being* of the Mishkan is represented by the light of the Menorah, which is kept permanently burning. Thus, enduring *being* of light in a state of Menuchah is a symbol of the spatial equivalence between the Mishkan and Shabbat.

The second point concerns the distinction that the Kedushat Levi makes between the Mishkan and the Mikdash. Here he describes the spatial parallel of the eighth day that transcends the Menuchah of the seventh day by permanently underlying all space. The idea that Menuchah refers to the eighth day appears in the commentary of the Sefat Emet on the creation story. The Sefat Emet writes,

> Before the first Shabbat the world was lacking Menuchah, and that is the Shabbat that includes all the six days of the week, and Shabbat unites them in the secret of "One"…[32]

As we already saw, the principle here is that underlying all time there is a permanent state of Shabbat that unifies everything in the sense that it discloses

---

32. Rabbi Yehuda Leib Alter of Gur, *Sefat Emet*, Parashat Bereishit (5631).

the *created-being* of everything that has its source in Havayah. In a later teaching the Sefat Emet returns to this theme, this time as follows:

> The world was lacking Menuchah.… On the six days of creation the existence (*kiyyum*) of the world came from the force of the Creator and from what He said on each day of the creation. But on Shabbat everything was complete and began to exist enduringly (*kayma*) even after the Holy One concealed His speech from the creations…but Shabbat is an act that enables nature to connect with what is above nature, and this is why it is called Shalom, which is the completion of everything that was created and of its establishment.[33]

Again, the principle of enduring *being* is connected here to the eighth day, which is referred to as the point of contact between the seven-day cycle of nature and the day that is beyond this cycle and hence beyond nature. This is the ongoing *being* of the world that here too is associated with the term *kiyyum*, which refers to the idea of establishing the world or setting up the *being* of the world to continue *being* after the process of Melachah is complete. In the *Kedushat Levi*, this idea is paralleled in space by the arrival of the Mishkan in Jerusalem. When he says that Jerusalem is an inheritance (*nachalah*) and not just a place of Menuchah, he means that it is the eighth day in space, where the temporary, portable sanctuary that represents the Menuchah of the seventh day, itself comes to rest. It is this final coming to rest that according to the Mishnah establishes Jerusalem from then on as the only place in which it is permitted to offer a sacrifice.[34]

The correspondence between the permanent Shabbat and the Mikdash in Jerusalem features also in the prayer Lecha Dodi. Lecha Dodi is a sixteenth-century hymn which is sung as the centerpiece of Kabbalat Shabbat.[35]

---

33. Rabbi Yehuda Leib Alter of Gur, *Sefat Emet*, Parashat Bereishit (5634).

34. The Mishnah in *Zevachim* (14:8) states, "When they came to Jerusalem the *bamot* (temporary altars for offering sacrifices) were forbidden and were no longer permitted, and it was an inheritance (*nachalah*)."

35. Kabbalat Shabbat is the special service instigated by the mystics of Tzefat in the sixteenth century and designed to welcome the Shabbat. See Lawrence A. Hoffman,

It is packed with mystical and rabbinic metaphors that echo the structure of *ashan* – i.e., the correspondence between the self, space, and time – that we have been following. Lecha Dodi was composed by Rabbi Shlomo Alkabetz, who regarded it as a meditation inspired by the Song of Songs, the purpose of which is to welcome the Shabbat while focusing on uniting the masculine Nefesh with the feminine Neshamah or Neshamah Yeteirah. As in the Song of Songs, these are metaphorically represented as a bride and groom who also correspond to the people of Israel and God, all seeking to unite with one another. The third stanza of this prayer is of particular interest to us here:

> O sanctuary of the king, royal city, arise and depart from amid the upheaval, too long have you dwelled in the valley of weeping. He will shower compassion upon you. Shake off the dust – arise! Don your splendid clothes, my people. Through the son of Jesse, the Bethlehemite! Draw near to my soul – redeem it! Wake up, wake up, Your light has come, rise and shine. Awaken, awaken; sing a melody. The glory of God to be revealed upon thee.[36]

This stanza begins a shift in the focus of Lecha Dodi away from the bride and the groom and toward the sanctuary and Jerusalem.[37] The Mikdash and the royal city of Jerusalem stand in here for Shabbat and the bride. The temporal theme of Shabbat is thus connected to its spatial representation in Jerusalem. The permanent Shabbat is the equivalent of the Mikdash in Jerusalem that discloses to us the permanent holiness embedded in the dimension of space. Similarly, the people, described here as the clothes that the awakened Shabbat

---

ed., *Kabalat Shabbat: Welcoming Shabbat in the Synagogue* (Jewish Lights, 2004) and Reuven Kimelman, *The Mystical Meaning of 'Lekhah Dodi' and 'Kabalat Shabbat'* (Hebrew University/Magnes Press and Cherub Press, 2003) [Hebrew with English Introduction].

36. For a translation and discussion of Lecha Dodi, see Hoffman, *Kabalat Shabbat.*

37. I want to thank my student Adina Shine who studied with me at the Rothberg International School at the Hebrew University in 2019. Her paper, entitled, "An Ontological Reading of Kabalat Shabbat," was helpful in clarifying some of the ideas in this section.

must don, are the social or political equivalent of the permanent Shabbat within human society.[38] This idea is one that we need to look at more closely.

The Problem of Jewish Chosenness from the Perspective of Survival and System

As we continue to consider the meaning of the structure of *ashan*, we reach the challenge of explaining the special status of the Jewish people in Jewish thought. Broadly speaking, it is fair to say that in the Torah-texts that we have been considering, the status of the Jewish people is built on exclusivist and ethnocentric beliefs. Most notably among these is the twofold claim that the Jewish collective is "chosen" and that this "chosenness" grants Jewish people a divine right to the land.[39] For separate but connected reasons, both ideas are fiercely contested in contemporary liberal discourse. Following the establishment of the State of Israel in 1948 and most particularly since the Six-Day War in 1967, Israel's right to the biblical land has been contested by Palestinians and the Arab world. And, given the current shift from a world in which Jews were the persecuted underdog to one in which the State of Israel is a cultural, military and economic world power, the demand for territorial compromise, the end of "occupation," and the establishment of a Palestinian state has called into question the legitimacy not only of the Jewish claim to the land conquered in 1967 but even to the borders established after Israel's War of Independence in 1948. International law distinguishes very clearly between the two, but the line between them is becoming harder and harder to defend while the national ethnocentricism of the Jewish state has become a subject of considerable controversy.[40]

---

38. Ibid.

39. For a wonderful discussion of the meaning of chosenness from a contemporary perspective see, Jerome (Yehudah) Gellman, *God's Kindness Has Overwhelmed Us: A Contemporary Doctrine of the Jews as the Chosen People* (Boston: Academic Studies Press, 2013).

40. This question was severely debated when the Israeli Knesset passed the Nation-State Law in May 2018 as a "Basic Law" of the State of Israel. This law stated the land of Israel is the historical homeland of the Jewish people, that the State of Israel is the nation-state of the Jewish people, and that the right of national self-determination in the State of Israel is unique to the Jewish people.

At the outset of this book we argued that certain Jewish ideas are distorted by being under water. What this means is that values championed by Zionism (such as the special right of the Jewish people to a national identity, self-determination, sovereignty over a historical homeland, and the right to self-defense, for example) only ever stood in for ideas and concepts – such as Jewish chosenness and the divine promise of the land – whose more concealed meanings lie beyond the confines of Survival and System. We argued that a paradigm shift was necessary, because these ideas malfunction when they are run as "programs" on the "operating system" of Survival and System and they can only really be appreciated in the paradigm of Segulah. We suggested that as the immediate aftershock of the Holocaust fades, it becomes harder to defend Israel's legitimacy on the grounds of Jewish victimhood. These claims are challenging to maintain in an era in which Israel's political, financial, and military power has surpassed all expectations. As Israel shifts from David to Goliath in world opinion, the memory of the Holocaust, though not forgotten, is most certainly difficult to marshal in defense of specifically Jewish, rather than universal humanist, concerns.

This is not just the result of the Israeli-Palestinian conflict and the balance of power between the two peoples; it is the heart of an internal crisis that Jewish identity and Zionism are facing inside the Jewish world. If Jewish identity and the justification of Zionism are predicated upon post-Enlightenment humanist principles, many Jews who wish to remain faithful to those humanist principles have a hard time continuing to pursue ethnocentric goals even when these have nothing to do with the political conquest of the land. Values such as in-marriage, which, strictly speaking, do not come at the expense of other people, nonetheless represent a kind of ethnocentric racial Puritanism that is excruciatingly difficult to defend in the terms that Survival and System understands. It should be noted that the philosophical quandaries involved in justifying the particularist Jewish or Zionist cause have adverse effects not only on those who distance themselves from Judaism and Zionism but also on those whose identities are most vehemently entrenched in them. Many are easily sucked into a kind of hawkishness or even fanatical fundamentalism that covers over these difficulties by amplifying the passions with which traditional convictions are held. This does not tackle the root of the problem, and what it can often do is compromise the moral and ethical validity of the very convictions they seek to defend. Beyond the moral crisis here, this alienates even those Jewish humanists who remain most sympathetic and loyal to the basic historical cause. The crisis between the right and the left is as rife and complex inside the Jewish world as it is externally. Indeed, it is at the heart of the rifts that divide Israeli political debate and Jewish identity discourse from within.

As we suggested in our introduction and indeed throughout, this problem is only the most politically acute version of an overall challenge that faces Jewish identity in the world today. The problem, as we have diagnosed it, is the distortion of key Jewish ideas on the right and on the left when these are understood in the paradigm of Survival and System. This paradigm is more than a worldview. If the Jewish collective is going to survive while holding on to its moral foundations, ironically it is the "brain" of Survival and System that must be identified as a serious obstacle.

We want to illustrate just how acute this situation is with an extreme but nonetheless instructive little thought experiment. In chapter 9 we briefly mentioned the speech that George Steiner puts in the mouth of his fictional version of Adolf Hitler in his book *The Portage to San Cristobal of A.H.*[41] The fictional premise of the book is that Hitler managed to survive the war and escape into hiding. Years later he is captured (Adolf Eichmann style) by an elite team of Mossad agents in the jungles of South America who then bring him to trial. In a first tribunal which appears at the close of the book, Steiner's fictional character A.H. is given his first opportunity to justify himself. He makes three key points,

> Erster punkt. Article One: Because you must understand that I did not invent. It was Adolf Hitler who dreamt up the master race. Who conceived of enslaving inferior peoples. Lies. Lies. It was in the doss house in Mannerheim that I first understood.... It was there that I first understood your secret power. The secret power of your teaching. *Of Yours.* A Chosen People. Chosen by God for His own. The only race on earth chosen, exalted, made singular among mankind....

---

41. Steiner, *Portage to San Cristobal,* chapter 9. This book was briefly mentioned above (see chapter 9, note 28).

From you everything. To set a race apart. To keep it from defilement.
To hold before it a promised land. To scour that land of its inhabi-
tants or place them in servitude. Your beliefs. Your arrogance.[42]

This is A.H.'s first point. His disturbing first line of defense is that Nazism
is modeled on the Jewish idea of the chosen race. His second point echoes
the arguments made in *Bluebeard* concerning the blackmail of transcendence
and which we have already discussed above.[43] Third and finally, A.H. suggests
that he is the true father of Zionism,

> The strange book Der Judenstaat. I read it carefully. Straight out
> of Bismarck. The language, the ideas, the tone of it. A clever book,
> I agree. Shaping Zionism in the image of the new German nation.
> But did Herzl create Israel or did I? Examine the question fairly.
> Would Palestine have become Israel, would the Jews have come to
> that barren patch of the Levant, would the United States *and* the
> Soviet Union have given you recognition and guaranteed your sur-
> vival, had it not been for the Holocaust? It was the Holocaust that
> gave you the courage of injustice, that made you drive the Arab
> out of his home, out of his field because he was lice-eaten without
> resource, because he was in your divinely ordered way.... Perhaps
> I *am* the Messiah, the true Messiah…whose infamous deeds were
> allowed by God in order to bring His people home. The Holocaust
> was the necessary mystery before Israel could come into its strength.
> It is not I who said it: but your own visionaries, your unravelers of
> God's meaning when it is Friday night in Jerusalem.[44]

In conclusion, A.H. sums up, saying,

> Gentlemen of the tribunal: I took my doctrines from you: I fought
> the blackmail of the ideal with which you have hounded mankind.

---

42. Ibid., 161–63.

43. See chapter 2 above.

44. Ibid., 169–70.

My crimes were matched and surpassed by those of others. The *Reich* begat Israel.[45]

When the book was first published this speech stirred up vehement opposition and outrage. In an afterword to the second edition, Steiner insisted that the centerpiece of the book is not A.H.'s speech at the end, but rather it is another speech that appears midway in which the head of the Mossad transmits a radio message to his agents in the field. In this deeply moving transmission he speaks about the victims of Hitler's tongue cautioning the agents not to let him speak. Alongside deeply moving and passionate descriptions of the pain, torture, suffering, and death endured by Jews in the Holocaust, the transmission warns the Mossad agents in the field to keep their distance from the man with the diabolical tongue who conjures deceit, death, and destruction with his words. This, Steiner insists, is the principal purpose of the book and as such, A.H.'s speech at the end should be taken as nothing more than a heinous example of his diabolical, manipulative tongue in action.

One might well question Steiner's sincerity here. It is tempting to imagine that his true intention was to use this moment in the book to slip in a highly provocative critique of Jewish chosenness and Zionism. One way or the other, our experiment hinges on the possibility that people reading this speech today might find it considerably less outrageous than Steiner's original readers did in 1981. There is much in it that echoes the rhetoric used even by Jews and Zionists who struggle to align their Western values with the ideas of chosenness and the promise of the land. If our little experiment has worked, it might help illustrate the attrition that we have been talking about, since the arguments put forward by Steiner's A.H. are used not only by extremists in today's world. Our purpose is not to take sides with moderates or radicals, but rather to underline the claim that the corrosion of Survival and System and the attrition that this has caused to the most basic claims of Jewish identity and Zionism is a crisis that cannot be addressed satisfactorily from any position on the scale that extends from radical liberalism to ultra-conservatism. For this, we must return to our efforts at rehabilitating the perspective of Segulah.

---

45. Ibid.

The People of Israel as Shabbat in the Dimension of Humanity

As with our previous discussions, our method will be to consider the meaning of Jewish chosenness from an onto-theological perspective that is based upon the negation of Heidegger. However, in the interests of intellectual honesty, it is important to acknowledge that some of the texts that are relevant to this topic are indeed quite disturbing. It is therefore essential not to distort the fact that religious Jewish texts normatively make qualitative distinctions between Jews and non-Jews. Some of the most obvious examples appear in the regular prayers, such as the Havdalah blessing recited at the end of Shabbat: "Blessed are You, God, our Lord, King of the universe, who separates between the holy and the profane; between the light and dark; between Israel and the other nations; between the seventh day and the six days of the week. Blessed are You, God, who separates between the holy and the profane."

While, as we have said, the distinction between the Jewish people and others poses powerful challenges to the paradigm of Survival and System, this problem perhaps may seem all the more acute when presented, as we intend to, in ontological terms. Indeed, from a post-Enlightenment perspective, there is no greater culprit than ontological essentialism for the moral perversions that we tend to associate with white supremacists, xenophobes, racists, colonialists, misogynists, homophobes, and of course, Nazis. Put simply, Jews should know better, and it is patently embarrassing (if not worse) to discover in their hallowed texts that they seemingly do not.

Our contention is that in the paradigm of Segulah, the negation of Heidegger does indeed redeem Jewish thought from this accusation. But this does not mean that Jews and even great Jews have never got this wrong. What it does mean is that the ontological system of the Torah gets it right though the line that it draws between Jews and Gentiles is subtle and regrettably easy to misconstrue. All the same, our argument is that when the very notion of ontology is moved away from Heidegger's brand of death-obsessed humanist essentialism, the chosenness of Israel as it appears in the structure of *ashan* emerges as the very opposite and indeed the absolute negation of the xenophobia and prejudice that Jews have borne more than any other people in human history.

To see this more clearly, we first need to understand what the onto-theological meaning of chosenness is and then we will be able to understand how the identity of the chosen people relates to the rest of humanity. Without trying to make things easy for ourselves, we will begin with an extremely challenging text in the hope that – using the terminology of our lexicon – we might manage to explain the fundamental distinction between Jews and non-Jews that the idea of chosenness points to even when it appears in its starkest and most troubling form. Our example (chosen among many others like it) is the following passage in the *Tanya*,

> Rabbi Chaim Vital wrote…that in every Jew, whether righteous or wicked, are two souls, as it is written, "The Neshamot which I have made" (Isaiah 57:16), alluding to two souls. There is one soul which originates in the Klippah of Sitra Achra and which is clothed in the blood of a human being, giving life to the body, as it is written, "For the life of the flesh is in the blood" (Leviticus 17:11). From it stem all the evil characteristics deriving from the four evil elements that are contained in it…. From this soul stems also the good characteristics which are to be found in the innate nature of all Israel, such as mercy and benevolence. For in the case of Israel, this soul of the Klippah is derived from the Klippat Nogah which also contains good as it originates in the esoteric "Tree of Knowledge of Good and Evil" (*Zohar* I, 12b). The souls of the nations of the world…emanate from the unclean Klippot, which contain no good whatsoever, as it is written in *Etz Chaim*, portal 49, chapter 3, that all the good that the nations do is done from selfish motives. So the Gemara (*Bava Batra* 10b) comments on the verse, "The kindness of the nations is sin" (Proverbs 14:34), stating that all the charity and kindness done by the nations of the world is only for their own self-glorification, and so on (*Tanya*, chapter 1)….The second soul of a Jew is truly a part of God above…. So, allegorically speaking, have the souls of Jews risen in the divine thought, as it is written, "My firstborn son is Israel" (Exodus 4:22) and "You are the children of the Lord your God" (Deuteronomy 14:1). That is to say, just as a child is derived from his father's brain, so – to use anthropomorphism – the soul of each Israelite is derived from His thought and wisdom, blessed be He. For He is

wise – but not through a knowable wisdom, because He and His wisdom are one.[46]

This is undoubtedly a disturbing text. But we do not intend to defend it apologetically. There is of course room here to consider that this formulation of the theme of chosenness is perhaps beyond the pale. The easiest thing to do might be to simply censure it or mark it down as an example of how some great Jews "got it wrong," as we mentioned above. Maybe its author's historical circumstances might be called upon to explain away his attitude. Alternatively, one might simply look at the author's disciples in the world today to see how their love, charity, and kindness toward Jews and non-Jews must somehow disabuse us of any wrong impressions that we may have about the intentions of their great teacher. But such defenses, as tempting and comforting as they might be, would miss the point here, which is to try to transpose the discourse into a different paradigm, one in which the foundations of the many disturbing distinctions that Jewish law undoubtedly makes between Jews and Gentiles can start to make morally plausible sense.[47]

So if we now try to enter the inner workings of the text, we can start with the observation that what it appears to be saying is that there is an ontological distinction between Jews and non-Jews on the level of both the Nefesh and the Neshamah. While the key characteristics of the body and the Nefesh are shared by Jews and non-Jews (as well as animals); there is one specific aspect of the Nefesh that is present in Jews and not in gentiles.[48] Moreover, the dis-

---

46. *Tanya*, chapter 2.

47. There has been some controversy in the past about the efforts of some scholars to blur the stark reality that many classical Jewish texts make clear distinctions between Jews and Gentiles. See, for example, Rabbi David Bar Chaim, http://www.come-and-hear .com/supplement/so-Da'at-emet/en_gentiles1.html He writes there, "It is clear that views presented by certain personalities, including [former] Knesset member Professor A. Shaki, Rabbi Lichtenstein and Rabbi Amital, and Mr. Yochanan Ben-Ya'akov, do not represent the truth of the Torah. Simple and clear Halachic laws, whose foundations are in the words of the Living G-d, clearly state the difference 'between the two bloods' (in the words of Ms. Huberman) – between Jew and Gentile. There is no escaping the facts: the Torah of Israel makes a clear distinction between a Jew, who is defined as 'man,' and a Gentile."

48. This is what the *Tanya* refers to as the distinction between Klippat Nogah and Klippat Sitra Achra in the passage cited above (note 46).

tinction made on the level of the Nefesh is compounded by a second point, which is the *Tanya's* claim about the uniqueness of the Neshamah, which is possessed by Jews alone. How are we to explain these differences?

Our approach will be to define the meaning of these terms through the specific negation of Heidegger's immanent metaphysics, which means that the differences between Jews and non-Jews described here point toward different ways of *being* as an act of reflexive consciousness. In this sense, the different levels of Nefesh and Neshamah correspond to different degrees of "ownmost-ness" in reflexive consciousness, all of which are contained within the structure of Tzelem Elohim. As we have seen, these different degrees are often described as being either higher or lower than one another. On several occasions, we have already suggested that this scale can be described more effectively in terms of internality and externality. Hence, the dimension of Neshamah is the innermost dimension of *being*, while the Nefesh is more external. It is lower in the sense that it is closer to the functions of the body. The point is that the flattening of hierarchy that this formulation offers is of intrinsic (and not simply apologetic) importance here, since the objective of the inner Torah is not the domination of one of these by another but rather the alignment of the two so that the more physical level of human *being* can function as an extension, externalization, and concretization of the inner level. Thus, despite the appearance of hierarchical language, the different components are in fact of equal importance and value (in the sense that we have referred to frequently as the reversible relationship between *peshat* and *sod*) since it is only through the combination of the two that the consciousness of Havayah extends into the external, concrete, physical reality of Dasein's *being-in-the-world*.

This has significant implications for the way in which we understand how this hierarchy determines the relative value of Jews and non-Jews. The fundamental principle that emerges from this is that if there is an ontological distinction between Jews and non-Jews, it must be discovered in terms of the difference between Jewish and non-Jewish ontological activity. Although there is indeed a sense of higher and lower here, this is not an ontological distinction in the social-Darwinian sense but one that distinguishes between more internal and more external forms of what Heidegger refers to as *care*. Thus, it is the content or the object of the act of *being* that defines the difference in the Nefesh between Klippat Nogah and Klippat Sitra Achra as well as defining the overall difference between Nefesh and Neshamah. Klippat Nogah, Klippat Sitra Achra, and Neshamah are all, therefore, more and less internal forms of *care*. Perhaps we can get closer to this idea by considering the following passage in the *Kedushat Levi*:

> For it says (Song of Songs 7:5), "Your eyes are pools of Cheshbon." And here, the root of the evil eye is like that of Balaam, for everything he gazed upon he cast a curse upon it because of the evil with which he looked at it. And thus he separated it from its higher root, which is the source of life…because he did not look upon it with the energy of God that is within it. But regarding the seed of Israel it is written, "Your eyes are pools of Cheshbon," even in things which are reckoned and accounted for according to their numbers and quantities; their gaze does no damage, because the man of Israel sees in all things the force of the Creator which is within it. And since he causes what he sees to cleave to its root from this gaze, blessing and abundance flows from the highest source upon that object. And this is what is meant by "your eyes are pools," that your eyes become like pools from which abundance flows.[49]

While in the literal sense, the word "Cheshbon" in the verse from the Song of Songs is perhaps nothing more than a place, the Midrashic reading of the text pays attention to the meaning of the place's name, which is "accounting." In this reading, "accounting" is a manner of viewing the world in which the quantification of things underlines their separateness. This way of looking at the world is referred to as the gaze of Balaam, which detaches the phenomena of the world from their roots in the unified total *alive-being* of Havayah. In short, Cheshbon connotes an external form of *care* for *being-in-the-world*. In contradistinction to this, the gaze of the Tree of Life is the more internal gaze that unites superficial separateness with the inner unity of Havayah. This unifying gaze is one that sees the *being* of Havayah in everything, and as such it turns the eyes into "pools of abundance." The abundant gaze that sees the

---

49. Rabbi Levi Yitzchak of Berditchev, *Kedushat Levi*, Parashat Pekudei, 235.

force of the Creator inside the *being* of everything is the gaze of the Tree of Life, and it is the specific purpose of Jewish life. Jewish life sees the world, *is* in the world, in the sense that it "devours the *being* of the world" in a way that consumes the lower expressions of Dasein's everyday *being* and converts them into expressions of the *being* of Havayah. This consuming gaze is a Jewish gaze in that it is the gaze of those who cleave to the Tree of Life, meaning the Torah. It is the gaze of those who direct the ontological activity of *care* toward the recognition that the *being-of-the-world* is *created-being*. Coming back to the specific context of this commentary, the point that the Kedushat Levi is making is that "Cheshbon" has a purpose in the Mishkan, because it is the purpose of this aspect of the Avodah to align the gaze of "accounting" with the Tree of Life.

The ontological meaning of the hierarchy between Jews and Balaam in this text is therefore based upon different levels of *care*. Measurement and quantification belong to the everyday condition of Dasein's *care* for *being-in-the-world*, whereas the gaze of the Tree of Life has the power to transform this into the gaze of the Neshamah. Thus, the distinction between the ideal of the Jewish people and Balaam is their gaze; it is the ontological directionality of their *care*. The Jewish people are separate not for racial reasons but because of their choice to accept the Torah, which obliges them to cleave to the Tree of Life. With the gaze that this grants them, even things that are quantified in their selfness are extensions of the *being* of Havayah, because "the man of Israel sees in all things the force of the Creator within it."

If we bring this back now to the *Tanya*, we can identify the gaze of Dasein as the Sitra Achra, which, in its illusory extreme self-deceitful selfness, is the source of evil. As we said above in our discussion of Churban, this is because Dasein's desire to *be* is overwhelmed by anxiety and conscience, which deceive Dasein into accepting the idea that the kernel of its *with-world* is its *being-with* itself alone. Even the most carefully concealed lair in which the Sitra Achra operates under layers of presumed virtues cannot conceal from view the existential self-deceiving, egotistical self-absorption that lurks within. In the world of the inner Torah, the gaze of the Tree of Life is capable of redirecting Dasein's *care* about *being-a-self* toward the *created-being* of everything that *is*. But this is possible only for those who cleave to the Tree, which is the Torah. Thus, the source of sinfulness or evil that is present in Dasein's gaze is not something that Jews are immune to, but it is a condition of *being* that their obligation to cleave to the Tree of Life seeks to redeem.

It is here that we reach the most challenging and difficult category, which is the middle position of Klippat Nogah. At first glance, this is the idea that is most disturbing because it seemingly dissociates Jews from the guilt of Sitra Achra by very virtue of their birth. It is important to point out that the idea that Jews can be implicated in the gaze of the Sitra Achra is not beyond possibility in Jewish texts. All the same, the idea of Klippat Nogah requires some explanation.

Klippat Nogah is a state of *being* that follows upon the obligation – even if it remains unfulfilled – of cleaving to the Tree of Life. Klippat Nogah is another kind of gaze, which we might define as the gaze of the Tree of Life in a deficient form. Like Klippat Sitra Achra, Klippat Nogah is the gaze of the unaligned Nefesh, which allows the *being* of Havayah to remain covered over or distracted by the illusory selfhood of *beings*. But Klippat Nogah which literally translates as the shell or concealment of the moon, is a form of *care* in which the light or consciousness of Havayah is not completely absent. Rather, it is presumed to be a misrepresentation or distortion of the *being* of Havayah. Good and evil are mixed together. Klippat Nogah is a deficient or distorted version of Havayah just as the light of the moon is only ever a distortion of the sun. Klippat Nogah is a distorted type of *care* for *being* that has its source in the being of Havayah.

What distinguishes Klippat Nogah from Klipat Sitra Achra is the obligation to cleave to the Tree of Life, which is the onto-theological definition of Jewish collective identity. The idea here is not that the Jewish people were formed and then chosen but that the "formation" and the "choice" are one and the same thing. To *be* Jewish is to *be* chosen, and to *be* chosen is to *be* Jewish. Both refer to the act of *being* that expresses itself in the choice to *be* the people defined by its collective obligation to cleave to the Tree of Life.

The idea that the obligation to see the world with the gaze of the Tree of Life defines the ontological distinction between Jews and non-Jews is central to the overall perspective that the Sefat Emet gives in his commentary on the Torah as well. It features specifically in his discussion of the dietary laws in Leviticus, chapter 11, which determine which "living things" can be eaten and which cannot. In his words,

> And this is the living thing – Rashi comments: "Because these animals cleave to life".… And here we know that the children of Israel when they received the Torah cleaved to the Tree of Life, and on account of this all sin should have been healed. However, this was damaged because of more sin, but all the same we each remained with our portion in the Torah, which is the Tree of Life. This is why we must avoid the mixture of good and evil. And in truth, in all creations there is aliveness, and it is constricted. But the children of Israel have a hold on the Tree of Life.[50]

The distinction between Jewish people and the rest of the world is captured in the dietary laws because the life of the "living thing" (i.e., the animal that is permitted) is defined by its alignment with the form of *care* that the Torah demands of those who are obliged to observe it. Hence, Jewish people can eat only certain animals because these animals cleave to life in the same way that the Jewish people must cleave to the Tree of Life.

What the Sefat Emet is saying here is that the purpose of the dietary laws in the Torah is to confine the consumption of animals by the children of Israel to those animals whose relationship to other animals is equivalent to the ontological relationship between Israel and the rest of humanity. The substance or the content of this difference concerns the ontological direction of *care*. The Jewish people are obliged to direct *care* toward the Torah and thus to cleave to the Tree of Life. By way of extension, in the same way that Israel is commanded to cleave to the Torah, which is the Tree of Life, they are commanded to eat only animals that cleave to life. While the specific reason that determines why an animal is pure or not need not concern us here; the general principle is clear. The Sefat Emet identifies a pointing capacity in the symbolism that the Torah attaches to pure animals. Since they are animals in which the aliveness that emanates from the Tree of Life is less constricted, they cleave to life in the same way that the Jewish people are commanded to cleave to the Tree of Life. Restricting the consumption of meat to these animals alone therefore serves the purpose of pointing out the directionality of

---

50. Rabbi Yehuda Leib Alter of Gur, *Sefat Emet*, Parashat Shemini (5645).). See also Rashi, Leviticus 11:2: "And this is the living thing."

the *care* that the Jewish people must attach to the Tree of Life. In other words, the Sefat Emet constructs a parallel here between the "objects of attention" that the Torah prescribes for the ontological consumption of *being* through *care* and the types of animal that the Torah prescribes for the physical consumption through eating.

In another commentary on the same verse, the Sefat Emet extends this principle into the four-tiered, onto-theological structure that we encountered in the *Tanya*:

> There are minerals, vegetables, animals, and those that can speak. And Adam rules over them all. And just as Israel has been chosen among humans because they speak the words of the Torah and of holiness, which is why Ezekiel says, "And you are called Adam" (Ezekiel 34:31), for there is no advantage to those who speak when he does not speak holiness. This is why the most important thing depends on the power of speech given to Israel. It is the same way with minerals, vegetables, and animals, that there are special species from the aspect of holiness which can be raised up by virtue of the speech of Israel, whose speech goes up to heaven. This is why no differentiation is made concerning what Gentiles may eat, and this is what is meant by the midrash that says that the mitzvot were given to Israel only so that they may join them with all creations. What this means is that Israel can raise up and connect every creation, mineral, vegetable, animal, or speaking (human) by virtue of the mitzvot that are in everything.[51]

Again, this passage is based on the idea that the people of Israel are separated from others by the intentionality that the Torah attaches to the direction of their *care*. As the addressees and recipients of the Torah, the Torah obligates them to cleave to the Tree of Life. This is what determines the substance and content of their gaze upon the world. One might say that the Torah is an external technology (a version of the Tree of Life that is wrapped in the Tree of Knowledge) that gives those who it addresses a set of practices and

---

51. Rabbi Yehuda Leib Alter of Gur, *Sefat Emet*, Parashat Shemini (5634).

a way of *being* that potentially endows them with the capacity to disclose Havayah as the *being* of everything in the world through their ontological consumption (*being-in*) of the world. This capacity is like a new stage of human development made possible by the alignment of the Nefesh and the Neshamah. The Torah gives the Jewish people an ontological capacity that is not yet fulfilled in everyday human experience. It is deposited outside of the body in the Torah, which activates the parallel perspective or gaze on the world that is concealed inside the ontological experience of *being-alive* in the higher residues of Ruach and Neshamah. To have access to Ruach and Neshamah is to be like Adam before the sin. Thus, when the texts of the inner Torah describe Jews as Adam (human) and non-Jews as animal, this does not refer to the humanity of humanism and the inhumanity of animals but to being like Adam before the sin. In other words, it refers to achieving the unfulfilled evolution of humanity into the being that reclaims the consciousness that was Adam's before it was contaminated with the fruit of the tree that propelled Dasein forward in its unholy quest to be a self. Thus, the consumption of the world by the consciousness of the Neshamah is unique to the Jewish people, who are addressed by the Torah and defined by their being the recipients of its commandments. The Torah directs Jewish consumption of the world – whether this consumption is through the ontological condition of gazing, eating, speaking, touching, smelling, or anything else – in a way that discloses the *being* of the world as Havayah. Jewish life permutates through conditions of *being* that are prescribed by the Torah and which allow the Jewish people to engage with everything in the world through the prism of the Tree of Life. This "raises the whole world" and makes the *being* of Havayah (which has the form or shape of mitzvot) explicit.

In another passage, the Sefat Emet returns to this theme:

> For in everything in the world there is the will or desire of God, blessed is His name, as it says that everything He created is created in His honor. But it is concealed and it requires Avodah to find it in the inner level.... The Avodah of Israel is to bring this light into the world of doing...this is the inner point in each act.... Through the Avodah of the Mikdash everything can be raised up to God, since this is how the divine presence below is made visible...as it

says…and every person in the world is like the seven days of the week, for there are seven Middot in humanity…which are drawn toward the inner level, which is the light of the seven days. This is the meaning of Shabbat and of the children of Israel, who are a testimonial that God created and enlivens everything. To show that the aliveness of the act is also from God….but through creation, light was given to every creation according to its quantity, and the children of Israel must uncover the inner aliveness. This is what is meant by the verse "And it was on the eighth day"…. And this is the alive animal which you may eat but could it not also refer to the alive animal that you may not eat? It must be clear that all life comes from God, but the kosher animals come from the side of holiness, and these are called the life that can be eaten, whereas the forbidden animals are the ones for whom His will is that Israel not eat from them, and these are called the aliveness that we may not eat. That is because this aliveness comes from the "other side" (Sitra Achra), which is the side that we must reject. The honor of God is revealed by man's overcoming his desire for the other side, and this is His aliveness.[52]

Much of this passage echoes the themes that we have already commented on. But there is one significant addition here that essentially brings us to the point of this whole analysis. The Sefat Emet comments here that the direction of *care* that is specific and unique to the Jewish people by virtue of their being commanded by and obligated to observe the Torah is the equivalent of Shabbat in the dimension of humanity. If we apply the structure of *ashan* to this, we gain the following insight: In the same way that the temporality of Shabbat as the seventh day to which all days face reveals the underlying Shabbat that is the inner meaning of all time, and in the same way that the Mishkan represents the Shabbat of space that points to the inner meaning of all space as sacred space, the Jewish people in their ideal state of *being* or *care* (i.e., when they cleave to the Tree of Life) are the dimension of Shabbat in the overall consciousness of humanity. The Jewish people declare to the whole

---

52. Rabbi Yehuda Leib Alter of Gur, *Sefat Emet*, Parashat Shemini (5631).

of humanity by nature of the ontological activity that defines their collective identity that all human life is sacred. This brings us back to the text of the Havdalah with which we began. What is the meaning of the separation of the Jewish people from the nations of the earth? What is the justification of their chosenness? In the words of the Sefat Emet,

> The purpose of the Exodus from Egypt was to know that I am God (Da'at Hashem), as it says, "And you will know that I am God" (Exodus 6:7). This is why there is a separation (Havdalah), because the purpose of the Exodus was to heal the sin of the mixing of good and evil caused by eating from the Tree of Knowledge of Good and Evil…and there are distinctions between space, time, and soul, which is why the children of Israel are separated from the nations, as it says, "Between light and dark, between Israel and the nations."[53]

The structure of *ashan* is explicit here, most especially in the phrase "There are distinctions between space, time, and soul." In space the Mishkan is Shabbat. In time, the seventh day is Shabbat. In the soul, the soul of the children of Israel is Shabbat. All these Shabbatot are set aside as *signs* whose *being* is the *being* of *reference*. In their set-aside-ness they point to the underlying Shabbat in which all space, time, and humanity are reconciled to the Tree of Life. This is how beginning with separation leads to unity. This is the outer rim and ultimate purpose attributed by the inner Torah to the architecture of Segulah.

---

53. Rabbi Yehuda Leib Alter of Gur, *Sefat Emet*, Parashat Shemini (5658).

~

The State of Israel from the Perspective of Segulah

Returning to Our Initial Two Questions

In our prologue we began with the two key questions that Ze'ev Mankowitz (and of course many others) had identified as definitive of both twentieth-century Jewish history and the challenge of contemporary Jewish-identity education. He asked how the Holocaust was humanly possible and how the no-less-mysterious Zionist energy displayed by so many of its survivors was humanly possible too. As we draw our conclusions from the analysis that we have offered so far, we want to return to these questions, to show how we tried to tackle them throughout this book, and to consider the implications of our answers going forward.

Conventionally, the Holocaust and the establishment of the State of Israel are coupled in Zionist thought in a way that one can hear year after year in the speeches of Israel's presidents, prime ministers, and military chiefs of staff on Holocaust Remembrance Day. The message is that only the State of Israel, with its Jewish sovereignty, its army, its moral justification after the Holocaust, and the refuge it offers to the Jews of the world, can provide the assurance we need that Jews will "never again" be the passive and helpless victims of murderous persecution by another nation or faith. This message, which landed on the fertile ground of Zionism's reaction to modern antisemitism, became a staple part of Israel's meaning and moral justification for Jews and non-Jews alike. It was an essential part of the new contract that allowed Jews the world over to pick up the pieces of their shattered institutions and reassemble them in the postwar world order.

531

At the outset, we suggested that this message has grown thin. While the return to prominence of those who advocate the mass persecution of Jews is always a threat, the military and economic strength of the State of Israel seems to have accomplished its goal, and the vulnerability of Jews to this threat has indeed been significantly reduced. However, in the new world that emerged after 1945, the humanist liberalism of the postwar democracies, followed by the steady move from liberal nationalism to an individualistic liberal internationalism led many to draw more universalized conclusions from the Holocaust that did not always celebrate Israel's success. The new approach contextualized antisemitism alongside a long list of other evils that included all forms of persecution, racism, sexism, homophobia, colonialism, and occupation, and indeed the suppression or oppression of a whole range of ethnic and sexual identities, all of whom were served in the same way by the famous slogan "never again." As far as attitudes to the Jews were concerned, the State of Israel placed them on the side of the Goliaths and not of the Davids, and the possibility emerged that the lessons of the Holocaust could be marshaled against them and not only in their defense. As inconceivable as this may have seemed in 1945, this is a reality that has tightened the slack that the Jewish people were given by the rest of the world to pursue their own particularist concerns without facing accusations of indefensible and unethical ethnocentricism.

This is a challenge that faces Israel in the international arena, but it is one that also ironizes the separatist or particularist tendencies of Jewish identity anywhere in the world. Among its many results, the most disastrous from our perspective has been the demographic depletion of the Jewish population in the liberal West through cultural assimilation and intermarriage. Our argument has been that the paradigm of Survival and System that emerged after the Enlightenment and has continued to dominate Jewish life since 1945 has no real answer to this challenge. For the most part the answers that have been developed either contribute to the corrosive process itself or tend toward forms of Western conservativism that associate Jewish identity with the dark side of ethnocentric nationalism. This is what liberal Jews justifiably fear most, and when faced with a choice between this form of Western Judaism and perhaps less resilient forms of Jewish liberalism, they choose liberalism with its universalist (and hence "assimilationist") tendencies every time. In this impasse, the State of Israel has built and sought to defend the meaning of its Jewish identity in the modern world. But its strength, its ethnocentric nationalist identity, and the moral complexity of the Israeli-Palestinian conflict have made this immensely complicated.

In order to face these challenges, we have proposed what we referred to throughout this book as a paradigm shift from Survival and System to Segulah. One way of looking at this shift is to see it as part of the effort to reframe the meaning of the Holocaust/Israel copula. In this reframing, the Holocaust is seen as a call for the disentanglement of Jewish and Western identity so that a different relationship between these two civilizations can be established. In the paradigm of Segulah, this idea of disentanglement is connected to a profound shift in attitude toward the inner dimensions of the Torah. More specifically, our primary argument has been that the inner dimension of the Holocaust/Israel copula is made accessible by bringing together (through negation or inverse mirroring) the ontological Nazism of Heidegger's analytic of Dasein in *BT* and the inner onto-theological dimensions of the Torah. We argued at length that despite Heidegger's Nazism, the philosophical portrayal of the self in *BT* should be taken very seriously. Returning to Mankowitz's first question, we suggested that essentially *BT* takes us on a remarkable journey through the inner landscape of the human psyche to a point at which the idea that the Holocaust was and always has been humanly possible seems eminently plausible. Regarding the second question, we noted the significance of a steady process that has gradually brought the inner dimensions of the Torah closer to the surface. Mysterious and esoteric as they are, their plausibility is emerging into view, and along with this we can begin to glimpse an understanding of the inner consciousness of the Jewish collective that explains the no less remarkable Zionist energy displayed by so many – survivors and others – after the Holocaust. In this concluding chapter we shall try to wrap up everything that we have said so far about the inner and outer dimensions of the Holocaust/Israel copula in order to make the meaning of our proposed answer to Mankowitz's second question a little more explicit.

Galut, Churban and the History of Mentality

As we have said, in our reframing of the Holocaust/Israel copula these events have both an inner and an outer dimension. In this model, major events that occur on the outside are linked to – perhaps caused by or cause – internal processes in which human consciousness is reconfigured. These two dimensions are inseparable. Whatever happens on one will always have implications for the other, and lessons learned in each must be applied to both.

The idea that history traces the internal processes of how human consciousness has evolved over time is not a new one. It was perhaps most famously articulated by the Annales school of European medievalists such as Marc Bloch and Lucien Febvre, who argued that the study of the past requires historians to reconstruct the mentality of the people who lived in the past.[1] The historians of the Annales school asked how scholars can choose between factual and unreliable historical sources when the medieval authors on whom they rely make no distinctions between their accounts of battles or political treaties and the influences of pixies, demons and sorcerers. They insisted that the only way historians can understand the events that took place in the past is to reconstruct the mentalities of the human beings upon whose accounts they depend. This method was called the "history of mentality" and it clearly rests on the methodological assumption that at different periods across time, the mental perceptions of reality that people have do not stay the same. As such, historians must come to terms with the idea that in different spatial and temporal contexts, human consciousness of the world can and does change.

If the calibration of human consciousness is something that does not stay the same, it is clear why religion, philosophy, psychology, physics, biology, and many other disciplines have all asked for generations whether or not there is an authentic or desirable state in which people can see the truth about the world and/or know enough of that truth to achieve happiness. If there is such a human state, then surely we must ask whether history is

---

1.   The term "Annales school" refers to the historians who contributed to the journal *Annales d'histoire economique et sociale*, which was founded by Marc Bloch and Lucien Febvre in 1946. Examples of this approach to historiography in other publications include Marc Bloch, *The Historian's Craft* (New York, 1953); Bloch, *The Royal Touch*, English translation (London, 1973); and Bloch, *Feudal Society*, English translation (London: Routledge, 1961); J. Huizinga, *The Waning of the Middle Ages: A Study of the Forms of Life, Thought and Art in France and the Netherlands in the XIVth and XVth Centuries* (New York, 1969) [Leiden 1924]; Aron Gurevitch, *Medieval Popular Culture: Problems of Belief and Perception*, translated from Russian by J. M. Bak and P. A. Hollingsworth (New York, 1990); P. Aries, *Childhood* (New York, 1980); and J. Le Goff, *Time* (Chicago, 1980).

indeed moving toward it. What can we do, if anything, to get there? More particularly, what does this mean for the evolution of Jewish identity and the different ways in which the Torah has been understood across Jewish history?

The history that we have told in this book is essentially an attempt to overcome the challenges and obstacles posed by post-Enlightenment consciousness to the accomplishment of the inner transformation that the Torah proposes. We discussed Kant and others who believed that the truth about the world was to be found in rational consciousness and that this was almost self-evident in the scientific breakthroughs of their time. Kant cemented what we referred to as the victory of epistemology over ontology and essentially provided the philosophical foundations and arguments that explained how human consciousness could be calibrated to recognize not only truth but also morality, peace, prosperity, and happiness at the pole of the object.

Kant's articulations of this vision acknowledged that the natural state of human consciousness was not rational. As such, when people look at the world, they do not naturally see what science or reason tells them is true. Similarly, their natural inclinations do not necessarily steer them toward morality, peace, or justice. But Kant and the other humanist philosophers and theorists of the Enlightenment argued that rational, scientific consciousness is something that can be learned by all human beings, and though the path is long, the effort to attain the rule of reason on a global scale can ultimately succeed. When this happens, the world will know peace, truth, morality, justice, and progress. Arguably, Kant's essay "Perpetual Peace"[2] offered the first systematic articulation of the modern order of international politics that saw the world divided into republics and centralized nation-states with dealings between them. From Kant's perspective, this order was designed to cultivate rational consciousness and reward reasonable behavior, thus improving the lives of all citizens who live in states on a global scale. The object was to use the power provided by the state to cultivate an international benevolent civil consciousness through state-controlled institutions of governance, law, education, culture and economics for the benefit of all. Aligning Jewish life

---

2.   Immanuel Kant, "Perpetual Peace: A Philosophical Sketch," in H. Reiss, ed., *Kant's Political Writings*, 2nd ed., trans. H. B. Nisbet (Cambridge: Cambridge University Press, 1991).

with this worldview is the key project of Survival and System, and this was the context in which the modern idea of establishing a Jewish state emerged.

In our discussion of Galut, we looked at reactions to this worldview that essentially came to rein in the Enlightenment's ambitions but without offering any alternative to them. What these reactions do is to call into question the basic idea that rational consciousness is indeed a stable state of mind. They do this by underlining the ironic dependence of rationalism on power that maintaining a stable society in this unstable state of consciousness requires. We can divide our discussion of this point into four subgroups:

The first subgroup was made up of psychologists such as Daniel Kahneman and Jonathan Haidt, each of whom in his own way called into question the viability of the Enlightenment's claim that human behavior can be dominated by rational consciousness. We looked at the different ways in which they configured the relationships between what Kahneman called System 1 and System 2 and what Haidt referred to as the elephant and the rider. We saw that while the possibility of scientific rational thought is certainly a human capability, the likelihood of society achieving its dominance over human decision making and moral conduct is extremely low, while the project itself carries undesirable consequences. For example, we saw how rationalism comes to defend conclusions that have already been reached but which were not conceived rationally. Thus, the ex post facto rationalizations that we provide for our intuitions function more often as weapons in a conflict than they do as a mechanism for reaching true peace.

In the second subgroup we included a range of Jewish thinkers such as George Steiner, Hannah Arendt, Theodor Adorno, Max Horkheimer, Ernst Cassirer, Abraham Joshua Heschel, and others who experienced the Holocaust as a definitive failure of the Enlightenment's claims about the benefits of rational consciousness. In different ways they reacted to the World Wars and the Holocaust, seeing them as grounds for retracting (or selectively retracting) the faith that had been put in the mythologies and institutions of the modern consciousness. Though the conclusions drawn by most if not all the members of this group were far from Zionist, this school of thought is one that can be compared to political Zionism's basic claim that post-Enlightenment antisemitism is a flaw in the system that proves that Jews can no longer live at the mercy of others and therefore need a Jewish state of their own.

Our third subgroup comprises predominantly Christian religious thinkers such as William Cavanaugh and Charles Taylor, who called into question the legitimacy of rational humanism's imposition of secularism on the institutions of public life. Taylor calls our attention to the deconstructive role of religion, placing a great deal of value on a kind of awareness that he calls "beyond life." Cavanaugh underlines the irony of how scientific rationalism surpassed religion by declaring war on it. Perhaps one might suggest that this argument can be connected to the post-colonial critique that sees the world dominance of the rationalist mindset as the product of the unprecedented political, military, economic, and technological advances that enabled the Western world to force its preferred mentality upon others (sometimes and in some places at the expense of millions of human lives).[3]

In our fourth subgroup we focused on Michel Foucault, Jacques Derrida, and Bruno Latour. We saw them as indicative of a much wider range of thinkers, all of whom might be seen as the pioneers and practitioners of "deconstruction." In our analysis, we distinguished between two forms of deconstruction that we dubbed "Deconstruction" and "De-con-struction." We did this to highlight what we see as the two genealogies of the approach that these thinkers adopted to the Enlightenment's ideal of rational consciousness. The first, "Deconstruction," is grounded in Ludwig Wittgenstein and in his warning that the truth claims of rational thought cannot be considered universally valid because they are not compatible with the way in which human beings use language. Given this, the whole project of rationalist philosophy that seeks to describe the world "truthfully" is valid only to the extent that it fits with the way in which language relates to the world. Henceforth, if the foundations of language and its connection to meaning cannot be explained rationally, language itself must be used to destabilize and expose the exaggerated ambitions and truth claims of rational thought rather than to support and ground them.

---

3. The extent of this phenomenon is documented by Adam Jones in his book *Genocide: A Comprehensive Introduction*, 2nd ed. (Routledge, 2010). See in particular part 2, "Genocides of Indigenous Peoples."

"De-con-struction" was our name for the aspect of deconstruction that is basically a reaction to Heidegger. Heidegger's critique of the Enlightenment was that the rational consciousness that it proposed was grounded in an inauthentic perception of the self that is therefore unstable. Foucault, Derrida, and others basically accepted this idea but, as opposed to Heidegger in *BT*, they distrusted Heidegger's ambitions. De-con-struction therefore acknowledges the inauthenticity of rational consciousness while trying to prevent Dasein from attaining the authentic state that Heidegger considered its true form. They offered the method of deconstruction to maintain an admittedly unstable sense of permanently vigilant deconstructive skepticism, which they preferred to the horrors that they believed Heidegger's notion of authentic Dasein would inevitably unleash.

What all these positions share is an insistence on the idea that the rational consciousness proposed by the Enlightenment could not live up to the ambitions that the philosophers, scientists, and political theorists of the "age of reason" had pinned on it. It is at this point that we saw an opportunity for reversing the devastating effects of this consciousness on our ability as Jews to discover the meaning of the Torah. We saw our chance for moving forward in the inner dimension of the Holocaust/Israel copula and in the tools that it gives us for rehabilitating the perspective of Segulah.

Our primary argument here was that having an answer to the question of how the Holocaust was humanly possible is essential to the inner understanding of the self, because the external history is an inner event in the evolutionary history of human self-understanding. Moreover, we argued that feeding this understanding into the Holocaust/Israel copula might uncover the inner meaning of the inexplicable forces that brought about the establishment of the Jewish state. In this inner copula, what is disclosed in *BT* is a gateway to a lost dimension of human historical consciousness that corresponds inversely but very precisely to a dimension of the Torah that Rabbi Kook referred to as the Torah of the land of Israel (or the inner Torah). In this framing, the external events are *signs* or *referents* in the ontological sense that point inward. What remains is for us to say more about the inner mentality that the Jewish return to the land of Israel represents so that we may see more about how the dimension of Torah that it reveals points the way forward for Jewish history and the State of Israel.

Inside Out or Outside In

As the possibility of establishing a Jewish state in the land of Israel began to take form on the stage of history, there were those like Rabbi Yehuda Ashlag, who cautioned that the inner drama of Rehabilitation must be complete before its external expressions could take a healthy form. Rabbi Ashlag argued that only after a cosmic peace between the human Nefesh and the Neshamah had been secured could the people establish Jewish sovereignty in the land.[4] Indeed, this was perhaps the argument that in many different forms and articulations moved most of the Orthodox establishment to express their vehement opposition to the Zionist idea.[5] This path is the one that insists that Rehabilitation must take place from the "inside out."

Conversely, the Gaon of Vilna and later Rabbi Kook suggested that Rehabilitation can also take place from the outside in. Rabbi Kook, who lived in the era of Zionism, envisioned a path to Rehabilitation that began with the secular Zionist movement that he saw around him. He identified the inner or hidden dimensions of history,[6] and saw the light of the Neshamah shining in secular Zionism crowning the institutions of the emerging secular state with sacred status. His spiritual vision began with the political and cultural accomplishments of secular Zionism on the stage of history. In his eyes

---

4.   Rabbi Yehuda Ashlag, *On World Peace: Two Essays by the Holy Kabbalist Rabbi Yehuda Ashlag*, ed. Michael Berg (Kabbalah Centre, 2012).

5.   Ultra-Orthodox opposition to Zionism is a broadly documented and studied phenomenon. Perhaps the most influential attack on Zionism written during the formative years of the State of Israel's history was composed by the leader of the Satmar Hasidic court, Rabbi Yoel Teitelbaum. The treatise, entitled *Vayoel Moshe* [Hebrew], published in 1961, cites the ways in which Zionism is both a violation of Talmudic law and a crime against the well-being of the Jewish people. See Aviezer Ravitzky, "Munkacs and Jerusalem: Ultra-Orthodox Opposition to Zionism and Agudaism," in *Zionism and Religion*, ed. Shmuel Almog, Jehuda Reinharz, and Anita Shapira (Hanover, 1998), 67–89.

6.   It is interesting to note that in all his writings, Rabbi Kook spells history (*historia* in Hebrew) using the letter *tav* instead of the more common spelling with the letter *tet*. This spelling connects the word *historia* with the three-letter root *samekh, tav, reish*, which spells *seter*, meaning hidden or secret and is synonymous with the concept of *sod*. In this way, Rabbi Kook suggests that history is the unfolding of the dimension of *sod*. See, for example, Yosef Avivi, "History for the Sake of Heaven," in Moshe Bar-Asher, ed., *Jubilee Volume in Honor of Mordechai Breuer: Articles in Jewish Studies* (Jerusalem: Akademon, 1992), 709–71 and Ronen Lubitch, "The Concept of History in Rabbi Kook's Writings" (Jerusalem: Yeshuat Uzzo, 1996), 413–36 [Hebrew].

these were the body and Nefesh of the Jewish people, and it was the secular Zionists who were bringing them back to life. Only afterward would these be filled with the ownmost awareness of the Ruach and Neshamah that by their very nature were *always already* there. Famously, he referred to these two stages as two messianic eras. The first was the era of Mashiach Ben Yosef (outside); the second would be that of Mashiach Ben David (inside).[7]

If we accept that the history of the State of Israel is indeed only the outside of something internal, the question is: How is Israel's internal dimension to be discovered? And if we have no answer, is it possible that Zionism lacks the ability to discover the light that is supposed to shine from the land of Israel when the Jewish people return to it?

There are of course those who argue that this light is shining all the time. And in many ways, they are right. Israel is an incredible country. Its accomplishments in so many fields of life are breathtaking. From agriculture to science, from business and technology to culture and of course security, Israel is a shining beacon. In all this Rabbi Kook might well have seen the *always-already*-ness of the Neshamah in action. But Israel is so many other less desirable things as well. Is the land of cherry tomatoes and start-ups that claims with pride to be the only Western democracy in the Middle East enough for those who yearn for the light to shine? Is this enough for the world? If not, is there a way forward, or have we reached a dead end?

Outside In from the Perspective of Survival and System

The possibility that we are knocking on a door with no key to open it is perhaps reinforced by many of the ways in which the religious Zionist community in Israel has sought to achieve its spiritual goals from the outside in. After all that we have written thus far, we hope we may be forgiven for simplifying matters and painting the picture of this in very general terms alone. Broadly speaking, then, we might say that Rabbi Kook's response to Zionism can be characterized by three distinctive efforts on his part. The first was his effort to be the rabbi of the secular Zionists; to embrace them, to challenge them,

---

7.   This distinction is central to the eulogy that Rabbi Kook delivered for Herzl in 1904. For a full version of this text and a detailed analysis of it, see Rabbi Yehuda Leon Ashkenazi (Manitou), *A Eulogy for the Messiah?!*, ed. Israel Pivko, Itai Ashkenazi, and Elyakim Simsovic (Bet-El: Chava, 2006) [Hebrew].

and to be part of the momentous enterprise in which they were engaged. The second was to provide the infrastructure in institutional, ideological, and halachic terms for religious Jews to play a part in the process of rebuilding the land of Israel and the Jewish state. The third was to discover, write, and teach the unique Torah that he referred to as the Torah of the land of Israel. This Torah, which he described as deeply embedded in the collective soul of Israel, is the spiritual wind that plays the fourfold song of Havayah on the strings of David's lyre.[8] This Torah is the light that shines from the land of Israel to the world, and Rabbi Kook could see it when others could not – even if in his time the light was only a glimmer. The Torah of the land of Israel is the inner Torah that can shine bright from the land only when the people return to it. But when it shines it is a fountain of living water that invigorates the Torah itself and the inner soul of Israel's national spirit. Broadly speaking, the first two of these can be connected to Rabbi Kook's image of how the redemption will take place from the outside in. Our argument is that the third cannot.

In the early years of the state, the relatively small community of those religious Zionists who saw themselves as Rabbi Kook's disciples sought to build a bridge between the world of Torah and the world of Israel's predominantly secular politics by participating in public life, sharing the national burden, and serving in the military. On the outside, they were fully integrated, but as a community they had their own spiritual ambitions which – perhaps because of their small size or on account of their proximity to Rabbi Kook' s lifetime – they kept far away from power politics. They cultivated their own institutions, collaborated with the secular majority, and perhaps anticipated the day when the example they set would turn the hearts of others to the Torah. When this effort seemed hopelessly defeated by the internal divisions that followed the Six-Day War, the Yom Kippur War, the peace with Egypt, the Oslo Accords, and the disengagement from Gaza, the strategy gradually changed. In the late sixties and early seventies, settlement in the West Bank/ Judea and Samaria afforded the national religious community an opportunity to cultivate more of the holy land, but it also created a new sociological reality which enabled them to further consolidate the inner strength of their

---

8.   See Rabbi Kook, *Lights of Holiness*, vol. 2, 444–45, and *Eight Collections*, 7:112 [Hebrew].

communal and political identity. Moreover, opposition to the withdrawal from Sinai, the Oslo Accords, and the disengagement from Gaza lent clarity to their political platform, which was now firmly saddled to the political effort to settle the land and strengthen the Jewish identity of the state's institutional commitments.

High birth rates, a robust education system, clearer political and economic platforms, and an increased effort to attain political influence were aided by an overall shift to the right in Israeli politics which placed the national religious political leadership inside a succession of coalition governments that were already tied to the accommodation of ultra-Orthodox religious interests. This constellation afforded the right wing of the national religious community the opportunity to influence the constitution and cultural identity of the secular state through prominence in the army, the press, the legal system, and the Knesset. They were now able to begin the process of institutionalizing their alternative to the progressively universalist liberal tendencies of the secular left.

Our argument is that as long as the method for implementing the strategy of spiritual and religious Rehabilitation from the outside in belongs to the paradigm of Survival and System, this path will inevitably lead to a dead end. As long as it is implemented with the use of power and amid controversy, even if the ideas and dreams that fuel the energy of this path are rooted in the teachings of the inner Torah, when they are translated into political strategies and policy proposals they cannot have their desired effect. Even where the deepest dimensions of the Torah are truly understood, they lose their luster the moment the strategy for their dissemination becomes mixed with the anxiety-ridden selfhood of Dasein's yearnings for authenticity.

A common solution to this problem is the separation of religion and state. And this has indeed been advocated not only by the secular liberal camp in Israel but also by many significant figures within the religious community. This is indeed the solution offered by the paradigm of post-Enlightenment humanism and – as we saw in our reading of Cavanaugh – what it means is the separation of the outside from the inside and the exclusion of religious concerns from the public sphere. It goes without saying that this is not what we are advocating, since it contradicts our basic premise, which – as we have said on numerous occasions – is modeled on the inevitable interrelationship between *peshat* and *sod*. What we wish to propose is a path ahead for Segulah that lies in the recognition that we have reached a point where rehabilitating the Torah of the land of Israel requires us to work from the inside out. The institutions of the state cannot be used for this process because they are the children of the wrong paradigm. But they must not be threatened or undermined by it until such time as the paradigm of Segulah is truly ready to emerge from its shell.

Cracks in the Shell

Before we can say more about what needs to be done from the inside out, we need to observe the processes that suggest we are indeed reaching a point in time when the effort to rehabilitate the Torah of the land of Israel has a chance of success. If we look at the demographic trends of the last hundred years, the underlying ideology of Survival and System is that Western liberal, progressive, democratic societies are the ones in which Jews will most naturally prosper. This is evidenced by the fact that the vast majority of the Jews in the world today live in liberal democracies such as Israel, the United States, France, Canada, and the United Kingdom. Beyond the questions we have already raised about the philosophical viability of this, we seem now to be living through remarkable processes of historical change that are opening up cracks in the shell of this ideology that create new opportunities for the paradigm of Segulah to emerge into view. The first signs of these cracks have been visible on the surface for decades, and we do not presume to know how they will develop. That said, at the time of writing there is definitely a sense that we are living through the tremors of a subterranean tectonic shift in the Western world, the meaning of which we wish to incorporate into our ontological analysis of the relationship between Survival and System and Segulah.

The international politics upon which the Jewish paradigm of Survival and System depends seems to be going through an alarming period of instability that is connected to our understanding of the Holocaust/Israel copula. Following our reading of *BT*, we can reframe Nazism's pathological hatred of the Jews as a result of the belief that the Jews – for a whole range of twisted reasons – were the ultimate promulgators of inauthenticity. From conspiracy theories about clandestine Jewish global domination to claims about the

Jewish bourgeoisie's detachment from their grounding in soil and purity of blood, the Jews were identified as a demoralizing and contaminating force that posed an existential threat to the German Volk's chances of fulfilling its historical destiny in authenticity. Given this, we propose that Nazism should primarily be understood as a cultural and political revolution against the inauthenticity of the Enlightenment's portrayal of the self.

When viewed in this way it becomes clear that despite the extraordinary opportunities that the postwar liberal regimes opened up for Jews, they are not a remedy for the human ontological aspirations that Nazism expressed. In fact, they do little more than put the genie (i.e., Dasein's suppressed desire for authenticity) back in the bottle. As we argued at length, the Deconstruction that followed the Holocaust provides no stable alternative to inauthenticity, while it is beyond the power of De-con-struction to maintain its deliberately inauthentic self-awareness over time. One way or another, authentic Dasein inevitably seeks to "break out."

What we called "cracks in the shell" more specifically refer to the crisis with inauthenticity that is coming back. We are living in a time in which Dasein is struggling with itself. There is no new Hitler on the horizon, and the primary expressions of this crisis are not necessarily antisemitic (though some of them undoubtedly are). But what we can see is a slow and complex shift from a veneer of stability to a disclosed instability in Western politics which in our view is an event in the post-Holocaust history of Dasein. On the "outside," this instability seems to be caused by the inability of democratic regimes to deal with the vast array of competing identities that live within them. Governments have a hard time representing the people when the rival interests of citizens are so complex. The frustration that this has caused has destabilized the balance between the executive, legislative, and judiciary branches of government as well as the contract with the electorate and the press. This has been further exasperated by the economic instability that governments have inflicted upon their own populations as a result of the COVID-19 pandemic. The struggle for power between the populations and institutions of the state is taking place in multiple settings all over the Western world. The United States, the United Kingdom, France, Germany, Hungary, Austria, Spain, and Israel are each examples of this in their own way.[9] Mark Blyth has eloquently explained why the polarization between the liberal left and the conservative right in each of these countries is characterized by a kind of antiestablishment tendency which he argues is calling into question the viability of the political and economic system itself.[10] In his opinion this is why more and more people cast protest votes against establishment interests instead of voting for their own beliefs. It is this turn in voting trends that accounts for the election of a man with no political experience to the presidency of the United States in 2016 and for the British decision to exit the European Union in the same year. Similar protests can be traced in the surge of support for Marie Le Pen in France, for Viktor Orban in Hungary, the AFD in Germany, the Golden Dawn in Greece, the Vox party in Spain, and others.[11]

This instability is not caused solely by the populist right. The shift to the right is counterbalanced by the rise of ultraliberal lobbies and parties and by the general polarization of political systems that are moving into chronic situations of political deadlock.[12] A cursory summary of the literature that has documented this process is characterized by book titles like A. C. Grayling's *Democracy and Its Crisis*,[13] David Runciman's *How Democracy Ends*,[14] and John J. Mearsheimer's *The Great Delusion: Liberal Dreams and International*

---

9.   These are processes that have been portrayed in multiple studies by the Scottish American political scientist Mark Blyth, beginning with his *Great Transformations: Economic Ideas and Institutional Change in the Twentieth Century* (Cambridge University Press, 2002) and his book coauthored with Eric Lonergan, *Angrynomics* (Cambridge University Press, 2020).

10. See Mark Blyth, *Austerity: The History of a Dangerous Idea* (Oxford University Press, 2012).

11. See Blyth and Lonergan, *Angrynomics,* "Dialogue 1: 'Public Anger and the Energy of the Tribes.'"

12. Consider, for example, the protracted instability in British politics following the decision to leave the EU in 2016, which included a parliamentary stalemate that was resolved only by the third in a rapid succession of general elections in May 2015, June 2017, and December 2019. Under different circumstances and for different reasons, Israel experienced a similar record of instability, when voters went to the polls in a general election three times between April 2019 and March 2020.

13. A. C. Grayling, *Democracy and Its Crisis*, updated edition (One World Publishing, 2018).

14. David Runciman, *How Democracy Ends* (Profile Books, 2018).

Realities.[15] In each case the overwhelming message is that liberal democracy is in crisis and it needs somehow to be salvaged.

From the outside there is much to be feared in all of this political dysfunction, and as we have repeatedly said, it is not our intention to undermine democracy or to promote any kind of antidemocratic behavior that might agitate the situation and make it worse. We are interested in looking at what this process can tell us about the work that needs to be done from the inside out. We want to suggest that the Western world, the Jewish world, and indeed the State of Israel are all polarized by political identity conflicts that are ontological in their nature. Divisions between the left and the right, between liberals and conservatives, religious and secular, globalists and nationalists, etc., appear to be the historical externalization of an inner conflict between two acute forms of ontological anxiety. Conservatives fear the endless exile in inauthenticity that deconstruction has imposed upon them. They openly and vocally struggle against the cultural, moral, and epistemological relativism that constantly moves the goalposts of legitimate social norms further and further away from the *world* that they (perhaps anachronistically) think of as traditional and authentic. They are on the move in a concerted effort to shake off the hegemony of inauthenticity and confine the boundaries of Dasein's *concern* to the concrete boundaries of its interactions. Consequently, their political rhetoric oozes with authentic Dasein's yearning to break out of inauthenticity, as is evidenced by such phrases as "taking back control" and "making America great again."[16] To this worldview, global concerns are less important than local ones, and developments such as nuclear proliferation or the pollution of the planet are not seen as the primary causes of political anxiety. Global concerns of this sort are easier to dismiss when the trade-off is economic or military strength, the benefits of which are felt much closer to home.

On the other hand, Liberals fear the essentialist, nationalist, decisionist, militarist, ethnocentric ambitions of authentic Dasein and seek a way

---

15. John J. Mearsheimer, *The Great Delusion: Liberal Dreams and International Realities* (Yale University Press, 2018).

16. "Taking Back Control" was the slogan of the "leave" campaign leading up to the Brexit vote in 2016, while "Make America Great Again" (similar to "Let's Make America Great Again," used by Ronald Reagan in 1980) was the slogan of Donald Trump's election campaign in 2016.

forward by evolving Dasein's *they-self* into a being whose sense of *being-with* assumes global proportions. The energies of everydayness have constructed a global economic community that consciously barricades Dasein from its ambitions of authenticity by permanently bombarding its *care* and attention with moral claims that lie beyond the confines of its perceived selfhood. Every form of "otherness" that is compliant with an expansive and progressively hybrid ideal of the *they* is absorbed within the network of concerns that struggles against the regressive forces of authentic Dasein, saturating its sense of self with seemingly boundless new *cares* that deconstruct its capacity to believe that its ownmost authenticity is still within its reach. This is De-con-struction at work as the dominant moral force in the ultraliberal left.

While the enmity between these two competing forms of existential anxiety is playing out in a political conflict that is characterized by polarization and exacerbated by fear, in Heidegger's analysis, inauthentic and authentic Dasein are only ever two sides of the same coin. Though the lobbies for and against nuclear weapons, climate change, and globalism compete with each other on the surface, as events within Dasein, its fantasies about the kind of power that can ensure its ability to *be* – whether this is achieved through military arsenals or the possibility of implanting artificially intelligent prosthetics in the human brain[17] – hail from the same source. The *being-in-the-world* of Dasein's spatial and temporal devouring self in both of its forms is seeking to harness the political and economic power of the entire network of international politics in the direction of conflicting existential concerns. By pulling it to and fro, it is causing the shell to crack in ways that recall the words of Rabbi Kook:

> In Mashiach Ben Yosef, the particularly Jewish nationalism is revealed. However, the final goal is not seclusion into national

---

17. The futuristic warning that the combination of nanobiotechnology and artificial intelligence is likely to create a bigger gap between humanity as we know it today and humanity in thirty years' time than the gap between human beings today and chimpanzees has famously been promoted by the historian Yuval Noah Harari in his best-selling book *Sapiens: A Brief History of Humankind* (London: Vintage Books, 2011), 453–66.

peculiarity but unification of the world's creations into one family for all to invoke the name of God. And by the time the world moves from centering upon the national toward the common goal, there will be a destruction of the thing that took root during the phase of limited nationalism, the nationalism that is full of the ills of selfishness. This is the reason Mashiach Ben Yosef is predestined to be killed and that the genuine, lasting realm will be that of Mashiach Ben David.[18]

In our analysis the individualized universalism of everyday Dasein and the collectivist, self-based nationalism of authentic Dasein are one. Together they represent the selfishness or self-ness that Rabbi Kook attributes to the collective identity of Mashiach Ben Yosef. The struggle that we are witnessing today is essentially the internal struggle of the ego and its ownmost self-ness that is in Rabbi Kook's words "the destruction of the thing that took root during the phase of limited nationalism." It is this struggle that is cracking the shell of the postwar world order and of the Judaism of Survival and System that depends on it. As if things weren't shifting fast enough, the coronavirus has acted as a catalyst that shifted the pace of this process up a gear. It is significant that this Western struggle is just as obvious inside the State of Israel, which on the surface appears to be no different from anywhere else. The shift toward globalism is cracking the shell of Israel's nationalism, and the question is whether Israel indeed has a unique inner dimension that, if illuminated, can point the way forward – not only for the Jewish people but for the whole world.

With the cracking of this shell, the plausibility of its alternatives can perhaps begin to emerge. On the outside, the possibility of a new international political system has yet to appear. But, on the inside, postmodernism's uncertainty about modernist rationalism has certainly precipitated new sentiments about the vitality of religious faith, its inclusion in the public sphere, and the viability of non-rational human perception.[19] Popular culture is saturated

---

18. Rabbi Kook, "The Lights of Israel," in *Orot* (Mossad HaRav Kook, 2005 ed.), 150 [Hebrew].

19. See, for example, John Micklewait and Adrian Wooldridge, *God Is Back: How the Global Revival of Faith Is Changing the World* (Penguin, 2009).

with fantasy, superheroes, magicians, and hyper-evolved human beings with telepathic, telekinetic, and other capabilities. Human imagination and science seem to be pushing us in the direction of Taylor's "beyond humanity" toward an era in which human beings as we know them will have capabilities that we can only imagine today. While many of these imaginings are horrific and monstrous, from the perspective of Segulah there is a repressed *always already*-ness about them that, put biblically, points to a human desire to regain access to the capabilities that Adam willfully suppressed when he chose to fuel human history with the mortally anxious energy that grew on the Tree of Knowledge.[20]

Similarly (though perhaps not obviously so), Jews all over the world seem to harbor a kind of irrational anxiety about antisemitism even where there is no real threat to Jewish life. The idea that the State of Israel is a safe haven that they will need some day in the future has been compelling for many since 1948 and even before. What we want to show is that these sentiments disclose the answer to Mankowitz's second question. We want to suggest that in this underlying feeling of insecurity there is a repressed *always-already*-ness that, put simply, points to a Jewish desire to return to the land in order to transcend the boundaries imposed upon humanity by the fruit of the wrong tree. This is a desire that active integration and assimilation, Survival and System, and indeed the politics of the State of Israel as they appear on the surface all repress very powerfully. With the cracking of this shell, the idea that the desire to evolve beyond humanity as we know it and the desire to return to the land are one and the same is the one that the journey from the inside out must make plausible.

The Politics of Tikkun Olam

So far our discussion of Rehabilitation has introduced us to the fundamental principles of the architecture of Segulah. We argued at length that the fundamental flaw of the politics of Survival and System is its lack of awareness or denial of the inner dimension of *being* that transcends the body and the

---

20. This is a reference to the kabbalistic understanding of Adam's sin in the Garden of Eden that sees the choice as one of profane technology or humanly wielded power over the choice to be aligned with divine *being* that is represented by the Tree of Knowledge. This idea is summarized by Avraham Sutton in *Spiritual Technology*, 41–56.

Nefesh and reaches inward to the Neshamah. Since the body and the Nefesh are the everyday ways in which we experience ourselves, this flaw presents a formidable challenge to those who would overcome it, since the very plausibility of Segulah's most basic premise – the existence of the Neshamah that bears witness to Havayah – is in question.

Using the terminology that Heidegger developed in order to map the horizons of Dasein's *with-world*, we have sought to portray an inner world that lies beyond the self-knowledge of Dasein's anxious *being*. We argued that when viewed from the ontic philosophy that Heidegger "destroys" in *BT* (the perspective upon which the Judaism of Survival and System is predicated), the inner dimension of the Torah should carry little appeal. It appears to be little more than a mythological world that one can enter only with a Kierkegaardian leap of faith. If it exists at all, it lies beyond the boundaries of Kantian phenomena and as such only the "will to believe"[21] and "practical reason"[22] (that measures and depends upon the utilitarian benefits of the enterprise but not on its intrinsic value) can justify the efforts and indulgences that the mastery of its landscape requires. When viewed ontically, this inner world is under water, out of reach, covered over by Structures of Concealment that keep it in a state of Galut.

Using the imaginative and creative capacities (which, in addition to rationalism, phenomenology recognizes are central to our self-awareness) in order to peer through the cracks in the shell of Klippat Yavan, we have sought to grasp the reality of this inner world, portraying it as an imminent onto-theological system that can be experienced plausibly because it emanates from a dimension of human consciousness that the Torah actually makes accessible. As the Jewish people return from Galut to the land of Israel in the great drama of history, Galut itself is deconstructing the conceptual constraints that block the door, like a spinning sword, to the inner Garden where the Tree of Life awaits. On the level of the macrocosm, the ongoing impact of the Holocaust points to the destruction of "selfish nationalism" that casts off the shell of Galut. On the inner level, this Churban is the lesson that we

---

21. William James, *The Will to Believe and Other Essays in Popular Philosophy* (New York: Dover, 1956).

22. Immanuel Kant, *Critique of Practical Reason* (1788), trans. Mary Gregor (Cambridge, 1997).

have tried to learn by reading Heidegger from the perspective of Segulah. The lesson – which once again we saw in the teachings of Rabbi Kook – is that the body and the Nefesh must despair of their desire to *be a self* in order to glimpse the way that leads beyond them.[23] What lies beyond is a different kind of politics, a spiritual collectivism that must be built, not from the outside in but only from the inside out. We referred to this system as the politics of Tikkun Olam.

The central characteristic of this system is that its institutions are *signs* and *referents* rather than holders of power. In the ontological sense that we discussed in our analysis of the Mishkan's symbolism, these *signs* or *referents* are not arbitrary. Rather, they are "set up in a definite way with a view toward easy accessibility."[24] The *sign* makes Dasein's *being-in-the-world* accessible, while the *sign* itself is a specific *referent* that gives access to the potentiality of *being* that Dasein discovers in it. Thus, the *sign* has a pointing capacity somewhat like that of a mirror in which Dasein sees a reflection of its *being* in the mode of *being* that the *sign* specifically discloses.

According to the system of thought that underpins the politics of Tikkun Olam, the disclosure of Dasein's *with-world* as an expression of the mode of *being* of Havayah is made accessible by what we referred to as the architectural structure of Segulah. The shape of this architectural structure is like a blueprint that allows the inner structure of Tzelem Elohim to align. This is because the same shape characterizes all the *signs* and *referents* of the Torah and its mitzvot. It is therefore recognizable to (i.e., can be aligned with) the structure of Tzelem Elohim in the state of conscious *being* that we have referred to variously as Devekut, Da'at Hashem, and Gadlut. This state corresponds to the inner level of the structure of *ashan* in which the matrix of human self-conscious *being*, spatial *being*, and temporal *being* are all aligned with or oriented toward (Kavanah) the total *being* of Havayah.

The highest or innermost level of this structure is represented in the Torah by the numbers 8 and 50. These numbers, which can be broken down into 7+1 or 7x7+1, disclose a dimension in space, time, and human consciousness that lies beyond our regular experience of *being* on the level of the

---

23. This is a reference to the theme of "generality," or *klaliut*, discussed in chapter 16 (above).
24. Heidegger, *BT*, 79.

Nefesh. As we have discussed at length, this structure is called Shabbat, and it applies to spatiality, temporality, and the Neshamah. In this structure the seventh day of the week "is a *sign* of Olam,"[25] i.e., of the concealed infinite dimension of time, space, and consciousness that are a totality of *being*. All being as we know it is therefore a constricted or reduced version of this whole that is Havayah. In time Shabbat is potentially a *referent* or a gateway to the eighth day which, as we saw in the *Sefat Emet*, is an "inner point" that shows how all the days of the week combine in an inner unity that *is* all of them. The seventh week of the Omer[26] (the counting of which starts "on the day after the Shabbat,"[27] i.e., 7 +1) is also potentially a *referent* and gateway to the beginning of an eighth week – a time in which the Torah is received – that represents the inner unity of all weeks (Shavuot).[28] Finally, the seventh year of the cycle of Shemittah is potentially a *referent* and a gateway to an eighth Shemittah or Jubilee year that represents the underlying unity of all years. This temporal structure is closely connected to the people and the land of Israel, first because the Omer, Shemittah, and Jubilee are observed only by the people in the land but also because the land of Israel, the people of Israel, and the language of the Torah are themselves associated with this structure through the number seventy. In the numerology of the Torah, the land of Israel is the seventieth land among the nations of the world; the Hebrew language is the seventieth language among the languages of the world; and the Jewish people are the seventieth nation among the nations of the world.[29]

---

25. This is a reference to Exodus 31:17, which says that the Shabbat "is a sign forever." In this phrase, the word usually translated as "forever" is *le'olam*, which can be translated and understood to refer not only to eternal time, but to the eternity of the world and the concealment of the Divine, as we explained.

26. The counting of the Omer refers to the seven weeks between Pesach (Passover) and Shavuot (Pentecost) as described in Leviticus 23:15–16.

27. The Bible designates the day for beginning the counting of the Omer as the day after the Shabbat: "And you shall count from the day after the day of rest" (Leviticus 23:15).

28. The Hebrew name for the festival of Shavuot (Pentecost) literally means "weeks." This is a festival with no special commandments and is thus understood as a symbol of time itself. See *Kedushat Levi*, Kedushat Mesamchei Lev Edition, 288–98 [Hebrew].

29. The idea that there are seventy nations in the world is based on the biblical enumeration of Noah's male descendants after the flood (Genesis, chapter 10). Each name mentioned is understood in rabbinic literature to refer to the founder of a separate nation. Genesis (10:32) describes the division of the sons of Noah into nations, while the Tower of

The land of Israel, Hebrew, and the Jewish people are all *signs* of Shabbat. All of them are potentially pointers, gateways – institutions of the politics of Tikkun Olam – that as *signs* and *referents* disclose the *being* of all the lands, peoples, and languages of the world as Havayah.

The institutions of political Zionism are indeed those of Survival and System. But as the cracks in their shell begin to show, the work that needs to be done from the inside out – and only from the inside out – is to disclose the plausibility of the idea that underneath the Jewish state as we know it today lies a rich network of alternative political institutions that the Zionist movement began to rehabilitate but which do not belong to the paradigm upon which it consciously operates. In this sense, the institutions of the secular state are the *peshat* of which the institutions of Tikkun Olam are the *sod*. Conversely, the politics of Tikkun Olam are the *sod* of which the politics of Survival and System are the *peshat*. These institutions of *sod* are the seventieth land, the seventieth people, and the seventieth language, all of which have

---

Babel story in the following chapter describes the division of the world into the speakers of different languages. Rabbinic tradition connects these two, inferring that the each of the seventy nations had its own language. See, for example, the discussion of the Tower of Babel story that appears in the Jerusalem Talmud (*Megillah* 1:9). The idea that Hebrew was the language spoken before the division of the nations appears in this passage, while the idea that Hebrew was the seventieth language after the division and dispersal appears in the Midrash Aggadah (Genesis 50:5). See also *Bereishit Rabbah* (37), in which each one of these nations is ruled over by an angel. In this list the people of Israel are singled out as the seventieth nation, who rejected the rule of the angel and instead chose to come under the direct provenance of God. The significance of this rabbinic distinction to the national identity of the Jewish people and hence to the State of Israel is discussed by Martin Buber in his essay "The Spirit of Israel and the World Today," in Martin Buber, ed., *Israel and the World: Essays in a Time of Crisis* (Syracuse: Syracuse University Press, 1997), 183–96. This principle is also recorded by the medieval commentator Rashi in his commentary on Deuteronomy 32:8. The verse says, "When the Most High gave the nations their inheritance, when He separated the sons of Adam, he set the borders of the people according to the number of the children of Israel." Rashi states, "When He scattered the generation of division (i.e., the generation of the Tower of Babel), He could have removed them from the world. But He did not and instead set their borders and did not destroy them." The verse continues, "According to the number of the children of Israel" and Rashi comments, "In accordance with the number of seventy souls of the children of Israel who went down to Egypt, He set the borders of the seventy nations and of the seventy languages." Thus, there is a correlation here between the seventy souls of Israel, the seventy nations, their seventy allocations of land, and seventy languages.

been built up, championed, and literally revived by Zionism in the last 150 years. What remains is to continue digging deeper in the effort to understand how these and other institutions that remain in obscurity can organize collective spiritual life from the inside out.

The call to engage in this challenge is ultimately the conclusion of this book, and the work that lies ahead is immense if not daunting and better left in the hands of those whose powers and mastery of Torah are greater than ours. What remains to be said is really only an appendix in which (in addition to what we have already said about the lexicon of Segulah in the previous chapters) we will try to say a little more about the meaning of the land and the language from the perspective of Segulah.

The Segulah of the Land of Israel

In our contemporary political reality, the historical or moral claim of the Jewish people to the land of Israel is deeply contested in a conflict that the politics of Survival and System seems powerless to resolve. At the core of this conflict is the legitimacy of the Jewish claim to the land that (without suggesting any actions that use political power to make changes to the situation from the outside in) needs to be further clarified from the perspective of Segulah. The meaning of the land in the Torah is indeed a deep and confusing mystery. Why is the land of Israel holy? What can the holiness of the land mean that somehow justifies not only the modern settlement of the land but also the biblical conquest described in the book of Joshua?

In his "Lights of the Land of Israel" Rabbi Kook writes,

> The land of Israel is not something external; it is not a national possession that serves as an instrument for the general unification (of the people), or for their physical or even spiritual maintenance. The land of Israel is an entity of our nationhood that is organically bound to its very life and inner being, which is tied with inner Segulah to its (the people's) reality. And because of this, the content of the Segulah of the holiness of the land of Israel cannot be grasped, neither can its preciousness be brought from the depths to the surface by way of any human reason. This can be achieved only with the *ruach Hashem* which rests on the nation

in its entirety by virtue of the natural spiritual stamp which is in the Neshamah of Israel.[30]

These words and many others that Rabbi Kook has written about the land are indeed deeply puzzling because of his insistence that the land of Israel is a reality that cannot be grasped by way of any human reason. He seems to suggest that there is a dimension of collective self-discovery that the Jewish people can achieve only together in the land, and conversely, there is a life energy in the land that can be disclosed only when the entire Jewish people settles it. This connection is alive and binding in the same way that the energies that tie the body to the soul are alive and binding. Rabbi Kook's son Rabbi Zvi Yehuda also emphasizes this body/soul relationship in which the people are the soul of the land and the land is the body of the people's soul.[31] Transposing this idea into slightly different terms, we might say that Israel – as a people - can only *be-in-the-world* in the land that "fits" them, and the land can only *be* as an extension of Israel's collective *being*. When the *alive being* of the people and the *alive being* of the land are aligned, the body and soul are united, and in this unity the land itself somehow comes to life.[32]

This ontological articulation helps to clarify the relationship that Rabbi Kook is describing, but it does not explain its substance, which remains puzzling and mysterious. What does it mean that the land and the people fit each other,[33] and in what sense can the land be described as alive? Many have pointed to the "reaction of the land" to the return of the people in modern times as a way of explaining this. But the remarkable agricultural, political,

---

30. Rabbi Kook, "The Lights of the Land of Israel," 1:1, in *Orot* (Mossad HaRav Kook, 2005 edition), 9 [Hebrew].

31. Rabbi Zvi Yehudah Kook, *Sichot HaRav Tzvi Yehuda* (5 vols.), ed. Rabbi Shlomo Aviner, vol. 5, 137–40, 150, 155–56, 160 [Hebrew].

32. Ibid.

33. One very interesting approach to this question can be found in Tamar Weissman's book *Tribal Lands: The Twelve Tribes of Israel in Their Ancestral Territories* (Renana Publishers, 2015). This book essentially offers the reader a guided tour through the different tribal territories described in the Bible. Weissman suggests a correlation between the traits and characteristics of each tribe as it is portrayed in biblical and rabbinic texts and the scenery, natural conditions, and characteristics of their corresponding portions of the land.

and economic revival of the land brought about by the Zionist pioneers and the State of Israel does not explain the mystery away. Many lands and countries have prospered as a result of attention, technology, investment, and economic development. There is nothing in this version of the land's aliveness that provides ex post facto justification for its conquest from the perspective of international law and human rights. From that perspective, despite the Israeli Declaration of Independence's frequent references to the biblical heritage and spiritual attachment of the people to the land, it is still the vote passed in the UN on November 29, 1947, that ultimately legitimizes the construction of the state in its 1948 borders and nothing more. But Rabbi Kook insists that this is not enough, since the relationship between the land and the people belongs to the dimension of Neshamah that rational consciousness cannot grasp. How can ideas of this sort provide the moral foundation that justifies the prices paid by others for today's physical and political conquest?

Rashi seems to have struggled with this problem when he commented on the first verse of the Torah that the whole purpose of the book of Genesis is to preempt the accusations of those who claim that the Jewish people stole the land.[34] The answer that Rashi offers is that Genesis begins with creation and the stories of the patriarchs in order to prove that the land was in the gift of the Creator, who promised it to Abraham, Isaac, and Jacob. As powerful an argument as this is in theory, in terms of modern politics, it belongs to a paradigm that is under water. It seems to say nothing that stands up in the courts of today. This is perhaps what Rabbi Kook means when he continues to say that the profound faith with which the Jewish people has yearned for Israel has been the life force of Israel in exile. Beyond the simple meaning of this is the deeper idea that not only the people but the faith itself as it functions in Rashi's answer is faith in a state of Galut (in the sense that it is faith that makes sense only on the other side of a Kierkegaardian leap). Similarly, the idea that the land of Israel is a national possession that serves either the physical or even the spiritual maintenance of the people is faith in a state of Galut. Rabbi Kook continues, "The unity of the people in the land of Israel is not a means of any sort to the attainment of salvation. Rather, it is salvation itself." If so, *being-in-Israel* is a form of *being* that the self in Galut cannot

---

34. See the commentary of Rashi on Genesis 1:1.

know. In Galut, the Jewish connection to the land is a matter of tradition, of dreams, and of prayers. But the idea that the land is salvation itself is more than that. It is not a rational concept. It is a reality that can be glimpsed only from inside the boundaries of the land where there is *ruach Hashem* and the spiritual stamp of the Neshamah of Israel.

It appears that writing in the early twentieth century, Rabbi Kook saw the Enlightenment and the modern nationalist movements that it generated as a crack in a paradigm that concealed from view this inner dimension of Israel. What he so famously saw through this crack is the holiness and potential of Survival and System. He envisioned the vital and sacred role that secular nationalist politics could play in revealing the meaning of the land by creating the conditions for the people's return to it. But he also saw through to the stages that still lie ahead. The Enlightenment's faith in reason was for him the vehicle that allowed the dreams, covenantal promises, and prophetic visions of the Neshamah to take a step closer to the surface of human experience. In this framing, Israel was the national homeland for a secular movement, and he was its rabbi. Israel was the religious homeland for a religious community, and he was its leader. But ultimately, Israel is none of these. The inner reality of Israel is visible only to a dimension of human consciousness that cannot emerge above the surface until the age of reason runs its course. In Rabbi Kook's worldview, reason is to be replaced by Da'at Hashem, by the Torah of the land of Israel. Here Rabbi Kook was a teacher and prophet standing at the edge of Exile; peering ever more deeply through the cracks trying to experience in his soul the *always already*-ness of the still implausible reality of salvation that lay ahead.

Today these cracks are showing more clearly, so that those of us with lesser powers can dare to sit on the shoulders of giants and dream some more. What can we see when we do? What is the vision and where is the consciousness to be found that will disclose the mystery of Israel's sanctity?

We have explained at length why we believe that Heidegger's immanent metaphysics is a key that, when appropriately inverted, opens the door to seeing more of the Torah's meaning. We have suggested that this key opens many doors in the language of Torah, finding the Torah of the land of Israel that hides within. We have argued at length that the language of inner Torah – whether we find it in the kabbalah, the Maharal, in the *Nefesh HaChayim*, or

Hasidic exegesis – is especially close to this system and functions as a powerful discloser of the ontological dimensions that lie within. Though the lexicon we have developed can be applied broadly to a wide variety of sources, we wish to return once again to the *Kedushat Levi* and the *Sefat Emet* to see how the body and soul that Rabbi Kook describes are joined and how this view from the inside can help us to imagine the dimensions of Israel's *being* that still remain obscure.

In his commentary on the book of Numbers, the Kedushat Levi discusses the spies whom Moses sent into the land to prepare the way for the people's conquest. Rather than portraying the military purpose of their mission in external strategic terms he – typically – grounds the military and strategic significance of their mission in its internal or spiritual purpose. As we saw in his discussion of the people of Israel's wanderings through the desert, the Kedushat Levi explains that the spies were supposed to pave the way for Israel's conquest of the land by raising up the sparks of light or Middot Neshamah that were concealed there within Klippot. However, when they entered the land of Israel their mission encountered a unique challenge. In his words,

> The rule is that a place where the sparks have been raised is easy to conquer and a place where the sparks cannot be raised is impossible to conquer. This is why it says, "Do not leave any *neshamah* alive" (Deuteronomy 20:16) for this they had to strip off all layers of physicality.…And here Moses sent them to the land where it is impossible to raise any spark, which is why they must strip themselves of all physicality, and this is the meaning of "send," which is to strip; to strip themselves of all physicality is to send for themselves people.[35]

This commentary, which is actually based on Rashi's reading of a verse in the book of Joshua, is essentially trying to explain how the spies were supposed to have enabled the physical conquest of the land. The "normal" practice of raising up the sparks was not available to them, since the land of Israel does

---

35.   Rabbi Levi Yitzchak of Berditchev, *Kedushat Levi*, Parashat Shelach, 103–4.

not allow it. Thus, a different approach was required, which was that of stripping themselves of all physicality.

To understand what this means, we must see how the Kedushat Levi focuses here (as in several other commentaries that he offers on the same verse) on the three Hebrew words *Shlach lecha anashim*. These are the words that God uses when he commands Moses to send the so-called spies into the land. When translated literally, this phrase means "send people." But the word *lecha*, meaning "for you," connotes God's commandment to Abraham, *Lech lecha*, "Go for you...to the land that I will show you."[36] The additional word *lecha* suggests that there is an internal dimension to this journey into the land that the Kedushat Levi seeks to explain. In his reading, he establishes a connection between the word *shlach*, which literally means "send forth" but which can also mean "discard," and the word *peshat*, which in this context means to strip off or discard the surface. In this sense, God's commandment to send forth men into the land is a directive that these men must discard the surface of their human physicality in order to enter the land. This reading is supported by the third word, *anashim*, which literally means "people." The commandment does not mention spies or scouts or leaders or generals. It is their humanity that is sent into the land and the form that it must take there is one of being stripped of its physical surface. These men are there in order to *be* people *in* the land who must discover the inner dimensions of their humanity in a place where only this and not the raising up of sparks can prepare the land for conquest. The Kedushat Levi continues,

> And many [commentators] have noticed [literally "screamed"] the word *lecha*, and it seems that the primary intention of the blessed Creator was that people who are spiritually complete and filled with *yirah* (awe of God) and whose whole purpose in life is His service should be sent into the land and not, God forbid, people who come to survey the physical aspect of the land. They were sent so that they could leave the mark of their service of God on the land that is through Torah and prayer, so that the energy from the higher land may be brought down to the lower land and the

---

36. Genesis 12:1.

land itself will desire the children of Abraham, Isaac, and Jacob to come into it. And this is the meaning of *shlach*…that is, that they will draw forth their inner humanity and reach the level of Moses our teacher. And this is the meaning of *shlach lecha anashim*, that they will send forth their external humanity, that is, they will strip themselves of physicality till they come to "you" [Moses], meaning, to your [Moses'] level; in other words, they will come to the land of Israel not to survey (*yatur*) its physicality, God forbid, but rather they come to the land "to survey it" (*yatur*) in the sense of "Torah," that is, that they come to the land because of the Torah. And the principle here is that when the Jewish people engage in the study of Torah and the practice of mitzvot they have a portion in the land of Israel beyond the portion that they inherit from their ancestors. What this means is that when the people of Israel engage in the study of Torah and the practice of mitzvot, I give the land to them, but this is not what fools think. They think that Moses sent the spies to survey the land in its physicality.[37]

As we have already argued on so many occasions, our suggestion here is that an ontic reading of this text and the religious assumptions that it seems to make is not capable of accessing the system of cause and effect that connects its different elements. What is the upper land and how is it connected to the lower one? Why should the practice of Torah and mitzvot give the people a portion in the land, and what is the nature of the role that the Kedushat Levi ascribes to God in all this? How can we make sense of a justification for the Jewish people's claim to the land that rests on the idea that it somehow is the land itself that wants them to be there?

Before we begin our ontological analysis of this, there is one more passage here that we would like to include. The Kedushat Levi continues,

For it says that God said to Moses, Send for yourself people and they will survey the land, and in the book of Deuteronomy Moses says that they were sent to dig into the depths of the land. And

---

37.   Rabbi Levi Yitzchak of Berditchev, *Kedushat Levi*, Parashat Shelach, 103–4.

it says in the Midrash (*Kohelet Rabbah* 1) that the 248 limbs and 365 tendons in the human body correspond to the land, as it says, "the nakedness of the land," "the navel of the land," "the eye of the land." And we know that the 248 limbs of the human body correspond to the 248 positive commandments and the 365 tendons correspond to the 365 negative commandments, and each limb and tendon is obliged to observe its commandment. In the same way, the limbs and tendons in the land are obliged to observe the 613 commandments, and when the people of Israel observe the commandments in the land, the land desires for them to be there to observe the commandments of the Torah. This is why Moses sent twelve men into the land and commanded them to survey it (*vayaturu*, "to survey," is linguistically close to the word Torah), meaning that they will study Torah and keep its commandments in [the land], which will make the land easy to conquer, because the land desires them to be there since they will be a source of spiritual plenty to the land and the land will be the recipient. And this is the meaning of the word "to dig" [the root *chafar* means both "dig" and "shame"]…that the land will be ashamed before Israel that they bring spiritual plenty to the land and the land is its recipient, which is its ultimate desire…[38]

The reading that we wish to propose here is perhaps still fantastical and far removed from our normal or everyday experience of reality. It is perhaps even essential that it should be, since what we are trying to glimpse here is a dimension of reality that is not (yet?) plausible to us. The challenge then is to describe the ideas outlined in this passage in "relevantly fantastical" terms – to somehow touch a fantasy that, like science-fiction, captures an inner yearning of the human spirit whose reality and plausibility is determined not by how it corresponds with the world as we know it but with how we truly and deeply wish the world to be (which in turn – from the perspective of Segulah – corresponds with how the Torah teaches us to wish the world to be).

---

38. Ibid.

From the perspective of the inner Torah, our deepest yearnings are primordial memories of what was lost in the Garden of Eden. In the Midrash, this collective historic sense of loss is also the experience of every individual, who experiences it again when the Neshamah enters the body and is thus born into the world. If we reverse-engineer the Genesis narrative, what is lost is the ability to separate good from evil. Without this separation all human actions, good or evil, are always both. As the saying attributed to Samuel Johnson goes, "The road to hell is paved with good intentions" and conversely, "There is not righteous person in the land who does good and does not sin."[39] So progress, kindness, discovery and holiness are always accompanied by a dark side and by negative consequences that make the ongoing effort of human beings to attain a stable state of happiness and prosperity so elusive. To paraphrase Dickens, all times are the best of times and the worst of times.

This situation in which good and evil are saddled to each other is the one that kabbalistic literature describes in terms of "sparks" (Nitzotzot) and "shells" (Klippot). Sparks and shells are complicit with each other, because sparks are contained within shells in the same way that the Neshamah is contained within the body. Without the shells, sparks would not be a thing of this world. It is the shells that enable the sparks to *be in the world* in the same way that the body enables the Nefesh and the Neshamah to take a physical form. The spark is the element of the *being* of Havayah that *is* the *being* of everything and the shell or Klippah is the physical form that it takes in the world, which both enables it to *be in the world* while simultaneously concealing the *being* of Havayah from the world. Thus, in a world infected with the impression of the Tree of Knowledge, all revelation is made possible by concealment or constriction, since pure *being* is clothed in the bodily form of the shell that carries it or extends it into the world.

As we suggested above, the politics of Tikkun Olam rests on the assumption that the primary institutions of Jewish life as prescribed by the Torah are placeholders for the *being* of Havayah. They are *signs* and *referents* rather than holders of power. In their *being* they disclose a dimension of human *being* that is recognizable to the Neshamah-self when it is appropriately *attuned*

---

39. Ecclesiastes 7:20.

and aligned. Unlike other lands, the land of Israel is designated by the Torah as an institution of the politics of Tikkun Olam and in this capacity it too is a *referent* that discloses the *being* of Havayah in all spatiality. It is the land of the Torah given to the people of the Torah and as such it is part of the network of *referents* and *signs* that we described above as conforming to the structure of *ashan* and the architecture of Segulah. This is the underlying principle that explains the way in which the Kedushat Levi presents his understanding of Moses' 'strategy' for conquering the land.

The Kedushat Levi begins his discussion of the conquest of the land by returning to a basic idea about sparks and shells. We already saw above that he understands the wanderings of the people of Israel in the desert with the Mishkan as equivalent to the six days of the week, whereas their entry into the land is equivalent to Shabbat. In this framing, the presence of the Mishkan and the people in each place functions as a *sign* that points to the form of the *being* of Havayah that is the underlying reality of that place in the dimension of Shabbat. However, in this passage he teaches that this principle does not apply to the land of Israel. In Israel, the land itself is a *referent* and a *sign*. It is already a *referent* of Shabbat. It is an institution in the politics of Tikkun Olam, and in this sense it is not a spark concealed in a shell. *Being* as the *being* of Havayah is therefore disclosed in the land of Israel in a different way.

The Kedushat Levi insists that the commandment *shlach lecha Anashim* is addressed to the appropriate *attunement* of Middot Nefesh (Yirah or awe of God) and to stripping off bodily physicality. In Israel the land is a *referent* for Shabbat, but the Nefesh of the people who entered it is not sufficiently aligned (is not sufficiently in the ontological mode of Shabbat) for the people to enter appropriately. It is the self that must attain the dimension of Shabbat for the door to the land of Israel to open. This is the purpose of the spies' mission. They must enter the land and be able to see the land as an expression of the *being* of Havayah. Their failure to do so is what forced the children of Israel to spend an additional generation wandering the desert in the place that represents the six days of the week. It is in this context that the Kedushat Levi connects the word *latur*, meaning to survey, with the root of the word "Torah," concluding that only fools associate the purpose of this episode with the physical surveying of the land. What the so-called spies should have sought in the land is the opportunity to transform their own physicality, to embody Shabbat in their own *being* by studying Torah and keeping its commandments in the land, so that the three dimensions of Shabbat (in place, time, and Nefesh) could be aligned. This alignment is alluded to in his reference to a theme that we have already discussed at length, i.e., that the architecture of Segulah corresponds in its shape to the number of positive and negative commandments in the Torah. We have seen this applied to the correspondence between the human body and the Torah and suggested how in the temporality of Shabbat/Netzach this accounts for the discovery of the mitzvot by Abraham even in a time that preceded the revelation at Sinai. Here, the intuitive ontological *being* of the land is connected through the Torah to the people in the same way, suggesting that the land is the natural habitat of the dimension of the self that discloses the architectural structure of Segulah in the self. As Rabbi Kook said, this self "fits" the land that, by virtue of its being the spatial *referent* of the *being* of Havayah, is the only geographical arena or context of *being* in which a land can be the physical embodiment of the self in its form as an expression of the Torah.

The anthropomorphic themes associated with the land (such as the eye and the navel of the land) therefore point toward the idea that concealed within the physicality of the land there is a dimension of the land's *created-ness* that is made specially accessible or recognizable to the Neshamah-self by virtue of the connection between the land and the architecture of Segulah. As the place of the Torah, the place in which the mitzvot are to be practiced, the land aligns to the spatial dimension of *ashan* and discloses through its relationship with the mitzvot the essential aliveness of all *being* as the *being* of Havayah. In this sense the land calls the people to *be* in the shape of the Torah by being the people of the land who recognize that it, like them, is a *referent* and a *sign* alive with the *being* of Havayah. The land functions in this way as the context of *being-in,* in which the people disclose this dimension of its spatial meaning.

Again, this is a theme that we can articulate more explicitly using the language provided by the Sefat Emet in his commentary on the same biblical passage. He writes,

> For in truth the land of Israel is prepared only for the people of Israel and to them the inner light that is concealed within it is

revealed…because the people of Israel are formed by the land and the land is formed by them…thus even though the holiness of the land is concealed, it is the people of Israel who are the vessels to bring it into the light…and this is why the spies saw that it is a land that eats those who dwell in it. They were supposed to have understood that the land is prepared only for the children of Israel. And Caleb and Joshua, who said the land is good, understood that it is its desire to reveal the good that is concealed in it to us. And thus the land of Israel is like the Shabbat, that is, a day in which the manna cannot be found and all blessing depend upon it, as it says in the holy *Zohar*. In the same way, the glory of the land of Israel cannot be seen from the outside but the source of all blessing is dependent on it.[40]

In this description of the relationship between the people and the land, the Sefat Emet echoes here the phenomenologically circular structure of *peshat* and *sod*. The people are the people of the land and the land is the land of the people, and in the intrinsic connection between them they together make accessible to the world the dimension of Torah or Havayah that they both embody in space and in the Nefesh. Thus, the land without the people is in Galut as are the people without the land. It is the embodiment of the land of the Torah by the live consciousness of the people of the Torah that discloses the *alive-being* of Havayah. In fantastical terms, when the land and the people align, the land will present itself as having awoken into explicit aliveness: thus the land comes to life;[41] the earth will rejoice;[42] the sea will roar with praise;[43] the fields will exult and the trees of the forest will sing;[44] the rivers will clap hands and the mountains will join together in song.[45] This is how space declares that the whole world is the alive *being* of Havayah and underneath it all space in its entirety is *always already* Shabbat – an event in

---

40. Rabbi Yehuda Leib Alter of Gur, *Sefat Emet,* Parashat Shelach (5661).
41. Psalms 97:1.
42. Ibid.
43. Psalms 96:11, 98:7).
44. Psalms 96:12.
45. Ibid. 88:8.

God. The aliveness that only the Torah discloses in the people of Israel is the aliveness that the people of Israel disclose in the land of Israel. This aliveness is the concealed beauty of the land of Israel that the people of Israel aligned and *attuned* see through Torah, transposing the visibility of this *aliveness* from fantasy to human possibility. But the possibility of this gaze when disclosed in Israel is not only the beauty of the people and the land; it is the beauty of all people, all time, and the whole world – Tikkun Olam. The Sefat Emet continues,

> And the point is that God made a covenant with Abraham our father, as it says, "And He found his heart loyal (pure)…and He made a covenant with him," that he was able to appreciate the inner meaning of the land of Israel since his heart was loyal. But this covenant was given even to the decedents whose hearts are not pure and who do not follow the ways of their ancestors, which is why it says twice to give the land to his descendants, since it was not the descendants who merited the land they were not able to see the inner glory of the land of Israel.[46]

What Abraham saw, his descendants do not. In this regard, the people of Israel in Galut are no more capable than anybody else. By framing ontology as activity, the ontological distinction between the gaze of Israel and that of the nations is what Abraham discovered but could not pass on. It remains deposited for the people of Israel as a fantasy, a memory, a hope for the future, an implausible vision and a dream yet to be fulfilled – but when fulfilled to be realized by Israel and through Israel for the entire world. If political Zionism has brought us closer than ever before to this vision from the outside-in, the task of embracing and realizing the fantastical oddity of its weird implausibility is the work that, going forward, the people of Israel must now do in the land. The quietly spiritual discovery of the Shabbat that lies within was the task of the spies. Like Abraham, their entry into the land was not a military conquest but a spiritual one (which is how the conquest of Joshua is seen in

---

46. Ibid.

Hasidic texts as well[47]). This is work that, as the Kedushat Levi says, must be done from the inside out: *shlach lecha anashim*. It cannot be achieved with force or power. The land is "conquered" through the accomplishment and dissemination of a new dimension in human consciousness that discloses the land and the people in it to the world as aligned *attuned* expressions of the *being* of Havayah. It is this that will resolve the two challenges (seen in the paradigm of Survival and System as contradictory and mutually exclusive) of bringing bring both peace and unity to the land. The rivers and the mountains will clap their hands and rejoice. Thereafter the nations of the world shall flow unto the land[48] to discover those inner dimensions of their own *being* that know how to witness the spectacle of the land as a living *referent* to the alive *being* of Havayah.

The Hebrew Language and the Architecture of Segulah

To bring this book to a close, we want to share some thoughts and ruminations about the significance of the Zionist revival of the Hebrew language. Volumes have been written about the history of this remarkable process and its linguistic, social, political, and cultural implications. The different ways in which the rich variety of specifically Hebraic hermeneutic principles shape the reading and interpretation of Jewish texts (Midrashic, halachic, mystical, Hasidic, exegetical, poetical, etc.) fill vast libraries of both classical and modern books and essays devoted to the subject. From the writings and teachings of rabbis of the Mishnah and Talmud, *Sefer Yetzirah*, the Bahir and the *Zohar* to Maimonides, Nachmanides and Abraham Abulafia; from Rashi, Rashbam, and the Gaon of Vilna to the Hasidic teachers; from Ahad Ha'am, Eliezer Ben-Yehuda, Chaim Nachman Bialik, Rachel and Zelda to Rabbi Yehuda Ashlag, Rabbi Kook, Gershom Scholem, Moshe Idel, Meir Bozaglo, Haviva Pedaya, and the tens of thousands of other men and women across Jewish history, culture, poetry, and scholarship, who have noticed the special qualities of the Hebrew language, Hebrew has been central to everything they write. Since Judaism in its entirety is intimately intertwined with the particularities

---

47. See, for example, the Hasidic writings of Rabbi Shalom Noah Berezovsky, *Netivot Shalom* on Genesis, where he discusses the seven Middot Nefesh that correspond to the Tikkun of the Seven Nations in the land.

48. Isaiah 2:2.

of the Hebrew language, it is not our intention here to summarize, comment on, contradict, or even add to the great discussion about Hebrew in any formal way. Our purpose is to fantasize a little. The following is not research or a systematic study of sources. It is rumination and reflection and perhaps even a confession and a prayer designed simply to say a few words about the personal meaning that we have attached to language in the composition of this book.

In a famous essay entitled "What Is Philosophy?" Heidegger argues that philosophy is a practice that is intrinsically connected to the Greek language.[49] To philosophize is to think in Greek and to be guided by the lines of investigation that the specific linguistic structures of this language dictate or disclose. As we discussed above, Heidegger insists in *BT* that other than Greek, no language is better suited to philosophy than German and it is therefore through the neologisms that German makes uniquely possible that he formulates the lexicon of terms that map the landscape of his ontological system. Heidegger's attitude to German and Greek philosophy is but one example of the opinion that certain languages are uniquely suited to certain cultural practices. Such opinions insist that a great deal is lost when these culturally specific practices are performed in translation.

The Jewish tradition makes similar claims about the Hebrew language, and the thought occurs that Judaism cannot really be understood in any language other than Hebrew. The idea that Judaism cannot be understood in translation perhaps explains why we fast and mourn on the day that the Targum of the seventy was completed.[50] The Torah as it appears in the seventy languages of the nations is a Torah dismembered and lost in translation. It is a Torah scattered in Galut with the *alive-being* of its Neshamah concealed (and perhaps protected), awaiting in trepidation and anticipation the Churban and Tikkun – its literal burning on European soil and its rehabilitation and replanting in the land of Israel in a state where people live, read, and

---

49. Martin Heidegger, *What Is Philosophy?*, translated with an introduction by Jean T. Wilde and William Kluback, New Haven (1956). See page 29, where he writes, "Now the word "philosophy" is speaking Greek...the word *philosophia* tells us that philosophy is something which, first of all, determines the existence of the Greek world."

50. The special passages that are added to the regular liturgy on the tenth of Tevet explain among the many reasons for fasting on that day that it is the historic date on which the translation known as the Septuagint was completed.

think in Hebrew. The State of Israel has revived an ancient language. Modern Hebrew is perhaps a language like all others, serving Israeli society merely as the language of its Survival and System. But it is also perhaps the Torah and the name of God in Galut waiting to come alive and become the seventieth language of the world that fully discloses the *alive-being* of the world to the world.

Hebrew is a language whose alphabet (*alef bet*) comprises only consonants. As a result, identical sequences of letters with different vowels can produce different words whose meanings can be obviously related to one another, altered only by the conjugations and declensions that the different vowels form. But these same sequences of letters can also suggest connections between words that we would not think of associating with one another outside of Judaism, like *shemen*, meaning "oil" and *shemonah*, meaning "eight," both of which connote the burning of oil for eight days that we celebrate on the festival of Chanukah. Many homophones are antonyms and many words are connected by the root letters that comprise them, by the interchangeable letters they share, and even by numerical values and sequences, all of which contribute equally to the overall construction of meaning.[51] The graphology of the letters combine to form other letters; the names of the letters have not only numerological values (that explain the sequence in which they are arranged in the *alef bet* which ascends from one to four hundred)[52] but also the names of the letters have meanings as words. Even their appearance has a kind of hieroglyphic significance. All the letters, numbers, meanings, symbols and vowels interchange, interconnect, and associate. All these meanings are equally expressive but can only seem so when they are understood as reflecting different linguistic dimensions. All are *referents* to each other and to the underlying whisper – the *yud*, the *heh*, the *vav*, and the *heh* – that every word and letter in Hebrew contains and conceals.[53] Hebrew is the language

---

51. For a rich and enlightening discussion of these linguistic dimensions of the biblical text and their meanings, see Friedrich Weinreb, *Roots of the Bible: An Ancient View for a New Outlook*, trans. N. Keus (Merlin Books, 1986), 14–15 and especially 36–41.

52. Ibid., 36–37.

53. This theme is central, for example in the classical kabbalistic text *Sefer Habahir* or the *Book of Illumination*. See *The Bahir: Attributed to Rabbi Nehunia ben Hakana, Master of the First Century Esoteric School*, translated and edited with an introduction by Aryeh Kaplan (Samuel Weiser, 1979).

of a journey that crosses a boundary in time, place, and the self. It is the journey of those who follow Abraham the "Hebrew," who crossed the river and entered the land.[54]

If all of this is so, we cannot avoid the thought that something essential in this book has inevitably been lost in translation. It might be the case that the transition from Survival and System to Segulah that takes us to a dimension of the Torah that lies beyond the West can only be completed when the languages of Klippat Yavan (English, French, German, Spanish, Italian, Latin, and ultimately Greek) are left behind. Even though the lexicon of ontological terms that we have been developing is comprised almost entirely of Hebrew words, our reading of them and our attempts to grapple with their inner meaning have all been in English. We have translated words and concepts moving to and fro between languages, seeking out the disentangled meaning of these Hebrew terms. But in doing so we have relied – ever so ironically – on the English translations of Heidegger's German neologisms.

What sense can this make? It seems that our journey has involved our moving forward by also moving backward. We have moved toward the perspective of Segulah by backing away from the perspective of Survival and System. The fact that Hebrew is read from right to left forces us to think about the difference between right-left/left-right directionality whether we think of this in terms of the geography of the planet as portrayed on a two-dimensional map, the different wings of our politics and parliaments, the sides of our bodies, of our minds, or of our Supernal Minds. We have moved toward Hebrew by backing away from German and English. We have moved toward the Torah by backing away from the West, away from places where words and sentences are read from left to right to a place where they are read from right to left. This is a journey that forces us to switch between these two directions like an alternating current. We have begun from the left or the West because this is who we most naturally are. But we must also know how to trace our steps back so that we can make peace between two directionalities that we have sought to disentangle but which we have insisted from the outset must ultimately have their conflict resolved. It is this movement from

---

54. The three-letter root of the Hebrew word for "Hebrew" – *ivrit* – literally means to cross-over a boundary or river.

the left to the right of the page that we associate with everyday Dasein's search (the Nefesh's search) for the Neshamah. But it is the movement from right to left that can ultimately reflect the Neshamah's entry into the Nefesh through alignment, thus assuming a bodily presence in the world.

The two-way directionality that we seek can be associated with the ascent and descent of Kavanah and with the cyclical interactions of *throwness, projection, understanding, interpretation, created-ness,* Chochmah, Binah, and Da'at; with the movement from Middot Nefesh to Middot Neshamah; from our ontic perceptions of the world to the state of mind in which we live our mortal lives as episodes in the temporal dimension of Netzach where death itself is negated by Devekut, Da'at Hashem, and the recognition that all is Havayah. It seems inevitable then that we must begin in translation in order to leave the need for translation behind. We must first make our peace with entering the *pardes* from left to right (from *peshat* to *sod*) in order to make our journey from right to left (from *sod* back to *peshat*) peaceful in return.[55] It is in this sense that we pray that the two civilizations who remain so alarmingly unaware of the conflict that endures between them can return their hostages to each other and begin negotiating the peace between them but this time in two languages and with interpreters in the room.

---

55. This is a reference to the famous passage that appears in the Babylonian Talmud (*Chagigah* 14b) which describes four scholars who entered the *pardes*. Only Rabbi Akiva succeeded in entering in peace and returning in peace, while the others – Ben Azzai, Ben Zoma, and Acher – were killed, driven to insanity, and driven to apostasy, respectively.

Personal Note

This entire book except for the preface has been written in the plural voice for reasons that we outlined there. But as its sole author, I believe it has also been a reflection on the meaning of my Hebrew name. This name, which I use only when I am called to the Torah, is "Alexander Chayyim." And so, I am called to the Torah with two names, one of which is read from left to right, the other from right to left. One represents Klippat Yavan, the other Havayah, and I am the alternating current that journeys perpetually between them.

עברי אנוכי ואת יהוה אל השמיים אני ירא.[1]

---

1.   Jonah 1:9.

Bibliography

Alter of Gur, Rabbi Yehuda Aryeh Leib. *Sefat Emet* [Hebrew].

Ameriks, Karl. "The Critique of Metaphysics: Kant and Traditional Ontology," in Paul Guyer, editor. *The Cambridge Companion to Kant.* Cambridge University Press, 1992.

Arendt, Hannah. *Eichmann in Jerusalem: A Report on the Banality of Evil.* Penguin Classics, 1963.

———. *The Origins of Totalitarianism.* Benediction Classics edition, 2009.

Ashkenazi (Manitou), Rabbi Yehuda Leon. *Misped Lamashiach?!* [Hebrew]. Edited by Israel Pivko, Itai Ashkenazi, and Elyakim Simsovic. Bet-El: Chava, 2006.

Ashlag, Rabbi Yehudah. *On World Peace: Two Essays by the Holy Kabbalist Rabbi Yehuda Ashlag.* Edited by Michael Berg. Kabballah Publishing, 2013.

Avivi, Yosef. "History for the Sake of Heaven." In Moshe Bar-Asher, editor. *Jubilee Volume in honor of Mordechai Breuer: Articles in Jewish Studies.* Jerusalem: Akademon, 1992.

Bakst, Joel David. *The Secret Doctrine of the Gaon of Vilna.* Vol. 1, *Mashiach ben Yoseph and the Messianic Role of Torah, Kabalah and Science.* City of Luz Publications, 2008.

———. *The Secret Doctrine of the Gaon of Vilna.* Vol. 2, *The Josephic Messiah, Leviathan, Metatron and the Sacred Serpent.* City of Luz Publications, 2009.

Becker, Ernst. *The Denial of Death.* New York: Free Press, 1973.

Beinart, Peter. *The Crisis of Zionism*. New York: Times Books, 2012.

Ben Attar, Chayyim. *The Light of Life* [Hebrew]. Venice, 1742.

Ben Ezer, Ehud. "Zionism: Dialectics of Continuity and Rebellion – an Interview with Gershom G. Scholem." In Ehud Ben Ezer, editor. *Unease in Zion*. Quadrangle/The New York Times Book Company and Jerusalem Academic Press, 1974.

Rabbi Levi Yitzchak of Berditchev. *Kedushat Levi*. Mesamchei Lev Edition [Hebrew].

Berezovsky, Rabbi Shalom Noah. *Netivot Shalom*. Jerusalem: Slonim, 1985–95 [Hebrew].

Berkeley, George. *A Treatise Concerning the Principles of Human Knowledge*. Hackett Classics, 1982.

Biale, David. *Austerity: The History of a Dangerous Idea*. Oxford University Press, 2012.

Blyth, Mark. *Austerity: The History of a Dangerous Idea*. Oxford University Press, 2012.

———. *Great Transformations: Economic Ideas and Institutional Change in the Twentieth Century*. Cambridge University Press, 2002.

———. With Eric Lonergan. *Angrynomics*. Cambridge University Press, 2020.

Bokser, Ben Zion. *Abraham Isaac Kook: The Lights of Holiness, Lights of Penitence, The Moral Principles, Essays and Poems*. Paulist Press, 1978.

Boyarin, Daniel. *Border Lines: The Partition of Judaeo-Christianity*. University of Pennsylvania Press, 2004.

Buber, Martin. *Israel and the World: Essays in a Time of Crisis*. Schocken Books, 1963.

Buxbaum, Yitzchak. *The Light and the Fire of the Ba'al Shem Tov*. Bloomsbury, 2006.

Buzaglo, Meir. *A Language for the Faithful*. Keter Books, 2009 [Hebrew].

Cantor, Norman F. *Inventing the Middle Ages*. New York, 1991.

Caputo, John. *The Prayers and Tears of Jacques Derrida: Religion without Religion*. Indiana University Press, 1997.

Carter, John Ross. *Dharma: Western Academic and Sinhalese Buddhist Interpretations: A Study of a Religious Concept*. Tokyo, 1978.

Cassirer, Ernst. *Myth of the State*. Yale University Press, 1946.

Cavanaugh, William T. "A Fire Strong Enough to Consume the House: The Wars of Religion and the Rise of the Nation-State." In J. Milbank and S. Oliver, eds. *The Radical Orthodox Reader*. London: Routledge, 2009.

Chatterley, Catherine D. *Disenchantment: George Steiner and the Meaning of Western Civilization after Auschwitz*. Syracuse University Press, 2011.

Chesterton, Gilbert. *The Book of Job: With an Introduction by G. K. Chesterton*. London, 1907.

Christianson, Gale E. *Isaac Newton and the Scientific Revolution*. New York: Oxford University Press, 1996.

Cohen, Hermann. *Das Prinzip der Infinitesimal-Methode und seine Geschichte*. Berlin: Dümmler, 1883. Partially translated as *The Principle of the Infinitesimal Method and Its History*, by D. Hyder and L. Patton, NKR.

Cooper, Levi. "The Assimilation of Tikkun Olam." *Jewish Political Studies Review* 35, nos. 3–4 (Fall 2013).

Dawkins, Richard. *The God Delusion*. Bantam Press, 2006.

Derrida, Jacques. *The Beast and the Sovereign, Volume 1*. Translated by Geoffrey Bennington. Chicago University Press, 2009.

———. *Of Spirit: Heidegger and the Question*. Translated by Geoffrey Bennington and Richard Bowlby. Chicago, 1989.

———. *On the Name*. Edited by Thomas Dutoit and translated by David Wood, John P. Leaver Jr., and Ian McLeod. Stanford University Press, 1995.

———. *Writing and Difference*. Translated by Alan Bass. University of Chicago Press, 1978.

Douglas, Mary. *Purity and Danger*. Oxford: Routledge Books, 1966.

Elbogen, Ismar. *Jewish Liturgy: A Comprehensive History*. Philadelphia: JPS, 1993.

Eliot, T. S. *Notes Towards a Definition of Culture*. Faber and Faber, 1948.

Elson, Christopher, and Garry Sherbert. "A Religion of the Event." In *In the Name of Friendship: Deguy, Derrida and Salut*. Brill-Rudopi, Leiden, 2017.

Etkes, Immanuel. *The Gaon of Vilna: The Man and His Image*, University of California Press, 2002.

Fallada, Hans. *Alone in Berlin*. Penguin, 2010,

Farias, Victor. *Heidegger and Nazism*. Edited by Joseph Margolis and Tom Rockmore. Philadelphia, 1989.

Faye, Emmanuel. *Heidegger: The Introduction of Nazism into Philosophy in Light of the Unpublished Seminars 1933–1935*. Yale University Press, 2009.

Fisch, Menachem. *Rational Rabbis: Science and Talmudic Culture*. Indiana, 1997.

Fishbane, Michael. *The JPS Bible Commentary: Song of Songs*. JPS, 2015.

———. *Sacred Attunement: A Jewish Theology*. Chicago, 2008.

Foucault, Michel. *The Archaeology of Knowledge and the Discourse on Language*. Translated by A. M. Sheridan. New York: Pantheon Books, 1971.

———. *The Birth of the Clinic: An Archaeology of Medical Perception*. Translated by Alan Sheridan. Tavistock, 1973.

———. *Discipline and Punish: The Birth of the Prison*. Translated by Alan Sheridan. Vintage Books, 1995.

———. *The History of Madness*. Translated by Jonathan Murphy and Jean Khalfa. Routledge, 2006.

———. *The History of Sexuality*. 4 vols. Translated by Robert Hurley. Random House and Vintage Books, 1978.

Freundel, Barry. *Why We Pray What We Pray: The Remarkable History of Jewish Prayer*. Urim, 2010.

Friedman, Milton, with Rose Friedman. *Free to Choose: A Personal Statement*. Harvest, 1980.

Fristche, Johannes. *Historical Destiny and National Socialism in Heidegger's Being and Time*. University of California Press, 1999.

Gadamer, Hans Georg. *Hegel-Husserl-Heidegger*. Tubingen, 1987.

Garb, Jonathan. *The Chosen Will Become Herds: Studies in Twentieth-Century Kabbalah*. Yale University Press, 2009.

Gellman, Yehuda (Jerome). *God's Kindness Has Overwhelmed Us: A Contemporary Doctrine of the Jews as the Chosen People*. Academic Studies Press, 2012.

Ginsberg, Asher Tzvi Hirsch (Ahad Ha'am). *The Jewish State and Jewish Problem*. JPS, 1897.

Gordon, Peter E. *Continental Divide: Heidegger, Cassirer, Davos*. Cambridge, MA: Harvard University Press, 2012.

Green, Arthur. *The Language of Truth, The Torah Commentary of the Sefat Emet*. JPS, 1998.

———. *Seek My Face: A Jewish Mystical Theology*. Jewish Lights, 2003.

Guitérrez, Gustavo. *On Job: God-Talk and The Suffering of the Innocent*. Translated by M. J. O'Connell. Orbis Books, 1987.

Guyer, Paul, and Allen W. Wood, eds. *Immanuel Kant, Religion and Rational Theology*. Translated by Allen Wood and George di Giovanni. Cambridge, 1996.

Habermas, Jürgen. *Philosophical-Political Profiles*. Translated by Frederick G. Lawrence. Cambridge, MA. MIT, 1983.

Haidt, Jonathan. "The Emotional Dog and Its Rational Tail: A Social Institutionist Approach to Moral Judgment." *Psychological Review* 108 (2001).

———— . *The Righteous Mind: Why Good People are Divided by Politics and Religion.* Vintage Books, 2012.

HaKohen, Rabbi Chayim, and Rabbi Reuven Sasson. *Talelei Chayim: Introductions and Gateways to the Inner Torah and the Service of God.* Ana Bakoach, 2003 [Hebrew].

Halbertal, Moshe. *Commentary Revolutions in the Making: Values as Interpretive Considerations in Midrashei Halachah.* Magnes, 1997. [Hebrew].

Harari, Yuval Noah. *Sapiens: A Brief History of Humankind.* Vintage Books, 2011.

Heidegger, Martin. *Being and Time.* Translated by Joan Stambaugh. SUNY, 1953.

————. *Kant and the Problem of Metaphysics.* Translated by Richard Taft. Indiana University Press, 1997.

———— . "Letter on Humanism." Translated by Frank A. Capuzzi and J. Glenn Gray. In *Martin Heidegger: Basic Writings.* Edited by David Krell. New York: Harper, 1977.

————. *What Is Philosophy?* Translated with an introduction by Jean T. Wilde and William Kluback. New Haven, 1956.

Heinrich, J., S. Heine, and A. Norenzayan. "The Weirdest People in the World?" *Behavioral and Brain Sciences* 33 (2010): 61–83.

Hertz, Joseph. *The Authorized Daily Prayer Book with Commentary, Introductions and Notes.* Revised American edition New York: Bloch, 1948.

Herwig, Holger. "Geopolitik: Haushofer, Hitler and Lebensraum." In Colin Gray and Geoffrey Sloan, eds. *Geopolitics, Geography and Strategy.* London, 1999.

Heschel, Abraham Joshua. *Israel: An Echo of Eternity,* 1967.

————. *Man Is Not Alone: A Philosophy of Religion.* New York: Farrar, Strauss and Giroux, 1951.

————. *The Prophets,* New York: Harper Collins Perennial Classics, 2001.

———. *The Sabbath.* New York: Farrar Strauss and Giroux, 1951.

Hirsch, Rabbi S. R. *The Collected Writings of Rabbi Samson Raphael Hirsch.* Vol. 3. Feldheim, 1984, and Rabbi Hirsch. *The Pentateuch with Translation and Commentary*, Judaica Press (1962). Isaac Breuer Institute Edition. Jerusalem, 1989 [Hebrew].

Hoffman, Lawrence A., ed. *Kabalat Shabbat: Welcoming Shabbat in the Synagogue.* Jewish Lights, 2004.

Horkheimer, Max, and Theodor Adorno. *Dialectic of Enlightenment: Philosophical Fragments.* English Translation. Stanford: Stanford University Press, 1987.

Idelsohn, A. Z. *Jewish Liturgy and Its Development.* New York, 1931.

Isaacs, Alick. "The Concept of Peace in Judaism." In Georges Tamer, ed. *The Concept of Peace in Judaism, Christianity and Islam* Key Concepts in Interreligious Discourses. Vol. 8. Berlin/Boston: De Gruyter, 2020.

———. *A Prophetic Peace: Judaism, Religion and Politics.* Indiana University Press, 2011: 10–12.

———. "Shlomzion." In *Common Knowledge* 20, no. 1. Duke University Press (Winter 2013/14).

James, William. *The Will to Believe and Other Essays in Popular Philosophy* (1896) New York: Dover, 1956.

Johannessen, Kjell S. "Rule Following, Intransitive Understanding, and Tacit Knowledge." In *Essays in Pragmatic Philosophy II.* Norwegian University Press, 1990.

Jones, Adam. *Genocide: A Comprehensive Introduction.* 2nd ed. Routledge, 2010.

Kahneman, Daniel. *Thinking, Fast and Slow.* Farrar, Strauss and Giroux, 2013.

Kant, Immanuel. *Critique of Practical Reason.* 1788. Translated by Mary Gregor. Cambridge, 1997.

———. *Critique of Pure Reason.* Translated by Marcus Weigelt. Penguin Books, 2007.

———. *Grounding for the Metaphysics of Morals: On a Supposed Right to Lie because of Philanthropic Concerns.* 1785. Translated by James W. Ellington. Hackett, 1993.

———. "Perpetual Peace: A Philosophical Sketch." In H. Reiss, ed. *Kant's Political Writings,* 2nd ed. Trans. H. B. Nisbet. Cambridge: Cambridge University Press, 1991.

———. "Religion within the Boundaries of Mere Reason." In Allen Wood, George Di Giovanni, eds. *Kant, Religion within the Boundaries of Mere Reason and Other Writings.* Cambridge Texts in the History of Philosophy. Cambridge University Press, 1998.

Kaplan, Aryeh. *Inner Space.* Moznaim Publishing, 1990.

———. *Sefer Yetzirah: The Book of Creation in Theory and Practice.* Weiser Books, 1997.

Kaplan, Lawrence. "Time, History, Space, and Place: Abraham Joshua Heschel on the Religious Significance of the Land of Israel." *Journal of Modern Jewish Studies* 17, no. 4 (2018): 496–504.

Kaplan, Mordechai. *Judaism as a Civilization: Toward a Reconstruction of American Jewish Life.* JPS, 1981.

Kimelman, Reuven. *The Mystical Meaning of "Lekhah Dodi" and "Kabbalat Shabbat."* Hebrew University Magnes Press and Cherub Press, 2003 [Hebrew with English introduction].

Kohn, Hans, ed. *Nationalism and the Jewish Ethic: Basic Writings of Ahad Ha'am.* Schocken Books, 1962.

Kolitz, Zvi. *Yosl Rakover Talks to God.* New York, 2000.

Kook, Rabbi Abraham Isaac. *Iggerot HaRayah.* Vol. 1. Letter 43 [Hebrew].

———. *Lights of Holiness.* Jerusalem: Agudah Lehotza'at Sifrei HaRayah Kook, 1938 [Hebrew]..

————. "The Lights of Israel," in *Orot*. Mossad HaRav Kook (2005 edition): 150 [Hebrew].

————. *Lights of Repentance*. Edited by Rabbi Z. Y. Kook. Or Etzion, 1986 [Hebrew].

————. *Musar Avicha and Middot Raayah*. Jerusalem: Mossad HaRav Kook, 1985 [Hebrew].

Kook, Rabbi Zvi Yehudah. *Sichot HaRav Tzvi Yehudah on the Torah*. 5 Vols. Edited by Rabbi Shlomo Aviner [Hebrew].

Koslowski, P., ed. *The Origin and the Overcoming of Evil and Suffering in the World Religions*. Netherlands: Springer, 2018.

Kuhn, Thomas. *The Structure of Scientific Revolutions*, University of Chicago Press, 1970.

Rabbi Chayyim lckovits of Volozhin (1749–1821). *The Soul of Life: The Complete Nefesh Ha-Chayyim*. Translated by Eliezer Lipa (Leonard) Moskowitz. Teaneck, NJ: New Davar Publications, 2014.

Laitman, Michael. *Self-Interest vs. Altruism in the Global Era: How Society Can Turn Self-Interest into Mutual Benefit*. Toronto: Laitman Kabbalah Publishers, 2011.

————. *The Zohar: Annotations to the Ashlag Commentary*. Laitman Kabbalah Publishers, 2007.

Latour, Bruno. *We Have Never been Modern*. Translated by Catherine Porter. Harvard University Press, 1993.

Levenson, J. D. *The Universal Horizon of Biblical Particularism*, New York, 1985.

Levi, Primo. *Moments of Reprieve*. Translated by Ruth Feldman. 1985.

Levinas, Emmanuel. *Time and the Other*. Translated by Richard A. Cohen. Pittsburgh. 1987.

————. *Totality and Infinity: An Essay on Exteriority*. Translated by Alphonso Lingi. Pennsylvania: Duquesne University Press, 1969.

Lewis, C. S. *The Problem of Pain*. London: Collins, 1966.

Lorberbaum, Yair. *In God's Image: Myth Theology and Law in Classical Judaism.* Cambridge University Press, 2015.

Lubitch, Ronen. "The Concept of History in Rabbi Kook's Writings." *Yeshuat Uzzo*, 1996, 413–36 [Hebrew].

Luft, Sebastian, ed. *The Neo-Kantian Reader* (NKR). Routledge, 2015.

Luzzatto, Rabbi Moshe Chaim. *Derech Hashem.* c. 1730. Section 3, 1 [Hebrew].

Maharal (Rabbi Judah Loew Ben Bezalel of Prague, The Maharal of Prague). *Netivot Olam* [Hebrew].

Maimonides, Moses. *The Guide for the Perplexed.* Translated by M. Friedlander. 4th edition. New York: E. Dutton and Co. Press.

Mankowitz, Z. *Life between Memory and Hope: The Survivors of the Holocaust in Occupied Germany.* Cambridge University Press, 2009.

Melamed, Rabbi Eliezer. *Pninei Halachah.* "The Laws of Prayer." Chapter 15, section 8 [Hebrew]. Also available in English translation at https://ph.yhb.org.il/en/category/tefila/.

Mendes-Flohr, Paul, and Jehuda Reinharz. *The Jew in the Modern World: A Documentary History.* Oxford University Press, 1980.

Meyerhoff Hieronimus, J. Zohara. *Sanctuary of the Divine Presence: Hebraic Teachings on Initiation and Illumination.* Vermont: Inner Traditions Press, 2012.

Milchman, Alan, and Alan Rosenberg. "Michel Foucault and the Genealogy of the Holocaust." In *Post-Modernism and the Holocaust.* Radopi, 1998.

Mitchell, Andrew J., and Peter Trawny, eds. *Heidegger's Black Notebooks: Responses to Anti-Semitism.* Columbia University Press, 2015.

Monk, Ray. *Ludwig Wittgenstein: The Duty of Genius.* Penguin Books, 1990.

Morgenstern, Arie. *The Gaon of Vilna and His Messianic Vision.* Jerusalem: Gefen Publishing House, 2012.

Neumann, Jonathan. *To Heal the World: How the Left Corrupts Judaism and Endangers Israel.* New York: St. Martin's, 2018.

Ott, Hugo. *Martin Heidegger: A Political Life.* Translated by Allan Blunden. London, 1994.

Pedaya, Haviva. *Expanses: An Essay on the Political and Theological Unconscious.* HaKibbutz HaMeuchad, 2011 [Hebrew].

———. *The Return of the Lost Voice,* HaKibbutz HaMeuchad, 2016 [Hebrew].

Perl, Jeffrey, ed. Editorial preface to *Peace and Mind: Civilian Scholarship from Common Knowledge.* Davies Group, 2011.

Pöggeler, Otto. "Heidegger's Political Understanding." In *The Heidegger Controversy: A Critical Reader.* Edited by Richard Wolin. New York, 1991.

———. *Martin Heidegger's Path of Thinking,* New Jersey: Atlantic Highlands, 1987.

Ramon, Einat. "Abraham Joshua Heschel's Critique of Modern Society." *G'vanim* 6, no. 1 (2010): 28–41.

Ravitzky, Aviezer. "Munkacs and Jerusalem: Ultra-Orthodox Opposition to Zionism and Agudaism." In *Zionism and Religion.* Shmuel Almog, Jehuda Reinharz, and Anita Shapira, eds. Hanover, 1998.

Reif, Stefan. "Jewish Liturgical Research, Past, Present and Future." *JJS* 35 (1984).

———. *Judaism and Hebrew Prayer, New Perspectives on Jewish Liturgical History.* Cambridge, 1993.

Ricoeur, Paul. *Evil: A Challenge to Philosophy and Theology.* Translated by John Bowden. New York: Continuum, 2007.

Rockmore, Tom. *On Heidegger's Nazism and Philosophy.* University of California Press, 1997.

Rorty, Richard, ed. *Essays on Heidegger and Others: Philosophical Papers.* Cambridge University Press, 1991.

———. *The Linguistic Turn: Recent Essays in Philosophical Method.* Chicago University Press, 1967.

Rosenak, Avinoam. *Cracks: Unity of Opposites, the Political and Rabbi Kook's Disciples.* Resling, 2013 [Hebrew].

———. "Hidden Diaries and New Discoveries: The Life and Thought of Rabbi A. I. Kook." In Shofar: *An Interdisciplinary Journal of Jewish Studies* 25, no. 3 (Spring 2007): 111 -47.

———. "Modernity and Religion: New Explorations in the Light of the Union of Opposites." In *Rabbinic Theology and Jewish Intellectual History,* 2013.

———. Prophecy and Halakha Dialectics in Rabbi Kook's Meta-Halakhic Thought." *Jewish Law Annual* (2011).

———. *Prophetic Halachah, The Philosophy of Halachah in the Teaching of Rabbi Kook.* Jerusalem: Magnes, 2007 [Hebrew].

Rosenak, Michael. *Tree of Life Tree of Knowledge: Conversations with the Torah.* Westview, 2001.

Rosenberg (Shagar), Shimon Gershon. *Faith Shattered and Restored: Judaism in the Postmodern Age,* Maggid Books, 2017.

Rosman, Moshe. *Founder of Hasidism: A Quest for the Historical Ba'al Shem Tov.* Littman Library of Jewish Civilization, 2013.

———. *From Identity-Based Conflict to Identity-Based Cooperation.* Springer, 2012.

Rotenberg, Mordechai. *Jewish Psychology and Hasidism: The Psychology behind the Theology.* Open University, Ministry of Defence Publications, 1997 [Hebrew].

Rothman, Jay. *Resolving Identity-Based Conflict in Nations, Organizations and Communities.* Jossey Bass, 1997.

Rouzati, Nasrin. "Evil and Human Suffering in Islamic Thought – Towards a Mystical Theodicy." *MDPI* (2018).

Safranski, Rüdiger. *Martin Heidegger: Between Good and Evil*. Translated by Ewald Osers. Harvard University Press, 2002.

Sanders, E. P. *Paul, the Law and the Jewish People*. Fortress, 1983.

Schmitt, Carl. *Political Theology: Four Chapters on the Concept of Sovereignty*. Translated by George Schwab. University of Chicago Press, 1985.

Scholem, Gershom G. "Bemai Ka'Mipalgi." In *Od Davar*. Am Oved, 1987 [Hebrew].

———. *Major Trends in Jewish Mysticism*. Schocken Books, 1946.

———. *On Jews and Judaism in Crisis: Selected Essays*. Schocken Books, 1976.

Sheehan, Thomas, ed. *Heidegger: The Man and the Thinker*. New Jersey, 2010.

Sherwin, Byron L. "The Assimilation of Judaism, Heschel and the Category Mistake." *Judaism* 53, no. 3 (June 2006): 40–50.

Shklar, Judith. *Ordinary Vices*. Cambridge, MA: Harvard University Press, 1984.

Shneur Zalman of Liadi. *Likutei Amarim, Tanya*. Hebrew with English translation. Brooklyn: Kehot Publication Society. 770 Eastern Parkway, 1981.

———. *Likutei Torah*, "Drushim for Shabbat Shuvah." *Otzar HaHasidim* 128 [Hebrew].

Simon, Ernst (Akiva). "Are We IsraelisStill Jews?" *Commentary* (April 1953): 357–64.

Sluga, Hans. *Heidegger's Crisis: Philosophy and Politics in Nazi Germany*. Harvard University Press, 1995.

Soloveitchik, Rabbi Joseph Baer. *Halakhic Man*. Translated by Lawrence Kaplan. Jerusalem: Sefer VeSefel Publishing, 2005.

———. *The Halakhic Mind*. Seth Press, 1986.

Stanovitch, Keith, and Richard West. "Individual Differences in Reasoning: Implications for the Rationality Debate." *Behavioral and Brain Sciences* 23, no. 5 (2000): 645–65.

Steiner, George. "Heidegger Again." *Salmagundi*, nos. 82/83 (Spring/Summer 1989): 31–55.

———. *In Bluebeard's Castle: Some Notes towards the Redefinition of Culture.* Yale University Press, 1971.

———. *Martin Heidegger: With a New Introduction.* University of Chicago Press, 1989.

———. *The Portage to San Cristobal of A.H.* University of Chicago Press, 1979.

———. *Tolstoy or Dostoyevsky: An Essay in the Old Criticism.* Yale University Press, 1959.

Sutton, Avraham. *Spiritual Technology*, 2013.

Taylor, Charles. *A Catholic Modernity?* Charles Taylor's Marianist Award Lecture with Responses by William Shea, Rosemary Lulling Haughton, George Marsden and John Bethke Elshtain. Oxford University Press, 1990.

Tyrer, Haim Ben Solomon. *Be'er Mayim Chayim*, Exodus 19:1–8. Jerusalem: Even Yisrael Institute.

Waxman, Chaim. "Messianism, Zionism and the State of Israel." *Modern Judaism* 7 (1987).

Weil, Simone. *Waiting for God.* London: Harper Perennial, 2001.

Weinreb, Friedrich. *Roots of the Bible: An Ancient View for a New Outlook.* Translated by N. Keus. Merlin Books, 1986,

Weissman, Tamar. *Tribal Lands: The Twelve Tribes of Israel in Their Ancestral Territories.* Renana Publishers, 2015.

Wiesel, Elie. *Night* (1960), NY Hill and Wand (2006)

Wittgenstein, Ludwig. *Culture and Value.* Edited by G. H. von Wright, with Heikki Nyman and translated by C. G. Lukhardt and Maximillian Aue. University of Chicago Press, 1982.

———. "Lecture on Ethics." First published in *Philosophical Review* 74, no. 1 (1965): 3–12.

———. *Philosophical Investigations.* Translated by G. E. M. Anscombe. New York: Macmillan, 1953.

———. *Tractatus Logico-Philosophicus.* Translated by D. F. Pears and B. F. McGuiness. London: Routledge, 1972.

Wolfson, Elliot. *The Duplicity of Philosophy's Shadow: Heidegger, Nazism and the Jewish Other.* New York: Columbia University Press, 2018.

———. *Heidegger and Kabbalah: Hidden Gnosis and the Path of Poiesis.* Bloomington: Indiana University Press, 2019.

Wolin, Richard. *The Politics of Being: The Political Thought of Martin Heidegger.* Columbia University Press, 1990.